D0364172

CL
MO

Two on the River (photographs by Stan Grossfeld)

King of the Cats: The Life and Times of Adam Clayton Powell, Jr.

The Haygoods of Columbus: A Family Memoir

IN BLACK AND WHITE

IN BLACK AND WHITE

The Life of Sammy Davis, Jr.

Wil Haygood

Aurum

First published in Great Britain
2004 by Aurum Press Ltd
25 Bedford Avenue, London WC1B 3AT

This edition published by arrangement with Alfred A. Knopf, a division of Random House, Inc.

A catalogue record for this book is available from the British Library.

ISBN 1 84513 013 8

1 3 5 7 9 10 8 6 4 2
2004 2006 2008 2007 2005

Designed by Anthea Lingeman
Typeset in Minion by North Market Street Graphics, Lancaster Pennsylvania
Printed by MPG Books, Bodmin, Cornwall

CONTENTS

Marvelous tunes you rang
From passion, and death, and birth,
You who had laughed and wept
On the warm, brown lap of the earth.

Now in your untried hands
An instrument, terrible, new,
Is thrust by a master who frowns,
Demanding strange songs of you.

God of the White and Black,
Grant us great hearts on the way
That we may understand
Until you have learned to play.

DuBose Heyward
Porgy

IN BLACK AND WHITE

YES HE CAN

By the ever twisting light of fame, he has lived a life both mesmerizing and distinctly peculiar. Since childhood he has wowed audiences across America as well as in many European locales. He is a veteran of night-clubs, radio, television, and film. Once the star of a trio dance act, for the past six years he has gone solo. There are many from the 1940s and 1950s who watched him grow up—onstage—and feel a kind of surrogate connection with him. His name often drops warmly from their lips. Like kin.

Sammy.

He has worked like a demon at familiarity. There have been a great many benefits for social causes. He'll do anything for his pal Frank Sinatra. Likewise for Reverend Martin Luther King, Jr. He won't turn away from any Jewish cause, either. He works fifty weeks a year. He suffers from insomnia—not in the sense of a medical malady; he simply abhors sleeping, for there is so much on his mind, so many things he wants to do. He considers idleness a curse. Born of vaudeville, his peripatetic life has come to explode within the slippery parameters of the stardom he has chased ferociously for so many years. He has known it all: fear, pain, love, and hatred. Behind him lie thousands and thou-sands of motherless nights. He has learned to hoard his raging insecurities, for if onstage he is commanding and confident, offstage he carries a wobbly sense of self.

It is 1965, and Sammy Davis, Jr.'s America is afire. There are riots, marches, sit-ins. Assassins have come upon the land. No one blames him for the loaded pistol he carries. Or the umbrella he sometimes strolls with: it can be opened in an instant, exposing a knifelike point capable of inflicting a lethal wound. He is a Negro married to a white woman. The death threats are common. His booking agents rarely send him into the Deep South; he has a colossal fear he will be murdered in either Alabama or Mississippi. Whenever he travels, Joe Grant, his black-belt, karate-kicking bodyguard, accompanies him. But right now, Sammy is ensconced on Broadway, starring in Clifford Odets's *Golden Boy* at the Majestic Theatre. (Grant can sometimes be spotted in the theater basement, breaking wooden boards with his bare hands.) The lines are long for *Golden Boy;* the show is a smash. It is Sammy's second turn as a Broadway star. This time around, Sammy is portraying a boxer, a fighter. Onstage he is also in love with a white woman. His stage name is Joe; hers is Lorna.

> JOE TO LORNA:
> But you don't know how I feel? Lorna, when I'm not with you I—bleed, I got a hole bleeding in my side nothing can stop but being with you because the other half is you, rotten, beautiful, the other half is you!—and I'm here on my feet, bleeding—for you—

It is, true enough, Odetsian stage speak, the rush of words and emotions and strange syntax, but it is also in some way a mirror of the times. America, having a bellwetherlike year, is herself constantly onstage. Every day there is an angry new protest, and new fears—in Selma, in Los Angeles, in Harlem. The bleeding occurs in a lot of places. Sammy himself is quite aware of the danger in the streets. He hates it when fans rush up to him on his left side. His left eye is sightless from a decade-old car crash, and he worries whether he might, in an instant, have to pull his gun. His heroes are cowboys, and he is extremely adept, as many in Hollywood know, at the quick draw. He has been known to dash off to Connecticut, home of Colt, the firearms maker, to have yet another set of guns—pearl-handled—made especially for him.

"Sammy and I wound up with the reputations of being the fastest draws in Hollywood," says comedian Jerry Lewis, Sammy's longtime friend, whom Sammy sometimes bested in mock showdowns. "And I was fast."

"Is his gun faster than Wyatt Earp's?" a magazine article once asked of Sammy.

In his dressing room, in front of the mirror, he sometimes practices his quick draw. Two seconds: the hand snatching the gun out, then twirling it back into the holster. Two seconds. Don't fuck with Sammy.

The big, wonderful, and edgy *Golden Boy* production—Sammy has already sent some of the proceeds down to Selma, to aid in "the movement"—suits him just fine, with its mixture of race and sex. With Sammy, there are always new dramas to battle old ones. And always a drama inside the ongoing drama, whatever it happens to be. Thunder in the soul delights him.

So: a twirling gun glints in a dressing-room mirror.

Draw!

Draw!

Draw!

But who is Sammy Davis, Jr.? What forces propelled him into being? How has he come to be proclaimed—by many, even in his own ego-ridden profession—"the world's greatest entertainer"? And why have there been so many motherless nights?

Eleven months into his *Golden Boy* run, Sammy's autobiography was, at long last, ready for publication. The book—*Yes I Can: The Story of Sammy Davis Jr.*—had been more than five years in the making. An almost cultlike curiosity had grown around it. That the country was rife with turmoil could hardly stop the book's publication now. But there lay, around the creation and publication of this book, hundreds of hidden little dramas. And those dramas, like much of Sammy's life, veered from the comic to the tragic, from the sweetly sublime to the ashes of vaudeville. They illuminated Sammy's ferocious determination in how he wished to present himself to the American reading public—a motherless Negro absent a culture, more white than black. *Yes I Can* was a stunning performance. And it was the making of that book—more than the book itself—that was a crystallization of everything Sammy had thus far mastered in life: shrewdness, guile, survival, fearless determination, and the switching of masks. *Yes I Can* had everything—except the real Sammy. As a *New York Times* reviewer would ask of the book: "Can it be that it is now permissible to reveal everything except thought?"

The book's beginnings date back to the late 1950s, in a series of Manhattan nightclubs, amid the jumpy voices and smoke and clinking of glasses. It began in the brain of Burt Boyar, Sammy's new sidekick. They had first met when Sammy made his Broadway debut, in 1956, in *Mr. Wonderful.* Boyar, a newspaperman, wanted to write a book. Newspapermen were wont to dream of such things. Boyar's book would be a novel. A novel about a Negro entertainer who rises to the top of the entertainment world. Included would be all the travails along the way, up and around the obstacle course that meandered through white and Negro America. For Boyar—dark-haired, handsome, tweedy—it would be fun, a thrill, an added hobby to life with his elegant and always fashionably attired wife. (Jane Feinstein met Burt in 1954, when she waltzed into his Madison Avenue press agent's office. On their first date, while strolling down Fifth Avenue, he told her he was going to marry her. Two years after they were married, the Boyars met Sammy. So much about them intrigued him: not least that they were young and attractive. They were also Jewish, and Sammy, who had converted to Judaism, was shameless in his courting of Jews.)

The novel would be based on Sammy's life, with Sammy as its hero. Burt and Jane did not consider themselves literary purists, by any means. They sometimes read Ayn Rand aloud to each other in bed at night, but that was for fun. Their novel would be done quickly—they couldn't imagine it taking more than a year. They'd just bang the thing out, have a romp with it.

Inside the nightclub on the evening they pitched the idea to him, Sammy listened as raptly as he did to any promotional idea that involved him. Which is to say he listened and, between interruptions, he half-listened, and between additional interruptions, he listened some more. There were so many schemes; they came and they went. While he listened, there went the quick jerk of the neck toward the door, following the new arrivals, Sammy waving maniacally, then the head yanking back to Burt, back to this book idea, the tapping of ash in the cigarette tray, the blowing of smoke, and then, a blonde, and another, all strolling by just to say hello, their perfume hanging in the air like bubbles.

Sammeeee! Sammeee!

What the hell. A novel. A book. One night, in another nightclub, another belligerent doorman looking him up and down like a new convict arriving at the state penitentiary, Sammy turned to Boyar and said: "If people could just know what it's like!" He meant the indignity, how you could be made to feel low and hurt even if you had crisp one-hundred-dollar bills in your pocket. And suddenly, drawing in all of Sammy's pent-up pain in that comment—it was as if Boyar's mind had taken on a new engine—Burt Boyar realized that Sammy was talking not about the joy, but about the slights and the pain, the sometimes awfulness of a life lived high one moment, then dragged to the depths of despair the next by doormen who were making a tenth of your salary. Who knew, out there in the hinterland, that beyond the opening nights, the champagne, the Vegas lights, the beautiful small-waisted blondes, the raw sweet sexual escapades, that he, Sammy Davis, Jr., cried? That he hurt? Boyar wrote entertainment columns for a horse-racing paper, and now, as he listened to Sammy vent, imagining new layers for his unwritten novel, the writing juices in him began to gallop. Burt Boyar knew next to nothing about racism or the pain of the Negro. He never marched with any protesters, never arched his back over any social ills. Racism was something over there, something in the history books, in another city. Now Sammy was telling him that there was rot in Manhattan as well. Burt Boyar had an epiphany. If Sammy felt it—racism—Burt would have to start, if not feeling it, certainly trying to under-stand it. "He was very despondent. Racism was absolutely deflating, so totally unkind, unnecessary," says Boyar.

Burt and Jane began to run alongside Sammy. They were at his New York apartment. They whizzed in and out of the nightclubs with him. Sammy was driving them—only they couldn't easily see it; he was pushing and goading them, telling them they were authors, writers; he had met Hemingway, at Ciro's, in Hollywood, and he frequently sprinkled his chats with journalists and writers with the story about the time he had met Papa. Sammy wanted a book, needed a book, believed a book would get him into the living rooms of middle-class (read *white*) America. By 1960, Burt and Jane had spent two years with Sammy, a great amount of that time at night. They were writing with their eyes, just looking, taking everything in. "In the early days Sammy found attraction in us," recalls Boyar. "We were the wholesome, well-dressed white couple. We moved very comfortably in the world he should have moved in. Although I'd think there were much more exciting people than us."

At one point the Boyars moved to Hollywood and lived with Sammy for three months. They saw the rarefied world of the Negro in early 1960s Hollywood.

There was Sidney Poitier.

There was Harry Belafonte.

There was Dorothy Dandridge, who had lived across the street from Sammy before her death, on September 8, 1965, from an overdose of antidepressants.

And there was Sammy.

It was a world of oneness: One Negro on the movie lot. One Negro folksinger. One Negro sex kitten. One Negro star on Broadway.

Burt Boyar had been a child actor himself, beginning with radio. Stars hardly intimidated him, though they still sent warm shivers through him. He knew the trapdoors they had to avoid to stay on top. Boyar could see that Sammy had the jauntiness of a star before he really was one. The quality charmed Boyar. "We were in a cab once," he says. "I take out a five-dollar bill, all I had. The bill was about $1.25. Sammy says, 'Give him the five, baby, I'm a star.' It was a lot of money to me."

The Boyars traveled by train to meet with Sammy. They flew. They drove. They were sycophants; they were novelists. Sammy was their prey and their novel. It was a strange and tricky tightrope. Boyar knew there were trade-offs. "I did his pimping for him," he says.

The white women would come to Boyar and slip a note to give to Sammy. And he would slip notes to the white women who caught Sammy's eye. But that was just life, the whiff of celebrity and fame. Burt didn't mind the pimping. The book idea drew them—Sammy, Burt, and Jane—so much closer. Their friendship deepened.

Jane and Burt Boyar were naive about the book-writing business. They didn't have a literary agent, they'd just write the thing—"It didn't occur to us to write an autobiography," he says—and try to sell it. Luck sailed through the window one day when Scott Meredith, a literary agent, phoned Boyar out of the blue. Meredith wanted to know if Boyar—whose occasional writing for *TV Guide* Meredith knew about—wanted to write a book about TV censorship. Meredith had big-time clients, among them P. G. Wodehouse. "I was flattered," Boyar recalls. He sat and pondered. He now suddenly had to imagine two book possibilities: a novel about a Negro entertainer—though in reality what was it but a kind of exuberant pipe dream?—or a genuine offer, in which there would be money up front to write a book about TV censorship? Burt and Jane liked to live well. They were winsome, carefree, childless. In a way they seemed a couple frozen in time, that time being the 1940s, when couples dined out, listened to Tommy Dorsey music in elegant restaurants, dressed well. They were seldom seen without each other. They swiveled easily into pricey eateries and nightspots. Money did not grow, they certainly knew, on the edges of rose petals, and it cost money to live the way they did. The novel would have to wait. Sammy would understand. Anyway, just another idea out the window, just another scheme gone with the cigarette smoke.

To write a book about TV censorship, Boyar knew he'd have to fasten himself down. He'd have to sit in dusty libraries and pore over records. He did not look happily upon such demands. And it wasn't long after Boyar signed a contract with Macmillan that he began feeling he had made the wrong choice. He realized he had no passion for such a book. It was dry, a colorless project, something, perhaps, for an academic. And he missed Sammy, the nights floating about Manhattan, mentally scratching up the novel. So he told himself he would not do it. Boyar confided to his agent his new feelings about no longer wanting to do a censorship book. He told Scott Meredith that what he really wanted to do was write a book about Sammy Davis, Jr. "If you can get that," Meredith quickly responded, "it'd be great."

Scott Meredith wasn't talking about fiction, though. He was talking about a nonfiction book, real life. Real blood. No matter how pretty it was, or how experimental, fiction couldn't hold a pearl-handled gun to reality. Ask Frank Sinatra, knocked loopy by critics and his love affairs, only to rise again, higher than ever; ask Jack Kennedy, murdered in the glow of his own promise; ask an old vaudevillian by the name of Will Mastin about real life—born before the automobile, before the plane, before the movie projector, now gliding along backstage at the Majestic Theatre, visiting with Sammy, to whom he had taught so much.

Suddenly, real life excited Boyar as well. He thought about a real book. He talked to Jane about it. The idea excited her too. To hell with the novel. "We only thought of it as a novel because we had to figure out a way to tell the story," he remembers. If they were to write a biography, the Boyars wondered if there might be those who felt they were too close to Sammy to write the book objectively. They also had worries that if it was an autobiography, there would be those who would wonder if they had enough distance to bring critical insight to the task. "Then we thought, what the hell, we'd just write the book," says Burt Boyar.

They told Sammy they now wanted to write it as autobiography. And there went Sammy: the eyes widening, the mouth forming into the circus smile, all followed by the Sammy hug. "Great," he said, "let's do it." They laughed long and hard. A trio again. Jane on one end, Burt on the other, Sammy in the middle. He viewed it as yet another performance. The Sammy Davis, Jr., Story. What did he know about book writing? He never went to school a day in his life.

Meredith got the trio a book contract with the publishing house of Bernard Geis Associates for $25,000. Sammy laughed some more: he was broke, he needed the money. They'd have to split it three ways, though. A third to Burt, a third to Jane, a third to Sammy. The same old curse delivered unto Sammy: two thirds of the dough gone before it came to rest in his pockets. Just like in the days when he danced with his father and Will Mastin.

Geis had no illusions about the type of books that intrigued him. In 1959 he published *Groucho & Me* by Groucho Marx. He was just now courting Lita Grey Chaplin, who was in the throes of writing a titillating tell-all about her marriage to and divorce from Charlie Chaplin. Never mind that the divorce had taken place more than two decades earlier. (*My Life with Chaplin: An Intimate Memoir* was published by Geis in 1966. That very year, old Charlie Chaplin himself was in England making *A Countess from Hong Kong,* billed as a romantic comedy. It was his last film. Despite an intriguing cast—Marlon Brando, Sophia Loren, Tippi Hedren—the movie was labeled a disaster.)

After the Boyars signed the contract in his office, Geis took them out that evening for a celebration. He squired them through the doors of the Waldorf Astoria, up to the Starlight Roof, everyone in a wonderful, lighthearted mood. There was an orchestra, music rising. Geis asked Jane—her black hair so long, so lovely—for a dance to celebrate it all. But Jane and Burt were Old World: they had long ago made a pact that they did not dance with anyone except each other. It was a kind of Elizabethan-era vow, and they very much realized it. Given the occasion, of course, one might have thought Jane would make an allowance. She would not. Geis looked befuddled. He was asking for a simple dance to celebrate something special. "Jane looked at me like, 'What should I do?' " recalls Burt. "I said, 'Mr. Geis, I hope this is not offensive, but Jane and I have a thing that we don't dance with other people.' It was very uncomfortable to tell your new publisher that. But that's how we set it up, and that's how we played it."

The "Associates" in the Geis company were TV variety-show host Art Linkletter and the Goodson & Toddman Agency. The thinking behind Geis publishing was to promote the books Geis signed on the TV shows that Linkletter and Goodson & Toddman had a stake in. The publisher was in bed with the TV shows. It was far from highbrow; it was just this side of P. T. Barnum. Write a book, the Geis folks seemed to say to prospective authors, and we'll hawk it on TV for you.

Sammy bought Boyar a fancy tape recorder and tossed it on a nightclub table. The Boyars would ask their questions, and Sammy would just start talking into the tape recorder. Just words, and the words unveiled memories, which unveiled hurts. He riffed, like a jazzman, the words just flowing and flowing.

The tape-recording sessions were done all over, in moving automobiles, in dressing rooms, in nightclubs, in hotel rooms. They were in El Morocco one night, "21" the next, and the Copa another, Sammy bouncing around, Burt sticking the tape recorder down in front of him, the thing whirring and swallowing up the words. Sammy called Jane and Burt "scribes," the old English word for newspapermen. "We didn't know what we were doing," Boyar recalls. But they kept doing it. Other Negroes would come around, and Sammy would introduce the Boyars to them, telling them the Boyars were writing a book about his life. And there would come those looks from the just-arrived Negro guest: a white couple writing a book about white-obsessed Sammy. Ha ha ha. It made for jokes, kitchen-table ridicule. "They were fascinated with him," remembers Evelyn Cunningham, a Negro writer for the *Pittsburgh Courier* who was based in New York City and met the Boyars. "They were not real hip—but they were hip enough."

There was something else that Cunningham noticed about the Boyars when Negroes were around Sammy. The Boyars would retreat, either from the room or the conversation. "They were a white couple who knew how to stay in their place in a large black gathering."

The Boyars, completely untested in the world of book writing, had no doubt about the kind of chance Sammy had given them. "When you think about it racially, Sammy gave us an opportunity," says Burt Boyar. "Here was a black man giving whites an opportunity. Sammy always dealt with the best— the best trumpeter, the best light man. So, with us, he took a big chance."

The more the Boyars heard of Sammy's life, the more fascinated they became. Stories about the road, about nightclubs, about being broke, about climbing up on the marquee. Stories about women, about white women, the angst of love. At night, Jane, and sometimes Burt, transferred the words from the tape recorder to paper in a typewriter, the tapping of the keys echoing off the walls of their apartment. Then they'd pack and run to Las Vegas, or Los Angeles, or Chicago, or wherever Sammy might be, for more tape-recording sessions. They enjoyed every second of it, reaching for new tapes as yet another tape ran out.

Sammy, into the tape recorder, recalled a show he gave while in the army:

> We played the show for a week and when I was on that stage
> it was as though the spotlight erased all color and I was just
> another guy. I could feel it in the way they looked at me, not

in anything new that appeared in their faces, but in something old that was suddenly missing. While I was performing they suddenly forgot what I was and there were times when even I could forget it. Sometimes offstage I passed a guy I didn't know and he said, "Good show last night." It was as though my talent was giving me a pass which excluded me from their prejudice.

Sammy recalled a musician who he felt didn't appreciate a book about Jewish history:

> Baby, you'd better read it again. These are a swinging bunch of people. I mean I've heard of persecution, but what they went through is ridiculous! There wasn't anybody who didn't take a shot at 'em. The whole world kept saying, "You can't do this" and "You can't do that" but they didn't listen! They'd get kicked out of one place, so they'd just go on to the next one and keep swinging like they wanted to, believing in themselves and in their right to have rights, asking nothing but for people to leave 'em alone and get off their backs, and having the guts to fight to get themselves a little peace.

The Boyars sat with Sam Sr., fond of playing the horses now, and he was as helpful as he could be. They went and found Will Mastin, head of the vaudeville trio that Sammy had begun his career in as a child performer. Mastin was cautious and weary on a good day; other days he was moody, distant, uncommunicative. White folk had always made him weary. Mastin listened to the Boyars' questions. He shared a few memories—names of theaters, names of old vaudevillians. Not a word, however, about his own life, his own roots, his own past. What was in it for him? What percentage of the cut? He didn't know why they wanted to drag up the past. It was useless jawboning. It was over with; life had gone on. They came back again, and it started to wear on him, and he wanted to know why it was taking so long to write the book, to gather the information, and he wondered if anyone was going to read a book about Sammy anyway. A couple of white kids—mere children!—cornering him like that. They stopped coming around, and he was happy when they did.

Nathan Crawford, Sammy's valet, was also bewildered by the Boyars, by their questions and their tape recorder. He said not a word to them: "Nathan had no use for us."

The Boyars approached Charlie Head, another member of the entourage, the passenger in the car accident in 1954 when Sammy lost his eye. Certainly he'd have some insights to offer—vivid memories of the accident and that near-death experience. Charlie Head waved them off. "Can't tell you why," says Burt Boyar.

Still, they were awash in Sammy stories. They believed what they heard. A bourbon and Coke in his hand, a cigarette in the other—the hour late, then later—Sammy gabbed and gabbed, and they took all the gabbing as truth.

For Sammy—in addition to tapping unused performance juices in the arena of storytelling—the whole enterprise was cathartic. So many whites didn't understand him. So many Negroes didn't understand him! He couldn't understand why; the Boyars couldn't understand why. But they asked no penetrating questions. They did not force Sammy down roads he did not wish to go. The Boyars knew no Negroes. They knew no Negro authors, no Negro teachers. They knew only Sammy, and his world—his dresser, his wife, his father, Will Mastin. To them, Harlem—Sammy's birthplace—might as well have been across the seas, in Peking. So they avoided Uptown.

Harlem unnerved Sammy anyway. Let Wilt Chamberlain and Willie Mays and Harry Belafonte rub shoulders with the denizens of Harlem's Hotel Theresa, where they were often seen; Sammy preferred the Waldorf—yes, the Waldorf downtown—its large rooms, its menu, its ornate setting. And if Sammy preferred the Waldorf, then what in the world would the Boyars be doing in Harlem? Sammy, into the tape recorder:

> I'm not going to run up to Harlem and hang around to keep up appearances, either. And I know now what's gonna happen. The mass Negro's gonna bitch, "He's not a corner boy." And they're right. I don't go up to Harlem and just hang on the corner of 125th and Seventh. I never did it when I was a kid and there's no reason for me to do it now. I'm not about to con my own people into liking me by making regular visits to Harlem and hangin' around like "Hey baby—I ain't changed. I'm still old Sam. Still colored."

The Boyars sat transfixed listening to Sammy. At times he'd alter his voice. He'd sound like a child. Then like a beatnik. Next an English aristocrat. He could sound like Amos 'n' Andy, which is to say he could sound like a semiliterate hick crawling out of a cotton patch. On and on it went. He took the Boyars into the bygone world of vaudeville. They listened like hostages.

He was seducing them, and at seduction, Sammy was phenomenal.

"Jane and I were probably platonically in love with Sammy," says Boyar. "You fell in love with Sammy without having a romantic or sexual relationship."

Boyar, who by now had taken a leave of absence from his column-writing job, began to get worried about Geis Associates. He wasn't getting the necessary feedback and editorial guidance. "It was a schlock operation," he would conclude. "It wasn't the class operation Sammy deserved." The book-advance money had run out. Three years had gone by. And at the end of those three years—plenty of laughter, plenty of good southern soul food (collard greens, fried chicken, black-eyed peas, corn bread, all of which Sammy's grandmother Rosa introduced them to; Sammy preferred Italian, like Sinatra), plenty of wonderful wine and lovely parties—there was no finished book and no money left. "I realized we didn't have the best contract in the world," says Boyar. He fretted but realized he had to go back to Meredith, his agent.

"I went to Scott and said, 'We're with the wrong publisher.' He said, 'No, no, you're not.' I said, 'No, Scott, Sammy's left this with me and I can't do this to him.' I said, 'I have to talk to Bernard Geis and extricate myself from this.'" Meredith told Boyar that if he talked to Geis in an effort to get out of the contract, he would no longer represent him. Boyar, naive enough not to realize the possible ramifications of Meredith's threat, gathered his nerve and went to see Geis. He didn't want Geis to think he was bolting because it was a "schlock" operation, so he told the publisher he didn't have enough money, that he needed more, that it was costly to keep up with Sammy Davis, Jr. Geis told Boyar he could give him no more money. So Boyar told him he wanted out of the contract. Geis said that would be fine, that he understood, and would release him from the contract. But there was a caveat. Boyar would have to return the entire $25,000 advance. Unfamiliar with book deal making, Boyar was stunned. He didn't have the money. His palms got sweaty. He rushed to Jane, and it was Jane who rescued the both of them: she borrowed money from her father to repay Geis.

By the time 1963 rolled around, Burt and Jane were obsessed with their unsold book. They now had no publisher, and they had no agent. "By the time we broke from Geis we had a thousand pages written," recalls Boyar.

A thousand pages. It was starting to feel like the *War and Peace* of a Negro entertainer. "It was our work, our love," Boyar confesses.

They took to carting the thousand-page untitled, unclaimed, and seemingly unwanted manuscript with them around Manhattan, fearful if they left it in their apartment it might be stolen, ruining them. "Jane and I are now deeply, emotionally involved in getting this story told," says Boyar. A hatcheck girl once stopped them at the St. Regis Hotel. She told them she'd be happy to take the suitcase they were carrying so it would be out of the way of the diners. They protested vehemently: their book rested inside the suitcase, and under no conditions would they let it out of their sight. Perhaps if they had been solo writers—Burt alone, or Jane alone—desperation might have set in, a feeling that the walls were closing in. But they were a team, a unit. They leaned on each other. Their finances might have dipped precipitously low, but not their confidence.

When they were ready and feeling confident they had done the best they could, they flew out to Los Angeles to show Sammy the manuscript. "Jane and I wrote three pages of anti-Winchell stuff, because Winchell had been hard on Sammy," recalls Boyar. By 1963, Walter Winchell's potent column-writing days were coming to an end. The *New York Mirror,* which ran his column, had folded. Winchell was dodging several libel suits. Younger newspaper editors looked on him as a relic, as out of fashion as the fedora that he wore. He was an old man now, trying to cadge press credentials to get to some faraway place called Vietnam. Still, none of that mattered to Sammy. He believed in comebacks. Winchell—a former vaudevillian—might make a comeback. He might rise again. So what if he was, figuratively, dead: Sammy wasn't about to tap-dance on the grave of a former powerful newspaper columnist. He might need Walter someday. On the margins of the pages where the material critical of Winchell appeared, Sammy scribbled—"Hot. Oh hot. Too hot."

"That's the only thing we took out of the book," says Boyar.

The Boyars made their way back east after sharing the mostly finished auto-biography with Sammy. They eventually found another agent in Carl Brandt. Brandt was part of a Manhattan literary agency that his father and mother owned. The agency—Brandt & Brandt—was noted for its large backlist of specialized books, most notably the cowboy novels written by Max Brand. Davis's life story intrigued the young Carl Brandt, who had worked in Mississippi in the mid-1950s for the *Delta Democrat Times,* a bravely liberal newspaper owned by Hodding Carter, Sr. Sitting in New York City on the cusp of the explosive 1960s, Brandt sensed something about the hoped-for publication of the Sammy Davis manuscript: "I thought it was perfect timing." He was confident he could sell the book.

He and the Boyars hit the pavement in New York City. "We went with Carl to every publisher in New York," Boyar remembers. And every publisher in New York turned them down. Harcourt Brace said they would not even care to read the manuscript. Brandt and Boyar were perplexed.

Publishers were in the business of making money. And they needed to see, and imagine, how they would make their money. They could not exactly see their way to categorizing the Sammy Davis book. Was it a tell-all? How much about Sinatra? Was it biography masquerading as autobiography?

Carl Brandt, fearing he had absolutely nothing to lose, invited Boyar and Roger Straus of Farrar, Straus and Giroux to join him at the Copacabana one night so he could introduce them. "Who else has he published?" the naive and ill-informed Boyar asked Brandt about Straus, whose firm had published some of the more esteemed authors in the world of literature.

On the surface, the Davis autobiography would not seem an easy fit for the literary house of Farrar, Straus and Giroux. But it was exactly that cut-against-the-grain approach that fascinated the agent. "It occurred to me," remembers Brandt, "what would be more illogical than to have Roger [Straus] do it?"

Brandt had an in with Straus. Brandt's mother was Carol Hill. Hill—dynamic and smart—had been the East Coast story editor for Metro Goldwyn Mayer before she married Carl Brandt, Sr. In 1948, while with MGM, Hill hired a scout in New York City to look for book properties. That scout was Roger Straus. Hill later ran her own literary agency—"a Tiffany-like agency," as Roger Straus would remember—before merging with Carl Brandt's agency after their marriage. The marriage yielded a son, Carl Jr., who was now squiring the Boyars around town.

Brandt found himself very much intrigued with not only Sammy but the Boyars as well. They appeared obsessed with their unpublished manuscript. They deemed themselves writers; they deemed Sammy a writer. A troika of writers. "The whole notion of having an autobiography written by three people was interesting," Brandt recalls. "This wasn't an 'as-told-to' book."

Farrar, Straus and Giroux had eclectic tastes and an intriguing history. Its reputation began to soar in 1949 following publication of Shirley Jackson's *The Lottery*. In 1950 the house published *Look Younger, Live Longer*, by Gaylord Hauser. It wasn't a literary book at all, but it sold a bundle—450,000 copies—proving that literary aspirations could coexist alongside commercial winners. The company had undergone various name changes—Farrar and Rinehart; Farrar, Straus and Young; Farrar, Straus and Cudahy—and on September 21, 1964, became known as Farrar, Straus and Giroux. The publishing house—located in Union Square, in rather grubby quarters—had produced the likes of T. S. Eliot, Jack Kerouac, Flannery O'Connor, and Randall Jarrell, books and authors whom Roger Straus admired. Straus was partial to ascots and drove a convertible Mercedes-Benz. However, he was not a denizen of nightclubs. "I'm not a nightclub boy," Straus would admit years later. "I wasn't a Morocco or Stork Club aficionado." On the night the Boyars and Brandt took Straus to the Copacabana, Sammy was—but of course!—performing.

And there he was, crooning, the hips swiveling, his gaze going from table to table, the voice changing in octave, the pure entertainer singing "Hey There" and "Black Magic," then doing his mimicry. Roger Straus had never seen anything like it. He sat in astonishment. Sammy simply cast his spell. "This is," Straus said, leaning over to Boyar, "a tour de force, isn't it?" And in that moment, that moment of nightclub performance and literary imagination,

Roger Straus, distinguished publisher of Henry James, thought he might be able to publish a book about an entertainer—who just happened to be a Negro. Straus was falling under the Sammy spell, just as the Boyars had done. "He was charming," Straus says. "He made friends fast. He liked people and showed it."

When Straus finally got his hands on the manuscript to read, he deemed it publishable. "It was a helluva story," Straus would remember. "It needs cutting here and there," is all he told Jane and Burt.

The Boyars now had a publishing home and—as improbable as it seemed—had gone from Geis to Farrar, Straus and Giroux. Straus understood why other publishing houses had turned the manuscript down. "If you're doing a celebrity book, the celebrity book most likely is going to be of the type, 'Did Marilyn Monroe fuck John Jones on Saturday night?' But here was a book by and about a celebrity that wasn't a muckraking book, but was a portrait about a talented man who led a hard life."

Straus told Brandt he would commence negotiations.

The drama, however, was hardly over.

Carl Brandt wanted to have a larger voice in the literary agency and became entangled in a battle with Carol, his mother. At the same time, Carol had grown weary of Carl and his unpublished manuscript about Sammy Davis, Jr. In fact, she got tired of the whole enterprise, the way it seemed to be engulfing her office. "There are times when families shouldn't be in business, and that was one of those times," Brandt recalls. Just before negotiations were to begin with Farrar, Straus, the Boyars received a telegram from Carl's mother, informing them that Carl no longer represented the book. "She said, 'You will get rid of this book. It will not be in this office,' " recalls Carl.

Jane and Burt, just like that, went from having an agent to not having one. The Boyars became nervous. Roger Straus calmed them. He also offered $40,000. The Boyars and Sammy split the advance three ways. And finally they were in the Farrar, Straus fold.

Straus went about the business of finding the right person to edit the book. The first editor he selected removed the first-person narrative structure. The Boyars were aghast and fired off an angry telegram to Straus. Straus sensed how flustered they were; he said he'd find another editor. The Boyars were far from mild-mannered when it came to their Sammy.

The book then went to Robin Pitchford. Upon the completion of her editing duties, Burt Boyar accused her of taking out "all of Sammy's grammar." With Sammy's nightclub-speak gone, he sounded like "an English professor" to Boyar. Touchy and protective, the Boyars felt they had no choice but to demand the book be taken away from Pitchford as well—and so it was.

Straus began to raise an eyebrow at the Boyars' peculiar demands, but then figured he'd put the matter to rest by assigning Henry Robbins—his very well respected editor in chief—to edit the book.

Robbins was known around literary circles to have enormous insight. Reading the Davis-Boyar manuscript, Henry Robbins saw and smelled things he did not like. Changes would have to be made, and, as the editor, he'd make those changes. After all, he was dealing with two writers—three, counting Sammy—who had never written a book before. Surely they would appreciate his candor. Robbins did not like the story of Davis's conversion to Judaism, which had been made not long after Sammy's car accident. It sounded immature, Robbins told them; it lacked depth. In fact, the story of Davis's conversion—the more Robbins thought about it—pained him. Boyar defended Sammy. "Here's this Jewish editor, and he decides he knows what Sammy Davis is all about," recalls Boyar.

There was something else about the manuscript that rubbed Robbins the wrong way. He felt Davis had been far too quiet in the book about civil rights. He wanted anger, heat on the page. He wanted to know where Sammy's heart lay. "Henry said, 'Sammy's got to fight back sooner. Everybody's going to think Sammy's a coward. Sammy's got to hit back sooner.' "

The Boyars sat and listened to Henry Robbins. And they didn't like what they were hearing. It was their Sammy, and they felt Robbins simply did not know their Sammy. Never mind that they were unpublished, that this was their first book; they still could not abide by Robbins's suggestions, his blunt orders. Robbins grew irritated. "If you don't," Robbins said to the Boyars about positioning Sammy as more of a rebel in the book, "people will see Sammy as a coward." Burt Boyar felt Henry Robbins was talking about a Sammy Davis, Jr., that simply did not exist. "Don't try to change the nature of this man," Boyar finally told Robbins. "He is what he is."

Robbins was not finished. He thought he might be able to get the Boyars to understand him if he got them in less formal surroundings, so he invited them to his apartment, where—through a meal and the flowing of wine—they took up their discussion anew. But Robbins could sense something: there was very little movement on the part of the Boyars. Finally, Burt Boyar had had enough. He did not want to discuss it further. He feigned near drunkenness and made his way to the door, Jane in lockstep with him.

Robbins simply "didn't understand" Sammy, says Boyar. "He was not editing; he was trying to write. He was trying to write Sammy instead of edit him."

Inside the publishing house, there was a sense that the Boyars were becoming oddly obstinate. "They were like two parakeets in a cage," remembers Roger Straus.

Peggy Miller, assistant to Straus, sensed Robbins's irritation. "He threw up his hands and said, 'I can't deal with these people,' " she says. Miller asserts that the Boyars were well liked and quite charming, but they had a flaw that could stymie a publishing house: they were obsessive about every little change—commas, semicolons—that might be made to the manuscript. Why, they had been to the nightclubs! They had whirred along in the limo with Sammy through the streets of Manhattan!

Despite the problems, Roger Straus announced plans to publish the (still-untitled) book in 1964.

The manuscript was passed from Henry Robbins to Sigrid Rock. Rock had been a writer at the *New Yorker* before turning to editing. "She was a tough-looking blonde," Straus later remembered of Rock, whom the publishing house had not worked with that often. She began editing the book by making cuts, up to twenty-five pages by the time the Boyars had received her first version. The cuts astonished them, and they felt they were drastic. Actually, they were merely a few pages here and a few pages there, trimming the fat from a huge manuscript. But the Boyars had become too close to the material. Any cut seemed like an assault on their love for Sammy. The Boyars decided they would have to have a very serious discussion with Sigrid Rock. The discussion never took place. Rock, in the midst of editing the Sammy book, attempted suicide: she had been going through a painful romantic breakup. She survived the suicide attempt, but Farrar, Straus thought it best to take the book away from her. The Boyars hardly complained.

Straus was indeed charmed by the Boyars. They finished each other's sentences; they often wore his-and-her matching outfits in the manner of young fraternal twins. They were doubly obsessive about their book. But, in time, enough seemed to be more than enough. "Because they were together all the time," says Straus, "they always talked about the book, nitpicking."

"Having put this manuscript together, it was holy writ" to the Boyars, says Peggy Miller. "They were a strange pair," Roger Straus would have to admit, albeit with affection.

Every time the Boyars received the book back from an editor, they reread it. And after another reading, they realized they had more stuff to add! More words, more Sammy scenes, more Sammy! The manuscript ballooned from a thousand to twelve hundred pages. Finally, an exasperated Roger Straus told the Boyars that he'd edit it himself.

So the book had an editor. But the 1964 publishing season had already come and gone. Straus announced that the book would be published the following year.

With the head of the publishing house hovering with them, the Boyars finally relaxed, and they accepted Straus's editing. All, at long last, went much smoother in trimming a manuscript that at times reached nearly two feet high. Straus did not toy with the stylistic tone of the book. He made cuts, but they were not radical in any sense. "We went through about five editors and couldn't work with any of them," Boyar would recall years later, with not a trace of apology in his voice. He and Jane found Roger Straus much more to their liking: "We answered every question of Roger's, and it went great." Peggy Miller figured she knew why the Boyars were amenable to Straus: "He was the head of the company. They had no place else to go."

The book was still in search of a title. Among those thought of and discarded were *Troubled Man, Excuse Me for Living,* and, in honor of Sammy's favorite drink, *Bourbon and Coke*—the latter the silliest and offered by May Britt, Sammy's gorgeous, Swedish-born wife.

One finds, however, in the *Golden Boy* script—the play Sammy was appearing in during the behind-the-scenes selling of his book—a genesis for the eventual title. In the script, Sammy, as Joe, asks the stage chorus a litany of questions.

> JOE:
>   Can I get what I want to get?
> GROUP:
>   Yes, you can!
> JOE:
>   Can I have a car
>   With a built-in bar?
> GROUP:
>   Yes, you can!
> JOE:
>   And a color TV
>   And a Playboy key!
> GROUP:
>   Yes, you can!

Sammy liked that theme of fighting for his dreams to come true—in both the script and his own life. He had been told he couldn't be a mimic, couldn't mime white people, couldn't hop from the stage into the band and play all those different instruments, couldn't do Broadway. And he had been told that because of his height and his skin color, he couldn't enjoy the full benefits of being an American entertainment star. He had been told he couldn't be a Negro cowboy, couldn't date white women, couldn't date actress Kim Novak, couldn't marry May Britt. He had been told he couldn't spend money like Sinatra spent money.

"Yes, you can!"

For literary purposes, the title became *Yes I Can*. And it had muscle. It stood up. It had affirmation.

By the summer of 1965—Sammy was now in full flight as the star of *Golden Boy*—his book was listed as a fall arrival from Farrar, Straus and Giroux. Among other titles on the distinguished publisher's list were *The Old Glory,* by Robert Lowell, *The Bit Between My Teeth: A Literary Chronicle of 1950–1965,* by Edmund Wilson, *To Criticize the Critic and Other Writings,* by T. S. Eliot, *The Myth and the Powerhouse,* by Philip Rahv, and *Aura,* by Carlos Fuentes. The unpublished Boyars were suddenly swimming in very deep and warm waters.

It had been nearly six years since the book idea had been born. The Boyars were so excited that they made a special trip to the Greenwich Village bindery where the books were being printed, and they saw the first copies rolling off the press. "We were there the night they put dust jackets on them," Boyar recalls. They grabbed up as many books as they could carry and rushed for a taxi to get them uptown to the Majestic, where Sammy would be. Inside the theater, inside the dressing room, they gave copies of the book to Sammy, who shrieked with delight. May was also there. On the last page of the book, Sammy—or Jane, or Burt—writes, in a scene that allegedly took place beside May's hospital bed after the birth of their daughter, Tracey: "I'm going to build something good and strong and wonderful for us, and I'll never let you down. I promise." (Tender words—only by the time May held the book in her hands, Sammy was already letting her down, by sleeping with a couple of long-legged beauties from the *Golden Boy* cast.)

The book, at 630 pages, is massive for the autobiography of a forty-year-old. The cover design is in bold yellow letters: YES I CAN. The publishers, on the flap jacket, describe the book as "a fullblooded, serious, intensely absorbing autobiography, written with the vitality, brilliance and aggressive greatness of Sammy Davis Jr."

The opening pages of the book are designed as a Hollywood musical's credits might appear onscreen at movie's beginning.

There is an empty page:

Y   E   S

Another empty page:

I

Another empty page:

C   A   N

And then, on succeeding pages: THE STORY OF SAMMY DAVIS, JR., BY SAMMY DAVIS, JR. AND JANE & BURT BOYAR.

On the back of the jacket is a moody photo of our memoirist, seated. He is holding a cane and has his chin rested on the hand that grips the cane. It is a side portrait (from the right side, showing off the good eye), taken by Philippe Halsman, a much-admired fashion photographer. Davis is wearing a pinstripe suit jacket and a white shirt with cuff links. He is holding a cigarette in his right hand. He looks to be as deep in thought as Aristotle.

His story, his life, in black and white. At the book's beginning is an epigram:

> *We ain't what we oughta be,*
> *we ain't what we wanta be,*
> *we ain't what we gonna be,*
> *but thank God we ain't what we was.*

The four lines sound like they might come from a Negro comic on a stage late at night—Dick Gregory or, say, Godfrey Cambridge, perhaps—over in Atlantic City. Or perhaps at the Apollo in Harlem. Note the bastardizing of the language, the verve—"We ain't what we oughta be"—of street lingo. Actually, the author of those words is genuinely revered across America for his speeches, his verse. It is one of those rare instances when Martin Luther King, Jr.—in the book, his name is beneath the four lines—kneels down to embrace urban slang. The tone suits Sammy just fine.

Farrar, Straus announced it would publish *Yes I Can* on September 19. The galleys, copies of the book for reviewers, had already gone out. Roger Straus was enough of an industry insider that privileged information about his books came to him without much effort. "First of September, Roger Straus called us and said, 'Kids, don't get too excited, but I think you got the front section [the book review] of the *Herald Tribune*,'" says Boyar.

The kids couldn't help but get excited. They were in their New York City apartment when Straus called, sitting on the floor. Just a mattress and a typewriter and a chair is all they had. They had ordered new furniture but ran out of money. They had never written a book, thus they had never felt the thrill—or the agony—of being reviewed. "[Straus] called me back," Boyar says. "He said, 'I got it in my hand.'" Straus proceeded to read them parts of the *Herald Tribune* review. It was written by the newspaper's Eleanor Perry, and it was flat-out glowing. "He has written (or spoken on tape) a magnificent narrative. It is related with honesty, humanity, enormous intelligence, rage and humor," Perry wrote. "For this reader it is the definitive documentary of The American Dream in America now." Perry went on to praise Davis's guts. "After he's made it, after he has every glittering thing money can buy and an entourage of

devoted fans and a magnificent house in a white suburb, he attempts suicide."
The newspaper wasn't on the street yet; it was, in fact, days away from publication; Straus was holding an advance copy. The Boyars were beside themselves.
Giddily they asked about the *New York Times*. Could they dare think, dare
imagine, they'd get the cover of the *Times* as well? In New York City, such a
feat—the *Times* and *Herald Trib* on their respective covers on the same Sunday
featuring the same book—was known to rival the almighty hat trick. And it
was rare indeed to become the beneficiary of such an accomplishment. "Don't
be silly," Straus told them. "Count your blessings." The Boyars hugged and
kissed.

They planned to celebrate. Maybe the Waldorf, maybe "21," maybe the Carlyle. Everyone knew Burt at the Carlyle; hell, he used to do publicity for the
place. But before they could make a move, the phone rang again. It was Straus.
"Don't leave the apartment," he advised. "I don't want you to lose my next
phone call." Pause. "You might get the front page of the *New York Times*." The
Boyars couldn't believe it. They made goo-goo eyes. Laughter stretched their
faces. Roger Straus's prediction was correct: the book was indeed planned for
the September 19 *Times Book Review* front cover. Its own hat trick indeed.
Straus soon had an advance copy of the *Times* review as well. It was written by
Martin Duberman, a professor of history at Princeton. "We have recently
learned much of the Negro's mistreatment, but the trials of a single man, when
recounted as vividly as Sammy Davis Jr.'s are in his lengthy autobiography,
renew and redouble the shock," wrote Duberman. Duberman liked the book,
but he had misgivings, and it was deeper inside the review where those misgivings could be felt. "When one man's experiences are filtered (to any degree)
through someone else's prose, the experiences themselves are altered. To eval-
uate this book at all, we must proceed on what we know is a false assumption:
that every sentence represents Mr. Davis and no one else. If the portrait is not
a fair likeness, he must nonetheless abide by it, for he has allowed the book to
bear his name." Duberman quotes Davis: "Baby, I know everything wrong that
I ever do—and I don't need a psychiatrist to tell me why I keep doing it," and
immediately senses falsity in the claim. "If so," Duberman wonders, "why not
share the knowledge with the reader? Why be reticent in the area of how? Can
it be that it is now permissible to reveal everything except thought?"

Straus's sources had certainly done well in getting him advance copies of
the *Herald Tribune* and *Times* reviews. (The *Herald Tribune* review was titled
"What Made Sammy Run." It was accompanied by a drawing of Sammy sitting
at a piano looking skyward. He seemed melancholy, was wearing suit and tie,
with the tie askew. To the discerning eye, he had been sketched into a very
Sinatraesque pose.) There was more than enough, in both reviews, to start a
publicity campaign. But there was one problem, and it was hardly insignificant. For weeks there had been talk of another New York newspaper strike. The

114-day strike of 1961–62 was brutal, and the new talk, when it began, caught many by surprise. The powerful newspaper print unions—known as the Big Six—were yet again wielding enormous weight. As well, the city was in the midst of a full-throttled mayoral campaign—Congressman John Lindsay (another "golden boy") had caught the fancy of the *Herald Tribune* editorial writers. (The *Tribune* was also receiving huge plaudits for its series of articles titled "New York City in Crisis." "New York is the greatest city in the world—and everything is wrong with it," was the first line of the series.)

Another strike might cost the closing of other city newspapers—the *Herald Tribune*, even the *Times*, perhaps. "I don't think it'll happen," Straus told Boyar. But it did. And Burt and Jane Boyar and Roger Straus were mortified. They had a book to sell; they had advance copies of stunning reviews that now, it appeared, would not hit the streets. Reviews were not everything, but good reviews surely sold books. Calamity had struck.

Sammy cried upon hearing of the strike. It was showtime, and now it was as if an earthquake had hit the stage he was prepared to go on. To assuage his pain, he bolted town—off to Honolulu—for ten days. (His understudy in *Golden Boy*, Lamont Washington, suddenly became Joe.) Roger Straus broke out in a rash.

Burt Boyar, former child actor, former performer, was cool and steady. He called in chips. He called Milton Berle, who was a longtime Sammy admirer, whom Boyar, as a *TV Guide* columnist, had written about enthusiastically over the years. "Count on me, babe," Berle told Boyar. "Mr. TV" vowed he'd go on television and trumpet the book. And he did. Clay Felker, working at the *Herald Tribune*, had been Boyar's onetime roommate. Felker talked fast, seemed plugged in everywhere in Manhattan media circles, and was relentless when he wanted to promote something. No one had seen the *Herald Tribune* review of *Yes I Can*, but Felker made sure they *heard* about it. And he promised Boyar to do a feature on him and Jane and Sammy at strike's end. Corbett Monica, a comedian and Berle acquaintance, went on *The Tonight Show* and lauded the book. "I've just read the most wonderful book on entertainment," he said, going on and on about *Yes I Can*. The publicity machine kept cranking up, and the publisher took out print ads in Philadelphia, the closest big city to New York. "Meanwhile," adds Boyar, "on CBS radio, Garry Moore had a daily radio program. He had heard what happened. He was sympathetic. He plugged the book every day."

By the seventh day of the strike, there was a feeling that, perhaps this time, the unions had overstepped their boundaries. Both the *Times* and the *Herald Tribune* had suffered huge circulation losses from the 1962 strike. Mercifully, on the eleventh day, the strike ended, and the presses began to hum again.

Yes I Can—like other books scheduled for review during the strike—had been dealt a harsh hand. The reviews had been printed, true enough, but they hadn't been distributed. Walking along Manhattan streets after the strike's end, Boyar would notice bundles of newspapers. Wrapped around some of the bundles was the *Herald Tribune* book review section of September 19—the one with the glowing *Yes I Can* review—now being used merely as wrapper paper. The sight crushed him.

The year had already seen a rather eclectic book-publishing season. Norman Mailer, who hadn't published a book in a decade, was back in bookstores with *An American Dream.* (Boyar, for a fleeting moment, had something in common with the tough-talking Mailer: Scott Meredith was Mailer's literary agent.) Mailer's new novel was about a congressman—idealistic, charming, good-looking—and a murderer. "I met Jack Kennedy in November, 1946," began Mailer's novel. Kennedy continued to haunt deeply, like some big square-jawed ghost upon the land who had exposed, in his own assassination, its derangement. Theodore Sorensen (*Kennedy*) and Arthur Schlesinger (*A Thousand Days*) both had books out about the man and the mysteries inside him. The Sorensen and Schlesinger books were selling very briskly. Truman Capote's novel *In Cold Blood* was also garnering wide attention. Capote's book was a documentary account of a 1959 murder that took place in Holcomb, Kansas, a family of four killed by two drifters. The book, brilliantly reported, was dark and mesmerizing. A small, fey man, Capote was a genuinely gifted writer. He was also a product of the American South, and he possessed wild insecurities. "Something very nice happened to him while he was writing *In Cold Blood,* which was that he was getting more masculine—which was terribly important to him," Norman Mailer later commented. "It was much more important to him than any other homosexual I've known. He really wanted to be a most fearsome little man."

James Michener's book *The Source,* a sweeping account of the history of Judaism, was atop the *New York Times* best-seller list in the fiction category.

And then there was *Yes I Can.*

Harper's Magazine and the *Ladies' Home Journal* both ran excerpts of Sammy's book. The *Ladies' Home Journal* piece was about Sammy and May Britt, owing to the fact that feverish and voyeuristic curiosity about interracial marriages existed across the country. *Ebony* magazine, a favorite of Negro readers, bought an excerpt. The negotiations with *Ebony* got testy: Boyar demanded a cover of Sammy; the magazine refused. There were tense words, verbal exchanges, but in the end Boyar relented. Sammy's relations with the Negro press were already beyond prickly. In the upper-right-hand corner of the December 1965 issue of *Ebony* (the cover article was "Black Power: New Laws for the Old South") went the headline heralding the excerpt: "Military Ordeal of Sammy Davis Jr." His service, of course, was hardly the stuff of a Tuskegee airman, that crack all-Negro military unit that flew in World War II dropping bombs from the blue skies. In fact, not a gun was shot in Sammy's stateside military ordeal, save in training exercises.

Maurice Dolbier, dean of the *Herald Tribune* critics, invited Sammy to the *Herald Tribune* author/book lunch. It was a nice coup for Sammy and the Boyars. Only Sammy did not jump up and down. What made Sammy run? The Dolbier book invite did. "For him to stand up and talk to this literary group, well, it started getting him nervous," Boyar remembers. Sammy was forever insecure about his lack of formal education.

A couple of weeks before the scheduled luncheon, Sammy had been slightly injured in one of his *Golden Boy* fight scenes. And just days before the author/book lunch, he began reminding Boyar that he had been hurt. Something about his neck, his arms, his shoulders. He wanted Boyar and anyone else around to know that he hurt. And if they didn't believe him, it was too bad. He checked himself into Mt. Sinai Hospital. Boyar sensed something awry. The *Herald Tribune* had been running full-page ads about the upcoming lunch featuring Sammy. Boyar fretted Sammy might try to pull out of the event, feigning illness. "He used hospitals as excuses to not do anything he didn't want to do," says Boyar.

On the very day of the event, Sammy phoned Boyar and told him he wasn't going to attend. Boyar couldn't believe what he was hearing. He raced to Davis's apartment, the taxi zooming along, Boyar's blood rushing. "I'm not going to let you embarrass yourself," he told Sammy. But Sammy told Boyar he doubted he could talk well enough to address the audience. At such times, his childlike voice would return, tiny and heated. "You're talking to me," Boyar snapped. "You can talk to them just fine." May, in the apartment, allowed her lovely Swedish face to turn cold at Boyar's words. She did not want her husband doing something he did not want to do. She consoled him while Boyar bore on. "I've never been so forceful with Sammy," says Boyar. "I was in too much awe of him." Finally, rising like a wounded prizefighter, Sammy got dressed.

In the gleaming Cadillac limousine taking them over to the Waldorf, Sammy sat stiffly in his neck brace. May, who didn't understand the demands on her husband's time, fumed. "You're sucking my husband's blood!" she screamed at Boyar. She had always been so unemotional—and now this.

Sammy stiffly got out of the limousine. Boyar coaxed him along, comforted him with words as best he could. Roger Straus was in the audience. His assistant, Peggy Miller, was also there. Miller saw Davis and the brace around his neck. "We all said, 'What the hell is that about?'" she says.

Always, whenever he entered a room, there were stares. Always, finger pointing, elbows nudging sides, whispers. "He followed two very polished speakers," says Boyar. "One was Walker Percy. These people really knew how to talk. They're book people. Sammy is called to speak. Sammy said, 'I feel so diminutive.' He was using words I never heard him use. He did fifteen minutes. They were spellbound. He talked off the cuff for fifteen minutes to these two thousand people and pulled it off magnificently."

"Everybody screamed, yelled, and carried on," remembers Peggy Miller. May sat there and smiled her movie-star smile. That's why she loved him—the gift he had, the way he gave himself to the moment, how he rose. How other women looked at him so admiringly. She didn't understand America, but she understood admiration, and stardom.

In the limousine, heading home—the license plate had a mere five letters, SAMMY—Sammy tossed the neck brace aside.

The reviews kept rolling in. The *New Yorker* claimed *Yes I Can* was "an adroitly balanced mixture of show-biz humility (no truly humble man ever writes a book about himself) and cosmic egotism (Mr. Davis speaks of his talents, which are certainly multitudinous, as an 'awesome gift')." The magazine allowed, however, that "one is never sure, from page to page, which Sammy Davis will be on deck."

Burt Boyar began to feel momentum building around the book. The initial print run was twenty-five thousand copies, and already they were headed back to press for another twenty-five thousand.

Sammy gave a copy of *Yes I Can* to Sinatra. Sammy highlighted, in yellow marker—the way a college student highlights a textbook—all the passages about Frank. It was a smart move; Frank was busy. He might read the damn thing, he might not. The highlighted scenes were memories of when Sammy met Frank, raw and naked fawning:

> After the show I hurried around the corner to the stage door. There must have been five hundred kids ahead of me, waiting for a look at him. When he appeared, the crowd surged forward like one massive body ready to go right through the side of the building if necessary. Girls were screaming, fainting, pushing, waving pencils and papers in the air. A girl next to me shouted, "I'd faint if I had room to fall down." She got her laugh and the crowd kept moving. I stood on tiptoe trying to see him. God, he looked like a star. He wasn't much older than a lot of us but he was calm, like we were all silly kids and he was a man, sure of himself, completely in control.

Frank didn't read the fan magazines, and he didn't read books about himself. Nobody knew why. Nobody knew Frank's mind but Frank.

The *Los Angeles Times* and the *Philadelphia Bulletin* and a host of other daily newspapers praised *Yes I Can*. While reading the particularly good reviews, Burt Boyar was known to start sobbing, tears streaking his face. Seeing him like that, so emotional, only unleashed Jane's own tears of joy. And there they sat, holding hands, dropping salty tears all because of and for their Sammy. The *Christian Science Monitor* offered praise as well. But there were unsettling observations in the *Monitor* review: "So it does not matter that the writing of *Yes I Can* is sometimes pedestrian, that it reads in places like a grade-B novel, that it's melodramatic, and that its incidents seem now and then far-fetched. It contains some basic truths that override such flaws."

They wanted to do a book tour. Jane and Burt and Sammy. But Sammy couldn't because of his *Golden Boy* demands. Then Boyar realized something: "Sammy was a living book tour." Which meant, if cornered in a hotel lobby, dressing room, nightclub, or street corner, and the subject of his book arose, he'd sell a dozen books, then a dozen more, and a dozen more after that with his enthusiasm and exuberance. Roger Straus wanted to have a book party at the Lotus Club, but they still fretted about lost ads during the newspaper strike, and instead decided to spend the book-party money on new ads. There was one semiprivate signing in Manhattan. A couple came over to Sammy and complimented him on the writing of the book. "I didn't write it," he told the fans while pointing out the Boyars. "They did. Go compliment them." He could, in a charming way, be so brutally honest.

When the new *Golden Boy* ads were made up, Sammy made sure they mentioned the release of *Yes I Can*. Hilly Elkins, the *Golden Boy* producer, didn't mind one bit. He'd hawk the book with the same energy he was using to hawk his Broadway show. One merchandising paw scratching the other.

On October 31, six weeks after its publication, *Yes I Can* jumped onto the *New York Times* best-seller list, at number 7. The appearance on the list made Roger Straus look uncanny. The reading public became enamored of *Yes I Can*, and it stayed in the top 10 throughout the month of November. On December 5, the book reached number 4. *Yes I Can* also hopped onto the *Publishers Weekly* best-seller list. These were stunning feats for a book that, at one time, couldn't find a publisher. Pocket Books snapped up paperback rights for $300,000, at the time a whopping sum.

The success of the book couldn't hide its flaws, of course. A review in *Negro Digest* would wonder what wounds Sammy's "tiny rejected spirit" must have suffered from the absence of a mother. There is little, as well, about Sam Sr. or Will Mastin in the book. There is little about the Cuban blood that coursed through the family history. Even Jess Rand, the dutiful press agent cum advisor, receives scarcely a mention. There is next to nothing about Sammy's sister, Ramona. (He didn't tell Peggy King, the singer, that he had a sister until years after they had known each other!) There is nothing in *Yes I Can* about all the broken engagements—to Chita Rivera, to Peggy King, to Helen Gallagher, to Eartha Kitt. Kitt received a copy of *Yes I Can* in the mail; "I got a bad feeling when I touched it," she would say. "I put my hands on the pages and didn't have a good feeling."

There is nothing in the book about Sammy's lust for white women—save his wedding to May Britt, presented as an old-fashioned love story, absent, of course, Sammy's enormous psychic wounds around identity.

Cindy Bitterman, nee Bays, also doesn't appear in the book. "Sammy didn't put my name in the book because Frank would have killed him," she later confided.

Sinatra's animosity didn't have anything to do with suspicions of romance between Sammy and Cindy, because there was none. They were truly platonic. It was simply the way Sammy made Frank nervous with regard to Frank's former girlfriends, and Sammy's inability to stop himself. Frank hadn't forgotten the way Sammy once sent his former wife Ava Gardner diamonds. Kim Novak—also one of Frank's former intimates—was also a very touchy subject. (Sammy went out of his way in the book to deny a romance with Novak, but that didn't make their affair any less real.) Cindy herself used to be Frank's girl. Once, inside Danny's Hideaway, someone snapped a photo, an eye-patch-wearing Sammy—it was in the aftermath of the car crash—seated elbow to elbow with Cindy. When Cindy later showed the photo to Sammy, he took it and tore her from the picture, then gave the picture back to her. He told her he didn't want anyone to get the wrong impression. So—Sammy and Cindy? Not at all. But who knew how Frank's mind worked during those late-night hours when the wine was rolling around inside him and old sad songs were circling his brainwaves?

Yes, Frank was busy. He wasn't going to sit down and plow through some 630-page book about Sammy. Sinatra did take Sammy and the Boyars out to dinner to celebrate the book's publication. They went to Jilly's in Manhattan. Sinatra uttered hardly a word about the book. Fuck the book; he thought life was bigger than books. "Jane was sitting next to him," Burt Boyar says. "She wasn't eating. He turned to her and said, 'Eat your food, Janie.' " (He couldn't help it: Janie. He could be so condescending—so Sinatra.)

Yes I Can is a book about a child entertainer who grows to manhood on the stage. Written by a former child actor, by a newspaperman working for a horse-racing newspaper, it has a horse-racing motif: dust, gallops around the corner, setbacks, comebacks, the firing of guns, fans up out of the seats! It is an apolitical book, quite unlike another autobiography, Dick Gregory's *Nigger*, published less than a year earlier. The tone of *Yes I Can* is one of uplift, optimism. Where there is hurt, it is Sammy's own hurt. It is certainly not a book in which an individual makes an attempt to probe his own psyche. Sammy makes countless allusions to his life and important moments in his life by matching them with maudlin scenes from Hollywood movies. There is a tearjerker scene of his attempt at suicide, foot to the pedal, and an aborted drive off a cliff. A heartbreaking scene: only it never happened. His friends and colleagues recall no suicide attempts, ever. (Even in his darkest moments, Sammy still hungered for life.)

Sammy liked mystery, and he seemed to know just what to give the public. He had propelled Jane and Burt Boyar to write the book he wanted them to write. Sans introspection. He was so seductive that way. He had goaded his father and Will Mastin to change the dance act, to turn it to his strengths, and they did. He knew how to play to the audience. And the audience liked—no, loved—a tearjerker. So he gave them a tearjerker. And he gave them all the headlines—May, Frank, the Negro press—but little underneath. He gave them a book that skirted, only fleetingly, along the fault lines of race in America. It was on the best-seller lists. Folks were making money. Why complain? As a performance, *Yes I Can* was amazing. It wasn't literature, but it was being promoted by a literary house. It wasn't introspective, but it was hard to put down. It wasn't all the truth, but why bring a man to his knees over a few little lies? Or a few big lies?

Sharp-tongued comic Lenny Bruce had a routine that had him playing a judge and that ended with his passing a harsh sentence on Sammy for his distance from the civil rights movement: "Strip him of his Jewish star, his religious statue of Elizabeth Taylor—thirty years in Biloxi!"

Biloxi? Let Lenny Bruce go to Biloxi! Mississippi frightened Sammy, and not without reason: in June 1964, the Klan had murdered two whites and a Negro—one of the whites a Jew—down in Mississippi. When the three—James Earl Chaney, Andrew Goodman, and Michael Schwerner—disappeared, a lot of locals, whites, said they were probably just engaged in some prank to attract media attention. Turned out they'd been released from a Neshoba County jail and murdered on the evening of June 20. "Are you that nigger lover?" one of the Klansmen had asked Michael Schwerner. "Sir, I know just how you feel," Schwerner is reported to have said before the bullet tore into his skull.

The hell with Mississippi. Mississippi was otherwordly. Once, in Mississippi, Dick Gregory held up his memoir and said to a gathered audience, "Take a 'nigger' to bed with you tonight." There was laughter aplenty, but a lot of it was of the nervous kind.

Sammy's whole America—the America that he loved—was one big nightclub. He had to keep them in their seats. They'd hate him, they'd take away their love, they'd never come back through the nightclub doors. "Sammy could read an audience in two seconds flat," says his longtime friend Jess Rand. "It was amazing. He would know right away what kind of house it was." So why wouldn't he know what kind of reading public lay beyond the nightclub doors?

And why drag them through his family torments, or the obsession with white women?

Fifty thousand copies in print, and another twenty-five thousand on the way!

One reviewer castigated the book for not being full of indictments against society's ills. Actually, the book was full of indictments. There were indictments against hotel doormen—though not against Mississippi sheriffs. There were indictments against those who ridiculed Sammy because he was not more handsome. Couldn't the critics see he was standing up for the little man, for the man who lacked handsomeness, for the man with one eye? *Yes I Can* is an indictment against the bully in society. It is an indictment against anti-Semitism. It even has a square middle-class white couple as bookends, as coauthors.

Sammy, in the finished book, on page 251:

> I opened a new book about the Nuremberg Trials, but the Negro press rap kept running through my mind. Isn't it "my" life? Why should I have to live by other people's rules? Who am I living for—me, or some guy who sits behind a desk and wants to tell me how to live? What makes his rules better than mine? Why should I let myself be forced into a mold? I've worked all my life toward the day when no white man could tell me how to live—now the colored people are trying to do it.

Negroes may have been quite proud of the wave of independence that, in 1957, began sweeping through African nations. They could, in fact, find in that continent-away movement some seedlings of the American civil rights movement that was now under way. Sammy viewed Africa through a different set of lenses. He related to the Boyars a stopover visit to Africa on his way back from Australia. Sinatra had asked him to rush back to do a little event on behalf of Senator Jack Kennedy.

> Now, the plane lands in Africa and I figure, "Hot damn, I'm home. I'll go out and see the family." I start down the ramp and I see two rows of chieftains in their tribal clothes. I give 'em my smile and wave "Hey, baby, here I am." Well—them cats started mumbling and looking at me with such hate that I turned right around and got back into my safety belt! Hell,

Mississippi is rough but them cats in the Congo—they're mad at everybody. They don't never smile. They're still mad at us from old Tarzan movies.

Sammy goes from angst against Negroes to an Amos 'n' Andy–like reflection of a visit to Africa that could have been uttered by a Mississippi sheriff.

So he wanted it both ways.

He was the visible invisible man.

From Ralph Ellison's *Invisible Man:*

> It goes a long way back, some twenty years. All my life I had been looking for something, and everywhere I turned someone tried to tell me what it was. I accepted their answers too, though they were often in contradiction and even self-contradictory. I was naive. I was looking for myself and asking everyone except myself questions which I, and only I, could answer. It took me a long time and much painful boomeranging of my expectations to achieve a realization everyone else appears to have been born with: That I am nobody but myself.

The fuss about the lack of racial depth in the book? Well, Sammy, Jane, and Burt just didn't understand any of it. "We didn't write it as a racial book," says Boyar.

Roger Straus suggested to Burt that he open the book with the 1954 car crash. Sounded good, so he did:

> I turned on the radio, it filled the car with music and I heard my own voice singing, "Hey There." Oh God! What are the odds against turning on the radio to the exact station at the exact moment when a disc jockey is playing your first hit? For a second I was afraid that life was getting so good that something would have to happen to take it all away. But the car, the suite in Vegas, the hit record—and all they symbolized, were the start of a new life, and nobody had given it to me, so there wasn't anybody who could take it away. . . . We were building and any day now we'd really break wide open and I'd be a star.

He came back from the car crash. America liked comebacks. Hadn't Sinatra come back?

Between hardcover and paperback, *Yes I Can* remained on the best-seller lists for a full year. "It was different," Straus would admit. "It had legs." In a way, *Yes I Can,* one of the trickiest autobiographies ever written, legitimized Sammy even further. It is, however, a book without history. Written by two whites—accompanied, shall we say, by the Negro, Sammy, on piano—its very shallowness gave it a kind of slippery and escapist art. Sympathy-wise, it went for the jugular. He was just a Negro trying to partake of the American Dream. A converted Jew trying to love everybody. He loved blondes, but who didn't? Well, maybe those so-called Negro radicals H. Rap Brown and Stokely Carmichael and Dick Gregory didn't. But he didn't admire them anyway.

America liked moxie. America liked showmanship. Sammy might not always have liked what he saw when he looked in the mirror at himself, but he had a full vision of what America, on the other side of that mirror, liked.

Sammy, awhile back, before they decided on a title for his book, came up with one—*Don't Call Me Nigger.*

Call him anything else. White. Entertainer. Sammy. Smokey—which is actually what Sinatra called him. Jew. He so loved Jews. "He wanted to know what it was that made them survive," says Boyar.

Sammy was surviving. And he was surviving quite well in the suburbs of America. Out there, *Yes I Can* was hot. That is to say, it was being gobbled up in places like Waukegan, Illinois; Utica, New York; Bangor, Maine. "Out there"— in the suburbs, where the white citizenry resided—fascinated Sammy.

A whole year of the phenomenon of Sammy. Not only in the nightclubs— but in the high schools where teachers were assigning the book, and in those suburban households. Sammy was deliriously happy.

Draw!

Draw!

Draw!

"White folks loved him because he didn't threaten them," Dick Gregory believed. Roger Straus imagined some of the book's success was due to its fortuitous timing. "It's a story of America emerging from the postwar syndrome," he says. *Yes I Can* was indeed published during a time of turmoil in America's streets. "It came at a time when it was important for a black man to be a hero in his own time," Straus says.

Well, Frank Sinatra didn't have a book in the stores, an autobiography. Neither did Dean Martin or Peter Lawford. Nor Sidney Poitier or Harry Belafonte, for that matter. But Sammy did. Maybe they were too vain. Or maybe they weren't vain enough.

Jess Rand, living in the suburbs now, read his copy of *Yes I Can.* He had been with Sammy for years, had starved with him, shared the same hotel bed with him when the act was low on money. After reading *Yes I Can,* an upset Rand sent a telegram to Sammy. "No You Can't," it said.

Rand felt Sammy wanted everyone who read the book to feel sorry for Sammy Davis, Jr. "Bullshit" was Jess Rand's one-word opinion of little Sammy's book.

Rand was a huge fan of Clifford Odets. It was widely believed in Hollywood that Tony Curtis, playing the publicity maven in the 1957 film *The Sweet Smell of Success*—the script itself had been cowritten by Odets—adopted some of Rand's physical mannerisms, especially his incessant nail biting. Rand had no quarrel with the movie or with Curtis's screen portrayal. "My favorite line from that movie was," Rand says, "'The cat's in the bag, and the bag's in the river.'" The Odetsian line meant the secret—whatever it happened to be—was safe, having been drowned.

Months after publication of Sammy's book—with *Yes I Can* firmly on the best-seller lists now, prompting reevaluations all around—Rand bumped into Sammy. "I thought you were going to let me have first crack at a book," Rand said to Sammy, reminding him that the two had talked of an autobiography long before the Boyars' involvement.

"I couldn't lie to you," Sammy told Rand.

The cat's in the bag . . .

"There was so much we couldn't put in that book," says Burt Boyar, "because of the times."

Chapter 1

VAUDEVILLE DREAMS

lthough Sammy Davis, Jr., was descended from the dangers of the Negro plantation—this one located in rural North Carolina—it was the Cuban blood that would confuse him for a lifetime. Family members on the Cuban side would refer to it as "this Cuban thing." They meant the currency implied in a particular shade of skin color. And, linked to that, they meant the way love and resentment and distance and abandonment can infect any family, the way it could zoom in and out of mothers and sons and daughters, like a storm whooshing sideways on a horizontal force of its own, missing no one. So it was with his own family.

"My mother was born in San Juan," Sammy Davis, Jr., proclaimed. But it was a lie, and he knew it. She was born in New York City, of Cuban heritage. The Cuban ancestry, in the wake of the 1962 Cuban missile crisis, which saw President John F. Kennedy and Russian leader Nikita Khrushchev battle to a standoff over nuclear arsenals, made Sammy nervous. Anti-Cuban sentiment had swept the land. The Cuban-haters might begin to dislike him, and Sammy was not in the business of losing admirers and fans. So he flipped the Cuban history—telling relatives to keep quiet about it—with made-up Puerto Rican history. And what the hell, he used the invented history for a joke that made many laugh, all the while lancing piercingly into his own insecurities: "My mother was born in San Juan. So I'm Puerto Rican, Jewish, colored, and married to a white woman." A pause for the punch line: "When I move into a neighborhood, people start running four ways at the same time."

All his life, he hewed to a talent that enabled more than a few brilliantly tragic minstrel performers to endure: he had the mysterious gift to laugh away a deep, nearly unfathomable pain that finds one scratching for an identity while lost in the beguilingly lit world of make-believe.

· · ·

Sammy Davis, Jr.'s, maternal grandmother was born Luisa Valentina Aguiar on February 14, 1884, at 111 Thompson Street in lower Manhattan. Her father, Enrique Aguiar, had given her the middle name Valentina because she was born on Valentine's Day. Enrique, born in Cuba, often talked of family wealth and respect back home in his native land. He had handsome eyes, looked like a man who supremely believed in himself, and carried himself with a regal bearing. Connecticut-born Ida Henderson had a soft round face and long, lovely hair. Enrique first spotted her strolling past a Manhattan laundry and gave pursuit. The romance led to marriage. Both Enrique and Ida were extremely light-skinned and could have mixed with the white citizenry of Manhattan easily. They made a striking couple walking in afternoon sunshine. Her pregnancy greatly delighted both. Then came sudden tragedy: Ida died giving birth to Luisa.

Enrique Aguiar had been very much in love with his wife, and her death devastated him. He was now forced to ponder, alone, how he would care for his only child.

Enrique Aguiar vowed to hold on to Luisa, and was proud of himself for doing so. The dynamic imbued her with a fierce and independent spirit of her own. Over the years, Luisa's light complexion and flowing hair would come to strongly resemble her mother's. The two of them—Luisa would often talk of it in the decades to come—weathered the violent blizzard of 1888 in New York City. The city suffered $20 million in damages during that storm. Many, trudging home in feet-high snow, had been forced to find shelter in the city's jails.

Like many Cubans living in New York City in 1898, Enrique Aguiar couldn't have helped but notice the screaming newspaper headlines about the bombing of the U.S. ship *Maine* while it was anchored in Havana Harbor, on the night of February 15. In the blast, 254 soldiers died instantly; eight more died later. The *Maine* was in Havana on a fact-finding mission following constant reports of Cubans being abused by the Spanish. A little less than a month before the explosion, the Spanish military in Cuba destroyed the offices of four newspapers criticizing its presence. The attacks sparked rioting, which alerted American diplomatic officials on the island.

Spain had upward of 500,000 troops serving in the Philippines, Puerto Rico, and Cuba in a desperate attempt to keep its imperialist grip on the region. The infamous Alfonso Guards of Spain—who fancied wide-brimmed white sombreros—easily outdid the Cuban insurgents, and over the years, every rebellion was put down. There were times when the Alfonso Guards would line captured rebels up alongside a fort wall on bended knee—faces toward the wall, hands tied behind them—and raise their heavy rifles. The snap-crack of shots would fill the air, blood would color the dirt, and revolution would be stayed for a while longer.

When Christopher Columbus discovered the Caribbean in 1492, its lush vistas must have dazzled his senses. It was Diego Velázquez, however, who would, in 1511, conquer the island for Spain and launch the Spanish Conquest. In 1526, African slaves were brought into Cuba to work the coffee and sugar plantations. Throughout the decades there would be slave and Indian uprisings. The islands of Cuba intrigued antiabolitionists during the American Civil War. They had a peculiar dream of annexing it and turning it into a slaveholding state. Disease eventually vanquished the Indians of Cuba. (Sammy's maternal grandmother, Luisa Sanchez—née Aguiar—was still, as a centenarian, reminding family members: "I am Cuban—and Indian.") With the Indian gone—though still coursing through their blood—blacks and Hispanics made up the Cuban populace. The Spanish delighted in pitting darker-skinned Cubans against lighter-skinned Cubans, and in the Spanish press, there often appeared reports of dark-skinned Cubans plotting uprisings. It became known as *miedo al negro* ("fear of the black"). Light-skinned Cubans considered themselves members of the ruling class, and it was from that class that Enrique Aguiar, father of Luisa, hailed.

Spanish officials denied involvement in the bombing of the *Maine*. In the blast's aftermath, President William McKinley urged caution, but Theodore Roosevelt, his assistant secretary of the navy, did not. The hyperactive Roosevelt browbeat administration officials into readying for war. He sent cables, made speeches, and harangued those close to McKinley. The Hearst newspapers urged war. William Randolph Hearst had been lucky: Richard Harding Davis, a star American reporter, was in Havana when the *Maine* was hit. Davis wrote feverishly, and Hearst ran emotional headlines that all but urged America to action.

Hearst's headlines were one thing, the words of Vermont senator Redfield Proctor quite another. Politicians of both stripes respected Proctor. He was not a man to idly commit American forces to foreign soil. On March 17, Proctor—who was a close McKinley ally—addressed the Senate to report on his thoughts following a trip to Cuba in the explosion's aftermath. He talked of the presence of concentration camps in Cuba that were filled with thousands. He said the loss of the *Maine* was tragic enough, but went on to say that if any appeal were made for war, it must be made because of "the spectacle of a million and a half of people, the entire native population of Cuba, struggling for freedom and deliverance from the worst misgovernment of which I ever had knowledge." It was simple yet stunning oratory coming from a man of Proctor's revered caution. And it set loose whoops of war talk.

"*Cuba Libre,*" went one cry.

"Remember the *Maine* / To hell with Spain!" went another.

As screaming headlines merged with patriotic fervor, it was becoming clear that Americans now wanted the Spanish out of Cuba. Battleships were prepared, though the month of March fell from the calendar with guns still silent. Crisscrossing the nation's capital like a man possessed, Theodore Roosevelt predicted that the country would "have this war for the freedom of Cuba." Roosevelt rose before a podium at a Gridiron Dinner and saw that Senator Mark Hanna, who was steadfastly opposed to war, was in attendance. Roosevelt ran down a litany of reasons why it was necessary for America to enter into battle. He assailed business interests, who he felt were screaming against a declaration of war, and implied that Hanna himself was unduly sympathetic to those interests. Realizing the sentiments of those in attendance at the dinner were in his favor, Roosevelt turned to Hanna with a sneer and asked, sharply: "Now, Senator, may we please have war?"

Death pushes hearts in all directions. A man, any man, scarred by the unexpected calamity of family death might well seek a strange kind of adventure where the heat of life itself can be felt, minute by minute, hour upon hour.

On April 21 the United States declared war on Cuba. McKinley asked for volunteers. Enrique Aguiar, a widowed father, had to choose between country—Cuba—and daughter, Luisa. There were 125,000 who volunteered, and Enrique Aguiar was among them. He placed his fourteen-year-old daughter with a New York City foster family and promised her he would return. Then he left to go fight the Spaniards and free his countrymen.

We do not know if Enrique Aguiar fought at the Battle of El Caney, or at the campaign waged at Las Guasimas during the three-month Spanish-American War. We do not know if he was, at any time, in the vicinity of San Juan Hill with Teddy Roosevelt and his Rough Riders. We do not know if Enrique Aguiar, like other soldiers in the conflict, was felled by yellow fever or malaria while in a makeshift hospital on the island. But we do know this of Enrique Aguiar: he never returned home from the Spanish-American War to his daughter, Luisa.

For months after the campaign's end, Luisa Aguiar would gaze out windows and worry of her father's whereabouts. She would swear he was returning to her, as he said he would. She had no other family in New York City. Maybe he was arranging passage for her to Cuba. Or maybe the next knock at the door would be his knuckles rapping. Or maybe a messenger was on his way just now with tickets for her from New York to Tampa, where he was simply collecting himself in one of the city's hotels, as so many men did coming and going from Cuba. She hoped and wished and dreamed, and brushed away reports of his likely death. But there was no messenger, no telegram, even as young Luisa continued to tell acquaintances that she knew her father was returning to her. She was Catholic; she held to her faith.

But time passed, and it was as if Enrique Aguiar had vanished from the face of the earth without a trace. If Luisa Aguiar's world hadn't already cracked enough—boarding with a foster family she did not like—the presumed death of her father must have been an unimaginable blow. She couldn't quite let go, however, of the vision of her father striding into her eyesight. "My daddy," she would begin conversations in the years to come, before trailing off. The habit, according to her granddaughters, would remain with her into the tenth decade of her life. (Luisa Sanchez lived to be 112 years old.)

There was a powerful reason Luisa Sanchez did not like her foster family: they beat her. Welts and deep bruises appeared on her head. For her grand-daughters, listening to the horror stories became a huge part of their upbring-ing. First they would hear all about Enrique and his disappearance. "She never saw him again," says Gloria Williams, the granddaughter, "and that's the thing that made her cry." Then Gloria would be treated to tales of Luisa's sufferings. "She would point to her head, parting her hair, to show bruises. She would say, 'Look. Look!' " recalls Williams.

Fearful of running alone into the streets of New York City, young Luisa Aguiar—a beauty, her skin a soft milky white—couldn't help but hope she'd meet someone to take her away from her foster family. That person was Marco Sanchez, himself of Cuban ancestry. Marco Sanchez sold Cuban cigars. Some-times he bartered them for liquor, which he sold—and drank in heavy quanti-ties, as well. Their marriage was tempestuous. Still, Luisa gave birth to four children, but only two—Julia, born in 1899, and Elvera, born in 1905—survived beyond infancy. The heavy-drinking Marco Sanchez didn't survive long either—he died of cirrhosis of the liver, leaving behind a young widow and two daughters.

First her father, now her husband. Once again, feelings of being abandoned and left adrift washed over Luisa Sanchez. But she was determined that such feelings would neither overwhelm nor defeat her.

By 1915, Luisa had found an apartment in Harlem, at 47 West 129th Street. Waves of Negroes had recently started migrating to upper Manhattan. It wasn't that Luisa followed the plight—or the momentum—of the Negro in New York. In fact, Luisa Sanchez did not keep company with Negroes. Her move to Harlem was purely for economical reasons. The rents were cheaper than in lower Manhattan. Sanchez found work as a personal maid and dresser for Laurette Taylor, a much-admired Broadway actress. Born, like Sanchez, in New York City in 1884, Taylor had made her New York stage debut at the age of nineteen in a production of *From Rags to Riches*. For years she toured the country in stock companies, honing her craft. On December 21, 1912, she opened on Broadway at the Cort Theatre—it was that theater's grand

opening—in *Peg o' My Heart,* an Irish family drama written by Hartley Manners. Taylor played Peg, and the role made her a star. Sarah Bernhardt, the
great French actress, came to see it and predicted that "within five years" Taylor would become "the foremost actress" in America. The play ran for 1,250
performances. Taylor had other memorable roles, in *The Devil, The Great John
Ganton,* and *The Ringmaster.* Her reputation soared. Directors wooed her; she
was an incandescent presence on a stage.

Being a personal maid for Taylor came with perks: Sanchez traveled with
the actress, dined with her in fine restaurants. There was just enough color in
Luisa's complexion that there were times she'd be mistaken for a nonwhite—
perhaps Mediterranean. She took being called Negro or Puerto Rican as the
worst kind of insult. "We don't serve Negroes," a restaurateur once said to
Sanchez. "I don't speak English," she replied, unrolling her stock answer. "I'm
Cuban."

Meeting other actors and actresses—John Barrymore had seemed taken
with her beauty—delighted Luisa. Still, she was not one to swoon easily over
men or their advances. Her physical beauty was one thing, but inside she
seemed possessed of something hard and impenetrable. She did not have a
timid tongue, and she was noticeably temperamental. Suitors found out
quickly enough she was fiercely independent. Two men, on separate occasions,
had each provided Luisa Sanchez with the services of an automobile. Grateful
though she may have been, she married neither man, though both had hoped
their generosity might move her heart. Relatives believed she had been so
shaken by her first marriage that she forever lost faith in the institution.

Luisa Sanchez arrived home early evenings with stories of Broadway glitter,
sometimes bearing gifts from Laurette Taylor for her daughters. It is little wonder, then, that sisters Julia and Elvera became wide-eyed when it came to the
world of entertainment. They gazed longingly at pictures of show folk. Talk of
show business seeped inside of them.

By the time Elvera Sanchez celebrated her tenth birthday, it was apparent
that she was becoming the opposite of Julia, her shy older sister. In fact, the
characters of the Sanchez girls could not have been more different. Elvera
spoke her mind with an edge and in a rush of words. She cared not at all about
consequences. In temperament, she was her mother. Elvera went to PS 89, and,
from there, to a Catholic school. But school and teachers bored Elvera. She was
impetuous, a free spirit. In the eighth grade, she grew increasingly restless. "I
went to Catholic school and I was kind of bad and they put me out," she would
recall. Her sister, Julia, had a work permit. Elvera took the permit and forged
her own name on it. With that, she began looking for work. She figured the
theater—familiar territory to her because of her mother's work—was as good
a place as any to begin. Her hunch proved smart.

Elvera got a job as an errand girl, working for a makeup artist out of the Astor Building, located on Broadway. She delivered packages around Manhattan. And as she ambled along the streets, she couldn't help but notice the busy world spinning right before her eyes: big noisy streetcars rumbling by; the hustle-bustle of pedestrians, of businessmen and perfume-scented women. "One day I went all the way down to Fourteenth Street to deliver a package. On the way I stopped at the Automat and ate up all my lunch money because I knew I was going to get a tip from this lady on Fourteenth Street. Well, she fooled me! I walked from Fourteenth Street up to 137th Street! I didn't know that I could have asked a cop for a nickel." She'd sit alone in a dinette and order a slice of pie and gawk. She'd stroll the dark streets of Manhattan, a solo journeyer.

The Sanchezes' move to Harlem had come at a fortunate time. Shortly after their arrival—the community had recently gone from mostly Italian and Jewish to mostly Negro, in one of the more dazzling real estate upheavals in New York history—Harlem came alive with both Negro culture and pride. World War I unleashed some of that pride, as the young men of Harlem went off to Europe to fight. (At the war's outset, actress Laurette Taylor and her personal maid and assistant, Luisa Sanchez, found themselves stranded in London because of the conflict. Eventually they sailed home.)

America's doughboys entered World War I with nary a moment to waste. Germany had nearly broken the back of France before it was pushed back by American and European forces. It was the war of General John J. "Black Jack" Pershing, who had once chased the Apache through Arizona, and who had once led Negro soldiers in Cuba: "Black Jack" was meant as an epithet; he didn't seem to mind. It was the war of young Ernest Hemingway, far from famous yet, who served with the Italian army and got hit by shrapnel: by war's end, he'd have plenty of stories to put into the novels that would come. And it was the war of James Reese Europe, revered around Manhattan before the war as a society musician partial to wearing white suits and shoes to match. Europe signed up with the 369th Infantry Regiment from Harlem. (Among members of that outfit would be a vaudevillian by the name of Will Mastin, who was destined to discover Sammy Davis, Jr..)

The Germans referred to Harlem's soldiers as "bloodthirsty black men." The French were more delicate: "hellfighters," they called them. On February 17, 1919, the men, who had fought so gallantly—more than six consecutive months in the muddy trenches—staged a shoulder-to-shoulder march up Fifth Avenue into Harlem. They were thirteen hundred strong, and Lieutenant James Reese Europe—survivor of a German poison-gas attack in the war—was leading them. They came home having been awarded the Croix de Guerre by the French. They came home having led the Allied march through mud to the Rhine. And they came home highstepping down Fifth Avenue to a drum-roll and to women with tears in their eyes. Press baron William Randolph Hearst and a bevy of other dignitaries were among the onlookers.

"The tide of khaki and black turned west on 110th Street to Lenox Avenue, then north again into the heart of Harlem," a chronicler of that march wrote. "At 125th Street, the coiled, white rattlesnake insignia of the regiment hissed from thousands of lapels, bonnets, and windows. A field of pennants, flags, banners, and scarves thrashed about the soldiers like elephant grass in a gale, threatening to engulf them. In front of the unofficial reviewing stand at 130th Street, Europe's sixty-piece band broke into 'Here Comes My Daddy' to the extravagant delight of the crowd."

Before war's beginning there had been those who wondered—given the Negroes' low standing on the socioeconomic ladder—whether, if called to fight, they would give their all. There now seemed little reason to ponder again the Negro sentiment concerning patriotism. "Black Jack" knew it: the Negro fought. Harlemites talked about the march for weeks on end. They would also come to mourn the fate of James Reese Europe. Less than three months after his triumphant march into Harlem, Europe was stabbed in the neck with a penknife by a fellow musician, who had started an argument with him while in Boston. Europe thought the wound was minor, but he bled to death hours after the stabbing. He received a public funeral in New York City. "Before Jim Europe came to New York the colored man knew nothing but Negro dances and porter's work," a grieving man told the *New York Tribune*. "All that has been changed. Jim Europe was the living open sesame to the colored. . . . He took them from their porter's places and raised them to positions of importance as real musicians."

The downtown Negro churches that had relocated to Harlem after World War I—bringing their congregations with them—found opportunistic real estate agents, who began to welcome Negroes to Harlem in larger numbers than ever.

There seemed to be much to enjoy in the growing Harlem. In time, scores of musicians and dancers began to arrive. "The Negro race is dancing itself to death," a Harlem minister had earlier said of the goings-on.

It was the neon glare of the Harlem theaters, especially the Lafayette and Lincoln Theatres, that soon caught the eye of the young Elvera Sanchez. You could look up at the Lafayette and notice, against the darkened sky, the word "VAUDEVILLE" twinkling in white neon light. The Lincoln had previously hosted white vaudeville acts for its white customers, but when the Negro drama critic Lester Walton leased it, he opened the theater to everyone. It was the men who dressed in snappy suits and raccoon coats and the women who wore silk that made Elvera pause in her Friday and Saturday walks along Harlem's streets. In teeming Harlem there were garden-rooftop parties. There were tango teas. Spindly legged dancers were doing the Texas Tommy, the turkey trot. From every nightclub, music spilled forth. Elvera was mesmerized. Soon enough—and for the first time in her life—she found herself inside a dance hall. It was called the Hoofers Club. "I had never danced," she recalled. And now she was hooked. She had a dancer's lithe physique, long arms and long legs. She had large and pretty eyes, a prominent nose. At the Hoofers Club, Elvera became a habitué. The owners of the club were in the habit of sending out invitations to musicians to come and play. Their jam sessions were known to be exuberant. "You knew," someone remarked about Coleman Hawkins playing his saxophone at the Hoofers Club, "he'd come in to carve somebody." (The lingo simply meant Hawkins would dazzle everyone with his horn.)

The grapevine of Negro America was hardly brittle. It held fast and strong east to west, north to south. The word went out: Negro Harlem was alive.

Duke Ellington arrived in 1922 from the nation's capital. Born to middle-class parents, Ellington had been playing the piano since the age of seven. In New York City, he joined Elmer Snowden's band, a band he was soon destined to take over. Fats Waller was playing before the curtain rose on vaudeville shows at the Lincoln on West 135th Street. The Tennessee-born Bessie Smith was wailing. Smith, who drove her very own customized car, recorded for the Columbia Record Company. "Up in Harlem ev'ry Saturday night / When the high brows git together it's just too tight," went one of her ditties. A stretch along West 133rd—just four blocks from the Sanchezes—became known as "Jungle Alley," for its number of nightspots. One hot spot, known as the Clam House, featured a performer by the name of "Gladys Bentley." A young Harlem artist, not yet famous—although fame would find Romare Bearden, as it would find so many others beginning to gather—would recall: " 'Gladys Bentley' was a woman dressed as a man. You also had a male performer who called himself 'Gloria Swanson.' So Harlem was like Berlin, where they had such things going on in cabarets at the time."

It wasn't long at all before whites began cruising into Harlem, especially after the downtown clubs closed for the night. In the deep nighttime, Harlem opened like a flower. You might, on any night of the week, catch a glimpse of Tallulah Bankhead or Joan Crawford or Hoagy Carmichael or Artie Shaw emerging from one of the hip nightspots.

But the new arrivals—writers and poets and painters—seemed to be non-stop indeed. Langston Hughes showed up in 1921. W. E. B. Du Bois would publish Hughes's soul-stirring poem "The Negro Speaks of Rivers" that very year. From then on, it seemed, the Negro in America had found a new muse. Hughes, caramel-colored and possessing an easy grin, took to hanging out at the Harlem Y with a parrot atop his shoulder.

A young girl—a young Elvera Sanchez—waltzing along the streets of Harlem couldn't help but become intoxicated by it all, the whiff of culture, the aroma of a certain kind of exalted nightlife. Eric Walrond, another young Negro writer new to the scene, thought of Harlem as "a sociological El Dorado."

If there was one individual who might have touched the consciousness of every young and excitable Negro girl in Harlem who dreamed of show business, it was surely Florence Mills. Mills had broken numerous racial barriers in New York theaters. She was the first to headline a show at the Palace Theatre downtown. Daughter of former slaves, she performed as a pickaninny with white vaudevillians as a child. She endured backbreaking working conditions, but seemed suffused with a pride to uplift Negroes through her entertaining. In 1921 she had her breakthrough in *Shuffle Along,* a black musical written by the team of Noble Sissle—who had been a sergeant in the 369th Regiment—and Eubie Blake. White audiences had never seen anything like *Shuffle Along,* melding, as it did, Negro music and dance in a sophisticated manner.

But swoon as she might, Elvera was at war with her show-business dreams and her mother, Luisa, who felt smothered by Negro Harlem. Luisa Sanchez spent her time in the white world with Laurette Taylor. Luisa Sanchez traveled. She dined at the table with gifted thespians. These were not pastimes—travel and dining—she engaged in with Negroes. Negro New York with its theaters and salons might have spoken of culture indeed, but it was not Luisa's culture. She felt her culture much closer to white America than Negro America. And yet, Elvera Sanchez saw and heard so much of this growing Negro Harlem. It intoxicated her: "Right around the corner where the Abyssinian Church is now was the Marcus Garvey Building. They had a low building. I could get into my kitchen window and look into 138th Street and I could see all the buildings," she later said. She frequented the movie houses along Lenox Avenue with her girlfriends. "We'd go there on Saturday, and it was five cents. You could sit there all day long for five cents," Sanchez recalled.

A significant part of the Harlem scene was now a heady mingling of poets, dancers, writers. The unknown Arna Bontemps had a liberal arts degree from Pacific Union College in California. That got him a job in a Los Angeles post office. That is, until the grapevine touched him about Harlem. Bontemps quit the post office and came east. In time he would make his mark as a literary figure. Bontemps's first glimpses of Harlem dazzled him. "In some places the autumn of 1924 may have been an unremarkable season," Bontemps would rhapsodize. "In Harlem, it was like a foretaste of paradise. A blue haze descended at night and with it strings of fairy lights on the broad avenues."

It was in that blue haze of 1924 that Elvera Sanchez would get her first breaks in the world of show business. She joined the chorus at the famed Lafayette Theatre. Her sister, Julia, was already working the chorus-line circuit. They, like so many others, had their dreams, however brittle.

So now—unto themselves, without husbands or father—all three of the

Sanchez women found themselves earning a paycheck in the make-no-promises world of show business.

The Lafayette—with its admired Edwardian decor—was only five blocks from the Sanchez family apartment. It was widely known that the Lafayette played host to some remarkable talent. Ethel Waters had appeared on its stage, as had entertainers Bennie Moten, Fletcher Henderson, and Stepin' Fetchit. Fetchit was a curious talent, epitomizing, with a fey smile and a roll of the eyes, the passed-along stereotype of the pickaninny. Fetchit entered vaudeville in 1914, performing in medicine shows. His real name was Lincoln Theodore Monroe Perry; the names of past presidents enraptured his mother. He took his stage name from a racehorse ("Step and Fetch It"), then wrapped the name around his act: "Step 'n' Fetchit: Two Dancing Fools from Dixie."

"We worked with a man named Addison Carey and Charlie Davis," Sanchez would recall of her showbiz beginnings. "They had two choruses. One worked in New York, one went on the road." Carey and Davis were known to slip downtown to Radio City Music Hall and watch the dancers on its stage closely, all the while taking mental notes, then hustle back to teach their Harlem dancers the steps they had seen on the Radio City stage. Carey and Davis worked their chorus girls hard, sending them hopping between various theaters. From the Lafayette they might hustle over to the Harlem Opera House, and from there to the Apollo. The two men had created a road show in a ten-block area. The work for the showgirls could be backbreaking. "We would do a new show on a Monday and would do it Tuesday and Wednesday as well. We'd start rehearsing on Wednesday night and Thursday for the following week. But you had to remember what you were doing during the week," Elvera would recall. There was nary a moment to grab anything to eat between shows.

The chorus girls—some of New York's most beautiful young women—had to know a variety of dance steps, and Elvera did. But her specialty was the soft-shoe, a seductive glide across the dance floor in step with the other dancers. The girls in her chorus were doing eight shows a day, and yet, hardly anyone complained. The hours were long, but the work was thrilling. Thrilling to catch a glimpse of Ellington's smile, to see some Negro musicians lined up— your mailing address in their pockets—ready to hit the road, their long coats as kind on their backs as capes. Thrilling to wade into show parties, to hear the illicit whispers, to taste the chilled champagne. But most exciting to simply be upon the stage as the velvet curtains parted and the music rose.

It was all so much better, Elvera thought, than schoolteachers and books. It seemed the very flip side of her Catholic girlhood, and she relished it, believing she was getting important life lessons here, in Harlem, on its stages: "Show business teaches you," she said.

Many believed the Cotton Club—although its junglelike decor raised eyebrows—to be the swankiest club in Harlem. Negro boxer Jack Johnson had owned the nightclub when it was called Club Deluxe. Owney Madden, a gangster, was proprietor now. Elvera Sanchez would stand outside the club, and a tingle would come over her. She couldn't get inside, at least not as a patron: the Cotton Club had a whites-only policy for customers. Negro singers, dancers, and musicians could appear on its stage, but they could not go through the club's front door to see a show. Still, merely standing outside its doors mesmerized her.

In her dancing job, Elvera Sanchez made $18.50 a week. It wasn't much, but it was enough to keep a chorus girl's dreams alive. The girls walked the Harlem streets in twos and threes. They had a cachet there. They were ogled. And invited to nice restaurants. Sweet notes from suitors arrived in their mailboxes. You could have knocked Elvera Sanchez over with a silk scarf from one of Harlem's fancy stores. "I remember I used to work the Apollo," she recalled. "We'd leave, go to a bar. I'd walk from 125th and Eighth to 129th at night, by myself. Not scared one bit."

She worked with the Duke Ellington band, and the Jimmie Lunceford band. Sometimes eight shows a day. "At the end of one show you'd be downstairs and you'd hear—fifteen minutes!—and you'd have to get ready for the next show."

Not long into her life as a chorus girl, Elvera Sanchez met Will Mastin of Holiday in Dixie, a vaudeville troupe Mastin had organized. The Mastin revue consisted of singers, a comedian, chorus girls, and dancing boys. Mastin, a shrewd gatherer of eclectic talent who had been raised in and around minstrel shows himself, offered Elvera a tryout. She won a job in his revue.

Elvera's mother, Luisa, had long been skeptical of young girls leaving home to travel the show-business circuit. She had been in the company of show folk long enough to know that there were men who led young women astray. There were men who whispered and made promises while twirling fedoras in their hands, and who stood at the bottom steps of a brownstone and promised the world. "I don't want you to go in show business because you are going to bring back a baby!" her mother had warned her from the earliest. "If I do, I'll be married," Elvera promised her.

Who could have told the young Elvera Sanchez that she would go from running errands up and down Broadway to rubbing shoulders one day with the likes of Duke Ellington and Jimmy Lunceford and dancing just inches from them on a stage? That she would hobnob with actors and actresses and hear their tales of a life in lights? Men paid to see her shimmy on the stages of Harlem. She wore silky and satiny garments that made her feel rich. She floated between theaters, hopping from chorus to chorus with drink in hand and her lips painted red. It was her job to dance her nights away, so she did. It was just the chorus, true enough, but she had dreams of becoming a singer also. And who dared say she couldn't be plucked from the stage and wind up another Sophie Tucker or Florence Mills or Ethel Waters? Why, Waters— "Sweet Mama Stringbean," they called her—had once been a maid, scrubbing dishes and washing clothes before she became a vaudeville star.

Elvera Sanchez dreamed beyond Harlem. Preening herself in a mirror, she was as game as any chorus girl in allowing her imagination to gallop. So, as 1924 came to a close, Elvera Sanchez—a willowy and fearless dreamer— packed her bags and joined the assemblage of talent with Will Mastin and hit the road. She was nineteen years old.

They traveled throughout New York State, into Pennsylvania, along the eastern seaboard, wherever they could find work. Elvera wore a small close-fitting and elegant hat, and she carried a long wool coat for winter winds. She carried makeup kits, shoes, and as many clothes as she could bundle up. She had been in show business for all of one year, and here she was, out on the road, a trouper. "He played all the fine hotels," she would remember of Mastin. "When I was with them, the dressing rooms were beautiful." And the theaters were fine as well. "Little kids would come out and look at the comedians with blackface on. The people were so nice." Her heart was light and gay; she was happy.

In a way, all of the members of Mastin's revue were fugitives from convention. They were a vaudeville troupe roaring through the 1920s. They could have been slaving away in cotton fields, or factories. The men could have been swaying on a Pullman train instead of a stage. They were grateful to be hitched to Mastin, and he kept them working.

They rehearsed on cold stages, giggled themselves warm. They tried new dance steps on one another, added skits to their shows. They ate in restaurants that catered to Negroes and wrapped delicacies in soft napkins to carry away with them. They idled at the homes of Negro strangers when invited and shared gossip, show-business news. They nursed one another through colds and fevers and back pains. They wrote letters home at night by lamplight and lamented that they could not provide a return address because they were on the move. They sent money home when they could, the better to assure family all was fine on the road of show business. They kept an ear out for places where recent lynchings had occurred—Mastin phoning ahead in whispered tones or sending telegrams—and avoided those towns. When troupe members weren't performing, they read newspapers, ironed their stage outfits, strolled around the unfamiliar towns, window-shopped.

It was inevitable that members would get to know each other, that friendships would deepen. And, of course, the possibility of romance was real. Just months into her show-business journey, Elvera Sanchez began an affair with

Sammy Davis, one of Mastin's lead dancers. "Sharp as he wanted to be," she would say of dancer Davis.

Sammy Davis arrived in New York in 1921 from Wilmington, North Carolina, with an eye on show business. His exit from Wilmington had not been smooth. He was fond of hats, particularly fedoras. In Wilmington, in a men's clothing shop, he tried on a dress hat. A more obedient Negro male might not have done such a thing in a white-owned store in the South. Davis was immediately scolded and ordered to take the hat off. "The hell with your hat," he said to the owner, tossing the hat to the floor, striding out the door. "The man wanted to have him arrested," recalls Charles Fisher, Davis's cousin and a resident of Wilmington. Davis went home and told Rosa, his mother, that the police might come looking for him. His mother told him he had no choice but to leave town. There was urgency in her voice. Like many other Negroes in Wilmington, Rosa Davis knew well the events of 1898.

The town was an oddity of southern towns, inasmuch as many Negroes— their power strengthened by voting Republican and bonding with the Populist bloc—held important elective positions. Of the ten aldermen in 1897, five were Negro. White Democrats intended to oust Negroes at the polls in the 1898 election, voicing concerns that so many Negroes in city government "emboldens bad Negroes to display their evil, impudent, and mean natures." Alex Manly was editor of the *Wilmington Record,* which catered to the city's Negroes. He was not a shy man. "Our experience among poor white people in the country teaches us that the women of that race are not any more particular in the matter of clandestine meetings with colored men, than are the white men with the colored women." The column elicited visceral anger on the part of whites. Just before election day, it was reprinted and distributed all over the town. It had impact: Negroes were voted out of office. Tensions began to rise; such was the brewing fear of more backlash that Manly fled town. This was wise; a mob torched his office. Negroes armed themselves and, in the Brooklyn section of the city—where Rosa Davis resided with her family—came face to face with armed whites days after the election. The first to be injured was a white man, William Mayo. A volley of shots was then unleashed, from both sides. More whites joined, and Negroes found themselves quickly outnumbered. A state militia was summoned. Negroes who could get away fled into cemeteries, the woods, anywhere for cover. It was estimated that two dozen Negroes were killed. In the aftermath, scores of Negroes left town on trains. By 1900, all the elected officials in Wilmington were white.

Rosa Davis wasted no time in pressing money to her son's palm following the hat incident and putting him on an Atlantic Coastline train to New York.

In New York City, Sammy Davis found odd jobs—among them elevator operator—before entering and winning several dance contests. His reputation led him to Will Mastin. Onstage Mastin and Davis quickly recognized each other's talents. They were elegant dancers, doing quick steps, followed by a slowing-down process of feet movement, only to speed up once again. Onstage, Davis specialized in the Charleston, which had swept the country in the early 1920s. It had become so popular that Charleston contests were held in many cities, spindly legged men and women working themselves into a feverish sweat. (George Raft, a young Broadway dancer, was reputed to be the fastest Charleston dancer in the country in the early 1920s. Raft would go on to make a name for himself playing murderously suave gangsters in film.)

As heralded by Mastin as Davis may have been out there on the road, Elvera was not at all shy about introducing him to other dance steps. Davis was six foot three, with perfect teeth—the smile warm but show-business slick—and had a deep baritone of a voice. His skin was dark and smooth. He had a proud posture, but also relaxed—like a military man gliding loosely and knowingly around a speakeasy. He carried a lovely gray fedora. There was something of the cad about Sammy Davis, and he seemed to know it. Women came after him, and he welcomed the attention.

Elvera Sanchez and Sammy Davis talked and talked as they traveled down country roads, earth rolling beneath them and the countryside passing by, on the way to another town and theater. His smile fell across her like autumn light. Meals and laughter were both shared, as were tales of Harlem and its still-running popular stage shows. They thumbed through newspapers together. Elvera found herself watching him from the wings of yet another stage in yet another town. He'd sidle up close to her as they exited yet another theater. He'd bundle her up on chilly mornings, fetch food for her. They posed side by side as pictures were snapped. He looked handsome; she looked as carefree as a flapper girl.

Within months, Luisa Sanchez's premonition had come true: Elvera was pregnant, and the father of her unborn child was dancer Sammy Davis. Luisa Sanchez had never laid eyes on the man. To stave off some of the shame of being pregnant and unwed, Elvera eloped with the dancer. (It was not unusual for chorus girls to be spirited away for abortions while on the road, but Elvera's Catholicism forbade any consideration of an abortion.) The two quickly married in Washington, D.C., in a bare-bones courthouse ceremony. Mastin allowed her to continue to dance as long as she could: she needed the money.

If there was a consistent theme among the Sanchez women, it was independence—and their ability to survive. They tiptoed across no streams, choosing to run and splash where others might have gingerly stepped.

Only when Elvera could no longer dance because of her pregnancy did she return home to Harlem, leaving her husband on the road.

She returned as Elvera Davis. And when she came back to Harlem in 1925, Harlem was still in the swooning grip of its cultural renaissance. A new book was arriving in bookstores called *The New Negro*. Published by Boni & Liveright—publishers of Sigmund Freud and T. S. Eliot—the book, which garnered immediate national attention, featured an array of Negro writers and essayists, among them Langston Hughes, Jean Toomer, Jessie Faucet, Zora Neale Hurston, W. E. B. Du Bois, and Countee Cullen. It seemed nothing less than a gathering of the best Negro talent in the country. The book had its genesis in March of that year when the entire issue of *Survey Graphic*—an awkwardly titled sociology magazine—had been devoted to writings about race. The editor of the magazine, as well as the book, was Alain Locke. "Negro life is not only establishing new contacts and founding new centers, it is finding a new soul," Locke wrote in the book's foreword. "We have, as the heralding sign, an unusual outburst of creative expression. There is renewed race spirit that consciously and proudly sets itself apart. Justly then, we may speak of this book, embodying these ripening forces as culled from the first fruit of the Negro Renaissance."

There was a feeling that Locke and his literary brethren had, at long last, offered the keys to unlock the pent-up genius of a people. The birthing of such a movement seemed an almost mystical convergence of raw talent, liberalized theater owners, poets, protesters, and gadflies. The sublime was as beautiful as the irreverent. It was Zora Neale Hurston—the young Negro writer from Florida who would cull much from Harlem—who coined the beguiling term "Niggerati." DuBois, the social critic who had launched his own literary reputation with the 1903 publication of *The Souls of Black Folk,* had his own niche, editing the *Crisis,* the influential magazine of the National Association for the Advancement of Colored People (NAACP). Countee Cullen, Claude McKay, James Weldon Johnson, and Langston Hughes were all working on booklength projects.

The New Negro movement, to be sure, had its white patrons, none more iconoclastic than Carl Van Vechten. Van Vechten dressed beautifully, wrote novels, and contributed articles to *Vanity Fair.* A native Iowan, Van Vechten was both married and homosexual. He collected photos of Negro males in the nude and was rarely without his silver flask. His downtown apartment—adorned with eye-catching artwork—attracted the likes of Theodore Dreiser, Paul Robeson, Tallulah Bankhead, and George Gershwin. It was Van Vechten who brought Langston Hughes's poetry to the attention of *Vanity Fair* editors, and it was Van Vechten who introduced many a Negro writer to downtown publishers. He allowed as to how his attraction to Negroes and their way of life had been "almost an addiction." One Van Vechten party was notable for a much-talked-about outburst. Blues singer Bessie Smith was there. Generous amounts of alcohol had been consumed. Farina Marinoff, wife of Van Vechten, tried to kiss Smith as she was leaving. A simple, friendly kiss. "Get the fuck away from me. I ain't never heard of such shit!" Smith bellowed, twisting her body, making a fuss.

Harlem seemed a kind of loose and fevered narcotic. And everyone seemed to want a little piece of the place—to hear Ellington's band, to see Ethel Waters, to read Countee Cullen and Langston Hughes, to listen to big Coleman Hawkins blow his sax, to spy the wondrous chorus girls in all their beauty. "Damn it man," the white writer Sherwood Anderson wrote to H. L. Mencken of the mystique of Harlem, "if I could really get inside the niggers and write about them with some intelligence, I'd be willing to be hanged later and per-haps would be."

Elvera Sanchez would have to wait to partake of Harlem's glories now. She had a baby to deliver.

Pregnant women in Harlem went to Harlem General Hospital to have their babies. In the early 1920s the hospital, referred to as "the butcher shop," had come under attack by Negroes for what many felt was mistreatment. It was often overcrowded. At times patients lay for hours on gurneys in hallways. After heated protest, the hospital hired its first Negro doctors in 1925.

It was at Harlem General Hospital on December 8, 1925, that twenty-year-old Elvera Davis gave birth to her first child, a son. She named him Sammy, after his father. Shortly after the birth, Elvera took her son home, where she took up temporary residence with her mother. There was something rather strange about the newborn child of Elvera and Sammy Davis: he had facial hair. No one knew what it meant. Those who saw the oddity of it were both bemused and perplexed. There were superstitious friends of the Sanchez family who believed the facial hair meant the newborn was destined to become a prophet.

They were young parents, and they were hoofers. The father was out on the road, earning a living. Thus their first child was suddenly webbed between their dreams and—for the moment at least—suspended in the shadows of those very dreams: a Jazz Age baby.

Elvera Davis's sister, Julia, and their mother, Luisa, helped her during those early weeks of motherhood. But Elvera was not very keen on taking on the duties of a young mother. In fact, she itched to get back on the road. Will Mastin kept a spot in the revue for her, and, not long after the birth of her child, she went back out on the road. Her infant son was left with family friends in Brooklyn.

The Mastin vaudeville troupe kept moving. Mastin not only produced the shows—which meant, among other duties, he dispensed the pay and meal money—he acted in them. A production in 1927 was titled *Struttin' Hannah from Savannah*. In this particular production Elvera Sanchez appeared in the credits as "El Vera" Sanchez, a stylistic flourish having suddenly been added to the presentation of her name. *Struttin' Hannah*—featuring a sixteen-member cast (among them a contortionist and banjoist) and an eight-member chorus—was about a couple bickering over a particular number to be played in the numbers racket. The action took place in both New Orleans and Harlem. There was chicanery, an arrest, and marital discord. There was, of course, a villain. He was played by Will Mastin.

Back in New York, Sammy, the baby, remained with friends of Elvera's. The arrangement bothered Rosa Davis, the baby's paternal grandmother. Rosa—who knew very little about her new daughter-in-law—worked as a cook for a white family in Brooklyn. A large and stout woman, she was also no-nonsense. The streets of New York could be tricky and dangerous, so Rosa Davis carried a small pistol with her wherever she went. "I never saw Rosa without the little gold-plated pistol in her pocket," remembers Virginia Capehart, her friend. Her grandchild was now with strangers, and the more time passed—days and days, then weeks—the more pained she became concerning his whereabouts. So one day Rosa went to retrieve the child.

She spent a fretful amount of time knocking on the wrong doors. When she finally found the right apartment, she was aghast at what she saw. Little Sammy was on the floor. He was dirty. A dog jumped about. Rosa took the baby over to a sink, put her pistol on the countertop, warned that not a soul should interrupt her, and bathed the baby. Then she clothed him and took him home to Harlem with her.

Times were indeed hard for the North Carolina–born Rosa Davis. She was estranged from her husband and rarely mentioned the man. Now and then, friends of her dancer son would drop by to slip a little money to her. She hoarded her dollar bills and often struggled to make ends meet. But she stayed too busy to fret about financial woes. She sold moonshine on the side, at times strolling with the baby buggy—little Sammy inside—down the streets of Harlem with bottles of the moonshine noisily bouncing around beneath the child, where they were hidden.

Rosa hardly minded the presence of her grandchild. Matter of fact, she doted on him. There was a Victrola record player in her apartment. She would play records, and little Sammy, holding on to the bed, would try to catch a beat, to take a step. She would beam at the tiny child, his sticklike legs bending to the music's syncopated rhythm. When Rosa had to run a quick errand and had no one to watch Sammy, she would simply lay him down on the floor, nail his gown to it, grab her keys, then rush out, hurrying back as fast as she could.

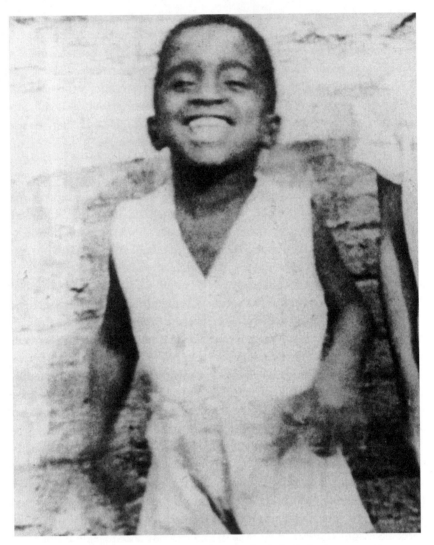

One of the few surviving pictures of Sammy Davis, Jr., before he was swept up into vaudeville. The smile seems so unrehearsed, so genuinely childlike. Yet, it also leaps at the camera.   (COURTESY STEVE BLAUNER)

During her forays back into Harlem to see her son, Elvera sensed a coldness from her mother-in-law. They never established a rapport. Elvera believed it had something to do with the prickly and quietly explosive issue of skin color.

Although no one born had any choice in the matter, skin color was a rich commodity in Harlem, and in many other Negro enclaves in America. The lighter the skin on a particular Negro, it seemed, the less threatening that Negro was seen in society. Elvera and the showgirls she traveled with often carried skin-lightening cream with them. During auditions, the eyes of the white nightclub owners seemed to land quickly upon lighter-skinned dancers. More often than not, it took a huge amount of poise to deal with the conundrum.

The arc of the dilemma could be traced back to slavery, when dark-skinned Negroes were, for the most part, resigned to field work, while light-skinned Negroes were given the "better" duties such as cook and maid on the plantation. (It all sprang, of course, from miscegenation, whites having had their fill of black women during slavery. Someone once asked President Warren Harding about rumors of black blood in his family: "How do I know? Maybe one of my ancestors jumped the fence.")

It was no coincidence that many of the chorus girls in Harlem—like Elvera Davis—were light-skinned. Advertisements appeared in Harlem newspapers—and in many other Negro publications across the country, such as the *Chicago Defender,* the *Pittsburgh Courier,* the *Baltimore Afro-American*—for skin ointments that promised to lighten one's skin. The ads often appeared near the theatrical pages. Likewise, it hardly seemed coincidental that throughout the years of Cuban revolution, many Cuban officers were light, while the dark Cubans seemed to be mired in brutish frontline work.

Negroes kept arriving in Harlem, and the arrivals made Luisa Sanchez nervous and suspicious. She did not link art and Negro, poem and Negro, literary renaissance and Negro. Luisa Sanchez, daughter of Enrique Aguiar of the light-skinned ruling class of Cuba, had no affection for the dark-skinned American Negro. "My grandmother was the family beauty," says her granddaughter Gloria Williams, "and Elvera was second." Like the Cubans in her father's native land, Luisa Sanchez had that *miedo al negro,* fear of the black. She had a name for the Negroes outside her Harlem doorsteps seen walking by. She called them "pickaninnies," remembers Gloria. She uttered the epithet quite often. The attitude could not have helped but infect—in ways casual or otherwise—her two daughters, Elvera and Julia.

Julia Sanchez never married, but she had an affair that yielded Gloria, her only daughter. "My mother did not know he was married," says Gloria of her father. Julia Sanchez's lover was so light-skinned that there were those in Harlem who believed him to be white. "He looked white, but he hung out in Harlem," explains Gloria. Luisa Sanchez hardly minded the man's ever-so-light skin color. Elvera, however, had married Sammy Davis, an extremely dark-skinned man. "She was rebelling against her mother," says Gloria.

Luisa Sanchez herself never remarried. "The first husband was traumatic enough," believes Gloria. "She figured marriage wasn't an easy institution." Gloria Williams, decades later, trying to interpret the maternal decisions of her grandmother and mother, seemed at a loss for words: "Families are strange," she would simply—or not so simply—utter.

Lorelei Fields, a grandniece to Sammy's mother who knew her great-grandmother Luisa quite well, laments that the women in her family seemed to lack a kind of gentleness. "It didn't start out as nurturing," she says, "and that filtered down through generations."

Whether political, cultural, or personal, the skin-color divide in Harlem was inescapable—and potent. Nowhere was that tension more prevalent than in the teachings and attitude of Marcus Garvey.

Garvey arrived in Harlem from Jamaica in 1916 and, swiveling his thick neck, surveyed all around him. Elvera Sanchez would remember watching as people rushed in and out of the Garvey building near her own family's apartment. Garvey did not like what he saw in America. Believing himself a prophet, Garvey dreamed of carrying the American Negro back to Africa. Never mind that few Negroes wanted to go back to Africa. Garvey still painted a picture of a wondrous and dreamy Liberia, his intended destination. It was the lack of rights that the Negro lived under that perplexed Garvey and drove him to map out such an exotic undertaking in his head. He asked: " 'Where is the black man's Government?' 'Where is his King and his kingdom?' 'Where is his President, his country, and his ambassador, his army, navy, his men of big affairs?' " Finding no answers to his rhetorical questions, Garvey deemed that the best chance for the American Negro lay an ocean away. In the exuberant community of Harlem, he found converts. Garvey tapped right into the Negro skin-color divide: huge numbers of his followers were dark-skinned. Garvey's first mass convention, held at Madison Square Garden in 1920, drew twenty-five thousand people. Soon there were Garvey parades, emotional speeches, and the formation of his United Negro Improvement Association. "Up, you mighty race!" was his motto. (Garvey had watched the 369th Infantry Regiment's march into Harlem following World War I. He was against Negro soldiers fighting in the conflict, and the procession angered him, so much so that he was seen sobbing.)

The Garvey parades were near-theatrical events: columns of men in pressed military uniform, the peek of white gloves from their belt buckles, African flags held aloft and flapping in the wind, mysterious medals adorning chests. Garvey himself wore a large plumed hat and starched military garb at such events. Among Garvey's well-wishers were members of the Ku Klux Klan, who delighted in the possibility of a back-to-Africa movement for Negroes. Luisa had a distaste for Garvey's politics, and she dismissed him and his pronouncements because "he was a race man," sniffs Luisa's granddaughter Gloria. A popular retort—believed to have been uttered by light-skinned denizens of Harlem—was that Garvey's UNIA merely stood for "Ugliest Negroes in America."

Garvey needed money to finance his grand plan. Harlemites became investors, offering five dollars to buy stock in his international dream. Ships were built and an armada readied to be set loose. But Garvey's shipping company—the Black Star Line—was beset with financial irregularities. While Garvey had thousands of followers, he also had drawn the interest of the FBI, and Negro undercover operatives had reported his activities to FBI director J. Edgar Hoover. The government prosecuted Garvey in 1925—the year of little Sammy's birth—for mail fraud relating to his stock offerings. There were Negroes from the beginning who had questioned his sanity. Now, seeing him wearing a long topcoat and being led away by Hoover's G-men, Garvey's doubters were supplied with reasons to snicker even louder, and they did. Many concluded he was but a con artist.

"Look for me in the whirlwind," Garvey told his followers, vowing that, with "God's grace," he would return to free the American Negro. His lofty proclamation made, Garvey was carted off to prison. President Calvin Coolidge freed him from an Atlanta penitentiary in 1927 following emotional appeals spearheaded by his wife. Upon release, Garvey was deported. His Falstaffian demise aside, Garvey had further let loose, beyond the confines of literature and nightclub job opportunities, the secret of the American Negro—the skin-color divide.

If the Sanchezes were haughty about skin color—and Rosa Davis and her son, Sam Sr., believed them to be—the Davises were just as haughty about their dark skin. They told Elvera that they were not intimidated by light skin color, that they would not bow before her and her ancestry. "I was that half-white bitch" to the Davises, Elvera says.

It was true that Luisa Sanchez—and her daughter Elvera—had no need for any hair-straightening concoction from hair magnate Madam C. J. Walker, and they certainly did not need Marcus Garvey to boost their self-esteem. "Luisa never thought of herself as black," says Lorelei Fields, her grandniece. "She was Cuban." Southern-born Rosa Davis, however, needed that hair cream, and many of the women whom Rosa Davis knew also did. Every time Elvera Davis looked in the mirror, she imagined ridicule from her in-laws. What she perceived to be the Davises' Garveyesque feelings toward her left her in pain: "There was jealousy." It did not go unnoticed among members of the Davis clan that Elvera sometimes mentioned that her son resembled—even after the hair had mysteriously disappeared from his face—"a little monkey." Playful as the comment might have been, it was uttered, the Davises felt, in the painful cauldron of skin color, and it would linger in family lore for years. There were also the quizzical looks members of the Davis family would cast in Elvera's direction when she would start lauding her family's Cuban heritage, which she knew very little of but clung to fiercely anyway. At times, it appeared Elvera could not win: Davis family members often believed the more she bragged of her Cuban ancestry, the more she was mocking American Negroes and their painful history.

In 1928, Elvera returned to Harlem and gave birth, on July 20, to another child, a daughter, who was named Ramona. Ramona would be taken to her aunt Julia, Elvera's sister, and raised by her. "My mother stopped going on the road when I was about two," says Gloria Williams, Julia's daughter. "She said she came home from the road once and she went to take me from my grandmother [Luisa] and I cried. She said, 'That's it. My child doesn't know me. I'm not going back out on the road.' "

For a long while, Ramona would believe that Julia was her mother. After she recovered from giving birth, Elvera hit the road again. But this time when she left, she went one way—joining another theatrical troupe—and her husband, Sam, went another. "Mother wasn't show business; 'Baby' was show business, and for her the whole world was fun," says Gloria Williams of Elvera, who was often called "Baby." "She stayed in it until the chorus lines disappeared."

Sam Sr. and Elvera knew, during their previous road separations, that something was amiss. There was no longing in the heart as they spent night after night apart. They no longer possessed the thread that would keep a show-business marriage stitched together, and so they separated. They had produced two children in three years while rumbling about in the rough-and-tumble world of the vaudeville opportunities Will Mastin had provided them.

"Will put everybody to work," Elvera, speaking of her family, would say many years later, gratefulness in her voice still.

Chapter 2

LONG
SHADOWS

Vaudeville—its name originating from the French phrase *voix de ville* ("street songs")—had its origins in European capitals during the mid-seventeenth century. In the years to follow, the term took on new incarnations—variety show, cabaret, minstrel show. By the early nineteenth century the word "vaudeville" was being bandied about in various American locales. English performers who had come to America left many would-be performers inspired. In 1824 an American impresario by the name of John Robinson was known to be the first to send a troupe out to perform in "packages." By the 1870s there were vaudeville companies spread throughout America. Sargent's Great Vaudeville Company, operating out of Louisville, had a contingent consisting of midgets, sword swallowers, contortionists, and female impersonators, the latter donning frightful-looking wigs. Soon enough, minstrel shows were drawing large crowds in the hinterlands.

The awfulness of slavery—lynchings, runaways, bloodhounds—was being played out daily in the backwoods and on the main streets of America. The institution, fraught with drama as it was, lent itself to another kind of drama: staged entertainments. Performers, in blackface, would show the country what really was going on in those secretive quarters of slavery.

The Virginia Minstrels—white performers in blackface—arrived in New York in 1843. They drew large and appreciative audiences. A year later they were abroad, onstage in Glasgow, heralding their show as a "true copy of the up and downs of Negro life."

Josiah Henson knew something of the "up and downs of Negro life." Henson was born a slave in 1789 in Charles County, Maryland. He saved up $450, the amount he was told by his owner would be enough to buy his freedom. When the owner upped the price to $1,000, Henson, sensing trickery, fled with his family to Canada. His story might well have disappeared had he not run into a little-known New England writer by the name of Harriet Beecher Stowe.

Stowe's family was involved in abolitionist causes. Incensed at the 1850 Fugitive Slave Law, Stowe began writing antislavery sketches in the *National Era,* known widely as an abolitionist journal. Her stories, presented as fiction, were emotionally driven narratives against slavery. A certain knowledge of slavery—which many found astonishing—appeared in her stories. Henson, whom she had befriended, was her secret muse. Stowe grouped her stories together, and, on March 20, 1852, they were published as a novel, *Uncle Tom's Cabin.* The novel—which was subtitled "Or, Life Among the Lowly"—told of the dehumanizing force of slavery. Abolitionists trumpeted the book. It took off, selling at a pace of ten thousand copies a week; at the end of its first year of publication, a whopping 300,000 copies had been sold. The country had never seen anything like it. Stowe became famous, a literary sensation. Show-business minds were already making plans around the novel. Minstrel-show producers saw great possibilities in *Uncle Tom's Cabin.* Rights were sold, casts were organized, road shows readied—and trains boarded! (Stowe herself was always ambivalent about the stage, owing to her Christian upbringing.)

In the beginning, the casts were all white. The first production of *Uncle Tom's Cabin* reached New York in 1853, a mere year after the book's publication. There was not a Negro among the cast. Uncle Tom was played by a white man in blackface. At first, Negroes could not even attend the play, a play ostensibly about them. The policy was relaxed—with caveats—and an ad was placed in the *New York Herald* later in the year:

> NATIONAL THEATRE—TO COLORED PEOPLE NOTICE—On and after Monday, August 15, a neat and comfortable parquette will be prepared in the lower part of the theatre for the accommodation of RESPECTABLE COLORED PERSONS desirous of witnessing the great UNCLE TOM'S CABIN—the front seats of which will be reserved for females accompanied by males, and no female admitted unless with company.

For years *Uncle Tom's Cabin* kept drawing audiences. Negroes were eventually added to the casts, apparently for authenticity. The advertisements promised "a passel of darkies and a brace of hounds." Yet another ad promised "genuine Negroes and real bloodhounds."

One road company, billed as the Comedy Company, made history. The troupe was run by Gustave Frohman. They became stranded in Richmond, Kentucky—thirty-five miles from Lexington—in 1877. The idleness apparently sent currents of newfound thinking through Frohman's mind: he decided to have a "real Negro" play Uncle Tom. Sam Lucas was given the part. Lucas, born in Virginia, made his first marks as a minstrel entertainer with the Plantation Minstrels in St. Louis. In 1873 he joined the Original Georgia Minstrels. A year later the company wowed audiences in New York. When Lucas stepped into the role of Uncle Tom, he did so as if his very theatrical life depended upon it. He drew raves. Harriet Beecher Stowe saw Lucas's performance and found it staggering. She lavished him with praise. After his Uncle Tom days, Lucas spent nearly twenty years in Boston as a single vaudeville act. From there it was off to England—where he received more raves—then back to America, where, along with his wife, he headlined Sam T. Jack's Creole Company. Next up: *A Trip to Coontown*. Lucas emerged as a huge star on the vaudeville circuit, spoken of, wherever he went, as an Uncle Tom for the ages.

Still, Lucas knew the wickedness of the profession he was in, how unpredictable it was, how wrought with sadness it seemed to be. Many Negro vaudeville performers—Lucas and the celebrated Billy Kersands among them—had little choice but to perform wearing blackface. On whites, the blackface makeup was a joke, something else to ratchet up the laugh meter by mimicking the Negro in look. On Negroes, it served as the cruelest kind of joke—reimagining themselves as imagined, in blackface, by white performers. On June 29, 1915, Billy Kersands, who had been a member of the Original Georgia Minstrels with Lucas, died in his private railway car following a stage performance. Lucas—now the sole survivor of that Georgia group—wrote a memorial to Kersands that appeared in a New York newspaper: "By some strange fate I stand alone, the last of that merry company which was the first of our race to amuse the fun-loving public," he wrote. "On Billy Kersands the curtain has now gone down for the last time."

The challenge to Negro vaudeville performers was to steal some of the limelight from Al Jolson. For many believed Jolson the greatest performer working the vaudeville circuit of his times.

The son of a rabbi, Jolson, born in Lithuania, began performing in 1897. Carnivals and tent shows were his milieu. In time he would be spending about forty-two weeks of the year on the road as a stand-up. And during those weeks, he smeared his face in burnt cork, achieving his notoriety as a blackface performer. It took him just ten minutes to apply his makeup, to go from white to "cooning" Negro in front of the mirror. White audiences came to revere him. At times Jolson wore dusty plantation clothes—straw hat and all—onto the stage. On bended knee, he played the minstrel role, and he played it for keeps. Women who sat close enough to the stage often burst into tears. They claimed Jolson's eyes were soulful and lovely enough to make them do so.

Jolson lived a good life, pampered on the road, theater owners catering to his every need. But mostly, the road of the vaudevillian—especially for the Negro—could be harsh. The Colored Vaudeville Benevolent Association was established to aid the indigent, but the organization itself was often strapped for funds. Many of those who suffered serious illnesses while on the road went without medical services and died. The deaths were quiet; the shows had to go on.

In 1918, Will Mastin was out on the road, doing what Sam Lucas had done before him—organizing shows, keeping vaudevillians working. Many vaudeville shows traveled with children, so-called pickaninny performers. The young Will Mastin, born in Alabama in 1878, had hitched himself to a pickaninny revue as a child. By his teenage years, Mastin seemed to vow—against odds not only daunting but seemingly impossible—that he was going to commit himself to a career in show business. The options were painfully limited: "coon" shows, "darkie" musicals, burlesque, tent shows, vaudeville. When times were especially fallow, he found work as a horse groomer.

The actors were most vulnerable in these shows, which could run one week, two weeks, or one day, depending on the vagaries of the public. Will Mastin aimed to hedge himself against the odds of being thrown out of work. So he hoarded his money and began putting together shows of his own, billing himself as both dancer and producer. Producers like Mastin relied on word of mouth and strategically placed advertisements. Pat Chappelle, based in Jacksonville and, like Mastin, another Negro producer, operated the Rabbit's Foot Company vaudeville revue. One of his ads was typical of the times. "State all that you can do in first letter and lowest salary," the ad advised. "Ladies send photos. Can also place advance agents, lithographer, bill posters and first class baseball players."

Vaudeville attracted a luminous array of performers. Will Rogers, the cowboy star, performed in vaudeville—at times behind the mask of blackface. He'd crack prairie jokes and twirl his rope. Harry Houdini became renowned as an escape artist. Handcuffed and padlocked in a box, dipped beneath water, time ticking, he'd work himself free and rise up at seemingly the last possible moment—beating back death. Onlookers would let out breathless gasps. Helen Keller, blind and deaf since early childhood, took to the vaudeville stage and gave readings in braille. The sight of her, waltzing across the stage in darkness, stilled audiences.

In 1915, Mastin had a vaudeville revue, *Over the Top*. In 1916 he had another show, *Mastin and Richards: Holiday in Dixie*. Roaming the country, coast to coast, he picked up all manner of entertainers. He was opportunistic and—for merely possessing the moxie to be a Negro producer—considered eccentric. One season saw Mastin with Bob Thurman among his assemblage. Thurman was said to be the fastest dancer in the country. Like the other dancers Mastin had with him, Thurman was known as a Texas Tommy dancer. The Texas Tommy was a swift dance, with feet crossing over, a blur of movement. Sometimes, however, the dancers were mistaken for something else: " 'Tommy' meant prostitute," Mastin once explained, "and when we presented the dance at a San Francisco theater—the place was jammed, lots of cops, too, expecting a riot—but nothing happened because there wasn't anything bad about it, just a kind of acrobatics, with every step you could think of added to it." Ida Forsyne, a onetime dancer for Mastin, remembers a peculiarly gifted contortionist and musician that Mastin had discovered and employed. A lit lamp was perched atop his head while he contorted. "His name was George McClellan, and he did his contortion work while he was playing, too."

And owing to Thomas "Daddy" Rice—a white actor who donned blackface—a potent character by the name of Jim Crow came upon the land. While in Louisville performing in 1830, Rice noticed a stable hand singing and shifting on his feet inside a livery stable. Rice could see the man was deformed, especially his left leg, and he walked with a painful limp. Rice heard the old Negro singing and caught a verse of the song: ". . . wheel about, turn about, do jis' so, an 'ebry time I wheel about I jump Jim Crow." The moment fascinated Rice, and he stole the verse—and the image of the man—for his show. ("Crow" was likely the owner's surname; "Jim" a common name given to slaves.) Rice acted the part of the shiftless coon, the illiterate stable hand. Jim Crow, in both image and myth, was born. Audiences loved it.

Mastin quietly rebelled against doing "Jim Crow" shows, making attempts to do shows that had style and plots as opposed to mere stereotype. In doing so, he separated himself and his shows from the likes of Bert Williams, who had become a Negro sensation with his "coon" act.

Born in the Caribbean—1874 has been widely accepted as the year of his birth—Williams was raised in Riverside, California. He spent his high school years in San Francisco, where he began performing in saloons. Soon thereafter he joined a minstrel company, and in 1893 formed an act with George Walker. Among the duo's early presentations was a performance called "The Two Real Coons." Walker played it straight; Williams was in blackface. Williams became a sensation at doing the cakewalk dance. He made it so popular it became something of a national craze. Williams also possessed remarkable skills as a contortionist. He and Walker made it to Broadway in *Son of Ham* (1900), followed two years later by *In Dahomey,* which itself would be followed in 1906 by *Abyssinia.*

When Walker retired, Williams went on to become the first Negro to join the Ziegfeld Follies. He seemed imbued with a searing common sense: fearing reprisals from hooligans regarding any type of sexual innuendo, he did not want ever to be onstage with one of the white Ziegfeld girls, and Ziegfeld operatives thought it smart to comply with the request. Williams's popularity soared so much that he became a draw on the private-party circuit. "Is we all good niggers here?" he was known to ask cryptically as he launched into his monologue. Williams had perfected the Negro stereotype, and he played the role—twisting it into a kind of pickaninny art—for keeps. "I have no grievance whatsoever against the world or the people in it; I'm having a grand old time," he once told a New York newspaper. "I am what I am, not because of what I am, but in spite of it." The strangeness of the comment seemed to echo a bruising melancholy. Williams found it impossible—like most—to turn away from the light of his fame. He once sidled up to a bar in St. Louis and ordered a shot of gin. The bartender seemed taken aback, had no intentions of serving a Negro, and decided to have some on-the-spot fun with him. He said a glass of gin cost fifty bucks. "Give me ten of them," Williams said, and smoothly laid five hundred dollars on the bar.

Being the possessor of two souls—pickaninny and man—exacted a huge price; Williams became an alcoholic. In 1922, he died. "Bert Williams was the funniest man I ever saw and the saddest man I ever knew," W.C. Fields lamented. "I often wondered whether other people sensed what I did in him—that undercurrent of pathos."

The blackface comedian Eddie Cantor—who had worked alongside Williams in the Ziegfeld Follies—perhaps caught that element of pathos in a comment he made about Williams that seems the oddest kind of compliment: "He was the whitest black man I ever knew and one of the finest artists the musical stage has ever had."

If Will Mastin was to keep a foothold in the world of show business, he would not be for hire—just some actor with a blackface kit under his arm—thrown out into the cold as a show closes. He realized he had peaked as a flash dancer. After all, he was forty-three years old at the time of Bert Williams's death. Mastin knew his success would lie in organizing shows, producing them, gathering talent. Who knew where there might be another Texas Tommy dancer like Bob "Pet" Thurman waiting to be discovered? He would have to look right into the eyeteeth of Negro vaudeville and minstrelsy—which sprang from something so savage and dehumanizing—and imagine ways to dignify it. "Pathos" was not a word in Will Mastin's vocabulary, but he would have to sail beneath it nevertheless.

Will Mastin liked a cane and top hat. He'd twirl both to keep his own shows together. If he could achieve a measure of independence, he figured he could keep the curtain from closing down on him. But even as he was imagining a route to his own independence, Mastin was being constantly challenged by the Theatre Owners and Booking Association, a phalanx of white theater owners who knew there was money, and plenty of it, to be made in Negro vaudeville.

In 1920 a group of white theater owners made their way to Chattanooga, Tennessee. Their intention was to form an organization that would give them full powers over the theatrical circuit, especially theaters that played host to Negro vaudeville. Each theater owner merely had to purchase $300 worth of stock to become a member. Individually, as owners, they were just names—Milton Starr, of the Bijou Theatre in Nashville; Charles F. Gordon, of the Star Theatre in Shreveport; K. W. Talbutt, of the New Royal Theatre in Columbia, South Carolina; E. S. Stone, of the Washington Theatre in Indianapolis—just men, showmen. But before they left Chattanooga, they were known as the Theatre Owners and Booking Association (TOBA). They decreed they would buy up Negro theaters where they could. They would stiffen performance contracts where they had to. And they would—by God—make more money for themselves.

News of their formation ricocheted through Negro circles. Some Negro businessmen who operated theaters wondered what the creation of such an organization might mean. *Billboard* magazine wasted little time in pondering the group's beginnings and brazenly hired a Negro writer, J. A. Jackson, to cover the group. Some found it fit to ridicule Jackson's beat as the "Jim Crow" beat. The *New York Amsterdam News,* in an unsigned column, came to Jackson's rescue:

> We greet you brother Jackson of the Billboard, and want to assure you that the position you occupy will occasion envy and malice in the hearts of the nincompoops as ninety-nine out of a hundred colored writers would welcome the opportunity to do "Jim Crow" work on any big white publication. At times we disagree with your attitude in certain things, but we have never forgotten the ability which attracted the attention of the *New York Globe* shortly upon your arrival in this city which made you one of the contributing editors to one of the oldest and most widely known journals in America. Minnows will nibble at the bait meant for sharks. Ow!

In the beginning there were reports of TOBA's being good for Negro vaudeville, with promises made by the new owners of plans to beautify theaters. But it did not take long for complaints to begin. Owners were accused of hiring unscrupulous managers and of engaging in nepotism—and, worse, of buying up Negro theaters, cutting Negro independence short. But the owners were deaf to the complaints. From on high, word came down that the profits were not enough. Actor contracts were stiffened. There was grumbling, and charges of bad working conditions. Clarence Muse, a gifted vaudevillian, traveled widely on the TOBA circuit and would later write a book, *Way Down South,* about his experiences. That the book itself survives—for only one thousand copies were initially printed—seems a minor miracle. Here is Muse describing the green room of the Booker T. Washington Theatre, in St. Louis:

> Many theatres have a "Green Room" where the select ones
> among the audience, friends of the actors and others of
> importance meet socially with the cast. The back alley was
> the Booker T. Washington's "Green Room." It was the most
> typical back alley in the whole world. A clothesline from
> which hung underwear, socks and pajamas, stretched directly
> across it. The coal man's wheelbarrow was propped up
> against one wall. Several big cans of ashes lined the other
> side . . . maybe there was a garbage can, too. A little soda pop
> place was on one side of the alley's end, a smoke shop on the
> other. Here the big shots of the Black Belt came to call on the
> chorus girls or visit with the principals of the show in
> between performances . . . here in this unique spot they held
> open court.

It is little wonder that in time Negro performers started referring to the
Theatre Owners Booking Association as something else—Tough on Black
Actors. (There was a cruder variation: Tough on Black Asses.) The bad publicity heaped on the theater owners kept building up. With it, many Negro
managers—working for the theater owners—lost their jobs.

Will Mastin—caught between the disenchanted Negro performers and
white theater owners—soon enough found himself in a game of life-and-
death survival.

It pained Sammy Davis that his son was being raised without either parent
around. So when he left Harlem in 1928 to rejoin Will Mastin, he had his little
son, Sammy Jr., with him. It was an emotional separation between the little
child and Rosa, his grandmother. Rosa wept. "It broke her heart," says Virginia
Capehart, Rosa's friend. Sam Sr. did not know how he would raise the child,
but there was more comfort in having Sammy close to him than fretting every
night about him back in Harlem without his natural mother.

Mastin kept his troupe working. They continued to work hotels and resorts.
They performed before the curtain rose on silent movies. But by 1928, there
were ominous rumblings in the entertainment industry: the talkies were arriving ("Garbo Talks!"). Vaudeville troupes were getting fewer and fewer bookings. Thousands of theater musicians began to lose their jobs. Radio brought
the vaudevillian right into the family home. In October 1929—the last Tuesday
of that dark and crazy-quilted month—Wall Street crashed. The plunging of
the stock market sent lives and careers into disarray.

New York had lived high during its Jazz Age; it fell hard during the beginning of the Depression. And where New York fell, uptown Harlem fell harder. Luisa Sanchez was better off than most, but there was now "five times as much unemployment in Harlem as in other parts of the city," as the *New York Herald Tribune* reported.

Breadlines began forming in Harlem. Negroes were soon living in the streets. There were people selling pies from open windows for a nickel. "By 1930," went one book-length report, "Harlem contained some 200,000 people. Half of them depended upon unemployment relief." Whites were hustling jobs they previously thought beneath them. Broadway theaters began closing. It seemed as if a deep bruising fist were flying across the land and knocking all in its path down. The perceptive writer F. Scott Fitzgerald wrote that it was "as if reluctant to die outmoded in its bed" that the decade "leaped to a spectacular death in October 1929."

Show-business deaths somehow seemed more devastating, imaginative minds convincing themselves that those deaths were premature, out of the ordinary. A'Lelia Walker, daughter of Madam C. J. Walker, the Negro hair-care magnate, died in 1931. A'Lelia wasn't an artist, but she played host to many Renaissance artists—Langston Hughes among them—at her Irvington-on-Hudson thirty-four-room family mansion. Hughes was among those who attended Walker's funeral. He recalled:

> A night club quartette that had often performed at A'Lelia's parties arose and sang for her. They sang Noël Coward's "I'll See You Again," and they swung it slightly, as she might have liked it. It was a grand funeral and very much like a party. Mrs. Mary McLeod Bethune spoke in that great deep voice of hers, as only she can speak. She recalled the poor mother of A'Lelia Walker in old clothes, who had labored to bring the gift of beauty to Negro womanhood, and had taught them the care of their skin and their hair, and had built up a great business and a great fortune to the pride and glory of the Negro race—and then had given it all to her daughter, A'Lelia.

Hubert Julian, one of the earliest Negro aviators—the "Black Eagle of Harlem"—flew over Walker's funeral procession and dropped a wreath from his aircraft. (The Depression didn't deter Julian: he flew off to Ethiopia and trained pilots in the army of Emperor Haile Selassie.)

But economic calamity was everywhere. The *New York World* newspaper folded in 1931.

W. E. B. Du Bois lost his home and fell into debt.

New York City began keeping a gruesome statistic: death by starvation. In 1931 it reported the number as forty-six.

In 1932 the Palace Theatre in New York—home to superlative vaudeville acts—closed. Flo Ziegfeld died that same year—penniless.

Jean Toomer, a celebrated writer, became unsure whether he wanted to be classified a Negro any longer. He was light enough to pass for white but had conveniently grabbed the Negro label in the heat of the Harlem Renaissance. Now he was jumpy about the skin-color issue and refused to be included in Negro anthology collections, fearing the inclusion would damage him. Publishers who had been excited about Negro authors during the Harlem Renaissance were now talking about the bottom line.

New York—like every other municipality—had to pay for its dreams. And the New Negro was, once again, suffering from old woes: unemployment, discrimination, hunger.

Many had no choice but to look elsewhere for work. "The West Coast, not the East, now served as funnel and expressive outlet for the vast, inchoate, violent impulses of the hinterland," a chronicler of the demise of 1920s New York has written.

There were theaters in the hinterland. And that is where Will Mastin was now holding forth. The economic malaise had forced him to let some members of his vaudeville troupe go. (Mastin had seen calamity before—he was backstage in a theater with Sophie Tucker during the great 1906 San Francisco earthquake.) Mastin's troupe was moving like other vaudeville acts, from city to city, taking what bookings they could get. In Mastin they were lucky: he had innumerable contacts with Negro preachers, morticians, teachers, educators, newspaper owners, barkeeps. He knew how to drum up publicity. Will Mastin did not so much arrive into a town as he flowed into it. The child Sammy was still in tow, and Mastin's showgirls took a fondness to him. "He was being tutored by one of the chorus girls," remembers Cholly Atkins, a dancer who worked with the troupe in those days. "He was very fond of the young lady tutoring him."

The girls pampered little Sammy backstage. They lay sweets in the palm of his hand. Mastin, a very private man, seemed to loosen a little himself around the child. From the wings, little Sammy began watching the shows, mugging and mimicking other performers. One afternoon—just another unbilled performance in Columbus, Ohio; Sammy himself would recall it as 1929—the little child ambled out onstage from the wings. For a moment, the boy seemed lost. But in the minutes that followed, he seemed to luxuriate in the light, to allow it to bathe him. The laughs, hoots, guffaws seemed to be the beginning of some awful kind of mockery upon the child, but as he began dancing and primping, those in the wings realized it was not mockery at all but praise, and healthy laughter at the way the child had begun to kick up his heels.

Will Mastin got an idea: add the child to the ensemble! Mastin allowed the scene to repeat itself in city after city. As Mastin and so many others knew, it was hard times in America, and yet, there remained the magic of a kid onstage and Mastin knew it. And that is how little Sammy received his training— watching from the wings, following others around onstage, scampering and doing his own manic version of the Charleston, the cakewalk, and the fox-trot. A shtick was added: the show would begin, and soon Monty, a male dancer out of Detroit, would feign anger and walk offstage. A grumpy Mastin would plead with him not to abandon the act, but Monty vanished. Then Mastin, looking befuddled, would peer out into the audience. Sitting out there, he'd spot a man with a child in his lap, the child asleep. "He'd say, 'Wake that boy up!' " remembers Cholly Atkins, the performer holding the child. "I'd be holding little Sammy and as soon as he said it, I'd turn little Sammy loose." And with that, the child would bound up, screech past the customers, hop up onstage, and begin dancing beneath the lights. It would bring the house down. "He'd do a little paddle and roll," Atkins remembered. "Then when he got through doing his dance, he took his bow and the music struck up and the three of them got together and did their exit." And with each performance, the child would become more and more confident. He was so eager to take to the stage. Set loose in the world of make-believe, little Sammy seemed happier than ever.

Timmie Rogers was another child performer who would grow up on the road and befriend little Sammy. Rogers traveled for a while in his youth with Ben Ross, a Jewish vaudevillian. With the lights down low onstage, Ross would approach the audience and tell them he wanted to introduce his son. When the lights would come up, they would be shining on little Timmie Rogers, a Negro. The audience would collapse in laughter. (Rogers was an impetuous sort. He once went up to a Negro who performed in blackface onstage and asked: "Would you still put blackface on if you were on the radio?" He got a strange stare but no answer.)

Rogers remembers the child Sammy as being obsessed with the stage. "He would learn things easily," Rogers recalled. He would watch Sammy onstage and simply marvel. "He would break audiences up. He would kill them." Rogers noticed that the child had questions for the other performers. He wanted to know how to do every dance. His whole body seemed to shake with questions, says Rogers: "How do you do this step? And how do you do this? He wanted to learn."

"For a child," dancer Billy Kelly says of Sammy, "he was a marvelous dancer."

Sammy turned five, then six.

In Boston, during an appearance at the Symphony restaurant, the six-year-old found a friend in Russ Howard, who worked as an emcee at the Symphony and sometimes jumped onstage to join the Mastin revue. "Sammy used to come home with me," Howard would recall. "We used to see that he got good meals. He was only about six years old and a real trouper. Stopping off at a Cambridge restaurant where the politicians gathered in the evening, Sammy would go into his act for the boys. He collected a good handful of dollar bills and would delight in showing them to his dad the next day." Howard sometimes sang a little duet—"Ain't She Sweet"—alongside little Sammy and the chorus girls.

For a child who desperately wanted to learn, standing in the wings of a Negro theater in yet another city could be something akin to getting a Harvard degree. You were apt to see anyone while anchored in the wings: the Berry Brothers, Bill "Bojangles" Robinson, the wondrous Jeni LeGon (she was being likened to a young Florence Mills), the gifted Bunny Briggs. And you could watch Will Mastin and Sammy Davis, Sr., tall and powerfully built men with nimble legs who moved about suavely. "I think the one thing that helped me more than anything else was just watching my father and [Will] perform while they played the vaudeville circuit," Sammy Jr. would recall.

DeForest Covan, another dancer on the vaudeville circuit, was astonished by young Sammy's precociousness. "He was like a sponge," Covan says. "Anything he could see, he could do."

Some nights, after shows, the child Sammy was too hyper to go to sleep. So his father and Mastin sat up with him and listened to radio shows—*Dragnet* was his favorite: cops and robbers, the apprehension of suspects, noirlike music humming from the radio and filling the motel rooms, the boardinghouses.

Mastin and Sam Sr. took little Sammy to meet dancer Bill "Bojangles" Robinson at the Hoofers Club in Harlem. Robinson had once been engaged in a barroom scuffle and Mastin came to his defense. (Robinson later began carrying a loaded pistol.) The brouhaha left Mastin with a scar on his cheek, which he carried for life, as he did the silver-tipped cane Robinson gave him as a gift.

Robinson—born a year after Mastin, in 1879—was revered by Harlemites. He got his start in a pickaninny chorus in 1892. He was an orphan, and the chorus became a kind of home. From 1902 to 1914 he toured the vaudeville circuit with George Cooper, playing the clown to Cooper's straight man. Robinson was tall, kindly, generous, and not without an ego. As a dancer, he was willowy. In top hat and tails, he looked like something that had just glided through an open window on wings. Robinson appeared on Broadway in Lew Leslie's

Blackbirds of 1928, emerging as a legitimate tap-dancing sensation. Taking a child to meet Bill Robinson was like taking a Little Leaguer over to Yankee Stadium to meet the great Babe Ruth. "Bill knew Sammy was going to be a star," recalls William Smith, a habitué of the Hoofers Club who sometimes served as Robinson's driver and man Friday. "Sammy used to like to steal steps from Bill." A pool hall was adjacent to the Hoofers Club. Whenever Robinson was sharing his dance steps, tutoring on the spot, the pool hustlers would drop their cue sticks. Everyone would become quiet. Smith and others would gather around and watch Robinson move. Robinson kept his hips stilled, as if they were in a cast; for him, it was all in the feet, which he moved furiously; the effect was astonishing. "Bill taught Sammy a lot of things," adds Smith. "Sammy loved coming around Bill."

The young dancer Fayard Nicholas, rising as half of a popular duo with his brother, Harold, remembers young Sammy, his eyes so very wide. "When we would go onstage, he'd be standing in the wings, looking at us, jumping up and down," says Nicholas.

To create the patina of family, little Sammy was told to refer to Will Mastin as his "uncle." Sam Sr. hardly minded.

They entered him in children's dance contests. He had his own suitcase, his own shoe bag. His own set of little drums. He had numerous outfits—a white suit jacket, a white hat, plaid slacks, and white buck shoes made up one dandy sartorial number. Another was a little-boy tuxedo, satin lapels and all. Onstage Will Mastin and Sam Sr.—in top hat and tails, each with a cane in hand— hovered over the child. Mastin grinned like a magician, as if the child at his knee had just sprung from inside the high hat atop his head.

"Will had all the contacts, knew all the people," says Cholly Atkins, on the road with the trio in 1932. "You'd live in rooming houses. Up in New England you'd get to stay at some hotels. Whenever we played the South, it'd be rooming houses."

They put white chalk around Sammy's lips, enlarging them. In blackface, he resembled a miniature Al Jolson. They pointed pridefully at him when others came backstage to see him, and instructed him to start dancing, and he would—the Charleston, the turkey trot, whatever emerged from within. There would be oohs and aahs and giggles. Times were hard; laughter was a tonic. They gave the child bright lights and dressing rooms. They gave him show business. They gave him pennies from heaven.

"This little boy was more than a cute child actor," says Evelyn Cunningham, a Harlemite who would go on to become a distinguished newspaperwoman and remembers the young Sammy. "That was clear. They were clearly very protective of him. You knew he was going to be somebody special."

He turned seven, then eight.

Little Sammy Davis, Jr., was basking in the performer's life. Eyeing train schedules like coloring books. Watching old vaudevillians slump into sleep on moving trains. Listening to the modulated tones of the Pullman porters, the names of cities spilling from their mouths like clipped music, their chained pocket watches glistening. Seeing snowflakes fall. Eyes widening at new automobiles gliding down the streets. Staring at leaves being windblown on autumn afternoons. Watching men slide nickels across countertops for the morning newspaper. Smiling at the pretty women who'd smile at him. Falling off to sleep as the covers were pulled up close to his shoulders in bed, all the while staring into the whites of the eyes of those who cared so much for him— his father, Will Mastin. The little boy was so free—and yet, so caged in the world of show business.

Will and Sam Sr. were as kind, as tender, and as attentive as they could be. In a way, they gave little Sammy everything. And with that, they bartered away his childhood.

They didn't hear much from Elvera in those days. She was a mother, true enough, but she hardly seemed strong or wily enough—even if she wanted to—to get her child from two dream-hungry vaudeville dancers. Maybe it was anger, or a deep kind of aching, but often when asked if she had any children, Elvera would mention that she had only one child—a daughter. Maybe she only meant she had one child whose address she knew. "They took the boy away from her," says Maurice Hines, a dancer who crossed paths with both Mastin and Sam Sr.

Elvera had continued to bounce around. She was in Philadelphia. She had joined another revue, *Hot Connors Chocolate*. But that revue disbanded. She joined another group; it was short-lived also. She wanted to sing. But she knew she had limitations, principally "I couldn't carry a note." It mattered little. She was going to launch a singing career. "She bought these long dresses," remembers her niece, Gloria. "She was going to try out an act." The act didn't work out. Who knows why, except a lot of acts didn't work out. She was in Boston. Someone said she was back in New York. No, she had left New York, was now in Montreal.

Look for her in the whirlwind, too.

Broadway actress Laurette Taylor, Luisa Sanchez's employer, had attended high school in Manhattan—though not for long. She was dismissed in her sophomore year. Her antics and hijinks bedeviled school administrators. Her father enrolled her in stenography classes. She loathed them. What she really wanted to do was act, to join vaudeville. A family friend told her and her mother about auditions being held at a vaudeville theater on Fourteenth Street. Taylor, barely fifteen, went and auditioned. Not long into her audition she sang—while holding a bouquet of violets in her hand—a song titled "You're Just a Little Nigger but You're Mine, All Mine." She sang another song with a French accent. Before her final rendition, she vanished backstage. Her mother applied burnt cork to her face. When young Taylor reappeared, she was in blackface and wearing a gingham dress, all to play-act as a "mammy." The vaudeville operatives didn't hire young Taylor that day, but they could see her versatility, her overwhelming need to please.

In the years ahead of her, Laurette Taylor would conquer stage after stage. In doing so, she seemed to gather a peculiar insight into the consciousness of the performer, and why the craft of acting had such appeal. In 1914—her fame continuing to cast a rich glow—she discussed the intrigue of the child actor:

> You see a queer little child, sitting in the middle of a mud puddle. She attracts you and holds your interest. You even smile in sympathy. Why? Simply because that child is exercising her creative imagination. She is attributing to mud pies the delicious qualities of the pies which mother makes in the kitchen. You may not stop to realize that this is what is going on in the child's mind, but unconsciously it is communicated to you. It is the quality of imagination that has held your attention.

Imagine, then: a little child backstage, being dressed up, adults towering above him, voices alternately soft and hard. Women fawning over the child, patting the child on the head, asking the child, time and time again, to dance, to do a little soft-shoe number. Home from the road, sitting among family and friends, Sam Sr.—a drink or two inside of him—would want to brag, to show off his little Sammy. He'd ask the boy to dance. Other children were around; the child wished to play, not dance. "Dance for your grandmother! Dance for your grandmother!" Gloria Williams remembers Sam Sr. bellowing to little Sammy during one holiday visit, then reaching for his belt to give the threat of a spanking. So the child danced.

Imagine that child, while out on the road, staring out a car window, without a mommy in sight, with a mommy a thousand miles away, or maybe, for all he knows, in the next town over, doing her own thing, trailing along with a bevy of other chorus girls, everyone chasing a dream.

Imagine that child tired, rubbing sleep from eyes. Imagine that child happy, because who would not like to play and play and play? But also imagine that child unmoored from home, swallowed by magic and the all-time hustle known as show business.

Imagine a child who must now save two men and a vaudeville troupe from time, from vanishing, from disappearing like some two-bit road show—from dying. Imagine that child smothered in the kind of tricky love that has money attached to each performance, and each performance attached to an adult's gratification or disappointment.

"One day when you're in show business and are a child, something clicks and you realize what you do is important to a lot of adults around you," says Bobby Short, a Davis acquaintance later in life who also performed in vaudeville as a child. "You are emboldened, and your childhood is over. It's not a happy circumstance. If you don't go on, you're going to hurt a lot of people."

Imagine the weariness. Short himself would remember it well in his own autobiography about vaudeville life as a child performer. "Sometimes on a weekend night at a roadhouse on the outskirts of town, I'd go to sleep at the piano during a lull, my head on my arms. When the lights of approaching cars were seen around the bend, they'd wake me, and before the customers got to the door, I'd be sitting up and playing 'Nobody's Sweetheart Now,' full tilt."

Imagine a child who must engage in furtive activities, hiding from truant officers, scampering on his little legs when told to run, to dash, all to escape them. Little Sammy became adept at the quick reaction. "He was always ducking truant officers. They'd put him in the closet and tell him to keep quiet," Timmie Rogers says of Will and Sam when the truant officers would come around. (The child did get schoolbooks from the Calvert School, an extension school in Baltimore that cost ninety bucks a year. They'd send the books and lessons wherever you were on the road. Extension courses were one thing. Another happened to be the cities where the truant officers warned Mastin and Sam Sr. about child labor laws.)

"Sammy would have schooling backstage," entertainer Al Grey remembers. But playtime often would interrupt: "I used to play cops and robbers with him. I'd catch him off guard—'Bang bang, I got you.' "

Will would notice which chorus girls were paying extra attention to the child. He'd slip them a couple extra bucks come payday.

Child performer Eileen Barton—who would cross paths with the Davises on the road—traveled in her mother and father's act. The act was called Bennie and Elsie Barton and Company. "I was the 'Company,' " Barton says. She was taking extension courses just like little Sammy. "My father wound up doing all my homework. I never looked at it."

Sammy watched newsreels and movies—Mastin still called them "talkies"—in movie houses. It was in Chicago, in 1931, when he saw his first movie. The movie was *Dracula*, in which Bela Lugosi, who had played the role on Broadway in 1927, starred. Sammy had snuck away to the theater. It wasn't difficult, inasmuch as it was attached to the vaudeville house where he and his father and Mastin were appearing. He sat in darkness, shaking, looking up at Dracula slithering across the screen. "My spine tingled, and the muscles in the back of my neck started making my head shake," he would later remember. "My mouth opened even wider than my eyes, and my body shook uncontrollably."

Sometimes he was accompanied to the movies by his father and Mastin, and he sat watching in the darkness of cinematic dreams as the two men dozed off into sleep, taking catnaps.

He did not participate in stickball, or softball, or the tossing of a football. He did not participate in sports of any kind—even as mere child's play. There was the fear of injury. Children at play filled his little-boy eyes with curiosity. Walking by knots of schoolchildren, he would point and wonder where they were headed. Small heads like his, bopping along in the sunlight. Then they were gone, with their giggling, leaving him the only child in sight.

He read comic books—Batman and Superman were favorites—listened to jazz, saw the flickering bulbs of red-light districts in towns everywhere: Detroit, Chicago, Norfolk, Washington, D.C., St. Louis. "We moved from New England into the Midwest, working steady, covering most of Michigan in theaters, burlesque houses, and carnivals, changing the size of the act to as many as forty people depending on what the bookers needed," little Sammy would later remember.

He danced in front of hotels on street corners, the nickels and dimes handed over to Will Mastin, money to survive on. It was boom and bust, weeks of work, then weeks of idleness. "When Sammy was growing up they played club dates—Portland, Seattle, Vancouver," recalls dancer Leroy Myers, who watched the act with awe. "Nice white clubs. You had to do a decent act to play them. If you were black, you had to be good to play them."

Mastin dreamed up yet another idea. Little Sammy as Al Jolson! Anything to keep the act fresh. With a cigar provided by Mastin in his little mouth, little Sammy played the great Jolson. So he—a Negro child—played a white man in blackface who was portraying a black man. Alternating masks and faces. He got laughs just as Jolson got laughs. (Will Mastin would admonish Sammy not to touch his face with the blackface on; it smudged.)

What does a Negro child think of seeing someone in blackface? What mental anguish—if any—might come of that? Here is Florence Mills, giving an interview in London in 1926, describing a scene when she was a mere four-year-old about to go onstage:

> When I was born, I was just a poor pickaninny, with no prospects but a whole legacy of sorrow. . . . One day, when I was playing in the street with a number of other children, a white comedian who was appearing close to my house saw me and took a fancy to my face. From him I learned my first song, "Don't Cry My Little Pickaninny."

> That was the beginning. At the age of four, I appeared
> with him on the stage with the proud intention of singing my
> little song. Half-way through I saw a black-faced comedian
> standing in the wings waiting to go on. His make-up was so
> startling that I broke off in terror and had to be led off the
> stage weeping bitterly.

Little Sammy himself was a mere four-year-old when he started donning blackface.

He slurped soda pop through straws. He ate Baby Ruth candy bars and wore a porkpie hat. In an automobile, he sat in the backseat like an urchin as the scenery—like frozen daguerreotypes come to life—passed in and out of his view.

Imagine staring fearlessly into the cameras, because he did that also. It was a little movie, *Rufus Jones for President,* shot in 1933 on a soundstage over in Brooklyn. Little Harold Nicholas of the Nicholas Brothers was first offered the part; he had other commitments. Will Mastin hustled the role up for little Sammy. (Will Mastin: now playing the role of Frank Capra.) The cast of *Rufus Jones* was eclectic. There was Ethel Waters, Hamtree Harrington, the Jubilee Singers, and the Will Vodery Girls. The movie is a dream in the mind of a little boy who wants to become president of the United States. His dream is realized in the movie; his mammy is vice president. Negroes in the White House—such a dream indeed for 1933. There is plenty of music, hijinks, and laughter. There are watermelon and pork chop jokes, the rolling of dice. A billboard in the movie says:

VOTE HERE FOR RUFUS JONES
Two Pork Chops
Every Time You Vote

The movie revels in racial stereotypes. In one scene, supposedly in the Senate chambers, there is a sign outside the Senate door: CHECK YOUR RAZORS.

Little Rufus Jones (Sammy) walks up to the microphone when he is introduced as president. He's got a pork chop in his hand. Even with all the racial baggage, watching the one-reeler decades after its release, one can see the clean and unmistakable talent of Sammy Davis, Jr., dancing and strutting, as jubilant around the camera as a child around a Christmas tree. In every scene he seems to be casting a kind of glow upon those around him. His signature song—"I'll Be Glad When You're Dead, You Rascal You"—is sung with gusto. The *Motion Picture Herald,* a Hollywood publication, calls little Sammy "talented" in the role. He's in the movies, just as little Shirley Temple is in the movies. Will

Mastin, however, is soon squinting his eyes. He is afraid. The studios might steal the child. That is what they do when they discover someone—steal them away, sign them to long-term contracts, own them. He can't let it happen. He won't let it happen. He needs little Sammy. Little Sammy will make one more movie as a child, something called *Season's Greetings,* which will star Lita Grey Chaplin. Her divorce from the great comedian Charlie Chaplin had been worldwide news. By the early 1930s she had spent much of her money from the divorce settlement on a lavish lifestyle and was forced to go back to work, joining a vaudeville circuit, and making, on the side, one- and two-reeler movies, one of which starred little Sammy. The Chaplin connection forces sweat to form on the brow of Will Mastin. He has no idea what Lita might tell studio operatives about little Sammy's gifts. Enough is enough: there will be no more movies, then; Will Mastin closes the curtain on little Sammy's film career.

"I never was a child," Sammy's *Rufus Jones* costar, Ethel Waters, would lament in the opening of her autobiography. "I never was cradled, or liked, or understood by my family."

So it must have been for Sammy. Everyone he met he seemed to be waving good-bye to a few days later, at the end of the show's run. Strangers onstage; strangers in memory. "Only the details changed, like the face on the man sitting inside the stage door, or which floor our dressing room was on," Sammy would remember. "But there was always an audience, other performers for me to watch, always the show talk, all as dependably present as the walls of a nursery."

So his life consisted of ephemera—rumor, correspondence courses, stage lights, back rooms, medicinal concoctions, superstition, comic books, trains, radios, hellos, good-byes.

His sister, Ramona, would recall—and sweetly—the dolls he brought home to give to her when she was a little girl. Some of them were porcelain. He was almost shy in the giving—as if handing something to a near stranger. In fact, he barely knew her. The dolls meant so very much to her. She cradled them. She placed them prominently in her bedroom. She had no other siblings. When he went back out on the road, she thought of him. She also wondered why her father was leaving her behind. She never had any idea when she might see them again. "I would ask my mother about Sammy and she'd say, 'I'm looking for him. I've called the Gerry Society.' "

The Gerry Society was established in 1874 in New York. Its agents' mission was to uncover child abuse; neglected children were found and delivered to orphanages. Gerry agents—who were authorized to arrest parents if need be—often put the fear of God into families. Mastin and Sam Sr. knew enough to fear the Gerry agents. In time they would avoid New York City as much as possible. They would have special codes to make contact with Ramona. "If the phone would ring twice, and stop, then I knew it was a clue. My brother was in town."

The strange and furtive relationship with her brother would haunt Ramona forever. She would blame much of it on her grandmother Luisa Sanchez, who Ramona felt encouraged Elvera to pay little attention to the children, because of skin color. "She was so bigoted," Ramona would say of her grandmother. "I couldn't have dark boyfriends. You understand how deep this goes? Sammy thought Mother raised me. My mother didn't raise me."

Ramona found the promises her mother made about contacting the Gerry Society bewildering. She never saw her do it. "The history of us being separated is about our grandmother," Ramona would say of her and Sammy. "My grandmother was a proper Hispanic—and a racist."

Sammy sometimes donned a porkpie hat and practiced his dance steps outside "Colored Only" restrooms while waiting for Will and his father. He saw his dancing shadow bounce off walls, and he grew proud of himself.

He watched as women whispered in his handsome father's ear, and as his father whispered back. His father was still married to his mother. He knew as much—the divorce wouldn't come until years later—but life was moving on.

He learned how to fold clothes neatly as napkins. He learned how to pack quickly, learned to scan the hotel rooms cleanly when it was time to check out—fewer items got left behind.

He stayed up late, past his bedtime. When other children were reminded of bedtime, he was reminded that it was time to go to work.

He hated sleeping alone. He hated *being* alone.

Sometimes Mastin or Sam Sr. told nervous show promoters—some were jittery about allowing a small child to work, because of labor laws—that the kid wasn't a kid at all, but a midget. Winks all around; chuckling in the air.

He saw his father drink, heard his father's voice rise in volume when he became drunk. Will Mastin, by contrast, seemed ascetic. No drinking, no women—just a fierce determination to find the next stage. Mastin was also a stickler for rehearsing; a craft had to be learned.

Sammy was inventive, seemed borne by his own inner light and energies. "Will was always disciplining Sammy," says onetime child performer Timmie Rogers.

In fits of little-boy angst, Sammy purchased comic books, dozens of them, as if storing up viewing material—always more pictures than words because he could not read—for the winter months.

He missed his grandmother.

Will Mastin, with the child in tow, couldn't imagine any fear, or sleepless nights, or pain, or motherless agony that a child might be having. That—or any kind of pathos—was far from his concern. He could only imagine what lay behind him: actors and vaudevillians thrown out of work overnight. That horrendous San Francisco earthquake; the terrifying Depression. Ida Forsyne, who had danced in one of Mastin's choruses, was now "coon shouting from twelve noon to twelve midnight" at Coney Island. And what of the great Sam Lucas—the first Negro Uncle Tom? Lucas was signed to play Uncle Tom in the first movie version of Stowe's novel. In one scene Lucas was required to dive into a pond of very cold water. Off-camera, he grew ill from that icy dipping. On January 15, 1916, Sam Lucas died from the pneumonia he caught while making the movie. Will Mastin was a nervous and fitful sort. It did not take much for him to imagine unemployment—or worse. He saw all of it. Old vaudevillians out on the road with a broken ankle, strep throat, begging money to get back home. And the representative from the Colored Vaudeville Benevolent Association nowhere to be found.

"The melancholy spirituals have been replaced by the equally melancholy, but less reverent, blues and the rhythm of the old plantation has vanished in the path of the weird and sensuous tempo of the jungle and the beat of the tom tom," the *Baltimore Afro-American* reported in 1933—seemingly in an effort to warn of change all around.

The world, then, was moving on.

Some of the young child performers who saw Mastin onstage were amused by his old-time dance steps. "Will was more of a strutter," recalls Timmie Rogers. "The strut thing was ancient. It was with Bert Williams's era."

If anything, Will Mastin was a survivor, and he believed he had found the new beat with someone who stood a mere four feet high.

Little Sammy was a queer little child, true enough, sitting and prancing around stage after stage, but he had genuine gifts, a currency. And he had Will Mastin. And he had a pair of toy six-shooters that he'd strap on backstage, and then he'd tug on anyone to play cowboys and Indians with him.

Draw!

Draw!

There were times—although now they were becoming less and less frequent—that little Sammy would return to Harlem with his father and Mastin. It was where his grandmother Rosa awaited him. She would get out her best dishes, her fine linens, in anticipation of his arrival. Inside the apartment, the child would run from adult to adult, tiring himself out all over again, talking about sights from the road. He would show off the small amounts of money that Will or his father had allowed him to carry around in his pockets. Rosa would delight in preparing a huge meal. The big woman would move about around the apartment as if light as feathers. Her little Sammy was back home, from places and towns they'd never heard of or seen. Then, as evening came on, she would have records spinning on the Victrola. "Momma, squeeze me till I hurt," the tired little child would finally say to his grandmother as he was being held close to her bosom. It was his way of asking her to rock him to sleep. And she would.

It was hardly the worst kind of life. There were cackling smiles from audiences, applause, hugs from strangers, a jawline smudged with lipstick from ladies. But it was a life without nursery rhymes. And it was a life without a mother in the kitchen baking pies. Sammy's sister, Ramona, believes he was forever scarred by his exhausting childhood: "That being given away never goes away."

Al Jolson, in his 1927 movie, *The Jazz Singer*—the first sound motion picture— cries out from behind the mask of blackface: "Mammy, don't you know me? It's your little baby!"

The focus of Will Mastin's life was simply to survive. "Those who have confined their activities to what we might term the Negro theatre exclusively have either vanished completely from the arena or are existing in mediocrity," the *Baltimore Afro-American* wrote in its January 1, 1933, edition. "The American black man honors only those whom the gods have chosen. The Negro theatre has not really progressed—it has merely been absorbed."

Absorption and death. Uncle Tom was dead: not the spirit, but the body. Bert Williams and Sam Lucas and Florence Mills—dead. Mills was a mere thirty-two when she died; 150,000 crowded the streets of Harlem for her funeral. Andy Razaf, the soulful lyricist, wrote and dedicated a poem to Mills, part of which reads:

> *Little Florence, so dear*
> *We thought so much of her*
> *Angels up above her,*
> *Wonder if they love her*
> *Much as we love her here*
> *Poor Little Blackbird*

The great Charles Gilpin, gone. At one time Gilpin—who had once been a member of the Perkus and Davis Great Southern Minstrel Barn Storming

Aggregation—had been the brightest of lights on Broadway. In 1921 he starred in the title role of *Emperor Jones,* Eugene O'Neill's Pulitzer Prize–winning play. One afternoon—out of costume, of course—Gilpin went to the ticket window of the theater where he was performing to purchase a ticket for a front-row seat. He could not purchase a front-row seat, he was told; Negroes sat in the balcony. He protested, to no avail. Gilpin could not get in to see Gilpin. Five years later he quit performing. In 1929, Gilpin suffered a terrifying nervous breakdown. He died a year later in Eldridge Park, New Jersey.

Jim Crow, an old deformed Kentucky stable hand, his life memorialized day by day in coon shows, never aware of his strange fame, was also gone. And did he too not have a heart, a soul, certain dreams before the shovelfuls of dirt were swung over his coffin?

It was in the long and deep shadows of those who had come before him that Will Mastin was operating. Time was fate, and fate was mystery. So many were gone. But he was still in the game, strolling the lobbies of dusty Negro hotels with Bill "Bojangles" Robinson's cane.

He had to create something new to keep going. And he did. When 1936 rolled around, Mastin had a whole new act: Will Mastin's Gang.

The sound of it had a circuslike ring, which is exactly what Mastin wanted.

There would be no women. There was something tricky about Negro dancers and the mingling of sex onstage. The innuendo—the whiff of Negro sex—could be viewed as unsettling to white audiences. The tragic comedian Bert Williams knew it all too well. Matter of fact, the "gang" wouldn't exactly be a gang at all—but less than half a dozen members.

Then Will Mastin thought of something else, his mind clicking hard now. The child had shown such astonishing fearlessness on the stage. The American public had a fascination with freaks onstage, with midgets, and, not the least, children. He decided to bump up a member of the act's billing, and the act's name was quickly altered:

WILL MASTIN'S GANG, FEATURING LITTLE SAMMY

Yes, that sounded so much better. More like vaudeville. Elvera would get reports from the road. Her son was doing what she was doing—working. "I liked Will," she would say, "because he took care of Sammy."

That year, 1936, dust storms were sweeping vast areas of the American West. So-called Okies were leaving the plains, bumping along in trucks. It was impossible to predict when the Depression might end. (No one kept a running count of how many vaudeville troupes had gone under, but everyone imagined the numbers were brutal.) Week after week folks were pitching tents on the sides of roads, financially destitute and driven from their homes. There was pain and more pain. Companies—General Motors, many others—hired Pinkerton guards to thwart the attempts of would-be union organizers. Goons hired by management engaged in nasty confrontations with workers. Blood spilled. "This land is your land," folksinger Woody Guthrie sang. It was hard to believe. Roosevelt—hearty, optimistic despite the Supreme Court's challenge to much of his New Deal legislation—swept to thunderous reelection by defeating Alf Landon. Roosevelt lost only two states—Maine and Vermont. "There is a mysterious cycle in human events," he said that year. "To some generations much is given. Of other generations much is expected. This generation of Americans has a rendezvous with destiny."

Jesse Owens, a Negro track and field star attending Ohio State University, won four gold medals at the 1936 Olympics. Adolf Hitler, the German chancellor, had no intentions of shaking hands with Owens, and abruptly left the Berlin stadium before the medal ceremony. (Hitler had broken the Versailles Treaty months earlier when his army marched across the Rhineland into France—an ominous portent of war that went largely unnoticed by the American government.) Owens returned to America a hero, though he couldn't find a job. He was soon seen at carnivals, out on the racetracks—being paid nominal fees to race by foot against horses. It was a shameful comedown from gold-medal celebrity. The track star seemed to take it in stride. "I wasn't invited to shake hands with Hitler," Owens would muse, "but I wasn't invited to the White House to shake hands with the president, either."

In Hollywood the Oscar nominations were announced. Frank Capra would win the Oscar for best director for *Mr. Deeds Goes to Town*. Gary Cooper would win the best actor award for the same movie. The gifted brunette Luise Rainer would be awarded the best actress statuette for *The Great Ziegfeld*. Ziegfeld had been dead four years now; his bones were still worth picking over.

Will Mastin was no Flo Ziegfeld. Ziegfeld would send a hundred legs sashaying across a stage. Will Mastin was just a flash dancer with a silver-tipped cane and a suitcase full of clothes and medicine for his nervous stomach and phone numbers of motels that catered to Negroes.

But he had the heart of a Ziegfeld.

Sammy turned eleven that winter. It was the same age Asa Yoelson—who would become Al Jolson—was when he ran off to join a carnival known as Rich & Hoppe's Big Company of Fun Makers.

Chapter *3*

THE KID IN
THE MIDDLE

They played roadhouses and gin joints, theaters with creaking stages. It was difficult to keep a vaudeville troupe upright in the mid- and late 1930s, and Will Mastin knew it. The unknown was everywhere. There would be a solid week's work, only to be followed by three idle weeks. The wicked economic times frightened theater owners; scheduled shows were sometimes capriciously canceled. Mastin felt he and his troupe were working twice as hard for laughs. The paychecks got smaller. Dancer Billy Kelly ran into the Mastin troupe in 1937 in Boston. "It was tough," Kelly recalls. "They weren't making much money. They borrowed from everybody. Naturally, they never paid back. The Depression was on." Even so, Kelly would sit watching the troupe, and just marvel. "It was a great act," he says. "A showstopper, with the boy," he adds.

When he could, Will Mastin would get to a telephone, always eager to confirm upcoming engagements to save the group travel fare in case of a cancellation. When engagements fell apart, the debt of carrying the act only deepened. With tight purse strings, Mastin began to jettison dancers. But not Sam Sr. His job was quite secure: little Sammy was his father's insurance policy. They were forced into subpar lodgings. At some of the motels, cold winds blew through cracked windows at night. Mastin and Sam Sr.—worrying more about the child than about themselves—were not above scrounging for fresh firewood.

In an environment where road acts were folding swiftly, Mastin must have pondered other alternatives to scuffling around the country. But what else could he do? An educated Negro might be able to get a job teaching in a Negro school. But Will Mastin had no education. And he was beyond the physical labor he performed in his youth working in and around horse stables.

So the vaudevillian held on.

Little Sammy—in the middle of it all—was such a natural. He had learned quickly. With bright and eager eyes, he seized stage directions and cues. He acquired the gift of improvisation. On nights when Mastin and Sam Sr. were weary, Sammy provided the needed shot of adrenaline. On the nights he wore white buck shoes, he moved so fast it looked as if there were white birds scampering across the stage's wooden floor.

Mastin had worked as part of a duet—Mastin & Richards, they were called—early in his career. And he had also put together shows featuring more than a dozen performers. But he had never worked as part of a trio. And yet, an ability to change had been his secret to survival. He looked around and found himself down to three dancers—and he wasn't even the most gifted of those three dancers! It didn't matter. He had the phone numbers, the contacts, the reputation. Theater owners trusted his word. That word had been built up over decades. He had his cane, his suitcases, his top hat, and his word. That was plenty.

So Will Mastin now found himself leading a trio. Six legs—and the most gifted among them the kid in the middle.

Nine or so meals a day. Food and train fare and bookings. Mastin figured it all out—when it would be best to head back to the West Coast; which train lines were friendliest to Negro performers. Every day he pondered questions and plotted strategies.

Another name change took place. This time little Sammy's name was folded into the whole act itself:

The Will Mastin Trio

They found work in Hank Keane's rolling carnival. Keane would put on six shows a day. You grabbed something to eat in between shows. Little Sammy would later remember hearing the echo of the carnival barker in his ears: "Hey! Here they come! Three little hoofers, hot from Harlem!"

Frank Bolden, a writer for the *Pittsburgh Courier,* remembers the trio when they unexpectedly arrived in Pittsburgh for a performance. "They weren't booked," he remembers. "I don't know if they missed the train or what. They stayed at the Bailey Hotel. That was the Negro hotel. They couldn't stay in the downtown hotels." Many had no idea, says Bolden, that a child was part of the Mastin trio. "We were looking for the other adult. Well, it was Sammy." Sam Sr. and Mastin told jokes, bracketing each other onstage. They also danced, though Bolden remembers Mastin and the elder Davis as being "kind of stiff." The show seemed to come alive when Sammy was turned loose, dancing and skipping with a ferocity across the stage. He drew whoops and hollers. Those who saw the child were amazed. "In tap dancing, usually one foot favors the other," says Bolden. "Sammy was good with both of his feet." Many who had been in the audience clamored afterward to meet the kid who had been onstage. But the kid had other interests. "He spent most of his time eating ice cream cones," Bolden says. When those who had seen him perform finally got Sammy's attention, they were full of praise.

Paul Winik, another dancer crisscrossing the country during the Depression, would remember the trio as tightly knit. Like Sammy, Winik was a kid with a pair of tap shoes and a chaperone on the road. "He used to stand in the wings and watch me dance," Winik says. "I'd stand in the wings and watch him dance." Sometimes, backstage, the two of them would dance until they were exhausted, then they'd keep on dancing. They'd practice like athletes, pushing themselves, creating new dance steps as they went along. "We were just two kids thrilled to be doing what we were doing," Winik recalls. "And he had such appreciation for other dancers' talents." Winik sensed the discipline that Mastin and Sam Sr. were instilling in young Sammy. "The father was very hard on him when he missed a step during the show. They were very serious dancers."

Any act—quartet, duo, trio—knew to keep on the move as much as possible. Acts competed against other acts, especially when it came to inventiveness and novelty. The more you moved about, the higher the likelihood of your act sustaining an element of surprise.

In Boston in 1937 the Mastin trio settled for a while in a rooming house on Columbus Avenue. A restaurant—Mother's Lunch—was located on the bottom floor, and they frequently ate there, the three of them waltzing through the door, little Sammy's eyes furiously darting about. Abe Ford, a booking agent, befriended the struggling trio in Boston. "They had trouble when they first started," Ford would recall. "There were a lot of vaudeville theaters in Boston. There was a woman named Mary Driscoll in charge of the licensing board in Boston. We used to pass Sammy off as a midget. She wouldn't let anyone perform under the age of twenty-one where liquor was sold." An act did not always get much time to prove itself. "If they did lousy, they wouldn't get another job," says Ford.

One of Abe Ford's booking assignments was for a show called *Round Up,* which consisted of a variety of vaudeville acts. "We used to put them in *Round Up.* The two of them would come out and they'd introduce Sammy and the house would go wild seeing a little kid like that hoofing the way he hoofed," Ford says. The agent could easily see that little Sammy's presence was potent: "It kept the other two guys working." Ford knew how desperate the times were. "There was no money around," he says. "Two, three, four dollars a day was a lot of money." Mastin was determined to keep his act a tap-dance act, and steeled himself against the exotica of other acts that featured contortionists, mind readers, and mystics—the kind of acts he himself had once been fond of.

Financial calamity may always have been a breath away, but Mastin managed to keep up appearances. "Sammy would be in dungarees on the street, but Will—onstage and off—was always a sharp dresser," says Ford. "Immaculate.

Always with the cane and high hat." Ford was impressed with the discipline Mastin demanded of the act. "The three of them were never yelling, screaming, like a lot of the acts," he remembers. "If Will Mastin said, 'We gotta do this,' they did it." Ford never knew how Mastin distributed the payment he received. "We used to pay Will Mastin," he says. "We'd agree on a price. What he did with it, we don't know."

Not long after he first met the trio in Boston, Ford ran into them in Auburn, Maine. "I went up there, to Priscilla's Ballroom, and who comes out but Will Mastin. They traveled all over New England."

They were still far down on show billings, but by 1940 they were certainly getting noticed. They appeared at the Metropolitan Theatre in Providence the last week of March that year. "A couple of jitterbugs billed as Jerry and Lillian appeared exuberantly and vulgarly, and the Will Marsten [sic] Trio, starring . . . Sammy Davis . . . added their fast tap routine." Mastin's name had been misspelled, but what the hell, they made the papers.

By the age of fifteen Sammy had started experimenting onstage. He'd start crooning a popular song. He'd mock the act that had gone on before—he was mimicking, becoming an impersonator. Mastin and his father sometimes shot him cold looks. His improvisations were not discussed. It mattered little to him; he was playing to the audience, and the audience was laughing, slapping their knees. Mastin never had to worry about Sammy getting any of the dance steps in the dance routine wrong. He had them down pat. But after he had finished the rehearsed routine, he'd keep dancing; it was his youthful energy; he simply could not turn himself off. Vaudeville was creativity and invention, and little Sammy instinctively knew it. He heard the whistles, the demands to come back out onstage. And he'd reappear again, and start dancing again. Will Mastin heard the applause—and so did Sammy's father. At performance's end, in town after town, on stage after stage, Sammy would do what his father and Will Mastin taught him to do: he would bow—lowering his head, then his waist, all followed by a bend of the knees—like an English prince.

Now and then the three dancers—especially when they were out of work— would find themselves back in New York City, where the booking agents Mastin needed to see were concentrated. Sam Sr. and little Sammy would stay with Rosa at her apartment in Harlem. Mastin—private and aloof when off the road—would find his own room in Harlem. The idea of him staying with the Davises was unthinkable.

Mastin and Sam Sr. could get sentimental about Harlem—its theaters, its speakeasies, its gambling parlors, its show-business veneer. Its churches were lovely, but they were not churchgoing men. As for Sammy, his childhood

Two dancers, entertainer and entertainer, father and son. Already little Sammy—as he is called—has seen America, has heard the great steam-rolling engines plowing across the land. When money is low, he taps on street corners, and dazzles. It is 1937; he is twelve years old. Clothing is an integral part of their presentation. Sam Sr. hunts Negro haberdasheries in virtually every town he arrives in; he will pass along the habit to his son.

memories were scattered around the places he had been, the towns he had slept in; so many had been far away from New York City. Harlem was just another piece of geography to him, a place where his mother's family resided—though not Elvera herself, who was still on the road.

Unlike his return trips when he was a mere child—and Sam Sr. and Mastin always nervous about him being out of their sight—now Sammy was older and could roam about the city that was his birthplace. Gloria Williams—Sammy's cousin—would accompany him around town when he returned to Harlem. "I'd ride the A train with Sammy," Williams recalls. "We'd sing on the train. He wasn't a star yet." Even fastened down on a train, Sammy couldn't stop himself from impromptu performance. He was always loose as a puppet anywhere. He and Gloria sang show tunes, tunes he had heard on the radio, his feet patting against the floor of the train, his head—large and oblong atop his small spindly body—always bopping and bopping. Luisa Sanchez, his tough and bitter grandmother, had little to say to young Sammy when he returned to Harlem. The two had never spent much time together, so to him she was another tall woman whom he did not know much about—just like his mother. Luisa did hang a photo of the trio on the wall in her home.

The visits to Harlem for the trio were always brief—those pesty truant officers!—then whoosh, the three of them, Will, Sam Sr., and Sammy, gone again, their backsides bending into a taxi, then a train, Sammy always moving quick, moving as if he were chasing grasshoppers.

With his father and Mastin, he moved about the country constantly now, unaware of what it meant to have roots. His place of identity would be the road. Al Grey, Sammy's childhood friend, remembers seeing the trio in Los Angeles. "I remember they stayed at the Morris Hotel on Fifth Street. Sammy would dance on the corner, had a hat he'd lay on the walk, and he'd get pennies and nickels." In all the years to come, staying put, being idle, would make Sammy nervous, fidgety. (In even later years—and with absolute glee—he would sign some of his very brief missives to friends as "Zorro": was here, but now gone. Fare thee well.)

Sammy continued to have no idea of his mother's whereabouts. All he knew was, like him, she was dancing; she was trying to make a living. Like him, she was moving back and forth across the landscape, a dream still inside of her.

Back in Boston for much of 1941, Sammy, his father, and Mastin moved into yet another rooming house in the South End section of the city. Mabel Robinson, a young singer and pianist, lived across the street. "They were lean days," she would remember. "Sammy would come over and we'd cook. Then he'd go to work with Mastin and his father." She sensed that the trio had financial woes. "His father borrowed money from me to get to work," she says. "I loaned them money. Sam Sr. seemed to be a ladies' man." There were times when Robinson and others would hear a pounding sound coming from the apartment where the Davises lived. "[Sammy] had drums," she says, "and he practiced them." She and other friends would sit and watch Sammy dance and just marvel. "Sammy Davis, Jr., was a beautiful dancer. Without Sammy, [Mastin and Sam Sr.] wouldn't have been anywhere." Sammy struck her as somewhat of a loner. He did not hang out with other teenagers. "Every day we'd feed him," Robinson says. "We didn't mind. We were all show people." Even though Robinson was only a few years older than young Sammy, he insisted on calling her "Mrs. Robinson." "He was well mannered," she says. When Robinson got a singing engagement in Harlem that year, Sammy asked her to go by and check on his grandmother. "I never heard him talk about his mother. I heard him talk about his grandmother a lot."

In 1941, Elvera Davis found herself in Boston, working on a bill with Buck and Bubbles, a renowned song and dance act that had been in vaudeville since 1912. In their early years the duo often donned blackface. Fred Astaire was one of their biggest admirers. Sammy was always eager—actually, he was ravenous—to watch other performers, and, being in Boston himself at the time, as soon as he heard Buck and Bubbles were in the city he hustled over to the theater to see them. He stood in the wings. He was always jumpy and loose and happy standing in the wings, watching other performers. While there, he saw her. Could it really be? It was indeed her. She was onstage dancing; he hadn't seen her in a long time; it was Elvera, his mother. Both were quite surprised. "Sammy would come specifically to look at Bubbles," Elvera would recall. "Bubbles was the dancer and Buck played the piano. If you were in a town and you could arrange it, you'd go see other performers. Well, one night we went to see Sammy's show. Sammy did his whole act based on what Bubbles had done. He'd copy anybody. Bubbles said to me later, 'I don't want him coming here standing in the wings watching me anymore.' " Sammy stole what he could and poured it into his own manic performance, jangling it to the point where it felt to him that his own originality overpowered what he had stolen.

There was no mother-son reunion between Elvera and Sammy in Boston, no evening chat in a hotel lobby, no meal shared in a diner. There were shows to do and other engagements, and before they knew it, both had packed and left Boston, gone their separate ways.

Elvera, however, was getting tired of the traveling and the rootlessness. She had been on the road nearly fifteen years now—all the years, in fact, of Sammy's life. She'd known chorus girls who had gotten out, taken their sore feet back home, found themselves a man, settled down and married. She knew her career was headed nowhere. The attempt to launch a singing career in Montreal had been a dismal experience. The motel rooms and boardinghouses and train depots started to seem meaningless. That same autumn—1941—

Elvera danced her last paid gig at the Club Paradise in Atlantic City. In Atlantic City, she met and befriended Grace Daniels, a Negro woman who managed the Little Belmont nightclub. Daniels offered her a job as a barmaid, and Elvera accepted it. She had no savings and was quite happy when her new employer advanced her some money to get settled. She aimed to stay put awhile.

She got herself a small apartment on Illinois Avenue. Her salary was twenty dollars a week. Sometimes she was able to double that with tips and pleasant conversation. "I used to get five-dollar tips from one person!" She could finally start saving a little money and buy herself nice clothes. "You had a sporting crowd," she would recall of the Little Belmont. "They would tip lavishly, and they knew how to live." As time passed, she realized how much she liked living near the ocean. She was all alone. Her son, Sammy, was out on the road, her daughter, Ramona, in Harlem. She and Ramona had never been close. As the years passed, Ramona would grow more curious about why her mother left her with relatives as she took to the road, about why her aunt Julia was always the one tucking her in as a child. Elvera was not one to stage reconnaissance missions of the mind; she didn't look back, so she had no answers for her inquiring daughter. She had the ever-ready smile of a barmaid; she had some clothes in a closet; she had some broken-apart dreams; and she had her toughness.

Now and then when Elvera returned home from work, bone-tired from standing all those hours on her legs and dodging the constant come-ons from strangers, she'd sit down with a pen and paper. And she'd compose a letter to her son. She had an address in Boston, one in Syracuse, New York, and she had his grandmother's address in Harlem. They were addresses she had on scraps of paper. All addresses where Sammy had stayed for short spells. "I would write Will Mastin, and Big Sam, to give my letters to Sammy—and my letters would be returned, unopened," she would say years later, a sliver of sorrow in her high-pitched voice.

So they drifted, Elvera and Sammy, mother and son, like ocean waves— farther and farther away from each other.

Will Mastin, constantly worrying about truancy agents in whatever locale the group played, knew there was vaudeville work up in Montreal, Canada. So he began venturing north of the border, hustling up work there during the early 1940s. The trips in and out of Canada would be supplemented by work in and around the New England states. In Montreal, they took a place on de Bullion Street. The area was in a red-light district populated by hustlers and schemers. Sammy danced feverishly before the Canadians. "Those were good days," Sammy would come to recall of Canada. "We had a little status because we were in show business." They played in French Canadian lodge halls, and they hardly complained about the pay. Some weeks they earned forty-five dollars among them. "And we were glad to get those gigs," Sammy would remember. During lulls in work he'd dance on street corners, an ear listening to the jangle of coins dropped into the hat at his feet. "My father had an after-hours club here in Montreal," recalls Randy Phillips. "Scalpers used to [sell] Sammy suits. They had no money. They wore stolen clothes." They played the Midway Theatre and the Starland. Young Sammy wowed the Montreal audiences. Sammy would remember the city as being "a mecca for vaudevillians."

One of the things Sammy witnessed in Canada was a far more relaxed attitude among the races, between Negro and white. For the most part the Canadian blacks were from the Caribbean islands; many were Jamaican. White Canadians had no psychological wound regarding the American Negro, and the revelation excited both Mastin and Sam Sr. Both men began dating white women. A whole new social world opened for the two hoofers. Sammy was still a mere teenager, but he had long lived in an adult world. He ate around adults, performed onstage with adults, poked his head in on their conversations. The idea of sex had started to enter his mind. He couldn't help but take notice of his father and Will Mastin and the Canadian women on their arms. His eyes glinted like a young wolf's.

White women. Interesting prey.

Will Mastin was a realist. He knew vaudeville was over. He'd arrive in yet another town, and yet another friend from days gone by would be out of the business—or dead. Yet another theater had posted a closing notice. He was not one to look to the past for sentimentality—it paid no bills. Mastin was more fortunate than most acts—he had a member of his trio who was already looking forward to the future. Sammy Jr. was beginning to imagine a whole new world opening before him. He had begun experimenting onstage, grabbing at instruments and playing them, singing songs, improvising. He convinced himself his homework was to watch, so on double and triple bills, he'd chat up the other acts. He'd sit between them during coffee breaks. He'd run to his room and practice what he had seen them do earlier onstage. He'd challenge them to tap contests, his whole body whirring across rehearsal stages. He was surprised at how little sleep he needed. He rushed through some days with candy bars in his pockets; he skipped down staircases using dance steps—just as Bill "Bojangles" Robinson had done in those movies with little Shirley Temple, and just as the legend had taught him in person—then he skipped right back up them.

He began reading audiences, studying their faces. When dancer Paul Winik ran into Sammy again, he could see that the boy had used his time on the road wisely. "Sammy had it all: a dancer, a musician, a singer, a drummer. I remember when either of us knew nothing about the future."

Two traveling show-business families who reek of royalty. The four gentle-men standing are the Ames Brothers. The Will Mastin Trio catches their show at the Copacabana in 1953. Seated in center on the left is Mastin. Directly across from Mastin sit Sam Sr. and his new lady, Rita, a Harlem nurse. Sammy has already begun telling acquaintances how "classy" Rita is.

(JESS RAND COLLECTION)

The trio would bound into a city and look for the cheapest lodging possible. Young dancer Prince Spencer met the trio for the first time in 1940 in Detroit. "That's when [Sammy] was wearing a zoot suit," he says. "He was living at the Carlton Hotel. I was living at a better hotel, called the Norwood, in Detroit. A lot of time I'd cook for him in my room. They put me out of my room for cooking for them. They wanted to save money."

On December 7, 1941, Japanese warplanes flew over Pearl Harbor in Hawaii, drawing America into the war in Europe. Draft notices arrived in mailboxes. At the time of the Pearl Harbor attack, Sammy was still weeks shy of his sixteenth birthday, too young, right now, for war. Will Mastin wasn't worried; he was, like Sam Sr., beyond age. Some nights they huddled together around the radio, listening to reports of war and shaking their heads in unison. Other nights they listened to *Amos 'n' Andy*, the popular radio series. Still other nights they listened to boxing, which was usually followed by gentle shadowboxing in the air around them, laughing and playing, but never too rough with Sammy, lest he strain a muscle, hurt an ankle. Then where would the trio be?

Let other boys chase athletic heroes. Let them sit in cold stadiums on Saturday afternoons rooting as their football gods galloped downfield. Young Sammy was inspired by tap dancers. He made mental notes of the best duets and quartets he saw. He listened to singers on the radio croon deep into the night. He celebrated unknown acts and musicians whom few seemed to know about save himself and small knots of others. His radar zeroed in on talent. And in 1942—ever a searcher, ever a dreamer—Sammy found his lifelong musical hero.

Frank Sinatra, a New Jersey–born singer, had made a name for himself in 1939 with the Tommy Dorsey band. "All or Nothing at All" was one hit; "I'll Never Smile Again" another. On December 30, 1942, Sinatra appeared on a bill at the Paramount in New York City with Benny Goodman. The young singer caused near riots. Teenage girls fainted. He stood at stage's edge and looked as if he might take flight like an angel; the shrieks only got louder inside that semi-darkened theater. At another Sinatra appearance—this one at the Capitol—Sammy took his grandmother Rosa to see him. It was as if he were showing her what he hoped to become. He clipped Sinatra articles and kept them in a scrapbook. And wherever he went—town to town—his Sinatra scrapbooks went with him. His father was his father, Will Mastin was Will Mastin. Money came between the three of them. It was different with a true hero. There was something mystical and mysterious about a hero. There must exist a great psychological gulf between hero and acolyte; that gulf is the carpet the acolyte rides in on.

A reed-thin singer, Sinatra looked nearly malnourished. But bobby-soxers fainted over him. He had a voice that seemed to be canyon-wide. And he had a mother back in Hoboken who loved him ferociously.

Sammy would be seen with one hand in his pants pocket, the other hand cupping a cigarette, a loose-fitting suit jacket on with one button buttoned. Just like Sinatra in all those photos. "His idol was Frank Sinatra," Winik recalls. "He worshiped that man."

Sammy sat up nights listening to Sinatra, rubbing the edges of his albums, dreaming. "The biggest excitement in the world for him was to hear Sinatra sing," says Winik.

He'd follow him. He'd honor him. He would even, in time, steal stylistic points from him—the butterfly bow ties, the overcoat slung over the shoulder. He'd send fan notes. Sammy's twin loves were now comic books and Frank Sinatra. Will Mastin and Sam Sr. let the boy dream, gave him money when he spent all of his own so he could buy fan magazines that featured Sinatra. They didn't give a damn about Sinatra themselves. Their vaudeville world was gasping for breath. They were rumbling around the country like well-dressed vagabonds.

One was from Hoboken, one from the road. One Italian, one Negro. It became a tender and tough love story, two performers, both fiercely competitive, pouring the juice of life at each other's feet. "You got your shoes?"
(AUTHOR'S COLLECTION)

· · ·

One afternoon, ambling around Los Angeles as he was wont to do—eyeing marquees, stargazing—Sammy met up again with Prince Spencer, the young dancer he had first met in Detroit. Spencer was now a member of the Four Step Brothers, an elegant quartet. (They were not brothers at all; it was merely a stage name.) Prince and Sammy were the same height, the same size. Around one another—and without any urging whatsoever—they'd break into dance steps; they laughed and clapped their hands at each other's inventiveness. Spencer, a native of Toledo, Ohio, was a phenomenal acrobatic flash dancer. He could jump in the air and touch the tips of his shoes with each fingertip. He was suave and always well dressed. "They had nothing going," Spencer would remember of the trio when he met up with them again. "They were glad to be in my company." Prince had money; he could treat the dancers to a meal. He remembers a particularly sad conversation he had with Sam Sr. "Sam Sr. had to go pawn something to get Sammy something for Easter," says Spencer.

As Spencer watched the trio, he found himself pondering how it all worked—exactly how Mastin meshed with the father and son; how the father knew when to halt Mastin from working his son too hard; when Sammy himself knew to pull back from the spotlight, lest in his youthful exuberance he vanquish his father and Mastin onstage. "Big Sam worked for Will," says Spencer. "This was all Will's ingenuity. Will would hustle up the work. Will's thinking was, 'Don't make this little kid bigger than my act.' "

Sammy couldn't get—except in his mind—close to Sinatra. But Prince Spencer was another matter. Spencer wore nice clothes, and nice jewelry. He let Sammy wear some of his fine clothes. Sammy loved it, trying on shirts, vests, pants, then preening in a mirror. Spencer learned soon enough that Sammy operated on seesawing emotions of competitive spirit and praise: he'd praise Spencer, then behind closed doors he'd swear he'd become a better dancer and performer. Spencer was insightful enough to recognize something about young Sammy: "He was very ambitious."

At first Spencer thought little of Sammy's peculiar need—or maybe it was a hunger—but in time what began to wear on him was Sammy's constant attempts to meet movie stars and singers. Sometimes, for hours on end, he'd want to hang around theaters, or loll outside movie studios blowing cigarette smoke and angling his neck for whoever might be approaching. Or—growing bored and unsuccessful in stargazing—he'd want to rush off to a nightclub or a movie premiere to see whom he might be able to pigeonhole there—maybe an autograph, a handshake, a contact for Mastin and his father. "He wanted to be invited where the top entertainers were," recalls Spencer. "But at fourteen, fifteen, no one knew him or went out of their way to be in the company of the Will Mastin Trio." But Sammy insisted, and he'd get to staring so forlornly at Spencer's jewelry that Spencer would feel sorry for him. "A lot of times when Sammy wanted to go someplace, I'd let him wear my watch and rings." Sammy would position himself to meet the stars—Danny Thomas, Humphrey Bogart, Milton Berle—and he would bow before them with graciousness and solicitousness. But it was off-putting to Spencer. He'd sit back and nearly recoil. "I saw Sammy 'Uncle Tomming' with white people, and I resented it. The Step Brothers, well, we knew our place was not to be in white people's company. He wanted to be in their company. I'd see it, and I'd try to block it out of my mind." While Will Mastin and Sam Sr. were sleeping, or playing pinochle, or soaking their feet in Epsom salts, their Sammy was pounding the pavement.

He has just performed at Bill Miller's tony Riviera nightclub in Palisades, New Jersey. It is 1953 now. The kid in the middle is all grown up. Sammmeeeee! they are beginning to scream. He will plead with the photographer, however, to never let this photo get in the hands of the tabloids—and it doesn't. Deep in the smiling, there is the whiff of sexual innuendo, of scandal—of black and white.   (JESS RAND COLLECTION)

"When Sammy was by himself," says Spencer, "he got mistreated, called 'nigger' and 'coolio.' " But Sammy could take the insults. They were nothing, just edgy and whispery words floating in and out of his ears. He wanted to make contacts, to elevate the trio. In self-promotion, he knew no shame. "They didn't infringe on entertainers the way Sammy did," Spencer says of Mastin and Sam Sr. "Sammy would make it his business to find out where the stars were and get their autographs."

It was becoming routine for the young Sammy: once a door was opened, he smiled his way through and then unleashed his talent on whoever would give him a moment. He'd corner nightclub owners and promoters and tell them he was a dancer with the Will Mastin Trio, a dance act, new to town. Mastin and his father didn't have the young legs anymore, and Sammy knew it, so he'd run for them, he'd be their legs, he'd pounce like a lion. He was their legs onstage, and he'd be their legs in the streets. He did not notice the shame in Prince Spencer's eyes. It was so very dim compared to the light of possibility.

But the Four Step Brothers were moving, far quicker than the Mastin trio, and Sammy worried about keeping up. He had no choice but to watch as the careers of the Step Brothers took off. In 1943 the quartet appeared in *It Ain't Hay,* an Abbott and Costello film. A year later they were featured in *Greenwich Village,* a Carmen Miranda and Don Ameche vehicle. No one was tossing any movie scripts in the direction of the Will Mastin Trio.

Given Sammy's competitive spirit, their ascendancy must have caused some kind of wound on his psyche. The laying down of a kind of ethos perhaps—to succeed, to run, to push, to climb and climb.

As much as he lamented that the trio's career was not moving faster, Sammy never stopped practicing. He practiced the speech patterns of movie stars, their mannerisms. He wondered how—and when—he and his father and Mastin would make it into the movies. Sometimes he became melancholy. He sulked in his small hotel rooms. He bought albums—Jimmy Lunceford, Ellington, Sinatra—and listened to them until he fell asleep. He read his comic books, fussed over his electrical gadgets. He fell behind in his correspondence courses and cried not one bit about it.

On account of the double-breasted suits he favored, young Negro boys looked at Sammy as if he were a minister's son. They smiled strangely at him, more out of mockery than admiration. He gave the same smile right back. Their games of throw and catch meant nothing to him. He was after the attention of their parents, who might pay a silver dollar to see him dance onstage. So he lived in his own world, between childhood and adulthood with no in-between.

He never seemed to get enough calcium. His teeth needed attention, cavities on both sides of his mouth. But there was no money to see a dentist, so he sometimes ate his meals in pain. He dreamed of Montreal. And dreamed of white girls. He had no interest in black heroes like boxer Joe Louis; he wanted to meet Sinatra. He listened to the singers on *Your Hit Parade* and lip-synched along. He dreamed himself to sleep, and dreamed himself awake.

Sometimes, in yet another city, he'd be dispatched to the store to get medicine for the small ailments that bedeviled his father and Mastin—rubbing cream and soaking salts to soothe the leg muscles. He'd sneak a cigarette, hand in pocket, the smoke curling above him while he took the pavement on his light feet.

Then it came, as it had come for so many thousands and thousands of others, and it stopped him, it quieted his tap shoes. It was his wartime draft notice. Psychologically, he was unprepared for it. Guns and blood and dying seemed but mere fantasy to him. Being a connoisseur of comic books, he believed in Superman. Now war and danger were as close as the blaring headlines. Abe Ford, the Boston booking agent, remembers talking with Sammy—they were zooming through Boston for an engagement—just before he went off to the army. Sammy seemed petrified. "I said, 'What's the matter?' He said, 'I'm scared stiff.' I said, 'Sammy, not only will you never fire a gun, you'll never see one, because of the talent you have.' "

Still, fear of the unknown gripped Sammy—just as it did his father and Mastin. The two hoofers knew men had gone off to war and not returned. Anything could happen. Will Mastin was old enough to remember that, in the aftermath of World War I, plenty of acts had simply fallen apart. And plenty of men had come home minus a limb—a foot, a leg.

Sammy found himself in San Francisco on the eve of induction. He was spending his last hours carousing with dancer Paul Winik and some friends in a hotel room—food, drink, memories, dance steps. Then the phone rang. Winik reached for it. It was the front desk calling. "We hear you got black people up in your room," someone from the front desk complained. They took their carousing elsewhere.

Next morning—August 19, 1944—Sammy Davis, Jr., entered the U.S. Army in San Francisco. Always ashamed of his lack of formal education, he put "high school graduate" for level of education on his induction form, which was quite far from the actual truth; he had no formal education at all.

It would be his first time away from the "home"—the hotels and motels, the trains and buses, the boardinghouses, the small towns and big cities—that had been provided by his father and Mastin. His father told him not to worry about his records and record player, his comic books, his nice clothes; he promised to take care of everything.

In a few months, Sammy would be nineteen years old. An interesting age, where there is still belief in possibility and even magic. His mother, Elvera, was nineteen when she first ventured out into the wide world to see what destiny awaited her.

After seeing Sammy off, Will Mastin and Sam Sr. made their way south from San Francisco by road and unpacked their bags at the old Morris Hotel in Los Angeles. Without their Sammy, they now had to imagine a different kind of act. Mastin hustled up a couple of jobs in burlesque houses, but the work quickly faded. Youth was not on their side, as it was for the Nicholas Brothers and the Four Step Brothers. Hardly anyone believed two male tap dancers—who were getting on in years—could keep customers in their seats. Bookings began to evaporate. Mastin brooded more than ever. The stack of bills that he kept inside the money belt he wore around his waist got smaller and smaller. "Will would come by every Friday, and I'd slip him a little something," remembers Paul Winik. "I was working and they weren't. When Sammy left they had nothing. I don't know how they survived. I gave them a few bucks, but what was that?"

Mastin was hardly going to take Sammy's absence without action. He would have to improvise. All his life he had been improvising. He needed to find another dancer, and he sent word around. Pudgy Barksdale asked for an audition. She hailed from St. Louis. She had originally come out to Los Angeles to dance in *Born Happy*, a show that starred Bill "Bojangles" Robinson. When she heard news that Will Mastin was looking for a dancer, she was eager for a tryout. "They weren't famous yet," Barksdale said. Mastin liked what he saw in Barksdale. She was small, five foot two—small like Sammy. Mastin and Sam Sr. welcomed her into the act.

Pudgy was amused by the two men, whom she thought of as from another era. "I thought of [Mastin] as old-time show business," she says. "I thought the routine he did was hokey. But Sammy's daddy was a good tap dancer."

Will Mastin had been living on "hokey" for a very long time now. "Hokey" had kept him in nice suits, nice shoes, felt hats, long overcoats come winter, linen come summer, silk at his pleasure.

Mastin concentrated on getting bookings in Los Angeles, mostly—he and Sam Sr. wanted Sammy to be able to find them if need be. He grinned tightly in the company of show promoters as he introduced his new dancer. "I was cute and little," Barksdale says, aware of how Mastin promoted her. "I had a costume." Her costume was "a little female tuxedo." She wore black shoes and stockings. "I was treated like a minor, really, even though I was in my twenties." Barksdale had played better venues than what Mastin offered. "They were working at nightclubs around Los Angeles," she recalls. "The clubs were so small that [some of the] seats would be at the bar." She'd watch Mastin and Sam Sr. onstage and, sometimes—surprising even herself—the hokiness got the better of her. "They looked good," she admits. Barksdale remembers one engagement where female strippers appeared onstage doing fan dances. Will Mastin was a dignified man, but the war was on, and money was tight, so he was not above playing burlesque houses and two-bit bars up and down Central Avenue. The old vaudevillian aimed to survive.

In time, there were fissures in the new arrangement. Pudgy Barksdale was young. She wanted to have a good time. She drank a little. Mastin was a disciplinarian. He did not brook tardiness. Sometimes there were cold stares, which made Barksdale chuckle. She kept her ears open for other dancing opportunities.

Barksdale got a job offer to join a chorus that impresario Leonard Reed was putting together. Reed was half Negro and half Cherokee Indian. Early in his career he had brazenly and successfully passed himself off as a white dancer. He was now preparing to take some dancers into Nevada and other western states on a tour. Knowing Mastin and Sam Sr. had an uncertain future with Sammy away, Barksdale asked Reed if the two hoofers could join up, and he told her they could. Will Mastin in a Leonard Reed show? Mastin didn't think so. He refused the offer, allowing that he did not fly—which he didn't—but the real reason was simple pride. So she left them. It was no leather off Will Mastin's money belt. He had seen dancers come and go for years.

Years before, Mastin had had cyclists and contortionists in his employ; he couldn't find either now, so he hired a roller skater instead. So there they were, Mastin and Sam Sr., two dancers in tuxedos twirling canes with a young roller skater zooming around and between them onstage. It felt and looked desperate, and they both knew it. Mastin let the roller skater go.

The Will Mastin Trio was down to two again.

Mastin was back to rubbing the money belt, jangling the coins in his pocket. He had to keep the tuxes cleaned; he and Sam Sr. had to eat.

As days rolled over onto weeks, the two men whiled away their time in and around the environs of Los Angeles, reading the theatrical trade publications, checking the desk in the lobby of the Morris Hotel for messages, eating greasy food, hoping for war's end. They were indeed resilient men, dancers who had traversed the country many times over: through the snows of Maine and the rains of Seattle; through the heat of Texas and the great mountains that humped in the middle of the country; along the Mississippi River and into dilapidated theaters; and into other evenings through doors of theaters constructed in the last century. And onward—often catching their breath in the falling-apart Negro part of town—playing the double and triple bills, sleeping with noise in the hallways; then, at sunrise, on a train's platform in coats and fedoras with the train whistle slicing the air, then gone, on the by and by: Harlem, the Catskills, the province of Quebec—they had seen it all. They had moved about the whole of North America like a tiny regiment. Three Negro dancers—six legs—counting on a juiced-up Sammy to dazzle.

Now, in the late winter of 1944, Will Mastin and Sam Sr. were just two nearly anonymous Negroes—albeit well dressed—putting one foot in front of the other, sometimes tilting their heads to the sky, on the lookout for bombers like so many others. They saw a new year—1945—come into view. Evenings in Los Angeles grew lonely and strangely quiet.

Without their Sammy, they felt utterly lost.

Following his induction, Sammy was shipped off to Fort Francis E. Warren, in Cheyenne, Wyoming.

In 1943—a year before Sammy became a part of Uncle Sam's army— America suffered through a season of explosive racial unrest. Whites and

Negroes battled in Harlem, in Mobile, Alabama, in Detroit, and in an additional three dozen other cities during that summer. The worst conflict erupted on June 20 in Detroit. As night fell, Negroes and whites began fighting on Belle Isle, a segregated municipal beach operated by the city. Tensions had been building over the Sojourner Truth Homes, a Detroit housing complex the federal government had constructed for Negroes but recently resegregated for white occupancy. By the time military police quelled the riot, twenty-five Negroes and nine whites were dead; 675 people had been injured.

With the onset of World War II, a great migration of Negroes from the South—more than half a million—took place. Negroes poured into northern cities in search of jobs. The exodus from the South would forever alter the social dynamic of the country. Negroes felt their allegiance to patriotism would also herald a call for active democracy. Campaigns were waged—using the war as backdrop—for better job opportunities and equal rights. The NAACP unveiled its so-called Double-V campaign, hoping for a double victory—abroad in the war and at home regarding equality. The organization was determined to "persuade, embarrass, compel, and shame our government and our nation into a more enlightened attitude toward a tenth of its people." The celebrated Harlem poet Langston Hughes asked a question wrapped in a poem:

> *You say we're fightin*
> *For democracy.*
> *Then why don't democracy*
> *Include me?*
> *I ask you this question*
> *Cause I want to know*
> *How long I got to fight*
> *BOTH HITLER—AND JIM CROW?*

The U.S. military had long had a peculiar and unsettling relationship with Negro America.

Many Northerners—at the instigation of Frederick Douglass and other abolitionists—began pleading that Negroes be used in the Civil War effort as Union casualties mounted. The idea made President Abraham Lincoln nervous, but the Union army needed help. Lincoln eventually relented. The Massachusetts Fifty-fourth Regiment—a group of Negro soldiers led by white officers—distinguished itself during the war, particularly during an attack on July 18, 1863, on Fort Wagner, South Carolina. The soldiers of the Fifty-fourth were well aware of their fate if captured by rebels: hanging—or slavery. The exploits of the Fifty-fourth may have been duly noted, but it did not mean Negro entry into future battles would occur easily.

Southern politicians railed in 1914 against sending Negroes into World War I, envisioning nightmarish scenarios in which Negroes might return to America and overtake white communities. But the possibility of Negro troops in that war energized the Negro thinker W. E. B. Du Bois. He believed Negro service in the conflict would result in "the right to vote and the right to work and the right to live without insult." But many Negro soldiers who returned home from that war soon met unsettling times as race riots erupted. "You niggers were wondering how you are going to be treated after the war," a New Orleans city official told a group of soldiers. "Well, I'll tell you, you are going to be treated exactly like you were before the war; this is a white man's country, and we expect to rule it."

The West—where Sammy was now stationed—was always tricky territory for the Negro soldier. There was plenty of proof in the infamous Brownsville, Texas, incident of August 13, 1906. In the darkness before midnight, a group of Negro soldiers stationed on the Brownsville base reportedly left their barracks and went into town. The soldiers had been complaining of being assaulted in town and not receiving service in the saloons. Once they were in town, shots were fired, and a white man was killed. Eventually, the soldiers retreated back to their barracks. (There had been rumors preceding the incident that a white woman had been sexually assaulted by a Negro soldier.) Many in the town feared Negroes had staged a revolt and might do so again. "We look to you for relief; we ask you to have the troops at once removed from Fort Brown and replaced by white soldiers." This was the end of an urgent telegram sent to President Theodore Roosevelt. There were emotionally charged stories in the national press. Roosevelt ordered the fort closed. Some of the soldiers were sent to a base in Oklahoma, others held under guard. There had been palpable fear a lynch party might attack them. During an inquiry the soldiers refused to answer questions. The silence angered Roosevelt and the Department of War. A day after his reelection—and absent any shame regarding the timing—Roosevelt ordered all 167 of the Negro soldiers dishonorably dismissed, without even a trial. Protests and demonstrations followed. The *New York World* referred to the Roosevelt order as "executive lynch law." Inasmuch as the soldiers never had a chance to testify in court, the case would forever be shrouded in mystery.

The Brownsville incident and others like it were dangerous and blighted tales kept far from the growing-up ears of Sammy Davis, Jr. For a little Negro child, Sammy had led a life with a certain protectiveness around it. From his years in vaudeville, Mastin had cultivated an underground world where he found dignity, respect, and certain manners. Over time, he had delivered the young Sammy into a world of soliticious theater operators; his father and Mastin's humble acquaintances; flashy but doting women who knew and respected both men. Mastin and Sam Sr. were shrewd and kept Sammy out of harm's way. "Sam [Sr.] and Mastin sheltered him, saying, 'Oh, we're staying with a family,' when the two old men knew they couldn't get a room in a segregated hotel," says Gloria Williams. Now Sammy was away from all that—the glue and the bookends of his father and Mastin—and in the war.

Fort Francis E. Warren had been an old and distinguished cavalry post established in 1867. Many of its troops had fought in the Great Sioux Indian Wars during the 1870s, when the installation was known as Fort Russell. In 1886 four Negro regiments were formed by Congress, and three of those regiments—the Ninth and Tenth Cavalry, and the Twenty-fourth Infantry—served at Fort Russell. The Negro units, roaming the West from the Canadian border to the Rio Grande, became renowned for their fierce skirmishes with Indians. In time they became known as "Buffalo Soldiers," a name reportedly given to them by the Indians in honor of the respect they held for the buffalo. The Negro units were hardly free of controversy. Henry Flipper, the first Negro to graduate from West Point and an officer with the Tenth Cavalry, was court-martialed. His crime: he had been spotted by white soldiers riding on a horse with a white woman. In 1930 the post was renamed Fort Francis E. Warren. It had long been noted for its harsh temperatures, and soldiers arriving knew to be prepared for the elements.

Sammy arrived to begin his basic training in the late summer, and cool air was already coming down from the mountains around Cheyenne.

The military still held its overall policy of racial segregation, but a month before Sammy arrived at Fort Warren, the army announced that its recreation and transportation facilities were to be desegregated. (Jackie Robinson, a young army officer at Fort Hood, Texas—son of sharecroppers and a native of Cairo, Georgia—had been court-martialed before the new ruling went into effect for refusing to sit in the back of a bus. Robinson, who had been a gifted multisport star at UCLA, fought the court martial and was reinstated. He left the army and joined the Kansas City Monarchs of the Negro American League in 1945, two years away from cracking the color barrier in modern major-league baseball.)

On his first day on base at Fort Warren, Sammy heard the word "nigger": "I ain't arguin' you're in charge," he overheard a recruit say to an officer. "I'm only sayin' I didn't join no nigger army." Sammy pulled his bags into the bunkhouse, got assigned a bunk, met another Negro soldier. A white soldier sneered at Sammy, telling him to shine his shoes. Sammy refused; the other Negro soldier did not. There was more sneering. Racial tension hummed all about. Every day, he seemed to be dropping down into a new temperature of reality. Owing to the cocoon his father and Mastin had kept him in, he was as surprised as someone new to America and unfamiliar with its racial history.

Following an exchange of racially charged words, Sammy and another white private exchanged punches. The scuffle—which ended when others intervened—left him bleeding and shaking. At night, in his bunk, he lay with his nerves on edge, wondering when the next fistfight might come. He was suddenly in a nightmarish world—the hurly-burly of army life and racism pressed into his eyes. He seemed shocked. "How many white people had felt like this about me?" he pondered. "I couldn't remember any. Not one. Had I just been too stupid to see it? I thought of the people we'd known—agents, managers, the acts we'd worked with—these people had all been friends. I know they were. There were so many things I had to remember: the dressing rooms—had we been stuck at the end of the corridors off by ourselves? Or with the other colored acts? That was ridiculous. Dressing rooms were always assigned according to our spot on the bill."

This was a different landscape from that of nightclubs and dressing rooms. These were soldiers in khaki. And while the American flag snapped over the base, the knuckle of a fist landed upon his chest because of the color of his skin. His father and Mastin were nowhere around to pull him to safety.

He was a dancer, in limber shape, and he made it through basic training. But he was not physical. Actually, he seemed almost too elegant to be a soldier. There was a feyness in his walk, something that made him seem vulnerable amid barracks and dirt. Army officers, unsure where to assign him, made him go through training a second time. The ropes, the calisthenics, the running, all over again. No one told him why, and he was too timid to complain.

He got assigned to latrine duty, which meant he was on his hands and knees scrubbing the toilet bowls in the barracks.

Another soldier crushed Sammy's wristwatch under the heel of his boot. Sammy recoiled, a shy nineteen-year-old, terrified. "Awww, don't carry on, boy," a soldier by the name of Jennings told him. "You can always steal another one." There was no hiding in the raw Wyoming wind. Just soldiers; some nice, some nasty and mean. "Overnight, the world looked different," according to Sammy. "It wasn't one color anymore."

It really hadn't ever been one color, but to a show-business kid, hustled and hustling from hotel to theater to train station—bags handed to the kindly Pullman porter—then repeating the process again, on end, for months, for years even, it might have seemed that way. Sammy's hands never touched cotton bolls; his feet never trampled across a sharecropping farm.

There was another fight in the barracks, and blood oozed from Sammy's face. He fought back, but with the same results, a beating. He dropped tears. He was in the army, and he was fighting, all right—but it was with an unexpected enemy: his fellow soldiers. He was not his father, Big Sam, who'd made threats against whites in Wilmington, North Carolina, before he had finally fled that town. He was just a kid, coming up on his nineteenth birthday.

He heard about the base band, the 352nd Army Band, and pleaded to join. A stage had been his lifelong home. He wowed the army officers.

As a member of the band, Sammy began to relax. Which meant he began to hop about wildly. There was no more idle time in the bunkhouse. "He had more things to do than the average black," Abe Lafferty, a member of that band, would remember.

His impersonations were riotously funny. He knew how to play several instruments. Over time, he would be allowed to organize musical shows. Gathered around musically inclined soldiers, he would yak into the blue moon about show business, about the theaters he had played, the cities he had seen. "You'd look on the bulletin board and it would say, 'Lafferty, Sammy Davis. Such and such a time,' " recalls Lafferty. "When a company was getting ready to be shipped out," he says, "we'd go give them a show."

Having band mates, being around those who were appreciative of his skills, made Sammy's confidence soar. He knew entertainment; no one could get him off a stage. "It was five of us who were always drafted to play a Sammy Davis show," Lafferty says. "He was always good for laughs. He'd come over to our barracks for a bite to eat. Can't remember any other blacks coming over there." Lafferty was amazed at how Sammy simply took over the shows—a comic, a mimic, a musician, a singer. "He'd emcee the whole show. He'd run the whole thing. It was his show." They were wowed—and stunned—by his impersonations. A Negro doing Jimmy Cagney, Boris Karloff, Edward G. Robinson, Frank Sinatra! (Frank was sitting out the war—a bad eardrum—and, with so many boys gone off to war, singing his velvety lyrics to a nation of lonely hearts.)

Sammy turned twenty in the army. There was no girl "back home" to send him perfume-scented letters. Still, his spirits improved greatly on account of the base shows, which gave him a measure of celebrity. He began to bounce back to where he was, regarding race, before he came into the army—race didn't matter; the world was colorless. He believed if he could perform, he could drive the racism away. The applause had ushered the return of his naïveté. "My talent was the weapon," he would believe, "the power, the way for me to fight. It was the one way I might hope to affect a man's thinking."

It can be traced to the mountains of Wyoming, where Sammy first felt and thought seriously about the sting of race upon his back. He couldn't decipher what it all meant. He believed that the quickness of his feet and the mimicry in his voice could defeat the hard glare of the redneck—any redneck—and he would, in their suspicious eyes, be transformed back to where he was with his father and Will Mastin: in the middle, juicing things up. "I dug down deeper every day, looking for new material, inventing it, stealing it, switching it—any way that I could find new things to make my shows better, and I lived twenty-four hours a day for that hour or two at night when I could give it away free, when I could stand on that stage, facing the audience, knowing I was dancing down the barriers between us," he would say.

By early spring of 1945, American forces had taken Iwo Jima, liberated Manila, then Paris. General Douglas MacArthur, in sunglasses, mythical and brilliant, had returned triumphantly to the Philippines. Momentum was clearly on the side of America and its allies. But then, on April 12, President Franklin D. Roosevelt—he was smoking a cigarette, doing work at his desk in Warm Springs, Georgia—suffered a cerebral hemorrhage. The death was announced at 3:55 in the afternoon. Next day, the train that bore him began its ride back to the nation's capital. Thousands stood alongside the railroad tracks. When the train reached a place near Gainesville, Georgia, a group of Negro women in a cotton field all seemed to drop at once to their knees, shrieking in awful cries of agony.

Sammy had been diagnosed in the army with a jumpy heart, and it qualified him for an early release. On June 1 he packed up his belongings and collected his release papers, his musician buddies guffawing in his ear, slapping him on the back.

He wanted to remember the army shows, the way he danced onstage, how he held the microphone, how he interacted with the other musicians. How the pristine Wyoming air felt hitting his face as he stood before his fellow soldiers. He wanted to remember the smiles that climbed from the soldiers and reached him as he mimicked someone. He felt so comfortable on those army stages. He wanted to remember all of that—Abe Lafferty's laugh and horn playing too— and not the sting of the fists that had floored him, fists that had come flying out of the darkness of history.

A train whistle blew, and the eleven-month army vet—who never rose above the rank of private, first class—was on his way back to Los Angeles, where he'd trade in the army boots for his old tap shoes.

Two months later, President Harry Truman would order the dropping of two atomic bombs on Japan, effectively ending the long and unmerciful war in which America had lost more than 290,000 men.

On the home front, Sammy's idol, Frank Sinatra, was bigger than ever. His wartime concerts were sellouts. "It was the war years, and there was a great loneliness," Sinatra would come to explain of it all. "I was the boy in every corner drugstore who'd gone off, drafted to the war. That's all."

Chapter 4

AND SAMMY SHALL
LEAD THEM

He had been too jittery to sleep on the train ride from Cheyenne to Los Angeles. On the train he was still in uniform. His army experiences aside, he was so very proud to wear it. Ever since Sammy had felt life—laughter and tears, the shift of seasons in the weather, the smell of food atop a stove—he had been in vaudeville. Being away from it had hurt, had torn at his sense of motion and self-esteem. Being back would provide a sense of balance.

His father and Will Mastin were at the train station to pick him up. Sam Sr. had beautiful and large white teeth; Mastin's teeth were smaller, but with gold; and there the two men stood, smiling their Sammy—in Uncle Sam's uniform—into their outstretched arms and back into show business.

They dined and they laughed, and they listened to Sammy's army stories. (Keenly aware of how emotional they both were about him, Sammy spared the tales of his fisticuffs.) They told Sammy about Pudgy Barksdale, how she came and went, and they laughed some more. Sam Sr. told Sammy that Pudgy, in fact, was back in town, was convalescing from an illness and staying over at the Morris Hotel. Sammy hustled over to see her. "He stood at the foot of my bed and did all of his imitations for me," Barksdale remembers.

There was news to share with Sammy. Mastin had signed with a booking agent, Arthur Silber, who had an independent agency in Los Angeles. Mastin had known Silber from his days in vaudeville when Silber was a traveling performer. Silber's best-known client was Big Jim Corbett, who was far from being famous. Sammy had never heard of Arthur Silber. Silber wasn't connected to the big agencies in town—his was a virtual one-man operation—and Sammy wanted to be with one of the big guns. But it was Will Mastin's show, and he couldn't complain. Silber got them work—a quick USO trip to Honolulu; sixty-six-year-old Will Mastin boarded a plane for the first time in his life—but it was a quick tour, and there they were, right back in Los Angeles.

In the late 1940s they were often on the edge of penury. Then would come the sudden notice of an engagement, and they'd have to borrow money to get their clothing out of the dry cleaners. The kindness of others helped them survive; agents and acquaintances occasionally slipped them small amounts of cash. Sammy never forgot such gestures. And there they'd be, onstage, the cane in Mastin's hand, Sammy in the middle, their suits— white mohair, in this instance, for Will and Sam Sr.—looking like a million. They had style like a bank has money. "Ladies and gentleman, the Will Mastin Trio—"   (JESS RAND COLLECTION)

Sammy beat the pavement. Every waking hour now he was but a dancer looking for a stage. He had always been driven and determined; he seemed more so now. The war was over; things were humming. He could not sit around and wait for a phone to ring. He bounced in and out of nightclubs as if scouting possible venues: the Moulin Rouge, the Mocambo, gliding along the back walls like a spy. (It was at the Mocambo that canaries whistled from cages, causing waiters to carry nets over the food trays in case of bird droppings.) Sammy's friends noticed his frenetic pace. Leroy Myers was another dancer in Los Angeles, just out of the war. He caught the Mastin trio as part of a large bill at the Orpheum in Los Angeles. "They were doing a bang-up job," he says. And of Sammy: "He was on his way."

Even though it lay years in the future, Myers says he felt Sammy had already begun calculating his solo adventure by incorporating new moves into the act. "He was able to exploit his talent by working with the trio. [The club promoters] just wanted you to do a hot nigger dance. They didn't want you to be clever." Myers watched carefully for signs of resentment by Mastin and Sam Sr. regarding Sammy's rambunctiousness. "I imagine they didn't encourage him. They probably gave him hell for stepping outside the act." Mastin and Sam Sr. had their pride, their honed skills. "Not that they were jealous of him," Myers says. "They were just trying to protect their jobs."

Ernest Cooke, another war veteran, had also seen Sammy perform before he went into the army. "When Sammy came out of the army," says Cooke, "he was even more sensational."

The act did a couple of weeks at the Cricket Club in Los Angeles. Sammy had started doing cakewalks. He'd dance on all fours. Then he'd hop up, place his hands behind his back, and move his feet furiously in front of him. Mastin and Sam Sr. were astonished by some of his improvisations.

Musician Tracy McCleary had toured the country with various bands before the war. After the war, he says, names of certain performers seemed to be on everyone's lips. One was Sammy Davis, Jr. "Everybody was so taken with Sammy," recalls McCleary. "He was just terrific. He would sing, dance, you name it. You couldn't help but notice this young guy was carrying these two older guys on his back."

Arthur Silber was Arthur Silber, and Abe Lastfogel was Abe Lastfogel, who just happened to be part of the team running the William Morris Agency. Behind Mastin's back, Sammy wormed his way into Lastfogel's graces, and there they were one afternoon at the swanky Hillcrest Club in Los Angeles, Lastfogel gliding Sammy around the room: meet Groucho Marx, meet Jack Benny, meet Al Jolson himself. Face to face, there were Sammy and Jolson; Jolson, the man whom Sammy had impersonated as a child onstage in blackface—whom he was still impersonating! After the war, and with Negro rights taking on more urgency, memories of Jolson's blackface routine were more hushed than loudly remembered. Still, Sammy couldn't contain the grinning, the exuberant hand-pumping. These were the men he listened to on the radio, the performers he had watched in darkened theaters in his youth. Marx, along with his brothers Harpo, Chico, and Zeppo, had risen to fame with riotously funny movies, highlighted by the spoof *Duck Soup,* in 1933; Benny had been a violinist in his youth and now had a popular radio program that featured Rochester, his Negro valet; Jolson was Jolson, aging now and desperately trying to hold on to the fame he had once known. All former vaudevillians, all born—as Will Mastin had been—in another century; all pressed into show business—as Sammy had been—in their youth. Sammy stood among them swooning, listening to their snappy one-liners, admiring the clothing they wore. Marx and Jolson were rather aloof, but Benny told Sammy he had heard his name around town. Sammy didn't know if it was true or not, but he liked hearing it. Lastfogel wanted to sign him, then reality set in for Sammy. He couldn't sign, because Will Mastin had signed him up with Arthur Silber. A part of Sammy was owed to Will Mastin, and Will Mastin had portioned off that part to Silber. It was akin to one of those tricky vaudeville contracts— a mirror and plenty of smoke.

But Abe Lastfogel, one of the cagiest operatives in Hollywood, had no intention of forgetting young Sammy Davis, Jr.

While onstage now, Sammy had begun working more seriously at singing. He had a clear voice, full of lung strength. Jesse Price, a drummer friend—in ten seconds flat Sammy could own you as a friend, hurling compliments, offering cigarettes—introduced him to the brass at Columbia Records. Sammy cut a single in 1946—"The Way You Look Tonight"—and no one exactly had high hopes for it, but it managed to catch on when it was released that year.

The first recognition of his breakaway talent came that year as well when *Metronome* magazine named Sammy "Most Outstanding New Personality." He didn't know what it meant, but he was so excited he went and found the magazine owners to thank them personally. One of the things it did not mean was an instant leap to more money; the Will Mastin Trio continued to scuffle. In any event, Sammy's fan base grew.

Elliott Kozak, a young William Morris agent, had begun hearing of the Will Mastin Trio shortly after the war ended. "It was word of mouth: 'You gotta see Sammy Davis, Jr.' "

The act now looked more lively and more animated. Sammy was rising, and he was taking the trio with him.

The *Metronome* honor brought Sammy to the attention of young Mickey Rooney, himself home from the war and trying to reenergize his career by taking to the nightclub circuit.

Rooney, born Joe Yule, Jr., five years before Sammy, had had a celebrated career as a child actor. Between 1927 and 1933 he charmed audiences while appearing in the *Mickey Maguire* two-reel comedy series based on the comic-book character. In 1935—now working as Mickey Rooney—he drew critical raves for his performance as Puck in *A Midsummer Night's Dream*. Two years later he made his first two screen appearances as Andy Hardy, a winsome young boy living a life of domestic sweetness alongside his father, played by a curmudgeonly Lewis Stone. Andy Hardy became every American boy, with a cowlick and a mischievous grin on his face. By 1939, Rooney had replaced Shirley Temple as America's number 1 box office star. His ego seemed a dangerous thing. In 1944, Rooney was drawing plaudits alongside Elizabeth Taylor in *National Velvet.* But wartime service seemed to have derailed his momentum. He made no movies in 1945 or 1946, so to reignite his career, he decided to take an act on the road. Rooney's manager, Sam Stefel, recommended the Mastin trio to Rooney as an opening act. It sounded fine to Mickey—he didn't ponder things very long.

Sammy, his father, and Mastin got themselves to Boston, where the tour would begin. Rooney said he'd meet the trio in the lobby of the Copley Plaza Hotel. He mentioned noon. And at noon he bounced in. "Now that's a pro for you," Mastin said to young Sammy. Rooney was always full of heat and anxiousness. He sized people up quick, then boom, he was off. He walked like a man fleeing the scene of a crime. Sammy said he'd like to do impressions. Mastin grimaced about the impressions, as they made him nervous. Nervous because Mastin sometimes felt Sammy was pushing the limits by mocking white entertainers as he imitated them. Stefel said his Mickey did the impressions, but Rooney overruled him and said it would be okay for Sammy to do impressions. And when Sammy did his impressions, the audiences loved it. Mickey himself cackled.

At night, on the road, Sammy and Mickey played cards, sang songs, wrote songs in their minds, sang those songs out. Sammy would watch Rooney, and whenever he watched someone he admired, he took mental notes. He liked Rooney's style and was determined to steal what he could from the performer. Dance steps weren't nailed down; a certain walk wasn't nailed down. Sammy was a mimic. He loved the way Rooney would just walk out onstage—boom, there he was, gliding toward the microphone, no announcement or anything—just whoosh from behind the curtains and there's Mickey, the Mick, Andy Hardy with the cowlick, in the raw flesh. Sammy liked the way the applause rose at such an entrance.

He and Mickey talked show business, movies; Sammy wanted to know all about Liz Taylor. Days rolled by, and Sammy was happy. Shooting the breeze with Mickey; Will in the dressing room, tugging at his French cuffs; Sammy listening to the pink-cheeked giggling white girls; reading the reviews over his father's shoulder; watching Mickey shoot by backstage, boom, just like that, just gone, and watching the applause drape over him out there onstage, and listening to the shrieks. Timmie Rogers—Sammy's vaudeville friend— remembers catching Sammy on the bill with Rooney. "The first show, Sammy did twenty minutes. The manager was mad at Mickey because they're paying Mickey all that money. Mickey said, 'Hey, this guy's got a lot of talent.' Sammy was on fire."

The two of them—Sammy and Mickey—had much in common. Aside from being dimunitive—Mickey was shorter than Sammy by two inches—

both were feverish and desperate for success. They'd grown up in show-business families, and so their childhoods had been radically disrupted. The word "love" was as tricky to them as invisibility. Didn't something have to first be visible to be invisible? "I don't know what psychologists would say about an infancy such as mine," Mickey himself would say. "Bad for the child, perhaps. Too much attention. Too little stability. Nonetheless, I know this. I had a hell of a lot more fun than if I'd been the son of a psychologist."

Back in New York, the Mastin trio got a gig at the Strand Theatre, opening for Billie Holiday. Sammy would dance hard, rush backstage to dry himself off, then rush back out into the wings to watch Holiday. Billie Holiday, born poor in Baltimore, was a heroin addict. She said she had been forced into prostitution at the age of eleven. Her childhood had clearly been full of torment. One of her most popular tunes—and perhaps her saddest—was "God Bless the Child." Holiday often wore a gardenia in her hair while singing. Dan Morgenstern was a young Manhattan jazz buff—he'd go on to head the esteemed Rutgers Jazz Studies program—who remembered seeing the trio with Holiday. "They were a very tight act," he says. "What I remember best were his imitations—of Crosby, Sinatra, Perry Como. The act had a real flair."

The trio next played the Apollo in Harlem, on the same stage where Elvera had once danced. A young singer by the name of Keely Smith caught Sammy at the Apollo. She was walking down the hallway where the dressing rooms were "and heard these impersonations," she recalls. Sammy was behind that door, practicing. She knocked on the door and went in. "And there was Sammy in a stocking cap and robe. He was so nice. He was quiet and shy." Sammy charmed her. "He did his talking through his impersonations. I got the impression he was not too happy with things. But he never knocked his uncle, his father."

Will Mastin gave Keely Smith a strange feeling. "He had an evil look about him. He just had a thing about him that you didn't get close to him."

But after seeing Sammy at both the Strand and the Apollo, Smith began to feel what others were feeling, that there was now "a buzz about Sammy."

Amy Greene, a young, dazzling Cuban-born New Yorker—and the wife of renowned photographer Milton Greene—also remembers seeing Sammy at the Strand. "He was the opening act for Josephine Baker," she says. "We had never seen a talent like Sammy. This little human being."

Greene not only became a friend to Sammy, she became a kind of muse and teacher, introducing him around Manhattan, sharing with him her love and appreciation of fine things—china, table settings, art.

Arthur Silber sent his son, Arthur Jr., to travel with the trio. A sidekick for Sammy, Arthur Jr. was a big strapping young man. He grew up in Mississippi and felt at ease around Negro culture. "I grew up on soul food before I met Sammy," he says. Once, he and Sammy were striding down 125th Street in

Harlem, Sammy always walking quicker than Silber. Sammy ducked into a diner, Silber right behind. "This white boy stole my wallet!" Sammy hollered out, just as Silber was squaring his shoulders. Silber froze. Heads swiveled. Silber thought he might be accosted. And then Sammy started cackling. "Just joking," he told everyone.

Sammy very much liked the idea of having someone white with the trio on the road. It stayed some of the natural suspicion in the world of segregation— of three Negroes idling at the local hotel.

There were hundreds of dance acts for any big-band musician to take on the road in the 1940s. Lionel Hampton plucked the Mastin trio. Hampton—who in 1936 had joined the Benny Goodman quartet, in what was considered a wildly progressive move on Goodman's part at the time—had great versatility. He played drums and piano, but his specialty was the vibraphone. By 1940 he had his own band, and, with the recording in 1942 of "Flying Home," his first hit. Hampton also had a keen eye and ear for talent. He told Sammy that he and the trio had thirty minutes. A half hour to shake the world. That was usually the curse of any opening act—you went on, got all heated up, shook up the audience, and then it was time to scram. Time limit notwithstanding, it was a good moment for Sammy. Hampton knew it as well. "We were big time," says Hampton of his band. "Sammy was in a good position."

Sammy opened, dancing up a storm as Mastin and his father two-stepped in the background. Bouncing from one end of the stage to the next, in a furious and fevered show, he offered as much animation as he could because, as he knew, the clock was ticking—the vaudeville clock—which was but a harsh rising arm in the wings telling you your time was up. Then he was off, his fingers still snapping, his legs still loose. After he got offstage, he'd dry off and run back out to the wings to watch Hampton. Night after night. And every night, after the show, he'd browbeat Hampton to teach him to play the drums, the vibraphone. He wanted to know what Hampton knew. "I played a lot of drums," says Hampton. "I taught him how to play drums. He was a fast learner. Whatever he attempted to do, he was good at." The bus would be rolling, and still, Sammy would be bombarding Hampton with questions. Will and Sam Sr. would be sleeping, glancing at roadsides, dozing, Sammy's voice still going in high gear full of questions—for Hampton or any other musician on the bus whose ear he could bend. He wanted to know everything about show business, about the big time. The land kept rolling. Hampton's wife would find places on the road for the caravan to sleep. "We were all like a big family," Hampton says. And yet, Hampton sensed a profound restlessness in young Sammy. "Sammy wanted to be a star, and that's what he was working toward." Will and Sam Sr. "were old show folks and welcomed the break they got," Hampton says. "But Sammy was climbing all the time. All the time he was climbing."

The more Hampton witnessed Sammy onstage, and the more his musicians began murmuring in his ear about the kid's talents, the more a funny kind of feeling began to come over him. Sammy, to him, seemed a nest of other personalities. Hampton couldn't imagine somebody being happy crawling in and out of their skin, somebody chasing vocal ghosts and shadows, because the further that person went into the mimicry, it seemed, the closer they stalked a kind of danger—laughing as Boris Karloff, as Cagney, as Bela Lugosi. "It was a great experience, and it was a great break for him," Hampton says of the tour. "But I told him, 'Don't imitate nobody. Go be Sammy Davis. Develop yourself.'"

Go be Sammy Davis? What did that mean? He *was* being Sammy Davis. The audiences were laughing!

When they got back to Los Angeles, Steve Allen, a local disc jockey who worked for radio station KNX, a CBS affiliate, wanted Sammy on radio. Allen had seen the trio perform in Los Angeles. "Ordinarily," Allen would remember, "one doesn't invite a tap dancer to appear on radio, for obvious reasons, but I solved that problem by having Sammy dance on top of my grand piano—with the top down flat, naturally—while I played piano accompaniment for him to dance to."

Allen was impressed with Sammy's "acute, quick sense of humor" and with his stunning array of impressions—Bogart, Edward G. Robinson, Cary Grant. Sammy would sing songs in the voice of Lionel Barrymore, and Allen would crack up. As for Mastin and Sam Sr., they befuddled Allen. "By the time I saw them, they were middle-aged and pretty run-of-the-mill as hoofers. Actually, without little Sammy, I don't think the other two would have had much luck in being employed."

They were on the road, in Portland, Maine, when the telegram arrived: OPEN CAPITOL THEATRE NEW YORK NEXT MONTH, FRANK SINATRA SHOW. THREE WEEKS, $1250 PER. DETAILS FOLLOW. HARRY ROGERS. It may as well have dropped from the sky. Sammy was going to appear on the same stage as Sinatra, his idol. He was beside himself, bouncing on his feet, giggly. Sam Sr. was happy because his boy was happy. "Frank Sinatra," Mastin told the two, as if, somehow, he saw it coming all along and was hardly ready to do cartwheels, "always has a colored act on the bill with him."

Frank Sinatra had a social conscience. It sprang from childhood, coming face to face, as an Italian, with words that cut. "I'll never forget," Sinatra once said, "how it hurt when the kids called me a 'dago' when I was a boy. It's a scar that lasted a long time and which I have never quite forgotten." He spoke, now and then, in his early rise, to children about racial tolerance. He once was on a high school stage in Gary, Indiana. A group of white kids had been rebelling against a school policy that allowed Negro students to play in the orchestra and swim—at an appointed time—in the school pool. There were some tough boys, sons of steelworkers, staring up at Sinatra, wondering just what he'd have to say. "I can lick any son of a bitch in this joint," he said to them, and he had them where he wanted them. They stared, and they listened. In 1945, Sinatra made a short film called *The House I Live In,* written by Albert Maltz. (The short was directed by Mervyn LeRoy, who had been one of the producers of *The Wizard of Oz.*) It was a touching and effective ten-minute documentary with Sinatra talking to a group of kids about racial acceptance. The film received a special Academy Award. So when Frank walked out onto the Capitol stage to introduce Sammy to the crowd, and tenderly threw his arm around him—the nigger and the dago, the house they sometimes both had to live in—there was something a little deeper than show business at play.

Onstage that night the young Sammy did it all, dancing around his father and Mastin in perfect syncopation, beautiful little dance numbers, long slides, the comedy routine, the impressions, more tapping. Frank's people shot cold looks from the wings; Sammy always ran long. But the audience was clapping wildly. It was on such nights that Will Mastin had touches of fear mingling with his joy. White power-brokers might see Sammy. They might steal him away. After the show, Sinatra had some advice for Sammy: "You sound too much like me, but you should sing." Sammy froze—not understanding the critical insight of the Sinatra comment—then a sheepish grin appeared on his face.

Frank didn't understand the inside-out hunger of Sammy, the Negro mimic. Sammy had been standing in front of mirrors for hours—weeks!— trying to sing like Frank Sinatra.

You sound too much like me . . .

Frank had given Sammy the highest of compliments.

After the Sinatra shows, Mastin, taking his pats on the back—and how many were slapping him as a tribute to the young horse, to Sammy?—would vanish into a taxi. Sore feet, a cane, a hat, a proud hoofer. As for Sammy, being in Times Square, feeling the hum of the place in the middle of the night, seeing all the lights twinkling, the Cadillacs gleaming, the jewelry on wrists, the honking horns, he had simply been part of a Sinatra scene. It was all like a bolt from his vivid dreams.

Dancer Maurice Hines believes that audiences took to the trio because they were "a very classy act." And, indeed, it had clearly separated itself from the so-called saloon acts. "They didn't do anything derogatory," Hines recalls. "No dirty jokes." And after the Capitol Theatre appearance, Hines says, there was a secret feeling—something akin to a subtle but powerful ocean wave—that

Frank, Frank Sinatra himself, who had thrown his arm around little Sammy so lovingly on that stage, and did it again backstage all for the cameras, "was behind them."

As he was swooping along in those early years, Sammy was recruiting his own showbizlike family—Amy Greene, for her lifestyle and sophisticated manner; now Sinatra, for his sheer power and clout. He began to send little thank-you notes to those he met, to those he felt, in whatever way, small or large, had helped him.

He plucked another recruit from the audience of the Strand Theatre in New York. Her name was Judy Balaban. Her father was the Balaban of the famous Katz and Balaban theaters, and on account of the family business, she was a frequent theatergoer, although she had never heard of the Will Mastin Trio. "They came onstage, and my socks fell off," she remembers. "I could just not get over this kid who I thought was talented beyond description in some magical way." After the show she got herself backstage. She had to meet Sammy. "It's not a denigration of whoever else was onstage that day. I can't remember who else was on the bill." She goes on: "We made a fan visit to the Will Mastin dressing room. The dressing room wasn't that impressive. I said to Sammy, 'You're the best thing to happen since Swiss cheese.' I was awestruck at his talent and told him so. He was genuinely grateful for the appreciation. We laughed, did some shtick back and forth." Something told her Sammy was just ravenous for success. "At that point in his career," she says, "people were not falling down over him. We were kids—talking to another kid." Will and Sam Sr. tensed at the gushing, which excluded them. She got the hint. "I remember consciously having to include them when I said, 'You're all so wonderful.' "

Hanging around Sammy, she got a bead on the trio. "From that moment on, I had a take on them: Sam Sr. was along for the ride, and Will was king shit. He was the power center, in his mind. Sam Sr. was an accessory. And Sammy was the goods. I remember that not from the act—but from the room. Will had a kind of grandiosity. It wasn't that it was evident. He was too shrewd for that. It was an aura, and he wouldn't have tried to show it."

Sammy gave Balaban her first Ray Charles records. "He came over to my house and said, 'You gotta hear this,' " she recalls. She fell in love with the trio, which meant Sammy. "If he was playing Camden, New Jersey, I'd drive to Camden to see him. Wherever he was playing, I'd go."

Paramount studios produced a good many musical shorts, features that appeared before the main movie in theaters. In 1947 the studio made *Sweet and Low*, starring Richard Webb. It was over in a flash, ten minutes' time. But right there, onscreen, was Sammy Davis, Jr., dancing and singing to "Boogie Woogie

Piggy" alongside his father and Will Mastin. It was their first national exposure to the moviegoing public, and Sammy danced—as he did in all of his stage performances—as if he would never get the chance to dance again. Like all shorts, against the backdrop of the main feature itself, it becomes blurry in the mind. Nevertheless, Sammy imagined it would make him famous. Maybe Sam Goldwyn or Louis B. Mayer would call. Maybe there would be a return invite to the Hillcrest Country Club. He had squeezed everything he knew into his moment on celluloid. Hardly anyone, however, seemed to take notice.

Chapter 5

WHITE SAMMY,
BLACK SAMMY

I t is an ancient art. Performers in open-air Greek theaters engaged in the practice of mimicry, cottony pieces of cloth draped around their shoulders, becoming someone else. The best mimics were great imitators, as were many of the earliest vaudevillians and silent-screen stars. There exists, in addition to the traditional definition of "mimic" ("To copy or imitate closely") a biological definition of "mimicry": "The resemblance of one organism to another or to an object in its surroundings for concealment and protection from predators."

To conceal the black Sammy, Davis became the white Sammy. There were no predators after the white Sammy. He was Al Jolson, blessed with the uncanny ability to turn the white minstrel performer inside out of his own self. He was Boris Karloff. He was the spangly Jerry Lewis. He was Jimmy Cagney, feet spread apart, hands cocked. Yew dirty ratttt . . . He was Barry Fitzgerald, the old Irish character actor—*How Green Was My Valley, The Naked City*—whose own accent often got mighty close to the ethnic Irish stereotype. Concealing one stereotype only to offer another, Sammy possessed a magician's confidence—and shrewdness. It took enormous skills to perform such feats, and he had them. He could be a southern tobacco auctioneer. He had the perfect auctioneer's shuffle. (Actually, he stole the shuffle from Stepin' Fetchit.) He could be Frankie Laine, the velvety-voiced crooner who made a reputation singing cowboy songs. (All things with a cowboy theme fascinated young Sammy.) And, of course, he could imagine himself and Sinatra. But he couldn't be Sinatra. He didn't have the right skin color. Only by turning himself inside out could he be Sinatra. Get up close to the microphone, just like Frank. Kiss the thing, breathe into it. Just as Frank had done at the Capitol Theatre. The white Sammy could do whatever he wanted to do. He could lose himself inside others. Prince Spencer knew why Sammy's appeal was on the rise. "Sammy came and excelled at what the white guys were doing. He excelled on their territory."

Will Mastin didn't understand the mimicry, just as Lionel Hampton didn't understand the mimicry.

Mastin wanted to bolt Los Angeles. Idleness made him nervous. But Sammy began to grow fond of the place. Once you got a whiff of the Hillcrest Country Club—even if some of those there had, during the walk around the golf course with Abe Lastfogel, thought you were just another Negro caddy—it was hard to let the place go from your senses. The sunshine, the homes, the big fat gates outside the movie studios, the lovely cars gliding into and beyond the gates—it all enraptured Sammy.

Sammy didn't have a car yet, so he hopped buses, bummed rides. And he walked a lot up and down Central Avenue, snapping his fingers, hi to everyone, rushing by, chasing glory.

He was desperate for Los Angeles friends of his own. He liked the way Sinatra had always had an entourage around him. Sammy spent his time with his father and Will Mastin's friends, men who were entertainers but far older than Sammy, men from another generation. He'd sit with them in hotel rooms and talk into the night; then, just like that, he'd bolt, go play his records. He had a certain fondness for these men, after all they were workers, hoofers. But they were on the way down—it was a cruel business—and he was on the way up.

On the nightclub circuit, he befriended Jeff Chandler, who introduced him to Tony Curtis. All had been born in New York; all were World War II vets. And all became fast friends. Chandler had been a radio actor who moved into movies in 1947, appearing in three that year—*Johnny O'Clock, The Invisible Wall,* and *Roses Are Red.* He had also been a nightclub performer. Nightclub acts intrigued him. He had looked upon Sammy with immediate fondness—the kid dancing with the two older men. Curtis had come to Hollywood in 1947 and signed a contract with Universal. Dark-haired and handsome, he began in small roles in studio movies. He and Sammy often talked about movies, about New York, about their individual hurts in life. Sammy could be a fan even of actors who had yet to make it. "I grew up in New York City," says Curtis. "I was a handsome Jew. I understood someone who had been picked on because of his color, size, whatever. That made us instant friends."

Curtis was born Bernard Schwartz; Chandler, Ira Grossel. Many actors changed their names, hoping the new name would sound better, easier on the tongue. The attitude didn't transfer to Negro performers. Their family names had been earned, they felt, taken from distant places, something dragged—yes—from slavery, but still, theirs. Belafonte was born a Belafonte; Poitier a Poitier; Paul Robeson a Robeson. "Sammy Davis" was as American as a name could be; the "Jr." gave it its extra kick.

Sammy Davis, Jr.'s name was just fine; it was his interior that would bedevil him: a Negro with his face pressed against the white world. "He felt inferior," says Curtis. "People treated him as inferior."

Except when he was onstage. Onstage was a different matter. The Hollywood nightclub crowd had never seen anything quite like Sammy, says Curtis. "He was unusual. There was not anybody around who could amuse and fascinate people like Sammy." Sometimes Curtis would scan the nightclub audience, grinning with his broad grin, his eyes bouncing from Sammy to the audience and back again. "He was very gifted," Curtis says. "He was able to do those things the white guys were doing—and better. I won't say he was accepted, but he was tolerated." To many in Hollywood, the trio was considered eccentric. "It was amusing and unique," says Curtis. "There was a guy with his father and [Mastin] and out dancing with them—but with graciousness. He wasn't trying to show them up."

Some of Sammy's long talks led to melancholy moments. He talked of the movies he wanted to break into—just the way Curtis and Chandler were doing—and he talked of the fancy nightclubs he wanted to appear at. "There was a lot of unhappiness there, sadness and pain," says Curtis.

Sammy seesawed between coasts now. A train ticket for either coast would bring a smile to his face. He liked movement. "I remember a couple times we'd take the train, the Super Chief, back to New York," Janet Leigh recalls of herself, Tony Curtis, and Jeff Chandler. Leigh was a young actress who began dating Curtis shortly after he met Sammy. "We'd have two compartments. We'd play Monopoly the whole trip. We ate in the compartment. We changed trains in Chicago. We changed to the Twentieth Century."

Sammy exhausted Mastin and his father, but he was determined to elevate the act, to take it where it had never been. And he was cultivating friendships wherever he could: he looked up Buddy Rich, a wickedly talented drummer; he hooked up with Billy Eckstine, a crooner, to see what he might steal. He hung out at the Brill Building in Manhattan, which a lot of singers and songwriters were known to frequent. "We did begin to have a rhythm of constantly bumping into one another around the Brill Building," remembers Harry Belafonte. "People hung out in restaurants. People hung out till two, three in the morning. Then we'd all gang up and go to some other place. I called us 'shepherds of the night.' Really all just show folk. In the late hour there'd be ham and eggs and girls. Finally you'd get home around five or six. It was in that environment that I kept running into Sammy."

The trio got a gig at the El Rancho in Las Vegas. It was a new town, right there in the desert, built by gangsters. But the treatment, off the strip, was terrible. Sammy told himself he'd come back someday with more respect. The city was harsh on Negroes; Sammy and his father and Will couldn't stay in the casinos, had to drive over the bridge, to the Negro side of town.

After Vegas, Mastin bought a big truck and sent his equipment ahead in it. There was an advertisement painted on one side of the truck: THE WILL MASTIN TRIO STARRING SAMMY DAVIS JR. Other drivers would see the truck, the advertisement, and could be forgiven if they thought it some kind of traveling carnival.

In a bewildering way, movement calmed Sammy. For it was in confusion and cacophony, in the everyday debris of old ideas he was trying to vanquish and new ones he was trying to foster, that he would find order. One day he'd be bypassing a wheat field, the next striding along the hard cold cement of Chicago, two old sturdy men beside him; and still days later he was back at the Brill Building in Manhattan hustling up recording contacts. The noise and disorder of his youth had washed inside him deeply, until his whole life, to have meaning to him, seemed worthwhile only if he was moving, galloping, scanning entertainment periodicals—eyes rolling right over the words he could not decipher—then tossing the periodical in the trash and moving onward. Never a stroll for the young Sammy, always quick-stepping. Sometimes ideas came to him like firecrackers—pop, pop—and he wanted to grab at something, then he'd look beside him, and there were the two old men. The Four Step Brothers were all in their twenties and early thirties. They, like Sammy, had youth; they flew like eagles. But Sammy had two aging men, and they could be heavy on his wings.

His looks bothered him. It was all the standing in front of the mirrors, practicing the mimicry, that showed him his face at long stretches. He did not like what he saw. He began considering plastic surgery. He thought all crooners— Billy Eckstine, Frankie Laine, Sinatra—looked far more handsome than he did. So he convinced himself a better nose would improve both his looks and his career: "I just don't feel like the type who can sing a romantic song convincingly," he said as he pondered the surgery.

Some nights, back in Los Angeles, Sammy would stroll by Ciro's, the swanky nightclub on Sunset Boulevard. Stars hung out there. It was like a movie set from one of MGM's dazzling musicals. He'd hang out front, blowing smoke, dreaming. Herman Hover was the king behind Ciro's. Nightclubs and entertainment had long cast a spell upon Hover. He had once been a chorus dancer in New York City's fabled *Vanities* show. (It was considered the strongest competition to the Ziegfeld Follies.) Hover graduated to manager of the show. In 1936 he came to Hollywood, forgoing studies at Columbia Law School, to take over another theater, not yet Ciro's, on Sunset Boulevard. Hollywood thrilled him. "Hollywood is booming!" he told his wife back in New York. "I'm coming to get you." In 1942, Hover leased Ciro's. He shrewdly capitalized on a heady mix of wartime spirit and glamour. On any given night one might see Clark Gable, Lana Turner, Marilyn Monroe, Lucille Ball. Hover liked class, and his club reeked of it. On the tables sat foot-high lamps, each with a velvet purple-and-green shade. Behind the chrome bar stood bartenders dressed in uniforms with military buttons. Gorgeous cigarette girls floated about the club. Rich men came just to ogle young starlets. (Hover hosted crooner Dean Martin's marriage to his wife, Jeannie, at his home in 1949.)

Hover was quite adept at coming up with little staged events, something unique to draw the media's attention. He was not above having a bathtub placed onstage and a sultry dancer rising out of it—barely clothed. For Academy Awards night in 1951 he decided to book Janis Paige, a rising Hollywood musical star who had more than a dozen films to her credit. Trained as an opera singer, she had been discovered as a singer-waitress at the Hollywood Canteen. With Paige signed up, Hover went casting about for an opening act to precede her. Arthur Silber suggested the Will Mastin Trio. Hover, who had seen the trio at Slapsie Maxie's nightclub and had a soft spot for old vaudeville acts, agreed. But then, before anything was signed, there was a tense bit of business about the fee. Hover offered $500, Mastin wanted $550. It went back and forth. Hover wouldn't budge; Mastin shook his head no, and kept shaking it: no, no, no. The vaudevillian was defiant. It wasn't about the fifty dollars—it was about Hover, another powerful nightclub owner, trying to take advantage of him and his trio, and not giving in, not budging at all, which, in the recesses of Mastin's mind, meant that Hover was quite possibly conjuring up a way to steal Sammy. Sam Sr. sided with Mastin. They were proud men, and would as soon hit the hustings again rather than give in. Pride was at stake; they were always ready to pack up and move on. But Sammy nearly cried. Ciro's was Ciro's. The neon of that club had flashed and flickered in his own eyes. He argued with his father and Mastin—to no avail. Silber sensed Sammy's anguish. He went back to the phone. He told Mastin that Hover had relented; $550 it would be. (The elder Silber actually had chipped in the extra fifty himself.)

It was a year, Oscar-wise, when Hollywood turned an eye on itself. *All About Eve* competed against *Sunset Boulevard* for best picture, along with *Born Yesterday, Father of the Bride,* and *King Solomon's Mines.* José Ferrer, for his portrayal of Cyrano de Bergerac, and William Holden, in *Sunset Boulevard,* were favorites in the best actor category, with Spencer Tracy, in *Father of the Bride,* the sentimental choice. Both Anne Baxter and Bette Davis were nominated in the best actress category for their performances in *All About Eve.* Judy Holliday had to be taken seriously for *Born Yesterday*—she had played the role to raves on Broadway—and Gloria Swanson, as an aging actress in *Sunset Boulevard,* gave a performance both wicked and sultry.

The Oscar event was set for the RKO Pantages Theatre on March 29, 1951. The stakes were high for Sammy, his father, and Mastin. They were booked on an "if come" basis at Ciro's, a famous term nightclub owners used when they were uncertain of an act. It meant, simply, that once the customers saw you on opening night, if they came back the next night and the next night, you'd stay on the card. So, in essence, you had only the opening night to pull them back—lest, the owners' thinking went, the opening act continue to be a drag on the featured act.

"I knew it that night," Sammy would remember, "this is my last chance to do it. Do it now if you're ever gonna do it. Or it's small time the rest of your life. You'll be workin' little joints around and never get that big opportunity, 'cause this is as close as you're gonna get."

Fred Astaire, so coolly elegant, hosted the Academy Awards. The two pictures that had garnered so much critical acclaim and publicity—*All About Eve,* and *Sunset Boulevard*—fared quite well at the ceremony. *Eve* won six awards, including best picture, director, and supporting actor; *Sunset* won three—best screenplay, best art direction, and best dramatic score. José Ferrer and Judy Holliday won best actor and actress statues. Afterward, there was a rush to the after-parties, the crowd beating its way over to Herman Hover's Ciro's. They'd be treated to Janis Paige, but first the Will Mastin Trio.

By the time Sammy slithered and skipped offstage, they were hollering for him. Mastin and Sam Sr. were already making their way to the dressing room, and Sammy had to stop and turn around and go back. The impersonations had floored them. Paige, in her dressing room, couldn't imagine what all the commotion was about. Joe Stabile—his brother Dick ran the Ciro's house band—was in the audience that night. "[Mastin and Sam Sr.] didn't want Sammy doing anything but tap dancing. They ruled the roost. It was, 'Hey kid, come on out!' But at Ciro's, Sammy started breaking out. The audience went crazy." Every time the audience broke into wild applause, Sammy would do something different. He had only so much time onstage. He would give them his whole damn arsenal—all the things he had done in Maine and Ohio and Pennsylvania that no one ever saw. All those things he had done in front of the mirror. He had waited years—years!—to get to one of the premier nightclubs.

When she finally stepped out onstage, Paige seemed tentative, still hearing the murmurings at the tables of the act that had preceded her. Herman Hover scanned the audience. He realized something had taken place. Mastin and Sam Sr. sat in the dressing room, cooling down, nodding to each other, nodding to Sammy the way you reverently nod in the direction of a great athlete. The impersonations had been a smash, his dancing had been a sensation, his instrument-playing had been a surprise. Tony Curtis and Jeff Chandler smothered him with adulation.

Next morning, the reviews were wonderful. "Once in a long time an artist hits town and sends the place on its ear," said the *Hollywood Reporter.* "Such a one is young Sammy Davis Jr. of the Will Mastin Trio at Ciro's." Word spread quickly, from Kansas City to Chicago to New York. "We knew about it in New York the next morning," Maurice Hines says. "The black guys in New York were jumping up and down. It was like Joe Louis had won the championship fight. Sammy had just opened another door for us. We all figured we got a shot, because the door's opening now."

Hover booked Sammy for eight successive weeks. The word of mouth was furious. One night a comic sat at a table, alternately waving wildly and staring intently. It was Jerry Lewis, himself a onetime child vaudevillian who had been, since the 1940s, appearing at nightclubs around the country alongside Dean Martin. "I was stunned at his whole body of work," Lewis would come to recall of first eyeing Sammy at Ciro's. "He did two hours of everything known to theatrical man. I'm thinking, 'He's a goddamn rocket.' I had to go backstage for theatrical common courtesy." There was something, once he reached backstage, that bothered Lewis. It was Sammy's stage dress: "He was working in a plaid jacket. After the show I said, 'Dump the jacket. You got too much talent.' "

Lewis became an instant fan. On another night during the Ciro's engagement, he took Jack Benny to see Sammy. "Jack Benny and I sat together and were flabbergasted," Lewis recalls. "I was there the night before, and Sammy did such a different show." And Sammy—constantly prowling for a way up the entertainment ladder—was eager to befriend Lewis. Not just as fan, but as something deeper, like kin. And Lewis accepted. "I advised him on contracts, and I helped him with business affairs," says Lewis. Lewis was relentless in taking on a role in Sammy's life. "He would call me 'the Preacher,' because I was always on him."

During his weeks-long Ciro's engagement, Sammy wowed the audiences. Hover gave the act a bump in salary to $750. The electricity surrounding the show brought William Morris's Abe Lastfogel—and his wife, Frances—out to see it. It was widely known in Hollywood that if Frances Lastfogel took a shine to you, you were a lucky soul. She would force her Abe to make things happen for you. Frances, raised in Italian Harlem, had once been a vaudeville star herself, a singer who sang in a variety of dialects. Watching Sammy onstage, she instantly became smitten, poking her husband in the ribs, laughing at the act, her eyes widening at Sammy's versatility. Abe went into action. He browbeat Silber to let the act go. Silber refused. He had a contract. And a contract was a contract. Lastfogel was hardly finished, and Silber knew he wasn't, because men like Abe Lastfogel hated taking no for an answer. Sure enough, Lastfogel came up with another offer: he'd give a percentage of the Morris agenting fee to Silber, providing the Morris agency could be the primary agent. It meant Silber would still get a fee—for doing far less work. Lastfogel wanted to take Sammy into television, into bigger nightclubs. Arthur Silber knew he couldn't take Sammy into those arenas, and finally he agreed. Mastin, having worked with Silber in vaudeville in years gone by, trusted Silber far more than the slick-eyed Morris agents whom he knew nothing about and who were always watching Sammy inside the nightclubs.

So now, William Morris was into Arthur Silber, who was still into the Will Mastin Trio—which owned Sammy Davis, Jr., who was starting to explode.

There were a million reasons why they called it show business.

There was often a little clicking sound coming from behind the door of Will Mastin's hotel room. Tap tap tap. Then long silences, only to start up again— tap tap tap. The old vaudevillian, all alone, would be tapping his cane on the floor of his room. He was a worrier. The German immigrant William Morris founded the agency that would bear his name in 1898. Will Mastin was twenty years old then, trying to bust his way beyond the pickaninny world of show business. And in 1932, when William Morris keeled over and died during a game of pinochle at the Friars Club in New York, Will Mastin was dragging a little seven-year-old kid around the country, trying to keep food in everyone's mouths. Now, in 1951, there were television sets with voices inside them in hotel rooms. Now there was someone by the name of Abe Lastfogel huddling with his Sammy. Will Mastin used to be able to control Sammy, guiding him across the stage while practicing the dance routines, then buying him dollops of ice cream. Things were lovely then. But now his Sammy was speeding like one of those automobiles screeching around corners and killing unsuspecting pedestrians.

Mastin's gnarly hand fit comfortably around the tip of his cane: tap tap tap. Sometimes Will Mastin, even with all that he had accumulated, not materially but spiritually—his pride and respect, his image, his little Sammy—worried that it would all get away. Sometimes, in fact, Will Mastin worried like a man on the verge of death.

His talent was the act. "Davis," wrote *Variety* in an August 1, 1951, review of the trio at Bill Miller's Riviera nightclub in New Jersey, "is a superlative hoofer, a suave gabber, a solid vocalist and a standout mimic—a natural. His only hazard is the possibility of burning himself out before his time in a long turn that requires him to go at a sprinter's clip." (The reviewer has no idea: Sammy rushed along as if the entire world of show business might be pulled out from under him, as vaudeville had been pulled out from under his father and Mastin, tossing them into penury.) The *Variety* reviewer had more to say: "That Davis has star potentialities is indubitable. The boy not only has a tour

Backstage, 1954, following yet another performance. He is on the road all year long; the theaters and back stairwells are a comfort zone to him. Yet to come is the auto crash, and the bone-deep fears that will shake him up during a black and white love affair. He is but a twenty-nine-year-old song and dance man, wrapped in terry cloth and his own wide-eyed gallantry in the face of racial segregation. (JESS RAND COLLECTION)

de force talent but a winning personality. That's demonstrated in his intros to each bit and in tributes to [Mastin and Sam Sr.] for breaking him into the business, the chatter being delivered with both polish and charm."

It was now time for Sammy to begin charting the act's direction. His moves had to be subtle—on account of Will Mastin—yet forceful. He was determined to make decisions. Nathan Crawford and Big John Hopkins were both Will Mastin hires. They were nobody to Sammy, a valet and a driver, two Negroes that Mastin and Sam Sr. felt sentimental about. Sammy now needed someone to promote the act, which meant promoting him. He needed someone willing to dream alongside him, who'd stay up past midnight imagining what new heights the act could be taken to. He wanted less sentiment and more shrewdness. He wanted someone out on the road with him who was white. He found his man in Jess Rand.

"First time I ever heard of Sammy Davis," Rand recalls, "I was doing publicity for Johnny Conrad and the Conrad dancers. Johnny Conrad said, 'Did you ever see Sammy Davis, Jr.?' I said, 'No, who's Sammy Davis, Jr.?' He said, 'There's this kid who dances with his father and uncle.' " Jess Rand also liked going to benefits because they featured a wide array of musical acts. He heard about another benefit, this one to take place at Madison Square Garden. If you arrived at most of the benefits early, you'd often get to see smaller, largely unknown acts, which would be warming up the audience before the bigger names came on. Rand was barely in his seat when he heard the announcer's voice introduce "The Will Mastin Trio Starring Sammy Davis Jr." "I remember the opening number, 'Put On Your Dancing Shoes.' Then Sammy started doing impressions. I couldn't believe it. It was a blast of energy like you never saw."

Leaving the Garden, walking fast, hustling, Rand accidentally bumped someone. Words were exchanged, a punch thrown in Rand's direction. A fight erupted, and Rand left with a bloody nose. He was walking slower now, wounded, in pain, and decided to go for a rest over at Child's, an all-night eatery. Approaching the eatery he spotted someone. He was holding his bloodied nose, so his vision was blurred, but it looked like the kid he had seen onstage at Madison Square Garden. "As I was walking past, I see Sammy Davis, Jr., walking with a whole handful of magazines. He looked at me and said, 'Why don't you get your nose fixed.' That's how I met Sammy Davis, Jr." Rand couldn't let Sammy get away, and soon they were engaged in conversation. They talked, about music, the benefit show Sammy had just been in, entertainers. Jess Rand was actually looking for a better job. He had publicity experience, and he had moxie. Sammy was looking for someone to go on the road with him, someone to help promote and market the act. Sammy as much talked it over with his father and Mastin—always careful to establish solid eye contact with Mastin when telling him something—as he told them it was going to happen. He was simply, as deftly as possible, beginning to exert a measure of power within the act. Mastin and Sam Sr. agreed with Sammy to hire Rand and promised him forty-five dollars a week, each member of the trio contributing fifteen dollars toward his weekly salary. (Sammy, growing in shrewdness, also hired a Negro press agent, Billy Rowe, who had worked for boxer Joe Louis, to keep his name bouncing in the Negro press.)

Jess Rand grew up in New York City, his mother a pianist. All around him was beautiful music. In his youth he had been quick on his feet, comfortable around artists. At DeWitt Clinton High School in the Bronx, he worked on the student newspaper, the *Magpie*. One of his fellow writers on the paper was a shy, large-eyed student by the name of James Baldwin, who would be destined for literary fame. After high school, Rand found a job running sheet music back and forth to various offices in Manhattan. His employer was Irving Berlin. There were days when Rand would find himself over at the Waldorf, delivering music to another musician — Cole Porter.

After wartime service, Rand — dark-haired, skinny, jazzy — returned to New York and got himself a job doing publicity for various musicians. When he had a little extra money to throw around, he'd go catch the acts swinging through town. He was wild about Sinatra and Ella Fitzgerald. There was nothing better to him than hustling through Manhattan's teeming streets on his way to another concert.

It took Jess Rand no time at all to feel the Sammy energy, the Sammy hunger. Sammy asked a million questions. He wanted to know how to get his name in the papers. He wanted to be on radio. He wanted publicity—now. "Sammy said to me, 'My grandmother won't believe I'm in show business until I have my name in [Walter] Winchell's column and my picture in Lindy's window.' "

Rand realized he was being tested.

He went and got a picture of Sammy, signed it himself ("To Leo Lindy, who feeds pastrami every night to the Broadway Army. Sincerely, Sammy Davis Jr."), framed it, and made a beeline over to Lindy's. He found Leo—whom he knew from hanging around Broadway—and he begged and cajoled him to put the thing in the window. Leo didn't know Sammy from beans, but he knew Rand and liked him, his eagerness. "Couple nights later I said, 'Sammy, you want to go to Lindy's?' " Sammy shrieked when he saw the picture right there in the window.

But now Rand had to get Sammy's name in Winchell's column. He pleaded with the acerbic columnist to come catch his client at Bill Miller's Riviera nightclub across the river from Manhattan. Winchell hemmed and hawed, put him off. "Winchell didn't like Sammy," says Rand. "He said, 'He's always chasing white women.' " Rand told Winchell he didn't know anything about the white women, he only knew that Sammy was one hell of an act. Winchell, beaten down, finally said he'd go. Then Rand got paranoid; he had to tell Winchell that it would be terrible for him if he mentioned only Sammy, that he must mention "The Will Mastin Trio Featuring Sammy Davis Jr.," because if only Sammy were mentioned, Will Mastin might get upset. "I said to Walter, 'Sammy's 99 percent of the act, but it's got to say, 'The Will Mastin Trio Featuring Sammy Davis Jr.' " Winchell thought Rand a little strange, but liked him nevertheless. "I said, 'Walter, I'll lose Sammy's account if you don't mention Will Mastin.' "

Winchell went—in coat, in hat, striking fear, the cigarette dangling, the smoke curling, the eyes darting—and watched, nonchalantly at first, then, as the show went on, with more focus. "I don't know what he's doing with those two older men," Winchell said to Rand afterward, but the way he said it—with such awe for Sammy—Rand suddenly knew Winchell would put it in the paper, and he did. "I got him into Winchell that fast," says Rand. "Sammy didn't believe it."

They hit the road.

Three Negroes and now Jess Rand. Jess was surprised by the act. It was the old—Mastin and Sam Sr.—and the new: Sammy. Rand found the clashing of styles almost comical. "Will never changed anything," says Rand. "They were still doing the same thing from vaudeville." Night after night Rand would spy Mastin "shooting the cuffs," while still standing onstage. It was an old vaudeville habit. Mastin wanted the audience to think he was giving secret hand cues to Sammy.

Rand found the two aging vaudevillians strange but delightful. He'd sometimes return to the hotel lobby only to spot Mastin in a chair, holding his stomach—he had ulcers—rocking back and forth, mumbling: "Something bad is gonna happen. Something bad is gonna happen." Sammy told Rand to ignore it.

They rolled on.

The four of them were in Boston, walking, checking out the city. Mastin had slept fitfully the night before. "Will passed out," says Rand. It was the ulcer, spitting fire again. Passersby gathered. Mastin, on the ground and in agony, suddenly told Sammy and Rand to hurry and take off his money belt—he was afraid the crowd would jump the entire lot of them. He quickly recovered on his own. Will Mastin was frightened of hospitals and preferred home remedies and store-bought medications.

Rand came to respect Mastin's reverence for show business. "He was always in the dressing room, polishing his cane."

They'd have a day off, strolling in a town, and Sammy would duck inside a store. He'd roll his eyes over shirts, scarves, hats. "I'll take two," he would say—one for himself, one for his father. "His father had style like you wouldn't believe," Rand says.

Dusk would turn to evening, and they'd stroll, loose and limber, Sammy humming a tune, snapping his fingers. Sometimes strangers—two or three, staring hard—positioned themselves in front of the group as if ready to start a confrontation. Sam Sr. always stepped forward at such times; he was responsible for his boy. "He'd say, 'You better watch out. You never met this nigger on the street before,' " recalls Rand. "It was a whisper." And it was enough to send the strangers on their way.

As press agent for Sammy and the trio, Rand always felt he was in the business of informing the public, of educating radio station deejays and magazine writers and newspaper writers, trying to get them to pay attention to this Negro act, to this kid with these two hoofers. "I'm a press agent in a country that doesn't know there's such a thing as a chitlin circuit." Chitlin circuit: those small theaters in out-of-the-way towns that didn't get much press, if any at all.

They got turned down for gigs, and it angered Rand. "I used to get sick [of the] people getting gigs we should have," recalls Rand. "Sammy would say, 'Baby, it ain't right. The timing ain't right.' "

Rand came to hate driving through the Midwest—Ohio, Illinois, Missouri. They got stopped a lot. "The police would frisk Sam Sr., and I'd lean against the car. We used to drive all through the night so we wouldn't have to stop in certain places. One police officer said, 'I don't know why you're driving this man around for.' I said, 'I work for him.' One time we mentioned Sammy Davis, Jr., and the cop said, 'How's that little spook?' "

St. Louis became a frightful place for the trio. Once a cop demanded Sam Sr.'s wallet, and he gave it to him. The cop lifted fifty dollars, right before their eyes. "You can go on now," he said, Rand watching, astonished. "Couple miles up, another cop did the same thing."

Rand wasn't accustomed to having to pick and choose places to eat. There were eateries along the roads that would not serve Negroes. "It was scary," says Rand. "You'd have to go to the Greyhound bus stations to get some doughnuts and something to eat." Some evenings they couldn't find a place to lodge: "We slept in the car." He and Sammy carried clothes in bags to wash. "We couldn't even go to the Automat—a black and a white guy—without people looking at us."

They stayed at places where you had to drop a quarter into a slot for the television to come on.

The two hoofers—Mastin and Sam Sr.—carried jewelry, just as the vaudevillians did before them. If their cash was stolen, they could pull their hidden jewelry out in the next town and pawn it. Good jewelry could be the ticket to keep rolling. Jewelry, then, was a kind of get-out-of-jail card—before you went to jail.

All that jewelry, for years and years, that had been gleaming in little Sammy's eyes.

Will Mastin wore a diamond ring. Offstage or in the car, he took it off. Or sometimes just turned it facing in. Onstage he turned it back up—so it glittered, like the gold tooth he had. The jewelry was Mastin's only indulgence.

Otherwise, he remained an ascetic. He hoarded his money. "Will used to take me in the bathroom," says Rand. "He'd get you in the stall, take out a bag of money, say, 'Thanks, you did a good job this week.' "

The sacrifices Mastin made for the trio touched Rand. Sometimes Mastin would skip a meal. Sometimes he'd just dine on Jell-O. "Will didn't eat, Sammy did. Will didn't get new shoes, Sammy did."

The nightclubs: "Some of them were toilets," remembers Rand. "We worked Harry Allman's Town Casino in Buffalo. Get a lot of Canadians there. The place in Montreal we played was called the Black Magic Room. Then the Three Rivers Inn in Syracuse. While we were traveling we picked up little nightclubs in the New York area."

Winter turned to spring, which turned to summer, which turned to autumn, which turned back to winter again. They stayed on the move, looking for fame.

Even as the nightclubs turned into big theaters, Sammy was hardly satisfied. "I've played every big theater in this country—but way down in the billing list," he noted rather sadly toward the end of 1950. "I'm not saying the Will Mastin Trio isn't fast and furious, but I'm working towards that graduation day when the people will like me well enough for me to fly solo."

He always talked about going solo out of earshot of his father and Will Mastin.

It was April 1939 when NBC heralded a milestone by becoming the first television network to broadcast on a regular basis. Initially, motion picture executives were not worried by the new medium. Movies were movies, bigger than life itself. But then the executives began to ponder the effects of television, because it was surely here to stay. However, with the onset of World War II, the production of televisions nearly came to a halt. After the war, however, TV—with new sets rolling off the assembly lines—became a cultural event. The 1948–49 season was a boon year for the medium. The first cable linkups between East and West Coasts took place. Some of the old vaudevillians were frightened of television, of all the wires, the machinery. But others, like Milton Berle and Arthur Godfrey, chewed on it with ravenous appetites.

On September 10, 1950, NBC premiered *The Colgate Comedy Hour,* a Sunday evening variety show done live that had been the brainchild of comic star Eddie Cantor. The show had a revolving door of hosts—Bob Hope, Jimmy Durante, Fred Allen, the comedy duo Dean Martin and Jerry Lewis, and Cantor himself. Before the show's premiere, Cantor's show-business career had been in decline. Born to Russian immigrants in New York City in 1892, Cantor was orphaned in early childhood. At fourteen he began working in vaudeville

Vice President Richard Nixon visits the Will Mastin Trio backstage in 1954 at New York City's Copacabana. Jerry Lewis is at far right. For Nixon and Sammy, it was the beginning of a beguiling friendship. Eighteen years later Sammy would campaign for Nixon's reelection. The decision would become a potent political drama in its own right, anchored to the forces of race, American history, and Sammy's naiveté. (JESS RAND COLLECTION)

and burlesque houses. He found success with the Ziegfeld Follies, and on Broadway in 1926 in *Kid Boots.* Cantor often performed in blackface alongside the Negro performer Bert Williams. He had odd performing tics; he began rolling his eyes wildly—the whites flashing at the audience—and became known as "banjo eyes." (Some Negro performers had been doing the strange minstrel eye rolling for years.) Cantor took his popularity to the big screen and in 1934 was the highest-paid movie actor in America, owing to the success of a string of movies he made for Sam Goldwyn, among them *Whoopee!, Roman Candles,* and *Kid Millions.* But after World War II his fortunes faded, as his act suddenly seemed outdated.

When Cantor would host *The Colgate Comedy Hour,* he was adamant about having exciting guests. "My format for the show was purely variety," he explained, "with a slight theme to take it out of the realm of vaudeville." He was proud of himself for introducing various new acts to national television. On February 17, 1952, he introduced Sammy Davis, Jr. to the first national audience that would see the tap-dancing sensation. Arthur Penn was working as the floor manager for the Cantor show. "Eddie Cantor came around and said, 'Wait till you see this kid,' " recalls Penn. "He was always a great one for finding new talent," says Penn of Cantor. "Of course he didn't have a lot of talent himself." Penn goes on: "[Cantor] knew he needed a lot of help. We had moved the show out of New York—to Los Angeles. Live show. No tape in those days. Went out live every Sunday—NBC." Cantor, onstage in a silk bathrobe and a white towel around his neck—he had just exhausted himself in a skit—said to the national audience: "The other night I saw the Will Mastin Trio and one of the greatest hunks of talent I've ever seen in my life, Sammy Davis, Jr." Mastin and Sam Sr. were in light-colored tuxedos, Sammy in a dark one. Sartorially, he stood out. Dancing—smooth, lovely, furious—they were wondrous. "It was an act," says Penn, "where the two older men would bracket Sammy. Sammy would cut loose with great dancing, good singing, great imitations." They all rolled offstage in perfect syncopation.

Barry Gray, a New York radio host whom everyone seemed to listen to, began talking Sammy up on his show, praising the Colgate appearance. "He was raving about the show, absolutely going out of his mind," remembers Jess Rand.

The trio's appearance was such a hit that Cantor asked them to come back several more times. Sometimes Cantor and Penn and other production staffers would just sit and watch Sammy off-camera. He'd be rehearsing. They'd just marvel. "At rehearsals he would do stuff that was not going to be on the show. At the rehearsal Cantor would say, 'Do Jerry Lewis.' Sammy would do this stuff, mostly for us."

Penn thought Sammy one of the more kinetic figures he had ever seen. "[Sammy] enjoyed himself a lot, and he enjoyed this new medium. Television was a perfect home for him. Television was like a miracle."

As for Mastin and Sam Sr., there was something a little mechanical about their television appearances. It was as if they were nervous about being watched by the camera's eye, by all those millions of viewers.

After his multiple appearances on the Cantor show, Sammy adopted a strange and odd habit: he began rolling his eyes, furiously, wildly showing the whites of them while onstage dancing. Why, he was mimicking Eddie Cantor! Banjo-eyed Sammy! From Cantor, it looked like an imitation. On Sammy, it looked painful, the return of the Negro minstrel.

He wished to be the pure entertainer. To succeed in the world of black and white, he would have to put his mimicry to full use. He had started practicing an English accent. By jove, he sounded like a white minstrel performer—in blackface! Jerry Lewis advised him to drop the accent.

He didn't hear Lewis.

He heard only the applause, the white hands clapping together in the audiences; the cackling noise from old wide-eyed Eddie Cantor in the rehearsal hall slapping his knee, and laughing, and laughing, and laughing. The hour-long format of the *Colgate* was actually a grind for Cantor. "It damn near killed me," he admitted. But what else was he to do? What old vaudevillian wanted to wind up behind the door of a hotel room tapping his cane on the floor with sickening worry? Eddie Cantor got his aching body to the NBC set, and there he saw Sammy—rehearsing, mimicking, giving a show before the cameras were even turned on—and he howled. It kept his own blood warm. And Eddie Cantor gave Sammy the same pitched laughter he used to give Bert Williams, his dear and sadly dead friend whom Cantor thought "the whitest black man I ever knew."

She was blond and she favored pearls, the kind that looped snugly around the neck. She had a movie-star gorgeousness about her. There was something also very tender about her eyes; a forlorn look, as if she prayed to herself that life would give her more than just beauty. Her skin was so proudly white it looked porcelain. He thought it nothing less than a miracle that she loved him back, that she was there, in New York, lying beside him. Helen Gallagher was like something he had seen in one of those beautiful picture magazines he was always thumbing through at newsstands.

He was outside his dressing room, in his billowy shirt, his tight pants, at Bill Miller's Riviera nightclub in New Jersey. The chorus girls—so white, so lovely—were milling about, getting ready to take the stage. They were adorned in snow-white outfits that had silvery sprinkles on them. Huge and birdlike feathered configurations sat atop their heads. In heels, they towered above him. "The Riviera Beauties," they were called. Men came from miles to ogle them. "He found me backstage," Helen Gallagher says. "He came backstage and said, 'Hi, I'm Sammy Davis, Jr. I just wanted to say hello.' " He always began like that, shyly. It was because he had to first get across the swinging bridge of race. Once that was traversed, however, he'd go in for the kill. He offered to take Helen and the chorus girls—the whole crew!—to a Broadway play. Really, he wanted only her, but the other girls could serve as his shields. There was safety in numbers. Sammy and a dozen pretty white girls.

Theatergoers thought he was the chauffeur. He didn't care. Thirteen Broadway tickets. He was always spending next week's paycheck. The Broadway play was *Me and Juliet,* a musical, directed by George Abbott. He laughed and she laughed and all the other girls laughed.

"He really wasn't a superstar then," Gallagher says. "I could go out between shows and watch him. He was incredible. He sang great. He was an incredible

She was a dancer, a Riviera Beauty, and Sammy's first love. Helen Gallagher kept their early 1950s romance a secret from her parents, until she could no longer hold it inside. They did not approve, the first of many such endings for Sammy's romantic interludes. (JESS RAND COLLECTION)

dancer. And he had such charisma with the audience. He had the audience in his hands."

Sometimes he'd stand still as a tree onstage, and then break into a sweet little soft-shoe number. It was as if he were dancing inside himself. She felt he was romancing her from the stage.

"He was good enough to perform at the hotels, but not to go into the dining rooms," Gallagher says. "It drove me crazy."

It was a funny thing about Bill Miller's Riviera. She never saw many Negroes in the audience. "[The doormen] could say, 'We don't have your reservation.'"

He was Negro, she was white, and it was 1953. It had to be a secret. She dared not tell her parents. "I was never uncomfortable with it," she says of her relationship with Sammy. "But it was an extreme departure for me. I was raised white, Irish Catholic. I must say people stared at us constantly." One night, feeling brave, he took her to Birdland, that jazzily toxic nightclub in Manhattan. He was wearing his hair processed, with little cowlick-like curls at the front. His Tony Curtis hairstyle. "People stared us down," she remembers. Sammy never took Helen to Birdland again.

His words, thoughts, ideas, and movement were all a rush of motion. She wanted, more than anything, for him to slow down. But he could not. "He was always on high speed, like he was rushing through life to the next thing."

At times, when the two of them were alone, he'd stare at her, her hair and her blue eyes, as if he were studying the interiors of a miniature castle. "He was just fascinated," she says, "by someone so absolutely his opposite."

He hustled her up to Harlem, to meet Rosa, his grandmother. It made him feel proud to show her that he had family. Not just Will Mastin and his father, Sam Sr., who were men, and who made up the act, but family, which meant women. "Rosa liked me. She thought I was good for him," says Gallagher.

As he stood beside her, a mirror nearby, looking at her and himself in profile, something would seem to drain away from Sammy. She would sense it, and it would pain her. "He thought he was ugly, and he wasn't, because there was so much charm." She saw a picture of Elvera, his mother, and noticed her beauty, and tried to reassure Sammy of his own looks, which obviously were connected to his mother's. "I said to him once, 'Your mother's very beautiful, and she cares about you.' And he said, 'She doesn't care about me, and she thinks I'm ugly.' " She was stunned by the comment.

Helen Gallagher grew up excited to watch tap dancers perform, and had studied tap as a child. She thought the Will Mastin Trio eccentric for merely existing and holding on. "The only other trio I remember at that time were the Dunhill Dancers. I didn't know any other trios." Mastin and Sam Sr. intrigued her—quiet men who cared for Sammy. "I once said, 'Your uncle . . . ,' and he said, 'He's not!' I guess that was a sensitive spot."

She wanted to hear of his life, of Harlem, of Negro life, and life on the road. But Sammy did not want to talk of Negro life. It was hard, sometimes unforgiving. He wanted, she felt, to talk of whites, of white people, white America. "He did so want to be white," she says. "I think he thought he would be accepted more."

Like Sammy, she knew of other Negro talents on the rise—Belafonte, Poitier, Eckstine. But she noticed how Sammy could wince discussing them. How easy it was for them—with their good looks, their height—to get the girl, the conquest, to disappear into the elevator with the lovely girl on their arm. "He wanted to be them—and white," she says. She never saw Sammy with Belafonte or Poitier or Eckstine—or any Negro male friends. "He hung out with the white guys."

When Sammy found out Helen had long had a girlish crush on actor Jeff Chandler, he smiled. A short while later Sammy appeared at the Riviera nightclub to surprise Helen; he had brought along Jeff Chandler, who was visiting from the West Coast. Only she wasn't there. It was her day off. "The next night Sammy says, 'Where'd you go? I brought Jeff to meet you.'" Chandler took everyone out to a party at the Sherry Netherland.

His crowd was Jeff Chandler and Tony Curtis and Janet Leigh. And Sinatra, when he was lucky enough to get close to him. "He was in absolute awe of them," says Gallagher. "You would have thought Tony Curtis and Janet Leigh were the biggest stars in the world. He was like a child."

One night he told Helen he had to split, and whoosh, he was gone. He had to tape a radio spot. "I want you to listen to the show," he had said to her. She sat listening. It was past midnight when she first heard him talking on the radio. "He said, 'I want to dedicate this song to the girl I love. She knows who she is.' And he sang 'My Funny Valentine.' He didn't say my name, and that was to protect me, not him. It's not a song we had ever discussed, but it's a song I loved."

He gave her things, gifts. At first it seemed charming, generous. Then it seemed strange and extravagant. "It was like a way of buying people," she says. "It was generous, but it was overboard. I mean, he used to buy Sinatra things. What the hell did Sinatra ever need?" She felt she knew precisely what Sammy himself needed: "He had a great need to be loved."

She was sitting in his dressing room one night at the Riviera. She was wearing pearls, a black sleeveless dress. He pulled his camera out—and flash. Her eyes were looking away from the camera's eye. Still—in the photo, saved all these years later—Helen Gallagher looks ravishing.

They talked of brave things, such as marriage. "He and I probably would have made it had it been a different time," she says. "He needed to be a star. I remember going to Brooklyn with Sammy and seeing Milton Berle. He said to Sammy, 'She's a nice girl, but you two will never be accepted, and she's going to ruin your career.'" Berle's bluntness shocked Gallagher; she thought Sammy might react with more emotion to the comment, but he did not, retreating behind chuckle and silence.

The subterfuge was painful, the furtive meetings. Helen Gallagher's parents still didn't know. Then she decided she didn't care if they knew. A friend of Helen's was giving a party on Long Island. She dragged Sammy along. Her parents would be there. "They were not thrilled," she says. "They just said, 'Helen, if you marry him you're letting yourself in for a lot of heartache.'"

She'd finger the jewels Sammy had given her, and her conscience would get the better part of her. "He gave me some wonderful jewelry," she remembers. "When we stopped seeing each other, I didn't think I should keep it. I took it [all] back to George [Unger] and said, 'Credit the account. I know he's always into you for thousands of dollars.' And he did." (Unger was Sammy's favorite jeweler.)

Sammy would find other loves—other funny valentines—and so would she. But Helen Gallagher was his real first love. And it is that love—if the poets and the balladeers are to be believed—that wounds the most, leaves the deepest scar. The kind of love that anchors itself inside you, even as you walk away with the memories: blond, blue-eyed Helen Gallagher, who wore pretty dresses, and pearls, and whose skin was so white, and who had small tap dancer's feet.

She had wanted the Negro in him, the black man. And that was something he couldn't give her. He wanted to give her the white Sammy, because his nose was pressed against the white world—Frank and Jeff Chandler and Tony Curtis showing him the view. It was a heaven and peek-of-hell existence. Being an impersonator and mimic, Sammy heard voices, and he gave those voices a home inside himself. Milton Berle: ". . . she's going to ruin your career." So he walked away. Friends could sense his sadness.

When in pain, Sammy listened to music for hours on end, jazz and bebop. ("And believe it or not," he told *Ebony* magazine, "I've got every record Frank Sinatra ever cut in his career.") When his friends convinced him to talk about something that had saddened him, Sammy's voice rose into its tiny, childlike register. He learned how to mimic emotions as well as voices. It was a deft ability—though not without a certain kind of danger.

Genes are mysterious and sometimes funny and inexplicable things. Inside the body, they are powered by forces both alien and intimate. Consider Sammy Davis, Jr., and his father and mother. His father was a quiet man. He had started out in life ambitious, winning dance contests. But once employed—more steadily than not—with the likes of Will Mastin, his ardor cooled. He had no more dreams to chase. He was a dancer, and he had a manager in Mastin, and that was good enough. He hummed along in life, his boy by his side, his good bottle of liquor tucked away. Where Will Mastin went, he went.

Elvera Davis was just the opposite of Sam Sr. She chased after her own future. She left home and family; the fires she started, she let rage. In pursuing her dream, she was possessed of a willful purpose. Her belief in herself was supreme. She packed her bags and climbed aboard train after train. A vision of her children crying out in the night did not slow her forward motion. She was all about execution. Of Elvera's two children, the one most like her—willful, determined, and with a messianic belief in self—was Sammy. In drifting apart, there was also something that fused them together. It is quite possible that a child dropped onto an ever-widening path of seeking constant approval never stops hearing a kind of hum, an echo from beyond. And that echo becomes the maternal knock against the conscience. *Can't you see me? Can't you hear me?* It becomes a sound that constantly escapes the width of the path, and the knock keeps echoing and echoing. Sammy had no idea that behind a bar in Atlantic City was the woman who obsessed him. Elvera Davis had driven herself out on the vaudeville road without a Will Mastin, without a father. For more than a decade she had been out there, searching, alone. That she never reached her goals was hardly any sin. She would certainly not be the last whose ambition outstripped her talent.

More than a decade, nearly four thousand days and nights, a woman searching, a woman alone. It took sheer will.

Elvera's ferociousness had become Sammy's.

By the end of 1953, Sammy, his father, Will Mastin, and Jess Rand had two homes: the Americana Hotel on West Forty-seventh in New York City, and the Sunset Colonial Hotel on Sunset Boulevard in Hollywood. The Sunset Colonial room made Rand nervous. You could pick the lock with a butter knife. But it was the one hotel on Sunset Boulevard that was friendly to its Negro clientele.

Rand was curious why Sammy always had a camera swinging. He found out soon enough as Sammy dragged him to the Hollywood nightclubs and he snapped pictures of the stars. "He'd take the picture, and he'd send them a picture," says Rand. Sammy once spotted Humphrey Bogart inside a Hollywood nightclub. "Pick up Bogart's check," Sammy instructed Rand. Bogie was impressed with Sammy's eagerness. "Bogart used to have Sammy over to his house for Christmas," says Rand, who became astonished at Sammy's ability to ingratiate himself into the lives of others. "Sammy was like Zelig—he always happened to be 'there.' I remember going to a party one night and Marlon Brando was sitting on the floor talking with Wally Cox. Sammy stepped over them and said, 'Mr. Brando, I'm Sammy Davis, Jr. I do impressions of you in my act.' Brando said, 'Stop doing it.' "

Sometimes Sammy said he'd pay the movie star's tab, only to slip out before the bill came. "Owners complained to me," says Rand.

Sammy was cultivating contacts. He was flattering. He was determined not to be forgotten. Rand would sit back, in the nightclubs, and just marvel—the way Sammy held the stage, gliding between his father and Will Mastin, bantering with the audience; bowing once, then again; a lovely wave of the hand in the direction of Will Mastin, then a wave in the other direction, to his father; then bowing yet again, the three of them, in perfect unison.

Rand couldn't figure where the low self-esteem offstage came from. "One time we were sitting around the swimming pool at Jeff Chandler's house. Sammy said to me, 'Wouldn't it be wonderful if everyone jumped into the pool and came out the same color?' I said, 'I think that would be bad.' "

A rare evening in 1947 when Sammy and his mother, Elvera—seated next to him—are out together. This is their first time together since his release from the army two years earlier. Elvera has been out of show business six years now, but still enjoys hobnobbing with showgirl acquaintances. The relationship with her son is ever strained. Her writing on lower right of photograph, "ME TO SAMMY," is notable for the "XXXX" scrawl—and not the one word he hungered his entire life to hear from her: love.

(COURTESY LORELEI FIELDS)

In every city, at every newsstand, Sammy reached for the showbiz magazines. Flat broke, he'd beg Rand to pay for them. "Sammy used to go to a magazine store at Fiftieth and Broadway," recalls Rand, "and pick up all these fan magazines. Then he'd turn to me and say, 'You got ten dollars?' " Sammy loved just standing there, flashing through them, almost furiously so. He had to know what Sinatra, Mel Torme, Tony Bennett, Harold and Fayard Nicholas (the Nicholas Brothers), and the Four Step Brothers were all doing. He could hardly sleep at night because thoughts of fame and celebrity—feelings that others were passing him by—filled him up so. There, in yet another magazine, was a picture of an entertainer. He'd never met her. She had an eager look in her eyes. She wasn't classically beautiful, but she looked ripe for the taking. And there was something as well a little different that Sammy noticed—she was Negro.

.   .   .

It was in San Francisco that Sammy first met Eartha Kitt. She was a young dancer and chanteuse. She was worldly, insecure, sexually aggressive, and domineering. Her hit Broadway show—*New Faces of 1952*—had given Kitt a name, and she was now on the road with the play.

Eartha Mae Kitt was born in a place called North, South Carolina, in 1928. Her parents, William Kitt and Anna Mae, were desperate sharecroppers. They abandoned Eartha Mae and her sister, placing them with a foster family. An aunt, feeling sorrow, invited Kitt and her sister to come live with her in New York City. Young Kitt arrived in 1936. She was artistically minded and liked dancing, at which she showed precocious skill. She was invited to join Katherine Dunham's admired dance troupe. Kitt traveled with the troupe around Europe and South America, where she began to make a name for herself. She branched off into nightclubs, her voice complemented with a husky sensuality. In Paris she attracted a following, including Orson Welles, the boyhood wonder of American cinema. In Paris, Welles cast Kitt in *Faust,* his much ballyhooed production. He and Kitt became an item—at least in the European gossip trades. In photos, she looked like a waif in Welles's giant arms. "We started in Frankfurt," Kitt would remember. "We had to work under a tent cov-

Rita and Rosa Davis. Rita became Sam Sr.'s second wife. Sammy adored his stepmother's panache and elegant manners. Rita was devoted to her husband and was quite happy to settle in California upon Sam Sr.'s retirement from show business. They liked tooling around Los Angeles in his convertible Jag. (JESS RAND COLLECTION)

Sammy wooed Eartha Kitt in San Francisco in 1952. She was a rising chanteuse—feral-like, blunt, fashionably sophisticated (note the buttons down the side of her pants leg), and, ultimately, too mature for Sammy.

(JESS RAND COLLECTION)

ering what was at one time part of a theater. The stage creaked and our moods were constantly broken, but we lived through it. I never knew what mood Orson was in until the moment [to] kiss. If he was gentle, then I knew his day had gone well."

By the time Kitt landed in San Francisco in 1953 with *New Faces*, she had played the Mocambo in Hollywood, the Village Vanguard in New York City, countless other nightclubs, and starred in Europe with Welles. She was sultry, had an arrogant manner, and a figure shaped like an hourglass. Sammy meant to charm the world traveler, and so he befriended Pat Warehauser, another member of Kitt's San Francisco production. Warehauser stood there with Sammy, at Kitt's dressing-room door. "I thought he was a gofer," Kitt recalls, "because that's where he was standing." She asked him to go get her a cup of coffee. He did. When he returned, Pat Warehauser reminded Kitt again that it was Sammy Davis, Jr., that he wanted to meet her. "I said, 'Who is Sammy Davis, Jr.?' The name didn't mean nothing to me. I thought he was just a boy from downstairs."

She knew Sammy would ask for a date, and sooner rather than later, because show-business people were on the move, always. Moments vanished.

"A couple nights later Sammy asked me out," she says. "Took me to a Chinese restaurant around the corner from the hotel. Everybody said, 'Ms. Kitt, come this way . . . Ms. Kitt.' He said to me, 'I've been in this business since I was four. Everybody knows you, and no one recognizes me!' "

They went on walks around that lovely city by the bay. Sundays were perfect for strolling. Both had the day off and could relax. "We'd be walking along the street and he'd say, 'You are such a big name. I'm gonna be bigger than you if it kills me!' He would be screaming this out," remembers Kitt.

She took Sammy to the apartment of a Mr. Maxwell, an art connoisseur she had befriended in the city. "He invited us over for breakfast," recalls Kitt. Afterward, Kitt and Sammy walked around the apartment, admiring the artwork. Maxwell mused as to how it might be interesting to do a bust of Sammy. Kitt immediately sensed Sammy was nervous because of his lack of art education. "All Sammy did was listen." What Sammy really wanted to do was scram, to take Kitt to his hotel room and show her where he lived, so he did.

His boisterousness charmed her, amused her. His hotel room made her chuckle to herself. "All he had were cameras, comic books on both sides of the bed, from floor to top of the bed mattress. I said, 'Sammy, you're really into comics.' He said, 'I'm into Superman.' " Eartha Kitt was into Proust, Chekhov, Dostoyevsky, Faust. She had seen the ruins of Italy with her own eyes. Now she was with someone she had never heard of who was wild about Superman. She managed condescending smiles, which Sammy could not quite interpret. "We got into a conversation about art. He said, 'I want to know what you know.' I said, 'Well, you can't read comic books.' He wanted me to take him to the museums."

Kitt's intellectual fervor hardly slowed Sammy's romantic pursuit. Actually, it had the opposite effect—he was inspired. He showed up at the Huntington Theatre one afternoon, where Kitt was performing, with a load of books under his arms. They were picture books—of Monet, Picasso, Renoir. Sammy was giddy, twisty on his heels. "He opens up the books. 'This is Degas! This is Renoir.' " Kitt stopped him: "I know the paintings," she offered. Then Kitt told him it was not good enough to get reproductions in picture books, she wanted him to read books, biographies of the painters. Sammy slumped. He did not know how to truly read. "Do I have to read about them?" he finally asked in exasperation.

She took him to museums, explaining sculptures and paintings, lecturing about what she had seen, by way of art, in Paris, in Rome. She drove him around the hills of San Francisco in her big yellow Cadillac; Sammy ogled the car. Finally he coaxed her to come to the roof of the Fairmont. He posed her and began snapping picture after picture. They kissed and groped; he took some more pictures. He screamed out that she had a beautiful body: so true. "We would go up on the roof of the Fairmont and he would photograph what he thought was the most beautiful body in the world," says Kitt. "When he looked at me, it was as if he were breathing me in."

Sammy invited her to come and see the trio perform. "He had not quite taken over the show yet," she recalls. "But I could see where it was going. He was dynamic. His father and [Mastin] trained him beautifully. They let him do what he could. It was as if they let him exercise his ability. I loved them as a trio. It was a little family thing, working beautifully." She felt warm in the company of Mastin and Sam Sr. "They were very gentlemanly. None of what Hollywood interpreted black entertainers to be and act like. They were very classy."

Kitt liked Sammy, but also had a feeling he suffered from low self-esteem. "Nobody made him feel important as a person," she felt, "not the community, or his family." Finally she convinced herself that Sammy's vaudeville years had left him badly scarred. "Before you realize you're a man, woman, or child, you're a *thing*," she says of the child performer.

Kitt was rootless, as so many performers are rootless, but she felt Sammy's rootlessness came with a price. "I'm an orphan, but I always felt I had a stabilized mind. I recognized my responsibilities."

The more Kitt probed—believing Sammy childish and immature—the more Sammy fled her conclusions. He wanted to show her his impersonations; he wanted her to listen to his jazz albums; he wanted to impersonate her voice, her sultry walk—he was a mimic! Will Mastin told her she'd make a good wife for Sammy, that she could discipline him. The comment made Kitt feel strange. "It's an embarrassment to think you can discipline someone, especially a man."

But Sammy had the curse of the romantic, seeing only what he wanted to see. He sent Kitt flowers, and more flowers. "Sammy was buying relationships," she says, "by sending too many flowers. When all I wanted was one petal. Eartha Kitt can't be bought. She *can* be earned."

Kitt was sure she and Sammy were simply not meant to be together. "The gods cannot be rushed. Timing is of the essence."

Kitt was more realist than romantic, but still found it difficult to cast Sammy away. And yet, even as Sammy's kinetic energy mesmerized her, one of the things that worried her was that he had never talked about his mother, his past, his childhood, special places. She felt sorrow for him. "Sammy never said, '*Je suis jesuis:* I am born as I am. There is nothing for me to explain.'"

Kitt left a heartbroken Sammy in San Francisco. She left to take an engagement at La Vien En Rose in New York City.

Sammy Sr. and Will had talked Sammy into pursuing Kitt. It wasn't a pursuit of the heart on Sammy's part when she left San Francisco; it became a matter of pride. His father and Will didn't think he could corral her. They had manly laughs about it. So Sammy chased her back across the country, all the way to New York City and her dressing room at La Vien En Rose. "It was opening night," Kitt says. "My dressing room was filled with people: Doris Duke, Gloria Vanderbilt. When I came offstage Sammy Davis came in with a little box in hand. He said, 'Come into the bathroom. I want to talk to you.' He gives me this ring. I said, 'Sammy, I can't take this.' It was gorgeous white and yellow—huge—a gold diamond. He said, 'Please.' I said, 'I can't put it on.' If I did, and walked out there, all the people would see it and would think we were going to be married. He said, 'Oh, please, please.' When I went outside, I had this ring on my finger. Gloria Vanderbilt looked at my hand. She realized Sammy Davis had asked me the question."

Men gave Eartha Kitt things. Being Eartha Kitt, she accepted those things. She was just a sharecropper's daughter from rural North Carolina, given up in her childhood. Even in the bright lights of La Vien En Rose, she was still a hurt child. She told Sammy—while admiring the diamond on her finger—that she'd ponder his proposal. He turned giddy, laughing inside himself. Monet and Picasso may have confused him, but not diamonds. Women liked diamonds. He didn't have to read books to know such things.

"The next day," adds Kitt, "I read in Earl Wilson's column that he had given me this ring. Now, how would Earl Wilson have known? Sammy had gone to the phone and called Earl Wilson. That put me off. It sounded like a publicity stunt—instead of sincerity."

Sammy had bought the ring from George Unger, his jeweler. Unger called Rand. "Hey Jess, I got a problem. The kid owes me a lot of money. He took this diamond ring from me.' I said, 'Diamond ring? What's he need a diamond ring for?' George said, 'He's getting engaged to Eartha Kitt.' " Neither Unger nor Rand knew that Kitt had huffily told Sammy that the engagement was off, but she'd keep the ring nevertheless. Sammy saw publicity in the whole affair, his name again in the gossip columns. But Rand didn't like it. He questioned Sammy, and Sammy finally agreed it would be nice to have the ring back; there were already high jewelry debts that needed to be settled. Rand scooted over to Kitt's hotel room. "It's a friendship ring," Kitt, cold-eyed, told him. Rand pondered the comment. "Ain't that kind of friendship in the world," he told her. Kitt, unrepentant, kept it. Jess Rand was hardly finished. He phoned Kitt's press secretary and told her he'd take the whole story to the press, and would make it seem as if Kitt had taken advantage of a gullible Sammy Davis, Jr. "We got the ring back," says Rand.

· · ·

Even when handling jewelry, rubbing his fingers across pieces of it, Sammy was caught between the old and the new: old vaudevillians used jewelry for currency, credit, safety—as he had seen as a little child in the backseat rolling along with his father and Mastin, when jewelry was bartered for freedom, to avoid arrest. But to the grown-up Sammy, jewelry—especially diamonds—was to be used for emotional currency and self-esteem. He believed that within the giving of it—the dazzling sparkle—lay the definition of love. Of that, he felt sure.

The contretemps involving Sammy, Eartha Kitt, and Jess Rand regarding the ring was not yet over. Both Rand and Sammy felt Eartha—having been shamed into returning the ring—might unleash a story line to the public that Sammy was immature, a word she often used about Sammy even to him. Rand, in the fever pitch of public relations, decided to preempt what they felt Kitt might do. So Rand, writing as Sammy, wrote an article—"Why I Broke with Eartha Kitt"—and tried to sell it to *Brown* magazine. A part of the contract, written by Rand, who was now billing himself as Sammy's "news agent," was indeed curious: "As Sammy Davis' news agent, I further agree that BROWN MAGAZINE is in no manner obligated to compensate either Sammy Davis Jr., the Will Mastin Trio or myself for this story which Sammy Davis Jr. is donating to BROWN MAGAZINE exclusively and free of charge." In addition, there was a rider attached to the contract: "No pictures of Sammy Davis Jr. & any white chorus or Copa girls to be printed in this article or any other." In Sammy and Rand's telling, it all came down to Sammy's busy-busy schedule—record deals, movie discussions, and so on—and there simply being no time for love, or Eartha. Alas, *Brown* took a pass on the article.

Abe Lastfogel's dream to get his client a television deal paid off in the summer of 1953, when ABC signed Sammy to a $150,000 contract to do a TV pilot. The money, of course, would only be paid out should the pilot sell. Considering TV's history with Negroes, the odds against success were daunting.

In 1939, the first Negro had starred in a television series. The medium was still fairly new; the star was Ethel Waters—Sammy's costar in *Rufus Jones for President*, his first movie. NBC named her vehicle simply *The Ethel Waters Show*. Waters, along with costars, performed sketches from *Mamba's Daughters*, a Broadway play she had starred in. "Results offered sharp contrasts," *Variety* would comment about the pioneering show, "all the way from deeply stirring drama to feeble slapstick comedy and not-too-effective scientific lecture. When it was good it was quite good but when it was bad it was capital B."

After just one episode, the Waters show, without explanation, was yanked. Years would pass before another Negro was featured in a starring role. In 1948, CBS hired Bob Howard, a Negro, who hosted *The Bob Howard Show.* On the show, Howard, a musician, played the piano, all the while stopping to introduce other programs on the network. Howard was not above singing minstrel tunes, such as "Dark Town Strutters." His show was also short-lived.

The DuMont network, which began airing in 1946, was smaller than the other networks and also more willing to take risks. The network had a progressive streak. In 1948, DuMont introduced *The Laytons,* a show starring a Negro maid played by Amanda Randolph. (Television—like the movies—had catapulted the Negro maid into a kind of backhanded cultural icon of the Negro race.) The high hopes for the Randolph vehicle never materialized, and the show lasted less than a year. The same year, CBS introduced *Sugar Hill Times,* a Negro variety show that featured, among others, Timmie Rogers. Rogers and others in the cast found steady work—at least for thirteen months, after which the show was canceled. Its setbacks aside, DuMont was not finished in its attempts to integrate the world of early television. The network offered a program featuring Hazel Scott. And there were those who suddenly thought that Scott, a pianist born in Trinidad and celebrated in New York City's swanky café society, might usher in a new type of show for the Negro woman. In 1950 the network gave Scott her own show. Scott, who was married at the time to Congressman Adam Clayton Powell, would simply play herself—a sophisticate in evening wear—tapping out tunes and singing. "Hazel Scott has a neat little show in this modest package," *Variety* would report. "Most engaging element in the air is the Scott personality, which is dignified, yet relaxed, and versatile." When Scott's name surfaced during an FBI investigation of communist sympathizers linked to the entertainment industry, the fate of her show seemed a foregone conclusion. Her husband, the enterprising Powell, encouraged her to appear before the House Un-American Activities Committee. Scott, a flinty personality, was eager to do so. "We should not be written off by the vicious slanders of little and petty men," she told the committee, speaking for herself and other artists. "We are one of your most effective and irreplaceable instruments in the grim struggle ahead. We will be much more useful to America if we do not enter this battle covered with the mud of slander and the filth of scandal." It was a brave appearance, but Scott failed to realize it was too late; the mud had already been thrown. Within three months her show was off the air. (Scott would spend much of the remainder of the decade in Europe.)

Television wasted little time in getting back to what it knew best when it came to Negro performance: the matronly maid hovering around the white family. Ethel Waters was summoned again, this time in 1950 to play the title role of *Beulah*. The show, which had originally been a hit radio series, quickly became popular. That did not, however, mean that Waters—both moody and blunt—was content. By the second season she said she was tired of the "white folks kitchen comedy role," and abandoned the part. Her replacement was Hattie McDaniel, who had been the first Negro to win an Oscar for her mammy role in the 1939 film *Gone with the Wind*. McDaniel, raised in Denver, had traveled alongside her father in her youth, performing with him in *The Henry McDaniel Minstrel Show*. By the time she took over the *Beulah* role, however, she was ailing. Hollywood's Oscar-winning maid—who had supported herself in her early Hollywood years by washing dishes—died in 1952 from breast cancer. Louise Beavers, whose movie career was launched in 1927 in *Uncle Tom's Cabin*, succeeded McDaniel. Beavers herself had played the mammy role in more than one hundred motion pictures. If Sam Lucas was an "Uncle Tom" for the ages, then Louise Beavers was certainly a mammy for the ages.

Blackface was now passé. Still, Negro culture—warped and presented with stereotype on both radio and TV—made audiences laugh. On the evening of June 28, 1951, American TV received a funny-bone jolt that proved powerful. That night CBS debuted *Amos 'n' Andy*, a comedy spinoff from the wildly popular radio series of the same name that had been running for more than two decades. On radio, Amos and Andy had been played by white actors with painful Negro dialects. The show's fans were legion—among them Harry Truman, Dwight Eisenhower, George Bernard Shaw ("There are three things," Shaw once said, "which I shall never forget about America—the Rocky Mountains, Niagara Falls, and *Amos 'n' Andy*"), Frank Sinatra—and all three members of the Will Mastin Trio. Before the show premiered on TV, the two white actors who had performed on radio pleaded for an opportunity to repeat their roles on TV—in blackface. Television executives nixed the idea. Who better to play the roles than Negroes—themselves starved for TV opportunities?

Actually, despite its two-character title, *Amos 'n' Andy* consisted of three primary players: Amos, played by Alvin Childress; Andy, played by Spencer Williams; and Kingfish, played by Tim Moore. The dialect was semiliterate, and the humor slapstick and stereotypical:

> Andy:
> I done told the clerk where I was goin', and he said he ain't never heard a nobody goin' to Arabia on vacation cause it's too hot over there. Does he know what he's talkin' bout?
> Kingfish:
> Well, ahhh . . . yes, and no, Andy.

ANDY:

What 'cha mean?

KINGFISH:

Well, I'll explain dat to you. At one time Arabia was the
hottest country in de world. But dats all changed now in
the past few years.

ANDY:

What 'cha mean, done changed?

KINGFISH:

Well, Andy, they opened the Suez Canal and let the breeze
blow into Arabia . . .

ANDY:

How could it do dat?

KINGFISH:

Andy Brown, I'm surprised at you, a man a your intelligence asking a crazy question like dat. I'll explain dat to
you. . . . Now one end of Arabia, they got dah Suez Canal
wit de gates open. And, den, on the other end, is dah Polish corridor.

ANDY:

Well, what about it?

KINGFISH:

Well, dere you is. Arabia is de only country in de world wit
cross ventilation.

ANDY:

I don't guess dah clerk knowed nothin' bout dat.

Amos 'n' Andy may have become a cultural phenomenon, but it was not
without its detractors, chief among them the NAACP, which had been waging
a long campaign to have the show canceled. Having the characters hidden on
radio was one thing; to have them shown to millions of television viewers on a
weekly basis was quite another. "An entire race of 15,000,000 Americans," the
NAACP proclaimed, "are being slandered each week by this one-sided carica-
ture." The pressure showed no signs of lessening and led CBS to cancel *Amos
'n' Andy* in 1953. It was the same year ABC signed Sammy to his television contract.

For months, television executives had worked on a format for Sammy.
Mastin insisted he and Sam Sr. have roles in the show. The request stumped the
executives. Finally, they came up with an idea. The show would be about a
traveling musical act, a trio—just like the Will Mastin Trio! There would be
skits and dancing, all revolving around the three show-business figures who

A gathering of vaudevillians. The legendary comic Jack Benny invited the Will Mastin Trio to go out on the road with him in 1953, then again in 1954.   (JESS RAND COLLECTION)

made up the Lightfoot family. Sammy would need a love interest. He told TV executives he had just the actress in mind.

He remembered the strikingly beautiful Frances Taylor, whom he had met at Ciro's when she was dancing with the Katherine Dunham dance troupe. Taylor was in Chicago, dancing as one half of Nicks & Taylor, when Sammy reached her and asked her to be in the pilot. She accepted without hesitation. Taylor was something of an ingénue herself, trained in classical ballet. She had been the first Negro ballerina to perform with the Paris Opera. Other cast members were Ruth Attaway and Frederick O'Neal. O'Neal, of course, had been one of the founders of the highly respected, Harlem-based American Negro Theatre. The producers came up with a name for the show: *Three for the Road*. Mastin didn't like it and had another suggestion: *Three for the Road— with the Will Mastin Trio*. The producers raised an eyebrow. Mastin reminded them that he had Sammy under contract, and threatened that he might bolt. So the producers relented.

There were problems from the beginning. "None of the actors liked the script," remembers Jess Rand. It was also obvious, from the beginning of taping rehearsals, that Will Mastin was out of his element. The television wires and equipment seemed to bedevil him. He was a vaudevillian, and vaudeville had consisted of much improvisation. This was television, and marks— positions where actors had to be—had to be hit. Lines had to be memorized, one's own lines as well as the lines of others. "Will couldn't learn his lines," says Rand. "And Sam Sr. didn't care." Rand says the two desperately wanted to get back out on the road, because, to them, "that's where the money was."

Sammy, sensing angst among cast members, approached the producers. "Would you mind if Jess did something with this?" he asked. The producers didn't mind, and Rand was quite game. "I rented a typewriter at the Ritz and rewrote the dialogue," Rand recalls.

The pilot was to be shot before a live audience. On the day of filming, Rand stood outside a New York City studio handing out tickets for passersby to come in and view the taping.

After the taping, Frances Taylor was convinced they all had done something special. It was not a show that put Negro stereotype on display. It featured Negro and white dancers. It gave her hope about the medium. But then, as time passed, no one heard when the show would be scheduled. The network approached Geritol to become one of the show's sponsors, but they declined. Other potential sponsors did the same. And some sponsors seemed confused about how to sell the show—as comedy, or variety? Sammy was the star, and television had never had a Negro male star singing, dancing, *and* acting. "We were all excited it would happen," Frances Taylor recalls. "Then came news it wouldn't. We were so depressed. I remember the dance scenes, and I said, 'How can they not want this?' The fact it was a 'first,' I couldn't accept. I was the first black ballerina to perform for the Paris Opera." Photographs from the pilot got out to the press. But by the time they were printed in some Negro publications—with all the fanfare of the belief that a new kind of Negro show was about to be unveiled—news had come down that the show had been dropped. ABC had spent $20,000 to make the pilot. It was a show without a mammy figure, and it was a show with a theme—struggling musicians—as opposed to slapstick and stereotype. Will Mastin was not Andy, and Sam Sr. was not Amos. They were gentlemen in high hats who wore monogrammed shirts and patent leather shoes. Onstage, next to Sammy, they were like silent- screen stars—seen and not heard. They were as bewildered by television as television was by them. But there they were, figures on a show that had been cast adrift before it had a chance to land on the schedule.

There were those who whispered to Sammy that his father and Mastin had stood in his way, that absent them the pilot might have stood a chance. The appeals to him to jettison the two grew even louder in the wake of the pilot's failure. "Everybody was trying to convince Sammy to leave his father and Mastin," says Rand.

Will Mastin and Sam Sr. and even Sammy shed no tears over the failed *Three for the Road* pilot. A naked stage with a microphone was all they had ever required to entertain.

Jess Rand came up with the idea to take out an ad in *Variety* showing a map of the United States. Superimposed over the map was a picture of the Will Mastin Trio. The message Rand sought to convey was that the trio traveled anywhere and everywhere. For quite a long time now, they had been three for the road.

Arthur Silber died on January 9, 1954, in Hollywood. He was seventy-five years old. The death freed the Morris agency from him—though not completely. Silber may have been a one-man operation, but he was not without a certain caginess. In the fine print of the contract he had signed with the Morris agency, it stipulated that, in the event of his death, the small percentage he had been getting from the Morris agency must continue to be paid—to his wife. So now, as long as Mastin owned a percentage of Sammy, Silber would continue to own a percentage of Mastin, who was under contract to the Morris agency, to whom he and Sammy both owed a percentage.

Sammy was now in debt not just to the living—but also to the dead.

Chapter 6

THROUGH A GLASS
EYE BRIGHTLY

Jess Rand thought it was a prank. Someone was on the phone from the
United States Treasury Department. He described himself as a secret
service agent. Rand later remembered the agent's request: " 'The vice
president and his wife would like to come to the Copa to see the show with
Sammy Davis, Jr., tomorrow night.' I said, 'Which show?' He said, 'Second
show.' Sure enough, the vice president of the United States walks in. Sammy
introduces the vice president." Nixon was dressed in a double-breasted suit, a
printed tie. Nixon, raised poor in California amid movies and make-believe,
always had an admiration for show business and actors. He chuckled throughout Sammy's performance. Now and then he'd nod his head, as if to catch the
beat. Pat Nixon, the vice president's wife, beamed. Afterward, Nixon asked to
be taken to the dressing room. Jules Podell, the club's owner, and Jerry Lewis
led the way. Jess Rand was busy hustling up a photographer. He wasn't about to
let such a moment pass. They all lined up: Sam Sr., Sammy, Nixon next to
Sammy with his arm around Sammy's shoulder, and Will Mastin and Lewis.
A flash went off. Rand knew publicity, and this was hot publicity. He got hold
of all the negatives. "I brought them down to every paper in New York—the
News, the *Herald Tribune,* the *Times.* Not one paper printed the picture." It is,
in a way, a thrilling black-and-white photograph: Will Mastin, a onetime pickaninny child performer, at the shoulder of the vice president of the United
States; Sammy, in his cummerbund and suspenders and pretty white shirt,
with a chin-jutting smile and his hair as wavy—as "white"—as Nixon's; Sam
Sr., the very picture of insouciance; Nixon, far more relaxed and at ease than
most photographs ever revealed him to be. Sammy swooned in the heat of
such moments. Sinatra was big, but Nixon was bigger because he was the vice
president. Sinatra might have traveled with men who carried guns, but so did
Nixon: those secret service agents! It didn't matter that the picture never made
the newspapers. Nixon had come to see him. Sammy never forgot. Nor did
Nixon.

Backstage at Bill Miller's Riviera, 1953, with, as they were billed, the Riviera Beauties. Will Mastin and Sam Sr. avoided the Beauties—owing to their own nervousness about possible racial backlash. Not so their Sammy.
(JESS RAND COLLECTION)

·   ·   ·

Sometimes, onstage, Sammy would cup a cigarette in his palm, light it—just like Bogie in so many movies—drag on it for a few puffs, all the while tapping, the heels clicking very slowly on the darkened stage as he moved about inside the coned spotlight. Curls of smoke rose. But then he'd drop the lit cigarette to his feet, crush it out, and start tapping, the seductive taps turning to fiery control, then outright abandon. Inside twenty seconds, upward of three hundred lightning clicks of the taps. It sounded like thin noise from a bell tower gone amok, and, metallically, it all sounded beautiful. His father and Mastin, in the wings, their eyes wide, nodding almost imperceptibly, had seen it so many times, sometimes in the hotel room, sometimes in the hotel hallway, where he'd practice, getting the guests, at first, riled, then, upon seeing him, curious and excited. Onstage now he seemed to be stamping out more than a cigarette. Sammy had reduced them, Mastin and his father—his teachers—to fans. And with each beautifully timed click of the heel, he seemed to be soaring away from them. But they were hardly frightened. In the haze of their own memories, and nostalgia, they convinced themselves they were looking at their former selves in him.

Imagine: a ship in a bottle; a dancer inside two aging men.

In the strata of upper-crust Negro society, one particular automobile took on a grand and psychic aura: the Cadillac. Moneyed Negroes—funeral directors, boxers, ministers, bootleggers, college presidents, Elks Lodge members—all cut supreme figures alighting from behind the wheel of a new Cadillac. The door would open, a leg would bend out, a shoe would touch ground, a body would rise up, and the heads of onlookers would swivel. Will Mastin of the Will Mastin Trio cut such a figure. He drove a Cadillac.

If well-heeled white America took the Cadillac for granted—just another comfortable car, from home to work and back home again—then Negro America took it for much more. It represented not only style, but one-upmanship. In a world where few luxuries fell from America's tree into the Negro's lap, the Cadillac was a purchase of quiet power, a victory in the commercial sweepstakes of the American dream. The 1954 ads in *Car and Driver* showed a family man and wife and their two children, all standing and smiling next to their Cadillac. The ads were handsome; the smiling and adorable members of the families always white. In 1954 America, a Negro driving a new Cadillac was a peculiar, even scintillating sight.

The '54 Caddy was quite a stylish machine. It was "lower and longer in silhouette," proclaimed the GM ad. Its features were seductive. "A great new 230-horsepower engine has added new power and explosiveness. A vastly improved Hydra-Matic Drive provides even greater smoothness and flexibility." The power steering was now said to be more "advanced"; the car featured a "more massive grille" and a more "distinctive rear deck," along with a "panoramic windshield." In the middle of the steering wheel was a decorative cone. Nothing overwhelming; you might like to know that GM paid attention to its ornamentation. "And what is even more remarkable, this great new Cadillac is as thrilling to drive as it is to see!" So it was actually more than a car; it was close to a dream. To the common man, it was automobile royalty. With those big whitewall tires, it seemed to be taking everything with it as it rolled by, hopes and whatever else was beating inside your very own chest.

Sammy never had a car of his own. But that year, that summer, Will and

Sam Sr. blessed him with his very own lime green convertible '54 Caddy, fresh off the assembly line. He jumped high in the air—like the dancer he was— when he first spotted it, turning with beads of sweat forming on his forehead, his yelp-yelp of a laugh filling the air, touching Jess Rand, standing nearby. Will got a bear hug, Sam Sr. got a bear hug; Sammy would have hugged the world if he could have. Climbing in, starting it up, he cruised up and down Sunset Boulevard. He felt special as a king. The car took the corners and the summer breezes—top down—so sweetly. At night Sammy parked it on Sunset while he grabbed something to eat. He was showing it off. A lot of entertainers had nice cars. Their female admirers expected them to. Now Sammy had his very own. Still, Diahann Carroll, an aspiring actress new to Hollywood who sometimes took a room at the Sunset Colonial and had caught Sammy's eye, wanted nothing romantically to do with him. Sammy frowned not at all; he was on to other conquests.

A new automobile might have sated the nervous energy of someone else, but not Sammy. Things—objects small and large—were toys, and toys only made him more eager, more hungry. Jess Rand worried that Sammy didn't have a driver's license. Rand went with Sammy, teaching him how to drive, mostly in the open lot behind a nearby Los Angeles warehouse. Sammy felt he knew how to drive well enough; he didn't have time to bother with taking a driving test.

Frank Military, who managed stage acts on both coasts, had an act appearing at the Mocambo. "Sammy came one night," he remembers. "I said to Sammy, 'Gloria De Haven and myself are going up to Nick Sevano's [a close Sinatra ally] house.' Sammy said, 'I'll follow you up.' Sammy was driving five feet behind me. I later said, 'Sammy, why were you driving so close to me?' He said, 'This is my second day of learning to drive.'"

Sammy hated hearing Jess Rand complain about his driving. He thought Jess worried too much.

In September 1954 the trio was in the middle of a gig at the Last Frontier in Las Vegas. They took a pause because Sammy had another commitment, in Los Angeles. He'd be gone a couple days. Will and Sam Sr. could enjoy the desert air—could gamble, eat good food, unwind over on the Negro side of town; have the tuxes for the act cleaned; do what old vaudevillians do: rest their bones.

Sammy had to drive back to Los Angeles to do a motion-picture sound track recording for his friend Jeff Chandler. Chandler could get Sammy into all the right Hollywood parties and all the swank private hotel soirees. They had glided in together to so many places, big blond Chandler, his smile soft but his

July 1954: Sammy has run screaming and yelping after receiving a gift from his father and Will Mastin: the brand-new lime green Cadillac convertible that sits at curbside. He has never owned a car. Come evening, he will drive it up and down Sunset Boulevard, top down, eyes roving, the palm trees swaying. Within a few short months, on a desert-touched San Bernardino roadway, he will lie shell-shocked, the Cadillac mangled— and his left eyeball loosened from its socket. (JESS RAND COLLECTION)

shoulders brusque, his walk hard as the Brooklyn he came from, daring anyone to stop him. And Sammy right beside him, limber as a jockey, his gaze darting about, taking the fill of rooms, of the blondes gathered about. Chandler could even pass along privileged knowledge about Hollywood casting— Sammy loved the gossip—but he couldn't get Sammy any movie roles. Overall, roles for Negro males were practically nonexistent in Hollywood. (There was a conversation with a Universal executive about Sammy doing a Bill "Bojangles" Robinson biopic. The possibility held such fascination: Sammy, onscreen, portraying the legendary tap dancer who had taught him more than a few moves back in Harlem. But like so much in the entertainment business, it all went to dust.) The studios couldn't see past color. Chandler knew it. There may have been color on the streets of Brooklyn, but not in Hollywood. Still, Chandler knew how eager Sammy was to have anything to do with a movie, so he got him hired to sing the title song to *Six Bridges to Cross,* a finished film that starred Tony Curtis, who was steadily rising in Hollywood since his magnetic title-role performance in *Houdini,* released in 1953. *Six Bridges to Cross* was a re-creation of the celebrated Brinks robbery in Boston. (The studio prepared to call the film *Five Bridges to Cross* until someone realized, before its release, that there were actually six bridges going into Boston.) Chandler, along with Henry Mancini, wrote the *Six Bridges* title tune. Chandler himself recorded on the Decca label, which owned Universal, the studio that released many of Chandler's movies. In Hollywood, Jeff Chandler had accumulated clout. If Chandler wanted Sammy, Universal—as long as it was an off-camera performance—was not going to go against his wishes.

So, on November 19, Sammy and his valet, Charlie Head, climbed into his Cadillac convertible and pointed it in the direction of Los Angeles. It was in the wee hours of the morning. Sammy was tired and stretched out in the back, curling up on the leather seat, while Head took the wheel. The car was so huge, Sammy might as well have been at home on a sofa—only, of course, he didn't have a home to call his own. The car's interior design dazzled Sammy; he had slept in motel rooms not much bigger than his Cadillac. It wasn't long before his eyes were closed. It was the old vaudevillian's curse: you learned to sleep anywhere—in a car rolling around the mountains and away from Las Vegas, taking you to another itty-bitty dream coming true on the road to stardom. He had never sung a film score before, and he aimed to sing this one with everything he had—not that he knew any other way. Chandler and Tony Curtis would be depending on him.

The big new Cadillac was out there now, between the mountains, whirring by earth and beneath the rolling sky, almost floating in the sureness of its 230-horsepower engine. Not long into the drive Charlie Head pulled over. He was tired. Sammy sprang up and climbed into the front seat to drive the rest of the way. Charlie stretched out in the back.

Soon enough, Sammy could see the sun rising. He was in El Cajon Pass now, ninety minutes from Los Angeles, cruising on the outskirts of San Bernardino, a little farming community where miles of land swept off into the distance. There were mobile homes and motels in view. The car window was rolled down; the wind was soft. Early morning, and there were not many cars on the road. A car passed on his left. He thought nothing of it. Two women— as he would later remember—in dress hats, humming along just like him. What GM promised in its ads was so true: plenty of power, plenty of luxury. He rolled and rolled, Charlie asleep. Then Sammy noticed that the car that had passed him—with the two women inside—looked to be slowing in the distance. He was coming up on the car now. Then the driver of the car inched it into the middle of the road. She was preparing to turn around. It was the damnedest thing, and so dangerous in the middle of a two-lane highway. He veered the Caddy into the left lane. Maybe he could pass her. No, he could not, for there were cars coming up ahead in the opposite direction. He quickly veered back to the right. And when he did, and before he could touch the brake, and before he could think another thought about singing a song for Tony Curtis's movie, and before he could wish himself anyplace else but inches from another car in the middle of the road with Charlie in the back sleeping, and before his heart had a chance to rocket right through his chest, and before he could think about all the times his father and Jess Rand had expressed concern about his driving abilities, he crashed his prized Cadillac—boom—right into the stalled car. His head snapped forward. Charlie bounced like a toy. In that instant, there was the fury of sound: metal upon metal, and glass, and the godawful feeling that life might be over, and land looking like sand through an hourglass, and out-of-control voices—his and Charlie's—and fear like a little child's in a dark cave at night, and the slamming of limbs into metal and the cone in the middle of the steering wheel finding his face, and the blood spurting like something out of a Hollywood B movie. He felt pain everywhere—the leg, the shoulder, the face.

"I had no control," he would recall later. "I was just there, totally consumed by it, unable to believe I was really in an automobile crash."

Everything was more vivid than normal reality. He was going to die. He was going to die on the road to stardom. He was already dead. A gifted but unlucky Negro. His road to Damascus. Maybe it was a dream. No, it was not. The day was real, and the wind was real, and the road was real, and Sammy Davis was real, and now he was stumbling from the car, blood streaming down his face, then turning in agony and reaching for Charlie in the back—and Charlie reaching his hand up to his own face and mouth and the teeth that had become pried from his gums.

It had all happened so quick; it was all so blindingly operatic.

Another driver slowed and hopped out and told the skinny little Negro that the two ladies up ahead were just fine—although one had a broken leg—and then Sammy and Charlie heard a siren and there were a couple of officers upon the scene.

Four months earlier the Eisenhower administration had announced plans for a massive and badly needed interstate highway system. But it was just a plan. The country had too many small roads; the roads were not keeping pace with the numbers of cars and travelers.

Sammy's Cadillac—dream car of the American Negro—sat there, a mangled mess on the side of the road.

Both Sammy and Charlie Head were rushed to County Hospital in San

Bernardino. It was the poor hospital, where any unknown Negroes might be taken. "The implication was that the police did not recognize Sammy Davis as a personality," recalls Dr. Fred Hull, "so where else would they take a black guy but to County Hospital?" But once at the hospital, word seeped out. It was Sammy Davis, Jr., the nightclub entertainer. Still, there was a dilemma: there were no beds available at the hospital. So Davis lay on a gurney. A cursory examination showed a serious injury to his eye and also an injury to a leg. Community Hospital was the better hospital in town. A County Hospital doctor phoned Dr. Hull, the best-known eye and ear specialist in town, who was on call throughout the county. "I got a phone call from one of the doctors at County Hospital," recalls Hull. "He said, 'We have Sammy Davis here. He has a major injury. They don't have a bed.' I said, 'Let's get him in Community Hospital.' "

Virginia Henderson was the head duty nurse on call at Community Hospital when the call about Sammy came in. She listened, and she knew she had no beds, but she kept listening, and as she was listening, she couldn't help recalling in her mind the talents of Sammy Davis, Jr. "I don't know why, but I had kind of followed Sammy's career," she says. "He intrigued me. So when he came here, I wanted to see that he had the best care he could get." Henderson's sentimentality was one thing, reality another. She knew to have Sammy Davis at the hospital would be a publicity coup. So what if there were no beds available? She'd make some available, quick. "I got to moving beds around and got a couple patients discharged," she would recall.

Word about Sammy's accident spread quickly. A reporter from the *San Bernardino Sun* was hustling over to the hospital. The wire services were alerted. Jeff Chandler and Jess Rand were on the Universal lot, awaiting Sammy, when they heard. And just like that, Chandler was already in his car—Cadillac convertible—zooming from Los Angeles to San Bernardino, Jess Rand in the passenger seat. Chandler's foot was heavy on the pedal. A policeman stopped him. Chandler, the easily recognizable movie star, explained the circumstances. The officer dashed back to his car, turned on his siren, and escorted them to the San Bernardino county line, where Chandler continued racing toward the hospital. He nearly galloped through the doors upon reaching them. He was wearing a pair of white duck pants. Tanned and silver-haired, Chandler looked like Hollywood. He and Rand raced to find their friend. "There was Sammy, a bandage around his whole head. He was moaning and groaning. Jeff and I were standing there, and didn't know what the hell to do," says Rand. Virginia Henderson, the admitting nurse, caught up with the pair. Chandler, upon seeing Sammy, suddenly looked hollow-eyed. "He took it very hard," recalls Henderson.

Sammy was in total darkness with head wrappings. He only heard voices. He had never been hospitalized before.

Tony Curtis had a different feeling of why Chandler had rushed out to San Bernardino. No one knew anything about the town. It was just someplace you passed on the way to Las Vegas. It was farm country; they grew oranges. There were not many Negroes in or around San Bernardino. Chandler worried what kind of treatment Sammy would get. "Jeff went out and patrolled and made sure Sammy wasn't going to lose another eye in the hospital because of [mis]treatment," recalls Curtis.

After spending time with Sammy—everyone holding to an optimistic outlook, the fate of the damaged left eye not yet decided—Rand asked about Charlie Head, the valet. "I said, 'Where's Charlie Head?' They said, 'Who?' " Rand found Head in another room. He was lying on a cot. And he was gurgling. Rand stepped closer. Head pointed to his mouth. He tried talking, but only gurgled. His bridgework had come completely loose and was gagging him. Rand reached into his mouth and removed the broken teeth.

As soon as Will Mastin and Sam Sr. got word, they raced to San Bernardino from Las Vegas, curving along desert roads fast as they could. When they reached the hospital, they made inquiries and were finally directed to Sammy. They walked along the hospital corridors—they were dressed casually but elegantly—with the smooth assurance of seasoned entertainers. Onlookers stared at them—two dandyish Negroes nearly glistening with worry. When they found him, he was on the gurney, heavily bandaged. They both grew sickened. They stood looking him up and down—his legs, arms, shoulders—worrying where injuries might be. They leaned over and whispered to him, trying to stay calm. They had had Sammy since childhood. They had protected him so, they had never seen him bloodied, in pain. This, now, was terrifying. This was Will's worst nightmare. Sammy, out of his sight, driving the California roadways, and crashing. Just when Sammy had his biggest hit, "Hey There," rising on the charts. Just when the act looked so unstoppable. Sam Sr. just stood, barely blinking. His Sammy, flat on his back. In bandages. The father did not want to break down before the son. He might instill more fear in Sammy than was necessary. So he was gentle, quiet, as reassuring as possible. Mastin was more expressive, seemed to be in more agony, showing a cross between commercial heartache—might this be the end of it all, the act?—and pain. "The doctor said it's going to be all right," Sam Sr. told Mastin in as sure a voice as possible. Rand and Chandler hovered near the two worried men. But Will Mastin seemed not to hear anything. Actually, he seemed to be going into shock. He stood looking at Sammy, at the star of his trio, at the only reason the trio still had currency coast to coast, and something seemed to spill right from him—life itself—like dark ink. For so long he had thought the world was trying to snatch Sammy. Showbiz agents whispering things to Sammy behind his back; Abe Lastfogel and his cheesy grinning; white women getting to Sammy, delivering notes from those very showbiz agents. Will Mastin believed wickedness was afoot in the cold world of entertainment. He was nobody's fool. Now this: calamity and disaster in the blink of an eye. The show must go on—only now the show would not go on. Sammy was the show, and the show was bandaged and bloodied. Mastin fell to the floor. Rand and Chandler and the nurses swiveled their necks and bent down to him, quickly reaching for him. "Will was on his hands and knees," recalls Rand, "saying, 'Jesus, just let him live.'"

The vaudevillian couldn't take it. From the Barbary Coast of San Francisco to the gritty streets of New York, he had seen so much in the performing world. But few things were as debilitating to him as the sight of his Sammy hospitalized. He had never invested so much time and energy in an act as he had in the Will Mastin Trio, nor in a performer as he had in little Sammy. Sometimes people laughed at him. The bobby-soxers and the nightclub promoters even snickered. He was the old man in the corner, hovering like a shadow. But he had grown immune to all that. At least he wasn't handing out tickets at some two-bit Negro theater. Nor was he on the unemployment line. Far from it: he was a Negro in a Cadillac with lovely dress suits and a trio to take care of. Will Mastin had nothing but the act. So in the hospital, he dropped to his knees and asked the Almighty to save Sammy. Jess Rand, whispering, asked a nurse for some sedatives to calm the seventy-five-year-old Mastin. "She gave me some Nembutal," Rand remembers. It was an antianxiety drug. "I told Will it was a vitamin."

There was a commotion back at the front door of the hospital. It was Jeff Chandler. He was verbally jousting with Jerry Lewis, who had just arrived and desperately wanted to see Sammy. Chandler—a very serious man, and one who did not take the young and often hysterically gyrating comic seriously—told Jerry that Sammy needed rest, that it might be wise to come back another time. Jerry's body began moving about like something suddenly wound up. "I tangled with Chandler," he would recall. "He stopped me at the door of the hospital. I said to him, 'If you don't have a white [doctor's] coat on, don't tell me what to do.'" Then Jerry Lewis raced down hallways until he reached Sammy's room. "It was devastating," he says of spotting the bandaged Sammy. Lewis pulled up a chair, and he sat down awhile, offering soothing words to Sammy. Of course, with the bandages, Sammy could not see him, only hear his voice. Quietly, very quietly, Jerry Lewis began to weep.

Fred Hull was a tall and gangly man. He had taken his medical degree in 1939 from the University of Southern California. The accomplishment made his father, a jeweler and a simple man, quite proud. In San Bernardino, Hull had acquired a reputation as a fine ear and eye surgeon. By the time Hull reached

Sammy at Community Hospital that Friday, the entertainer had been lying on a stretcher in a hallway, uncomplaining. Jeff Chandler wasn't so tight-lipped about Sammy lying on that stretcher. Chandler had, in fact, frantically gone about calling other hospitals for a bed, but had had no luck. "I examined him, and I found that the left eye had been ruptured and that some of the contents of the globe of the eye had been lost," Hull would recall decades later. "And in my judgment, the proper treatment was to remove the eye." Hull wouldn't even entertain leaving the dead eye in. To do so would risk "sympathetic ophthalmia"—a condition in which the damaged eye, over time, dilutes some of the power of the undamaged eye. "So the safest thing to do," says Hull, "is remove the damaged eye if it is irrevocably blind."

Having made his diagnosis, Hull went to tell his patient. Sammy listened with barely a movement. There was no howling, no expressions of verbal emotion, no self-pity. He took the news with amazing calmness; Hull was quite impressed. "He didn't carry on or anything like that," the doctor recalls. "I tried to explain in layman's language what had happened and that he would never be able to see with that eye." Sammy kept asking about his leg, pointing to it. There was a cut on his right leg, and pain. It wasn't just a leg, but a dancer's leg. His legs caused those nightclub-goers to rise and applaud him and take a sip of their drink and applaud him some more. Hull assured Sammy there would be no permanent damage to the leg.

Sam Sr. realized he would have to phone his mother, Rosa, Sammy's grandmother, and the realization of it jangled his nerves.

There was no time to waste, and Hull decided on surgery that very night. Both Henderson, the nurse, and Hull could see how pained Mastin and Sam Sr. were when told of the news. "I just told them," recalls Hull, "that he had a very major injury and his eyeball was destroyed and it had to be removed."

Janet Leigh, rushing from Los Angeles, arrived that very day, before the surgery. Thin, pink, lovely, she had been starring in a string of MGM movies years before her marriage to Tony Curtis. The marriage to Curtis, in 1951, rocketed both into the consciousness of the fan-magazine crazies. Tony had introduced her to Sammy, and she had been immediately taken with his talents and showbiz eagerness. "It's such a shock," Leigh would recall of arriving at the hospital to see Sammy. "You're not knowing what to expect." She found him, told him it was she, blinked back her tears at his appearance. She sensed how calm he was, but thought it masked something else: "I think he was in shock. That's almost too much to take." She sat by his bedside for a while. Yes, she thought, sensing his sunny disposition, it must be shock. She later huddled, away from Sammy, with Jeff Chandler and Jess Rand. Everyone worried about Sammy's future.

It was not a terribly old hospital—having been built in 1909—but it had aged quickly. Repairs were clearly needed. There had been talk of building another one, but the talk always evaporated because of the lack of money.

Nurses arrived in Sammy's room to prepare him for the operation. He was placed on a gurney, and hospital staff wheeled him outside, into the open air, because the surgery would be performed in another part of the hospital, accessible only by first going outdoors. As he was being wheeled, some staffers told him they knew family members who had seen his nightclub act; some told him they had only recently heard him singing on the radio. The adulation comforted him. Watching it all, Will and Sam Sr. kept shaking their heads. The whole scene—wheeling him about, nurses hovering, the coolish November air—looked rather ominous. Once he was inside the surgery room, the doors closed.

During the surgery, reporters found Will and Sam Sr. sitting out back of the hospital. The aging hoofers looked forlorn. The reporters wanted some reaction, something for the next day's edition; they had deadlines to meet. But the two entertainers were too somber to be voluble. They talked about Sammy having been a performer since childhood, how much he liked performing— simple reflections. They rubbed their hands, looked into each other's eyes, lowered their heads. They simply had little to offer. They rarely talked to the press anyway. Sammy had always done all the talking.

His surgical tools assembled, and with Sammy sedated, Hull went to work. "The eye was removed, and then we used what we call an implant to fill up the volume of the space in the orbit. You would do this to make better movement of the artificial eye," he remembered. The delicate surgery required the smallest of tools, and took forty-five minutes. "The eye was removed. An implant was inserted, muscles closed over the implant, and the incision closed. He had cuts through the lid of the eye. There you have to do plastic surgery repair. I'm as proud of the lid repair as I am of removing the eye."

All went well. In time, Sammy was wheeled back to his room, Will and Sam Sr. following every step of the way. It took thirty stitches to close the surgical incision.

News of the surgery was now out over the radio airwaves. The next morning, hospital switchboard operators began fielding calls, and the calls kept increasing. Sinatra called. So did Dean Martin and Joey Bishop. Eddie Cantor called. "Someone called me," remembers Eartha Kitt, who was in Chicago at the time, "and said, 'Sammy's in the hospital.' They said he was saying, 'Where's Eartha? I got to talk to Eartha.' I was doing an engagement. They explained to me the accident, and I screamed."

Strangers began calling. Flowers arrived, and they kept arriving. Will and Sam Sr. brightened at all the goodwill, but they really wished they could turn back the clock, that Sammy would never have climbed into his new Caddy and driven it across the desert. "They were pretty pessimistic about the situation—

but Sammy wasn't," says Virginia Henderson. "Sammy knew he had one good eye."

His friends back east were stunned when news reached them. "I was home," remembers Judy Balaban. "I was very pregnant. I was watching TV. I didn't know then he'd lost his eye. I remember my heart dropping. I remember getting on the phone. I remember having the name of the hospital and trying to call the hospital. I remember I had Sammy's mother's number and couldn't find it. I didn't know what to do."

His sister, Ramona, called from New York City. "A friend of mine owned a pub. I went to the bar. They kept giving me change to call the hospital all night until he came out of surgery."

In the hospital, Virginia Henderson was constantly trying to keep everyone calm. She could tell, however, that Jeff Chandler—back again the day after surgery—remained restless and agitated. "I invited him to lunch a couple of times," she would remember. "He was so upset."

The few Negroes who were employed at the hospital strained to get glimpses of the injured entertainer. They tiptoed by his room. And as they walked away, they shook their heads in agony and gossiped among themselves—as did others—that darker forces had been at work. That it wasn't an accident at all, but the work of men—possibly Mafia hoods from Vegas—who loathed Negroes who dated white women. But such dark thoughts were in fact far too fanciful and merely reflected the temper of the times. Ruffians who wanted to injure Sammy Davis, Jr., would hardly have sent two elderly ladies—one seventy-two, the other sixty-nine—out into the morning hours to stage a car wreck.

As the hours and days began to pass, Will and Sam Sr. couldn't help but think of the future. Onstage, minus Sammy, they were nothing. Before him, they were indeed something. But that was a long time ago, and a long time ago was gone.

"I just got word that Timmy French give up the ghost," Sam Sr.—apropos of nothing, save maybe the knowledge that the ghost, like time, was always on the move—had told Will Mastin one afternoon. "Let everybody go and he's runnin' a elevator at some hotel."

The ghost was the business itself—the shoeshine box you kept and the rack of suits you owned and the names of theaters you had committed to memory and the money you had saved and the celebrity you had earned and the way your ear pressed against the velvety curtains backstage, where, if you were a Will Mastin, or a Sam Sr., you could nearly guess the number of folks in the seats on the other side of the curtains just by the timbre of the noise. The ghost lifted you from bed in the mornings. No member of the Will Mastin Trio knew the ghost as well as Mastin himself.

You could love and loathe the ghost. But you loathed it only when it wasn't loving you properly. When all was going beautifully, when the square white boys in Spokane and Philadelphia and Syracuse were waiting in the wings and your name—Will Mastin of the Will Mastin Trio—was rolling off their tongues and echoing like meshed-together voices from a corner phonograph, when the name itself was up in lights, when you had crisp bills folded handsomely around the money clip and the ulcer wasn't spitting fire, you were made aware of the gift-giving gentleness of the ghost. And as the years rolled along, you didn't even have to move your body onstage much anymore because the kid, Sammy, the man-child, was moving around enough for a dozen men.

The ghost was the smooth road out of every town that had treated you right and with respect. The ghost was the Negro side of town, the folks who pointed to you as if you were some kind of hero, the ladies who had seen your face in some newspaper, or maybe even in one of those Negro periodicals like *Jet* or *Hue* that, more often than not, you could purchase only on the Negro side of town. The ghost was all the Negro ministers who had you into their homes— an afternoon supper of collard greens, yams, neckbones with gravy, a sip of liquor—and prayed over you when you hit the road again. Yes, the ghost was everything when everything was working right, the years—1950, 1951, 1952, 1953—rolling by, each better than the previous one.

The ghost was the soft bed in the good hotel. The ghost was all the edgy headlines of the day—Negroes on the march, Negroes jailed—which sailed right over you because you did not bleed from those wounds, you were moving across the land, you were on radio, on TV, Eddie Cantor himself sweeping you along down the hallways of the studio. You had a matinee in Pittsburgh, another gig in Vegas. The ghost had kept you away from your deep southern roots, where blood had roiled and men had been treated as less than men. To hell with Alabama: Mastins had died there flat broke and unmentioned in newspapers. Just died, gone, shoveled under.

The ghost was the diamond ring on your pinkie. It was the way you tipped your hat to the lovely lady walking toward you with a compliment about that evening's performance. The ghost was all of that, and more: Mastin with an "i," not "e," to the scribes; the Cadillac whirring up and over the mountains, up and right through the land of the free and the brave, right down Sunset Boulevard on a sunny afternoon. And so what if sometimes, when you ached, when you were tired, you couldn't figure anymore if the ghost was chasing you or if you were chasing the ghost? Or, worse, if both of you were at a standstill, peering into the beyond of bad dreams and nightmares? That was just weariness, a drink could solve that—and antacid medicine could tame the bubbling ulcer.

Will Mastin knew the ghost. And sometimes the ghost frightened him.

"Something bad is gonna happen," he'd say over and over to Jess Rand, even, bewilderingly, in the glow of a triumph for the trio, as if success itself held some underlying and dark forces.

Sometimes those traveling with him—Big John Hopkins, the equipment manager; little Sammy; Jess Rand; even Sam Sr., who had known him the longest—couldn't quite figure what had been poured into Will Mastin's eyes, into those vessels. They couldn't quite see in there what was beautiful, and what was unfathomable. The Depression had nearly clawed him under, but he had fought back; he had endured.

During the traveling vaudeville season of 1930, Mastin gave five-year-old Sammy Jr. the ghost. You couldn't always see the transferring of it. The same way you never saw how the ship got in the bottle. But it was there for the glazing glance: it was Mastin's hand on the little kid's shoulder while standing backstage and listening to the hum of audience members shuffling their way to their seats. It was the way he applied the child's makeup. It was the slow and precious way he picked up the child's strewn clothing. It was what Eileen Barton, child actress, saw when she looked at little Sammy, being tended to by Will Mastin, her eyes going over to Sam Sr., and Sam Sr. looking down at his boy, and Will Mastin looking over at Sam Sr., then the two hoofers looking at their Sammy. It was something deep and true unto itself. The child had been given the ghost, and it was inside him, and the years had gone on. They were men who drove Cadillacs and had money in their pockets. They were not men who wanted to give up the ghost. But here they were now, circling a hospital room with their Sammy half-blind and lucky to be alive. With their blood pressure rising. Never mind that the Negroes who worked in the kitchen would sneak glances at them as if they were the most important of Negro men, asking if they could get them anything—anything at all—to eat. They felt weakened. Watching as Sammy's hand groped to touch things, to find things—water, a tray—and bending to help him. Sitting and watching as the evening November light faded inside the room as nurses appeared to check Sammy's temperature, his vital signs. They grew tired; they felt more exhausted than they ever had on a stage. Their minds wondered dark thoughts. "They felt it was the end of his career," Virginia Henderson says.

"They knew they'd never do anything on their own," Jerry Lewis says. "What they had with Sammy was utopia."

Timmy French—someplace out there pushing the buttons of a damn elevator. Which, in fact, is exactly what Sam Sr. did upon arriving in New York City all those years ago.

The owners of the Last Frontier in Las Vegas had to quickly find a replacement for the trio's broken engagement. Tickets had been purchased; the people wanted to see someone on the stage. Jeff Chandler and Billy Eckstine both offered to perform. No appearance, however, was as unexpected as that of film star Betty Hutton, who would appear alongside Eckstine. Hutton—known lasciviously as "the blond bombshell" despite her multiple talents—had announced her retirement from show business two weeks before Sammy's accident. Betty Hutton was a feisty Hollywood figure. She was not at all shy about battling with studio heads when she felt she was either being mistreated or not taken seriously. She won wide kudos for her performance in *Annie Get Your Gun*, MGM's lavish 1950 musical. (She took over the role for an ailing Judy Garland.) Two years later she won the coveted lead in Cecil B. DeMille's *Greatest Show on Earth*. But thereafter she consistently argued with studio executives, walking out on a Paramount contract principally because the studio would not allow her husband, Charles O'Curran, to direct her films. Yet there she was—for one night only, it was to be understood—in Las Vegas, for Sammy. There were doubtless not many in the Last Frontier audience who knew about Betty Hutton's upbringing back in Battle Creek, Michigan. Her father died when she was a child. Little Betty June Thornburg took to standing on street corners and singing. She was, in as dignified a way as possible, begging for money. The Thornburgs had to eat. By the age of thirteen—which would have been 1934, the depth of the Depression—she was constantly on the road, singing with bands.

Little Betty Thornburg. Little Sammy Davis, Jr. Not just Depression-era children, but Depression-era workers: to hell with that tummy ache—sing, dance, move!

Betty Hutton, song-and-dance lady, took the stage of the Last Frontier dressed in a black evening dress, her shoulders bare. She looked tough and sexy, belting in a voice that had, years earlier, also conquered Broadway. Standing onstage that night—on behalf of onetime child performer Sammy Davis, Jr.— Betty Hutton looked quite proud.

He looked helpless and nearly pitiful in his hospital bed, his head wrapped up, his world gone dark. But he never complained, and he never turned bitter. There were three shifts of nurses, and on every shift, the nurses would take extra care in tending to Sammy. "All the nurses had to go in and say hello to him," says Henderson. He wanted some music, so Hull found a businessman in San Bernardino to donate some stereo equipment. And the whole hospital got wired with sound. Unable to have the bandages removed until more healing had taken place, Sammy was forced to use his ears as never before. "He loved people around him," recalls Henderson. "He wanted to know, 'Who are you and what do you do?' He identified some people by their voices." They brought his fan mail up in sacks and read him letters. He was touched. Some military guy called, said he'd donate one of his eyes to Sammy. Of course it was impossible, but they told Sammy anyway. News of his accident kept humming on radios, from Harlem to Los Angeles. In a way everyone listening belonged to him, just like the country, or so he made himself believe, because he really had no hometown. He was an itinerant. He knew everyone and he knew no one. He could call anyplace home. Anyplace from Syracuse to Chicago to San Francisco to Seattle, wherever there was a theater, the passing of a paycheck from Will's hand to his; wherever there was a blonde who wanted to slip beneath the covers with him. In a pinch—loneliness?—he'd take a Negro lady in Anywhere, America, and allow her to make him feel wanted and loved.

Virginia Henderson didn't get over to Los Angeles that much. It was just one big town with a million cars. And true, it was Hollywood, but you could see Hollywood—or at least what it produced—on the black-and-white TV set. San Bernardino was big enough for those who resided there. It had things to do: the annual San Bernardino National Orange Show, for instance. Dr. Fred Hull was crazy about the orange show. He once went and watched an up-and-coming Negro act—the Will Mastin Trio—perform. And he thought they were pretty darn stylish.

But now San Bernardino had something else. Jeff Chandler strolling through the hallways of Community Hospital. And Tony Curtis and Janet Leigh. And funnyman Jack Benny. And Eddie Cantor, with those wild eyes, grinning at the nurses. For years Sammy had cheered Hollywood on, slavishly saluting stars, sidling up to them, snapping their photos, his adoration shameless. Now it was being returned. Hollywood wanted Sammy to know how much they loved him too.

Cindy Bitterman and Eileen Barton were in a car in Los Angeles when the news of the accident came over the radio. "We turned around and went immediately to the hospital," Bitterman recalls. Once at the hospital, they raced right to his room. "It was one of the most horrifying days of our lives to see this kid you love and his head bandaged and he is shaking like a leaf," Bitterman says. "I had the shakes. One of the nurses had to go get me a pill. I thought this couldn't happen to one of our friends."

Cindy Bitterman, an ethereal beauty and Sinatra acquaintance, was one of the few women in Sammy's life who didn't want anything from him except to be a friend—a tricky word in the world of show business. She played mother, sister, wife, confidante. "I sat there and just held on to his hand. He had tears coming out of his other eye. I said, 'Don't worry, we're going to take care of you.' " There was one thing about Sammy that Bitterman found rather strange during his ordeal: "Sammy never mentioned his sister"—and his sister was someone she thought he might want by his side at such a time.

On the drive into San Bernardino with Bitterman, Eileen Barton couldn't help but think how desolate the town seemed to be. "We sat and talked for a couple hours," she would remember. "He was in the middle of nowhere at that hospital. He was lying there alone. So you can imagine how happy he was to see us."

Where were Harry Belafonte and Sidney Poitier? How come he didn't hear their voices from the side of the bed? Where was Nat King Cole? Couldn't Dorothy Dandridge get up off her butt and visit? Didn't she know how wonderful that would be for the photographers? Her lovely face, at bedside? Well, maybe they didn't love him. His mother couldn't come. She didn't have any money. She phoned, though, calling from the bar in Atlantic City, where she was working. Ramona, his sister, couldn't come either. No money. They couldn't just up and fly all the way to California. Sammy didn't have the money to send for them because he, as Tony Curtis knew, "was dead-ass broke."

And where was the Negro press?

As the days passed, and the time neared for his release, new waves of doubt washed over Sammy. He knew the act really had no money. Or, rather, they had money but it was spent. They owed nightclub owners dates on money they had borrowed in the past. Now there would be a huge hospital bill. Then Dave Duschoff, owner of the Latin Quarter in Philadelphia, flew in. He pulled Dr. Hull aside, told him he'd pay the entire bill, told him not to stint on the entertainer's hospital care. Then he left. The angels were coming forward. Sammy felt so much better.

But lying in the hospital bed, he realized he'd have to get back to work. He had to take care of his grandmother Rosa, because Rosa had taken such care of him. And he had to take care of Will and his father. Could he do that with just one eye? He wondered and wondered. "Everyone," remembers his friend Amy Greene, "said his career is finished, it's over. Who ever heard of a blind song-and-dance man?"

It was Cindy Bitterman who heard the deepest doubts coming from Sammy's hospital bed. "One night he had a nurse call me," she remembers. "He was in hysterics. I said, 'What's wrong?' He said, 'I have no place to go.' He said, 'Am I going to stay in a hotel?' " Bitterman didn't know how to answer. She herself was boarding with her uncle. But she told herself she'd figure something out. "I said, 'Get some sleep. You're not going to be on the street.' "

Sammy kept hoping for Sinatra. Just by visiting, Sinatra could make things better. Surely that was Frank coming down the hallway just now. Only it wasn't. It was someone else, and then someone else. Where was Frank?

Cindy Bitterman knew how hurt Sammy was that Sinatra had not yet come to visit. "I kept telling Sammy the reason Frank had not been out to see him was because he had a bad cold and didn't want to give him an infection." But then she couldn't take it any longer. So she got Sinatra on the phone—out of Sammy's earshot—and told him to go to San Bernardino because he was hurting Sammy every day he didn't show. And when she said it, there was an edge in her voice. She was one of the few women who had been in Frank's life who could talk to him like that.

She left the hospital to go home still angered at Sinatra's behavior. "When I got back, Frank's car was in front of my aunt's house," she remembers. "He was in a rage. I went into a bigger rage. He wanted to know what I was doing in San Bernardino with Sammy. I said, 'You don't understand what you mean in this kid's life.' He said, 'I'll go tomorrow.' But at five in the morning he comes back to Coldwater Canyon. He was drunk. I came running out in a bathrobe. He started sobbing—not about Sammy, but about what a mess he had made of his life. I said, 'I don't want to see you again, because you're so destructive.' The next day about two hundred flowers arrived. But what did it mean?"

First he wanted to see Sammy's doctor. Now. Word had spread that Sinatra was in the hospital. Dr. Hull was summoned. And Dr. Hull talked to Frank. Frank somehow made him feel inadequate. Asked him a lot of questions which put him on edge. Hull sensed condescension in Sinatra's voice.

"He was Frank," Hull would remember of their face-to-face meeting.

Just fill in the blanks—all the news clippings, all the horror stories, all the stories of Sinatra's mercenary ways, slapping folks around, bullying, threatening. The tantrums and the fisticuffs. There was that way he could look at you with that fuck-you-buddy look. And right then, you knew, he was already beyond you, in both thought and action, the legs beginning to walk away. Which is just how he was now beginning to look at Dr. Frank Hull.

He was Frank.

Damn right he was Frank.

Come to check on Smokey, on Sammy, on Charlie, on the kid—whatever name he wanted to call him.

And Sinatra wasn't finished with this Dr. Fred Hull. He was going to check him out. "He called around and found out my reputation was okay," says Hull, still snickering decades later about how well his reputation held up against Sinatra's snooping. Sammy was beside himself when Sinatra finally reached his room. All he heard was the Sinatra voice; his eyes were still bandaged. But it might as well have been a son reconnecting with a long-lost father. Sinatra didn't have long. He told Sammy he'd be staying with him in Palm Springs when he got out of the hospital. And just like that—a snap of the finger—Sammy had a place to recuperate.

Whatever other demons moved Sinatra, generosity was a genuine part of his signature. To Sinatra it was just a small deed, the least he could do. Nevertheless, the idea was not his; it was Cindy Bitterman's. ("[Frank] called me," Bitterman recalls. "I said, 'I'm going to ask you something. I want you to invite Sammy to Palm Springs, invite him to stay with you.' He paused. I said, 'You're playing for time. Say yes or no.' He said, 'Yes.' ")

Then Sinatra was gone, the soft patter of nurses' shoes trailing him. It was like a scene in a movie, and all that had been required of him was a cameo. In and out. Frank playing Frank. He had things to do.

After Frank left, Sammy wanted to call someone to share the good news. "So he called me," says Bitterman. "He was euphoric. I said, 'Oh my God, Sammy. I'm so happy. While you're doing that, we'll find a place for you to live.' "

Sammy hated to be left alone. It was worse than hearing no applause from the stage. But his head hurt and his eye hurt and sometimes he needed rest and sleep and the nurses would shoo people from the room. Sometimes, at night, he had problems sleeping. The radiators hissed. He worried about Will and his father. He worried how his grandmother Rosa was taking the news back in New York.

Hospital staff had hung new wallpaper in Sammy's room—"to pep him up" on the day the bandage was to be removed, says Henderson.

Hull began the process of removing the bandage slowly. An ugly scar swooped across the bridge of Sammy's nose. The left eye, of course, was gone, a deep dark socket now visible. On the dead eye, the eyelid was lower than the eyelid of the good eye. With the scar and the drooping eyelid, Sammy looked as if he had been in a terrible fight, perhaps with a knife. "Where am I?" he asked Hull, looking around, taking measure of the surroundings. Hull examined the eye socket, and then the good eye. He saw nothing to worry about and believed the healing process would go fine.

Much about Sammy's future now stood unknown, a fact echoed in the stillness of the room with the doctor and nurses and Mastin and Sam Sr. all focused on Sammy.

The scar would heal. But he would never quite look the same again. The left eye would forever appear askew. Dr. Hull instructed Sammy in the kinds of eye exercises that would be important to his recovery. He warned him there would be problems with depth perception, but he assured him that, in time, he would get used to working with just one eye.

The fear of rejection always crawled beneath Sammy's skin. He had an overbite, and he had crooked teeth. Now, facially scarred, he couldn't help but sneak peeks at himself in the mirror. Tony Curtis worried about what effect the loss of the eye might have on Sammy's psyche: "Sammy never started out as handsome. It was frightening for Sammy," he says. Poitier and Belafonte and James Dean—Sammy would stare at Dean at Hollywood parties with awe— had currency on good looks. As did Curtis. Female fans nearly dropped at the sight of them. They were not just handsome; many women found them gorgeous. Sometimes Sammy talked to Curtis about the years before the act found celebrity. "He said it was tough to get girls," Curtis recalls.

Talent, of course, was a beautiful thing. And it was talent—sheer uncontained talent, the singing and dancing, the all-around entertaining—that made Sammy beautiful. "Onstage he makes me think of Cary Grant," Marilyn Monroe said of Sammy.

The country had rumbled along nervously that year.

Senator Joseph McCarthy, the communist hunter, had his tent folded down via national TV—80 million had watched the McCarthy hearings that spring—when he shamed himself by making more ludicrous accusations. Boston lawyer Joseph Welch was army counsel during the hearings. McCarthy—sweaty, fervid—went after a member of Welch's staff. It was a severe misstep. "Let us not assassinate this lad further, Senator," Welch said, a TV audience watching. "You have done enough. Have you no sense of decency, sir? At long last have you no sense of decency?" At that, finally, a nation seemed to gasp.

Will and Sam Sr. never had to worry about any political goings-on. They weren't trying to be intellectuals or poets or writers or playwrights—all of whom had been victims in the McCarthy witch-hunts. Their politics was entertainment. The only subversive activity they engaged in was trying to get next week's pay a week early to settle some debts.

A young white kid down in Memphis with a shock of black silky hair and feminine lips was entering the consciousness of the nation's music scene. Disc jockeys were saying they had never seen anyone quite like Elvis Presley.

In November, Marilyn Monroe and Joe DiMaggio split. And there were so many who said they were so wonderfully matched when they married eleven months earlier. His baseball heroics, her film stardom, their good looks. But where he was private, she was a publicity geek, klieg lights and flashbulbs serving like some kind of strange oxygen to her. He couldn't understand it, any of it, so it was over. "The truth," Monroe would confide, "is that I've never fooled anyone. I've let men fool themselves. Men sometimes didn't bother to find out who I was, and what I was. Instead they would invent a character for me. I wouldn't argue with them. They were obviously loving someone I wasn't. When they found this out they would blame me for disillusioning them and fooling them." Maybe those words actually originated in Marilyn's mouth. Maybe some hack wrote them out for her, then she uttered them. Still, they were not without an admirable kind of perceptiveness. And so it was: DiMaggio, who had lived a dream, had been fooled by a dream.

Joltin' Joe climbed into his car, a navy blue Cadillac, and glided away from it all.

A new kind of TV news show premiered in the nation's capital the third week of November. It was called *Face the Nation.*

Many school districts across the country were still refusing to enforce the Supreme Court's May ruling striking down "separate but equal" schools. The Earl Warren haters—he was the chief justice—grew by the day.

On Broadway, a musical called *By the Beautiful Sea* was still running. It starred Shirley Booth as a softhearted former vaudevillian helping out actors on Coney Island. New York critic George Jean Nathan described the show in rather beguiling prose: "The show is largely of the kind that tries to boost itself into some life by periodically bringing on the routine chubby Negress singer who while rendering the routine saucy ditties pumps her avoirdupois up and down like a tureen of demented meringue to an accompaniment of the usual dental and ocular exuberance and that further purveys the usual cute little colored boy in dance steps with the leading lady." Another musical, *The Pajama Game,* was also still running on Broadway. One of its featured songs was "Hey There," now being sung from the airwaves by Sammy Davis and given an extra dose of sentiment from the deejays. The musical was about a strike in a pajama factory. Carol Haney was one of the stars. One night her understudy went on. The understudy was a smash. Her name was Shirley MacLaine.

Elia Kazan's *On the Waterfront* was in the can, being prepared for release. Studio executives were high on the picture. It was about waterfront shenanigans, mob intimidation, and broken dreams. The stars were Eva Marie Saint, Karl Malden, Rod Steiger, and Marlon Brando. (Kazan, Saint, and Brando would all eventually win Oscars.)

Down in Montgomery, Alabama, a young Negro minister by the name of Martin Luther King received a letter—as much a letter as a warning—from his father: "You see, young man, you are becoming very popular. As I told you, you must be very much in prayer. Persons like yourself are the ones the devil turns all of his forces aloose to destroy."

Eight days after entering the hospital, Sammy was discharged. He wore an eye patch. He walked gingerly, from weakness and the lingering effect of the bruise to his leg. Some reporter asked Will Mastin when Sammy might be ready to get back to work. "Whenever he's ready," offered the taciturn Mastin. "There's no rush. When his eye muscles are strong enough and when he says he wants to go to work, that will be the time." Mastin privately hoped sooner rather than later.

The act had no money coming in. And they had already had to cancel weeks' worth of work. Mastin knew that show business could be a cold affair. There were nightclub owners who'd forget you overnight, no matter what promises they made to a performer lying in a hospital bed flat on his back. There were other hot acts out there, climbing up the ladder just to snatch your billing. Why, hadn't the Will Mastin Trio shoved other acts to the side, into the background, farther down the marquee billing? Ask Janis Paige about Ciro's and Sammy Davis, Jr. Will Mastin worried what lay ahead.

Nurses loaded all of Sammy's fan mail into huge sacks. He told the hospital staff he'd be back. He felt they had saved his life. He was always over-grateful, his thank-yous always epic. When Henderson and Hull mentioned their hopes for a new hospital someday, Sammy said he'd like to help. They didn't exactly know what he meant, but it made them smile.

The Negroes who worked in the kitchen sought him out, to press their flesh against his. The world was dangerous; they wanted him to be careful.

He was alive. He had one good eye. His father and Will Mastin considered it divine. They loved him, and they needed him. Sometimes there were those who spent time with them who thought they needed him more than they loved him. Especially when an argument broke out among the three—more often than not the arguments were about Sammy's wasteful spending habits. But sometimes it was just family being family—argument and disagreement the flip side of unity and togetherness. But now, with him leaving the hospital, the two wanted to show him how much they loved him, so they had gone out and purchased a little something for Sammy. He saw it before he touched it. So what if they were getting older. Will Mastin and Sam Sr. could still produce magic: it was a Cadillac—convertible, lime green. Just like the smashed-up one. As if none of it ever happened. Sammy smiled. Will and Sam Sr. brightened.

A new car to take him forward, and an eye left behind, Sammy and the others climbed into the shiny Cadillac. Hospital staff members stood waving.

Then the Cadillac vanished down the road.

Dr. Fred Hull's work was hardly finished. He went about the work of ordering a prosthetic eye for Sammy.

The history of prosthetic eye making had been an arduous one, dating from sixteenth-century Europe. The first process involved metal and gold; those injured would have a metal ball painted, fastened to a rope tied around their head to keep it in place. Eventually, glass was put to use. Still, the fake eye was clunky and uncomfortable. In the nineteenth century, Ludwig Mueller-Uri, a German, revolutionized the process of prosthetic eye making. He had a strong

Days after Sammy was released from the hospital in San Bernardino, Jess Rand, on left, hosts a party for him. Film star Jeff Chandler is on Sammy's left. (The woman on Chandler's left was a party crasher; the host had never met her before.) Seated next to Marilyn Monroe is renowned photographer Milton Greene. Whenever Sammy found himself in a photo with Monroe, he would soon begin denying rumors that they were having an affair. The denial was Sammy's way of titillating the tabloids—inasmuch as the rumor found a life only in Sammy's breathless denial of it.

(JESS RAND COLLECTION)

impetus: his small son had lost an eye. Mueller-Uri's occupation was also quite fortuitous; he was a glassblower who sometimes made eyes for dolls. With his son's need of a model eye, he turned his hobby into a mission. He wanted to make an artificial eye that looked human, lifelike. He began to use "bone glass," which provided the useful effect of a glint to the eye. Later, the use of acrylic would make the eye even more authentic-looking. It was a pair of these acrylic eyes that blind and deaf Helen Keller—who would become a celebrated lecturer on behalf of the handicapped—took wearing. "No longer did Helen Keller have to be photographed in profile, and from then on, most photographs would show her gazing straight ahead," a Keller biographer would write. "She was often described in newspaper interviews as having 'big, wide, open, blue eyes,' few reporters realizing that such a luminous countenance came out of a box." But the glass that Mueller-Uri used could not be imported from Germany during and right after World War II. Still, Mueller-Uri's invention had inspired American technicians, who constructed their own plastic eyes for wide use.

"I went with him to the doctor who was doing the prosthetic," recalls Jerry Lewis. Upon seeing the eye fitted into Sammy's facial socket, Lewis immediately complimented him—lest Sammy become despondent over the way he now looked. "Sammy said to me, 'If the prosthetic looks so good, maybe *you* should have it done.' "

It lay 120 miles east of Los Angeles, just a spit of land, a desert oasis. The weather was nearly perfect. There were hot springs and palm trees and plenty of Mexicans to work the land, to tend the eucalyptus and mimosas that dotted the gardens. There was not much talk of Hollywood or movie deals. You came to Palm Springs to breathe the air, and you came to feel blessed of your good fortune.

Frank Sinatra much appreciated the resortlike feel of the place. There were often guests at his Palm Springs hideaway to keep him company. They were treated like royalty—lavish spreads of food, cheeses, innumerable wines, gift boxes in each guest room. The servants were smooth operators; everyone's privacy was highly respected, just as Frank demanded. Sometimes Sinatra had programs printed up: when to meet in the bar, what the evening's activities would be.

"He'd take armies out to dinner," says Roxanne Carter, a guest at the compound.

He didn't play much of his own music on the record player. He was too classy for that; he did, however, have a thing for Billie Holiday and Ella Fitzgerald, and their music often wafted through the house.

Recuperating in Palm Springs was a wonderful tonic for Sammy. He had never known such comfort, such pampering. He whiled away his time listening to music and idling by the swimming pool, where he fretted about his future. It was Sinatra who kept him calm and made him feel everything would be all right. Sammy's awe for Sinatra—already immense—only deepened. "He was so relieved that he was alive and that he could still work," Tony Curtis says. Sammy returned to Los Angeles following several weeks in Palm Springs. He was now wearing an eye patch. He got the idea from his memory of Wiley Post, a pilot who wore one and who died in a plane crash with Will Rogers.

"I told him, 'You got to use it to your advantage,' " Keely Smith says. She suggested he keep wearing the patch "and make jokes about it."

But he couldn't quite make jokes about it yet—nor could his friends. "I was devastated," Helen Gallagher would recall. "I felt terrible. He said, 'As if I don't have enough strikes against me, now I have this.' He was depressed."

Sammy already had two commitments lined up. Jess Rand was going to be getting married in December, and Sammy would be best man. He also had to begin rehearsals. Herman Hover, manager of Ciro's, had promised the act—at Sinatra's instigation—that they had a Ciro's engagement as soon as Sammy felt well enough to perform. The trio's appearances there with Janis Paige years earlier were still fondly remembered. There were, of course, those who began to wonder if the loss of an eye would diminish Sammy's ability. They wondered what toll it might take on his nerve. Hover would give him time to prepare, booking the act's appearance for early January.

On December 2, Jess Rand threw a birthday party for himself, his last as a single man. His wedding to pretty Bonnie Byrnes was a week away. Sammy liked parties; he showed at Jess's wearing his eye patch. Beneath it could be seen a large white bandage still covering his eye. It looked frightful, as did the scar across his nose. It seemed as much a coming-out party for Sammy as a birthday party. Many of Rand's and Sammy's friends were there, giving the evening a feeling of warmth and celebration for both of them. A surprise guest was Elvera, Sammy's mother, who had come in from Atlantic City. "She told me if I ever got married, she'd dance with me," says Jess Rand—and Elvera, the former showgirl, did. She could still cut a step. (She had had to borrow money from the owner of the bar she worked at in Atlantic City to fly to the West Coast. It was her first time seeing Sammy since the accident.) Jeff Chandler looked, as always, smoothly elegant. The breathless woman huddling near photographer Milton Greene was Marilyn Monroe. She wore a black dress with spaghetti straps, and looked both seductive and hazy. Sammy smoked and sipped his drink and chatted away the evening. He liked nothing better than to be surrounded by the famous, by fame itself, by those who had been and were still as hungry as he was for whatever mystical gratification lay on the other side of the magazines and on TV and radio. All they could do was deliver the superficial; they could show the homes and the money spent and the Cadillacs purchased. It was what the public couldn't see—the juice inside the body, the large appetite that never seemed to get filled—that he very much liked. Holding on to fame itself was far more valuable than any money resulting from that fame. Will and Sam Sr. never understood why Sammy spent money he didn't have. But it was because fame was sweeter than money in the bank. Will and Sam Sr., who had stared into the dark and challenging eye of vaudeville, who had cut their dance steps on the Depression, rarely thought along those lines. Money was tangible, money was safety, to be valued and kept secure in the money belt.

During that West Coast visit, Sam Sr. once again asked Elvera for a divorce.

He confided to her that he wanted to marry Rita Kirkland, his new lady friend. He had met Rita in his doctor's office in Harlem, where she worked as a nurse. A petite woman—her friends called her Pee Wee—she had caramel-colored skin and lovely social graces. Elvera said she'd give him a divorce, but the price would be $10,000. Sam Sr. scoffed, and Elvera flew back home.

On December 8, 1954, Sammy Davis, Jr., turned twenty-nine years old. He celebrated it in his new home, on Evanview Drive. It wasn't lavish at all by Hollywood standards—four bedrooms and a guest house—but it was quite comfortable. Jess Rand had to rent the house in his own name in order to outfox the real estate agents, who wouldn't rent to Negroes. Sammy celebrated in his first home by throwing a party. As soon as she arrived, Cindy Bitterman could tell how happy Sammy was to be there. "Judy Garland was there," Bitterman remembers. "Sinatra was there. The place was very crowded. I had gotten there with Bob Neal, a wealthy guy from Texas." Everyone admired the place, complimenting Sammy, who fussed over his guests, tending to the stars.

Friends and acquaintances began noticing little tics in Sammy, impersonations of Sinatra—in his walk, his selection of hat wear, clothing. He bought the same kind of raincoat that Sinatra wore. "When Sinatra started wearing the white raincoat, Sammy started wearing a white raincoat. But he wanted to outdo Frank—so he added a cane," says Jess Rand. There were even times when Sammy's voice would take on a bully's edge, just like Sinatra's. "I'll tell you something," says Rand. "It'll haunt me until the day I die. I never saw Sammy rehearse. The only thing I saw him rehearse was the Sinatra walk."

The Sinatra walk: languid but gritty, the back arched but the rest of the body loose. The walk of a man looking for tender music but easily annoyed in the search.

Mack Miller had been one of Sinatra's publicists. Miller was also Cindy Bitterman's uncle, a connection that Sammy was not about to let get by him. "When Sammy found out my uncle had been that close to Frank," says Cindy Bitterman—and in a voice with no bitterness at Sammy's obvious shamelessness—"our friendship became tighter."

There were many in 1954 who—like Sammy—might have wished to be like Francis Albert Sinatra. His was a story wrapped in family, Italian roots, magical lungs, and a critical understanding of the deep valleys where love traveled.

Born December 12, 1915, in Hoboken, New Jersey, Frank Sinatra worked as a copyboy for a newspaper in his youth. Natalie, his mother—known as Dolly to everyone—was a loving but forceful woman who exerted a powerful influence over her only son. She spoiled him, gave him the keys to a 1929 Chrysler. He started a singing group—The Hoboken Four. Then came amateur-hour gigs

Frank Sinatra and Cindy Bitterman. She played the role of blunt-talking sister to Sammy. It is December 8, 1954, Sammy's twenty-ninth birthday party. The pure joy of his survival from the car crash three weeks earlier can be seen in their eyes. Sammy hovers above them, playing both host and fan at his own party. He raises his camera: photograph by Sammy Davis, Jr.   (COURTESY OF PEGGY KING)

and radio appearances. Soon it was nightclub work. Harry James, the band-leader, heard about young Sinatra and signed him up. It was 1939—hard times. But Sinatra cut his first recordings that year. He moved on to sing with Tommy Dorsey, a fortuitous move that yielded a number 1 hit—"I'll Never Smile Again." Teenage girls and young women were soon swooning over him. He wasn't classically handsome. He was bony; he might have been any soda-fountain jerk. Except he was not. There was something velvetlike in his lungs; he had spent hours beneath water swimming to strengthen them. Onstage, his lips just inches from the microphone—as if it were a sweet and delicious woman—he was cool, confident, and serious. The eyes were blue and the voice sure. He was the top male vocalist in 1941, according to *Billboard* magazine. While singing, he seemed to be breathing the hurt of others. He listened to and admired Bing Crosby. But he seemed to put more medicine into his songs than

Crosby did. In Pasadena, California, in 1943, a line of police officers had to form a human shield to keep the bobby-soxers from getting to him. Standing before them—dressed in a light-colored suit, white shirt, and bow tie, pointy-toed shoes—he looked sweetly forlorn. An invitation came to him from the Roosevelt White House. "Fainting, which once was so prevalent, had become a lost art among the ladies," President Roosevelt told him. "I'm glad you have revived it." On October 12, 1944, Sinatra was back at the Paramount in New York City for three weeks. Times Square swarmed with fans, an estimated thirty thousand of them. He was hot, and he knew it. For two years—1943 to 1945—he was the lead singer on *Your Hit Parade,* the popular radio program that Sammy, along with millions of others, listened to. In 1940 record sales in America were estimated at $48.4 million. Five years later, in 1945, the take totaled $109 million. It was widely assumed that Sinatra sales played a prominent role in the increase.

It was a wonderful singer's life—that is, until the clouds rolled in. In 1947 a series of articles appeared in the press (mostly in the conservative Hearst newspapers), castigating Sinatra for a friendship with gangster Lucky Luciano. The articles were damaging. His record sales began to plummet. Conservative columnists bore in on him. He blamed it on politics, allowing that it was all happening because he was a Democrat. There were whispers he was a commie sympathizer. There were physical brawls with journalists. His marriage to Nancy fell apart. His movie roles had been light comedies, and he had shown promise in them. But now the studios stopped sending scripts. He fell into the arms of Ava Gardner, an undistinguished actress—but voluptuous Hollywood starlet—from tiny Grabton, North Carolina. Hers was a sharecropping family. She had been raised poor, and Hollywood only exposed her insecurities. She had terrible mood swings. Gardner's first marriage was to former child actor Mickey Rooney. Friends and acquaintances tried to tell Rooney—still riding the fame of his Andy Hardy serials—that Gardner was a gold digger, using him for his popularity, to help grease her way up the Hollywood ladder. At five foot three, the diminutive Rooney wasn't Clark Gable, but he was every bit a star. He was deaf to the talk that Gardner might somehow be trying to take advantage of him. They married in 1942. "Ava does strange things to men," Mickey would knowingly lament. It lasted less than a year. "The night we broke up, Ava said, 'Get the hell out.' It wasn't as dramatic as the night she threatened to kill me," Rooney would write. After Rooney she married bandleader Artie Shaw, and that union did not last long either. With two marriages behind her, there stood Sinatra in the doorway. They married in 1951. She was as domineering as his mother, Dolly, and the boomerang to his psyche was awful. There were public feuds, mutual jealousies. He cowrote a song—"I'm a Fool to Want You"—and everyone knew it was about her. The marriage lasted barely two years. After its demise he seemed to grow surly, even more temperamental. His agency dropped him. He seemed a man at curbside, in the dark rain. Now the affliction that he had once thought to have cured in so many others—a great loneliness—ailed him. He found it hard to distance himself from friends: he didn't give a damn about the gangster talk. Loyalty was like an elixir.

His mother, Dolly, was tough as iron. She loved him fiercely, even if she never coddled him.

He fought back. In 1953 he had started recording with Nelson Riddle. The voice was more mature now. An album, *Songs for Young Lovers,* was released at the beginning of 1954. It was a smash. With heartache—his own, not that of others—something rose inside his voice. Loneliness—like the roundhouse you don't quite see coming—seems to have made him a better performer. The movies did not come after him, he went after them, particularly one role, that of Angelo Maggio in the script from James Jones's novel *From Here to Eternity.* The studio wanted Eli Wallach, a much-admired Broadway actor, for the role. When Sinatra let his interest be known, the studio was silent. Clark Gable—so shrewd in the ways of Hollywood—told Sinatra to take a screen test, to show some humility. Sinatra said never. But then he relented, took the test, and won the role. His performance—sinewy and physical—drew raves and earned him a best supporting Oscar. The entertainment columnists characterized it as a great comeback. He seemed, right then, the essence of the American male id— fallen only to rise, stronger for inner pain. Gangsters may at times have had his ear, but love—the wicked power of it, for like everyone else he only wanted to be loved—had his heart.

Sinatra had Sammy out to his mother's house in Hoboken during the 1954 holiday season. Dolly—one could so easily see her Frankie as the mirror of her face—prepared a huge feast. "He'd talk about Frank a lot, the songs he sang, the look," says Frank Military, who was there during that particular visit. "Sammy was always there with a camera taking pictures of Frank." (Military sat in an audience at the Copa one night. Sammy had arranged a front-row table. "He'd sing a song and say, 'Do you think Frank would like this?' ")

Sammy was a decade younger than Sinatra. Not that he let the Sinatra powers lower his own competitive edge. "If Frank slept an hour, Sammy slept only fifteen minutes," says George Schlatter, who had worked at Ciro's. "Frank smoked Camels, so Sammy smoked Pall Malls—strong and longer."

Jess Rand remembers the recording session for "Hey There," Sammy's first hit. "Sammy turned to me—coldly—and said, 'When Frank hears this, he'll eat his heart out.' "

Those who entered Sinatra's private circle were either the dazzlingly talented or those whose ridiculous fawning he simply tolerated. Sammy was rare: he met both requirements. He found the Sinatra vibe hard to turn away from.

It was intoxicating. And in its web, he spun and spun. "Over the years, I watched Sammy dress like Frank, walk like Frank, smoke like Frank," says Cindy Bitterman. "He wanted to be a little Frank, which I found pathetic."

In 1954, Sammy was still boyish and childlike. He was not quite famous, but he was in the room where fame's candle certainly burned. His was a dazzling nightclub kind of fame. Movies still eluded him, though he had gotten onto the record charts. He moved across the country like lightning, picking up converts, singing, dancing, mimicking. And now, with an injury, he stood webbed between darkness and light, between achieving fame and, suddenly, the raw punch of misfortune. There now seemed nothing on earth—except death, which had touched him but not claimed him—that could slow him. He himself allowed for no dark thoughts, no dark imaginings.

His one continuing vice, if it can be called a vice, was relentless sexual pleasure. "Pussy is pussy," says Tony Curtis. "I don't care what color. And Sammy loved that stuff."

Especially if it was white.

Bonnie Byrnes—Jess Rand's fiancée—was a UCLA graduate. A petite and attractive brunette, she kept herself in wonderful shape by playing plenty of tennis, and she had the winsome smile of Audrey Hepburn. Rand met Byrnes in 1952 in New York; she was in from California on Thanksgiving vacation. In their early conversations, he thought she was being coy, distant; he imagined she would be a challenge to woo. He wanted to make an impression with the first date. Two tickets, him and her—"a deuce table right up at the stage," as he would remember—Bill Miller's Riviera: Sinatra onstage. In time Rand's courtship of Bonnie seemed always intertwined with his work and travels with the Will Mastin Trio. Bonnie never complained. She got a kick out of hanging out with the group. Sammy made her laugh, completely charmed her. "After the shows he liked to stay up all night," she would recall. "I was teaching school. He'd do things to make you want to stay up. He'd get everybody in pajama tops; he'd say, 'Put this on, be comfortable.' We'd start doing Shakespeare, *Hamlet, Macbeth*. By the time we got through, it was four in the morning. Then the next night Sammy would turn on the tape recorder [from the previous night]. You'd say, 'My God, that's me!' "

Whenever Bonnie could, she'd get on the road to see Jess. Actually, she found herself just as excited to spend more time with the trio. "He was a giant to me onstage," she says of Sammy. "We were so young." The more time she spent with the group, however, the more she noticed differences between Sammy and his father. "They were like night and day. Senior didn't have to prove himself. He knew he was a star. He knew he was a success as a man, a person. I think Sammy Jr. didn't have that confidence. One man was sure of himself, and one was not."

There was something else that Bonnie Rand noticed: "He was a homely little kid," she says of Sammy, "until he got onstage. And then he was beautiful."

Bonnie looked radiant on her wedding day—December 11—at the Brentwood Country Club. Best man Sammy huddled with Jess out of sight before the start of the ceremony. The eye patch was jolting to those who had not seen it before. Sammy's one-button tuxedo matched the black of the patch. The flower in his lapel looked like a puff of white smoke. Sammy—and not Rand—seemed fidgety, nervous. "You want to split? You don't want to get married," he told Rand. The groom thought Sammy was kidding, talking just to ease the nervousness. But he was not. "Sammy had a limo and tried to get me to walk out on the wedding," says Rand.

Sammy feared losing anyone close to him.

The wedding ceremony itself was a wonderful affair. Sam Sr. showed—but not Will Mastin. Sammy crooned—a microphone in his hand, his bow tie loosened at the neck—while couples swooned against each other on the dance floor. He sang "Hey There" and "Birth of the Blues," rummaging through his list. Jess had one special request—"My Funny Valentine"—so he sang that one too, and with much emotion. (When Jess finally got around to telling Bonnie of Sammy's attempt to hijack her wedding, she was not at all amused.)

Sammy returned to rehearsals for his upcoming Ciro's engagement. He kept outsiders and the curious away. Onstage he had to face the reality, and face it alone, that one side of his vision was missing. His energy was back, but his friend Amy Greene sensed his fear. "All that month it was unacceptable for anyone to come into the rehearsal hall," she recalls. "He had one eye now. He didn't know. Within himself, it was uncharted territory."

So he practiced in secrecy, his image bouncing around, against mirrors, the two men—Will and Sam Sr.—watching him as if he might stumble or faint from exhaustion.

One morning Sammy climbed into his car—he was fearless when it came to driving again—and headed back out to San Bernardino to Dr. Hull's office for a post-op visit. He had already been fitted with his glass eye. It was a good replica, but he was still uncomfortable when he took it out at night. He often wore the eye patch, but heading out to San Bernardino, he had discarded it. When he wasn't wearing the patch he wore thick eyeglasses, thick enough to conceal the false eye. When he reached the small town of Fontana, he started having engine problems. The car stopped. "I got a call from him," recalls Hull. "I drove out and picked him up. Brought him up to the house." Hull was impressed that Sammy showed no signs of depression or broken confidence. In fact, inside Hull's home—and after Hull had looked at the eye—Sammy regaled the family by entertaining. He did quick-draw tricks with a pair of six-shooters, wowing Hull's teenage son. Amazingly, he seemed fast as ever. He banged on a pair of bongos. He seemed to want to prove to Hull that he could see just fine. His right eye—as Hull had told him it would—seemed to be compensating for the loss of the left.

Sammy invited Hull to his upcoming engagement at Ciro's. Another driver came out from Los Angeles to fetch him, and Sammy bounced from the Hull home in a spate of energy.

At some social functions, friends of Sammy's—Jeff Chandler, Tony Curtis—would show up wearing eye patches. It was their way of showing camaraderie. The patch got him publicity, and Sammy didn't mind. Unlike Sinatra, he loved his name in the papers. "I read in the paper that we gave him a monocle," says Cindy Bitterman. "It wasn't true."

By year's end, there was something else profound in the life of Sammy Davis, Jr. It was religion. Sammy pronounced himself a Jew.

The announcement—the ricocheting word of mouth—startled his friends. He had never mentioned Judaism before. His own background had been one without religion. His mother was a lapsed Catholic, his father a lapsed Baptist. His adoption of Judaism could not really be called a conversion, because he had nothing to convert from. If pressed, he might well have answered "entertainment" as his religion. The decision had been made like many other decisions made in the life of Sammy—spur of the moment, a bout of light introspection, the mind working with a vaudevillian's quickness and agility, no turning back from an arrived-at decision.

Sammy had always been a fervent searcher. And where his mind was not intellectual, his heart was always vulnerable. The conundrum left him forever open to new gadgets, new ideas, new kinds of love. And whatever winds blew those new ideas into the soft recesses of his heart proved, more often than not, to be strong enough to push the ideas even further into his mind, where they fastened, and where he mistakenly thought they had originated with the weight of intelligence. So he came to Judaism quickly and romantically—as if electrical currents were guiding him.

"I never could figure it out," recalls Jess Rand. "It came out of left field."

"He came to me," recalls Jerry Lewis—born Jerry Levitch, and himself Jewish—"and said, 'I'm going to turn Jewish.' I said, 'You don't have enough problems already?' "

If we are to believe Sammy's autobiography, *Yes I Can*, the act of conversion had whipped itself around in his mind for all of two weeks. It involved the happenstance of coming across a book, *A History of the Jews,* and having a few conversations with rabbis. (During his hospital stay, Eddie Cantor had slipped him a Star of David, which he was now wearing around his neck.) There was no hunger, however, greater than Sammy's hunger for fame, for Hollywood. He watched movies, trailed the famous, snapped their pictures, hugged them, and hugged them some more. Fame was meat. He was its tiger. If, as the film historian Neal Gabler has proclaimed, the Jews invented Hollywood, then, in 1954, Sammy proclaimed himself—with the acquisition of an almost overnight spirituality—an appendage to that invention. Once seized by a notion, he could be relentless.

He found Max Nussbaum, a rabbi in Los Angeles and a refugee from Europe. In Germany, Rabbi Nussbaum's reputation kept growing. He had a gift. He was told he should be in that place known as Hollywood. His wife sensed his powers. "When he was young in Berlin, he was like a meteor coming on under Hitler," Nussbaum's wife would come to recall. "Everybody heard about Max Nussbaum in Berlin because he was such a novelty." The Jews of Berlin came to revere Nussbaum. He told wonderful Hasidic tales, spinning them out. He was, according to his wife—and others—"beautiful"; his mind was energetic. "When I met him," his wife recalled, "I didn't particularly like him, because he was much too glamorous for my taste. I made fun of him. I said, 'You belong in Hollywood.' That was 1937."

Nussbaum reached Hollywood in 1942, an escapee from the waves of persecution sweeping the continent. He headed Temple Israel. Five of the seven founders of the Hollywood-based temple were power brokers in the movie business. Nussbaum corralled actors and actresses for fund-raising benefits. Following one—where Bill "Bojangles" Robinson had been the featured guest—he squired everyone to the famous Brown Derby restaurant. The group was told that Robinson, a Negro, would not be served. Nussbaum and company turned and left.

When Sammy found Nussbaum, he was full of childlike questions. He grilled the rabbi as if he were a director moving huge camera equipment across impossible terrain and he needed Nussbaum to help him navigate it all—this very minute. The rabbi was suspicious and saw fit to warn Sammy: "Let me caution you not to expect to find Judaism in books."

Sammy opened his one eye wider. The comment perplexed him. He would find Judaism, then, in the clutter of his emotional heart.

There were, however, depths and undertows and crosscurrents that Sammy could not imagine that would intercut with his decision to convert.

The Jew and the Negro had a sometimes complex and always emotional history in America. Both groups, indeed, stood upon common ground: that of an oppressed minority. Bondage and suffering had shoved them together. Pain was understood by both. Several years before Sammy's conversion, a young writer and essayist by the name of James Baldwin, writing in *Commentary* magazine, said, "Though the notion of the suffering is based on the image of the wandering, exiled Jew, the context changes imperceptibly, to become a fairly obvious reminder of the trials of the Negro, while the sins recounted are the sins of the American republic. At this point, the Negro indentifies himself almost wholly with the Jew. The more devout Negro considers that he is a Jew, in bondage to a hard taskmaster and waiting for a Moses to lead him out of Egypt." Baldwin goes on: "It is part of the price the Negro pays for his position in this society that, as Richard Wright points out, he is almost always acting."

Judaism was cultural, a long thread in a family dynamic. Many who underwent conversions did it for reasons of marriage. But not Sammy. Sammy the actor—the impersonator!—would take the lore of Jewishness because he was Sammy. It was like a wonderful role—he needed the approval of no casting director. He could just do it—open his heart a little, read, entertain other Jews, sit at Rabbi Nussbaum's knee. Sammy, in the presence of intellectual vigor, sometimes simply wilted. Nussbaum, in the presence of Hollywood, sometimes became vulnerable. (The walls of Nussbaum's office were lined with photographs of Hollywood stars.) Nussbaum's warnings to Sammy aside, it was not his mission to try to dissuade him. They were two entertainers, and they were both in the business of pleasing, of soothing when necessary. Their eyes could easily tolerate the klieg lights.

Sammy did not care how Negroes would react to his conversion. He tried his best to operate above the emotional guitar strings of the Negro. Negroes were finicky—just like the Negro press. And Negroes were hardest on Negroes. He would merely endure their bemusement. Will Mastin and Sam Sr. uttered nothing about Sammy's conversion. It was beyond them, although Sam Sr.— as if to bond with his son—draped a Star of David around his own neck. He wore it like a trinket.

Jess Rand and Jerry Lewis were hardly the only Sammy acquaintances to cast a suspect eye upon the conversion. "That was a ploy," believed Amy Greene. "It was nonsense." She figured she knew why Sammy had gone searching for religion: "Boredom. That's how come he needed Judaism."

He became a Jew. He was a Jew. A Negro in Jew's clothing. It was tender, and it was strange. To Tony Curtis the conversion was also "a bit gratuitous."

Actually, it was just Sammy being Sammy—shrewd, opportunistic, heart-touched, and childlike. There had been no religion in his life, there had been no foundation, and so there was plenty of room for invention. And where there was the possibility of invention, surprise could occur. Maybe something decipherable only by a psychiatrist—or a mimic. Or just a desperately searching hoofer who had been spared death on a California roadway. Now the Negro in him was a Jew, and the just-created Jew in him was a Negro. Two Sammys, searching for truth and light. And love—and women, and sex, and money, and jewelry, and new clothes. The moguls had invented the town. And if Louis B. Mayer knew Sammy was a Jew, like Mayer himself, then great. And if Samuel Goldwyn knew Sammy was a Jew, like Goldwyn himself, then great. Hollywood was clannish. The gossip fell like rain. Sammy was now a Jew.

But he hardly escaped the guffaws. "When Sammy embraced Judaism I was doing the Milton Berle show," says Peggy King, a singer who would have an important relationship with Sammy. "Milton said, 'What are we going to do— Sammy became a Jew?' " King and others who were gathered around wondered what Berle expected them to say. The comic, recalls King, answered his own question. "Then he said, 'I know, we'll give them [the Negroes] George Jessel.' You never heard such waves of laughter. We were rolling on the floor."

Sammy—during a conversation with King—could see that she had concerns about his conversion. "He asked me what it means to be Jewish," she would remember. "I said, 'It means never doing anything to someone you wouldn't want done to you.' " He looked at her quizzically. When he did, she made her own conclusion: "Sammy wasn't Jewish."

He bragged about his newfound reading habits. He walked around proudly carrying a book—*Everyman's Talmud*—under the crook of his arm.

Before his accident, Sammy had promised to perform at a benefit in New York City for the Actors Studio. "He had been so thrilled he had been asked," remembers Judy Balaban, who would be attending the event. "He was jazzed out of his brain." But now, recuperating from his eye accident, Sammy decided he wouldn't go. He wanted out of the commitment. "He called me and said, 'I'm going to tell them I can't do the show,' " remembers Balaban. "I said, 'Why can't you do the show?' He said, 'Because of the accident.' I said, 'I hear you're out and okay. So why aren't you going to do the benefit?' He said, 'Because I don't know if I'm good.' I said, 'Do you think you're going to bomb?' He said, 'Judy, if I do it and I'm a hit, I won't know if they are applauding me because I was good or because I lost an eye.' "

Sammy instructed Balaban to pass along word that he would have to cancel. Balaban slept on it. The more she thought about the conversation, the more upset she felt herself becoming. She thought Sammy was being a coward. She phoned him back. The words were heated. "I said, 'Sammy, why can't you do this? You either have a career with one eye—or you don't. In my opinion, if you don't do this, you're not going to work again. And I'm not giving anyone any messages.' " The challenge stunned him.

Whether or not Judy Balaban thought she was using something akin to reverse psychology on Sammy, it worked. He came east; Balaban was so happy, she threw another birthday party for him in her apartment at the Hampshire House. "Larry Gelbart and Jay [Cantor] and I spent two weeks before the party writing parodies and songs for Sammy. They were all satirical things about Sammy's career. It was great. We invited all kinds of people. We had skits and parodies, Sammy was knocked out. His peers were there, up-and-comers. A lot of people to validate Sammy's sense of self. We made a Sammy tribute out of it. He loved it. He loved the evening."

The Actors Studio benefit took place on the roof of the Astor Hotel. Sammy sang, danced, and whirled in his first public performance since the accident. "He was brilliant," remembers Balaban. "Beyond brilliant. People were standing, shrieking, screaming. Marilyn Monroe, Leonard Bernstein—everybody from New York was there." Anthony Franciosa, a young New York actor and a member of the studio, remembers Sammy's visit. "He had a patch over his eye. He had that room rocking. He was so good. It meant a great deal to him. I remember how solicitious he was to the audience."

Before he left New York City, Sammy visited Balaban at her apartment. She always had enjoyed sitting and talking with him, about life, movies, show business. Because of the accident, Balaban suddenly wanted to talk about Sammy's family. Before, it had just never seemed appropriate. "I said, 'Sammy, tell me about your mother.' He said, 'No, tell me about *yours*.' I told him about my mother, who had given me this incredible gift of unconditional love. I remember tears coming down his face. At first I couldn't figure out if he was crying because of the story or what. I said I had this mother who would watch me make mistakes but still loved me." Balaban felt she had touched a nerve. Others might have backed away; she bore on; it was her nature. She really wanted to know about Sammy's mother, so she asked again.

"She's not like your mother," Sammy finally told her.

"And I'll never forget the way he sounded when he said it," she remembers. "I had said, 'Tell me about it.' He said, 'No!' "

Sammy made an emotional visit to Harlem to see his grandmother Rosa. She hugged him fiercely, examining his face, looking him up and down, fussing and fretting over him and insisting he sit and eat.

As soon as he arrived back in Los Angeles, Sammy huddled with Mastin and his father. His confidence was coming on. The legs were just fine. The eye socket still gave him occasional headaches, but he didn't cry about it.

On January 11 they climbed into the Cadillac and rolled through the night air to Ciro's. Will was quiet, Sam Sr. fatherly. They'd done this hundreds of times, all through the years. But never like this—the air alive with anticipation and curiosity. When they opened the door to their dressing room, they saw flowers everywhere. They'd never seen so many flowers before, with so many sentimental notes attached.

Herman Hover always sent out elegant, yet understated, invitations. The typical Ciro's invite was a beige card with the name "Ciro's" cursively written in the middle of the card, and in the lower left-hand corner, in dark lettering: "H. D. Hover presents the Will Mastin Trio."

Sammy, his father, and Will Mastin slipped inside the theater.

Automobiles cruised up to the front of the nightclub and valet attendants rushed to open the doors. Out stepped Cary Grant and wife. And Humphrey Bogart and Lauren Bacall. (A year earlier Bogart had had an amazing array of films in release, among them *The Caine Mutiny, The Barefoot Contessa,* and *Sabrina.*) Out stepped Edward G. Robinson and wife; and Mr. and Mrs. Gary Cooper. Another car door swung open and there was Spencer Tracy and wife. Out stepped Dick Powell and his wife, June Allyson, star of so many MGM musicals a decade earlier. Jimmy Cagney came with his wife, Billie. Flashbulbs were crackling. Dean Martin. Flash. Jerry Lewis. Flash. Jeff Chandler. Flash. And there, in the lights, alighting from the car as if rising up from the night itself—flash upon flash upon flash—Marilyn Monroe. The flashes caught her jewelry, her smile, her cleavage. Marilyn was accompanied by Milton Greene, the *Life* photographer, and Amy, his wife.

"There was a line on the Strip," remembers Jess Rand. "If a bomb would have dropped that night, it was the end of Hollywood. Everyone was rooting for him."

Inside the nightclub, Hover, dressed in his usual black tux, was floating about, nodding, instructing members of his staff, fussing with the table settings, making eye contact with Sinatra, checking up on his Sammy and Sam Sr. and Mastin.

Leading up to the show, away from Will and Sam Sr., worries had engulfed Sammy. He wondered how the eye patch would play. "When you take off the patch, it's got to be important," Jess Rand had told him.

The night before, he phoned Cindy Bitterman. "I spoke to Sammy," she would recall, "and he was terrified. I said, 'Don't worry, even if you sing flat, they'll embrace you.' "

The club had started to fill: chatter, handshakes, the curling of cigarette smoke; the aroma of perfume; the grin on Hover's large face because of a packed room.

Dean Martin and Jerry Lewis were seated at a table right below the stage. The two longtime gag artists joked with anyone who came near them. Dean pulled out a deck of cards and began shuffling them.

Outside the club, onlookers had gathered, ogling the arrivals. "There had to be a thousand people outside who couldn't get in," remembers Jerry Lewis.

Tony Curtis—pinup boy for a million screaming teenage girls—floated about with his wife Janet Leigh. "It was extraordinary," Curtis would remember. "There was the excitement of Sammy showing up with one eye. But it was a little bizarre from my point of view. I think the main purpose, for me, was that he was alive."

Charlie Head, injured in the car accident, was as dapper as anyone. Moving about, he smiled often; he too was happy to be alive. Jeff Chandler looked radiant, his blond head surveying the crowd, nodding to those whom he knew and to strangers as well. There was always, about him, the air of a man who decided fates and destinies. There was only a sprinkling of Negroes in the audience. One stood out: it was Rosa, Sammy's beloved grandmother. A large woman, she walked about slowly in a dress made of silk. She carried a small purse; her hair looked freshly fussed over. In her lay the river's source—both a grandmother's and a mother's love for little Sammy. The gilded surroundings of Herman Hover's nightclub did not intimidate Rosa Davis.

Sitting at her table, Amy Greene could not help herself; she grew even more nervous, wondering if Sammy might be overcome by fear. She had goose bumps. "You walked into this tension-filled atmosphere of joy and hope," she would recall. "Everybody who was anybody was in that place. They had ringside tables. There was the raised balcony. No one knew what we were going to see. It was totally an exploratory exercise."

The nightclub could hold six hundred, and when Hover reached that number—and a little beyond, truth be told—he had to start turning folks away. But not Fred Hull, Sammy's eye surgeon. Sammy had arranged for special seats for Dr. and Mrs. Hull, and they walked to their seats sneaking peeks at all the movie stars. The Hulls didn't care much for nightclubs. They were, in fact, making their first visit to Ciro's. The surroundings—the cigarette girls, the decor—fairly wowed them. The eye doctor could hardly believe his eyes—Marilyn Monroe, Gary Cooper, June Allyson; Jerry Lewis, Dean Martin, Tony Curtis. He felt a giggle rise up in him.

The newlywed Bonnie Rand couldn't help but keep swiveling her neck around the room. "It was Hollywood at its height. You were sitting with June Allyson, Jeff Chandler, [Humphrey] Bogart. Everybody was so much for him. Howard Hughes had a table reserved—and didn't show. [Darryl] Zanuck was there."

So was Judy Garland. Her brutal and sad decline—pills, alcohol, raging depression—was not far away, but it was rippling; those who knew her well saw the warning signs.

Sinatra sat smoking a cigarette—starlets all around. The dark times were over for him, and many dropped by to shake his hand. His smile had grown tighter these days. It was the past—the being forgotten, begging for a second chance like some Hoboken bum. The yin and yang of his existence: never forget a slight, and loyalty is all.

As the time for the show neared—Hover checking his watch, nodding at Sinatra—small waves of excitement began wafting through the crowd, from table to table.

There was something almost poetic—a kind of hard-won grandeur—in the way the Will Mastin Trio prepared. In the dressing room there would be small banter, talk about women, what was going on with other acts across the country—all those acts, chased by the ghost. In the dressing room, Will and Sam Sr. were like two old lions in the tall grass of celebrity: there was deliberateness in their movements; they had been at this for a long time; there was no need to rush. Sammy was like the eager cub still, at the grass's edge, peeking, poking, checking the hallways, reading the telegrams. Nathan, their dresser, laid out their tuxedos. They wore stocking caps on their heads to keep hair particles from falling, to keep their pomaded hair in place. After the suits, Nathan set the patent leather shoes out. The shoes gleamed like springwater. No matter how much Nathan brushed the suits, Will would have to brush his again. It was just his habit, and in his habits, he was meticulous. Their hats were placed in the corner, lest some visitor accidentally sit on one. They poked at their many pairs of cuff links, eyes gazing over which ones to pluck from the case. They took discreet puffs on cigarettes, careful not to allow ash to fly onto their garments, Nathan making sure the ashtrays were in place. They slipped their cuffs into their monogrammed shirtsleeves—WM, SDS, SDJ. Will shined his cane until his old bones told him that was enough. When they were ready, Nathan went from man to man, holding the pants before them. "He'd hold the pants up for each dancer," says Jess Rand, "and they'd step into them"—so no pants cuffs would touch the floor. "They were meticulous," adds Rand. First shirts, then pants, then shoes (the last particles of dust swiped from them), then bow ties, then the removal of the stocking caps. For years, just like this: if Cadillac had made human beings instead of cars, here would have stood three of them. They helped one another with the tuxedo jackets. They checked the taps on their shoes. They looked one another over, up and down, chest to chest, front and back. And there they stood—three men, a unit, a family, nodding in acclamation of one another. They smelled of mint and aftershave and talcum powder. Thousands and thousands of nights just like this; only on this night, of course, all was different. Sammy adjusted the eye patch. And both Will and Sam Sr. fixed their eyes on the piece of material. It too must look right. Will grabbed his cane; Sam Sr. raised his hat to his head; and they were out the door now, gliding, like geldings, to the stage, Jess having gone out to clear the pathway.

It was the Will Mastin Trio *Starring* Sammy Davis, Jr.! Sammy was the first to be seen, and right over his shoulders Will and Sam Sr., brought to the stage by Sinatra, who was introducing them.

Standing there onstage, they looked beautiful and satiny, the three of them, back from the brink, because where the kid went, the act went. Everyone knew it. Amy Greene immediately began to worry about the eye, and the smallish Ciro's stage. "He's going to fall off the stage," she whispered. The ovation—before he sang a song, before he danced a step—went on for five minutes. Then five minutes more. He looked out over the gathering, scanning. June Allyson's face was streaked with tears. Danny Thomas just stared. Dean Martin smiled, Jerry Lewis shrieked.

And then they leaned into the audience, shoulders outward, and began their show. "Sammy opened with a thirty-foot knee slide," recalls George Schlatter, who booked talent for Ciro's and stood watching in rapt attention that night. The knee slide elicited a cacophonous round of applause. "He did a tap routine. Tore up the stage. Did impressions of everybody in the audience. Danced some more. Then went into straight songs." Bonnie Rand sat mesmerized. "He just took the audience and sucked them in."

He sang "Glad to Be Home," segued into "Birth of the Blues." Mastin and Sam Sr. were in the background, doing gingerlike steps, "shooting the cuffs." But he was beyond them; he was stylistically dismissing them. Bartenders would pour drinks and glance up at the show and the pandemonium. Flashes were going off. "It was such an excess," says Amy Greene. "He didn't sing three songs, he did six."

He did spins. And twirls. "It was only one show that night, and it was an explosion," says Bonnie Rand.

He sang "Hey There." He sang "Black Magic" once, then he sang it again. He'd spot a celebrity in the crowd—Gary Cooper—and do a dead-on impersonation.

He sang "Stand Up and Fight," a rousing number from the *Carmen Jones* movie. He sang—this one for Frank—"I Get a Kick Out of You."

"He put the patch on his eye and came onstage and drove them crazy," says dancer Maurice Hines. "Wasn't nothing they could do after that except play " 'The Star-Spangled Banner.' "

He tapped and tapped; he grabbed for musical instruments and began playing them. He stood, soaking in applause, staring around the room. Then he'd look to his sides at Will and his father, his face having to swivel a little extra now because of the blind side. The band kept playing just the right kind of thumping music, music to keep up with his movements across the stage. He was giving them all he had. He was giving them more than Will and his father thought he had—and they believed he had more to give than anyone they had ever seen give. He would not, could not, let them or himself down on this night.

Sam Sr. was proud as a father might be proud of a son. But it went even deeper for Will Mastin—well-heeled white Hollywood saluting him like this. And how could any of them know from how far back in the woods he had come? This was better than vaudeville; this was better than running from all the ghosts of the past. This was redemption and salvation. He had founded this act, put it together, kept it together through lean times, blizzards, rainstorms. Hadn't he collected wood for fireplaces when they were cold? Hadn't he gone without decent meals at times? The stars out there who had met him and thought he was moody, distant, had to give him his respect now. This was show business. And he kept shooting the cuffs, moving his feet, seventy-six years old now. An old man living alone in a hotel. He felt tired but light as a butterfly. And on this Ciro's stage he'd dance as long as Sammy danced. Rosa was breathing and sighing heavily. She couldn't take her eyes off her little Sammy. She would look over her shoulders at the stars and feel warmth climb up inside of her.

Sinatra admired the sheer unrehearsed magic of the act. Hell, he had been noticing it for years. He looked around, saw the adulation. He couldn't help it if moments of sourness crept into his gut: Hollywood was two-faced, mercurial. He had tasted the whole buffet. But he didn't let it ruin the moment of the night. He smiled the way everyone smiled. Judy Garland teared up, her eyes bright as champagne. Sammy wouldn't stop. He sang some more and danced some more—all as if for dear life. Amy Greene did not have to worry about his falling off the stage. He had played a million stages. He knew where every square foot of the stage was located. He was smart that way—back and forth he went, kept going, kept sliding, twirling, dancing. Jimmy Cagney loved dancers; he'd gotten his Oscar for playing song-and-dance man George M. Cohan in *Yankee Doodle Dandy*. And he always told anyone who cared to know that he remained just a dancer. Cagney sat transfixed. Bogart felt proud, very proud, and he couldn't wait to see Sammy backstage because he actually had a little advice he wished to lay on him.

"The joy he had of doing impersonations of Gable, Cooper, Bogart, and seeing the stars' reactions of a black man impersonating them was something," says George Schlatter.

Sammy was onstage for an hour, then twenty minutes more, then twenty minutes longer. Allan Grant, the *Life* photographer sent to cover the opening, snapped away, even turning his camera on the audience. Sammy knew them all—at least, being a sieve of movies and movie trivia, he knew their movies and their roles, which meant, to his cinematic mind, that he knew them as well. They were his Hollywood, and he wished only to please them forever.

Then he was finished, and Dick Stabile's band lowered the volume, and Will hugged him, and his father hugged him, and the flashes were going off, and Marilyn was teary and Judy Garland was teary and Rosa was weeping. They clapped and clapped. And when the clapping died down, when it stopped, when there was just the rolling hum of gratification, looking from his father to Mastin, from Hover to Cooper to Sinatra, the faces blurring—he lifted his arm and reached around his head and pulled the eye patch off. Just like that. It happened so quickly no one realized what he had done. "I don't think I need this anymore," he said, and he threw it out into the audience. Ciro's erupted. "It was an explosion," says Bonnie. Whistles and applause as the black patch floated through the air. It was snatched by Jess Rand's outstretched hand.

Janet Leigh gasped at the removal of the patch. "Once the eye patch came off, I never thought about it again," she would remember. "He just overcame it."

He stood there, still. They had worried about the eye. Sammy knew he could defeat the loss of the eye. He had always been beautiful at compensation. It was the legs that he needed. His legs and his heart and his hunger saved him, as the combination always had. "People screamed, whistled, and hollered when he finished," remembers Hugh Benson, a TV executive who was in the audience and was already thinking of ways to get Sammy on network television. Surrounded by stars, he stood there. Stillness did not become him the way it did Sinatra or Nat King Cole; standing still, Sammy was just an explosion waiting to happen. As a kid he had found such comfort in dark movie houses, looking up at the big screen, at all the stars. Herman Hover started walking up on the stage, led by a bevy of people. And they surrounded him and started applauding some more. They grabbed him before he exploded again.

Sammy fairly floated to the dressing room. And it wasn't long before he was mobbed again. Sinatra and Jeff Chandler and Bogart and all the rest: his father, Sam, and Rita, Sam's lady. And Rosa, the big grandmother swishing right for Sammy. They made way for her, and she squeezed him tight, her eyes welling up. Charlie Head, the valet, grabbed him, then stood looking at him—two survivors of a car wreck—as if their very existence were nothing less than a miracle. Then Sammy began—as only Sammy could—congratulating *them*, all those around him, as if they themselves had gone through some kind of ordeal. Any praise he received, Sammy always felt compelled to give right back. He caught sight of Jess Rand. The eye patch was in Rand's pocket. He and Rand locked eyes and smiled. "It was all scripted," Rand would admit years later about Sammy's dramatic removal of the eye patch and tossing it to the crowd. Scripted: like some kind of great, thrilling, and wonderful movie moment, truly unforgettable, where the Negro wins, where the Negro rides off into a bright sun.

Well, hooray for Hollywood moxie. The Negro himself had helped write the script!

"That was an emotional night," Janet Leigh would remember. "He had tremendous courage and will. And a sense of humor."

Will stood mostly in silence in the dressing room, taking his congratulations. Now and then he could be seen cocking his head toward those whispering in Sammy's ear. He distrusted so many. He'd often eye Sinatra as if he were the competition for Sammy, but Sinatra had lavished Sammy with such affection—just as he was now doing—so Mastin kept silent about their bond. But Humphrey Bogart was gliding about. Mastin long believed that the roles actors played onscreen represented their true personas. So Bogart—Sam Spade, Captain Queeg, Duke Mantee in *The Desperate Hours*—was someone not to trust. Bogart was a villain come to life if ever there was one. Then there stood Bogart in Mastin's face. You are "too damned old for the business," he told Mastin. Mastin didn't know if Bogart was joking or not. Only if he had been joking, he would have broken the joke by laughter, which he did not. The look on Bogart's face was serious. Mastin was insulted and recoiled. The old vaudevillian, squared off against the criminal from the big screen. In another day, he might have thrown words back at Bogart. Or maybe more than words. The scar on Will Mastin's face wasn't there from frolicking in the grass. He had founded this act back in 1936. Humphrey Bogart didn't sign Sammy Davis, Jr.'s, checks; Will Mastin did. The old vaudevillian never spoke to Humphrey Bogart again. (Not that Bogie would have lost any sleep over it.)

Everyone rolled from Ciro's to the Villa Capri, site of the after-party. There was champagne, and more salutes. Amy Greene overheard someone say that watching Sammy perform that night had been like watching "a Charlie Chaplin movie." Amid the salutes, Sammy realized he had to get to a phone. There was someone he desperately wanted to call. Soon as he reached her, he started telling her all about it, about Sinatra's presence, about the stars who had come out to see him, about what he did onstage. He told her about the new spin moves he had come up with. And the sight of him doing spin moves even in her imagination made Cindy Bitterman shriek through those telephone wires. "Who knew he could do spins?" she says. "He called me at five in the morning. He was in heaven."

The press reviews were astounding. "It was Sammy Davis Jr.'s night," crowed *Variety*. "The lad who lost an eye came back in whirlwind style to pack Herman Hover's posh spot to the gunwales opening night and receive one of the greatest ovations ever handed a performer, any place." The review went on: "Singer, dancer, mimic, musician, whatever Sammy is for the moment he's entirely to the crowd's taste."

Sammy was a survivor. He had been wounded and come back. This was a kind of salvation.

Well-wishers greet Sammy following his boffo comeback performance at Ciro's on January 11, 1955. (He has temporarily slipped his eyepatch back on.) The man in sunglasses is Charlie Head, the valet who was in the backseat of the car Sammy was driving when he crashed. At far left stands Sam Sr., wearing a triumphant grin.

(JESS RAND COLLECTION)

Less in reality and more in the heartstrings, Sammy had entered the world of Hollywood reverence. It was as if he had vaulted over the sad and painful world of Hollywood and the Negro. Since Hattie McDaniel had become the first Negro to receive an Oscar, in 1939 for her mammy role in *Gone with the Wind*, roles for Negroes had not gotten much better. Lena Horne, a nightclub singer—and former Cotton Club chorus girl—was the first Negro to sign a long-term movie studio contract. But MGM was fearful of her—seemingly of both her beauty and her color; she was relegated to small roles in small movies and had her scenes clipped from movies that played below the Mason-Dixon line. She made *Duchess of Idaho* in 1950, then vanished from the screen for six years, believed to be a victim of the blacklist because of her associations with

Paul Robeson. Robeson, a Phi Beta Kappa graduate of Rutgers University, had reached acclaim on Broadway in two Eugene O'Neill plays, *All God's Chillun Got Wings* and *The Emperor Jones*. With astonishing range, he excelled both in recitals and dramatic stage work. There were film roles with all-Negro casts. But Robeson had an affinity to Stalinist Russia, and by the advent of the cold war, he too was blacklisted, his passport taken away. Negroes simply had no precedent for success in Hollywood. Many did not hunger to be of the place. But Sammy was an exception. And he skidded along the border of Negro Hollywood and white Hollywood—as if the Negro past meant nothing to him. With his talent, he killed his naïveté. Coming out of vaudeville, where stereotype had helped draw laughs and keep his family working, he looked past history and into the beyond, and in the beyond he saw James Cagney and Gary Cooper and June Allyson; he saw Dean Martin and Janet Leigh and Robert Mitchum applauding him. On his night at Ciro's he felt connected to those in the audience; he was theirs. To get to this place, he had survived a damaging childhood. He had carried two old men back and forth across the country. He had left blood on a highway. He had the grit of vaudeville in one pocket, and the hard coin of the future he hoped for in the other. The loss of the eye had been his crucible, and he had met it and soared above it. Adversity—as it had in the past and would do in the future—propelled Sammy forward.

The winds were shifting now. Herman Hover's phone was ringing off the hook. Everyone wanted tickets to catch Sammy's Ciro's engagement. Sammy was hot. Other calls came in; other nightclub owners wanted to talk. They had to talk with Will.

Mastin kept polishing his cane. He'd now have to watch Sammy soar—and still hold on to him. The old vaudevillian didn't want to die—not now.

Sammy, at long last, felt loved. Some of it was sympathy, he knew, but he was throwing the sympathy back at them every night, and giving them talent. Night after night. Every star in Hollywood seemed to be lining up to catch his show. It was fearlessness on display. Night after night, Will and his father stood behind him and watched; he was just a blur to them onstage now, though ever so gracious, turning to them, extending his arms, dripping them with applause meant for him.

Night after night he drew crowds to Ciro's. The lines were long, then longer. "Never dug you before," said the telegram from a famous young actor. "Dug you tonight. Marlon Brando."

Pulling the French cuffs on his sleeves to show a peek, adjusting his bow tie, looking at himself in the mirror through one eye, checking the taps on his shoes, nodding to Jess Rand, then to Nathan Crawford, he was ready. And he walked his father and Will Mastin onto the Ciro's stage to give Hollywood what it most respected—a star.

An eye for an eye, then—and an eye for fame.

"The eye didn't stop him," says Maggie Hathaway, the sometime actress whose home Sammy retreated to for many of his dalliances. "He kept on making love to white girls."

Shalom.

After Ciro's the trio flew east for an engagement at the Copa. Sammy loved the Copa. They packed the house. "In the main, socko," *Variety* magazine said about that engagement. *Time* magazine wrote him up in its April 18, 1955, edition: "In a time when entertainers are often shoved onstage as a result of a hit record, without any experience, Sammy Davis Jr. is a seasoned pro. His dancing is a study of fine rhythm and agility, his timing precise, his ad libs are deft." (*Time* would go on to describe Will Mastin as being "60-odd." In fact, he was seventy-six.) Sammy shared with the magazine his performing philosophy. "I never studied anything I do. I just wake up in the morning thinking it would be good to do Bing Crosby, and I can do him."

He took a suite at the Gorham Hotel for his stay in Manhattan. He began discussions with MGM to star in a musical, *St. Louis Woman*. (The discussions went nowhere because of the demands made by Will Mastin.) There were inquiries beginning to trickle in from Broadway impresarios. The world was opening anew, and he could feel it. *Down Beat* magazine named him one of its "New Stars" on the cover of its March 23, 1955, issue.

At times he was still struggling with the eye. He had taken to wearing glasses all the time now. They were thick glasses, the kind some beatniks and TV host David Garroway wore. Sammy owned several replacement plastic eyes. One had been designed a bloodshot-red color to match his good eye when it was bloodshot from overnight drinking.

Since television had come of age as he came of age, the medium fascinated Sammy. When he peered inside the box, he rummaged for people to meet. Sammy found it both easy and simple to fall in love with someone he had seen on the television screen. He often fell in love with voices and images. That way, before he met them, he told himself what he wanted to tell himself: they they might not covet his looks, but they'd adore his talent. With his newfound celebrity, Sammy could reach inside the TV screens and pull people out.

He became a fan of *The George Gobel Show*. Gobel's show premiered October 2, 1954, on NBC. The comedy variety show featured two appealing young stars—Eddie Fisher and Peggy King. King was an ingenue, many believed the next Judy Garland. Blond and adorable, she was totally at ease in front of the camera.

Born in Ohio, she sang with big-band leaders Charlie Spivak and Ralph

Flanagan onstage. She wore white gloves when she sang. In 1951 she heard that Mel Torme had signed with CBS to host a musical variety show. It would be among the first shows to be broadcast in color. She wangled an audition. "I knew every girl singer would be there." She got the role, had her TV break, and even signed a movie contract with Columbia. She couldn't resist the entreaty from the Gobel show producers. Her audition impressed them, and she had the part. In no time at all, fan letters poured in to the network. "Three weeks later I couldn't walk on the street," she says of the fame that followed her. She was commonly referred to as "pretty perky Peggy King." Sammy sent Ed Golin, a friend and press agent, to find pretty, perky Peggy because he just had to meet her. "He reeled off for me the last fifteen songs I had done on *The George Gobel Show*," when they first met, King recalls. "That's pretty flattering. And he had my albums."

Sammy invited King to the Copa to see his show.

"The first time I saw the act, I said, 'My God, I've never seen anything like this in my life.' You couldn't catch your breath. He was the best dancer outside of Fred Astaire." They talked through long evenings. She heard a wistfulness in Sammy's voice. "He told me, 'You're the girl I should have gone to the high school prom with' "—only, of course, there was never a high school, much less a prom.

Peggy King found herself falling in love. She had never met anyone like Sammy—so serious one moment, so silly the next. King's first album for Columbia was *Girl Meets Boy*—an album of sunny songs. Sammy memorized every single on the album; sometimes he'd break into song, singing those very tunes. Peggy could only break into a smile. She wanted to talk of serious issues, serious matters, and could get frustrated at Sammy's zigzagging attention span. "I tried to interest Sammy in the Civil War," King says. "He had a lot of excuses. I said, 'Do you know Lincoln's plan was to take all of the slaves and give them to Florida?' Burl Ives told me this. Burl was a Lincoln fanatic. I told Sammy. He started laughing. He said, 'You mean I would own the Fontainbleau [the chic Miami Beach hotel] and you would be working for me?' "

Manhattan was a city for nightcrawlers. Their meetings were all furtive, always out of the public eye. A rendezvous here, another one there. "He was very protective of me," she says. "I was everything white middle America represented to him. He was very careful not to be seen alone with me in New York. He thought it would be bad for my career." They'd sit in his room at the Gorham and talk and talk. They'd watch the moon rise. "I remember he said to me, 'You probably don't know what it's like to be poor.' I said, 'Wait a minute. We went through a whole winter on Relief.' He liked hearing that. That put us on a more level playing field."

She remembers a mostly private party for Edward G. Robinson. She and

After his breakup with Helen Gallagher, Sammy fell in love with Columbia recording artist Peggy King. He took countless photographs of her, including this one in Manhattan in 1956. King—an inveterate reader of social history—often worried about Sammy's lack of racial identity. She wondered why he preferred white to black. (COURTESY OF PEGGY KING)

Sammy were both Robinson fans and were happy to go. Sammy quickly introduced her to Sinatra, who was also there. A cameraman—as if from behind an invisible curtain—suddenly appeared, and positioned himself to snap the both of them, Sammy and Peggy, together. Sinatra saw it all unfolding—Sammy and Peggy King, click click click and right into the gossip columns. Frank knew about scandal. And he wouldn't let it happen. Striding across the room and bringing all of his guile and quickness and charm with him, he plopped right down right next to Peggy. The camera's flash went off. And that was the picture: Peggy and Frank—and Frank's friend, Sammy. Frank and two fans. A harmless snapshot. Frank would not let bad things happen to Sammy. Sammy was his acolyte. Sammy was the little Frank, the reflection in Frank's eye, and Frank liked that, seeing himself in another man, and that man climbing up the ragged edge of the mountain and Frank trying his best to control the weather on top.

But over time, Peggy King thought Sinatra had an almost unhealthy hold on Sammy. One night when she was with Sammy and a small group of other friends, the phone rang. Sammy picked it up. When he hung up, he turned to Peggy: "Can you stay here and take care of the people? Frank just beat up a couple hookers. I have to go.'" And whoosh, he was gone. It bewildered her. "He thought Frank was a god. Well, be careful who you pick for your god."

Sammy started posing her on couches and snapping her picture. Picture after picture after picture. They'd be eating, and down with the fork for Sammy because he was grabbing for the camera. "He could make his own reality," she says of the pictures. "For that moment, that person belonged to him. He always took pictures. It was compensation for his drawbacks. His way of making beauty."

In the aftermath of his eye accident, Sammy resumed his passion for photography—only now, ravenously.

"Photographs, which turn the past into a consumable object, are a short cut," Susan Sontag has written in *On Photography,* her perceptive chronicle of the subject. "Any collection of photographs is an exercise in Surrealist montage and the Surrealist abbreviation of history."

Surrealism: "A 20th-century literary and artistic movement that attempts to express the workings of the subconscious and is characterized by fantastic imagery and incongruous juxtaposition of subject matter." So says the *American Heritage Dictionary.*

Sammy—the Surrealist.

Oddly, Sammy took very few pictures of Will Mastin and his father. Or, for that matter, of any family members.

There was, forever in Sammy, the belief and conclusion that everyone wanted to be like someone else. Who could be happy as they were? "You don't have to look like anybody," he jauntily told Peggy King. "You look like Lana Turner." While posing her, he'd fret over the way she looked, until he felt she looked just right. Then: click. "The way he took it," she says of one photograph in which Sammy, to her, wasn't going for the Lana Turner look, "I look like Kim Novak."

Sammy introduced Peggy to Rosa, his grandmother. Rosa came to adore Peggy. Will Mastin and Sam Sr. did not. She could feel that she made them nervous and suspicious. "I was a new wave," she says. "I was away from vaudeville. I was TV. Vaudeville people didn't like 'new.' They did the same act for forty years—same laughs, same pratfalls."

Every time she tried to befriend Sam Sr. or Will, it went nowhere. "He didn't like me at all," she says of Will. "I don't know why. Maybe because I was encouraging Sammy to read. Sam Sr. didn't like me either. I was the girl next door. I was dangerous territory. I was everybody's sweetheart. I was Mary Pickford. I was the innocent. I wasn't some siren on the screen. Will and Sam didn't like a lot of Sammy's friends. I believe they felt Sammy was being pulled into another world—and they couldn't follow."

Sammy's celebrity always seemed to conceal something—that something lay behind his vulnerability—and King realized it. "I always wanted to take care of him. I didn't want anybody to hurt him." Her genuine joy came in introducing Sammy to books, the pleasure of reading. She realized he needed goading to read. "He hadn't read *Huckleberry Finn*," King says. "He'd seen the movie and pretended he had read the book. I made him do a list of about thirty books to read."

Sammy had fallen hard for *Wuthering Heights*, the 1939 William Wyler–directed movie that starred Laurence Olivier as Heathcliff and Merle Oberon as Catherine. But he fell harder for Emily Brontë's novel, originally published in 1847. "He called me 'Cathy,' from *Wuthering Heights*," says King. "That was my nickname."

The doomed Brontë lovers fascinated Sammy, how the two of them in the novel would keep going—and loving—in turmoil, in blackened storms, in deceit. Brontë's novel was the first classic that shook Sammy. Its powers overwhelmed him, as it had so many others. "It is as if she could tear up all that we know human beings by, and fill these unrecognisable transparencies with such a gust of life that they transcend reality," Virginia Woolf would write of Brontë's novel. "Hers, then, is the rarest of all powers. She could free life from its dependence on facts, with a few touches indicate the spirit of a face so that it needs no body; by speaking of the moor make the wind blow and the thunder roar."

Sammy and King recited, back and forth, in English accents, passages from the novel. Sammy liked reversing roles, and often he mouthed the beautiful words of Catherine: "I've dreamt in my life dreams that have stayed with me ever after . . . gone through and through me like wine through water, and altered the color of my mind."

So he loved Heathcliff and Catherine, the skies they lit—all for love—and darkened. He now came to words and poems as if they had just recently been invented. For Sammy, prose was a great discovery.

He tossed a little brown paper bag at King one day while in his Gorham suite. She imagined it might be candy, some mints maybe. "When I opened it, there was this Cartier watch. It said, 'From Heathcliff to Catherine.' "

All his life, however, he would remain self-conscious, because of his lack of formal education, about his ability to write. Not just prose pieces, but anything at all. "He would never attempt to write a letter," says King.

The word came out from his mouth one evening: marriage. It just dropped like some big object from a rooftop. He giggled, she giggled, then when her ardor seemed not to match his, he said something about both of them being pelted with if it ever happened, and the subject was changed.

Peggy King knew nightclub acts made decent money. But Sammy was often low on cash, and she never understood where his money went. "He was always saying, 'I'll pick up the check.' And he didn't have any money. Ladies used to carry a little money. I had to do it with him."

One night she had something personal to tell Sammy, something she wanted him to keep secret. Peggy King told Sammy that she had been adopted. Yes, her parents had left her to the vagaries of the cold world. "What difference does it make who your parents are?" Sammy asked her—and in a manner so blithe that she was immediately taken aback. It wasn't until years after they met that Sammy even told Peggy he had a sister. (Eventually she would meet both Elvera and Ramona. "They were so secretive and deceitful," King says.)

Hard as she tried, King could never get used to Sammy's moods, the child-like way in which he went in and out of emotions. Sometimes her phone would ring. It would be Sammy. "I need you, Peggy!" he would scream. She'd rush over, wherever he was; she wanted to save him from whatever bedeviled him at the moment; she loved him. She'd arrive, rush in, ask him in panted breath what was the matter, and he'd look at her blankly. He had forgotten, there was no problem; like a child, he had gone on to other momentary pursuits.

There was another bag with something in it from him to her. In the bag, a box. Inside the box, a diamond ring. Speechless, she blushed. She put it on, admiring it, then she blushed some more. (Later, she went to give the diamond ring back. "He would not take it back.")

There were times—sitting in another nightclub watching Sammy—when King would wonder to herself when he was going to go solo. She sensed the shifting tide of his emotions. "He knew there was this [solo] career out there," she says. "I told him over and over there were movies and Broadway shows in his future."

Like so many others, Peggy King became a part of Sammy's underground world. Operating in two societies, he had a romantic view of the white world—and why not, with Sinatra crooning, with Catherine still believing in Heathcliff? The black world could be so unromantic.

"I think Sammy was very cunning," King says. "I believe he tried to place himself with people he could learn from. I was 'America' to him."

She came to feel a kind of sadness about him. She couldn't help feeling that Sammy desperately wanted to be someone else. She'd often wonder about his past, where he had been, how he got from there to here. "It was like the little lost childhood, and he was the 'littlest' lost child."

How wonderful to be so deep in another culture, in the juicy world of white America. Sammy had already gone beyond Bert Williams; he had given himself another dimension, and with a camera around his neck, a copy of *Wuthering Heights* in his possession, he was outrunning the ghosts. It made no difference who your parents were—so he thought.

Sammy had to try several glass eyes before he felt comfortable. In between new fittings, he would don his eye patch. During an engagement at the New Frontier in Las Vegas in 1955, he tells Will Mastin (center) and his father that he is finished, once and for all, with the patch, that the eye he now wears fits quite well. Note the chromed traveling trunk in the background, in which are packed some of the accoutrements of the trio's trade: a written listing of dance numbers, spare taps for their shoes, medicinal lotions, hair tonics. Mastin wears a monogrammed shirt and specially designed cuff links that say "500 CLUB"—the name of the mob-connected Atlantic City nightclub where they have had success.

(JESS RAND COLLECTION)

It was just a small thing, a small shift in loyalties. Cindy Bitterman and Peggy King and Tony Curtis all noticed it. Sammy stopped hanging out with Jeff Chandler. "He stopped seeing Jeff and started seeing Frank" even more, says Tony Curtis. "It was another crowd. Through Frank he saw another career. He didn't see anything with Jeff. With Frank, he could see that Las Vegas was open to him."

Sammy's proclivities—the white women, the Judaism, the Sinatra worship—did not at all bother Will Mastin and Sam Sr. He was their baby; their boy; their life. Sammy's years were their years. If Sammy was wrong—about life, people—then they were wrong. And they did not believe themselves wrong. In wide-brimmed felt hats, white suits, and low-heeled patent leather shoes, they'd stand with their Sammy against the world.

. . .

When in Manhattan—or anywhere else—and not appearing onstage, Sam Sr. spent his hours gambling, going to horse races. Since he found Rita, his womanizing days were over. He steered clear of Elvera. As for Will Mastin, whenever he had idle time, he vanished. In Manhattan, no one knew if he spent his free time lolling in Harlem dining spots, or looking up old cohorts from his vaudeville days. Invited to parties in the city, he wouldn't show. He suffered nightmares and stomach cramps from the ulcers. The one constant thing in his life was the Will Mastin Trio.

Even if it had long been undeniable that Sammy was the whole show, Mastin, in a sweetly self-convincing and even humble way, began to tell others he cared little about Sammy's fame. He would tell them that his own performance continued to be important—in the organizing, the bookings, the traveling, the dealing with the promoters. Mastin conceded that the white promoters had powers, far more than he'd ever have. But he had Sammy. Whoever got a peek at the contract would still see one indisputable fact: Will Mastin *owned* the Will Mastin Trio, and he had little Sammy Davis, Jr., under contract until 1965. Sammy felt that to question that contract, well, he might as well have been questioning the love of his very own father. And who dared do such a thing?

Chapter 7

THE GREAT WHITE
SAMMY WAY

Few performers are without a competitive edge, and Sammy was no different. Although he was apt to heap slavish praise upon fellow entertainers, he also possessed an edgy, competitive streak. Not only did he want to be as good as Mel Torme and Perry Como and Frank Sinatra, and as funny as Eddie Cantor and Jerry Lewis—he wanted to be better. He had the nerve to stand before them—as a mimic—and bring them into himself, then spit them right back out into the rolling waves of laughter. Most mimics are swathed in the ethos of irony—even if they can't quite put it into words. "Nobody wants to be a mimic," says impersonator Will Jordan, who first met Sammy in 1952 in Pittsburgh. (Jordan was considered the craftiest of the Ed Sullivan impersonators.) "We want to be ourselves." As himself, Sammy knew how good he could be, knew that it would take more than the loss of an eye to stymie his gifts. The entertainers he looked up to had one thing in common: they were white. They traveled in many of the same circles he did. He was charmed by the very air they breathed. Peggy King concluded that Sammy simply wanted to be someone else.

"Sammy," says King, "wanted to be white—and pretty."

Cindy Bitterman held a similar opinion. "I don't think," she says, "he thought of himself as a black person."

There were, however, two Negroes in 1950s Hollywood whom Sammy deemed important enough for him to keep an eye on: Harry Belafonte and Sidney Poitier. Both were more handsome than Sammy, which unnerved him. "Sammy caught me on the balcony with Sidney at a party, and he gave me this killer B-movie look he affected," recalls King.

Poitier was born in 1924 in Miami and raised in the Bahamas, where his parents were tomato growers on Cat Island. He quit school by the age of thirteen and worked in a succession of dead-end jobs. He believed his future lay elsewhere—certainly not in picking tomatoes—and set his sights on New York

*Sammy in a 1955 recording session for Decca Records. The resulting album
was titled* Sammy Davis Jr. Sings Just for Lovers. *His voice was large, but
his phrasing, unlike Sinatra's, was too often mechanical.*

(JESS RAND COLLECTION)

City. When he arrived, he was nearly broke and forced to sleep on rooftops. He
found himself caught in the Harlem race riots of 1943, dodging bullets and
luckily escaping injury. After a stint in the army, he returned to Harlem and
saw an ad for auditions at the American Negro Theatre. At his audition he was
told his Caribbean accent was too thick. He rid himself of it by listening for
endless hours to voices on American radio. Finally accepted by the Negro
drama group, he rose in its ranks and made his Broadway debut in 1946 in an
all-Negro production of *Lysistrata.* His Hollywood debut came in 1950 in *No
Way Out.* His next film was *Cry the Beloved Country,* in which Poitier gave a
strong and noticeable performance playing—opposite the estimable Canada
Lee—a South African priest. There was a leonine grace in the Poitier walk,
strongly accentuated by cool dark features. In 1955 he created a character both
vulnerable and riveting in *The Blackboard Jungle,* an urban drama centered
around a high school; Glenn Ford starred. Even in a film career that was still
new, it was obvious by 1955 that Sidney Poitier would not be ignored.

Poitier and Belafonte—who was born in Harlem in 1927—met in New York
City after the war. The two long-legged actors cut an elegant path in Manhat-

tan. Raised by a single parent, Belafonte had joined the navy at the age of seventeen—joining as much to see the world as to escape poverty. While enlisted, he became a voracious reader, plowing through the works of W. E. B. Du Bois. Upon release from the military, Belafonte—as Poitier had done—joined the American Negro Theatre. He possessed beautiful, almost Valentino-like looks, and a husky voice. The potent combination landed him a theatrical agent. His first lead role onstage was in Sean O'Casey's *Juno and the Paycock.* In 1953 he appeared on Broadway in John Murray Anderson's *Almanac.* The only Negro in the cast, Belafonte received stunning reviews—and a Tony Award for best supporting actor. That same year he made his motion-picture screen debut in *Bright Road.* The two—Poitier and Belafonte—became fast friends, and when in Manhattan they took to hanging around Greenwich Village beatnik joints. Women ogled them. Belafonte also started forging a reputation as a folk singer. In 1954, Belafonte was teamed with Dorothy Dandridge in *Carmen Jones,* the Otto Preminger–directed film version of Georges Bizet's opera. The role established him—within the limited confines of Negro cinema—as a legitimate sex symbol. Bracketing each other, and within a few short years, Poitier and Belafonte had placed themselves at the front rank of what few starring roles were being offered to Negro males.

Sammy, a keen reader of the Hollywood trade papers *Variety* and the *Hollywood Reporter*—as well as the Negro press—could hardly ignore the two performers. Reading about them, noticing the attention they were getting, only unleashed his competitive juices. "Sammy used to say if he was as tall as Harry Belafonte, he'd run him out of the business," says Shirley Rhodes, who went to work for Sammy in 1956 as an assistant.

There was something else, aside from cinematic good looks and stage training, that both Poitier and Belafonte had in common that Sammy did not: they had been witness to a society—the Caribbean (Belafonte spent part of his youth in Jamaica)—where blacks had cultural ownership from within, where a spirit of fighting against colonialism existed that gave them both a political identity and a center. In 1950, when the British government of Nassau would not release Poitier's film *No Way Out,* there were widespread demonstrations by blacks in the Bahamas; Poitier had rushed home to join them. Belafonte himself had long been influenced by the social activism of Paul Robeson, whom he considered his hero, and was quick to join progressive causes. Granting them their feisty streak, friends of the duo sometimes referred to Poitier and Belafonte as "those two West Indians." Both Poitier and Belafonte meant to serve notice to Hollywood that they would not endure shuffling, stereotypical roles. They aimed to play fully drawn characters. Sammy came from the dusty aura of vaudeville. He took what was given to him; the play was not the thing—the thing was the opportunity to perform. His struggle lay in getting his name in lights. To that end, his nerves and pride pinched hard against each other only in the name of entertainment opportunities. Social activism did not—at least yet—move him. Sammy had not been running around Hollywood, cavorting with actors and producers, sidling up to them, schmoozing with them, so that, at the last minute, upstarts Sidney Poitier and Harry Belafonte could be seen striding through the doors of Hollywood—right by him. He would concede them their handsomeness—but little else. He had been in the business long before they even started scuffling up acting jobs in New York City. The American Negro Theatre wing in New York City did not teach him a thing: he learned on the road; he learned from the shrewdness and grace of Will Mastin; he learned from the giants of vaudeville. He learned from Eddie Cantor, who had come to visit him in his San Bernardino hospital bed—when Poitier and Belafonte had not.

Sammy prided himself on versatility. Poitier and Belafonte had Broadway roles to their credit—and he did not.

The gap would not last much longer.

Jule Styne was a Broadway impresario and bon vivant. He wore French cuffs with his monogrammed shirts, fine tailor-made suits. Jule played the horses—and he was addicted to gambling. One of his dreams was to get Sammy Davis, Jr., to Broadway.

Born in London, as Julius Stein, he came of age in Chicago. As an eight-year-old, he began taking piano lessons at the Chicago College of Music. At recitals, he wore Little Lord Fauntleroy outfits. His parents were amazed at his composure at the piano. He played Rachmaninoff and Mozart and Haydn. The dream of becoming a classical pianist, however, began to fall away when an instructor bluntly told him he would never become a great classical pianist because his hands lacked strength. Styne sulked, though not long. He bought sheet music on Chicago's famed Division Street and began playing ragtime at his high school. He got jobs in burlesque houses, playing "Mama's Blues" and "I Want a Girl Just Like the Girl That Married Dear Old Dad." In the burlesque houses he was teased by strippers and befriended by Negro musicians. He sat starry-eyed listening to the likes of Fats Waller and Louis Armstrong and Bessie Smith.

Enraptured by jazz, Styne graduated to mob-backed nightclubs. "More or less, musicians fed off the mob," he would recall. "They still do, to a certain extent, and before I got out of Chicago, I must have worked a couple dozen mob joints. But those people always seemed to like musicians, and I did my job and kept my mouth shut." When Gene Tunney fought Jack Dempsey in Chicago, Al Capone rented out the Metropole Ballroom for an after-fight party; he hired

Sammy, springtime 1956, in Manhattan. He is on Broadway, in Mr. Wonderful, *and ensconced in a suite at the Gorham Hotel. He sits on the rooftop of the Gorham, the city spread out below.*

(JESS RAND COLLECTION)

Styne to tend to the music. Capone tipped young Styne $2,500. Chicago was wicked, and Styne knew it: he was in the city when the St. Valentine's Day massacre happened. When other musicians began taking off for New York City, Styne felt the wave eastward. "The big-band day had definitely started, and it looked as if New York, not Chicago, was the place to be."

He fell in love with Manhattan, writing music, gigging in bands. Quick and voluble, he worked tirelessly. In 1942, Styne met songwriter Sammy Cahn—genius seems to find genius—and the two began a long and fruitful collaboration. Their first hit was "I've Heard That Song Before." A very skinny Frank Sinatra sang it in *Youth Parade,* a 1942 film. A string of Cahn-Styne hits followed, many of them World War II hits, speaking romantic love and gallantry. Styne soon formed an important friendship with Sinatra. They roomed at the Warwick Hotel together for a while, with plenty of hijinks—"sharing a bathtub together, that sort of thing," recalls Styne's widow, Margaret.

Styne worked tirelessly, never taking no for an answer regarding his projects and dreams. He was "impossible," actually, as his widow describes him. "Very funny. Loved to be the center of attention." Styne was the major force behind *Gentlemen Prefer Blondes,* which, in 1949, became a long-running Broadway musical and made a star of Carol Channing. Styne originally wanted Nanette Fabray to take the Channing role. "Please, Nan," he begged, scrunched-faced in her apartment lobby, "take it. It's going to be a great show." (Fabray didn't believe him; Channing did, and she became a star. The show ran for 740 performances.)

Always hunting talent, Styne kept a close eye on nightclubs, on who might be rising on its stages. Sammy caught his attention, and Styne saw his act on both coasts. "He adored Sammy," recalls Margaret Styne. "He was absolutely crazy about talented people." Before Sammy's car accident, Styne had approached Sammy on the West Coast—Sammy had been appearing at the Mocambo—and asked him about his interest in Broadway. Sammy listened; he was always easily flattered.

There had been Broadway impresarios and backers, like Styne, who had seen Sammy's alternately rambunctious and riveting nightclub act. They were quick to wonder: Was he an actor? Did he have the discipline it took for the legitimate stage? They'd answer no, of course he did not—only to go on marveling at his skills. But the fact was that few shows on Broadway had featured a Negro male in the lead role and succeeded. Broadway was cold terrain for Negro writers and performers, and Sammy knew as much.

In 1925, Garland Anderson was the first Negro playwright to have a production—*Appearances*—mounted on Broadway. Ten years later came Langston Hughes's *Mulatto.* There was a six-year gap between Hughes's play and the next production, *Native Son,* by Richard Wright, which featured Canada Lee in a starring role and was directed by Orson Welles. It lasted only 114 performances.

In 1944 there was some bright light with the opening of *Anna Lucasta.* It was the acclaimed production of the Harlem-based American Negro Theatre wing. It did not have a recognizable star, but rather was an ensemble production—although the beautiful Hilda Simms and estimable Frederick O'Neal would receive wonderful notices. *Anna* would run 957 performances, the longest for a Negro production on Broadway. Oddly enough, few considered it a "Negro" play, inasmuch as it had been written with a Polish family in mind, and it reached Broadway without any of the depth or emotional weight of

Negro history in it. The fallout from *Anna* was bitter: the Harlem-based theatrical troupe lost out on most profits because of tangled contracts with Broadway and its own theater.

She wasn't the lead, but Ethel Waters—Sammy's costar in *Rufus Jones for President*—returned to Broadway in 1950 for the first time since *Cabin in the Sky* a decade earlier. "Someday, somehow, I hope I can find a play in which I don't have to sing all the time," she said rather sadly during her *Cabin* run. "It's a long time now that I've been singing, and I'm getting tired." She got her chance in Carson McCullers's *The Member of the Wedding*. Her nonsinging role: the family cook. Another six years passed before Louis Peterson's *Take a Giant Step* opened on Broadway; it featured the Broadway debut of young Louis Gossett.

"It was apparent that no one wanted to handle the 'black' theme," a Styne biographer would write of Styne's proposed show for Sammy. "One writer, shocking Jule, said he could easily come up with a story that involved a black man raping a white woman."

But the eye accident had changed so much. With Sammy's popularity soaring, Styne struck again, returning to Sammy with a Broadway proposition. He caught up with Sammy in Los Angeles. This time Sammy not only listened to Styne's new intentions, he hurried them along himself, now dreaming of Broadway: "The sooner the better," he told Styne of a Broadway debut.

Jule Styne—the gambler—did not shrink from challenges.

He pondered show ideas, then hatched one quickly, firing off dictation into the ears of Dorothy Dicker, his secretary.

Styne's planned production for Sammy was a musical. Something about a singer, in Miami Beach, who has a nightclub act and rises to fame. It would, in a way, be tailored to Sammy's own nightclub act. Styne rushed around, looking for writers, lyricists, hustling in and out of the Brill Building on Broadway. He made phone calls, sent telegrams, held meetings with show financiers, among them Ruth Dubonnet. Dubonnet, of the wine Dubonnets, had long been charmed by Styne, whose productions, recalls John Barry Ryan III—about to become a Styne employee with his new musical—always "ran out of money." It didn't hurt that Dubonnet had a crush on Styne; she liked the Sammy pitch.

Styne cared not a whit about having all the particulars sorted out: Sammy wasn't signed, Will Mastin hadn't been consulted. As well, the Mastin trio was a nightclub act, with nightclub commitments lined up. Styne bore ahead anyway. He had written lyrics for Sinatra. He had little doubt he was going to get what he wanted.

Word went forth that Jule Styne was hunting talent for a planned Broadway musical that would star Sammy Davis, Jr. Some of the company he pulled together quickly because they had worked with him before. George Gilbert, a coproducer, had worked with Styne on *Hazel Flagg* and *Will Success Spoil Rock Hunter?* Lester Osterman, Jr., was brought aboard as another coproducer. Osterman, who had deep pockets, was a longtime Styne friend—and also a member of the New York Stock Exchange. Oliver Smith was being wooed to design the sets. Smith had done the set design for *Rock Hunter*. Smith's talents were so sought after that he also had signed on to do the set design for Alan Jay Lerner and Frederick Loewe's musical that was in rehearsal—a little something called *My Fair Lady*.

Jack Donohue was hired to direct. Donohue, who had started out as a dancer with the Ziegfeld Follies, was carving a career on both stage and screen. By 1956 he had directed dance routines in nearly two dozen Hollywood films and had worked with stars ranging from Shirley Temple (he directed the dance routines in five of her films) to Esther Williams.

Styne needed a lyricist for the show. He had a couple in mind. Jerry Bock and Larry Holofcener had met each other at the University of Wisconsin, where they began writing musicals together. In 1949 the duo arrived in New York City. They got jobs writing scores for a series of one-act musicals produced by Max Liebman. The Liebman work got them plenty of notice, and they were quickly labeled prodigies. They wrote for various TV shows—*The Mel Torme Show, The Kate Smith Hour, The Red Buttons Show*. The two also got writing jobs with Tommy Vallando's music publishing company. Vallando, after a year, was beginning to lose faith in the duo; to him, they were little more than unproductive gadabouts; they seemed to produce first-rate work for everyone except him. Tommy Vallando wanted results—now. The past was the past. He began thinking of firing them. But then Bock and Holofcener heard through the theatrical grapevine about Styne's planned musical. The two immediately went looking for Jule. Styne, meeting with them, was struck; he liked their energy and moxie. He hired them, convinced that "they were going to be the next Adler & Ross"—the eclectic music-writing team that had been responsible for *Pajama Game*, a 1954 smash. Bock and Holofcener rushed into Vallando's office and excitedly announced: "We're going to do a show, and we're going to do it for Sammy Davis, Jr.!" Tommy Vallando would be a fool to fire them now.

For years Vallando had been trying to break into Broadway. And now two kids were telling him they were going to get him there. Other Broadway music publishers always seemed to outfox Tommy Vallando, to always trot out new talent. So he found himself listening to the kids, who were now about to be teamed with the gifted Jule Styne. Vallando's future suddenly brimmed with possibility. "His chance had been thrust in his face," recalls George Davis Weiss, another writer who worked in the Vallando publishing office. "Tommy says to them, 'Get to work! Get to work! We can't drop this ball.' "

Styne already had Dubonnet as a financial backer; now he went after others. One evening, Dubonnet held a little cocktail party to introduce Styne's two young writers to potential investors. "Jule wanted them to play for the gathered people," remembers Weiss. Dubonnet was adept at throwing such affairs, mingling the money people with the art crowd: among her guests—"a gang of big people," recalls Weiss—were Ethel Merman, star of the smash 1946 musical *Annie Get Your Gun,* and Oliver Smith, the set designer. "At some point," recalls Weiss, who was also invited to the Dubonnet affair, "Oliver Smith drew himself up, haughtylike, and walked away from the piano silently saying, 'Are you kidding?' " Smith simply sniffed no magic in the compositions and was, in fact, aghast at what Styne's writers had produced. "It was a big flop," recalls Weiss. Styne, an emotional man, cringed. "The party was quickly over," says Weiss. "He wanted everybody out. He went into a rage with the two kids. Jule had no feeling for kindness. He would break out in screams, shouts. They didn't know what to do. They were stunned."

Styne—who felt Bock and Holofcener were trying to write "an opera"— phoned Vallando and told him to forget everything, crying that "the kids" had let him down. "I'm going to call the coast and get myself a couple great writers," he complained. "It serves me right to play with nobodies."

Vallando pleaded with Styne. "Give it a chance," he begged.

"Give it a chance?" Styne answered. "I had all these people in to see this new team, and I get egg on my face!"

Feeling desperate and sensing a prime opportunity slipping away, Vallando proposed adding another writer to the team, one of the seasoned writers on his staff—George David Weiss himself. When Styne finished fuming, the idea of adding Weiss seemed to calm him down. He had heard of Weiss. Weiss also wrote both words and music, Vallando told Styne—sure to be a valued contribution with the unproductive prodigies. Weiss—who would first have to meet Styne—secretly figured Styne was game for any new ideas from Vallando because he did not want to lose the opportunity to get Sammy Davis to Broadway. "He was an egomaniac," Weiss says of Styne.

Weiss had studied at the Juilliard School of Music. He had also done arrangements for Stan Kenton's big band and had a decade's worth of hits behind him, among them "To Think You've Chosen Me," "That Was My Heart You Heard," "I Ran All the Way Home," and "Let's Make the Most of Tonight."

Styne soon summoned Weiss—a rather formal man—to his apartment. "I went up to see him, scared to death," remembers Weiss. "I realized I had a chance at a Broadway show." After Styne got past complaining to Weiss that the writers on Vallando's staff were trying "to ruin me," he started, almost in the same breath, asking Weiss about ideas for the musical, about scenes, about what the beginning and middle and end would look like, all while simultaneously offering his own ideas about what would make the show work. Then he told George David Weiss to go home and start writing. Styne had exhausted Weiss.

Working furiously over the weekend, songs coming into his head and floating out, only to float back in a better version, Weiss finally had something he was ready to show Styne the following week. This time Weiss would be going to the Styne apartment with musical numbers. "I crawled—I did not walk—to Jule's apartment," says Weiss. "I showed him my concepts, ideas. I sat at the piano and played him a couple of melodic things. He gets all excited—to my shock—and says, 'Terrific! Terrific! Terrific!'" Jule was so excited, he began jumping around, playing the melodies over and over in his mind, allowing them to float in and out of his ears. He was smiling; he seemed happy. Maybe Weiss had the job. He looked into Jule's eyes, waiting for an answer. But Styne bid him good-bye. There was no handshake on a deal, which worried Weiss. He feared Styne, and in that fear, he was unable to figure him out. Time passed—fitfully. It took a few days, and then news came that Weiss had one of the coveted music-writing jobs for the Broadway show.

So it was: George David Weiss, son of a milkman, was going to Broadway. And Sammy Davis, Jr., was waiting for him.

Weiss and the two kids—Bock and Holofcener—began working furiously, composing *Mr. Wonderful*. (The book for the show was by Joseph Stein and Will Glickman.) In a short time, however, the creative process grew tense. Bock would disagree with Weiss; Weiss would disagree with Holofcener. There were too many writers, too much stirring of the stew. The arguments didn't seem to let up. Finally, the William Morris agent representing Bock and Holofcener asked everyone to come in for a meeting. "He said," remembers Weiss, " 'I can't take this bullshit. You guys have the biggest opportunity of your lives. This is Jule Styne—and it's gonna star Sammy Davis, Jr., who's going to be the biggest entertainer in the country.'" The agent went on to tell them that when there was an impasse, the writers should vote on it. Weiss told the agent it was nearly impossible to vote on such a creative venture. "He said, 'I don't care. Get the project written.'" The young writers huddled, and convinced themselves that egos must be put aside and the unnecessary arguments stopped.

The day soon came when Jule Styne told Weiss it was time to meet Sammy. Everyone would meet at the 500 Club in Atlantic City, where Sammy was performing. It was Skinny D'Amato's club.

It was no secret that gangsters hung out at Skinny's club, against a backdrop of swanky entertainment and fine bourbon. In the shadows of many high-profile nightclubs—sometimes not even in the shadows—sat mobsters. The mixture of nightclubs, entertainment, and the mob had long been a potent force in America.

America was born of revolution, of settlers and invaders, of slavery and immigrants, of action on the dusty plains. And of capitalism, which unleashed the shrewd work of financiers. The financiers had their games, and they played them for keeps. Liquidate, liquidate, urged financier Andrew Mellon. Mellon wished to protect the rich—those like him—and soak all others. Somehow, the common man pushed on. The country enjoyed its pastimes, its sporting events, its nightlife. Alcohol became a part of the enjoyment, a constant, like the sunrise. Early in the century, some began to shout pieties, believing moral decay was setting in. For years there were speeches, cavalcades led by fire-and-brimstone preachers, men and women screaming to the heavens and urging abstinence from alcohol. In 1919 they had their victory with the adoption of the Eighteenth Amendment, which outlawed the sale of alcohol.

The means to enforce Prohibition confused and bewildered many. Undercover agents caught drinking were fired. Mayor Fiorello La Guardia of New York City said it would take 250,000 officers to enforce Prohibition in his city, as well as "a force of 250,000 men to police the police." Prohibition would last for much of thirteen years, and during that time, there was danger and tomfoolery, all accompanied by a massive rise in bootleg joints and speakeasies, places where the bubbly could be consumed furtively. These establishments needed protection, a certain kind of muscle. Thus began the rise of the modern gangster, lethal henchmen to safeguard the interests of the nightclub owners, men who collected on outstanding debts. From New Orleans to Chicago to New York, there were gang wars, and the spilling of much blood. "Oh mama, mama, mama," bootleg gangster Dutch Schultz cried out as he was shot down in New York City on October 23, 1935, by a rival gang boss.

Certain names—Lucky Luciano, Meyer Lansky, Frank Costello, Mickey Cohen, Bugsy Siegel—would become synonymous with the melding of nightclub and gangster. The nightclub business could be a profit-making enterprise but was also very dangerous. Bugsy Siegel learned too well. Siegel borrowed money from mobsters to build the Flamingo Hotel and Casino in Las Vegas. There were huge cost overruns. It opened December 26, 1946, amid much fanfare. Jimmy Durante sang and cracked jokes on opening night. George Raft, an actor in gangster movies, boon buddy to Siegel, played the role of shadow host. The club was Siegel's dream in the desert. Siegel believed—not that he minded the tinhorns—that the film community from Hollywood would crowd the place, keep him swimming in dough. The prostitutes he hired were gorgeous, masquerading—lest he get cracked on a white-slavery charge—as "the help." But in the weeks and months ahead the Flamingo lost money, a lot of it. And it kept losing money. The dapper Siegel was inattentive to detail. And he was skimming off the top. The mob was quickly onto him. Six months after the casino's opening—a June night in Beverly Hills, the air sweet with jasmine—

Siegel, sitting downstairs in the home of his girlfriend, Virginia Hill, was shot dead, his face blown off.

On May 10, 1950, America got a gritty accounting of just how much crime permeated the country, when Estes Kefauver, a Tennessee senator, launched an investigation into organized crime. The Senate Crime Investigating Committee's hearings would last a year. Kefauver went all across the country—Philadelphia, New York City, Kansas City, Los Angeles, Chicago, St. Louis, other locales—gathering evidence. When the hearings reached television, they made for a riveting spectacle. The nation saw, up close, in black and white, an assortment of mobsters, gangsters, even their molls. Virginia Hill was called to testify. She wore a wide-brimmed hat indoors and told stories of European vacations with mobsters. She confessed, however, that she knew nothing of Siegel's demise. As the weeks passed, the committee was besieged with letters. "For hour after hour we watched in fascinated distaste the specimens of sub-human scum that squirmed in the glare of their notoriety," one letter stated. "A nationwide crime syndicate does exist in the United States of America, despite the protestations of a strangely assorted company of criminals, self-serving politicians, plain blind fools, and others who may be honestly misguided, that there is no such combine," the Kefauver committee would finally conclude. Kefauver's work touched a nerve, and the mail poured in. It was overwhelmingly positive, but there were exceptions. "Wish you were here," a postcard addressed to him said. It came from Alcatraz. The Kefauver findings left the country no choice but to fully recognize the extent of its criminal underground. "Infiltration of legitimate business by known hoodlums has progressed to an alarming extent in the United States," the committee stated.

Many of the nightclubs that flourished across the country were starry places, full of women, booze, and dream-makers. There was the Chez Paree in Chicago and the Coconut Grove in Miami; the Sands in Las Vegas; Bill Miller's Riviera across the Hudson in New Jersey; Sherman Billingsley's Stork Club in New York City (Billingsley had been a former bootlegger); and the Copacabana—some believed it to be the jewel of them all—also in New York City. Jules Podell ran the Copa. He came up in the bootlegging business, for which he had once been shot. He also had a prison record. The women who worked at the Copa were jaw-dropping beautiful. The long arm of the law was never far from the club's front door. At the Copa—as at many other nightclubs—there were constant probes by government investigators who believed the clubs were beehives of gangster activity. The LaGuardia administration believed there were behind-the-scenes operatives at the Copa masquerading as "part owners" who were "disreputable persons engaged in unlawful enterprise."

Nightclubs—often fronted by the mob—had to fill their seats, and those seats were filled by good entertainment. Frank Sinatra once tried to explain his link to gangsters: "I spent a lot of time working in saloons. . . . I was a kid. . . . They paid you, and the checks didn't bounce. I didn't meet any Nobel Prize winners in saloons."

Every time Sammy began to contemplate his independence from Will Mastin, he ran into something hard to get around—the contract that Mastin had him signed to, which was good until 1965. Will Mastin knew that in his silences—and in his waning physical abilities to perform—the world had come to believe him a fool. He had long conceded Sammy marquee billing—the Will Mastin Trio Starring Sammy Davis Jr.—but it remained Mastin's trio. And the contract stipulated that whatever the act earned, Mastin pocketed one third for performance, and this after the 20 percent he had taken off the top because it was his act.

To be fooled by the old fool: show business.

It was still agreed that Sam Sr. would get one third of the trio's earnings. The elder Davis held no illusion about his marquee pull. "Let's get down to the nitty-gritty," he said to Rand one night, as if assuaging the limits of his own ego. "I'm the only guy in the act who can't have billing."

The whole act was Sammy—and Sammy got blessed with just slightly more than 26 percent.

Mastin had learned well from other producers over the years. "Will Mastin used to tell me," says Norma Miller, a Las Vegas showgirl who befriended the trio in their early years, "that if it wasn't for the kind of contract he had, they would have stolen Sammy."

"They": that constantly moving word that always lurked behind the curtains—the big-time entertainment agencies, the smiling agents who ran all the other nightclub acts coast to coast, the likes of Frank Sinatra.

With the nightclub business coming in on the modern era, and with hand-shakes replaced by written deals, Sammy certainly realized the wisdom of being with the William Morris Agency. It only meant, however, that the agency would book the act, that Mastin would be relieved of that duty. The outlines of the contract would remain in place: Mastin agreed to the agency's 10 percent fee. It was little sweat off him; he was getting old.

But Sammy needed more money. So he went tugging on the sleeves of nightclub owners—shaking the tree harder—and time and time again, he borrowed money from them. It was money for gifts, for clothes, for women. He wanted money to throw around the way Sinatra threw money around. "I remember one night they played a club and the owner said, 'Sammy took a $3,000 advance on a $5,000 date,'" says Jess Rand. "That left $2,000 minus the

William Morris money. Sam Sr. grabbed Sammy and said, 'You want to blow your money fine, don't blow mine.' " (Sammy's FBI file is merely a toothless stack of paperwork. But there are some interesting nuggets—namely the number of death threats against Sammy the bureau had to investigate, because of his failure to repay loans. By the time the bureau leapt into action—and it is anyone's guess the level of energy they devoted to these threats, given the shadowy nature of it all—Sammy had wisely repaid. There is mention, for instance, in one file of "a Miami Beach gangster who had threatened the life of Sammy Davis Jr. The related comment indicated that the above individual [the name is blotched out] probably referred to [another blotched name] of Miami, Fla., and concerning a $7,500 debt which reportedly had been paid by Davis.")

Sammy's way to pay off his old debts was to commit the trio to future engagements—in the nightclubs whose owners he owed money. Mastin believed these future engagements were just business as usual, simple confirmation of the act's drawing power. The act's drawing power was indeed as potent as ever, but it had also been hijacked by Sammy. Finding no way to get out of one bad contract—with Mastin—Sammy entered into many handshake contracts with nightclub owners, most of whom had to answer to mobsters. It was the proverbial deal with the devil, one that often leads to the hallway and the clutches of the tax man. In due time, Sammy would be ushered down that hallway.

It wasn't long after Sammy's car accident that Harry Belafonte phoned and asked Sammy to come to Chicago. Having known of other Negro entertainers who had been unable to get out from under unsavory characters—and hearing of Sammy's piling debts—Belafonte came up with a plan for what he thought might alter Sammy's financial dependence. Being the most political of the three—Sammy, himself, and Poitier—Belafonte saw a duty born of history and insight to try to save Sammy. "He and I met," recalls Belafonte.

> I had a driver. We drove out of the hotel and went to a river in the middle of Chicago. We stood on the dock—a kind of walkway—and I said, "Sammy, let me tell you, if what I'm told the size of your debt [actually] is, let me pay it off. I'll buy your marker. And you'll have only one obligation. Let's cut a recording contract. That will be the only collateral. And proceeds from the record will go to pay off the marker. Then the rest will revert to you. This means I'll pay off your marker. Everything you earn in personal appearances is yours. You don't have to pay gambling points." I left him with that as a proposal on the table. He called back the next day

and said, "I can't discuss it, but the answer is, I can't." I said, "Why?" He said, "What's at stake is much bigger than that."

Will Mastin could hardly keep up with Sammy's offstage alliances. Gangsters, in all their dangerous grandeur, glided around Negro ambitions as if those ambitions didn't even exist. Gangsters owned the Negro boxer in America. And gangsters frightened the old vaudevillian.

Something bad is gonna happen . . .

Sam Giancana—a Chicago-based mob boss—liked Sammy. He used to call him, supposedly with affection, "Nigger weasel." Sammy, who had Giancana's private phone number, had had to call upon him more than once. Jess Rand remembers Giancana giving Sammy money to settle old debts. "I told Sammy he was making the biggest mistake of his life."

Sammy's friends—Peggy King, Cindy Bitterman, and others—also saw his dalliance with gangsters, and it made them very nervous. "I used to tell him," says King, " 'You can be in show business and not be involved with the mob.' "

Maybe not if you were trying to escape an ironclad contract and an old man—Will Mastin—to whom your father felt you owed everything in life. An old man who, at one time, had made it possible for your very own mother to eat and survive.

"Sammy never had enough money," says Bill Miller, who ran the Riviera in New Jersey. "He was a terrible spendthrift." Sammy once racked up a $35,000 debt at the Waldorf during an engagement. The Waldorf summoned Miller, hoping he could help settle things. "They said to me, 'See if you can collect it,' " recalls Miller. "I came in and spoke to Sammy. I arranged to pay half the price of the $35,000 debt." Which meant, of course, that Sammy would be returning to Bill Miller's Riviera because Bill Miller was into Sammy yet again.

Sammy's relentless spending angered his father. There were loud words, father-son fights. "He would lie about money, and his father beat him up a few times—rightfully so," says Cindy Bitterman. "He didn't know he was playing with fire. That's how stupid he was."

"If the act made a thousand dollars," says Jess Rand, "Sammy would spend nine hundred. It pissed everybody off."

The William Morris Agency—which had many of the hottest nightclub acts around—was happy to sign Sammy. He was assigned to Abbie Greschler, the agent for Dean Martin and Jerry Lewis. After Greschler he was assigned to Lenny Hirschan. But always, in the shadows, stood George Wood. Wood often handled business—when the word "business" was known to take on a rather dark edge—for Sinatra. And more times than a few, George Wood would have to intercede with underworld figures to extricate Sammy from conflicts.

Wood started out booking show-business acts in the hurly-burly days of

Prohibition. He was smooth, well spoken, and familiar with the ways of the underworld. He dined with gamblers and gangsters. When Prohibition ended, Wood took his unique skills to Abe Lastfogel, who, in 1930, was appointed to run the New York offices of the Morris agency. Lastfogel sent Wood into the nightclubs—familiar terrain—to scout talent. Wood went about his job, completely at ease in the shadows and the company of unsavory characters. One of his close friends was known to be Frank Costello, a gangster who had a stake in the Copacabana, and who had testified at the Kefauver hearings, and whose autobiography Wood was trying to sell. (A biographer of the Morris agency would come to describe Wood as Lastfogel's "emissary to the mob.")

The Morris agency's roster of nightclub acts was illustrious—Sophie Tucker, Milton Berle, Jimmy Durante were among them. One of Lastfogel's esteemed agents was Johnny Hyde, who discovered Norma Jean Baker, who became Marilyn Monroe. With his gift for dexterity, Lastfogel put Wood to work watching over his unpredictable clients, of whom Sammy was one. "He knew all the heavies," Jess Rand says of Wood.

When Sammy couldn't get out of debt fast enough, he called Wood, and Wood solved the problem. Sammy felt at ease with him. He even believed Wood might become a more equitable Will Mastin. Sammy went to Wood in 1953 because he needed money—$25,000. He pleaded with Wood not to mention it to his father or Will. Wood assured Sammy he would not mention it, simply because he was not going to give him the money. The agent then left town on a business trip. While he was away, Sammy made another appeal to the Morris office—not bothering to tell them of Wood's refusal to grant the $25,000—and got it. Sammy felt all-powerful. He felt like Frank.

While Wood was away, something else occurred: the MCA agency tried to pluck Sammy from the Morris office. Sammy so liked being wooed. He invited a group of MCA agents to see his nightclub act. But a group of Morris agents also showed and spotted the MCA agents on hand, sitting at Sammy's table. It was inelegant politics on Sammy's part. The MCA agents were embarrassed. When Wood returned to Los Angeles, he asked Sammy to come see him. He was angered at the $25,000 that had been given to Sammy. But he told Sammy he would not take it personally, as long as Sammy renewed his Morris contract for another five years. Sammy said he could not do it, that he was considering signing with MCA. It was a brutal affront to Wood, a very tough character in his own right. George Wood's face reddened. "Sign!" he said to Sammy, "or I'll throw you out this window." It was the forty-first floor; George Wood was not a man to be trifled with; Sammy signed. Then he tried to chuckle the imbroglio away.

In the nightclubs he played, Sammy—like Sinatra—didn't meet any Nobel Prize winners. But he met men who could give him money. He didn't walk shoulder to shoulder with mobsters as Sinatra did. But he often waltzed into the dark rooms. He played it with the giddiness of a mascot. And his name wound up in the FBI files with all the other hoodlums.

Stepping from the shadow of Will Mastin, Sammy stepped into another shadow—darker, wider, far more pernicious. Money and debt began to grease parts of the lining of his soul.

And Skinny D'Amato became a friend.

His real name was Paul Emilio D'Amato. He was a little over six feet, weighed around 185, wore glasses, and had a distinguished air. He was in the rackets as a teenager. He began pimping women. His stint in the big house—Lewisburg Federal Penitentiary—was for white slavery. Not long after the Depression ended, he was back on the streets of Atlantic City, a city so rife with corruption that President Franklin D. Roosevelt had once sent in federal forces to try to clean it up. Not long after his release from prison, D'Amato took a table at the hood-scented 500 Club. Soon enough he had a stake in the place. (And who knows, it's quite possible that during some of those nights he brushed shoulders with the honey-colored barmaid whose name was Elvera Davis over at the Little Belmont nightclub.) Skinny enjoyed booking acts for the club. Jerry Lewis and Dean Martin had had wonderful success there. And Sinatra: well, Skinny loved Frank; he couldn't do enough for Frank, a Jersey guy; he loved Frank the way he loved the smell of the salt air whipping off the ocean down by the boardwalk. Skinny didn't necessarily like the press, though. "He never let anyone point the camera at him," says Jess Rand.

A lot of entertainers knew that Skinny liked helping out performers, stuffing advance dollars into their pockets. It was so generous, so kind. It meant he liked you, he loved you—and he owned a part of your ass. Rand says Skinny's favorite line was always the same: "Need anything? Remember, if you do, come see me first—all right?"

Skinny liked Sammy. The way he performed, the way he sang, the way he aped Sinatra, which Skinny thought funny—very funny. Ha ha ha. And those tight purse strings Will Mastin had on Sammy—well, Skinny could certainly loosen those.

When Jule Styne and George David Weiss walked through the doors of the 500 Club, there sat Skinny, his criminal history sitting inside him like ink. Skinny always wore sunglasses—even indoors. Styne and Weiss just wanted Skinny to listen to their plea. And Skinny was game; he had nothing to lose. Skinny understood the need to listen. Skinny understood, because he had his claws into Sammy. Old debts.

And now the little nigger—that affectionate phrase the Italians used for Sammy—wanted to go to Broadway, take a pass on some old debts and promised nightclub appearances.

The Copa in New York City seated seven hundred; Skinny's 500 Club seated a thousand. Nighttime at Skinny's was such a fine time: overhead lights and drinking men, whispers in the corner and the flash of a cigarette case, the cigarette being brought up to some dame's red lips. Inside Skinny's, there was plenty of the plenty for everyone.

Styne and Weiss were beyond the doorway now, angling for the back, the table where Skinny sat, arms motioning them closer. Sammy sat next to the nightclub owner. He had one of those smiles on his face that read "God bless America and Skinny D'Amato is a great man."

Skinny ordered some drinks. His whole body posture said just two words: Need anything?

"Jule said Skinny wants to be part of the meeting," recalls Weiss.

> The reason for that was that Sammy Davis was under contract to the Mafia—a whole gang of them, club owners. They tied him up by giving him money. So he had to work where they wanted him to work. We finally have this meeting in one of the rear tables of the 500 Club. I was personally scared to death. Skinny was surrounded by five, six of his henchmen. You can see they're all carrying weapons. And there's Skinny sitting there opposite me without as much as a smile on his face. Jule Styne says, "Tell Sammy about the show."

Gangsters wowed Sammy. As did real guns. The gangsters around him at the 500 Club were surely real, and the scene itself surreal: Skinny transforming himself as background power broker, a kind of unbilled producer, outfitting his reputation with links to the legitimate theater; Jule Styne a character right out of *Guys and Dolls*, there to outwit the henchmen.

"All three of us start, off the top of our heads, telling [Sammy] about the show, how it starts," Weiss says. "Skinny is sitting there listening to it, absolutely without moving a muscle on his face. Finally, Sammy says, 'Whew, whew. Sing that song. Sing this song!' Sammy could get like a little baby voice. It was so embarrassing to us. Sammy would join in with us. He knew some of the songs. He had been working with Jule. Sammy seemed to get embarrassed because Skinny was so unresponsive. He began to feel that Skinny hated everything." There was awkward silence, eyes darting about, Sammy frozen in his childlike trance owing to the guns, the gangsters, the hope, Skinny, Jule. Someone finally asked Skinny what he thought of it all. "You got six months," he said to Jule.

And that was it: Jule had Sammy, thanks to Skinny, because Skinny had a deeper version of Sammy. (Even before coming aboard the play, Sammy hit Styne up for a financial advance of several thousand dollars.) Sammy owned his talent, but he did not always own the direction in which that talent would be pointed.

There was still the issue of money to mount the production. Styne figured a budget of $250,000. He knew he could count on Dubonnet, but others were skittish. He was alarmed and hurt. Many potential backers laughed, believing a Negro male lead in a Broadway show was a recipe for a flop. Styne forged on, accepting investments even in the $500 range. Eventually, he raised his money from a wide assortment of "angels," otherwise known as investors. Two hundred angels dropped money into Styne's Sammy bucket. Sammy's own salary was $3,500 a week, and 10 percent of the gross.

Styne began to assemble a cast and start auditions. Sammy had never been on Broadway, and Styne aimed to surround him with proven talent. He hired Jack Carter, a gravelly voiced stand-up comic who had already appeared on Broadway in *Call Me Mister* (produced by the gifted Melvyn Douglas) and *Top Banana*. Carter was also a veteran of early television, having made a reputation for himself on such shows as *The Colgate Comedy Hour* and *Texaco Star Theatre*. Then Styne went after and got Kay Medford, who had left Hollywood for the Broadway theater, where she distinguished herself in shows such as *Paint Your Wagon, Black-Eyed Susan,* and *Almanac;* in the latter she starred alongside the young Harry Belafonte. One of Styne's more interesting choices was Olga James, a young Negro actress with a soprano voice who had made her Hollywood screen debut in Otto Preminger's *Carmen Jones.* James's singing was so accomplished that she was one of the few members of Preminger's cast who did not have to have her vocals dubbed later. (*Carmen Jones* also landed its star, Dorothy Dandridge, on the cover of *Life* magazine, an honor never before accorded a Negro actress.)

For smaller roles Styne hired dancer Hal Loman—with Sammy's backing, since Loman had been doing choreography work for the Mastin trio; T. J. Halligan, a veteran Broadway actor who recently had been seen in the revival of *Pal Joey;* and a twenty-three-year-old ingenue by the name of Chita Rivera, who had been a knockout in off-Broadway's *Shoestring Revue.*

When Sammy landed in Manhattan on December 8, 1955, from a Miami nightclub engagement, Jule Styne took note it was his star's thirtieth birthday. There must be a celebration.

"What would you like to do tonight?" Styne wanted to know.

"I'd like to go to the '21' Club," Sammy told Styne, "but they might not let me in."

Jule Styne would not let Sammy down. He immediately began imagining

Sammy, his leading lady, Olga James, and Will Mastin, opening night of Broadway's Mr. Wonderful. *Sammy was eager to tackle Broadway, but he had to battle with Mastin, who believed the road was home.*

(JESS RAND COLLECTION)

how he could get Sammy into "21," which was so exclusive it had the feel of a private club. It did not have a "no-Negroes" policy, yet Negroes were not made to feel welcome. George Jessel once arrived at "21" with Lena Horne. The maître d' looked at them, coldly, then asked just exactly who had made the reservation.

"Abraham Lincoln," Jessel said.

Jule Styne put in a call to Pete and Jack Kreindler, the owners. Styne refreshed their memories about who he was, where he had been, his powers on Broadway—and told them he was bringing Sammy there because that's where he wanted to celebrate his thirtieth birthday. And later that night, there sat Sammy inside "21," his birthday rolling over him with champagne, a cake, and Jule Abraham Lincoln Styne slapping his back. If only Sinatra could see him; if only Belafonte and Poitier could see him now! "I didn't want anything negative to happen," Styne would recall of the evening. "The Kreindlers made certain that Sammy was treated casually, yet royally. An every-night occurrence was how it felt, thank God."

Styne announced that rehearsals would last for a period of three months. (Sammy had already informed Styne there had to be roles for his father and Will Mastin.) The show was given a title: *Mr. Wonderful.* Working out of his office, Jule Styne Productions, Styne had to receive unannounced visits by shady characters—Skinny's men, not to mention Styne's own acquaintances from the world of horse racing and betting. ("Are we casting *Guys and Dolls?*" Styne's general manager, Sylvia Herscher, once asked.) One of the guys was Will Mastin, who made sure he received proper billing—in addition to his normal cut of Sammy's salary.

The Broadway and theater veterans Styne had hired could be forgiven if they had reservations about Sammy Davis. A Broadway stage was not some nightclub populated by dreamers, backroom operatives, schemers, and hucksters. "I remember being a little snob," Chita Rivera says. "I was strictly from the theater. I heard that this fantastic nightclub entertainer was going to do a play and his nightclub act was the second part of the play. I wondered, 'What about the plot?' I wanted to know how a nightclub performer was going to fit in a book of a show."

It did not take long for the first controversy to begin brewing. Young Negro dancers were being screened, and for some reason, they were not being sent to the theater to meet the director and the producers. Albert Popwell, himself a young Negro actor, sensed injustice and threatened to lead a picket to get Negroes hired in the chorus. "I went up to the audition for *Mr. Wonderful* in rehearsal clothes," recalls Popwell. "I went up to the assistant choreographer. I said, 'Are you hiring any blacks?' I said, 'See those blacks out there? Some of them took their lunch breaks to be here.' I said, 'Tell you what. You get to Sammy Davis, Jr., and tell him if there's no black dancers in the show, there'll be a picket.' " Popwell led ten dancers down to Equity. It was not custom, but he had the Negro dancers who auditioned mark "C"—for "Colored"—on their audition cards. Four of the ten dancers who had marked "C" were hired: Jerri Gray, Tempe Fletcher, Claude Thompson, and Sally Neal.

Sammy did not bother with race, integration, or protest. Nor did Will Mastin, nor did Sam Sr. Their protest was against the ticking of time: other acts were right behind them; money was everywhere and it was nowhere and they wanted more of it.

One might wonder why Sammy took the risk of Broadway. His income would surely drop. Sammy, however, not only had competitive juices, he was shrewd. In 1950s America, Broadway was powerful, even golden. Already, in the first half of that decade, the actors who had appeared on Broadway constituted an astonishing array of talent. Among them were Paul Muni (*Inherit the Wind*), Gwen Verdon (*Damn Yankees*), Andy Griffith (*No Time for Sergeants*), Robert Preston (*The Male Animal*), John Garfield (a revival of *Golden Boy*),

Helen Hayes (*Mrs. McThing*), Audrey Hepburn (*Gigi*), Henry Fonda (*Point of No Return*), Hume Cronyn and Jessica Tandy (*The Fourposter*), Yul Brynner (*The King and I*), and Claude Rains (*Darkness at Noon*). Negro males in leading roles were largely absent.

In the firmament of the 1950s, nightclubs and Broadway were big. Someone who could make it in both venues would be a kind of king.

The rehearsals were going well. There were moments when Styne was genuinely pleased. Bock and Weiss were achieving excellent results. Styne would remember: "Sammy wanted to do an Astaire number, and in three days Bock and Weiss completed it . . . 'Too Close for Comfort.' Pure Astaire."

Sammy was ensconced in a penthouse at the Gorham Hotel. "It sounds great," remembers Jess Rand, "but it was a funky place."

While a Negro dance act and their featured performer prepared to take on Broadway, time rolled on.

Jazz saxophonist Charlie "Bird" Parker died in New York City March 12, 1955. He collapsed while watching a flickering TV screen at the home of Baroness Pannonica de Koenigswarter. The coroner estimated him to be in his late fifties, early sixties. He was thirty-four. Drugs had ground him down. He was buried in Kansas City, his home. There were ghostly sweet placards posted in Manhattan: "Bird Lives." Ralph Ellison believed that Parker's "greatest significance was for the educated white middle-class youth whose reaction to the inconsistencies of American life was the stance of casting off its education, language, dress, manners and moral standards: a revolt, apolitical in nature, which finds its most dramatic instance in the figure of the so-called white hipster."

Two weeks following the death of Bird, Tennessee Williams's *Cat on a Hot Tin Roof*—about a southern family embroiled in the dramatic flappings of sex and deceit—opened on Broadway. It starred Ben Gazzara and Barbara Bel Geddes. Burl Ives played Big Daddy; Big Mama was played by Mildred Dunnock. "Time moves by so fast, nothing can outrun it," Big Mama opined.

Children were asking their parents about the new color TV sets on the market. In California, something called Disneyland had risen from the ground up.

In San Francisco and in Greenwich Village—not too many places in between—the Beats were afoot, poets and rebels and dreamers. One of the more celebrated of the clan, Allen Ginsberg, credited yearlong sessions of psychotherapy with his insights. Lawrence Ferlinghetti, another Beat, had written a poem titled "Tentative Description of a Dinner to Promote the Impeachment of President Eisenhower."

There were those still predicting Elvis Presley would come and go.

The blunt comic Lenny Bruce was either angry or subversive. Many did not know what to make of him.

In Princeton, New Jersey, the genius Albert Einstein, who at times wore a Mickey Mouse hat and loved mugging for photographers, died at the age of seventy-six.

Marian Anderson became the first Negro to sing with the Metropolitan Opera Company in New York City.

In St. Bernard, Louisiana, eight couples were indicted by a grand jury. Their crime: interracial marriage.

In the Deep South, violence against Negroes had been unleashed. None had been more riveting to the media than the murder of Emmett Till on August 24. Till, a fourteen-year-old Negro youth, had been in Money, Mississippi, visiting relatives. He waltzed into a grocery store where Carolyn Bryant worked. (A French newspaper would later refer to Bryant as "a crossroads Marilyn Monroe.") Till was reported to have made a come-on to Bryant before leaving the store. When Bryant's husband, Roy, found out, he was livid and determined to find Till. He gathered a friend, J. W. Milam, and set about to find the youth. Milam and Bryant found Till and immediately took him away to a barn. The boy was tortured. "Mama, Lord have mercy, Lord have mercy," someone heard him cry out. Till was taken to the banks of the Tallahatchie River, where he was shot with a .45, had a seventy-five-pound cotton-gin fan roped around his neck, and dumped into the river, where he sank. It took three days to find the body. "Have you ever sent a loved son on vacation and had him returned to you in a pine box so horribly battered and waterlogged that this sickening sight is your son—lynched?" cried his mother, Mamie Bradley, to the press. An old and gnarly man by the name of Moses Wright stood up in court and identified one of Till's murderers. "Dar he," he had said, pointing, his words semiliterate, his heart heroic. An all-white jury acquitted the murderers.

The saga of Emmett Till spread everywhere in America. From library to bus stop, from schoolroom to college campus. It seemed but a prelude of things to come: On March 24 of that year, a fifteen-year-old Negro girl by the name of Claudette Colvin was arrested in Montgomery, Alabama, for refusing to move to the back of a city bus. Her arrest preceded, by nine months, the arrest of seamstress Rosa Parks, whose name, and not Colvin's, would be etched in the contours of history in the record of the celebrated Montgomery bus boycott.

Chapter 8

THE WONDER
OF IT ALL

John Barry Ryan III came from old money. His father and grandfather had never had to work. His great-grandfather—Robert Fortune Ryan—had been one of the robber barons. Young John Barry Ryan III was a rebel, and he was, indeed, constantly looking for causes. Thrown out of St. Paul's in 1947, he ended up at Yale. Yale lasted a year. "I resigned college," was his explanation. His parents knew people with connections—like John Wilson, an esteemed director. Wilson directed a musical that Jule Styne produced called *Make a Wish*. Ryan got a job on that show and befriended Styne. Theater charmed him, so he had finally found a cause.

Styne hired Ryan to stage-manage *Mr. Wonderful*. Ryan had just enough of the rich-boy bohemia pedigree to make Styne believe he would be a perfect man Friday for Sammy. "I want you to be with Sammy all the time," Styne told Ryan. "I think you guys will get along."

Ryan first encountered Sammy at the Gorham. Ryan arrived dressed in a preppy blue blazer and slacks. "I get off the elevator, and I start down the hallway," Ryan recalls. "This thug was sitting outside Sammy's room in a chair. I get in. Both doors fling open from another room. Sammy is standing there—bare to his waist—with blue jeans on with a gun belt with two guns in it. He screams 'Draw!' at the top of his lungs. I'm standing there looking at this guy. It was so weird. The apartment was full of girls and guys and jewelry dealers. They all start laughing. I'm looking down the barrel of these two guns and I'm thinking, 'Oh, my God, I'm spending time with this maniac?' " Ryan's eyes kept ricocheting from the guys to the girls, back to Sammy. The rich boy had suddenly been thrown into a carnival of hijinks, child's play, dames, shadowy characters. He grew to love it. "Jule paid me $420 a week, what I think was then the biggest sum of money a stage manager had been paid. In those days that was stunning."

When Sammy first arrived to meet the cast, he was with his father and

Mastin. Striding in together, they looked connected, inseparable. Three cats, new to Broadway, cool and confident, with money in their pockets. "I saw this guy come in with his father and uncle and I went, 'Whoo, okay,' " says Chita Rivera.

Claude Thompson, another dancer, young and Negro, was spellbound by Sammy and his father. "There were nice moments seeing Sammy hold on to his daddy," Thompson would remember of seeing Sammy walk across the rehearsal stage to touch his father. For Thompson and others in the cast, there sometimes seemed to be two productions going on simultaneously. Many afternoons, Sammy simply did not want to stop rehearsing. "Will would say, 'Come on, son, let's go eat.' I was envious. I had never had that kind of relationship with my family," says Thompson.

The cast of *Mr. Wonderful* had simply never been around a figure like Sammy. From the beginning, he gave it his all. His energy burned. "Sammy was odd for us because we had never met anybody like him," recalls Rivera. "His talent was unlike anything we had ever seen. And his stamina. And he came from nightclubs, and we didn't know what that was about." The cast, just like director Jack Donohue, looked wide-eyed at Sammy during rehearsals. He had never given the same nightclub performance more than once. He aimed to dazzle, even in rehearsals. "There was something new every day," says Rivera.

They were younger than he was, these dancers, but he exhausted them. They'd notice something about him during rehearsals: the unselfishness. He was full of compliments. But then he'd wow them with his own skills and gifts. He didn't go to the New York High School for Performing Arts, and he didn't go to Juilliard. He went out on the road when he was a child. That was his school. And if you cornered him, he could tell you some authentic stories about Bill "Bojangles" Robinson himself. He was a star, and yet, he never forgot the joy and giddiness of marching toward stardom, reaching for it, the craving it unleashed inside of him. He understood why they looked at him the way they did.

After rehearsals, Sammy would often invite cast members to his "funky" penthouse at the Gorham. And there, they'd party, talk, laugh. He was full of questions: Where were they from? What were their families like? A company of dancers charmed him—the closeness they seemed to share. Many had families in New York City. He did too—but not really. So he envied them. "I never was up so late in my life," says Rivera. "He'd invite the kids over to the apartment, and we'd sit up till six in the morning." They hung on to his words, his conversations about books, movies, singers, Sinatra. "Sammy was Sammy," says Ryan, "this brilliant, talented nightclub performer who could do everything."

The plot of *Mr. Wonderful* was straightforward. Sammy would play Charlie Welch, a small-time singer and nightclub performer who is afraid of the big time because of an inferiority complex. He finds a mentor, played by Jack Carter, and finally is on his way. By play's end, he is huge, playing a successful nightclub performer not unlike—voilà!—Sammy Davis, Jr., himself. Jule Styne was no fool: Sammy Davis on Broadway playing a nightclub performer rising against the odds had a certain kind of autobiographical ring.

Will and Sam Sr. would play subsidiary roles in the musical. Cast members were bewildered by the two aging men. "Sam Sr.," says Ryan, "was a kind of invisible man. He thought of himself as part of the furniture." Will Mastin, of course, was different.

For the first time in his life, Will Mastin had been taken off the road. He was a man accustomed to motion. Now he was being anchored. Still, he held his dignity aloft. "Will did not think of himself as part of the furniture," remembers Ryan. "Will thought of himself as the Founding Father of the whole thing."

Mastin and Sam Sr. seemed content with their small roles. The two men were too old to express overt excitement about things. Mastin had come from another century. Giddiness was not part of his repertoire. And these were kids, reckless youth. But when told that Jack Carter would play the role of Sammy's manager in the play, Mastin arched his back. He was the damn manager of Sammy Davis! "Will insisted on a meeting with Jule Styne because he was manager of Sammy Davis," recalls Dorothy Dicker, Styne's assistant. "He couldn't put together this was a fictional play." Mastin was reassured, but would remain wary of the entire enterprise. He felt he was in a sea of double-talkers. "He was paranoid about Sammy," says Dicker. "He didn't want to lose his meal ticket."

Ryan tried to befriend Mastin. The task was huge. "There was very little you could talk to Will Mastin about," says Ryan. "The idea—particularly to a white person—of Will thinking he and you had anything in common was very slight. You felt the presence of the bitterness that he carried around."

But Chita Rivera grew to love the trio of Sammy, his father, and Mastin. Whatever it was that had kept them together on the road all these years, she herself witnessed up close. "I'm Latin. We like our family, our support system. He came with his. Surrounded by support. I loved seeing him flanked by Will and his father. Oh, it was so chic and smart."

Two old men, led by Sammy's youthful power, all in from the wicked world of nightclubs and bistros, preparing for Broadway. "It was an amazing situation, watching it unfold," Rivera says.

They'd help one another with their suit jackets. They'd whisper among themselves—conspirators against the outside world. They'd give one another stage direction. They'd direct silent nods toward one another.

Sammy's leading lady, Olga James—she possessed a kind of Lolita-like beauty—was less than a year out of Juilliard. The world of the Negro performer was small indeed. James had actually gotten to know Sammy while staying at the Sunset Colonial in Hollywood. "The next time I encountered Sammy was in New York after the film [*Carmen Jones*] had come out," James says. "Somewhere in between Sammy had lost his eye. He struck me as extremely lonely." James came by her role in *Mr. Wonderful* rather fortuitously. Her New York City roommate—the two resided at the Devon Hotel—was Cissy Rose. They had both been performing during basketball-game intermissions. One day Rose ran into Jack Carter, who mentioned that Jule Styne was looking for a leading lady for Sammy's Broadway debut. The role was coveted, and James soon wanted it badly. She had already put together a nightclub act. A friend from *Carmen Jones* had a friend who knew Jule Styne; the friend happened to be Ruth Dubonnet, the fairy princess. Dubonnet came and heard James sing, was impressed, and helped put in motion her audition. Styne also found himself charmed, and James won the part. Aside from her talent, there was something else attractive about the pairing of Olga James and Sammy Davis: she was, like Sammy, diminutive in height.

If others in the cast were constantly being bowled over by Sammy's talent, James was not. She had already seen it. "I knew of Sammy's reputation as a big nightclub star from having worked in Atlantic City." Something, however, did still her: Mastin and Sam Sr. She couldn't help but notice the dynamics of the trio. Mastin and Sam Sr. struck James as being somewhat odd characters. "Will Mastin, by this time, is an old man. Sam Sr. is younger and more approachable. Will seemed to stay in the background and watch. I don't know what he was watchful of—whether it was Sammy or his reputation." Another performer, Albert Popwell, had similar feelings: "Will Mastin was a strange individual. He hardly ever smiled."

Rehearsals went on, as did rewriting by the day. Every day, paper flying, from Dorothy Dicker to Styne, then to Sammy, then back to Weiss and the other writers, then back to Dicker, sending her back to the typewriter. The first half of the show would be about Charlie Welch/Davis, trying to rise out of meager nightclub surroundings. The second half of the play would be a rendition of the Will Mastin Trio Featuring Sammy Davis Jr. At that theatrical device, the writers grimaced. "It was presented to us," Weiss says of the second half. "We didn't like it. That was the climax of the second act. It was deemed necessary. Sammy wanted to do it."

It did not take Sammy long to begin his gift-giving. He gave dancer Popwell—whose insights frightened Sammy—a piece of jewelry, a band to wrap around the wrist. Popwell turned the band over and noticed an inscription: "From Uncle Will to Sammy." Sammy had tossed him a gift from Will that he no longer wanted. Big deal. Ha ha. Popwell, however, did not find it funny. "I went to give it back to Sammy. Sammy was always giving."

It is not uncommon that many child actors come to possess a very sharp

The Great White Way had never seen anything like Sammy when he arrived in 1956 to star in Mr. Wonderful. *He took command of the musical, ignoring the critics, and lasted a year. His father and Mastin (in fezzes behind Sammy) were befuddled by the taxing nature of a Broadway show. They were aging; their Sammy was soaring. All they could do—they were old pros—was hold on, and they did.* (COURTESY SALLY NEAL)

insight. They are able to look beyond the surface. In a way, they are forced to become little adults. Like Sammy, Albert Popwell had been a child actor on the New York stage. There were times when Popwell would look at Sammy—and then right into him, with a kind of laserlike intensity. "I remember saying to Sammy one day, 'Why have you got your mother working in a bar?' Sammy broke down and cried."

Weiss, the lyricist, was Jewish. Sammy homed in on him. The homing made Weiss nervous. He smelled fakery. "Apparently he took a liking to me," Weiss says of Sammy.

> And apparently he believed I was not exactly the dumbest guy in the world. He loved to get into discussions about deep things with me. It was to convince me he was an intellectual. There was a time during our acquaintance he was going to do a show, *In the Spotlight,* emceed by Mike Wallace. It was a half-hour show. The star would sit on a stool in the middle of

a darkened stage. A light would come on and light up the star onstage. Everything else was dark. There was a whole thing going on in the country about religious conversion. Sammy told me to watch the show. "Sure," I said. I'm sitting there watching it, saying to myself, "Why does he want me to watch this?" After a minute or two, Sammy says, "Mike, look, you can ask me anything, but respect my religious belief and don't ask me about my conversion to Judaism." And he proceeds to use the entire program talking about his conversion to Judaism. That's what he wanted me to see. He had talked to me about this brilliant rabbi.

The company headed to Philadelphia in February for their pre-Broadway try-out. Styne and Sammy settled in at the Bellevue-Stratford. Sammy was in a Brooks Brothers suit–wearing phase. Everywhere he went, he looked like an elfin Negro banker or funeral director; the thick horn-rimmed eyeglasses completed the touch.

Sammy seemed completely at ease onstage, but the Philadelphia run was rocky. One critic pronounced it "a dazzling showcase" for Sammy, but overall, the reviews were bad. The *Philadelphia Daily News* referred to the musical as "a tedious two-hour build-up for a half-hour night club act." The words had to sting the production. "True," the *Daily News* added, "the floor show finale stars Sammy Davis Jr., one of the cafe circuit's most gifted and popular young performers." At play's end Sammy does a Jolson imitation—as in his childhood, in blackface. He relished the Jolson interlude. The *Daily News* critic took notice, with a sideways compliment. "Major innovation is the Al Jolson 'tribute' on the stage ramp, which is intended to be meaningful, but is merely another portrait in Sammy's extensive gallery of impressions."

"The book was trite, it was nothing," says cast member Jack Carter of *Mr. Wonderful.*

There were missed cues, rocky arrangements, and cast members knew it. Jack Donohue might have been used to working with Shirley Temple; Sammy was another matter. Sammy was quick, he improvised, he whirred. With tensions rising, knives were drawn, culprits looked for, bodies to point fingers at. "Jule Styne didn't want me," says Carter. "He was a snob. Sammy fought for me." It was to be expected that Olga James, making her Broadway debut, might be a little nervous. "I almost got fired on the road," says James. "When you have problems on the road, one of the rules is, 'Fire the ingenue.' I gather Sammy and Jule Styne took up for me."

Sammy remained cool. Damn the critics. He had other weapons: his nightclub denizens. In Philadelphia there was the Latin Casino; across the river in New Jersey there was Bill Miller's Riviera. He rushed from stage to nightclub, a one-man publicity machine. He lunged at radio microphones, imploring listeners everywhere to come see the play. He quickly took the company over; he let it ride on his shoulders, just as he had been doing for years with his father and Will Mastin.

Will Mastin wasn't happy. In the script, there were lines that seemed to mock him. In one scene, the Jack Carter character has to say he has taught Welch (Sammy) all he knows in the world of show business. A meeting was called. Will Mastin voiced his feelings about that line, unable, as Dicker noted, to separate fact from fiction. "I don't want Carter saying that 'I taught Sammy everything he knows,' " Mastin blurted. "How do you think my friends react to that line?" Styne would have laughed, aloud, but he peered into Mastin's eyes and saw how serious the old man was, saw that Will Mastin was confusing show lines with reality, saw that Will Mastin truly seemed pained. And the vaudevillian was hardly finished. "And we want more to say in this show. We're performers." When he finished, he left the hotel suite along with Sam Sr. Everyone in the room stared at one another.

The Mastin threat, however, was not to be ignored. Will Mastin owned the Will Mastin Trio, and Sammy belonged to the Will Mastin Trio. "Unless you listen to what he says, he'll pull Sammy," a William Morris agent who sat in on the meeting whispered to Styne. Sammy felt the hurt of the two old men, but he assured Styne that everything would be fine. "Don't worry," he said, "I'll talk to them."

Styne felt a need to keep Sammy out of the possible imbroglio, so he went to see Mastin himself. "In the show," Styne began explaining to the vaudevillian, "Sammy isn't playing himself. He's playing [Charlie] Welch. So you'll have to tell your friends that we don't have Sammy Davis, Jr., onstage. We have a character. You aren't playing Will Mastin, are you?"

All his life, show producers had talked down to Will Mastin. And a lot of them were now gone, right down memory's hill, where so many show-business acts tumbled—and Will Mastin was still around. He glanced coldly at Styne.

"I bet you think I'm dumb," he finally said.

Sammy huddled with Mastin and his father, and he finally settled things. Then it was hugs all around; now as ever, the trio against the world.

In Philadelphia, Jack Carter began an affair with Chita Rivera. Sammy had had his eye on the lovely dancer. "Sammy went bananas," says Carter.

The show opened on Broadway on March 22, 1956. The reviews were tepid. The show had shortcomings—the script, principally—and the critics knew it.

"The show was looked down upon like it was a piece of garbage," admits Carter.

Try as he might, John McClain, theater critic for the *New York Journal-American*, couldn't bring himself to give *Mr. Wonderful* much of a passing grade. "The youthful Davis is by all odds one of the most versatile and stupendous singer-dancer-musician-impersonators on view anywhere in the world today," McClain wrote, "but here he's been asked to achieve the impossible." McClain seemed to be rooting for Sammy's talents, but not the show itself. "Don't get me wrong—it's a monumental hunk of showmanship, but it doesn't belong in a theatre."

Sammy felt otherwise.

Styne had worried about both Mastin and Sam Sr. on opening night. He witnessed bizarre goings-on onstage: "On exit the opening night, they'd said hello to the drummer. They didn't understand a book show, I suddenly realized. To them, this was just a different approach to their nightclub act, where it was okay to greet the lead trumpet, have a dialogue with the audience."

Jule Styne, sure enough, had landed in the world of vaudeville.

A week earlier another show had opened, and to wonderful reviews. It was based on Bernard Shaw's *Pygmalion*. *My Fair Lady* starred Julie Andrews and Rex Harrison and was quickly on its way to becoming a raging smash. Alan Jay Lerner, who did the books and lyrics, would remark of the success of *My Fair Lady*: "The time was ripe for something gay and theatrical, something that was not two lonely people finding each other in a dark alley."

So it was Sammy against Rex Harrison.

Following the breezy first act of *Mr. Wonderful*—the eye-catching costumes looked like a cross between Indian sheikh and African royalty—it rocketed forth in its second act, with Sammy taking over and turning the production into the outlines of a one-man show. It was a thrilling spectacle. "Sammy," recalls Olga James, "could generate more electricity and hold an audience in a way I had never seen before."

Sammy constantly improvised, ad-libbed. He was giving his all, and all different versions of himself. "He was unbelievable," says Dicker. "I went to the theater almost every night. He would do different things every night. It was an undisciplined type of play, but he was magnificent in it."

Pat Marshall, the dancer, found Sammy's newness to Broadway charming. "Sammy had never been in the theater before. We were standing in the wings—this is sweet—and Sammy was so excited. He said to me, 'Look at them, it's "RSO." ' What he meant was 'SRO'—Standing Room Only. He was cute."

Word spread about *Mr. Wonderful*. Not about its being spectacular, or particularly riveting—word spread about Sammy. And the stars started to come.

"It was a very showbiz crowd," says dancer Thompson. "And blacks came. We were the only black Broadway show at that time. *South Pacific* had had one or two blacks, but that had closed. *Bells Are Ringing* had closed. This show had 75 percent blacks." (Actually, it was closer to 50 percent—but this was still revolutionary for Broadway.)

The crowds would line the hallway leading to his dressing room. "It was the first time I met Quincy Jones, Sidney Poitier," remembers Olga James. "You'd come backstage and there was Kim Novak. She really was glorious-looking."

Carl Green and Dean Green, young Negroes in Harlem—he would soon be playing basketball with the Harlem Globetrotters, she would become involved in Sammy's fund-raising for charities—couldn't help but notice the excitement Sammy was bringing to untraditional Broadway audiences. "It was great," Dean says. "I wasn't that sophisticated about theater then." She spotted many other Negroes milling about in the theater lobby and got the impression they, like her, were newcomers: "The reason they were there was because of Sammy Davis." She'd go backstage, and there stood Sammy, in a terry cloth robe, fans mobbing him, women slipping him notes, gifts. "He was so graceful, so wonderful."

Jack Carter and Sammy formed a fascinating bond. For Sammy, Carter served as a means to an end. "Wherever he was appearing he would have parties," Carter says of Sammy. "People would come to him. He wouldn't go out. He was afraid of rejection. Like the Stork Club. I would 'beard' for him and get him in." Sammy seemed to be clawing so ferociously that Carter began to form other opinions. He felt both an odd kind of pain and sensation percolating inside Sammy. "He always wanted to be white and Jewish. He was like a little Jewish kid. His speech, demeanor, everything was New York. He didn't do 'black' comedy like Buck and Bubbles."

Onstage, Carter and Sammy dueled, each measuring the laughter the other elicited from the audience. They competed, nightly. "We were strange fruit," says Carter. "We were outlaws." Carter, playing the Davis character's manager, would show the kid steps, moves, how to perform. Sammy, as Charlie Welch, would watch, listen, then do a number that would absolutely bowl Carter over. Inside the play, the revelation was simple: the ghost was catching up to the Jack Carter character. At times Carter and Sammy would become Jack Benny and Rochester, Benny's valet. The audience kept howling. The two would do Amos 'n' Andy, adopting southern drawls. The audience would keep howling. It was all so theatrical, so spontaneous, so gay. Will and Sam Sr., in the background, were shooting the cuffs, dressed in their costumes that made them look like Arabian sheikhs slumming as butlers.

One night Sammy broke free and did a rendition of Cyrano de Bergerac, the accent, just like that, going from southern-tinged Amos 'n' Andy to French de

Bergerac. Another night, he turned to Carter onstage and said, "Lightly, I toy my hat around, lightly they dwell onstage. Jack, I'm going to show you dramatics!" When stumped by a Sammy ad-lib, Carter would turn to the audience and say, in a drawn-out southern drawl of his Amos 'n' Andy voice, "Holy mackerel, what am I going to do now?" Night after night, the audiences felt these word duets between Sammy and Carter a hoot. "That is what kept the show going," Carter says. (Some of the Negroes in the cast were beginning to think Carter did the Amos 'n' Andy routine with a little too much gusto, and that Sammy accepted it with a little too much glee.) The show was just like vaudeville—no, it was better than vaudeville. Better because the money was better, the working conditions were better, the hotel was nicer.

Another night Sammy's glass eye fell out. He did a quick pratfall to retrieve it. "When he hit the ground, Will went crazy," remembers Carter of Mastin's screaming outburst afterward backstage.

And yet, on another night, the Carter character said "Bow!" to Sammy.

"I will not!" Sammy shot back.

Cast members detected an edge in Sammy's voice, as if he felt something demeaning had crept into Carter's tone.

There was something else profoundly amusing about *Mr. Wonderful.* During the second half of the show—the nightclub act truly come to life—known actors and actresses would walk up onstage and take a seat, part of the party at the nightclub. It became a show within a show. Yes, that was Rex Harrison up there. "People," recalls Jack Carter, "would say, 'Jesus, that looks like Rex Harrison and Julie Andrews onstage.'"

"I walked on the stage in the middle of his number, and the fucking theater came down," says Jerry Lewis.

The theatrical device kept astonishing audience members. "Everybody knew to come sit on the stage at ten-thirty, and Sammy would come out and do his nightclub act," says Ryan, the stage manager. "There was nothing else like it before or since."

Sammy would pause in the middle of the performance and give out baseball scores, or discuss the Democratic convention taking place. "They don't do this for you in *My Fair Lady,*" he rightfully quipped.

Never mind that critics blasted the show, Sammy kept them coming back, his sheer force boomeranging their knives. "It was a hodgepodge," confesses Jerry Lewis of the show. "But nobody could say anything negative about Sammy."

Columnist Walter Winchell—his own TV program, *The Walter Winchell Show,* had just recently premiered; Sammy had been one of his earliest guests—arrived one night to see the play. Winchell, so powerful as a columnist that when he mentioned a chorus girl's name in his column she had a good chance at seeing her salary rise—was a magnet for stunts. When he arrived to see *Mr. Wonderful,* he had a group of newsboys with him, and they drew stares when they paraded down the aisle to their seats. It hardly mattered to Sammy that Winchell remained on the outs with many Negroes owing to his imbroglio regarding Josephine Baker, the Negro chanteuse. Baker had been refused service inside the Stork Club back in 1951 and left in a huff. Winchell was inside the club and did nothing, though later he said he saw none of it and refused to assail Sherman Billingsley, the club's owner. The tempest boiled over nationwide: Winchell was attacked by the NAACP; Sugar Ray Robinson, a Winchell friend, expressed his anguish; TV host Ed Sullivan went to war with Winchell. Winchell had the heart and pen of the proletariat, true enough, but he was a gossip, and he was thin-skinned. When liberals attacked him over the Baker issue, he erupted into bouts of megalomania, using McCarthy-like tactics to smear the NAACP, other journalists, and many liberals. The backlash against Winchell was fierce, so much so that Winchell believed if he went sashaying through Harlem, his "blood would flow in the streets." But that was 1951, this was 1956. To Sammy, Walter Winchell was not a man on the outs with American Negroes, but a big-time, wide-eyed Broadway columnist who just might help him get fans into the seats to see his play.

Midway through the performance he attended, Winchell rose and strode right down the middle of the aisle with the newsboys trailing him. He climbed up on the stage and gave a rip-roaring speech about patriotism, about America and how wonderful she was, about Sammy and how great a performer he happened to be—and on and on and on. It was Winchell; it was theater; it was Sammy; it was *Mr. Wonderful.* (Winchell's TV show, alas, survived only a few months. On TV, wearing his fedora, smoking cigarettes, talking in a loud carnival-like voice, he looked strange, like an overwrought G-man on some kind of speed-me-up drug.)

There were times when Jule Styne sat in the theater with a puzzled look on his face, as if even he were not quite sure of what he had created. "My uncle was a fabulous man," says Buddy Bregman of Styne. Bregman—who had met Sammy earlier on the West Coast—liked hanging around the theater during the *Mr. Wonderful* run. "Jule would go get the shoeshine man right outside the theater and ask about the show. Jule would say to him, 'What do you think?' Jule would talk to people at Lindy's. He'd get little snippets from people." Even well into the show Styne was apt to adopt more changes. One week he announced some new changes, told Sammy they should rehearse them immediately. "They decide to try them at Wednesday's matinee when all the bar mitzvah ladies were there," Bregman remembers. "Jule is at the back of the theater. Halfway through the first act he realizes this is so fucking awful and says, 'What have I done?' The curtain goes down on the first act. Sammy goes offstage and grabs a cigarette. Jule's screaming, 'It's horrible!' Sammy says, 'God-dammit, motherfucker, we're going to finish it.' "

Mr. Wonderful would surely have closed with a leading man of lesser talents than Sammy's. He had not let the Will Mastin Trio fold, and he would not let *Mr. Wonderful* fold. There were lines at the ticket booth during the day, at the stage door seeking autographs at night.

"Sammy and Jule said, 'Screw the critics,' " recalls Amy Greene. "Sammy began to do local TV. He brought people into the theater. It was packed every night. He literally saved the show." Greene saw the effect the show had on Sammy. "It was like a child let loose in a candy factory. He was carousing all night long. He was young, talented, a rich celebrity. He had any woman he wanted."

John Barry Ryan had seen many a Broadway production, but nothing like this. "His success in what he was doing was so without parallel," he says of Sammy. "A young man who survived black nightclubs and a ghastly auto accident, and then Broadway—how much did it matter that the reviews were terrible? I don't think very much."

Cast members were awed and beguiled. "I was a little snot sitting there watching a nightclub performer in a Broadway show," says Rivera. "I thought the theater was being ruined. But I learned some things: genius is genius."

The show became so popular that Jule Styne went back to Skinny D'Amato and asked to have Sammy longer. It was all such fun; Sammy was sending hundreds into the nightclubs because he mentioned the names of friendly nightclubs in all the gossip columns he made it into. "You can have Sammy 365 days," D'Amato offered. "But on the 365th day he opens at the Chez Paree in Chicago."

Need anything?

Sammy couldn't stop himself from moving. He burned like weeds around the entire company.

Once the evening was over, it was out the stage door, signing the autographs, getting to the car, tugging at Jack Carter. "We'd go to Atlantic City on weekends," recalls Carter. "We'd drive and be there at midnight. We'd party until seven in the morning."

There were times during the show's run when he'd do "breakfast shows" at nightclubs over in New Jersey, an early-morning show for nightclubbers still awake—starting to repay some of Skinny's debts at the 500 Club. He'd take the whole cast on excursions. With no notice, Sammy was apt to announce to the kids in the show he was taking them out—they must hurry hurry hurry and get ready—to the Copa. And there he was, dressed in a beautiful suit, leading them, turning heads, talking, the voice fine and modulated, talking up his musical, slapping Jule Styne on the back, his strides faster than a kid scooting into Yankee Stadium, then finally, there, at the appointed destination, his head moving like a bird's, quick, in dartlike fashion, the one eye assessing the environs. Then pulling out chairs, ordering drinks, and more drinks. "People would do things like move tables ringside for his party," remembers Olga James. "It was exciting to have ringside seats."

Josephine Premice, a Haitian-born New York dancer, would see Sammy around the Manhattan nightclubs at the time. "He loved sitting with a table full of beautiful women," Premice would remember. Sammy seemed to adore Premice's French accent, which would make him erupt into his very own, quite skilled, British accent. He was, of course, doing what he had a peculiar gift of doing: sizing people up, claiming those he wanted to claim, engaging in mimicry. "Sammy," says Jack Carter, "collected actors and actresses. He loved them."

Yes, he loved them. And they loved him, because celebrity and fame are things to love. At least until they break your heart.

Dicker would stand watching as the play neared its end, with Sammy at the microphone singing "Birth of the Blues." Women swooned. Dicker had a twin sister—Charlotte—and she was often present at the theater as well. At times both of them—unmarried—would stand ogling Sammy, a habit not unnoticed by other cast members. "I don't know if it was sexual," Dorothy Dicker herself says of Sammy's attractiveness to women, "or if he was just so damn talented." The Dicker twins were also identically disheveled. They looked like down-on-their-luck beatniks. "They never took care of themselves," says Buddy Bregman, Styne's nephew. "Sammy paid attention to them purely out of kindness."

Not everyone fell under the Sammy spell. Dancer Sally Neal—who had studied at the esteemed High School for Performing Arts—would often find herself wondering about Sammy's conscience. "We did this number in *Mr. Wonderful* called 'Miami,' and I put my hands on the white guy's shoulder. Afterward, Sammy called a meeting, right on the stage, and said, 'We live in discriminatory times, and white and Negro can't be holding hands.' But I thought this was Sammy's way of just disciplining me because I wasn't with his group of people. Sammy was a weird kind of person. If he couldn't have you, he didn't want no one else to have you."

Sammy indeed believed love was for sale, backstage, coast to coast, everywhere. And: "He was blonde-infatuated," Jack Carter says.

True, but he made exceptions.

Chita Rivera was brunette. And Sammy loved her and just knew she loved him, so he bought her a diamond ring. He'd marry her, just as he had thought of marrying Eartha Kitt, and just as he had thought of marrying Peggy King.

He was free to dream, and the brighter the diamond, the higher the dream. About marriage: "Sure we talked about it," says Rivera, a beauty who sported a bobbed hairdo. She was in love too. "Everything about him was so much bigger than the fact that he had only one eye, that he was five foot four. He was so big you got swept away by him."

Chita and others in the cast were curiously beguiled by the Sammy–Will Mastin relationship. Mastin seemed to see beyond the glitter and gossip-column notices, seeing not forward but backward, into the past. "I think Will's presence for Sammy was both hugely difficult," says stage manager Ryan, "and yet a constant reminder to Sammy that he came from a world which Will had always struggled with and driven himself through and held this act together despite discrimination, wars, segregation, and God knows what."

Whereas Mastin and Sam Sr. were always at the theater early, it wasn't always so for the star. One late Sammy arrival stands out. "This kid—the second assistant stage manager—was checking people in at the stage door," recalls Ryan.

> The kid, looking at Sammy, said, "Where have you been, little black Sambo?" If Sammy had had one of his guns on, he'd have shot him. Sammy started chasing this kid. He starts chasing this kid down Broadway. Eventually, Sammy comes back to the theater. About fifteen minutes later, this kid drags his ass to the theater. I said, "You better stay out of sight until I tell you it's all right." Five minutes later, I was standing at the desk. Will is in a knotted stocking cap, bathrobe, dress pants. And he got in front of me. He spoke in a voice that would have shattered glass. He said, "There'll be no show today!" I said, "What's the matter?" He said, "There'll be no show unless that white boy apologizes to Sammy in front of the whole cast!" It had pushed a button in Will. Every scrap of rage and bitterness he had was standing in front of me. This was a man who had spent his life being manhandled by the white nightclub world. Up until that moment, it had just been small stuff: Will had said Sammy's dressing room was not big enough. But this was something we were not going to get out of by making small talk. Before the curtain went up, the kid came up and apologized in front of the whole cast.

To Ryan, it represented a painful and yet tender moment. "This was Will saying, 'I'm in charge here.'"

. . .

Steve Blauner, who would become singer Bobby Darin's manager, was in the military, on a base near Buffalo, and constantly dreamed of how he could meet Sammy Davis, Jr. In his room—he lived in the Officers Club—were pictures and clippings from *Mr. Wonderful*. Blauner admired and studied the lost world of vaudeville. He kept a scrapbook on Al Jolson. Blauner himself did some performing, small things, children's hospitals. They were comedy routines. Sometimes Blauner—white, tall, and hulking—brazenly did his act in blackface. "I didn't know better." By the time 1956 rolled around, he was deeply under the spell of Sammy. On a three-day weekend pass, he traveled to New York City and got a ticket to see *Mr. Wonderful*. But first he went to take in a show at the Copa. At the Copa, seated at a table—Blauner can't believe it—is Sammy Davis, Jr., himself. He couldn't just keep still. "I walk across the lounge, and say, 'Mr. Davis, the way you feel about Frank Sinatra is the way I feel about you.' He stands up for twenty minutes. He says to me, 'I got a table, second show, every night of the engagement. What night do you want to be my guest?' " (Sammy was referring to Sinatra's upcoming Copa engagement.) Like Frank, Sammy giveth. Sammy gave Blauner his secretary's phone number and told him to call her. He said the next time he was in New York City they'd hang out together. But of course he must have said that to everyone, Blauner thought. It was such bullshit. Such wonderful, magical, amazing, unbelievable, thrilling bullshit. Nevertheless, Blauner was game enough to call the secretary weeks later. A meeting was set up. "I'm supposed to meet Sammy in front of the stage door," he recalls of his arrival back into New York City. "I say to myself, 'He's not going to remember me.' And here comes Sammy walking down the alleyway wearing a Chesterfield coat above the knees, and he must have been carrying six cameras. He says, 'Come on, Steve,' like he's been knowing me."

Then Sammy turned to Blauner and asked him if he'd seen *Mr. Wonderful* yet. "Six times," the starstruck Blauner answered.

Sammy introduced Blauner to the cast. Then he got dressed as Charlie Welch—he wore a sequined vest and tight black pants and looked like a matador—did the show, and quickly ushered Blauner into the waiting limo. They were returning to the Copa! To see Sinatra himself! Blauner couldn't believe it. Hazel Scott, the glamorous pianist, was seated at Sammy's table, along with Billy Rowe, one of Sammy's press agents, and a dancer from the chorus of *My Fair Lady* who happened to be one of the few Negroes (she was light-skinned) appearing on Broadway other than those in Sammy's show. "In the Copa I'm looking around," says Blauner. "It seemed every white woman in the club wanted to fuck Sammy. Onstage Sammy was ten feet tall." After the show, Blauner, summoning the nerve, asked Sinatra for an autograph. It was always tricky with Frank—depending on the moon, the stars, how his last drink went down, his attitude. "He signed it, which was a lot of class."

Sammy grew up listening to cowboy Tom Mix's radio shows in the 1930s, and he loved twirling six-shooters. After the loss of his eye in the 1954 automobile crash, Sammy deemed his return to quick-drawing the ultimate proof to himself that he was back to form. Here he demonstrates for the son of eye surgeon Fred Hull at his San Bernardino home.

(COURTESY FRED HULL)

Everyone got dropped off. There was just Sammy and Blauner in the limo. Sammy directed the driver to the Colony Records store, then he vanished inside. He reappeared with stacks of albums under both arms. He gave Blauner one of the stacks, the one with all the Sinatra albums. The tender Sinatra album—*In the Wee Small Hours*—quickly caught Blauner's eye. And with that, Sammy had Blauner, another recruit to the Sammy cause, the Sammy train.

Blauner would return to New York City in the weeks ahead and go straight to the Gorham. He was *in* now, with Sammy and his gang. "We'd play nickel-and-dime poker. There were always people around Sammy. A lot of his generosity had to do with trying to buy love. I never smoked a cigarette in my life. He gave me a solid gold cigarette case from Dunhill."

Jule Styne was an ardent Democrat, like his friend Sinatra. It was Styne who introduced Sammy to Jacqueline Kennedy and Senator Jack Kennedy at a Manhattan party. Sammy couldn't resist: if the Democratic Party was good enough for Jule and Frank, then it was good enough for Sammy.

Adlai Stevenson was running for president against Eisenhower, who had beaten him in 1952. Stevenson was a poetic man, but poetry did not win national elections. Hard knuckles did, and many believed Stevenson lacked them. Phoebe Jacobs, once the secretary to Sy Oliver, the celebrated music arranger, was working in New York City for Columbia Records when *Mr. Wonderful* was playing on Broadway. She joined the Stevenson campaign as a volunteer in New York City. At Columbia Records she worked directly for Mitch Miller. "Mitch told me Sammy was an Adlai Stevenson fan," she recalls. Jacobs had secured use of a mansion for a Stevenson fund-raiser, and she felt Sammy would be a terrific draw if she could snare him. She went to the theater, once, then again, leaving notes for Sammy, information about the event, where it would be held, all the particulars. But no response. She went back three times. Finally, someone called: "Sammy's coming. He'll bring a couple of people." And there he was, walking into the mansion, with a busload of friends and *Mr. Wonderful* cast mates, moving like smoke, drifting here and there. "Everybody was so thrilled. This man chartered a bus and brought the entire company up and made them do a number. Sammy stayed until two or three in the morning, signing autographs, posing for pictures."

Stevenson lost the presidential race in 1956, just as he had in 1952. He took the defeat coolly and went away as quietly as someone stepping back behind a curtain.

There were other events besides presidential politics that found their way into the newspapers.

Down in Alabama, the segregated city bus system—by virtue of a Supreme Court ruling—had come to an end. Before year's end, Martin Luther King, Jr. climbed aboard a city bus near his Montgomery home.

"I believe you are Reverend King," the bus driver said.

"Yes, I am," King replied.

Nine innocuous words exchanged between them. And yet, something gigantic seemed about to roll in Montgomery other than those buses.

Stevenson may have lost, but King rolled. And on Broadway, Sammy kept rolling too. A Negro was drawing the theatergoers to their seats. The show—even if Sammy had bastardized a Broadway musical—seemed to liberate, at least a bit, the thinking of Broadway producers. The reality had to be acknowledged that a Negro could carry a Broadway musical. Lena Horne was being wooed for a show for the upcoming Broadway season. (*Jamaica* would bow in 1957.)

It was a good time—and a good year—for Sam Sr. He was on Broadway with his boy—and he was deeply in love with Rita, who had also brought three children along with her in a rather discreet bit of adoption.

Rita had a dear friend, Eleanor Carter, who did domestic work, scrubbed floors, whatever she had to do to care for her three small children. Rita fretted about the children, the long hours their mother was away from home. When she worried, Sam Sr. worried. Eleanor Carter wound up in Harlem Hospital. "My mother got sick. I wound up in the ambulance," recalls her son Pierre. The illness was serious. And it was painfully clear to everyone at the hospital that Eleanor would no longer be able to care for her kids. At the hospital, Pierre looked up, and there was Sam Sr. standing next to him.

"You're going with me," the older man said. "I said, 'I can't leave my sisters.' " So Pierre found himself in the blue Cadillac, which soon parked outside the apartment building where he lived with his sisters. Sam Sr. told him to go get the two girls.

Pierre and his sisters moved into a large apartment in the Gorham. Upstairs was Sammy's suite. The echo of children seemed to delight Sam Sr. "I been hungry," he once explained to young Pierre. "I won't have a kid around me who's hungry. If a kid wants a cup of milk, I'll get him a cow." The children felt like they were in a fairy tale. "I'm a boy from 145th Street. Now I'm riding around in limousines going to Danny's Hideaway for breakfast," remembers Pierre. "That Christmas I must have had gifts from half the people on Broadway."

That Sam Sr. suddenly had a new family with children seemed not to draw much attention from the *Mr. Wonderful* cast. "That was an era when you didn't ask questions," says Chita Rivera. "My ears would be open, but one doesn't ask questions."

Cast members began noticing a change with Sammy Jr. as the *Mr. Wonderful* run lengthened. There were sparks of rebelliousness, something they hadn't seen before. The rebellion that was directed at his father seemed to be typical father-son squabbling. But with Will, the arguments were deeper, raw man-to-man confrontations. "The world was changing, and Sammy was changing," says James, the leading lady. "At one point during the production, Will and Sammy had a big argument that you could hear all over the theater. Will said, 'Boy, do you know who I am!' Sammy stormed out, hollering for Chita."

Chita loved him still. And Chita was still so beautiful. She was more beautiful than Eartha. Or was Eartha more beautiful than Chita? Eartha was pre-crash, so he had seen her beauty with both eyes. He had seen Chita's beauty with one eye, but the one eye was now sharper than two eyes, just as the doctors had told him. Marriage to Chita? The idea had sounded so warm and sweet and tender in those midnight conversations, as they saw the moon rise over the East River. But none of it could hold a candle to the long leg of fame. And in his pursuit of fame, Sammy was as relentless as a barracuda. He let Chita keep the ring. It angered Sam Sr.

The year-long Broadway run had imbued Sammy with newfound powers, and with a streak of independence. The midnight nightclub shows he escaped to do gave him the chance to practice solo performing. In a way, *Mr. Wonderful* was the beginning of the end of the Will Mastin Trio. The night-after-night grind wore upon them, though more so on the elder Davis than on Mastin. Sam Sr. had started whispering to his son that he was going to quit. There was a woman in his life now. Sammy seemed torn. His father had the knack of catching things people said to the trio that Sammy didn't catch: little inflections, body movements, letting Sammy know who meant them well, who did not. Sammy would feel lost without him, and he knew it, but he would not debate his father about staying if he wanted to give up his tap shoes. However, the wording of the playbill attested to Mastin's continued power:

Mr. Wonderful
A New Musical Comedy
with
The Will Mastin Trio
starring
Sammy Davis Jr.

But Mastin, with the cane of a dead man ("Bojangles" Robinson died in 1949), seemed to believe he would live forever. He would hear no talk of his quitting the act. The warm and deep truth was that they were not rolling any more Will Mastins off the assembly line. He was not just of another time; he was of another world.

While in New York City just before the end of 1956, Sammy made his way over to the Friars Club. The club consisted of an avuncular group of popular comics, singers, and stars, and had been formed by George M. Cohan and William Collier. Sammy was given a pair of gold cuff links, presented to him by the legendary comic Joe E. Lewis. It meant that Sammy was now "in"; he was a Friar. Sinatra was a Friar, so was Dean Martin. Eddie Cantor was a Friar. And of course Mr. Television, Milton Berle, was a Friar. Sammy was one of them now; he had another tentacle of a family to claim. He must take not only their kindnesses, but their jokes. He must accept that the color of his skin was now open for laughter and hilarity.

Maybe he got in because of Sinatra, who pulled some behind-the-scenes strings. Maybe he got in because he nearly died on that roadway. Maybe he got in because of all of his combined gifts or his newfound religion. Bill "Bojangles" Robinson had performed for the Friars Club members years earlier, but he wasn't invited to join. Sammy, in 1956, was the first Negro to be inducted into the Friars. Sam Sr. and Will were there, grinning like two fathers.

To be a Friar. To be a Jew. To be loved by Chita. To be loved by Skinny. Ha ha ha. So much love.

By the time Sammy left New York City at the end of the *Mr. Wonderful* run, it was obvious that he had started to control the destiny of the Will Mastin Trio—if not the purse strings. The trio went out on the road with the Ted Firito tour. Sammy had hired George Rhodes as their new bandleader. Rhodes hailed from Indiana and had made his name as musical director for Joyce Bryant, a torch singer notable for both her voice and an ever-prominent blond wig on her head. Rhodes—who was married at the time—brought along an assistant. Her name was Shirley Vest, and Rhodes found himself falling in love with her. Shirley's father, a Negro booking agent, had known plenty of show people in the Midwest. He anchored his business from Detroit. As a little girl in the mid-1930s, running around Detroit's Norwood Hotel, one of the city's Negro hotels, Shirley would often play with one of the guests traveling with his father—little Sammy Davis, Jr.

Shirley, who soon became Shirley Rhodes, rose in the ranks from assistant to road manager. Sammy trusted her. Like him, she was young. And she was very businesslike, formal and intimidating. Out on the road, she enjoyed herself and never looked back to Detroit, or Mansfield, Ohio, where she had graduated from high school. "I left Mansfield as quick as I could," she would recall. "I told my mother the day I graduated, 'This diploma is yours, and I'm out of here.' "

She was quite charmed at Sammy's infatuation with his father. "He idolized his father. He was clean, dapper, knew how to act. His father took him when his mother didn't want him." She'd sit talking to Sammy. His life seemed to enthrall her. "He regretted he never went to school. He never played baseball. His father didn't want him to get hurt." She wanted to tell him that she had done those things, and yet, she was happier out on the road; but she did not, because she detected so much unhealed sadness about his childhood.

On the bus, other members of the troupe would snicker at Will Mastin, sitting alone, staring out the window. They'd stop in towns and wonder if Mastin had enough energy to get off the bus and get back on. It was the wheezing, the coughing, the slow walk, the way he'd touch his stomach—the ulcers. Sam Sr. had hoped he'd choose to retire to the West Coast. But there he was, climbing back onto the bus. Then another town and another theater, still polishing his shoes, brushing lint from his tux. The old man did not have a clue why the kids looked at him so strangely. "It was the joke of the road that Will came on the road with us still, and laid all his makeup out in the dressing room," says

Shirley. In show business, she had found most performers gregarious, quite available to the all-night gabfests. She had never met a man more private than Mastin. "In all the years I knew Will Mastin—from the time I was a little girl— I never saw him with a woman," she would recall. "Whatever he did, he did behind closed doors."

He was an old man with suit bags and an encyclopedia's worth of memories. Yes, it was tender and even sweet if you were prone to gentle adjectives in describing Will Mastin. But the kids on the bus with him were not so reflective. They were kids, they lived for the moment, there were not enough hours in the day to be reflective. They were chasing and living their own dreams, catching what glitter they could from Sammy's big-time dreaming—catching a glimpse of Sinatra here, of Ava Gardner over there, of Jerry Lewis backstage. Will had only himself to lean on now. He was deaf to the guffaws coming from behind closed doors. He heard what he had always heard: the footsteps of theatergoers; the sweet little drumbeat signaling the arrival of his Sammy, which had always put him at ease, delivering him from the fear that whirred inside his mind about what catastrophe might befall Sammy, which hustlers might try to steal him in the night while his eyes were closed to the world. And applause— he certainly heard the applause. He also saw what he had always seen: the smiling and excited faces, the sparkle of jewelry out there in the darkness.

Even when Sam Sr. couldn't go on—his own nagging ailments trailed him town to town—Will Mastin didn't let it stop him. There he was on some nights, tap-dancing behind Sammy, onstage, shooting the cuffs, absent a sickly Sam Sr.—a trio performing as a duo. It looked strange—so strange that to deliver his son from the embarrassment of it, Sam Sr. told Shirley and others he was going to fake a heart attack backstage. The only words Will Mastin had for Sam Sr. in the aftermath of the faked heart attack was that he should take better care of himself.

Will Mastin was still touching members of the company on the shoulder, directing them to follow him to the bathroom. There, in secrecy, he would pull out wads of cash—the payroll. Will Mastin paid off in the toilet. Sammy used to joke about it—but always out of Mastin's earshot.

Shirley and George, who had gotten married ten months after joining Sammy, intended to devote themselves to each other and to Sammy. They would stay on the road with him. Sammy seemed to be putting together another family, one distinctly different from his father and Will Mastin. Even if his father and Mastin did not always seem to, Sammy himself paid particular attention to the march of time. "He was torn between those two guys," Tony Curtis says. "He saw he was headed to another level. Will took offense to that, being made to feel he was just a part of the act. The daddy was willing to do whatever the son wanted."

The jokes about the two aging hoofers stung. There was one little joke going about that if folks knew how old Will Mastin really was, why, they'd come out not to see Sammy—but the seventy-eight-year-old man onstage, hoofing! Will Mastin wanted to hold on. Keep the cane in hand; the ghost at bay. Sammy wanted to fly solo, and the prospect excited him even as it frightened him. "He said to me one night," recalls singer Keely Smith, "that he couldn't wait until the day came when he could walk out onstage by himself."

Annie Stevens—wife of conductor Morty Stevens—knew Sammy felt perplexed. The world was cold, and the two men were his family. "Emotionally," she says, "it was eating at Sammy, but he knew he had to be out on his own."

On January 14, 1957, Humphrey Bogart died at his home in Los Angeles. His last screen appearance was a year earlier, in *The Harder They Fall*, a Budd Schulberg–written boxing drama in which he played a cynical press agent. For more than two decades, he had been—along with James Cagney—the signature tough guy in American film. The death was from lung cancer; he was fifty-eight. During his last days alive he still smoked; the shots of morphine stayed some of the pain. The last movie he saw on television was *Anchors Aweigh*, which had starred his friend Frank Sinatra; the lyrics for *Anchors*, a musical, were written by *Mr. Wonderful*'s Jule Styne. (Another signature of the gifted Styne was generosity toward other lyricists—thus he had eschewed writing duties on *Mr. Wonderful* in favor of giving the opportunity to Jerry Bock, Larry Holofcener, and George Weiss.) Bogart's passing not only took away a riveting screen persona, it also stopped the evening get-togethers he had long held at his home in the Holmby Hills section of Los Angeles. Among those who gathered were Judy Garland, Lauren Bacall (Bogart's wife), Sinatra, musician Jimmy Van Heusen (if many believed Sammy patterned himself after Sinatra, there were those who felt Sinatra patterned himself after Van Heusen), Irving "Swifty" Lazar. Once, when they were all gathered together in Las Vegas to see a Noël Coward show, all sleeping off the aftereffects of a night on the town, Bacall told them they all looked like "a rat pack." The Bogart cohorts had a simple goal: "the relief of boredom and the perpetuation of independence. We admire ourselves and don't care for anyone else." The only Negro who got to peek at the group's goings-on was the occasional maid or butler.

Bogart had always liked Sammy. It was a tough and tender kind of admiration. A visit backstage at Ciro's in '54; an invitation up to his home, where there was talk about show business; yet another invitation to a holiday party. He could see Sammy coming on. Humphrey Bogart was not an emotional man, but he had always been known for his candor, his nasal-soaked words delivered quick, as if they had been lined up so his tongue could knock them down like miniature bowling balls. Bogart had always whispered—aloud, even in the face of Will Mastin himself—that the kid should go solo.

The tough-guy movie gangster would not live to see the solo flight of Sammy—nor Sammy's being welcomed into a quicker, sleeker version of the rat pack Bogie himself had stirred into being.

Christmas week of 1957 found Sammy back at the Sands in Las Vegas. "Sammy Davis Jr. uncorks another supercharged show in his latest Copa room appearance, this time reshuffling his repertoire considerably since the last time around," *Variety* noted in its review. But deeper in the write-up there were hints of the fragility of Sammy's partners, his father and Will Mastin: "Davis Sr. is still out of the act because of illness, but Will Mastin is on hand with his consistently fine softshoe routines."

In Chicago eight weeks later, critics picked up on a report in the *Chicago Tribune* that Sammy was about to permanently go solo. A rift ensued; Sammy accused the press of misquoting him. The press was hungry for a story, and the possible breakup of the Will Mastin Trio was news, even if gossip rather than fact. Sammy called a press conference. To the sharp ear, there was ambivalence in his denials. He "definitely" intended to work as a solo act in the future, he told the press—"but it won't be the result of any [family] rift."

Imagine: a friend in every city. In Cleveland her name was Betty Isard. They met in 1959. She was lovely and, of course, blond.

> He was playing—we had a theater in the round in Cleveland—and the owners were friends of mine. Every night Sammy wanted me to go where they all went [after the show]. He loved this one restuarant—Corky & Lenny's. He loved Jewish food. We'd go there. He would come to my house in Shaker Heights. My husband had a Ford agency. We gave Sammy a little Thunderbird to drive around in. He'd come to my house and bring his play guns. He would practice drawing. Frank Sinatra gave him a silver goblet. He wouldn't drink out of anything else. He loved to play, and he loved to go to movies. I'd go to the movies with him in the afternoon. He loved Louis Armstrong's *The Five Pennies*. We went to see it twice.

The movie merely featured Armstrong. Its star was actually Danny Kaye. It was a biopic about jazz trumpeter Red Nichols. The critics thought it too sentimental. Sammy must have made mental notes: In 1966 he would make his own jazz-themed movie. *A Man Called Adam,* and would cast Armstrong in a featured role.

Isard would stare at the Jewish star Sammy wore on his chest. She wondered what prompted his conversion. "He said, 'I need all the help I can get.' He said he liked Jewish people because they helped him the most. He said he wouldn't be where he was if it weren't for Jewish people."

She fell for him and didn't know why. She did not think he was particularly handsome. "One night we went to a big nightclub. We were at a long table. He turned around and grabbed me and pulled me into the kitchen. He said, 'I would love to give you a kiss like you never had.' Then he said, 'Forget it,' and went back to the table."

He was Sammy, which meant he was soon gone. "I was so unhappy when he left," she remembers.

Chapter 9

A HITCHCOCKIAN AFFAIR

With his wading deeper and deeper into the consciousness of America, Martin Luther King, Jr., began to attract celebrities and stars to his cause. With celebrities came media attention. On May 17, 1957, King starred at a "prayer pilgrimage" in the shadow of the Lincoln Memorial. More than twenty thousand showed. Among them were young actors Ruby Dee, Harry Belafonte, Sidney Poitier—and Sammy Davis, Jr. Sammy—as always—was going places where Mastin and his father lacked the desire to go. Belafonte had formed an almost brotherly bond with King. "I became very central to this theme pointing directly into the heart of black culture," says Belafonte. "I began to debate folk, hit on folk. I tried to assuage their fears and place their fears in the agenda of dignity." Of the Negro stars at the pilgrimage, both King and Belafonte realized that the one who had the easiest rapport with whites was Sammy. It was the cachet of his powerful and intoxicating nightclub act, his success on Broadway. In his pursuit of equality for the Negro, the young minister decided Sammy could definitely help. Belafonte knew as much: "Sammy could sing, and dance, and do one-liners. He was the torch."

In time—on those occasions when his Southern Christian Leadership Conference needed a quick infusion of cash, needed someone with star power to appear at a fund-raiser—King would often turn to Belafonte and utter just two words: "Get Sammy."

That Sammy had an affinity for white women was hardly of concern to King. King himself—as the FBI duly noted—partook of the same pleasurable pursuits.

The Morris agency had a revolving door of agents assigned to Sammy. The latest was Sy Marsh. It took Marsh himself little time to recognize Sammy's appeal to white women. "The women used to say to me, 'Sy, when he walks out onstage, you realize how unattractive he is, but one and a half hours later he's six feet tall, and handsome.' "

Buddy Bregman—Jule Styne's nephew—had been raised in a well-to-do family in Chicago where there were servants and a private plane for the family's use. In Hollywood, as a musical arranger, he quickly became something of a prodigy. On NBC's *Eddie Fisher Show* in 1957, it was the Buddy Bregman Orchestra providing the music. Young Bregman drew the attention of the likes of Ella Fitzgerald, Jane Powell, Bobby Darin, Sinatra, and, among others, Sammy. (Sinatra had one word for Bregman: "Genius.") After the *Mr. Wonderful* run, Bregman was happy to bump into Sammy again out in Hollywood. They both dressed like surfer kids in their Sunday best—argyle sweaters, khakis, loafers; Sammy in horn-rimmed glasses to complete the look. One thing Bregman had in common with Sammy was their mutual fascination with blondes. Sammy wooed and won; Bregman less so. "I hated him for it," says Bregman. "It used to drive me crazy." Bregman believed Sammy took the black-white color scheme to extremes. "Sammy had black silk sheets. It was the 'white girl on the black silk sheet' thing."

Ever since his childhood, Sammy dreamed cinematically, in movie time. Practically raised in movie houses—his head tossed back, his eyes wide—he let movie stars and bits of dialogue guide the sweep of his imagination. The films of the 1950s touched him deeply. Many were high-minded melodramas, and they featured a stunning array of talent: Brando, James Dean, Paul Newman; inventive directors like Nicholas Ray, Douglas Sirk, Alfred Hitchcock. Sammy loved the clean whiteness of those films—the sparkling jewels, the mink coat, the shadows, the love both thwarted and won. And he adored the women in those '50s dramas: Janet Leigh, Barbara Rush, Rhonda Fleming. Sammy carried his cameras everywhere; he imagined himself someday producing gorgeous photo books of all the actors and actresses. He knew them all—sometimes personally, like Janet Leigh—but always their movies. Deanna Durbin. Kim Novak. Of course a Negro male could not get close to one of those screen sirens, not in the flesh. It was unheard of, even unimagined. And yet, there was an innocence to Sammy's dreams. They were as romantic as they were gallant, and they served to lead him down unimagined roads.

Kim Novak first caught the public's attention in 1955. That was the year the twenty-two-year-old starred opposite Frank Sinatra in the Otto Preminger–directed *Man with the Golden Arm*, a gritty tale about a heroin addict (played by Sinatra). Then came her appearance in the screen version of *Picnic*, based on the William Inge play of the same name. She played a Kansas girl who gets swept off her feet by a drifter, portrayed by William Holden. The small-town girl wants to be appreciated for more than her looks, and hopes the drifter will whisk her away, praying that he sees more in her than the myopic denizens of her little town. Inge, having been born in Independence, Kansas, knew the midwestern milieu well. When the Novak character dances with Holden—her hips moving with silky and raw seduction—it becomes one of the greatest heated moments of a dance duet ever filmed.

The wide CinemaScope screen quickly turned Kim Novak into a sex symbol. Blond and big-boned, Novak also possessed an airiness, not unlike that of Marilyn Monroe, to whom some were quick to make comparisons—even to the point of ridiculing her talent. (Novak's given name at birth, in fact, was Marilyn; to Hollywood, "Kim" sounded better.) Novak, however, was not weighed down with Monroe's self-absorption. Soon enough she was on magazine covers. There were lavish photo spreads—the hot young Hollywood actress drove a bone white convertible Corvette. There were studio publicists assigned to her, and they kept the star-making machine humming.

Studio executives at Columbia Pictures, where Novak was under contract, sought to put tight reins on her social life, but she dated willfully—whom she wanted and when she wanted.

In her first three years in Hollywood, Novak starred opposite the likes of Jack Lemmon, Fred MacMurray, Tyrone Power, and both Holden and Sinatra. There had been a romantic affair with Sinatra; Cary Grant was bewitched and wooed her as well.

In the summer of 1956, NBC premiered *The Steve Allen Show*, a variety show timed to compete against *The Ed Sullivan Show* on rival CBS. Allen gathered an eclectic group of stars for his show's debut: Vincent Price, Dane Clark, Wally Cox, Kim Novak—and Sammy Davis, Jr. Sammy fell hard for the young actress with the soulful brown eyes. He could not take his eyes off her. But an open courting of Novak was out of the question. He would have to play by a discreet set of rules. He was hardly intimidated; rather, he was quite determined. When odds were wildly stacked against him, he only sensed additional thrills. "The white-woman thing was his way of saying, 'I'm just a little shorter than Sinatra,' " says Cindy Bitterman.

Kim Novak's reviews for her performances onscreen were not always positive. There were those who believed she often glided along merely on the arch of her beauty. But she managed to outrun the reviews. And it certainly mattered little to the public, or to Hollywood, that she lacked formal training. She had Harry Cohn behind her, and Cohn, the powerful head of Columbia studios, was determined to make her a star.

She was born Marilyn Pauline Novak on February 13, 1933, in Chicago. Her family was close-knit and Catholic. After high school she worked a series of jobs, among them elevator operator and clothing salesgirl. By her teen years young Marilyn Novak had sprouted up. Her height made her feel gawky. She was besieged with feelings of insecurity. At home she posted a sign in her bedroom window: "Bring your sick animals to me." She spent a great deal of time alone, writing emotional poems, ruminating about the outside world, its mysteries and secrets. Her mother, Blanche, worried about her, so much so that she took her daughter to see a psychiatrist. Apparently, the visits proved fruitful enough to boost young Marilyn's self-esteem. She sought out modeling jobs. The modeling agents quickly saw potential; her gawkiness had turned to sexiness.

At first the modeling assignments, in and around Chicago, were small. But she had a presence, and striking features. She was selected "Miss Deepfreeze," a plum honor for an aspiring model. She traveled the country, posing in front of gleaming new refrigerators. While she was in California, talent scouts from Columbia studios took notice, and did so at a propitious time.

Rita Hayworth had been a longtime star at Columbia. In the 1940s she compiled a string of memorable screen performances, among them *My Gal Sal, Gilda, The Lady from Shanghai, Cover Girl,* and *You'll Never Get Rich.* In the latter, she held her own dancing—very nicely, having been a professional dancer since the age of twelve—opposite Fred Astaire. Hayworth, red-haired and beautiful, had a sweet sexiness. Her picture in *Life* magazine on August 11, 1941—sitting upright on her bed at home, dressed in nighttime silk, cleavage showing, plenty of light in her eyes—made thousands of doughboys swoon and became an instant pinup classic. "Love Goddess," she was called. (World War II soldiers would affix the picture to one of the atomic bombs dropped on Japan. When told of it, she could think only of the death and dying, and broke down in tears.) Harry Cohn, feeling that he had made Hayworth's career, rebelled when she started wishing for a public life less intrusive than what the studio imagined for her. Cohn, one of the original founders of the studio, and a man with a notorious temper—he had been given the nickname "White Fang"—did not approve of the men she dated and slept with, who were often her costars. Nor did he approve of the men she married. When Hayworth left her first husband, she became engaged to pretty-boy Victor Mature. But she fled the engagement to marry, in the fall of 1943, another lover, Orson Welles. She found much in common with Welles, whose own independent streak was legendary. But Welles's appetites—in matters of the flesh as well as art—were huge. There were infidelities, tears in her lonely bedroom. In 1949 she married again, this time Aly Khan, a playboy and a prince. Khan merely pushed her toward despair again, and the marriage unraveled. In 1953, Hayworth married Dick Haymes, a singer. Cohn howled at his minions about Hayworth, who, amid the breakup of her marriages, kept demanding more money for the roles thrown her way. She was a tough lady, and yet, it is a wonder that Hayworth held to her sanity. The early years of her life had been torturous. Her father had forced himself upon her in her youth. She was all smiles and composure for the cameras, but the pain inside was unbearable. She felt no one seemed interested in getting to know *her,* her soul. Over time, she grew depressed. Cohn began to feel that Hayworth was a flighty actress, a star ungrateful for his hav-ing guided her through the tricky lights toward stardom. Time and time again she willfully exasperated him. And Harry Cohn was not a man to exasperate. He often threatened legal action against her. Finally, he told studio executives he would replace her.

Harry Cohn giveth, and Harry Cohn taketh away.

Kim Novak would be his new love goddess, his new Rita Hayworth. Cohn told Novak to hurry along those voice lessons, dance lessons, and singing lessons. She was a star; the public had anointed her; now she must make an attempt to become an actress.

It did not take long, however, for Harry Cohn and others to realize that Kim Novak had not quite left her insecure Chicago childhood behind. On movie sets she cried and threw temper tantrums. She seemed befuddled by her own fame. In a 1956 exhibitors poll, she was the number one box office attraction. She had looks, certainly, and mystery, but it was a mystery created by the stu-dio. Becoming a star before learning how to act was hardly a sin, but it could take a toll. The train was hurtling along, leaving her no time to catch up to it. In the tunnel of Hollywood magic—soundstages and whistles—she was already aboard. Mindful of the ease in getting the ticket, she was forever wary.

Still, the more one looked at the Novak phenomenon, the more perplexing it could appear. She seemed to breeze between intensity and nonchalance about her career. Ezra Goodman, a *Time* magazine writer, was assigned to write a profile of the actress during her meteoric rise. When he had gathered what he deemed enough material, he still felt confused about her, so he took his notes to a Beverly Hills psychoanalyst. A curious detour for sure, but he had a story to write. The psychoanalyst studied Goodman's material, then finally confided to him that Novak was much like Marilyn Monroe and Jayne Mansfield, products of the 1950s, buxom beauties best left beyond the yard-stick of intellectual probing. In essence, they were all dreams, the fancies of men, images upon the screen. "And in the Fifties," came the report from the psychoanalyst, "with their pronounced loss of identity, the most popular movie stars are pudding-faced, undistinguished girls, not particularly talented—like Monroe, Mansfield and Novak. Their undistinguished back-ground appeals to most people. These girls have no father or mother, figura-tively speaking, and sometimes literally. They seem to come from nowhere." The assessment seems too brittle, overlooking, as it were, one fact: they were gorgeous women, and gorgeousness played like honesty on the big screen. Such beauty couldn't be a lie!

Kim Novak had a father, all right. He lived in Chicago, and he put movie posters of his daughter on the basement walls. Harry Cohn wanted to be her father—figuratively speaking—her Svengali. She would not have it, even if she was a creation of the public and Cohn, the twin forces that had turned her into such a seductive presence in the rococo theaters of America. Onscreen, Novak seemed tough yet vulnerable. Her eyes told stories. Richard Quine, a onetime actor turned director—he cast Novak as a gangster's moll in his 1954 film *Pushover*—believed Novak possessed "the proverbial quality of the lady in the parlor and the whore in the bedroom."

She sent money she made from the movies back home to her family and asked her parents to keep her life as private as they could. Fame had been pushed upon her as with a velvet pitchfork. She rented a house in Malibu. Evenings she could listen to the ocean. And she also pondered the low pay scale female stars suffered under compared to male stars. She considered it unconscionable to keep quiet about the disparity. So she complained to Harry Cohn.

Against the mirror of self-deceiving Hollywood, her strength was believed to be but naïveté—the young lass taking on the great and feared Cohn.

For public consumption, she was known to be dating a quiet man who had construction interests and eshewed the limelight. But at night she was gliding by the palm trees on her way to yet another secret rendezvous with Sammy Davis, Jr.

With Sammy, there was plenty to talk about. He also had a Cohn-like figure in his life, Will Mastin, and he couldn't shake him. So they talked about breaking free of the forces that hemmed them in. The world was often cruel, small-minded; together, they commiserated. They fortified each other. She loved that he was part of a trio, that blood ties were always with him. She snuck into his home often disguised and wearing gaudy wigs, which were easily obtained from studio makeup departments. "There were columns upstairs at Sammy's house," says Annie Stevens, wife of Morty Stevens, who arranged music for Sammy. "All of a sudden, you'd see Kim doing a sexy pose around a column." She remembers another visit: "Sammy and Kim had been in the kitchen, on the floor, making out. Kim's wig fell off."

Novak sat and ate collard greens and pork chops prepared by Sammy's grandmother Rosa, who was now happily moved to the West Coast and living with her Sammy. For Novak, the word "family" carried precious weight, and even if Sammy didn't quite understand his, he tried to honor the majesty of it by pulling his grandmother close to him. Since she came from inner-city Chicago, the world of Negroes was not foreign to Novak. Around Sammy and his family she beamed. Rosa adored her, thought she was down-to-earth, without airs. Sammy spun records for Novak, pulling them from his vast album collection, bopping about his home like a nightclub host. The actress folded her legs beneath herself and listened as he riffed, on and on, about life, movies, music, her Chicago, which he knew, the way he knew so many cities across the great vast American landscape. She told him he must meet her family.

It was, nevertheless, a dangerous liaison.

Arthur Silber, Jr., sometimes drove them around on their furtive missions

All his life he swam toward dangerous waters. Kim Novak was exactly someone Sammy was not supposed to have. The things he saw with one eye would have blinded the nocturnal ambitions of others. So there they were, on the beach in Malibu, at nighttime. Here is proof that the movie camera adored Kim Novak.

and getaways. They ducked in the backseat of the car, giggling, kissing. The home of Janet Leigh and Tony Curtis was always a safe haven because Leigh and Curtis were friends, and always discreet. "They were very much 'together,' " Leigh would remember. "And very compatible."

And so they carried on their underground affair. Her movies; his famous nightclub act. They had much to smile about. Novak told certain friends secrets. If they betrayed those secrets, she never spoke to them again. There was a Garboesque quality about her. (Sammy addressed the affair in *Yes I Can*. But it was a mere four pages, and much of that a mixture of his sometimes Sinatra-like machismo and his anger against Negro newspaper columnists who had tried to expose the affair.)

"He was so enamored of her," remembers Jerry Lewis. "I said, 'They'll cut your knees off and you'll never dance again. Do you understand what you're doing?' He said, 'Yes, she's the best thing in my life.' I said, 'You can have any blonde out there. Why her?' He said, 'Because I didn't ask for it.' "

And, of course, that was true: everything he had, he had to claw for, chase down. But there she was, Kim Novak, pursuing him, wanting to be with him, lying next to him. He did not have to woo. He did not have to send the jewelry. She wanted him. Not Poitier, not Sinatra, not Belafonte. *Him.* The little weasel. The little nigger. Ha ha ha.

In 1957, Novak won the coveted role of Jeanne Eagels in the movie of that name. Her name would appear above the title. Eagels, born in 1894, had been onstage since the age of seven. She was a stunning Hollywood beauty and an admired actress. She was also a heroin addict. In 1929, she died from an overdose. There was haunting drama in the life of Eagels, and for Novak to be offered the opportunity to portray her spoke well of her rising stature in Hollywood. "George Sidney wanted Kim to do *Jeanne Eagels*, a very demanding role," says Luddy Waters, who would become Novak's dialogue coach. "We had new dialogue every single day. I used to meet her at five-thirty every morning. She was living in Malibu."

Alfred Hitchcock—the British filmmaker who had directed such recent films as *To Catch a Thief, The Trouble with Harry, The Man Who Knew Too Much,* and *Rear Window*—usually got the actors he wanted for his movies. In 1957 he wanted Vera Miles, so memorable in John Ford's 1956 Western *The Searchers,* for a crime thriller he was preparing. It was based on the French novel *d'Entre les morts,* by Pierre Boileau and Thomas Narcejac. But Miles was in the first months of pregnancy and declined the role. Hitchcock then turned to Novak. He had to enter negotiations with Cohn because he was making the movie for Paramount and not Columbia. Hitchcock had already decided on his male star. It would be Jimmy Stewart, who, in 1954, had turned in a shrewd performance—opposite Grace Kelly, another Hitchcock blonde—in *Rear Window.*

Hitchcock would ultimately change the title of his new movie to *Vertigo.* Not long after filming began, in San Francisco, Sammy arrived to watch the film's daily rushes. He frequently used his movie contacts to visit film sets, spry as a kid around cranes, movie cameras, and lights. On the set, he'd silently glide around Novak, letting on to no one that she was his reason for being around, until he befriended Luddy Waters as his "beard." (Sammy soon hired Waters's husband, Jim, a lowly actor, to become an assistant on his staff.)

Steve Blauner, who had befriended Sammy during the *Mr. Wonderful* run, had now gone on to take an agent's job with GAC (General Artists Corporation). Sammy excitedly told Blauner about his relationship with Novak. Blauner froze. "I grab him by the throat," Blauner remembers. "I say, 'You stupid son of a bitch! How long you think it'll be a secret? They'll kill you.' "

Blauner did not mean literally, but figuratively. They—the men in the shadows of the big studios, the men who had to keep the secrets inside the secrets of a Hollywood secret—would ruin little Sammy's career. But Sammy heard none of it, none of the words raining from the mouth of big hard-edged Steve Blauner. He was in love. He had pulled Kim Novak down from the big screen and into his life. Blauner feared that news of Sammy and Novak could only lead to tragedy, certainly for Sammy, possibly for Novak.

Kim Novak liked what so many other women had liked in Sammy—the way he rose in a nightclub, how his mind searched and searched, the genius gathered inside him. "I happened to be one of the females in the world," says singer Keely Smith, "who thought Sammy Davis was one of the sexiest men alive. Sammy had an animalistic thing about him that was sexy. If you're a woman in the audience and watched him, you'd think he was the sexiest man alive." Kim Novak had been, for a spell, Sinatra's girl, and yes, Sammy wanted what Sinatra had had—and why not? Sinatra had the best things in life. So Sammy did what came naturally to him—he gave her things, things to make her like him, or love him, or think of him. Kim Novak received what Peggy King and Eartha Kitt and Chita Rivera all had received—flowers, gifts, sparkling jewelry. His friends could tell how happy he seemed to be, both for the furtiveness of the relationship and for the fact it was Kim Novak. The lady in the parlor; the whore in the bedroom. "I remember being in his room," Bonnie Rand says of Sammy. "He had just hung up with Kim. He was so happy."

Sammy and Sinatra and singer Keely Smith were sitting around one evening. Just three singers, awash in the joy they were all having, talking about singing, songs, life. Sammy told Sinatra he'd have to leave early, couldn't hang around. Sinatra couldn't understand what might be more important than hanging around with him. So he wanted to know why Sammy had to leave, and those blue eyes pressed for an answer. It was Kim Novak; they had a date. A little smirk crawled across the Sinatra face. He told Sammy he could get Kim to break the date. Sammy thought Sinatra was kidding, but he wasn't, the blue eyes steady and hard. Keely Smith sat listening, looking between both men. Sammy against Frank. She knew who would win. "I said, 'Frank, don't do that.' He went into the room, called Kim [said he wanted to see her], and she broke the date with Sammy to go with Frank. It broke Sammy's heart. And Frank never went to meet her."

Sammy, by conveying to Sinatra that he could swim in the same romantic waters, had toyed with the famous Sinatra ego. He had sinned. And to sin against Frank Sinatra carried consequences.

Gossip columnists—Walter Winchell, Dorothy Kilgallen—began sniffing around. Sammy and Kim Novak? It sounded preposterous—but also rich with scandalous possibility.

This was not like Sammy's other affairs with white women, which were quiet, hushed dalliances. This was Kim Novak. She was the property of a major movie studio, Columbia, which had invested heavily in her. This was box office, part of a studio's future. This was Harry Cohn. Movie studio operatives were savvy in the ways of handling scandal, but not Negro and white scandal that had the lightning bolt of sex attached. This was explosive and uncharted territory.

But Jerry Lewis saw the mutual affection. It struck him as something deeper than a fleeting affair. "There was no question that the two of them were insane over one another," Lewis says. He'd watch Novak's eyes peering into Sammy. "She looked at him like she had just gotten the gold ring."

At the time Sammy was secretly seeing Novak, Cindy Bitterman was working for Columbia Pictures in the publicity department. "They told me Kim Novak was coming to town," she remembers. "I was to take care of her." It was just a chaperone assignment, two young attractive Columbia employees out on the town. During the outing, Sammy's name was never mentioned.

A short while later Bitterman was invited to dinner with a group of Columbia executives. Harry Cohn himself was at the table. The mogul showed off a bottle of pricey perfume he had purchased for one of Columbia's starlets. The junior executives effusively complimented their boss about his taste in perfume. "At dinner," recalls Bitterman, "the names of Kim and Sammy come up. Cohn has no idea of my relationship to Sammy. He asked somebody at the table, 'What's with this nigger?' My stomach started cramping. 'If he doesn't straighten up,' he starts saying about Sammy, 'he'll be minus another eye.' I went to the bathroom and threw up. I threw up out of fear and greed and Hollywood moneymaking."

Sammy and Kim Novak's romance unfolded in 1957 against a brooding cinematic summer and autumn.

In April, Hollywood producer Darryl Zanuck started talking up his new film, *Island in the Sun,* even though the movie would not open until July. Among the film's stars were Dorothy Dandridge, Harry Belafonte, Joan Fontaine, and John Justin. The setting was the West Indies. The film marked the return of director Robert Rossen. Six years earlier Rossen had appeared before the House Un-American Activities Committee. He refused to name names and was blacklisted. So he went back and named more than fifty colleagues who had been, according to his testimony, either sympathizers or members of the Communist Party. Friends were aghast. Rossen left Hollywood. Eventually, with the dimming of McCarthyism, he found work again, but it was abroad, in foreign locales. But Zanuck did not have to worry about Rossen's past. The heated insinuation of black and white romance in his film was a far more potent flame, so much so that it all but vanquished Rossen as a concern. In South Carolina, two months before the movie's opening, legislators debated levying fines against theaters that planned to show it. Politicians across the South threatened organized boycotts and picketing because of the film's suggestion of sex across racial lines.

There was picketing in Arkansas that autumn, but of a different sort.

On the morning of September 4 in Little Rock, the Arkansas capital, nine Negro schoolchildren—they and their families had been winnowed from a larger list—were scheduled to integrate Central High School. It had been three

years since the *Brown v. Board of Education* decision outlawed school segregation. But Little Rock officials had yet to enforce the ruling, just as many others
across the South had not. Rumors of possible violence against the children
frightened their parents, and the planned integration was called off. Elizabeth
Eckford, one of the nine students, did not receive the message (her family had
no phone), and she went to school. At the school she was taunted by a white
mob. Epithets flew; cameras clicked all around her. "Lynch her! Lynch her!"
someone cried out. For all the world to see, she was just a young Negro student,
clutching her school materials, trying to reach the classroom. She never made it
inside, as she was forced to turn back. Governor Orval Faubus had decided
none of the children would integrate the school and ordered the Arkansas
National Guard to block their planned entry. News of the event quickly reached
the White House. Eisenhower officials made appeals to Faubus to remove his
guardsmen. Eventually the governor was summoned to the president's summer
retreat in Newport, Rhode Island, where talks continued. Faubus, a shifty operator, finally did remove the troops but left no protection for the children against
the massing mobs. On September 23 the nine Negro students had to be hurried
out of the school for fear of violence. Members of the media kept arriving in
Little Rock; two Negro reporters were beaten up by the mob. The White House
felt tricked. A day after the children had been whisked from the school, an infu-
riated Eisenhower ordered the quick deployment of one thousand paratroop-
ers from the 101st Airborne Division to Central High to protect the children.
Never before had television cameras swooped over and around such an event. A
state was pitted against federal forces. The phrase "forced school integration"
entered the nation's vocabulary. One had to harken back to the dangerous days
of Reconstruction after the Civil War for such an example of federal troops
demanding order in the aftermath of racial strife. The Little Rock crisis ended
without loss of life, though a military presence—federalized National Guard
troops—would have to remain at the school for much of the year.

Against this backdrop of paranoia and violence, it wasn't difficult to imagine the challenging and potentially dangerous odds of tackling an interracial
love affair on a movie screen.

Evangelist Billy Graham staged a two-month-long crusade in New York
City that year. One of his fellow ministers issued a paper—"No Color Line in
Heaven."

Hollywood—where Sammy Davis and Kim Novak resided—was quite a
long way from heaven.

In Chicago in 1957, visiting her hometown, Novak took her family to see
Sammy's nightclub act at the Chez Paree. As expected, he got them one of the

best tables in the house. Novak herself seemed oblivious to the possibility of gossip. But already Harry Cohn had studio flatfoots trailing her, snooping.

Sammy's dancer friend Prince Spencer—who had had such an influence upon Sammy—was in Chicago at the time. "We were walking down the street with him," Spencer says. "He was talking; he was in love. He went to a public telephone, called her, and let my wife and me talk to Kim Novak." The phone conversation made his wife, Jerri, nervous. "[Sammy] wanted our approval," she says, "and we said, 'No, you can't do that.' "

After Chicago, Novak returned to the West Coast to continue film work. Jess Rand was summoned by Harry Cohn to come and see him on the Columbia studio lot. Rand was under no illusion of what the studio boss wished to talk about. Led into Cohn's office, Rand walked up to the chair in front of his desk and prepared to take a seat. "Sit over there on the couch!" Cohn yelled. Rand, startled, backed toward the couch, wondering if Cohn was joking. He was not. The aging mogul—so paranoid he often recorded the conversations of visitors to his office with a hidden microphone—began to rant about Sammy and Kim Novak. He threw the remnants of a smoked cigar at Rand, who ducked. "I was scared to death," Rand would remember of the blistering verbal assault against Sammy. "I know the right people," the mogul threatened, glaring. "I'll see he never works in a nightclub again."

When Rand left the Columbia lot, his heart was beating furiously. He feared Cohn's reach. "Hollywood was a small town." Indeed it was: Sammy's friend Jeff Chandler had filmed *Jeanne Eagels* alongside Novak. Rand talked to Chandler about the affair. "Jeff told Sammy he was crazy" to continue seeing Novak, says Rand.

Rand boarded a plane and flew to Chicago to see Sammy, to tell him about the meeting with Cohn. Rand found Sammy in his hotel room, talking with a man he had never seen before. Sammy looked agitated; the man sitting on the edge of the bed facing him appeared quite calm. The discussion going on was about Sammy and Novak; the eye being talked about was Sammy's. Rand quickly—and rightfully—figured the man came from the underworld. "If you fuck with my right eye," Sammy told the man, "I'll kill you." Sammy's threat astonished Rand. He was surprised to hear Sammy talk with such uncharacteristic bravado; it sounded as if he were onstage, mimicking Bogart. After the threat, the room got quiet; you could have heard feathers floating. The man slowly rose from the bed. He pulled back his jacket and showed Sammy a flash of the gun he was carrying. "Don't ever say that, kid," he began, leaning over Sammy, the words coming slowly, "unless you mean it." Sammy was stilled, as was Jess. The man left; they had no idea who sent him.

Was it a death threat? Was the man just fooling? Sammy and Rand had no idea. Word began to filter among Sammy's friends, and they themselves began to worry and play host to dark thoughts. (For years to come these mob-linked imaginings will play around in Sammy's mind-set, as well as the public's. In a succeeding decade Sammy will revel in the Chicago company of Sam Giancana, a known mobster. But Sammy's connection to the mob underground was all surface: the loaning of money, the *heh-heh-heh* of his friendship with Sinatra, his own wobbly sense of self, which took him through various doors in life. Sinatra and Dean Martin both had financial stakes in Las Vegas properties, and those arrangements often had mob fingerprints upon them. Sammy's skin color prevented him from being involved in such deals. As his financial fortunes improved, he had no need for his mob connections, and so they faded.)

Amy Greene felt the affair was Kim Novak's way of rebelling against Harry Cohn, and that her fight with Cohn had placed Sammy in the middle. "It was just a blatant, sexual, fun relationship," she says. "Her entire life was programmed by Harry Cohn. All of a sudden Sammy came into her life." Greene worried that Cohn operatives might try to hurt Sammy simply "because he was banging Kim." The relationship worried Tony Curtis as well. He felt Sammy was swimming in very troubled waters. "He didn't know how to protect himself," Curtis says. "You needed someone to help you organize that type of lifestyle: where to show up, what time. It had to be two or three people aiding you in that area."

Sammy—the converted Jew—had no rabbi. At least not the kind called on in such situations.

"Harry Cohn wanted him dead," believed Jack Carter, Sammy's Broadway costar from *Mr. Wonderful.*

Sinatra would not help. Not regarding a former lover. Frank only sang for the lonely; he did not advise them.

"What he was cocking around with was the mob," says Jerry Lewis of Sammy. "They had a lot of money in Columbia—namely Harry Cohn—and I knew it."

Sammy sweated, had terrible dreams. Arthur Silber, Jr., was also quite nervous. "There were no random shootings in Las Vegas," he would say. "They wouldn't allow rampant gangs. People were just dead." Will Mastin and Sam Sr. were beside themselves with worry. They were vaudevillians; they believed most anything could happen in life. Mastin's mantra—something bad is gonna happen—rang in Sammy's ears just as it rang in the ears of Jess Rand.

To be tucked away in hotel suites with white women was one thing. To have one of those affairs oozing out into public—when that white woman is attached to the economic dreams of others—was something else. The need for subterfuge was real; possible exposure served only to unleash notions of conspiracy, studio intimidation, racism, Chicago gangsters—the whole narrative world that sometimes circled Negro and white America. Sammy was now caught in the boiling cauldron of it all.

America was splattered with examples of the repercussions of what could go wrong when minds raced back through the time zone of black and white sex. Negro boxing champion Jack Johnson went into the eyeteeth of it, and he paid a dear price. In 1911 he married the first of his three white wives, Etta Terry Duryea. A year after the marriage she committed suicide, the general feeling being that the pressure of being married to a Negro was too unbearable. In 1912, Johnson married Lucille Cameron. In 1913 he was convicted under the Mann Act for traveling across state lines for "immoral purposes"—the act of making love to his wife. Johnson did not wait around for his sentence and skipped to France. In France he boxed and wrestled. They were exhibitions, and he looked foolish. In 1915 he traveled to Cuba to defend his title against Jess Willard. He lost. He returned to America in 1920 and served a year in prison. The dethroned champion married Irene Pineau, the last of his three white wives, in 1924. On June 20, 1946, Johnson—now retired from boxing and dabbling in business affairs—died in a car crash in Raleigh, North Carolina. His life, to some, had seemed devoted to striking fear in the minds of whites from the boxing ring to the bedroom. There was yet another incident in the racial-sex narrative as potent as the Jack Johnson narrative, though this one touched more lives.

They referred to them as the Scottsboro Boys. On March 25, 1931, in Paint Rock, Alabama, nine Negro youths were pulled off a train and arrested. A group of whites had claimed that the boys had scuffled with them. There were two white women in the train compartment with the youths. Later, under pressure, the white women claimed the Negroes had raped them. Lynch mobs formed in Scottsboro. The case, written up in feverish newspaper accounts, unleashed raging fears across the South about Negroes and white women. Eight of the youths were sentenced to death. There were appeals. In 1934, Ruby Bates, one of the accusers who had gone on to recant her story, joined nearly three thousand marchers to the White House to make a plea for their release. The case gnawed on the conscience of civil rights officials for nearly a decade, becoming a cause célèbre. Charges were dropped against the youngest of the nine, but the others served a total of one hundred cumulative years before the final accused was freed in 1950.

Sammy's predicament was dangerous—as quietly dangerous as the groaning echoes in movie theaters in 1957 when Harry Belafonte reached over to touch the arm of Joan Fontaine in *Island in the Sun*, the whiff of sexual foreplay whirring around both of them. In Atlanta alone, upward of five thousand— egged on by southern politicians—protested the movie's showing.

"The joke was that Sammy didn't start walking until he was two," says his mother, Elvera, "and the first person he walked toward was a white woman."

Judy Garland—although their relationship was merely platonic—seemed awed by Sammy. "He came into the Dunbar [a Los Angeles hotel] one night with Judy Garland," says actress Maggie Hathaway. "They said, 'Oh, no.' My husband said to Sammy, 'Come over to our house. We have a guest room.'" Any white woman had to cross barriers to get to him—history, race, his looks. Garland sailed past his color, and he became, right before her eyes, just Sammy, his only history that counted not Negro but show-business history.

"The black girls wouldn't pay him any mind," says dancer Maurice Hines. "The white girls looked at the money—not color. The white girls were aggressive." Being caressed by a white woman made him feel soft and loved. He could not help himself. White womanhood is what he wanted; it thrilled him so. But it rattled bones in the American psyche, and those bones made loud noises.

"Big publicity for Sammy," says Jess Rand, "was if he was dating a black woman."

Steve Blauner was worried enough to make a trip to the Columbia studios. He knew someone there, and that someone was Abe Schneider, one of the founders. "I said, 'Abe, I know you don't know what's going on. Sammy Davis is having an affair with Kim Novak. If anything happens to Sammy, I'll blow the whistle.' "

Sammy found it hard, as days passed, to shake the scene in that Chicago hotel room with the mysterious gentleman, the way the man had shown him his gun, the cold look he had in his eyes. There was something else he couldn't shake: what Harry Cohn had also blurted out to Jess Rand. Cohn said that Sammy needed to marry a Negro woman. "You get him married!" Cohn had yelled. Rand put no significant meaning to the rant, until Sammy told him about a mysterious phone call. "I hear you like white women," the unidentified caller said to him. "You should marry one. Her name is Loray White, and she works at a casino in Las Vegas." Then the caller hung up.

Loray White? He knew her, only to have seen her, to have shared drinks with her—as there were so few Negro girls working in the Vegas clubs. She sang in the lounge at the Silver Slipper, down on the far end of the Las Vegas strip.

Sammy's own vaudeville mind began to go into overdrive. He saw it all slipping away, his entire future—records, movie deals, the nightclubs. What would become of his father, of his grandmother Rosa? It was as if he himself were in a Hitchcock drama—the imagination knifed by whispers and bizarre phone calls, visits from strangers. And all because of the beautiful blonde curled up on his sofa: Kim Novak.

Besieged with worry, Sammy inexplicably told Jess Rand he was going to marry Loray White. Rand was stunned. But then everyone—Rand included—began thinking of their careers. Hollywood, in fact, was so small that you could disappoint the wrong people and the place could suddenly become smaller than a dot. And that dot could engulf you. Rand went along with Sammy's wishes.

Sammy went and met with White and pleaded with her to marry him. She was dumbfounded at first. When she saw how strangely earnest Sammy seemed to be, she became giddily flattered, a going-nowhere Negro singer in Las Vegas. Her first marriage—to a piano player who happened to be white—went badly right off and quickly ended. She had no inclination to toss away this fairy tale, so she agreed to marry Sammy. Will Mastin and Sam Sr. tried to talk Sammy out of it, but they could not; and because they could not, they began to feel he knew more than he was telling them. The two old men still believed that evil men onscreen were evil in real life. Nothing was more important than survival. And it was Sammy who had seen the gun in the hotel room, and Sammy who had heard the strange voice on the telephone.

Sammy well knew men were buried in the sands of Nevada. They were buried out there for crimes no one—save their perpetrators—knew about. In the shadows, and in the imagination—or maybe in both—there lurked dark figures: Harry Cohn, who knew George Wood, who knew the gangster Frank Costello, who knew other gangsters.

"The gossip," remembers Annie Stevens, "was already backstage: Sammy has to get married—or he'll be killed."

Jerry Lewis believed Sammy had little maneuvering room regarding his plans: "He was told to do it." Lewis felt the dark shadow of mobsters behind it: "You don't say *no* to them! I grew up with these people. One thing you don't do is ignore them."

Sammy and Loray went, accompanied by Rand and Arthur Silber, Jr.—Rand having tipped off the Las Vegas press—over to the district court county clerk's office to apply for the marriage license. Bureau clerk Helen Bunting accepted the application; Sammy raised his right hand to swear that all the information he had given was true. He was dressed in a plain cardigan sweater, a dark shirt underneath, simple slacks. He looked distracted. His fiancée wore a long dress, pearls, high heels. She looked to be swooning. Outside the courthouse they posed on the steps. Flashbulbs went off. He had bent a leg on the step just above the flat surface of the ground. He had tried to raise himself up as the flashes went off. Loray was taller than he was; her high heels only further reduced him in height. At times she bent down to his ear to talk.

Sammy hustled to introduce Loray White to his friends. "Sammy took us over to the Silver Slipper to see her sing," remembers Annie Stevens. "She was an okay singer—but very, very beautiful. That night he got up onstage and introduced her as his fiancée."

Once the wedding date was announced—January 10—it seemed impossible to pull it back in.

"Sammy didn't even like her," admits dancer Prince Spencer. It seemed to matter little. The invitations were liberally sprinkled about: every stage act along the strip was invited. Jack Entratter, president of the Sands, put his publicity staff to work. Sammy assured Entratter he would stick to his appearance schedule at the Sands, even on his wedding night.

One afternoon Sammy turned to a gathering of friends—Annie Stevens among them—and made an announcement.

"Annie is going to be the matron of honor," he said.

"How can you do that," Stevens shot back. "I don't even know Loray."

Kim Novak had appeared on the cover of *Look* magazine in its November 12, 1957, issue, eight weeks before Sammy's scheduled wedding. She looked golden, and lovely, wearing a straw hat with a lavender ribbon wrapped around it. Her face—one eye in shadow from the brim of the hat—dominates the photo. In the accompanying article, there are references to her past, mentions of her love life. For months, her secret affair with Sammy had been humming along inside the edges of Hollywood. And yet, in the article, there is not a single mention of Sammy, of the Negro entertainer. He'd been sufficiently erased.

Loray White went shopping the day before her wedding. Bonnie Rand thought it an odd diversion. She jauntily breezed in and out of the Las Vegas stores. "She bought about fifty pairs of shoes" at I. Magnin, remembers Rand.

On January 10, their wedding day—it all took place at the Sands with Jack Entratter hosting, which meant that Entratter footed the bill and thus would own a little more of Sammy's ass—all the stars of Las Vegas showed. There was Joe E. Lewis, the old Borscht Belt comedian; Donald O'Connor, the dancer; actor Gordon McRae; Eydie Gormé; a bevy of tall and exquisite chorus girls. Will Mastin and Sam Sr. looked elegant, as always. They brought along Rosa, Sammy's grandmother, and members of Sam Sr.'s new family, Rita and the adopted children. Best man Harry Belafonte—a feline presence with his butterscotch complexion—was coolly attired in a black suit.

Amid the subterfuge of Sammy's wedding day, Belafonte arrived as a Byronic presence: he was a dash of Negro Hollywood—but he also staved off what he perceived as Sammy's deep pain. Belafonte was more knowledgeable than most about what had occurred behind the scenes. "I knew he was having a romantic interlude," he says of Sammy and Novak. As small as Hollywood was, it was considerably smaller for the Negroes working in its employ. Belafonte was too conscientious to abandon Sammy in his time of need. "Sammy was in an excruciating place in his life," Belafonte would remember.

He had come off a hard experience with Harry Cohn at Columbia. Whites in the country were upset with his intrusion into their private realm—Kim Novak and all that. When they got through beating up on him—and he on himself— he came to me and said, "I want to move to another place in my life. I want to have children and I want to get out from all this. I've met someone and I think I'd like to marry her. I'd like very much for you to walk with me to the altar." I told him if he was making the decision to marry as a response to social pain, that that was hardly a base in which to enter a marriage. I had not heard him define the element of "love." He imparted to me it wasn't all about love, that that was only part of it. I accepted that. I wasn't his warden. He's a man responsible for himself.

Sammy's mother, Elvera, was not in attendance, unable to take the quickly arranged marriage seriously. She stood behind the bar where she worked in Atlantic City and let an assortment of scenarios flow in and out of her mind about why her son was about to get married. "He married her because if he had not, they would have broken his legs," she would say years later.

The drama reached Madelyn Rhue, an insightful actress who, in the past, had peered deep inside Sammy. (Rhue, who was white, had briefly dated Sammy. Her mother was aghast, and it all ended.) Now Rhue felt for Sammy. "He was left out there on the hook, and no one came to help him."

Inside the Sands on Sammy's wedding day, it was as if a camera were rolling and no one could stop it. Sammy had picked a near stranger to marry. Everyone was slightly bewildered, but the champagne flowed and flowed. When the bride finally arrived—forty minutes late, after having been fussed over by her happy mother—she was attired in a two-piece dress with a raised collar and a paper-thin hat that lay almost flat upon her head. It was fashionable, in an avant-garde way. It was her wedding day, and Loray White was smiling. She had plenty of reasons. As if overnight, Loray White was now in the arms of one of the biggest Negro stars in America. Why, a mere month earlier, she had no idea he cared about her—let alone loved her! It was a wonderful world. After the ceremony, Loray fed Belafonte a piece of wedding cake—Sammy standing between them, his face contorted like a clown's, and wearing his too-thick glasses—and the cameras clicked away. "Harry was the token black," says Bonnie Rand. "That whole wedding was staged."

A whole wedding, acted out, not at all about love or genuine heart flutterings. All of it floating by as if a dream, Sammy jumping up and down like the vaudeville kid he had been.

Sinatra didn't show: the foolishness of it all.

The reception for the 150 guests was held in the Emerald Room of the

Sands. There was glitter, the blowing of kisses. It all had the panache of a shot-gun wedding merged with a nightclub soirée.

Sammy was no fool. This was a unique opportunity for publicity. He had a Negro bride, so a call had been placed to *Ebony* magazine. Something for the Negro readers, to build up much-needed positive Negro sentiment.

The bride and groom's families posed behind the three-tiered wedding cake. There were plastic ducks in the middle of the cake. There was one word stretched across the front of the cake: "HAPPINESS."

Sammy gave his new bride a mink coat—white—as a wedding gift. It was a Sinatra-like move—and it cost him three grand.

"Wedding of Sammy Davis Jr., Loray White surprised entertainment world," *Ebony* would report in an understated headline.

After the wedding, and nightfall, and the completion of his performance, Sammy sat with Jess and Bonnie Rand. The hour grew late, then later. Loray White—Mrs. Sammy Davis, Jr.—had retired to their bridal suite. It seemed, to the Rands, that Sammy was paralyzed with fear. He did not want to go to his wife. When he finally did, it was nearly three a.m., and he returned just hours later for breakfast. There was no joy on his face.

Jess Rand uttered not a word about the behind-the-scenes maneuvers and fears that had precipitated the wedding. He knew the cat was in the bag, and the bag was rolling away in the river.

Sammy told former lover Helen Gallagher that he had gotten married. "Yeah, to someone you knew for two days," she snapped to him. He felt ashamed and told her that he feared Harry Cohn was going to have someone kill him if he didn't marry White.

"There was a wedding, but there was no consummation of a marriage," record executive Joe Delaney, a Sammy acquaintance, said. "It served its purpose. It took the heat off Sammy."

Heat, mystery, bad dreams, guns.

Draw!

Draw!

Harry Cohn died of a heart attack on February 27, 1958, a mere six weeks after Sammy's wedding. The funeral was on the lot at Columbia. Playwright Clifford Odets—*the cat's in the bag*—who had done script doctoring on some of Cohn's pictures, wrote the eulogy; Danny Kaye delivered it. More than two thousand attended, among them comic Red Skelton. "Well," said Skelton, "it only proves what they always say—give the public something they want to see and they'll come out for it."

And five months after Sammy's wedding, *Vertigo* was released. Kim

On January 10, 1958, Sammy married Loray White, a Las Vegas lounge singer, at the Sands Hotel. It was an arranged marriage for reasons owing to gangsters, a Hollywood mogul, and Sammy's beguiling relationship with actress Kim Novak. Sinatra avoided the wedding festivities but played host to the couple at the Villa Capri in Hollywood two days after they married. Sammy and his new bride—as Sinatra was aware—barely knew each other. (JESS RAND COLLECTION)

Novak—guided by Hitchcock's swooping camera work and a moody Bernard Herrmann musical score—would receive some of the best reviews of her young career. The movie is awash in double-dealing and trickery, lies and whispers, movement in the shadows. It revolves around a retired detective, played by Jimmy Stewart, trying to transform a living woman into the image of his dead wife. It is a heartbreaking grasp for elusive beauty. It is about the wicked trickery the imagination can play on itself in the name of love. The film has a kind of poetic madness to it. In one of the more intriguing movie posters created for the movie, Stewart is sitting in a chair, his arms folded tightly around a blonde. Her lips are gently kissing his, her eyes closed. Behind the chair in which Stewart is seated, there is another woman, this one a brunette, a dark mole on the left side of her lovely face. Our retired cop, already suffering from vertigo—a fear of heights—has been bedeviled by beauty. Both women are played by Novak. A dual-roled performance—not unlike her secret affair with Sammy, an affair that she had to pretend did not exist.

Vertigo would have been anathema to Sammy. He craved heights.

"When audiences left a Hitchcock movie, they would often translate those fears to the dark shadows cast across the streets where they lived." Those words were written by a onetime child vaudeville performer who loved movies and Hollywood and white flesh and life itself. They were written by Sammy Davis, Jr., in a gushy little book, *Hollywood in a Suitcase*, he wrote in 1980 that no one bothered to notice.

Before their breakup, Kim Novak knitted a stuffed llama and presented it as a gift to Sammy. He nearly choked up. He would keep it for the rest of his life.

In the end, their relationship simply seems to have run out of energy. It was never for public consumption, and the breakup before his marriage was just as quiet, akin to a movie-screen fadeout—the two lovers in shadow in the distance. And yet, now and then, when Loray had come and gone, Novak would be spotted at Sammy's home.

In high school back in Chicago, young Marilyn Novak, just a few years before she became Kim, wrote a poem. She composed it while sitting at a train station, all alone. It is a plaintive piece, titled "A Train Makes Me Lonely," and speaks of love, loss, even hope. It seems to echo, as well, bravery versus fear. It partially reads:

> *I'd proud board the train*
> *That's not the express.*
> *The worth not the price*
> *Would be more and not less.*
> *But every stop I'd get out and see*
> *And maybe I'd find the right home for me*
> *And somewhere out there*
> *He'd hear my plea*
> *Bring me his love and then marry me.*

Chapter 10

ON TO CATFISH ROW

ammy himself desperately wanted to break into movies. It took an invented Polish family to get him there.

In the summer of 1936, twenty-three-year-old Philip Yordan—born in Chicago and educated at the University of Illinois—made his way to Los Angeles. It was the Depression; he thought he had nothing to lose, a young man pulling up stakes. He had shifted his career plans from wanting to be a lawyer to wanting to be a writer. In Los Angeles, he sat down with his type-writer. The story that flowed from him was about a girl he'd known back in his native Chicago. Her name was Elizabeth Halley. She had a foul mouth and was absolutely gorgeous. She also had to prostitute herself at times to make ends meet. Yordan took her out on dates. He had no business with her, and knew it, but he fell deeply in love. He'd sit in virtual silence listening to her life story. "She was a very sad person," Yordan would recall. She had been raped, and a child was born. She fell in love with the doctor who delivered the child. But the doctor himself had a tortuous history: he had his medical license revoked for participating in plastic surgery on the face of gangster John Dillinger. "She was hopelessly in love with the doctor," says Yordan, himself hopelessly in love with Elizabeth Halley. It was the stuff of drama. "She was the inspiration for the play," he says of *Anna Lucasta*, which he wrote and finished during those first months in Los Angeles.

Yordan found an agent, and his play began making the rounds. Antoinette Perry, the revered actress and director, optioned it. But she couldn't get it produced, and it languished. Some feared its themes of prostitution and explosive family entanglement were scaring away producers. Yordan had to make a living, and he soon turned his attention to writing screenplays; one about gang-ster John Dillinger was building inside him.

Meanwhile, his unproduced *Anna Lucasta* found its way east, landing, oddly enough, atop the desk of Frederick O'Neal at the American Negro Theatre in Harlem. All the white theatrical troupes had turned it down. The American Negro Theatre was considered avant-garde, a unique blend of idealism and financial sacrifice. O'Neal founded it along with Abram Hill, a writer, in 1940. One of the goals of the theater was to "portray Negro life as they honestly saw it." It was a financial cooperative, meaning everyone shared in expenses. Those members who found work outside it were asked to donate 2 percent of their earnings back to the theater. In 1942, the company added a training program, and among its early graduates were the young Sidney Poitier and Harry Belafonte. It was Yordan's agent—knowing that the ANT was a kind of experimental theater—who had sent *Anna Lucasta* to O'Neal. O'Neal was at first nervous, knowing that the play had been written about a Polish-American family. He asked Yordan what he thought of staging it with an all-Negro cast. "Go ahead," Yordan told him, "do anything you like."

The troupe soon began rehearsals in its home—the basement of the Harlem public library. Ruby Dee, a young college student and actress, was witness to the transformation of the Yordan play from Polish to Negro. "I remember watching [director] Harry Gribble and some of the actors during rehearsal as they improvised on the script—making up dialogue on the spot, throwing out scenes, and creating new ones. There was much writing, rewriting, then hopping up onstage to try it all out."

The ANT production opened June 8, 1944, in Harlem. The audiences grew, and it became a hit. Night after night, crowds flocked to the library basement to see *Anna*. O'Neal was as surprised as anyone. "People began to come up to Harlem to see it, and eight people were bidding for the rights to present it on Broadway," he would recall.

The space in the basement of the Harlem library could hardly accommodate demand for the play. The all-Negro version of *Anna Lucasta* opened on Broadway on August 30, 1944—less than three months after its off-Broadway premiere. O'Neal starred, and the beautiful Hilda Simms played Anna. The drama was still running strong at the end of its first year. With its themes of family drama and sexual dynamics, *Anna* had struck a nerve with audiences both Negro and white, but its all-Negro cast had a prideful appeal to blacks. Road companies were formed. Sidney Poitier joined one of them; his travels with the cast—to Ohio, Missouri, Indiana, Pennsylvania—introduced him to the American landscape. "In St. Louis all the female members of the cast checked into the Phyllis Wheatley Home for Girls, a kind of resident hotel for colored women, while all the men checked into a local colored hotel," Poitier would recall.

Another young and gifted actor, Ossie Davis, also joined a road company of *Anna*. Davis was raised in Waycross, Georgia, and had attended Howard University, where he studied under Alain Locke, who had been so influential dur-

ing the 1930s Harlem Renaissance. But after Howard, Davis sojourned to New
York City and suffered mightily. He spent time sleeping on the streets. In 1946
he won the lead role in *Jeb,* a play by Robert Ardrey. But not until *Anna* could
he even dream about the possibility of making a living in the theater. He found
himself in Chicago with an *Anna* touring company. "Chicago, at that time
always in short supply of theater, took its theater more seriously than New
York," Davis would recall. "The black community had pounced on *Anna* like a
leopard from ambush, hungry to make a kill. Actors were treated like
demigods—we could do no wrong." Davis had no complaints with the traveling accommodations for the *Anna* company: "The company had a Pullman
sleeping car, just for us, and each actor had a berth in the sleeping car. When
we moved from one city to the next, that Pullman would be hitched up to a
train that happened to be going in that direction. Some of us had trunks as
well as suitcases, all of which were carried along with the set and physical
properties for the production." They reached Los Angeles, where, initially,
Davis was exuberant about the Hollywood reception given to *Anna.* There
were bouquets and curtain calls; Charlie Chaplin sat in the audience one
evening. Davis's exuberance was short-lived. He recalled: "Hollywood's lavish
opening-night welcome did not extend to hotel accommodations. Some
members of the cast were from Los Angeles, and they had no problem. The rest
of us were parceled out among various black families, who were glad to rent
their guest rooms to entertainers on the road. I wound up on San Sedro Street,
down near the railroad station, where there was lodging for railroad sleeping
car porters."

Still, with Hollywood figures so enamored of the play, Davis just knew that
a movie version was in the planning. And a movie did get made. In 1949, Irving
Rapper directed a screen version of the Yordan play—but the cast was all
white. "At the time," recalls Yordan, who produced the movie, "there was strong
prejudice. They said black films had no audience." "Opportunity's golden
door," Ossie Davis now felt, "which was to have led us all to fame, glory, and
stardom, had closed before it opened." Paulette Goddard won the role of Anna.
(When casting got under way, Yordan approached Ingrid Bergman's agent,
who was aware of the Negro play. "What do you want, Bergman to play it in
blackface?" the agent asked. Yordan was aghast.) In addition to Goddard, *Anna*
starred John Ireland, Broderick Crawford, Will Geer, and Oscar Homolka.
"They paid Paulette $175,000," recalls Yordan. "The picture was a flop."

The playwright Langston Hughes wrote a letter to a friend passing along
gossip about another potential movie: "He told me they are thinking of doing
St. Louis Woman in white face in the movies—like Anna Lucasta."

In 1958, the screen rights to *Anna Lucasta* reverted back to Yordan. That very
year, Longridge Enterprises, a fledgling film concern, decided to make an all-

Negro version of *Anna Lucasta*, believing that Negro audiences' fascination with it still held. It would surely be one of the more intriguing routes a dramatic play had ever taken. Written for—but never performed by—a Polish cast, *Anna* was now about to travel full circle: from its staging by an all-Negro cast, to its all-white film version, now finally back to its original all-Negro presentation.

"They wanted names," Yordan says of the film company about to make the Negro *Anna*. Both female and male leads—Anna and Danny—would have to be able to sing. For Anna, Yordan wanted Hilda Simms, who wasn't a big name but surely a unique talent, as she had shown in the Broadway version of the play. The studio nixed Simms. Lenny Hirschan, a young William Morris agent, went over to the La Jolla Playhouse one afternoon to talk to Eartha Kitt, one of his clients, about playing the lead. Kitt was appearing onstage, playing the Tallulah Bankhead role in Thornton Wilder's *Skin of Our Teeth*. There were few Negro actresses in the country who hadn't heard of the Anna role. Kitt quickly pounced, and Hirschan convinced the studio to accept her. The choice did not make Yordan happy. She had appeared in three other films, her most recent the 1958 vehicle *St. Louis Blues*. "The camera," says Yordan, "couldn't conceal the fact that Eartha was not a beautiful woman."

The male lead had been played on Broadway by Canada Lee, an actor whose career had been both brave and haunted. Lee—born Leonard Lionel Cornelius Canegate and raised in Harlem—had once been a boxer. The sport cost him an eye. He turned to acting. His first significant role was as Banquo in an all-Negro version of *Macbeth* that was staged by the Negro Federal Theatre Project in 1936. In 1939, Lee appeared on Broadway in *Mamba's Daughters*, alongside Ethel Waters. When Orson Welles cast his Broadway version of Richard Wright's *Native Son* in 1940, he chose Lee to play Bigger Thomas. (There were plenty who considered Welles's interracial casting scandalous.) Three years later Lee appeared in Hitchcock's *Lifeboat*. But his career came fatefully apart when he was hounded by the House Un-American Activities Committee for his outspokenness on racial stereotyping in films. In 1952, Lee journeyed abroad to make *Cry, the Beloved Country*, a movie based on Alan Paton's acclaimed novel set in South Africa. Sidney Poitier was also featured in the cast. Lee never made it back to America; he died in London, at the age of forty-five, and various reports claimed he died penniless. Lenny Hirschan suggested William Morris client Sammy Davis, Jr., for the role Lee had made famous on Broadway, and the studio quickly accepted. It would be Sammy's first starring movie role since childhood. As well, it would be a sort of déjà vu: in the movie, he would be chasing after Anna, as played by Eartha Kitt, the woman he had once chased after in real life in San Francisco.

The studio selected Arnold Laven to direct. Like Yordan, Laven was a native of Chicago. His best-known film had been *The Rack,* which appeared in 1956 and starred Paul Newman, along with Walter Pidgeon, Anne Francis, Lee Marvin, and Cloris Leachman.

Filming of *Anna Lucasta* began in May 1958 at the Samuel Goldwyn Studios in Hollywood. Sammy was eager and excited, as he was embarking on one of his rare creative ventures without Will Mastin or his father. In the movie, Anna is a prostitute who hangs out around the San Diego naval station. "I wish someone would find me," she utters in one of her memorable lines. Sammy arrived on the set with all his lines memorized. Yordan watched him whir around. "He had a lot of energy," he says. Yordan owned a grainy tape of Canada Lee's Broadway performance as Danny, and he shared it with Sammy. But they were distinctly different actors. Lee was a formal actor. And while he had presence, there seemed to exist in him the insecurity of an athlete turned actor. He acted on direction, not instinct. Sammy was a loose performer; instinct was everything to him, and direction a sort of nuisance. He and Yordan developed a friendship, and after long hours of filming, they often went out to eat together. "The dinners I had with him were at Lucy's restaurant," Yordan recalls. "They had private booths, and they were three-quarters concealed. Sammy would mainly talk about all his troubles, his difficulties. That he was so small with all this talent. He felt he always had to fight to measure up to Sinatra."

Kim Novak's name came up during their shared meals together. Yordan knew the actress, from Chicago. "He was quite bitter. Harry Cohn had threatened him. He brought that up. Cohn had affiliations with the Chicago mob, and he had them contact [Sammy]. He told me, very bluntly, they threatened to put out his eye if he continued going with Kim."

As filming continued, Yordan sensed that Kitt, who possessed a fierce competitive streak, was attempting to chew up all the scenery around her—even Sammy, when he got in the way. "But he carried his role, and she couldn't tower over him," says Yordan. "He stood up to her."

The low-budget film completed shooting in less than thirty days. Even before its opening, there was controversy. The Motion Picture Association harrumphed about the movie posters and the way they presented Kitt—in a tight-fitting yellow dress that left little to the imagination. According to the *Hollywood Reporter,* the MPA felt that the ads "blatantly portray the femme lead as a prostitute," and further noted that the artwork "emphasizes her posterior." (Kitt, grateful for any publicity, uttered not a word.) It is clearly Kitt's picture, and she claims the screen every chance she gets. Sammy's performance as Danny is fairly loose, but there are times onscreen he does not seem fully focused. (During filming, he had intermittently flown to Las Vegas to give evening performances.) Critics were kind, if not effusive. "The story has none of the so-called comic cliches usually associated with Afro-American drama but it is rich with the humor and common sense wisdom of the Negro point of view," the *Hollywood Reporter* wrote. "There is no particular feeling that this is a 'Negro film,'" said *Daily Variety*. "The racial character dwindles as the human characters come through. The people are not humorously Negro or pitifully Negro, but people, funny and sad."

But the Negro film version of *Anna*—which had created such expectation because of its legendary Broadway following, and which had unleashed a torrent of excitement in large urban Negro communities around America—suffered a fate similar to the white version: it flopped. "It was early for an all-black picture," says Lenny Hirschan, the agent. "It was a family story. It was a modest film." In one of the more riveting and talked about moments in the movie, there is a furious montage of Sammy on drums—with echoes of his nightclub act. Geography was not kind to the movie: it suffered below the Mason-Dixon line, where it was shown in a scant number of theaters despite the fact that Sammy and Eartha wrote letters to southern theater owners pleading with them not to dismiss the movie based on "racial grounds."

The year 1958 saw the beginning of an increase in school and church bombings in the Deep South, due to school integration measures. Earlier that year, the young minister Martin Luther King, Jr., embarked on a pilgrimage to India. He aimed to study the depths of Gandhi's nonviolence movement, which had shaken the British during India's battle to wrest itself from colonialism.

With a powerful agency behind him now (never mind the continued intrusiveness of Will Mastin, who turned seventy-nine in 1958) Sammy decided to become one of the first Negro actors to have his own Hollywood office—a shrewd and daring move. It was a small affair, with Jess Rand, Luddy Waters, and her husband, Jim Waters, a not-so-successful actor who had taken on the title "assistant to Sammy." Having his own office made Sammy feel quite proud. Sidney Poitier and Harry Belafonte didn't have offices. But Frank Sinatra had an office, and now Sammy had one. (Will Mastin had never needed an office. His office was the hotel room, the train depot, the bathroom stall, the road.)

Looking around Sammy's office, one of the things one noticed was that there was not one Negro face in sight. The staff was segregated—all white! (Shirley Rhodes was part of the road crew.) Sammy's father wondered about the wisdom of that, so phone calls were made. "A friend of mine in Chicago said, 'Sammy needs someone to work in the office,'" recalls Jean Flemming, who was hired. "They needed a black face."

Flemming eagerly packed and headed for Los Angeles. She felt a tinge of cultural pride. Soon, however, her mood shifted, and worries began. Hollywood was sending not scripts to Sammy Davis's office but something else. They were bills, stacks and stacks of them. Nothing now made Sammy feel better than gliding into a nightclub—the Crescendo, Ciro's, the Mocambo—sitting down with friends, ordering food and drink, and more drink, then rising, turning to the manager, and telling him to send the bill to "my office." And sure enough, those bills came, and Jean Flemming opened them. "We were forever late paying the bills," she remembers. Sammy blithely shrugged it all off. In and out of more nightclubs he went, racking up more bills. He loved reserving tables, then having bottles of Scotch lined up on the tables for his arriving guests. Flemming went to Mastin, who began a struggle to keep the trio's debts separate from Sammy's. "Will had the money. You'd go to Uncle Will for the money. Sam Sr. was a gambler. My paycheck used to bounce. I was only getting sixty dollars a week." Sammy thought the Hollywood glitter in Flemming's eyes might calm her, but, she says, "I wasn't interested in meeting Judy Garland. I just wanted my check to clear." One of many times her paycheck bounced, she told her husband in a forlorn voice that it must be a mistake. "My husband—and I'll never forget his words—said, 'You're goddamn right it's a mistake.' "

Sammy had astounding clothing bills that Flemming winced at as well. "He was always having stuff made up that he couldn't pay for."

Now and then Sammy and Loray were seen out in Los Angeles, her fur rubbing against his cheeks. Into the flash of the cameras she smiled and smiled. One evening Sinatra was the escort—his way, perhaps, of making up for missing the wedding. Flemming was bewildered by the marriage, principally because, as she knew, it was a sham. Sammy lived in one house, Loray in another, on Sunset Plaza Drive, where Sammy was obliged to pay the rent as well as other bills. They led separate lives. "Loray would call her boyfriend at night and go to sleep with the phone off the hook," says Flemming. "The first phone bill I saw there were thirty-nine [long-distance] phone calls. I asked Loray, 'How can you talk that long?' She said, 'I fell asleep.' The bill was five hundred-something dollars. That was 1958!"

A marriage made in fear was bound to boomerang. "She had a sweet deal," Flemming says of White. "But she went crazy. She [had been] making minimum wage at the Silver Slipper. Sammy bought her a convertible Ford. He bought her a ring nice enough to photograph. He got her a house on Sunset overlooking the city." If Flemming wasn't opening restaurant bills for Sammy, she seemed to be opening shopping bills for Loray. "Loray's bills were coming in, and they were overwhelming."

In September, nine months after the marriage, Loray White announced to the press she was going to file for divorce. The drama had gone on just long enough to make the press think it had been an honorable attempt at marriage. "Sammy gave her $10,000," says Sy Marsh, one of Sammy's agents. "He never even lived with her one day. He had so much pussy he didn't need her." Flemming sensed, before White's rehearsed announcement to the press, that White suddenly had misgivings, that she wanted to veer from the script and try a genuine marriage. "She decides that she's in love with Sammy. She was only in love with Sammy because she couldn't have him."

"It was doomed from the start," Sammy would come to reminisce about the marriage—like Emily Brontë exposing the fate of Heathcliff and Catherine.

Now and then, long after the announcement of the divorce, Loray would drop by Sammy's Los Angeles office. She was a curious sight. Sammy had missed sending a support check, and she needed the money; she was thinking of writing a book about her marriage; perhaps someone they knew was looking for a singer. Mostly—with all the flashbulbs dimmed, with the fantasy evaporated, with Sammy himself gone—she just seemed lonely. Such a malady hardly afflicted Sammy. "After his divorce from Loray," says Maggie Hathaway, "Sammy was being introduced to all the blue-eyed, blond white girls."

In all her time watching and working for Sammy, certain feelings began to overwhelm Jean Flemming about her employer. She began to feel a strange kind of pity about Sammy. "He was different in black," she says, "than he was in white. He thought he *was* white."

During those times, hardly a season passed that the country did not experience a violent racial murder. In May 1959, Mack Charles Parker was pulled from the Poplarville, Mississippi, jail where he was being held on charges of raping a white woman. His body was found a short time later—disfigured—in the Pearl River. His mother, Eliza Parker, fearing for her own safety, was forced to flee the state.

Racial unrest veered from the deadly to the absurd. When the Boston Red Sox sent its only Negro player, Jerry Green, down to the minors in the spring of 1959, protestors gathered outside Fenway Park. They had company. "We want a pennant, not a white team," one of the signs supportive of the Negro player said. Joe Cronin, the American League Baseball president, defended the Red Sox and its owner, Tom Yawkey. Yawkey, Cronin announced, was not prejudiced, because he had "colored help on his South Carolina plantation and takes excellent care of them, pays good salaries, and they are all very happy." Then from the absurd to the bizarre: An eerie chuckle came from the stacks of the Alabama public library system. Segregationists demanded that *The Rab-*

bit's Wedding, a children's book, be removed from the open shelves. Their complaint: interracial marriage—among rabbits! Garth Williams, the author, was dumbfounded. "I was completely unaware that animals with white fur were considered blood relations to white human beings."

In the year of the white rabbit, acquaintances of Sammy's who stopped by his house in the weeks after his divorce were surprised at whom they would see, frequently eating Rosa's delicious meals: Kim Novak. Theirs was the longest of movie fadeouts. "She was up there eating collard greens," says Flemming, who saw Novak there once.

"She was quite simple," says Philip Yordan of Novak. "Nothing complicated about her at all. She was a star. She did what she wanted."

There would be many film roles in the career of Sammy Davis, Jr., but none would he bring to life so electrifyingly as one born in the mind of DuBose Heyward.

Heyward was a white Charleston, South Carolina, insurance salesman struck by the plight of Negroes who lived on the darker edges of society there. Born in 1885 to a family long removed from its once comfortable position in society, Heyward was a sickly youngster—he had polio—and a high school dropout. His first decent job was working in a steamship warehouse in Charleston. He saw Negroes everywhere: "Negroes in long lines trucking cotton on the wharves; dim figures in a deserted warehouse squatting over a crap game; spirituals bringing me up short to listen against the wall of a dilapidated church that I had to pass on the way to work." Though the job lasted only one year, the work was colorful, and the presence of so many Negroes seemed to fasten to his mind. Afterward, he went into the insurance business and did well. Having saved some money, he spent more time writing short stories and poetry. Negro life fascinated him, and tales of the southern Negro threaded his work. In September 1925 his first novel, *Porgy,* was published. It told the story of Porgy and Bess, two Negroes, and their lives on Cabbage Row amid schemers, hustlers, and gamblers. Porgy is crippled and fights robustly—using his great upper-body strength—for his Bess. One of the novel's more sinister figures is Sportin' Life, who wears a derby and sells "happy dust"—cocaine. The book would become a critical success ("The best novel of the season by an American author," said the *Chicago Daily News*) and land on many bestseller lists. Cecil B. DeMille was interested in Heyward's novel for a movie, but plans fell apart. George Gershwin entered the picture, determined to turn it into an opera. Instead, first came a theatrical play, which opened on Broadway on October 10, 1927. Reviews were favorable; many thought Heyward's depiction of what he referred to as "an unfortunate race" was generally sympathetic. Al

Jolson bought the radio rights and dreamed of taking the drama to the big screen, where he'd play Porgy in blackface. (Alfred Lunt and Lynn Fontanne, a great acting duo, also desired to play Porgy and Bess in blackface, but theater operatives dissuaded them from the idea.) It took the stock market crash of 1929 to send Al Jolson off in other directions.

Heyward had a fascination with family in his novel, with the pains engulfed within. "Hush, little baby, don' yo cry," he would write. "Mudder an' fadder born to die."

Gershwin never lost sight of *Porgy,* and in time he and Heyward were at work on the operatic adaptation. Gershwin even made a trip to some of the sea islands surrounding Charleston to view the Gullah population, Negroes descended from slaves who had never left the islands; anyone attempting to create something of the Heyward novel would certainly benefit from trying to understand them. Gershwin sat one evening with a throng of Negroes singing spirituals around a fire. He became sweaty and inspired. DuBose Heyward was with him. "I think he is the only white man in America who could have done it," Heyward would remark. While in South Carolina, Gershwin began composing at a feverish clip.

By mid-1935, Gershwin had his opera finished. The first premiere was staged in Boston. It met with resounding success. "You've done it—you're the Abraham Lincoln of Negro music," J. Rosamond Johnson, a Negro assistant conductor, told him. A critic for the *Boston American* would write: "When the cries of genius subside, George Gershwin's *Porgy and Bess* will take its place indubitably as the 'first' American opera." It opened in New York on October 10, and the reviews were stunning. Gershwin had melded, for all to see, the rhythms and folklore of Negro life in the South. In time the word "classic" would become attached to *Porgy and Bess.* Negroes would rise to fame among its ranks—Leontyne Price ("a Bess of vocal glory"), William Warfield (Porgy), and Cab Calloway (Sportin' Life), to name a few.

Over the years, there were world tours arranged, none more notable than those led by Robert Breen, general director of the American National Theatre and Academy. Breen—who once directed John Barrymore in *Hamlet,* in a staging performed at the Hollywood Bowl—was an admirer of experimental theater, and thought theater belonged on the international stage. In early 1956 he took a *Porgy and Bess* cast to Moscow. The company was eighty strong, and included Truman Capote, a young writer on assignment for the *New Yorker.* Capote wore a yellow scarf as protection from the Russian winter winds, and everyone was amused at his fey accent. He looked askance at the Negro cast, wondering why they would laud a production that, in his mind, mocked them, especially with the song "Oh, I Got Plenty o' Nuttin'." In turn, the Negroes believed that, behind their backs, Capote was disparaging them as "Uncle

Toms." Soon enough, cast members and administrators alike believed Capote, with his scathing comments under his breath, had come along to sabotage their production. The writer appeared in the lobby of the Leningrad Hotel one day, a throng of Russians buzzing about. At his colorful clothing and rather feminine walk, heads swiveled. A Russian's voice—speaking in accented English—rose above the din: "Ve have dem like dat in de Soviet too, but ve hide dem."

Over the years, nearly ninety film producers had shown interest in *Porgy*, but nothing had ever materialized. Harry Cohn had gone so far as to say Al Jolson would play Porgy, with Rita Hayworth as Bess, and Fred Astaire as Sportin' Life—all in blackface. But since the premiere of *Porgy*, America had undergone some significant changes. For one, blackface was no longer acceptable.

On May 8, 1957, an announcement came from Hollywood: Samuel Goldwyn had purchased the screen rights to *Porgy and Bess*. He promised a lavish production. With roles for Negroes in film so scarce, every role—especially the principal roles of Porgy, Bess, and Sportin' Life—would be coveted.

The Hollywood branch of the NAACP, however, would have quite a bit to say about the DuBose Heyward novel that Goldwyn planned to bring to the screen.

Was there really a Porgy? a Bess? a Sportin' Life? Well, an old Kentucky stable hand may have died anonymously, having sprung "Uncle Tom" into the vernacular, but DuBose Heyward was a touch more generous in acknowledging his inspiration for Porgy. While reading the *Charleston News and Courier* one morning, Heyward noticed an item:

> Samuel Smalls, who is a cripple and is familiar to King Street, with his goat and cart, was held for the June term of Court of Sessions on an aggravated assault charge. It is alleged that on Saturday night he attempted to shoot Maggie Barnes at number four Romney Street. His shots went wide of the mark. Smalls was up on a similar charge some months ago and was given a suspended sentence. Smalls had attempted to escape in his wagon and was run down and captured by police patrol.

The item fascinated Heyward. "Just think of that old wreck having enough manhood to do a thing like that," he uttered to his sister. As far back as 1928, Heyward gave recognition to Smalls in the form of a dedication: "To Smalls, I make acknowledgment of my obligation. From contemplation of his real, and deeply moving tragedy, sprang Porgy, a creature of my imagination . . . upon whom, being my own creation, I could impose my own . . . conception of a summer of aspiration, devotion and heartbreak across the color wall."

DuBose Heyward died in 1940, and thus did not live to see *Porgy* make it to the screen. Much of his writing life had been spent pondering the fate of the Negro. He cowrote the screenplay for *The Emperor Jones,* a 1933 film in which Paul Robeson starred. He also wrote *Mamba's Daughters,* which Ethel Waters appeared in onstage. Taking more than his white southern upbringing would seem to have allowed him, Heyward wrote of Negroes with an unexpected tenderness and understanding.

Sportin' Life became history's flamboyant hustler; Bess, its brokenhearted sweetheart; Porgy, its prideful beggar. "Porgy lived in the Golden Age," Heyward would write. "Not the Golden Age of a remote and legendary past; nor yet the chimerical era treasured by every man past middle life, that never existed except in the heart of youth; but an age when men, not yet old, were boys in an ancient, beautiful city that time had forgotten before it destroyed."

Samuel Goldwyn brought in an assortment of writers to take a crack at the screenplay for *Porgy,* and he finally settled on the version written by N. Richard Nash. Nash had scripted *The Rainmaker,* a well-received 1956 drama that starred Burt Lancaster and Katharine Hepburn. (Nash also wrote the play, for which he won a Pulitzer Prize.) When Goldwyn had an acceptable screenplay, he sought a director. Frank Capra and Elia Kazan both passed. He finally chose Rouben Mamoulian, who had directed the first staged *Porgy and Bess.* Mamoulian was Russian-born and had acquired a reputation for directing complex operas in Rochester, New York. Casting got under way. And once that began, the NAACP went into action.

The civil rights organization castigated *Porgy and Bess,* drawing attention to its tales of Negro drug use, fornication, gambling, and murder. Harry Belafonte, politically sensitive, turned down the lead role. "I rejected it," Belafonte says. "DuBose Heyward wrote a very racist story. The leading man was on his knees. The second leading man was a cocaine pusher. The third man was a hustler. The leading lady was a prostitute. What makes *Porgy and Bess* work is the remarkable music. But the images were highly distasteful."

The leading role was next offered to Sidney Poitier. Poitier also declined. "I had a considerable aversion to *Porgy and Bess* because of its inherent racial attitudes." Goldwyn asked Poitier for a private meeting; Poitier agreed to meet but still refused the role. The few Negro stars in Hollywood seemed to be running from the movie. Pearl Bailey said she might accept a role—but not if any of the female cast members wore a bandanna, which reeked of plantation dress. Finally, after Poitier's agent put fear into him by telling him Goldwyn could blackball his career, Poitier signed on for the lead. Goldwyn, obviously sensing possible trouble and believing that a "quiet boycott" existed among Negro talent, donated $1,000 to the NAACP. Dorothy Dandridge, the most visible Negro female star in Hollywood, agreed to play Bess. Still, the third largest role in the movie, that of Sportin' Life, remained to be filled.

Belafonte remained steadfast in his sentiments that the movie not be made. "In a period of calm, perhaps this picture could be viewed historically. But skins are still too thin and emotions still too sensitive for a lot of Uncle Toms in *Porgy & Bess* to be shown now," he told an interviewer.

Sammy convinced himself that the role of Sportin' Life was his and his only. He practiced all the Gershwin songs from the *Porgy and Bess* songbook. He skipped around his home singing as he practiced drawing his six-shooters. When he heard of a party Judy Garland was giving, and that Goldwyn would be in attendance, Sammy Davis, Jr.—the newly minted Jew—went to meet Samuel Goldwyn, the old Jew. (Goldwyn privately considered Sammy just a Negro comic who spent all his time aping Jerry Lewis onstage.) When Sammy arrived, not only was Goldwyn there, but so was Lee Gershwin, wife of Ira. Sammy bopped about, shaking hands, spotting Goldwyn. He got himself near the piano and sang several Gershwin tunes, with Garland hovering nearby.

"Swear on your life you'll never use him," Lee Gershwin said to Goldwyn, out of Sammy's earshot.

"Him?" Goldwyn said. "That monkey?"

The phone from the Goldwyn studios did not ring in Sammy Davis's Beverly Hills office. Goldwyn wanted Cab Calloway—who had starred as Sportin' Life on its road tour—for his movie. Sammy was worried, but fiercely determined. "Sammy knows one thing," says Jess Rand. "He wants to be Sportin' Life. I was a Gershwin fanatic. I saw the original *Porgy and Bess* with Avon Long. I knew this [role] was Sammy." The Morris agency began thinking of ways to get Goldwyn's attention.

Abe Lastfogel called Sammy's office, and told Rand to reserve the Earl Carroll Room (private, but with a view of the stage) at the Moulin Rouge, where Sammy was performing. "I'm going to bring Goldwyn and his wife," Lastfogel said. Goldwyn begged Lastfogel not to tell Sammy he was coming. But, of course, Sammy was prepared. "They come in," Rand remembers.

> Sammy begins pulling out all the stops. Doing the longest show you ever seen in your life. Then he stops. He says, "Ladies and gentlemen, you can't see them, I can't either. But

Samuel Goldwyn and his wife are up there." Sammy says, "Mr. Goldwyn, I'll do the role of Sportin' Life for nothing." Goldwyn looked at Lastfogel and said, "He's a vaudevillian. I'm looking for an actor." Frances, Abe's wife, looks at Goldwyn and says, "Sam, listen to Abe." Sam said, "All right, call me tomorrow."

Samuel Goldwyn had his Sportin' Life.

Rand fired off news of the signing to the newspapers, the white as well as the black press. All done, of course, at Sammy's energetic urging. But the Goldwyn people didn't like it: "We do the publicity," one of Goldwyn's boys quickly told Rand.

Sammy, so happy, went out and bought Goldwyn a wristwatch to show his gratitude. The watch had gadgets on it. Jess Rand watched Sammy present it to the mogul. Goldwyn fingered it, peered at it, squinched his face. "It's too complicated," he said. He took the thing anyway.

The fittings for costumes began. Sammy was given a plaid suit, a derby, a cane—not much different from the clothing he wore in vaudeville. A controversy erupted during fittings, for someone had obviously ignored Pearl Bailey's dictum: she looked around the costume room and began to scream. "No one is going to wear a bandanna in any picture I'm in!" She didn't get her way totally; a small number of bandannas were handed out.

On the first day of filming, Sammy gave everyone on the set gifts. Then he turned himself into Sportin' Life—a drug pusher on Catfish Row who spreads his "happy dust" all around and insinuates himself into the life of Porgy and Bess.

On July 2, 1958, a fire broke out on the *Porgy and Bess* set. It was calculated that damages totaled between $2 million and $5 million. But Samuel Goldwyn was accustomed to having his way; the old mogul would not be deterred from making the movie. "So go replace it!" he snapped to his minions when told of the movie-set damages. And of course there were those who wondered—given the controversy surrounding the film—if Negro arsonists had engaged in an act of sabotage. If arson crossed his mind, Goldwyn kept such thoughts to himself, while conceding there would be a two-month delay in filming.

Before filming began again, there was another distraction: Goldwyn fired the director, Rouben Mamoulian. Mamoulian said Goldwyn had been too intrusive, and had made "trespasses upon my private and professional life." The mood was strange and bewildering. Goldwyn quickly hired another director, the estimable Otto Preminger. Leigh Whipper, a cast member—and president of the Negro Actors Guild of America—blasted Preminger's hiring and abruptly quit the production. "I believe that the proposed *Porgy and Bess* is now in hands unsympathetic to my people," Whipper said. "I have first-hand information concerning the new director which brands him, to me, as a man who has no respect for my people." Sammy uttered little, save a statement, along with Pearl Bailey and Brock Peters, applauding Preminger.

Let other Negroes—Harry Belafonte, Whipper, members of the NAACP—complain and commiserate about a German director making a movie about Negroes written by a white Southerner in Negro dialect. Sammy was in heaven. Shameful material? Not to Sammy Davis, Jr. He was hungrier than all the heated protests of all the stereotypes of Hollywood cinema combined. "I went to visit Sammy," Keely Smith recalls of a trek to the *Porgy and Bess* set. "Sammy was happy as a lark."

It wasn't always so for others in the cast. When Preminger screamed at Poitier one afternoon, Poitier calmly removed the knee pads he had to wear portraying the crippled Porgy and walked off the set. The mood was tense, the silence forboding. He agreed to return only after Preminger apologized.

Both Poitier and Diahann Carroll—young, very beautiful, and cast as Clara in the film—were married. But they fell in love on the set, and it would cause turmoil in both their marriages. Sammy added to the production's overall turmoil.

"I won't be here on Monday," he announced to Preminger at the end of one workday.

"Why not?" Preminger demanded.

"It's Rosh Hashanah," Sammy said. "It's the Jewish New Year."

Preminger didn't care; he had a movie to shoot. "I'm Jewish too, Sammy, I'll be here on Monday."

"There's a difference," Sammy shot back. "You're an old Jew. I'm a new Jew."

The tough German director seemed taken aback, but he granted Sammy his wish.

Before *Porgy and Bess* completed filming, Sammy had another engagement to fulfill. It may have taken him four years to deliver on his promise, but on November 15, Sammy climbed into a bus—he had commandeered three of them—with a bevy of handpicked stars to return to San Bernardino. Ever since his eye surgery there he had vowed to go back to raise money for its hospital. By the time he returned, in 1958, a new one had been built, but the proceeds from his concert would go toward buying needed medical equipment. "He said he would do it," nurse Virginia Henderson recalls, "but when he left, we said, 'He'll forget.' "

On the buses were, among others, James Garner, a onetime traveling salesman who, a year earlier, had become a TV star playing a cardsharp in *Maverick;*

SAMUEL GOLDWYN

PORGY and BESS

SIDNEY POITIER · DOROTHY DANDRIDGE
SAMMY DAVIS, Jr.· PEARL BAILEY

Music GEORGE GERSHWIN · Libretto DuBOSE HEYWARD

Lyrics: DuBOSE HEYWARD and IRA GERSHWIN (Founded on the play 'Porgy' by DuBOSE and DOROTHY HEYWARD)
Produced by the Theatre Guild · Screenplay: N. RICHARD NASH

Regie: OTTO PREMINGER

TODD-AO° · TECHNICOLOR° · STEREOPHONIC SOUND

Never mind the scorn heaped upon it while being made, Porgy and Bess *showcased a cinematic Sammy of remarkable range. Some saw a mammy musical, but he saw gold, and he twirled and high-stepped onscreen in spats. It would be the high mark of his uneven movie career, even as his dream of an Oscar for playing Sportin' Life went unrealized.*

(AUTHOR'S COLLECTION)

Zsa Zsa Gabor, a former Miss Hungary who had parlayed her smoldering looks—as opposed to acting talent, of which evidence was scant—to make herself a Hollywood celebrity; Lindsay Crosby (one of Bing's sons); Buddy Bregman, the young musician (Sammy had brought Bregman along as music conductor, but he also wanted to secretly discuss with him—out of earshot of Sam Sr. and Will Mastin, who had stayed behind—musical possibilities for his solo career); Tony Curtis; Sidney Poitier (Porgy himself!); Diahann Carroll; Luddy Waters; Warren Cowan, the powerful Hollywood figure who handled Sinatra's public relations; and Judy Garland. It was an eclectic mix, owing to Sammy's reach across Hollywood.

"Sammy was intrigued by celebrity," says Cowan, the publicity agent. "And Sammy just didn't know he was the biggest celebrity of them all."

While rolling along, Sammy regaled his busload with stories of his auto accident, shrieking like a child who had escaped a terrible misfortune in some darkened cave. "I remember him stopping at a drugstore on the way," recalls Luddy Waters, "and running in and coming out with all of these outrageous little gifts for us."

The townsfolk of San Bernardino eagerly awaited Sammy's appearance. A month earlier tickets for the benefit had gone on sale, and a frenzy had ensued. A ticket could be purchased at Krause Pharmacy, Wilson Mortgage Company, or the Arrowhead Springs Hotel—where a good many of those arriving on the buses would spend the night—and also Howe's Shoes. In no time at all, the benefit sold out, to the tune of seventy-five hundred tickets. Posters were all around town:

San Bernardino Community Auxiliary Hospital
presents Sammy Davis Jr. and Company
Benefit/Show Sat. Nov. 15 8:00 PM national
orange show SWING AUDITORIUM $5.00 and
$3.00 and $2.00 each (tax) Call TU-8-0211
SAN BERNARDINO

San Bernardino's finest came out to the Swing Auditorium on Mill Street on the evening of November 15, along with Sammy's doctors and many of the nurses who had been there the day of the surgery. Virginia Henderson was in a lovely printed dress; Fred Hull, Sammy's eye surgeon, put on a tux. They were all enormously excited knowing so many celebrities would be in their midst. No one could remember such a large number of people ever before fitting into the Swing. Many of the women were in fur, the men in long wool coats.

Sammy bounded onto the stage in a tuxedo and glasses following his introduction by Virginia Henderson. The city presented him with a scroll, of the type the mayor gives to a lot of visiting dignitaries—only this one had a little feature: it highlighted Sammy's musical career in words. Sammy eyeballed the thing as if it were the Magna Carta.

Then the show: he sang and danced. He introduced his friends—the other stars—his arms rising out to them with such reverence. A slight bow; a step back from them in his patent leather slip-ons. He reminded Henderson of a fast-moving master of ceremonies. He did a gun-drawing duel with "Maverick"—James Garner.

Draw!

Draw!

Draw!

Both were lightning fast. Oohs and aahs from the crowd. Sammy won.

He did some mimicry, some tap dancing, some singing: his anthemlike "Let Me Sing" reached a fevered crescendo, and thunderous applause followed. Henderson and Hull were amazed. All this just because in the wee hours of a quiet morning, on a desolate roadway, a rising-fast singer crashed his lime green Cadillac and lost his eye and lived to tell about it. His friends sat and watched him and loved it—their Sammy, so magnanimous, so giving. Then he turned the stage over to others.

"Judy Garland was here," says Henderson. "Poor ole Judy. She wouldn't go onstage until I got her a bottle of vodka. I had to get one of the security officers to go down to the liquor store. She sat on a stool, dressed in a woman's tuxedo. She gave a performance like you wouldn't believe. She sang one song after the other. But she was higher than a tick." Garland—her booze in a nearby flask—couldn't stop singing: "Day In and Day Out," "The Bells Are Ringing," "Clang Clang Clang Went the Trolley." Young Buddy Bregman watched wide-eyed. He remembers the auditorium being so crowded he "couldn't see the end of the audience." Garland seemed ready to quit, but Sammy egged her on to do more, and she did: "Rockabye Your Baby with a Dixie Melody," "Swanee," and, of course, "Over the Rainbow." "She punched me in the ribs with her elbow," remembers Bregman, who was conducting the orchestra, "and kept saying, 'Cut to "Rainbow." ' " After she finished the tender and haunting ballad, the song's lyrics seemed to hang in the air. Many had been near tears, as if they were sensing a kind of personal coda for Garland's own torment.

Danny Thomas—star of TV's *Make Room for Daddy*—was there, but he didn't arrive with the others on the buses. "Danny Thomas gave a terrific performance," remembers Henderson. "He drove up with his chauffeur, performed, got in his car, and took off."

Sammy had more to offer. He brought out Nita and Pepe, an acrobatic dance act—ever the touch of vaudeville—that had been opening for the Mastin trio. Sidney Poitier introduced John Carroll, a baritone singer who gave a rendition of "O Sole Mio," and followed that with "The Lord's Prayer."

Afterward, there were hugs all around, and much kissing. The reception was right next door. Some local college kids, attending San Bernardino Valley College, had served as ushers for the event. Sammy told them to come to the VIP reception. They backed off—they had no money. So he insisted they come as his personal guests.

The event raised more than $20,000.

Next morning, Sammy was gone, back to Hollywood.

Those reading that morning's *San Bernardino Sun* saw that the reviewer had referred to Sammy's benefit gala as "undoubtedly the greatest vaudeville show ever to be presented in San Bernardino."

Porgy and Bess premiered on June 24, 1959, in New York City. Amid flashbulbs, Sammy showed up with an entourage, and Elvera, his mother, was also there. For weeks there had been buzz about Sammy's performance. The reviews confirmed them. "In previous stage productions of this folk opera," Bosley Crowther wrote in the *New York Times,* "Sportin' Life has come through as a sort of droll and impious rascal with the bright, lively quality of a minstrel man. . . . But there's nothing charming or sympathetic about the fellow Mr. Davis plays. He's a comprehension of evil on an almost repulsive scale." Justin Gilbert of the *New York Mirror* would write: "The most articulately fascinating figure is Sammy Davis Jr. as Sportin' Life. Let us say that with his tight little derby, high buttoned shoes and twitching cane he exhales sulphur and brimstone as the devilish dope peddler. In two words HE'S GREAT." And the *Saturday Review of Literature:* "Sammy Davis Jr. is a source of constant fascination as he twirls and springs and minces through the role of Sportin' Life, lively as a rubber ball, evil as the 'happy dust' he leaves in his wake." In white gloves, spats, and a checked suit, Sammy is riveting. Onscreen he appears to be unleashing—pirouetting, strutting, singing—all of the inventiveness he has learned from a life on the road. (Only Sammy and Pearl Bailey did their own singing in the film; other voices were dubbed.) Goldwyn may not have wanted a vaudevillian, but he got one, rolled into a mimic, rolled into an actor. Sammy had felt hemmed in on the *Anna* set; but on *Porgy,* with its Gershwin music, he let loose. Now, at last, he was as tall as Sidney Poitier—maybe taller, even. Never mind that Negroes had complained bitterly of the stereotype in Heyward's novel. In playing the role colorless, but colorful, Sammy soared. In a way, *Porgy and Bess* was the last of the old mammy musicals produced by the Hollywood studios. And it was also the last movie made by Samuel Goldwyn. Sammy blazed through a movie the critics saw rather indifferently. He was a kid come to life, giving a brilliant performance that mattered to no one save himself and his own blinding and impossible-to-fill hunger. He told Jess to start thinking up an Oscar campaign. Jess took out a full-page ad in *Variety* showing Sammy frozen in pose—his white-gloved hands outstretched, the derby shielding his eyes. He resembled an elegant snake outfitted in dashing threads.

All his movie dreams finally came true: He was but the gifted and rootless son of vaudevillians, and he had stolen the biggest, most beguiling Negro movie of the year.

The resemblance was so astonishing that one did not even have to look close. Sammy met her in Montreal, during an engagement at the Bellevue Casino in late 1959. Joan Stuart was a young Toronto native who had danced with Canada's National Ballet Company, and made her living singing and dancing. With her blond hair and round face and gorgeousness, she was a dead ringer for Kim Novak. At long last, Sammy had finally found his blonde. They went out, gliding about wintry Toronto, the Canadian scribes close behind. He gave her jewels. In two weeks he was in love, she was in love. He could not see what Negroes were complaining about. His life was so sporting. He told Sam Sr. he had found true love. Big Sam beamed. White women. The prey of little Sammy's heart—and one now captured. Big Sam called Elvera to tell her the news of their Sammy. "The phone rings," Elvera remembers, and Sam Sr. went on to tell her that their Sammy was now engaged. Then he told her she was a white woman.

"Tell me what other kinds of girls he knows?" she said.

The engagement was announced on November 5. The plan was to marry the following March.

Word seeped out in Canada that young Joan Stuart's parents were opposed to her marrying Sammy. "It's hard for them to appreciate that we want to marry after knowing each other only ten days," she said, sounding wonderfully innocent. "I love her very much and we want to get married," Sammy insisted.

In America, the year 1959 ended with the young minister Martin Luther King, Jr., vowing to continue the fight for equal rights. "I can't stop now. History has thrust something upon me from which I cannot turn away."

Sammy was in Toronto in January 1960, going, for the first time, to meet the parents of his fiancée. The meeting did not go well. Joan Stuart's father strongly objected to the marriage. He told the couple that he could not sanction an interracial union for his daughter. Stuart's mother appeared flexible, having made the initial announcement a month earlier about the engagement.

At the time she was merely happy for her daughter, as any mother might be. But now she bent to the will of her husband and was forced to listen to her daughter's lamentations.

A woman is a sometime thing, George Gershwin had written in his mind while waltzing along the waterfront of Charleston, South Carolina, researching the life of "the unfortunate race" that DuBose Heyward had portrayed.

Like a bantamweight Jack Johnson, Sammy would go on searching for his eternal blonde. And he hardly felt unfortunate knowing so.

Sammy left Toronto with a grin upon his face.

Chapter 11

THE SANDS OF LAS VEGAS AND BEYOND

J ust inside the door of the new decade—the 1960s—sat the ghost, and the ghost was waiting for Will Mastin and Sam Sr. Sammy could not take them any farther. The men who had ironed his clothing, wiped his nose, taught him so much about show business, dragged him back and forth across the country, and stood him right before the eyes of the great Bill "Bojangles" Robinson himself, had become relics.

Sam Sr. had grown painfully tired. His heart genuinely was ailing; Rita, now his wife, wanted him home so she could care for him with her nurse's training. In those last months on the road—the winter of 1959, the cold like knives on the flesh of old men—Sam Sr. was more determined than ever to leave the act. But if he left and Mastin stayed, it would look bizarre to audiences, as it had on previous occasions when Sam Sr. was sick and Mastin still went onstage. Mastin also now had a wife—Germaine Doust, a white Canadian: he had bested Sammy in the sweepstakes!—but she was back in Montreal. The old vaudevillian preferred the road—the glitter of his cuff links and diamond ring, the sheen on the lacquered stage floor, his name in lights, his backside against the seat of the Cadillac—to a soft bed beside his wife. He had recently been moving about with a studied pantomime motion. His ankles, knees, and shoulders hurt. His blood pressure was high; sometimes he was a man swimming in his own dizziness. Nevertheless, he wore his ailments like badges of honor. Damn them all—their stares and their asides. The two of them—Sammy and Sam Sr.—would listen to Will behind his hotel-room door. That tapping of the cane had started up again—tap tap tap. And that only made it harder for the two to say anything. There were still moments, to be sure, during those last months when there was something tender, and indomitable, about the two, Sam Sr. and Will Mastin, standing in yet another dressing room, the glow of the bulbed light touching them just so. But then another telling moment: Will reaching for Sammy's shoulder—to swipe lint from the jacket, as was his habit—and Sammy gone, hardly feeling the swipe, hungry for the solo life now.

So one day, Will Mastin called a meeting. (That was another thing: Sammy had grown impatient with Will's meetings.) Will said he thought it wise if he went back to the West Coast to manage the act from there. And Sam Sr. breathed a sigh of relief, and announced his retirement also. And just like that, the Will Mastin Trio was done. Twenty-three years of nonstop performance, radio, television, Broadway, nightclubs.

No one knew how many club dates they had played—thousands upon thousands. How many strange beds they had slept in; or how many police officers walking the beat in some small town they had had to explain themselves to.

Sam Sr. had his own home in the green hills of Hollywood, and that's where he went. He drove a lovely soft-top Jaguar, and kept busy playing the horses all over—Del Mar, Santa Anita, across the border in Mexico. Sammy always heard the talk: that his father was a careless spender, that wads of cash just vanished from his pockets and palms like birds let loose skyward. But what could he do? Like father, like son. Big Sam was the old black man walking along the rows of freshly cut hedges in Beverly Hills, his pants creased beautifully, his shoes shined to a gleam, his hair swept back in little waves, his life a miracle. It had been a long journey from the fields of North Carolina.

Will Mastin realized—despite what the *Porgy and Bess* ad that trumpeted Sammy's rave reviews said in the lower right-hand corner ("Under the Personal Management of Will Mastin")—that he was no longer needed as manager. He retreated into himself. Now and then he could be seen walking alone up and down Olympic Boulevard in Los Angeles—anything to keep his legs moving. He invested some money in real estate up in Fresno. He poked his head in and out of church on Sundays. And sometimes he came over to Sammy's office. That was, in its own way, quite special. An office to go to. A place to sit and be remembered and let the mind wander. The great Bert Williams and the great Sam Lucas—the legendary minstrel performers— never had an office to go to. Before she died, Bessie Smith never had an office to go to. Neither did Billie Holiday. Generosity was part of Sammy's signature; he kept his father on the payroll. Mastin's contract didn't run out until 1965. Now and then, when someone would come into the office and spot Mastin, and mention the act, having seen it one place or another, he'd rise, slowly, and do a little two-step. He looked old—and proud. But then, moments into the routine, he'd sheepishly lower his eyes, as if he suddenly realized how much the memories hurt.

As the 1960s dawned, Sammy was as happy, and as free, as any Negro in America could possibly hope to be. He never cried over lost love. He swam, instead, into the jaws of the sharks—there were already rumors of yet another white actress he had fallen in love with; he had outstanding debts to nightclub owners; the IRS was coming after him and Sam Sr. for a $56,000 payment. But he could care less. Money wasn't really money unless it was getting away from him. When he had to claw and hustle to get it back, to run from city to city, stage to stage, scratching and sweating to retrieve more of it, when he was threatened with penury, is when his adrenaline would start to rush. Only then would he realize the preciousness of money, the sharp and undeniable connection of it to his lifestyle. "He never had enough money," recalls Bill Miller, the Riviera's manager, who would front Sammy thousands of dollars over the years. "He was a terrible spendthrift." Spending habits mattered little to Sammy. The deeper the water's danger and depth, the better he swam. When he needed money, he could—and on short notice—make bucketfuls of the stuff.

So Sammy was smiling now.

His grandmother Rosa—the onetime servant herself—had servants of her own! Rosa still liked doing her own shopping, tugging on Rudy, the valet, getting him to drive her to the market out there on Central Avenue, where she'd carefully inspect the produce—only the best fruits and vegetables were good enough for her little Sammy.

Now, without his father or Will Mastin, the nightclub marquees said just one word:

SAMMY

Glittery little lightbulbs circling the marquee where his name appeared. Long lines of men and women—the men in fedoras and coats, the women in dresses and pearls—looking up at his name, then whispering about him the way they whispered about prizefighters. The lines were mostly always all white because, to many Negroes, those tickets to see Sammy were just too pricey.

Alone now, without the two old men who had bracketed him and danced beside him for so long, he performed like someone let loose from body restraints. He seemed to have more energy than ever. He was unstoppable.

He was rising like flames in the night.

Television producer Aaron Spelling wanted him for a General Electric drama in 1961. Sammy was playing at the Sands. Filming would take place during the day, early morning. His shows at the Sands sometimes didn't end until the wee morning hours. There was no shuttle plane service, so he'd have to pull out of the drama. Only there was no way he'd pull out. His hunger precluded his doing such a thing.

"No one thought he could make it after the show," remembers Warren

Cowan, the Sinatra publicity maven. But Sammy wanted the role badly, and he assured Spelling he'd be on the set every morning. He hired an ambulance and driver, and every night, the ambulance took him from Las Vegas to Los Angeles. He slept in the ambulance. He never missed a day of filming. "I always thought that was brilliant," says Cowan.

The road crew was all Sammy's now. He was bending them to his will. Shirley and Rudy and Murphy no longer worked for Will and Sam Sr. They worked for him. They were not blood family, but they had made him their life. They were the ones who constructed the wall around him, the ones who put him to sleep at night, who closed the door gently. He was in the third decade of his life, and there were many nights when he still loved being tucked in. What did loyalty and love mean anyway, if your own mother had abandoned you? He had stood in a mental hospital in Connecticut—quiet, lovely, expensive— and said to his sister, Ramona, "Don't let the hate kill you." She had suffered a nervous breakdown; she wondered if their parents even cared for her. Sammy told her that she had to survive, as he had survived. Then he quietly paid the hospital bill and rushed back to the coast. Sometimes—even though there was still much of the child in him—he could sound so wise. Well, he had been on the road since childhood. He knew life was strange; there were people who had honest faces but cruel hearts. Shirley and Murphy and Rudy would protect him from the cruel hearts of others. He could not depend on the red blood of family. "I remember being in Atlantic City with Sammy," recalls Cindy Bitterman. "Sammy said, 'I have to go see my mother tomorrow, so round up the gang.' I said, 'What do you mean. Can't you go see your mother by yourself?' He said, 'No, once you meet her, you'll see why.' Then he said, 'And after five minutes or so, you have to say, "Okay, let's go, Sammy, you've got a radio interview to do." ' "

So to survive and keep going he'd depend on the family who surrounded him now, rolling across the great and gift-giving American landscape with him. Pots and pans jangling on the bus, Shirley and George in love and on the road, Murphy drowning his own dreams of singing to be by Sammy's side, the country flashing by them all like postcards. It was, in its own way, as lovely and gritty as vaudeville—but without the desperation.

Sometimes they found themselves flying, floating through the clouds. There were not many Negroes up that high. And Sammy would be cackling, hungry as ever to prove himself. He just couldn't wait for the plane to land, to take the city below, the stage that awaited him.

Let the decade close. Sammy was happy. He had broken nightclub records. It mattered little to him that he had to slip through backdoors and side doors as he was playing those first-class clubs.

He had so much now: a cook and a valet and an administrative staff and endless bookings. But there was something missing. He wanted a wife. The attempts at marriage had gone so wrong; diamond rings out the window. He wanted a real marriage, with love, unlike the farce with Loray White, and the hole in the wake of Joan Stuart. As the decade came to a close, as luck would have it, Sammy had a new lady. Like so many of the others, she was willowy, beautiful, and blond. She was May (pronounced "My") Britt, a Swedish-born Hollywood actress. The romance had been quick, and already Sammy was swooning about the future. Marriage plans had been discussed. "It won't be a mammoth affair, I assure you," he told some reporters while relaxing in his hotel suite in Windsor, Ontario, that summer, "but I've a lot of friends who I am sure will want to attend when I set the definite date."

With the black-white wedding sure to unleash protests, and feeling he would need a more powerful figure to handle media relations, Sammy—with a nudge from Sinatra—coldly dropped Jess Rand. Theirs was a relationship fostered before the Will Mastin Trio saw its name in lights. Rand had not only worked for Sammy in press relations and publicity, but had helped guide the trio by plotting strategy as they moved back and forth across the country. Sammy hired Warren Cowan, the powerful Los Angeles public relations figure. Cowan had plenty of clients. His best known: Frank Sinatra. Rand never forgave the brutal dismissal by Sammy, and their relationship would never be mended.

Sammy decided to introduce his new fiancée abroad.

"Here she is, fellers," he said to a contingent of goggle-eyed English reporters—even more sharklike than the American press—while in London. He sounded like a cowboy, mocking the scribes in the land of the King's English. Once again, however, a cunning Sammy: in London, he was far from the American press, and he was even farther from the prickly American Negro press, which had no full-time correspondents based abroad. At the London press conference to introduce his fiancée, he was grinning, all teeth and victory, his legs moving across the room as if they were oiled. The reporters' necks were swiveling like chicken necks. Britt strolled in in spiked high heels, wearing a hot-pink summer dress. She had a hypnotic gaze and gave the reporters yet another sensational Sammy story to report. They would report the hell out of it. Before nightfall, the hecklers were on the streets of London. How so many Londoners had loved him onstage! And how so many were in the streets reviling him now—saliva dripping from the corners of their mouths, eyes red, fists balled. At a restaurant, dining with Britt's parents, he tried smiling away the nervousness and fear on their faces: Nazi marchers had assembled outside the restaurant, protesting announcement of the engagement. It was all just a simple confession of love. A year ago the Canadians had been so kind, so understanding, when he posed for pictures with Joan Stuart. But this wasn't Canada. The anger stunned May, and she bolted for the States.

He had seen it all before. It was like an old newsreel—white and black and secret sex—and he was both projectionist and star. Friends would wonder where all the hurt went after it got deposited inside his small frame. For Sammy, so much of it was entertainment. He couldn't help but enjoy it. Still, the one eye was working overtime in and around London now. He had to beware the crazies and the nuts and the pistol-packers. Why, couldn't they see how lovely she was? How fine a body she possessed? They just didn't understand. Neither did Britt's mother, who thought her daughter was only inviting unnecessary danger into her life.

Yes, Sammy was still a happy man. He had a new blonde, and she was wearing his engagement ring. "Sammy Davis to Wed May Britt," the *New York Times* reported. There was now the possibility of having a real family: a wife, kids. Let the IRS take their damn $56,000. It was a few weeks' pay. Chump change. And if he couldn't come up with it fast enough, there was always Skinny D'Amato, or Bill Miller, or Dave Duschoff at the Latin Casino. Nightclub work was lined up for months and months. The movies were calling—actually, it was Sinatra calling. He had sent over a script, something about hustlers robbing the casinos in Las Vegas, easy work, with the filming to be done right there in Vegas. And, of course, there was music, the fingers snapping. A new Sammy album would be landing in the record stores soon. "I Got a Right to Swing!" he would proclaim on it.

Back on American shores in 1960, Sammy, following a string of nightclub appearances, began a Los Angeles engagement at the Huntington Hartford Theatre. Steve Blauner, the MCA entertainment agent, couldn't resist seeing Sammy perform. He'd seen him a hundred times, from Buffalo to Vegas, and he'd see him a hundred more times if possible. Blauner would marvel at the fact that Davis never seemed to give the same performance twice, that he seemed, onstage, to rebirth himself every night right before the audience's eyes. The spontaneity could be hell on Sammy's band members, but the audience members never caught on to that. What Blauner didn't know, of course, was this: there'd always be a need for Sammy to prove, to himself and the audience, that he was worthy of the lights, the high stage. He had seen so many entertainers fall off the stage, unable to find their way back up. He kept a running list in his mind of which performers were hot, which cold, who was out and who was in, who was on the radio, who was on TV. Who was—to use that old and shameless word of the business—*loved*.

Blauner arrived at the theater in a tuxedo. He went inside and made his way to Sammy's dressing room. "I go backstage to wish him well," recalls Blauner. With Sammy, there was always the bear hug, given and received. But once back out in the theater, Blauner heard noises in the lobby and beyond, in the direction of the front door. An imposing man at six foot five inches, Blauner could always see over the heads of others in front of him. He made his way toward the commotion, and there, right out the front door, he saw the whole scene. Picketers had gathered, and they were parading, men in brown shirts and brown pants. They wore armbands with Nazi insignia. One held a barking black dog on a leash. There were gawkers, and theatergoers wanting to purchase tickets, all joined by the small group of Nazis. In London, Sammy had bragged to the British press that Americans would not protest his marriage to Britt, that there would be no picketers as there were on the streets of London. Now George Lincoln Rockwell had sent out a quartet of "soldiers" from his American Nazi Party to tell Sammy Davis what they thought of his engagement to the beautiful, blond May Britt. By the time Blauner reached the picketers on the sidewalk—one of their placards said "Sammy Davis Jew-nior"—his emotions had escalated. "I go crazy. I take my glasses off and go for them. I knocked one over a car and took the poster he was carrying and broke it over my knee." The gawkers stumbled backward, forced to make room. There were shrieks, hands cupped over mouths, bodies flying. Blauner had big arms, big hands, and he was swinging, one man against four. One huge and suddenly perspiring emotional military vet who loved little Sammy—whaling against four stunned Nazis. Word raced back to Sammy to stay inside. He didn't resist. Blauner pinned one of the Nazis on the ground. The other Nazis lunged for him, but a small, elderly man blocked their path, sacrificing his body so Blauner could continue to throw his thick fists at the Nazi beneath him. "Next thing I know," Blauner recalls, "the police knocked me off of him." The crowd, on Blauner's side, began yelling at the police, and during the commotion, Blauner was shoved inside the theater, staving off an arrest. The Nazis went home. Sammy went on, and gave every patron their money's worth. "Mob Routs Nazis at Davis Show" said the *Los Angeles Mirror* headline.

After Los Angeles, Sammy found himself back in Las Vegas. Sinatra had corralled him, along with Peter Lawford and Dean Martin and Joey Bishop, for twenty days of performances at the Sands. Sinatra had a small stake in the hotel. They arrived in a private jet. There'd also be a movie, *Ocean's 11*, to shoot after the shows. Studio publicity didn't say it, but they might as well have: casting by Sinatra. Dean, Peter, Joey, and Henry Silva were all part of the cast, along with Sammy and Angie Dickinson. It was Sammy who had suggested to Sinatra that he cast Dickinson: he'd gone wild for her performance in the cowboy picture *Rio Bravo*—she played John Wayne's love interest—released in 1959.

It is hard, nearly impossible, to redirect the course of a relationship between men away from its beginnings. Sammy was hungry, chasing Frank for advice, for any type of assistance, so happy to beg all those years ago. Frank was cocky and fulfilled, gracious enough to have lent a hand and assisted Sammy in his rise. But, forever thereafter, Sinatra was on top of the relationship, and Sammy beholden.

Up onstage, the lights catching their pretty white shirts and the sheen in the lapels of their tuxedo jackets, they were enormously watchable. Dean moved like an old man. Sinatra moved like a man happily watching himself in the mirror. As for Sammy, he moved with the quick and unexplainable movements of something feral, something suddenly set free. "Here," Dean says onstage to Frank one night into their Sands engagement, having lifted Sammy, holding him in his arms like a hurt fawn, "this award just came for you from the National Association for the Advancement of Colored People." Liquor was sliding down throats, laughter and spittle just flying, Sammy cackling almost orgasmically. There would, sure enough, come a time when the jokes, especially the watermelon jokes, would start to sound a little mean to Sammy's ears. His emotions—kept hidden in those little out-of-the way eddies where hurt flowed and stored itself in the dark, waiting to explode—would eventually erupt. There would come a time when he would loathe the word "Frank," and the word "Sinatra," when he could no longer keep anything hidden.

But not now.

Now there was only the stage of the Sands, and good sweet tingling and wild laughter. There was, to be sure, much beauty to Sammy and Sinatra's relationship. So much in it, and of it, was right: Sinatra ignoring the casino owners, the naysayers, who didn't want the Negro around, all the talk falling from lips about Sammy chasing white women, which threatened the white men. And Sinatra never-minding all the southern Democrats and the whispers about Sammy possibly marrying that white actress, and how would that look, now, right now, with the senator from Massachusetts, Jack Kennedy, brother-in-law to Peter Lawford, running for president and, in fact, sitting in the audience at the Sands. No, Sinatra would worry about none of that; he'd just sing "High Hopes," and the others would croon in, laughing, the high rollers in the audience slapping themselves, tobacco smoke rolling over them like lazy gray bubbles, all of them, Frank, Dean, Peter, Joey, and Sammy, bouncing around onstage like men on a floating mattress: the Rat Pack. The owners, the bellhops, the women, no one could do enough for them, but they tried, and they tried hard.

And there they were, a portrait frozen in time, as if age would never catch them, right beneath the giant SANDS lettering in front of the hotel: Sinatra on the far left, hands in pockets, looking like the richest man on earth, with that I-own-the-men-in-this-photo smile on his face; Dean, to the right of Frank, looking as if he has just rushed into view, looking impatient, as if he'll give the photographer one click—fuck what Frank says—and bolt; and, panning to the far right, Bishop, almost invisible and just happy to be there; and, on Bishop's right, Lawford, taller than everyone else, looking as blocky as a nightclub bouncer. And there, smack in the middle, in a double-breasted suit, the only one with tie loosened, the only one with a little cock of the knee, the smile looking so easy, as if it's melting right into the lens, stands Sammy. His waist looks about as wide as a silver dollar. He looks itchy, because he has always been itchy, wanting to go, to run someplace. They seem, especially the three to the left—Frank, Dean, and Sammy—to be plotting something inviting, something secretive. They look as if they are on the deck of a ship, and it is on the verge of sailing backward, away from everything normal and quiet and serene, into something better, and riskier, into a whole other America, into something that didn't even have its catchall name yet: the sixties. There are many, in living rooms across Negro America, who believe Sammy to be the most gifted of the group, but they will never tell him because they loathe him for his acquaintances with white women. Sammy now alternately floats into consciousness as Negro America's gift and, at times, her shame. He had already seen Negro life from down off the stage, where troubles and heartache brewed, where life was unpredictable and totally separated from the white world. Onstage, life looked wonderful and seductive. Sammy could look out of the good eye and see how life, up high, looked so good for Frank. Life up onstage was a feast, Negro life in segregated America a chore. His singular passion did not lie in wanting to be a Negro, but in being a wonderful, always-hungry, and unforgettable entertainer.

Filming of *Ocean's 11* went smooth enough. Sammy played the garbageman who picks the loot up and drives it away from the casinos. He also sang the title song, "Ocean's 11," his voice sounding, as always, too epic for such a small body.

Sammy was the youngest member of the Rat Pack. Sinatra was ten years older, Martin eight, Bishop seven, and Lawford two. In their midst, Sammy was all athlete. He imbued the group with a sense of movement and motion. Without Sammy, they'd have looked about as nimble as a barbershop quartet. He'd glide across the stage of the Sands, doing Fred Astaire poses—arms wide, knees bent, head cocked—yanking the attention of the audience, imbuing the pack with youthful bursts of energy. He looked like something from a Roy DeCarava photograph. He could not steal the spotlight every night, not if he wanted to keep Frank happy, so just as often he subsumed himself, crawled inside himself, allowing his talents to languish, merely offering the one-liner, or the opening lyrics of some song that would be quickly and comically interrupted by Dean or Frank. He had the ability to bust the evening wide open, just as he had done for years on stages with his father and Mastin. But Frank was moody, and Sammy chose his moments carefully. What price to disappear? Especially for the vaudevillian—a known klieg light snatcher? What price to dilute oneself? When he had picked a moment, when he could no longer contain himself, Sammy just went, soaring, like some skinny penguin, right by Frank and Dean and Peter and Joey. He'd freeze at one end of the stage—then, like something shot out from a painting, he'd bolt back across to the other end. He gave the Rat Pack dimension. Without him, they were four white guys carousing on a stage. He gave them edge. He gave them black and white.

Sammy was on a carousel now, going around and around. Harry Belafonte was watching, and so was Sidney Poitier, his only rivals as superstar Negro entertainers. They did not like what they saw. "Harry, Sidney, and Sammy were very close," says Shirley Rhodes. "But they took umbrage at Frank putting his arms around Sammy. They felt Sammy had defected to Frank."

There were currents of protest in Las Vegas that summer. Two months after Sammy and Frank and the others had departed the Sands, the nightclub owners relented and began allowing Negroes into the clubs on the strip. The NAACP had threatened to send marchers over if the casino owners would not open their doors to Negroes. The owners hardly wanted that kind of publicity. In the end, the old civil rights organization—and not the Rat Pack—had the last laugh. An integration decree was signed on the west side of Las Vegas, at the Negro-populated Moulin Rouge nightclub itself. They called it the Moulin Rouge Agreement.

After Vegas, Sinatra, Sammy, and the crew arrived in Los Angeles by train. They arrived just in time for the Democratic National Convention.

Sammy's support of politicians went back years, all the way to Adlai Stevenson, up to and including Governor Edmund Brown of California. But it was Kennedy's expected Republican foe, Vice President Richard Nixon, who had first invited Sammy to the White House, in 1957, searing Sammy's memory as he sat in Nixon's highback chair. And how could he forget the moment with Nixon backstage at the Copa—with his father and Will and Jerry Lewis? But Kennedy was Lawford's brother-in-law, and Lawford was in the pack, and Frank just had to whistle, and Dean and Sammy and the others were lining up to do what they could do for him. Sammy would hardly be alone at the convention as entertainer, as star. Janet Leigh was there; so were Gina Lollobrigida and Norman Mailer and Christopher Isherwood and Gore Vidal, among so many others.

John Kennedy did not naturally appeal to American Negroes. His refusal to castigate Joe McCarthy hung in the air, as well as his cordial relations—many thought too cordial—with southern Democrats, who habitually blocked civil rights legislation. Negroes were fond of Hubert Humphrey and Stuart Symington, two senators representing, respectively, Minnesota and Missouri; both men were considered progressive. Kennedy could not match their liberal credentials.

It was Sammy's first convention. He was excited. For months, he had been playing go-between for Sinatra with Kennedy and the King camp, Frank threatening King about his lackluster support for Kennedy. (Deep in the darkness of that convention, the FBI and CIA were both wiretapping rooms: there were fears of the Kennedy and Sinatra connection, because of the Sinatra and Sam Giancana connection.) When Sammy took to the stage along with Sinatra and Peter to sing, the Mississippi delegation booed. They were booing Sammy's skin color, his engagement to May Britt, just the fact he was before them; boos and boos. Sinatra rolled his eyes. They were bigots. In such a public arena, there was nothing they could do, except sing, and they continued singing the song they were singing when the booing began: "The Star-Spangled Banner."

Senator Kennedy won the Democratic nomination on the first ballot.

The following winter months were not kind to Jack Kennedy when it came to Negroes. They remembered well his endorsement from James Patterson, the segregationist Alabama governor, and how warmly he had accepted it. There were also many old Negro southern ministers who still cozied warmly to Republican sentiments, owing to Lincoln's legacy. Kennedy stood staring out at black ministers at one appearance, and many of them were wearing "Nixon Now" buttons. Nixon, in private, could be sincere, even charming ("if Richard Nixon is not sincere," Martin Luther King, Jr., would write to a confidant, "he is the most dangerous man in America"). Kennedy's call to King in a Georgia jail, where he was being held, may have been coldly political, but it was also quite shrewd. Many Negroes believed it was a sign foretelling what kind of president he would be. Kennedy squeaked into the White House that November.

There still remained nothing more combustible, more dangerous, for an American Negro to do than to choose to marry a white woman. It was also illegal in many states below the Mason-Dixon line.

Two weeks after Kennedy's election—Sinatra had asked Sammy to hold off until after November—Sammy took another bride, adding to his numbers of haters, both Negro and white. But Sammy could not help himself. He loved white women, loved the sight of one on his black silk sheets. His American dream.

She was born May Wilkens in Lidingo, Sweden—a sliver of a Stockholm suburb—in 1933. Her father was a postal employee, her mother a housewife. She grew tall, fancied a pageboy haircut, island-hopped, swam, sailed with family. It was a rather typical middle-class European upbringing. Young May had catlike eyes and high cheekbones. Following finishing school, she worked in a photography studio in Stockholm. Surrounded by the beauty of Sweden, she wanted to become a photographer. Not long after the war, Carlo Ponti, an Italian filmmaker, began roving the European continent in search of young beauties. He'd breeze in and out of photography studios, studying the pictures of models, of beautiful women he felt could be in pictures. Once recruited, they were trained, instructed in how to become even more beautiful, sexier, and then they were put onscreen, where, suddenly, their beauty seemed as extravagant as it was precious. Some would fade away, not hungry and resilient enough for the tricky business of movies. Sofia Scicolone—dark hair, darker eyes, voluptuous figure—was one of those who did not fade. Ponti had discovered her in 1951 in a small Italian village and put her in the movies. Sofia Scicolone became Sophia Loren, who became an international star. She also became Mrs. Carlo Ponti.

Ponti waltzed into a Stockholm studio where young May Britt was working as a photo assistant. He was prowling through the daylight for his Yolanda, the lead character in a movie he was planning. Ponti wanted an unknown. Unknowns could be full of surprises; there was magic in the true discovery. Ponti saw magic in May Britt. Fourteen days after he laid eyes on her, May Britt found herself in Rome. She was all of sixteen years old. And she was going to be in the movies.

Her screen debut came in 1952 in *Yolanda, Daughter of the Black Pirate.* The ingenue took easily to Italian life. Over the next several years, she averaged two movies a year. Movie acting did not seem to intimidate her. Buddy Adler, the chief at Twentieth Century–Fox, spotted Britt in a small role in *War and Peace.* Director Jean Negulesco was on his way to Europe to make a movie, and Adler asked the director to stop off in Rome and screen-test the young Swede. The test went well. And there she was—in Hollywood. There were comparisons to Garbo. But where Garbo was distant and her beauty icy, Britt was approachable and warm, at least on the silver screen. She took an apartment in Beverly Hills. A clotheshorse, she shopped as if it were an avocation. Her lithe frame showed sweaters and slacks to a lovely effect. She was hardly naive: she told the studio, in one of those limp and self-serving biographical portraits, that she'd like to marry a doctor and have five or six kids.

She was a young actress, and she was sucking on dreams and ideas like candy.

Her first American movie, in 1958, was *The Hunters.* It starred Robert Mitchum. Critically, save for her beauty, she went unnoticed. Next she was cast in *The Young Lions,* the adaptation of Irwin Shaw's flinty World War II novel. The movie starred Marlon Brando, Dean Martin, and Montgomery Clift. Britt played a Brando love interest. She had more screen time, and there were teasing hints of her seductive powers. But it was in a remake of *The Blue Angel* that Britt finally had her breakout role. (Hollywood widely thought the part would go to Marilyn Monroe.) She played Lola Lola, a sleep-around singer, and she played it to the hilt. (In 1930, the role had ignited German actress Marlene Dietrich's career.) With *The Blue Angel*, moviegoers could truly see what separated Britt and Garbo: Britt appeared warmer; she did not appear as if she might slap you for saying hello.

In Hollywood, you always wanted what you didn't yet have: scripts, movie roles, the lovely new female starlet in town.

May Britt might have dreamed of marrying a doctor, but she settled, at first, not on Sammy but on a socialite and would-be actor by the name of Eddie Gregson. Gregson, whose father ran an investment company, was also heir to millions. May Britt's beauty carried currency, and she knew it: she married Gregson in Mexico on February 22, 1958—one month after she met him.

On August 17, 1959, Britt appeared on the cover of *Life* magazine: "May Britt: Star with a New Style." *Life* was enamored of film beauties and would often feature them on its cover: Kim Novak, Liz Taylor, Sophia Loren. The beauties were a good magnet to draw you to the serious fare: "Nixon Wows Warsaw," said the cover that featured Britt. The *Life* article referred to Britt as "strange and lovely," and went on to describe her life as a Hollywood ingenue and new bride: she plays tennis in the mornings in a see-through nightdress, she gulps coffee, she likes riding motorcycles, and she strolls with her husband on the Stanford University campus, where he is a student.

At first, her quick marriage to Gregson was good and it was true, but ultimately it was too good to be true. The couple split after nineteen months. Britt then fell in love with an Academy Award–winning cinematographer, Leon Shamroy. But he did not fall in love with Britt; he let her know he was married. Britt went looking for love again.

Sammy was always looking for love.

May Britt had no knowledge of American history, least of all its volatile racial history. She did not know of Frederick Douglass and Jack Johnson, who suffered for their marriages to white women. She did not know of the Scottsboro Boys. She did not know of all the states, in 1960, that had laws on the books banning interracial marriage. And she certainly did not know of two Negro youths, ten-year-old James Thompson and nine-year-old David Simpson, who had been sentenced to reform school in North Carolina in 1959—the very year of her engagement to Sammy—for kissing a white girl. She knew none of this. She confessed she had met no Negroes while growing up in Europe. In a way, the less she knew made her marriage to a Negro all the sweeter, absent—at least in the early going—the residue of racial paranoia that lay across the land.

It was not lost on many entertainment watchers that Sammy—unlike Belafonte, unlike Poitier—lacked matinee-idol looks. And yet: "He was an absolute genius," says actress Barbara Rush. Rush accompanied her husband, Warren Cowan, around the country in the 1950s, watching Frank and Sammy and Dean perform. "Women like to be around men who are fascinating. And Sammy was a fascinating man."

There were times, even when he was not appearing in a film, when Sammy would make his way out to one of the Hollywood film studios to have lunch at the commissary. He was always hustling, always angling. It was at Fox studios one afternoon in 1959 that he first spied May Britt. She was there filming *The Blue Angel*. Sammy knew her face from her movies. But now, seeing her in the flesh, he became wildly smitten. He had to devise a way to meet the Swedish actress off the studio grounds.

Singer Dinah Washington was in Los Angeles, appearing at the Cloisters. Sammy decided to throw her a closing-night party. He invited Britt; the rising young actress, happy for party invitations, showed with a male acquaintance and her mother. In time, Britt caught on to Sammy's interest and showed no hesitancy—even though she had never been involved in an interracial affair—in embracing the furtive manner in which they had to date. They went boating together out in Encinitas, plenty of Sammy's friends along for obvious reasons. Britt resided in Malibu, where she rented a guest house. Sammy would come visit her under the cover of darkness, quiet as a spy. He started the jewelry-giving. And he began snapping pictures of her, and, once they were developed, admiring them in his home, his eye widening at her beauty. She asked no penetrating questions about race and America. Her naïveté gave her a blanket sense—false, as it happened—of security. Sammy was emboldened that his white male friends—Sinatra, Jim Waters, Buddy Bregman—were always available to "beard" for him. Britt began flying into Las Vegas—as a "guest" of Sinatra's, the nosy reporters were told—and catching Sammy's performances. In 1960, when May went to New York City to film the crime caper *Murder Inc.*, Sammy missed her terribly. His marriage proposal was blurted out over the phone; she accepted just as quickly; and there they were, Sammy and his golden blonde, sipping wine in her suite at the Sherry Netherland.

Britt had no idea she had become a capstone of Sammy's long and enduring white-blonde dream. Unaware of his inner dramas, she believed the fast courtship was sweet, and simply their private business. She did not bother to concern herself with the omens laid out on the dust tracks of history when it came to black and white matrimony.

In Manhattan, news of their pending nuptials had leaked, and the scribes were already hustling down Fifth Avenue to the hotel for peeks of the couple. Anytime they were surrounded by the press, an impromptu press conference seemed to form. Sammy would grin sheepishly, looking like the nerdy (those glasses!) and shy high school kid who, unbelievably, gets to take the most beautiful girl to the prom.

A week before Sammy's wedding, a group of his friends—Dean, Frank, Peter Lawford, Milton Berle, Buddy Bregman among them—treated him to a stag party at the Villa Capri in Los Angeles. "We had the backroom," recalls Bregman. "I was sitting in a booth with Sammy's posse, and the biggest names in the business were there. Sammy Cahn threw the whole thing. Sammy [Cahn] wrote parodies for Dean and everybody else. The evening was so funny. It was so fitting." Berle vanished during drinks, then reappeared dressed in drag—as May Britt. Sammy howled. When everybody caught their breath, Berle sang a song parody to the man of honor: "Have a lot of luck / Especially when you fuck / Hopefully he's not a midget down there." Sammy howled some more.

The wedding took place November 13, 1960, in Sammy's Los Angeles home. Britt's parents flew in from Sweden. Her mother, tall and shy, wore long white gloves. Sinatra was best man, Lawford one of the groomsmen. Luddy Waters, Sammy's former assistant—who had also been Kim Novak's former assistant—was the maid of honor, giving the proceeding a kind of unwhispered incestuousness. Shirley Rhodes was quite noticeable as the only Negro bridesmaid. Sam Sr., always natty, wore a tux; against his white shirt lay a white silk tie. (Will Mastin was a no-show.) There were white chrysanthemums, which the bride and groom strolled beneath. Rabbi William Kramer pointed out instructions. A gaggle of photographers had assembled. Looking around, seeing all the faces, Hugh Benson, a producer, realized something about the groom: "He wanted to be white. His close friends were white. Deep down in his heart, he wanted to be white."

May looked lovely. The expressions on Sammy's face alternated: at times he looked startled, as if he had just fallen through the roof and landed on his feet in the middle of a gala wedding affair. At other times he looked as if he might cry—and then, strangely, he did. He was wearing a three-quarter-length tuxedo coat and his square, thickly rimmed glasses.

Outside, ten bodyguards stood watch. The death threats against Sammy had been coming more often leading up to the ceremony.

And there they were now, married, together, their love out in the open. In her high heels, she towered over him. In his giddiness, he warmed her soul.

They settled into Sammy's home on Evanview Drive. May decided she wanted to learn about Judaism, so she went to Hebrew school. When they were asked if Britt's movie career would be hurt because of her marriage, studio producers were too polite to answer, but it spoke volumes when she began to receive fewer and fewer scripts. She didn't seem to mind; she was happily married. She said she looked forward to raising children, to settling down.

But May Britt had married Sammy Davis, Jr. Settle down? He could hardly stop moving.

Sammy rarely slept.

Well, he did sleep, but hardly anyone saw him sleep. He imagined himself accomplishing as much in the night as during the day. He could sleep in cars, on airplanes, on trains. He slept for five minutes, three hours, any amount of time—and it was deep sleeping—then he'd rise and bolt like a man afire. Ideas would come to him—about entertainment ventures, movies, TV shows—and he'd leave a room, to think to himself, leaving other guests perplexed.

To Britt, his lifestyle was dizzying. He had never considered himself stationary. He had been moving since he was a child. May was surprised at his nonstop motion. He packed enough luggage to shame a dozen women. She was startled at the things he dragged with him. Just like that, they left Los Angeles in 1961—they'd keep their home—and moved into a New York City apartment.

In New York, fans trailed him on the street. He hated when they walked up to him on his bad side, where the world was invisible, and he'd yank his head suddenly when he heard a voice, felt a nudge at his elbow, saw May out of his good eye speaking to someone. Many times the autograph-seekers made him nervous. Janet Leigh visited the couple there. "I remember we were walking in the street to their place. We were talking about this movie idea—about a black man and a white woman—and Sammy said, 'You have no idea how hard it is with me and May. You see this?' He showed me the umbrella he was carrying. You could press it and the tip could become a knife. He said, 'This is how hard it sometimes gets.' "

Sammy huffed on Mike Wallace's *Nightbeat* radio show that his wife didn't need American movies, that she was highly sought after in Europe. Sammy was wildly overestimating his wife's overseas allure. During the course of their marriage, she'd never make another movie in Europe.

Sammy was constantly hunting properties. Producers and directors did not come to him nearly as often as he would have liked them to. So he looked for material on his own. He looked at mediocre movies late at night and imagined remakes, casting himself in leading roles and interesting character parts that

Greeting wife May in 1965. His Golden Boy *shenanigans had caused rumors of a separation. Sammy holds daughter Tracey. Pictured also are the couple's two adopted sons, Mark and Jeff, and, in the center, the children's nanny, Lessie Jackson. The adoptions seemed to bewilder Sammy. Fatherhood was the one role he would never master.*

(PHOTO UPI)

he felt had originally been miscast. He talked, animatedly, with his friend Amy Greene about a remake of *The Scarlet Pimpernel*, the classic 1935 film that starred Leslie Howard, leading a double life, and Merle Oberon.

Sammy as the British Pimpernel! He talked and talked; his Hollywood friends listened and listened.

The theater frightened many Hollywood actors. The stage judged immediately, and it could also judge cruelly. But Sammy was comfortable onstage, so he considered Broadway properties as well. In 1962—in a tale based on actual events—Sammy started dreaming of playing Glenn Griffin.

Griffin, along with another ex-convict, had broken into a suburban New York home and held a family hostage, terrorizing them. The context of family, sexual threat, murder, was, as drama, irresistible. *Life* magazine wrote evocatively of the real-life event. It wouldn't be long before a playwright weighed in: Joseph Hayes's drama was titled *The Desperate Hours*. It premiered on Broadway in 1955 and had a healthy, admirable run. Among its skillful cast were Karl Malden and, as the young hoodlum Griffin, Paul Newman. (It was also made into a movie starring Humphrey Bogart, Martha Scott, and Fredric March and directed by William Wyler.)

In his revival of *The Desperate Hours*, Sammy—having used his name to mount the production—surrounded himself with unknowns. But he was savvy enough to recruit Lloyd Richards, the celebrated young Negro director, to direct. Three years earlier, in 1959, Richards had directed Sidney Poitier in Lorraine Hansberry's electrifying drama *A Raisin in the Sun* on Broadway. That play had heralded, for the first time, white America into the living room, kitchen, and hearts and souls of a breathing, striving Negro family. On the eve of its March 11 opening, playwright Hansberry would write to her mother from a Connecticut hotel room: "Mama, it is a play that tells the truth about people, Negroes and life and I think it will help a lot of people to understand how we are just as complicated as they are—and just as mixed up—but above all, that we have among our miserable and downtrodden ranks—people who are the very essence of human dignity." (On opening night, Poitier pulled Hansberry up and onto the stage. The applause was deafening.) Hansberry—who favored Beat sneakers, who lived in Greenwich Village, who hailed from Chicago, and who, like Sammy, had married white—became the youngest woman, and first Negro, to win the New York Drama Critics' Circle Award for best play of the year. It seemed, almost overnight, that American theater had suddenly crossed a threshold. Negroes had unleashed a kind of cultural juiciness into the American theater. There had not been as much talk about Negroes onstage, in fact, since Sammy's wild and slapsticky romp in *Mr. Wonderful*.

"What I was intrigued by," recalls Richards about Sammy's mounting of the crime drama, "was Sammy's desire to do a straight play. He wanted to establish himself as an actor and not just a pure personality. I knew this was not just a frivolous event on Sammy's calendar. He had a purpose in doing it."

Sammy moved out to Long Island for rehearsals. The play would open at the Mineola Playhouse, then go to the Westport Country Playhouse, and, if there was enough buzz trailing along the way, perhaps Broadway. Sammy sent a car into New York City every day to pick up Richards. The young director thought that was classy.

Sammy already greased and straightened his hair—oh, to have hair like Tony Curtis! Now he dyed it red for the production. Richards was impressed with Sammy during the rehearsal period. "He was completely disciplined, which I assume came from his training in the business. You don't get to be a singer, dancer, performer of that magnitude without a hell of a lot of work."

Billie Allen, a New York dancer who had once spurned Sammy's romantic overtures but became a friend instead, drove out to Long Island to see the play. "He had dyed his hair red, a red conk," she recalls. "He said, 'I think it makes me look younger.' He wanted so much to be a straight actor, a serious actor." Allen was mesmerized by the different incarnations of Sammy Davis, Jr. "He didn't put himself in a category. That's what I loved about him. You couldn't box him in."

If Richards began the production wondering which Sammy he'd be witnessing—celebrity entertainer or Vegas nightclub act—by play's end, his opinion of the performer's gifts had soared. There were also tinges of sentiment, for in getting to know Sammy, Richards would find himself admiring Sammy's quest. "He was in no-man's-land," Richards says. "Nobody had encountered the things he had encountered. He was a big person, and he was in a big world—trying to find a way to live with dignity, and survive, and progress."

The Desperate Hours closed without Broadway's interest. Davis shrugged his shoulders. His mind whirred like a child's mind: there were a million ideas in front of him, and a million days left to do them. There would be no tears for things that failed to materialize. His shell was hard.

An invitation arrived for Sammy and May from the White House, and it made him brighten. He suddenly felt loved by the most powerful man in the world.

Once in office, President Kennedy had begun striking positive chords with American Negroes. Negroes were hired—in tiny numbers, to be sure, but they were hired—in high-placed government positions. For once, there were Negroes working for the president of the United States in positions other than valet, cook, butler, maid. Andrew Hatcher, a Negro, became a presidential deputy press secretary. But with the passage of time, those White House and federal jobs seemed rather insignificant compared to the plight of Negroes in many southern states who were still kept from voting by threat of intimidation or even murder. Waves of students across the South were continuing their sit-ins. Louis Martin, the shrewd black Chicago operative and a Kennedy advisor, sent a missive to the president on January 31. Its direct message implied that, as far as Negroes were concerned, all was not well along the shores of Camelot. "American Negroes through sit-ins, kneel-ins, wade-ins, etc. will continue to create situations which involve the police powers of the local, state and Federal government," Martin warned Kennedy.

Southern Democrats had been instrumental in Kennedy's thin victory over Nixon. But the Dixiecrats, as they were known, were loath to support civil rights, and Kennedy stepped gingerly around the issue of Negroes and their battle for rights. However, Martin's memo struck a nerve in the young president. Kennedy told Martin to plan a meeting with Negro leaders. It would take place on February 12, Lincoln's birthday. (There would, however, be no publicity, a highly unusual decision but one owing to Kennedy's nervousness.)

Martin had contacts in every corner of the Negro world, from politics to sports to entertainment. He went about making his calls with enormous pride, knowing that such an event had never taken place at the White House before.

So on the Great Emancipator's birthday, a stream of prominent Negroes were ushered through the southwest gate into the White House. The guest list was indeed eclectic: There was Langston Hughes—it was the great poet's first visit inside the White House—and Dick Gregory, the comic, who had never imagined such an invite. There were NAACP officials and National Urban League officials. Louis Martin was beside himself. "It looks like Uncle Tom's cabin around here," he quipped. Sammy and May walked hand in hand. Getting Sammy there was a coup for Martin: White House officials kept scratching Sammy's name from the guest list, fearful of repercussions of having him and his white wife at the gathering. But every time they scratched it off, Martin wrote it back on. As Kennedy began his descent downstairs from the White House to join the reception, his scanning eyes stopped cold on Davis and Britt. "What's he doing here?" he heatedly asked an aide, an edge in his voice. "Get them out of there!" he ordered, and then he realized some form of tact would have to be adopted. Kennedy told aides to tell his wife to usher May Britt out of the room before the photographers arrived. Jacqueline Kennedy, however, became distraught at the idea and refused to tell them. She rushed upstairs, angry at the president. Others ushered the couple along before any photographer saw them. (That very day—just hours before the meeting with Negro leaders at the White House—the U.S. Civil Rights Commission delivered a report to Kennedy on the condition of the Negro in America. Among its findings was that freedom for the Negro was "more fictional than real.") Sammy Davis and May Britt left the White House that evening deeply aware of the awkward treatment they had received. The man who many believed the top entertainer in the world—Negro or white—would not forget what had happened.

On February 25, two weeks after the White House affair, union stalwart

A. Philip Randolph announced in New York plans for a march on Washington. The same Randolph had used the threat two decades earlier with the Roosevelt administration until they had capitulated to his demands for antidiscrimination legislation. The Kennedy White House paid little attention to the new threat.

By now Sammy had, along with Frank and Dean, shot a movie, *Sergeants 3*, and had it in the can. (It was, like *Ocean's 11*, really Frank's movie.) During the shooting Sammy had to fly back to Las Vegas for performances. He complained of the small plane, bitterly, until Howard Koch, the movie's producer, hired a private plane. "We paid for him to fly in a big plane, six-hundred-seater—a black man sitting on the plane all by himself."

In addition to his not wanting to fly in small airplanes, there was something else that Sammy needed to talk to producer about. "He had one major problem. He always needed money," recalls Koch.

Dean Martin, during the early '60s, had an onstage joke that drew howls: "At night we say, 'Smile, Sammy, so we know where you are.' "

A. Philip Randolph, Martin Luther King, Jr., and labor and Jewish leaders had finally secured permission to hold a massive rally in August 1963 on the lawn of the Lincoln Memorial to rally for Negro rights in America. President Kennedy and his brother Attorney General Robert Kennedy did not welcome the event, imagining chaos and disaster right under their noses.

Indeed, fear gripped the nation's capital during the weeks leading up to the planned march. In an article that hit newsstands before the event, *Life* magazine said that Washington was agonizing about "its worst case of invasion jitters since the First Battle of Bull Run." The government had made preparations for what they imagined would be a possible insurrection: nineteen thousand troops were at the ready. Hollywood showed in force: Marlon Brando, James Garner, Charlton Heston, Eartha Kitt, and Sammy were all there. Sammy had on a Nehru outfit—jacket and slacks—and his oddly hip Buddy Holly spectacles. He waded through the throngs, touched, acknowledged, his lower chin working in greetings. "I remember," recalls Julian Bond, working the affair as a young NAACP media assistant, "going to get a Coke for Sammy Davis. He said, 'Thanks, kid.' " Dancer Billie Allen couldn't take her eyes off Sammy as he paraded about. "He was fervent and into it," she recalls, immediately sensing that his civil rights fervor was now more alive than it had ever been. "He was a chameleon. I feel he changed group to group, environment to environment. He had a profound need to." Allen served as chaperone to Josephine Baker, the

Negro chanteuse, who had come from Paris to take part in the event. "Josephine wore her uniform from the army of the French Resistance, this wool thing," says Allen. "Didn't sweat a drop. That's discipline."

The Kennedys listened in the White House to the speeches from the Lincoln Memorial. They were fidgety. King's sweeping and lyrical oratory, delivered in the hot sun, ushered in a new way for America to think of herself. It was nothing less than a moral call to arms, delivered sermonlike with the cadences of a gospel hymn. More than 250,000 were listening at the Lincoln Mall, "all God's children, black men and white men, Jews and Gentiles." The event marked a potent culmination of a Negro and Jewish alliance that had long been tackling social ills in America. And there stood Sammy Davis, Jr.—Negro by birth, Jew by choice—the very embodiment of King's oratory. If King's words had immediately been adopted by all, Sammy would have stood as a shining example of brotherhood rather than as a cultural oddity—a Negro and a Jew, a man colorless to himself, who happened to be married to a white woman.

Afterward, Sammy, the fans rushing him, hustled toward his limousine. In the flesh he elicited squeals and curiosity and wonder. He was a one-man parade gallivanting across the boundaries of race and sex; a singing and dancing figure in Sinatra's shadow, true enough, but riveting on his own; a television personality, a Broadway veteran; a familiar face to the grandmothers and grandfathers of America who remembered him growing up onstage, the little Negro in the middle of that trio. Up close, in Nehru suit and horn-rimmed glasses, he was a star, and a star was like lightning to the senses. The eyes of those crowding around him went from Sammy to the limousine, and then back to Sammy again: power. Sammy had an after-party to get to. He spotted Josephine Baker—he was ever the sycophant—and yelled at her to hop in his limo. But the fans were rushing and crowding, and she couldn't get close enough, and the limo was getting more crowded, and the driver was getting nervous. The great Josephine Baker was left standing as Sammy's driver pulled away.

Sammy went on location to shoot his next movie, *Robin and the 7 Hoods*. It was a gangster spoof with music, all Frank's show again. Sinatra played the leader of a Chicago gang. Dean was in it, and so was Bing Crosby. Edward G. Robinson had a cameo. The beautiful Barbara Rush played the female lead. Sammy, as a member of Frank's gang, wore a derby and a long coat. Beneath the coat, he wore a pearly pair of six-shooters. Sammy dazzled cast and crew with not only his voice but the way he handled his guns. "I was in awe of him," Rush says of Sammy. "I think he was the most talented man I had ever seen perform." Edward G. Robinson is killed in the movie, and the grips had set up the cameras for his funeral scene. "We were in the cemetery burying Edward G. Robinson, who played my father," recalls Rush. "Howard Koch drove into the cemetery and said, 'I want you to know President Kennedy has been shot.' " Heads dropped. Sinatra closed down filming for the day. He had a mind to close down the whole damn production. "High Hopes" suddenly seemed just a sad, sad song.

They all wanted to get away to retreat someplace. It was but the beginning of a time of assassination, and no one could see such a thing coming. Frank took his crew and retreated to Palm Springs. Sammy took his crew and headed east, to New York City. The Gucci luggage, the Tiffany jewelry, the beautiful tailor-made suits, everything was packed up. And how he loved traveling, moving across the country, free as a bird, just him and the sky, the sun, and the moon, whirring and whirring, unable to stop, just the way Sam Sr. and Will were unable to stop. The song of vaudeville lay deep in his mind. He'd show May's mother and father that Sammy Davis, Jr.—never mind the death threats—was the best thing for their daughter in all of America. "He always liked to say, 'If we ain't going first class,' " recalls Shirley Rhodes, " 'the boat don't leave the dock.' "

If one thing bothered Shirley Rhodes about Sammy, it was his relationship with his mother, which was virtually nonexistent. "I used to push him: 'Call your mother. It's your *mother*,' " she says.

During the second week of June in 1963, Sammy, back in Los Angeles, had to board a flight quickly. His mother, Elvera, lay in a hospital, having been viciously assaulted. "Sammy Davis' Mother Beaten," screamed one headline. The story said that she was "brutally beaten by a Harlem bartender described as her boyfriend." Reporters had gathered at the New York hospital where Elvera Davis was being treated. On his arrival, they all lunged in Sammy's direction, but he refused to speak with them. He was shaken enough at the sight of his mother that he canceled a scheduled appearance on *The Ed Sullivan Show*.

Chapter 12

SAMMY AND HILLY

Hilly Elkins had been chasing Sammy since 1961, and Sammy had been hard to catch. But there were not many, no matter which side of the Atlantic Ocean, who could elude the grasp of Hilly Elkins for long.

Elkins was a New York City theatrical producer. Brooklyn-born, he was a rebel as a child, too mischievous for his own good. He ran with gangs and "was knifed a couple of times," he would recall. There were confrontations with juvenile authorities, but he brushed them away, and let their dire warnings float through his ears. Teachers wondered if the bravado might not be concealing deeper, more productive talents. Hilly was dimunitive but hardly shy. He had a gift of gab and could entertain and enthrall with words. He also loved books; he had been seduced by the lyricism in Thomas Wolfe's *Look Homeward, Angel.* In his mid-teens Elkins found himself in a radio workshop for talented students. Microphones and stages, which rattled so many, seemed to calm and soothe Hilly Elkins. By his senior year of high school, he had already written, directed, and performed in a play. Like so many born of the Depression, Hilly Elkins concluded the world would not give him anything. He would have to browbeat, hustle, take. He would have to have fire under his heels.

By the age of nineteen he had talked his way into a job at the William Morris Agency. Office boy. The job description was laughable, because as soon as he got inside, he started kicking his way up the ladder.

Theater, when he started out in the early 1950s, was still its own king and had its own kingdom. There were genuine talents—José Ferrer, Judith Anderson, Helen Hayes, Burl Ives, Montgomery Clift, and Paul Muni among them—appearing on the New York stage. Elkins gravitated toward the theatrical department at the Morris agency. Now and then he'd peek into TV and motion picture work—he discovered a young Steve McQueen; in time he counted Mel Brooks and Gypsy Rose Lee among his clients. Television could be lucrative, but his love lay in theater.

There was an army stint, after which he left William Morris and bided his time with another agency. But he seemed to burn with too many ideas, and the more ideas he offered, the more he kept hearing the same words: no, no, no. So he began his own New York agency, set up shop on East Sixty-second Street. Self-educated, Hilly Elkins started producing plays. He also dated beautiful women, wore fine clothes, and drove fancy cars. He was five foot seven, but he stood much taller. It was the way he carried himself, as if a hurricane were at his back, in his mind, pushing him every which way, forcing belligerent words to sometimes spill from his mouth. A picture of Napoleon hung in his Manhattan apartment. Visitors got the impression it wasn't merely hanging there for decorative purposes.

Hilly Elkins finally caught up with Sammy at a midnight matinee at the Prince of Wales Theatre in London. Midnight matinee performances were for theatrical folk who couldn't get off to see the hot shows in London because of their own stage commitments. Among the thousands to catch Sammy's act was a floppy-haired rock band, the Beatles. "There was no place Sammy couldn't draw a crowd," remembers Elkins. Sitting in the elegant theater— there were twelve hundred seats; Sir Lew Grade owned it along with his brothers; Sammy sold the place out night after night—and listening to the cries of applause rushing over Sammy, accompanied by shrieks and giggles, and Sammy, as always, unable to leave the stage until he had exhausted himself, Elkins grew nostalgic and sentimental, remembering the legwork he had done when he was one of those young Morris agents sent through the revolving door to look after the Mastin trio when they were on the road. But Hilly Elkins did not cross the Atlantic because of sentimentality. He had a theatrical idea on his mind. "I was anxious to find something that would work for Sammy," he says. After the final curtain—and it was now hours past midnight—Elkins bolted from his seat.

"I went backstage and said, 'Sammy, I got an idea. It's *Golden Boy*.'"

A rabid movie fan, Sammy was familiar with the movie version of Clifford Odets's play. But Hilly Elkins was not talking about a movie remake.

"What do you mean?" Sammy asked.

"I said, 'If we can get the rights, it can be a great story. About a guy coming out of his neighborhood who uses boxing to break out of his environment.'"

They talked and talked. And Elkins promised Sammy he would get the rights; it would be no problem; he'd rush back to California and see Odets himself.

Sammy was flattered. Eye to eye with each other, the two men seemed to connect: two onetime kid performers, Sammy dripping in his own sweat, their chests heaving now with excitement, the autograph-seekers waiting to see Sammy, only now they'd have to wait a little longer because Sammy liked listening to Hilly Elkins, and, most of all, Sammy loved being wooed. He told Elkins he liked the idea, but he would not yet make a commitment. Sammy had learned from disappointment. More than one producer had tossed an idea at him, only to have it vanish in the wilderness of flattery. There were producers who could not deliver. There were producers who produced more beautiful words about productions than productions themselves. Hilly Elkins might follow through with his intriguing idea, and he might not. Sammy hugged him anyway.

Elkins rushed back across the ocean. There were two young musical talents he had under his wing, Charles Strouse, a composer, and Lee Adams, a lyricist. Both had worked on *Bye Bye Birdie,* the 1960 musical starring Dick Van Dyke, that was a spirited mockery of an Elvis-like figure and all the teenage hysteria he had set loose. Their reputations soared. Hilly asked, cajoled, and pleaded with them to join his *Golden Boy.*

Strouse's background was eccentric. In his youth he had traveled the Deep South as a pianist with Butterfly McQueen, the Negro actress who appeared in *Gone with the Wind.* Some bigots spat on him in Alabama as he was attempting to buy food for her in a whites-only restaurant. After her movie career, McQueen had had trouble finding work. She washed dishes. She clerked at Macy's. She bent her back in a factory. Eventually she went on the road and closed her eyes and sang as Strouse, the white kid, tapped out tunes for her. Barely out of college, the kid cowrote the score for *Bye Bye Birdie.* That musical also featured Chita Rivera, her talents from Sammy's *Mr. Wonderful* now in full flight. *Birdie* ran for 607 performances. Strouse had friends going to graduate school, and other friends working ordinary jobs. And suddenly, he was famous, his name on Broadway billboards. He did not mind the money, because the money was fine. But fame, rolling as fast it did toward him, was a scary thing. "It was as if I got a limousine and didn't order it."

When Hilly Elkins cornered Strouse and Adams, he told them he had Sammy Davis's commitment for *Golden Boy.* Strouse's face lit up; he marveled at the possibility of working with Sammy. Elkins had lied, of course. He had Sammy's enthusiasm, but not his full commitment. But it was a Hilly Elkins lie: rather charming because it was so energetic, so energetic because he fully intended to make it all come true. Then it wouldn't be a lie anymore.

All along, Hilly had been zigzagging. First he got to Sammy. Then Strouse and Adams. But now he had to go to the playwright. A less confident producer—guarding against calamity—might have started with Odets himself. But Hilly Elkins, child brawler, did not lack confidence. He dragged Strouse and Adams aboard a plane. The destination: Beverly Hills. They'd have to go to Odets. Odets wouldn't come to them. He hated flying.

When Elkins reached Odets, the playwright had been out of the public limelight for years. He was, in fact, penning silly TV scripts—one even for Elvis Presley. He was raising two children alone; the kids had to eat. Writing TV scripts, however, was a mighty comedown for Clifford Odets.

Born in Philadelphia and a high school dropout, by the mid-1930s Clifford Odets had established himself as one of the riveting talents of American drama. He began as an actor but grew frustrated and started writing. Poetry came first, then the dramas. *Waiting for Lefty* opened in New York in 1935; Odets was twenty-nine years old. Another play, *Awake and Sing,* premiered that same year. His plays mocked corruption and heralded the little man who was being crushed by the Depression. Odets's work hissed with a social conscience. "Strike! Strike! Strike!" came the chorus line in *Waiting for Lefty.*

His face peered from the cover of *Time* magazine. There were those who called him a genius. From the tree of fame, fruit dropped: Odets married Luise Rainer, the beautiful Austrian actress.

Odets's *Golden Boy* opened in 1937, performed by the Group Theatre, a gifted and eclectic outfit of performers that included Elia Kazan, Jules (later John) Garfield, and Lee J. Cobb. Directed by Harold Clurman, the drama ran for 250 performances. *Golden Boy* became a movie a year later, starring William Holden and Barbara Stanwyck. Many thought the material played better on stage than screen; critics dismissed the movie while Odets happily pocketed his Hollywood money. There was a New York stage revival of *Golden Boy* in 1952, which Odets himself directed. John Garfield, back from the movies and Hollywood, played the lead role of boxer Joe Bonaparte. Garfield found solace in Odets's work: he starred in another Odets play, *The Big Knife,* in 1949, this one about corruption and greed in Hollywood. (The film version opened in 1955 and starred Jack Palance, Rod Steiger, and Ida Lupino.)

But with the rise of the communist scare, Odets's career began an ominous slide. Subpoenaed to appear before the House Un-American Activities Committee, he swore that he had abandoned the Communist Party when they tried to trifle with his plays. He was summoned a second time, and this time he had a name for the committee, and he coughed that name up: J. Edward Bromberg. That was bad enough to Odets's friends; even worse was the fact that Bromberg was dead. He had been an actor, appearing in some of Odets's plays, and had died of a heart attack shortly after being called before the committee. Many never forgave the playwright. In the end, the committee still thought Odets belligerent and sarcastic; he served three months in a West Virginia penitentiary.

In January 1955, Odets left New York for Hollywood. He was going there to work on a movie for mogul Harry Cohn. The playwright kept his New York apartment, but years rolled over him in Beverly Hills. One year turned to two, two to four. He avoided New York: he had an aversion to flying, and the ghosts still whispered there. He had no complaints about the Hollywood weather, either.

Odets sat them around a table covered with magazines, scripts, and cigars, listening to Hilly Elkins and his companions during their visit. He was a towering man, with broad shoulders, deep eyes, and hair like electric wires. Strouse and Adams were in awe of the legendary playwright. Odets prepared a meal. "Fish, which he grilled beautifully," remembers Elkins. Odets listened, but the playwright wondered about the vicissitudes of the American theater— Odets had often commented that of all his plays, he had made money from only two, *Golden Boy* and *Country Girl*. Odets wondered if anyone cared about him and his vision anymore. But soon enough, Elkins began noticing a rising interest in the writer's voice. Odets began sharing ideas about the kind of music he envisioned—it would be Brechtian, dark and heavy. Without making a commitment, he kept talking, offering ideas. Strouse sat enthralled. "I thought he was one of the great men of the American theater." But Strouse was surprised when Elkins bragged to Odets that he already had Sammy. And, for all the positive signals circling at the meeting, Strouse noticed something else: Odets seemed fidgety, bothered by something, perhaps sadness. It left Strouse, young and impressionable, feeling a bit blue himself. "He made you feel he had ruined his life, ruined his days," says Strouse. "I never met any man more guilt-ridden than Clifford. One got the impression that right away he felt he was doing something immoral by being out in California." Odets, veering from talk about *Golden Boy* to talk about Hollywood, began regaling his guests with tales of his sexual prowess, which both Strouse and Adams thought weird. "He would talk to us all the time about his sexual exploits," says Strouse, adding that the bragged-about exploits mostly involved young would-be starlets performing oral sex on Odets. Listening, Strouse felt uncomfortable. Elkins didn't. Hilly Elkins had heard far darker things in life than a onetime famous playwright bragging about his sexual romps with young California nymphets. Elkins, pouring on the flattery, believing he himself could reinvigorate Clifford Odets, began sensing victory. (Being human, Odets was hardly immune to flattery.) By the time the afternoon ended, Odets had given Elkins the right to mount a new production of *Golden Boy,* and there were hearty hugs all around. Strouse and Adams were overjoyed. There would, they all knew, have to be rewrites, revisions. The play, after all, had been written for an Italian American; now it was to star the hottest Negro entertainer in the world. Then in a gush of enthusiasm, Odets solved the rewriting problem: he volunteered to do it himself. The lion was coming back to Broadway.

Leather briefcase in hand, Elkins was out the door, smashing through the sunshine, heading back east, giddy with excitement, ideas, plans. He was beside himself. Just wait until the critics got wind of this, of what he had assembled.

Not the theater critics, but the Hilly Elkins critics, because he had them, plenty of them, back east, and they sometimes called him a hustler, a shyster even. But wait til they saw this Hilly Elkins–produced lineup:

Clifford Odets

Sammy Davis, Jr

Charles Strouse

Lee Adams

Broadway

They'd have plenty to cackle about at Sardi's, that beehive of a Broadway restaurant.

Back in New York City, Elkins feverishly began assembling his team. And never mind that Sammy himself had yet to sign. "Of course, the thousand-pound gorilla was always Sammy," as Strouse put it. Elkins saw the revival as having social impact. There were so few opportunities on Broadway for Negro performers. This version of *Golden Boy* would be highly integrated. The leading lady would be white. The combination could be explosive and tricky, which is exactly why Elkins liked it. It could also be viewed as mischievous, inasmuch as large segments of the public were still nervous and twitchy about Sammy's interracial marriage. Elkins signed up Donald McKayle, who was about to become the first Negro choreographer on Broadway. Adams and Strouse were on board to do the score and the lyrics.

In time, Adams and Strouse began to get nervous; they could not work without Sammy's input. They needed to know what he liked, what he didn't like. Musically, they needed to know which songs he could take and fly away on. Like Elkins before them, they would have to chase Sammy. They would have to chase him all around the country, from Bill Miller's Riviera to Danny's Hideaway, from Sardi's to the steamroom at the Sands in Las Vegas. "The year before we opened, I think I saw him three hundred times," Elkins says of Sammy. "I brought Odets to Harrah's. I brought Strouse to Buffalo. I went to Rochester."

Strouse—soft-voiced, thin, and shy with a collegiate look—worked hard on scoring the new version of *Golden Boy.* When he felt as if he had accomplished something—something that might please—he'd hop on a plane to go to the star.

All his life, Sammy had been sizing people up: tutors when he was a child; tap dancers when he was a teenager; nightclub managers when he needed money in advance. There was no neutrality in his world. Acquaintances would be sized up, measured, and, according to how much he needed them, either embraced or dismissed. In his world of human relationships, he moved fast.

Sammy sized up Strouse quickly and had his way with him. "I was very shy, and playing songs for Sammy Davis rattled me," Strouse would recall years later. On one visit Strouse caught Sammy at a Las Vegas casino, regaling waiters and waitresses, drinking, the Sammy laughter bouncing off walls, the shoulders rolling like pinballs. Strouse was too nervous to interrupt. So he lay back, soundless as a kitten. Then Sammy turned and spotted him. Sensing the awkward shyness, Sammy pounced and demanded to know what the young scrubbed-faced musician had brought to share with him. "In Las Vegas I had to play in front of the waiters and chorus girls. I would be hanging around and Sammy would say, 'Let me hear that new song!' " Away from Sinatra, Sammy could become Sinatra. Sammy wouldn't budge, playing the big shot, needling young Strouse. And then Strouse would start humming, finger-tapping, explaining, pausing, trying to retain Sammy's attention. He never knew if he was pleasing Sammy or not. His impromptu performance over, he'd leave, only to return, days or weeks later, when a new version of a score was ready, one that Sammy might like a little more, and repeat the process all over again.

"I met Frank Sinatra and Dean Martin in the steamroom in Vegas," says Strouse. "Everybody was naked. I went down there, security was heavy. I finally went in there. I noticed Frank was bullying Sammy. Frank would tell him a joke and hit him hard, and say, 'That's funny, Sam!' " Strouse would wince. Later, unaware of where he found the gall to do it, Strouse spoke to Sammy about the roughhousing Sinatra had enjoyed at his expense. "I told Sammy I thought he was letting Frank bully him. I asked him why. He told me it was because Frank was so loyal and loving to him when he had needed it."

Elkins's creative team began settling on musical numbers. All day long, often at night as well, jingles would be floating in and out of the heads of Adams and Strouse. Odets was busy doing rewrites—or, at least, that's what he kept telling Hilly Elkins. Elkins didn't see the rewrites, nor was he demanding to see them. After all, Odets had written the play, and who better to update it than Odets himself? Elkins plowed forward. He lined up his investors. He reminded the doubters that Sammy had kept the mediocre *Mr. Wonderful* running on Broadway a full year—and it could have gone on longer if he hadn't had to get back to nightclubbing! There were casting calls—dancers, supporting actors and actresses to be hired. The all-important leading lady had to be hired. In between it all, Elkins, Strouse, and Adams had planes to catch—Philadelphia, Los Angeles, Las Vegas, Paris—that would take the creative team to wherever Sammy happened to be at the time. They were all working hard, around the clock. They were all in a dark tunnel. Sammy was the light at the end. But there was fear in the tunnel. Fear about Sammy's real commitment. "The goal was so magical," recalls Strouse. "There were a couple years we worked with him, but there was always, in the back of my mind, the nightmare he wouldn't do it."

In nightclubs, Sammy's salary was a princely sum. Broadway was Broadway,

Both Albert Popwell and Sally Neal—caught here by Sammy's camera during a rehearsal—were dancers in his Golden Boy. *They were from a younger generation and were quick to challenge Sammy's politics, which they thought were too timid. How were they to know that Sammy was one of the secret financial weapons in the civil rights movement?*

(COURTESY SALLY NEAL)

but to Sammy Davis, Jr., Broadway was a financial sacrifice. His agents balked while Sammy danced from nightclub to nightclub as Hilly charged on. Sammy was smashing records at the Copacabana. "Sammy wouldn't sign the dotted line," remembers Strouse. "He was making $40,000 a week. His agents did not want to give that up."

Without Sammy, there would be no *Golden Boy*.

The thousand-pound gorilla was playing coy. But Elkins was relentless. He began putting his production in place as if Sammy were all but signed. Potential directors were contacted. Casting notices had been placed in the theatrical trade publications. It didn't matter that there was still nothing in the mail from Clifford Odets. Great playwrights were moody, they worked on their own clock. Hilly waited to hear from Odets, and Hilly could be patient. He would not bother the great man.

Sammy's agents tried to steer him away from *Golden Boy*. But he found the idea of a return to Broadway intoxicating. It would be his show, his stage—no more Will Mastin Trio Starring Sammy Davis Jr. A boxing musical built around him. It could be fun. As well, there were movie studios in New York City; he might get movie work. Maybe even some TV work. There would be ways to make up the financial loss of appearing on Broadway. Besides, May had been complaining about his moving around so much, every week away from home, working and working. On Broadway, Sammy would have to stay put.

Finally, convinced there was little to lose, Sammy Davis went to the William Morris office in New York City, along with Elkins and Clifford Odets, to sign the contracts. He was now officially returning to Broadway for the 1964 season. There was a party at Sardi's to celebrate the announcement. Inside the restaurant, amid the clink of champagne glasses, Sammy and Hilly donned boxing gloves. They posed as if each were getting ready to square off. May stood in the middle, in a black sleeveless dress, separating the two. She looked winsome, and loomed taller than both men. Cameras clicked away. "Sammy Davis Jr. As Golden Boy," the cake made up for the occasion announced.

Hilly had circled the globe trying to make *Golden Boy* a reality. He never once complained of exhaustion. It took him two years to make the deal, but he'd done it.

It was Hilly, more than Sammy, who could sniff the political winds, the changing racial climate in America. When he thought of this *Golden Boy*, Hilly Elkins dreamed of producing something unforgettable.

May had been, from the beginning of the marriage, quite eager to start a family, and in 1961 gave birth to the couple's first child, a daughter they named Tracey. She was a beautiful child, cinnamon-colored (May and Sammy had often joked about having "little brown babies") and had a Bobbsey hairdo. The idea of children intrigued Sammy, but shortly after Tracey's birth, he hit the road again. May had a nanny, Lessie Jackson, but still, raising the child alone was hard. Sammy implored her to come join him in Philadelphia, in London, in Miami, in Chicago—wherever he happened to be! He himself had been a child on the road! But May would have none of it. She had no intention of ferrying her daughter around the country; children were susceptible to colds and fevers when traveling; children needed a home. When she constantly reminded Sammy of their daughter's tender age, Sammy seemed befuddled. When he was actually at home, he would allow photographers to snap pictures of him, May, and Tracey, but then he'd be gone again, hearing that siren—Sammy! Sammy! He loved his daughter, and saw proof of it in the bundle of toys he purchased for her from F. A. O. Schwarz. But toys were toys, and a father was a father. May was bewildered as well as crestfallen, and confided to Shirley Rhodes that she wished Sammy were home more so he could see his daughter grow.

Two years after Tracey's birth, May decided she wanted her daughter to have a brother. She told Sammy, in no uncertain terms, that she planned to adopt, and when he came off the road, she had already arranged the adoption. Rudy Duff, the new valet Shirley had hired for Sammy—Duff had been working in the local post office and suddenly found himself behind the wheel of Sammy's Rolls!—drove Sammy and May to the courthouse in Los Angeles for the paperwork. "When I went to the courthouse with them to adopt Mark," recalls Duff, "I was told to stay outside. They went in a private office." The new child was also interracial. A year later, liking the noise and feel of a family, May decided to add to it again and adopted another interracial boy, whom they named Jeff—after Jeff Chandler. The adoptions had been so sudden that it was obvious to Sammy that May was steering the domestic ship of their lives. With or without Sammy, she aimed to fill a house with children. Sammy watched it all unfold like a wide-eyed child himself. Now the Davises had three children. At times Sammy eyed them as if he were watching a movie screen—with glee and surprise. In reality, they seemed to puzzle him. He once ventured out to a Little League game to watch Tracey play softball. He picked up a ball to throw with her before the game's start. Sy Marsh had accompanied him. Marsh felt Sammy was tossing the ball strangely, almost spastically. Then he suddenly realized something: Sammy didn't play softball as a child. He could barely toss the thing with any form at all. Sy felt embarrassed for Sammy. "I said, 'Save your energy. Let me do it.' If you don't think that tore his heart out!"

To raise children, one had to fasten oneself down at times. Sammy's sister, Ramona, had known the curse of the vaudevillian. Now Sammy's own children would.

Sammy came east—the staff trailing—and anchored himself in a rented brownstone on Ninety-third Street. Tracey and Mark were enrolled in the tony and private Dalton School. Jeff was not yet school-age. May was happier than ever to be seeing her husband every night.

Finally, pages arrived from Odets, but they were incomplete pieces. Hilly Elkins couldn't mount a play with bits and pieces of dialogue and sketchy scenes. Odets swore he was coming east, that he had more material to show. But weeks came and went, and still no Odets. Elkins began to harangue the great playwright. Odets gently reminded Elkins of his hesitancy to fly. Elkins's voice would rise through telephone wires; he had money on the line; he had

Sammy Davis lined up, a theater booked, rehearsals to begin! Odets finally boarded a plane and flew to New York.

They tracked Sammy down at the Latin Casino in Philadelphia, where he was appearing onstage. Sammy arranged for everyone to have a table right up front, and he was proud to introduce them to the audience. Strouse and Adams and Elkins watched Odets watching Sammy. It was clear to them that the playwright was bowled over, that he could suddenly see his Joe Bonaparte in the body of Sammy Davis, Jr. After Sammy's performance, Odets—towering over tables—rushed over to Sammy. "I'm going to write this in your *mouth*," he proclaimed. His finger was poking Sammy's scrawny chest. What Odets had just told Sammy meant simply that he had every intention of jazzing the play up, giving it a new texture and language that would fit Sammy Davis, Jr. And from that moment on, Odets was energized. He had seen Sammy live; now he could see his play as a musical. Sammy hugged Odets—hugged the man so that the promise would come true, hugged the man so he would be true to his word, hugged the legendary playwright for coming. They shared drinks. Then they talked into the night. Then they all went their own ways, the dream alive and real now.

Hilly Elkins still had no leading lady. The role was widely coveted. But it was Odets who kept prolonging the audition process because his rewrites were not coming in.

Lee Grant was interested. So were Tuesday Weld and Lee Remick. They were all beautiful. They were all ingenues. It was Strouse who suggested Paula Wayne come in to audition. Strouse had first seen Wayne on Broadway in *Best Foot Forward*. Wayne was, like many a struggling actress, looking for her breakout role. She made extra money dubbing Italian movies into English. She lived in a small apartment on West End Avenue. Another struggling actress by the name of Liza Minnelli was her roommate. Liza's mother, Judy Garland, hadn't paid her daughter's rent at the Barbizon, so Liza had to hustle up a place to stay. She was appearing in a play with Wayne, who offered her housing. Theater folk liked Wayne's energy. Vincent Sardi, owner of Sardi's restaurant, would feed her when she was hungry.

"They brought in every star they could think of," Wayne would recall about her audition. "I never dreamt I'd get that part. It was almost too big to contemplate."

Wayne was superstitious. Every time she auditioned, she wore the same clothing. One by one, actresses were eliminated. The process could be gutwrenching. Again and again, Wayne—who had also sung in nightclubs—was called back. "Then came the great day I was going to sing for Sammy Davis. This day, there was nobody but me. I can feel it like it just happened. I got up on the stage, standing in the middle of the Majestic Theatre. And Sammy

Davis starts walking toward me. My throat closed. I started to cry. I ran out of the theater. I ran into Sardi's. I was crying my heart out."

The sight of Sammy had unnerved her, and she suffered a panic attack. Those in the theater—Sammy, Hilly, others—froze. The stage manager gave chase.

"I was overwhelmed. I'm from Oklahoma. I had never met a great star."

The maître d' on duty at Sardi's tried calming her down. The stage manager went back and told Sammy she was at Sardi's. And then there he was, the great star, the slicked black hair, the tiny giant. Show business was a killer, and at such times, he could be so understanding, so touching.

"He said, 'What happened, hon?' He sat there with me, ten to fifteen minutes. Everyone was sitting in that theater, waiting to see if Ms. Wayne would calm down. Sammy held my hand. Then he said, 'You ready to sing?' "

Paula Wayne, led by Sammy Davis, Jr., walked back across the street, into the theater, up on the stage, and started singing. She wowed them all.

After auditioning 236 hopefuls, Sammy and Hilly had finally found their leading lady.

"I thought to myself," Wayne would recall, "I've got the part of the decade."

Who didn't notice, who couldn't see, who dared mention it, lest it seem a little impolite, that Paula Wayne was as beautiful—and as blond—as May Britt herself?

There was another interesting role to be cast in *Golden Boy,* that of a female Negro dancer who ultimately catches the eye of the Sammy character, the second female lead. Sammy thought of Frances Davis, who, before her marriage to the brilliant jazz trumpeter Miles Davis, had been Frances Taylor and had filmed Sammy's long-ago 1954 television pilot alongside him. Miles, aside from being complex and moody, was dangerously controlling. Sammy went to Philadelphia and told Miles he thought Frances would be wonderful in *Golden Boy;* nodding, Miles listened behind his dark glasses. Sammy kept talking and Miles kept listening—in silence. "Miles didn't give him an answer then," says Frances Davis. "We were leaving the next day. Miles still didn't answer. Normally, we would leave around noon. We left at nine the next morning. That was the answer. I was heartbroken again."

Hilly selected Peter Coe, an Englishman, to direct the play. Coe had won raves for his direction of the Broadway musical *Oliver!* The rising young Harlem-born comedian Godfrey Cambridge was cast in the featured role of Sammy's brother. Cambridge received a Tony nomination in 1961 for appearing in Ossie Davis's *Purlie Victorious,* a farcical look at southern life on a plantation that had skirted nervously around the issue of sex. The *New York Mirror* described it as "burlesque without the strippers."

Sammy went down to Puerto Rico. He sat in a nightclub and watched his friend Billy Daniels, the singer, perform. Of course he couldn't just watch. He hopped up on the stage, did a number on the drums, a cigarette in his mouth, the elegant Daniels waving his hands like bird wings. Daniels, renowned for his version of "Black Magic," had never played Broadway. Sammy was trying to convince him to make his debut in *Golden Boy*, playing the role of Eddie Satin, the smooth and mysterious boxing promoter. (It was clear that Sammy, as much as Hilly, was putting this production together.) Daniels joined the production.

The promised rewrites were still not coming fast enough, and Hilly grew angry. Odets would sit and chat for hours about wine, offering long discourses, then veer off into chatter about Hollywood, and Hilly would wait him out, until finally he realized something—Odets was afraid. Even the lyricist Lee Adams could feel it. "Odets was aware that making a musical was a different animal than a play," says Adams. "His biggest problem was writing concisely. He'd do a scene of fifteen fine pages. We'd say, 'Cliff, we need three pages.' He'd say, 'Oh my.' "

The great playwright of the 1930s, the onetime boy wonder, was wracked with fear—of New York City, the critics, his play. Would *Golden Boy* still stand up? The leading man was no longer white and Italian, but a Negro. There would be interracial themes to explore. And there was the real-life drama of Negroes, from Harlem to Mississippi, going on the march for their rights and freedom. In one of the early meetings, Sammy had said that race wouldn't matter in the play. He drew strange stares. Hilly Elkins knew, better than anyone, that a play about black and white without backbone would surely be attacked. Hilly demanded rewrites from Odets now on a daily basis.

Inside the rehearsal hall, there was a feverish energy. Cigarette smoke was everywhere. Sammy flitted about, sometimes in a tweed suit jacket with a corncob pipe poking from the breast pocket. Many thought it was a strange outfit, and they only stared harder as he made his way to the dressing room. He was getting carried away with his British affectations and could not help himself. The young Strouse, who favored argyle sweaters, tapped his fingers, hummed, worked on the music. Some days May silently watched rehearsals in the dark, Sammy's assistants checking on her, keeping her comfortable. Hilly sat like a general struggling with battle plans for war. He cursed; he smoked; he dreamed of opening night; he cursed some more. Odets had come out of the sunny climes of Beverly Hills for this—a kinetic leading man whom he wasn't sure he could write well enough for; a producer barking in his ear; and race riots brewing across America as a backdrop to his play.

But they were professionals, and they forged on. From the beginning, Sammy and Hilly let it be known they wanted to make the musical look—and feel—as authentic as possible. There were weekends when Strouse, Adams,

When Golden Boy *opened on Broadway on October 20, 1964, Sammy was happily married to white actress May Britt. But within months, he was romantically linked to one of the black beauties in the play, Lola Falana (left), seated alongside fellow cast member Sally Neal. What must Sammy have been thinking as he snapped this photo? The cultural upheaval across the country changed him. His marriage began to collapse. Fade to black . . .*   (COURTESY SALLY NEAL)

Sammy, and Coe would check out the boxing matches at Madison Square Garden. They wanted Sammy to move like a pro in the ring onstage.

Women were arriving through the stage door—leggy, beautiful—to audition for dancing roles. They'd quickly change into their leotards and take to the stage. Sometimes Sammy himself had summoned them. "Sammy would bring a lot of girls in who were pretty—but weren't technically trained," recalls Sally Neal, one of the dancers who was cast in *Golden Boy* and who had performed with Sammy in *Mr. Wonderful*.

Sammy, still the camera freak, aimed his lens everywhere, and at everyone, during rehearsals. It was as if he could stop the world for that nanosecond it took for the camera's shutter to click; otherwise he might lose forever what his one good eye had just seen flash by—something beautiful, something soulful.

So he aimed his camera and stopped what he saw. The competition on Broadway for dancing roles was stiff, and doubly so for Negro dancers, who had so few opportunities. The chorus dancers were known as gypsies. In order to stand out as a gypsy, to catch the eye of director or star, you had to do something provocative. You had to shine every day, until you were no longer just shining, you were becoming indispensable. One of the new dancers—tall and aggressive—was shining every day. She caught Sammy's eye. He believed he had spotted his ingenue—the role that he had first offered to Frances Davis. He raised the camera. Click, click.

Her name was Lola.

Lola Falana hailed from Philadelphia. As a schoolgirl she was quite determined about her future plans. "Even in high school I had said I wanted to be like Sammy Davis, Jr., when I grow up." Shortly after high school, she had begun talking of going out on the road, of leaving home. It was just the kind of talk that frightened many parents. One night, the house quiet, she began to pack. Her mother stopped her on the steps, three o'clock in the morning, panting: she begged Lola not to go, told her how upset her father would be. "This is a done deal," she told her mother. "I'm gone. The hour has come."

She was headed to Atlantic City, where she joined a chorus revue put together by Larry Steele. She took a room in a boardinghouse. Lola Falana became known as a workhorse of a dancer. Her sexiness was potent. She heard about a Broadway-bound musical being cast starring Sammy Davis, Jr. She got herself into Manhattan. And during the *Golden Boy* auditions, she stood out.

"We put her in a pair of gold pants," Hilly Elkins remembers. Her body—"a hell of a build," says Elkins—froze the eyes of men. And the eye of Sammy.

Chapter 13

GOLDEN

One of the rewards of returning to New York City for Sammy was the chance to renew old acquaintances. He hadn't lived, really lived, in the city since *Mr. Wonderful,* and that had been nearly a decade before. He invited musicians, journalists, jewelry salesmen, and hangers-on to the *Golden Boy* rehearsals. They came, and he hugged them as if they had all been survivors of a sinking ocean liner. Magazine writers sent their requests to interview Sammy to Murphy, his assistant. Murphy was in no rush to reply.

While in New York City, Sammy—just as he had hoped—was going to make a movie. He rented an office, and Shirley Rhodes quickly turned it into a production office. Sammy had secured a movie deal with Embassy Pictures. He'd star in and produce *A Man Called Adam,* a tough-luck drama about a jazzman coping with the ups and downs of his life. If Sinatra could both star in and produce a movie, then so could Sammy. Shirley kept visitors without appointments away from the office, stopping them at the door, her face going cold in the presence of nonsense. Negroes were watched warily by whites. She knew it. Any missteps, and there was bad publicity, a rise in the number of Negroes doubting other Negroes. She would have none of it heaped on Sammy. So: a movie and a Broadway play! Sammy's kind of pace; he'd film around the play.

Meanwhile, with Strouse, Coe, and Sammy working hard on *Golden Boy,* Odets fled back out to California, promising finished rewrites today, tomorrow, anyday. Hilly fumed. Then there was the matter of the production having to adjust to Sammy's New York City schedule. "He was consistently late," recalls Strouse. "He was the first person to use the expression to me 'CPT' [colored people's time]. He was so complicated that when he was late, I felt guilty. I never felt totally at ease with him." During rehearsals, Strouse realized Sammy was unable to read music. Sammy had developed an extraordinarily tuned ear. To compensate for the lack of reading, he'd pounce on whatever didn't sound right. The process unnerved Strouse. "I was doing a lot of bowing and scraping."

On August 14, 1963, Clifford Odets died in California. He had been sickly off and on, bravely keeping it from Hilly. It was cancer. Hilly was sent reeling.

Odets, only fifty-seven, was saluted in the press, remembered for his early glories as a playwright by the likes of Lee Strasberg and Harold Clurman, two big guns of the American theater. But there were also the reminders of his shameful House Un-American Activities Committee testimony. In the end, as a playwright, Odets seemed a man frozen in that dangerous territory of being unable to transfer the words and ideas from his quick eyes and brain to the empty page. He had been told to write *Golden Boy*—once again—and lift it even higher this time. Always a man who came alive at night—he slept during the day—he had begun to find solace in darkness, far away from Hilly Elkins and his golden dream. What had sounded possible in Hilly's mind proved stifling to Odets. He had taken on the assignment for the best of reasons—to support his children. Following his death, one of Odets's former students, who had met him in the 1950s, referred to him as "an archangel who had fallen."

Hilly wouldn't hear of retreat. He'd certainly miss Odets, but the world was going to keep spinning. He and the *Golden Boy* company would hash the play out, trying to imagine where Odets might have taken it. They'd rehearse longer. They'd take the notes and rewrites, skimpy as they were, that Odets had left behind. They would keep going. Sammy displayed not a bit of concern. For a child in vaudeville, potential disaster lay around every corner. This—the death of Odets—was life.

So they kept going. However, tension started to pervade the production. Hilly's voice grew louder, edgier. The opening of *Golden Boy* would coincide with the opening of *Fiddler on the Roof,* another big musical, starring Zero Mostel. Hilly's investors started to worry.

At times it appeared Sammy—seen jumping rope one moment in rehearsals, puffing on a cigarette the next—and Peter Coe were not on the same page. Everyone in the rehearsal could feel it. Everybody in the production seemed to be offering suggestions now. "One time," recalls Strouse—still feverishly reworking musical numbers as well—"I went to Sammy's dressing room with a notepad. Sammy said, 'What's that pad?' I said, 'I took a few notes.' He said, 'Get the fuck out of here.' "

Sam Sr. had come east to visit. He was worried, and it had nothing to do with the death of Clifford Odets. "The big deal was that the leading lady was white," says dancer Lola Falana. Sam Sr. warned Sammy of possible backlash.

Hilly had lined up the cities and theaters for the out-of-town tryouts for *Golden Boy.* They'd begin in Philadelphia, go from there to Detroit, and then on to Boston. And from Boston, to Broadway. As he looked around at his cast before they hit the road, a tinge of pride overcame Hilly. He had assembled a genuinely integrated company. "Because of the fact that, outside from the Negro Ensemble Company, there were so few opportunities on Broadway for blacks, I was able to put together the most extraordinary company."

As the forty-one-member company set out, the belief in success, fueled by Hilly's optimism, was rising. Odets was dead, but Sammy was very much alive.

Privately, there were cast members—particularly Negro—who still thought that long swatches of the play's dialogue felt dated. But the road was for repairs and adjustments, and they knew every day would count.

In Philadelphia the reviews were tepid and troublesome. But the reviews were not the only problems. Outside the theater, there were hecklers, bigots shouting at the actors and actresses as they emerged, making references to the interracial romance onstage between Sammy and Paula Wayne. "For the first onstage kiss we had bodyguards," says Elkins. It was something no one expected. Paula Wayne was rattled. Sammy ignored the protests, as if he had seen it all before—which he had—and as if life was just life, which it was. The fighter in Hilly wanted to tussle with the bigots. Instead, he settled for police protection. After Sammy received the first of several death threats, a bodyguard—in addition to Joe Grant, his personal bodyguard who always traveled with him—was positioned outside his stage door. It is a rather lovely phrase—"the Philadelphia Negro"—and it had been coined by W. E. B. Du Bois. Well, the Philadelphia Negro just now had no intentions of staging protests on Sammy's behalf: he'd as soon cast his emotional glances in the direction of the Deep South, where church bombings and the murders of civil rights workers were going on.

Cast members found themselves leaving the theater at night and glancing over their shoulders. "Being on the road with *Golden Boy* was one of the more painful experiences of my life," says Strouse.

At the end of the Philadelphia run, they headed for Boston. Before arriving, Sammy waxed sentimental with the press about his memories of that city, where he had spent time with his father and Will Mastin. "All of the old burlesque houses! They were schools for vaudeville performers. There's no school like them for variety performance," he cried. "There's no way left for a boy to learn the business. There's nowhere left for a boy to learn how to bow!"

Those cruel, unpredictable, poverty-stricken, dark, and sad days of vaudeville. Sammy sometimes missed them.

He talked to another group of reporters, and someone asked about the Rat Pack. Sammy did not want to dwell on that: "a joke can only go so far, and it's over now," he said about the group and the movies and fun times they had. "Besides, most of us have too many commitments in the future to be able to get together again."

They each—Frank, Dean, Sammy, Peter, Joey—had had their own kind of fame. And when they were together, that fame had taken on a kind of electricity of its own. But now they were just too famous to be famous together again. The Rat Pack. Done in by fame. It was the old Hollywood story.

Someone asked about Barry Goldwater, whose presidential campaign was scaring liberals and Negroes alike. "I don't have to think," Sammy answered. "I'm a Democrat."

Just after arriving in Boston, Sammy busied himself with his traditional duties. He shopped. He bought camera equipment, clothes, gifts for cast members and stagehands. The fans and autograph-seekers only caught glimpses of him, ducking in and out of the backseat of his silver-colored, convertible Rolls-Royce. "In Boston, a great many young fans once caught up to the Rolls," remembers Strouse. "These kids started climbing all over the car. There were fifty kids on the windshield of the car. I was scared—I'm claustrophobic."

The first preview audience in Boston streamed to the Shubert Theatre to see *Golden Boy*, right alongside Elliot Norton, the city's esteemed drama critic. Norton, a Harvard graduate, wrote for the *Boston Herald American*. In his youth, Norton had seen Paul Robeson onstage playing Othello in a theater near Harvard Square. When the foot stomping began, Norton could see that Robeson was nervous, fearing trouble because of his white Desdemona. But it was just the Harvard kids' way of showing their appreciation of the performance. Sammy wasn't Othello, and Wayne wasn't Desdemona. But Norton sensed a schizophrenic leakage in the play, as if they weren't sure they truly wanted to tackle the racial angle. Norton also felt the play needed more action, and that Sammy's character, Joe Wellington ("Wellington" had now replaced "Bonaparte" as the last name of Davis's character, the former a Negro-sounding name, the latter Odets's Italian name), wasn't quite credible. The review virtually dismissed the production. Hilly was livid. He felt Norton was trying to sabotage his play. Hilly had to take action. He went on Jerry Williams's Boston radio program publicizing the play; he did fifteen hours' worth of radio in Boston, trumpeting it.

Hilly Elkins was wise enough to know he had work to do before *Golden Boy* reached New York. He phoned Paddy Chayefsky, the renowed playwright, who was a friend, and asked him to come take a look. Chayefsky came, sat, and watched. "At the end of the performance," says Elkins, "Chayefsky said to me, 'Hilly, I'm your friend. Close the fucking show. You ain't got a show.'"

Hilly heard every word Chayefsky said, and he heard them loud and clear. And they angered him, but only a little. What they really did was propel Hilly Elkins forward. He had no intention of closing "the fucking show."

Still, more and more, Hilly and Sammy realized their *Golden Boy* continued to have huge holes in it. Hilly stretched rehearsals, and he grew antsy. Godfrey Cambridge—whose wit could be biting, who was a raconteur, who was an edgy and sarcastic presence in the company—began expressing doubts about the durability of the production. It did not go unnoticed that he was spending time on the telephone, talking to his agent, his voice quite audible, trying to line up another job. That was enough for Hilly, and he fired him.

Johnny Brown, the garrulous young actor who was Cambridge's understudy, now had the proverbial break. Still, Cambridge's firing only highlighted the tension coursing through the show. There began a creeping feeling of desperation. Sammy grabbed understudy Brown and took him under his wing. Suddenly, it was Sammy playing Will Mastin.

Hilly, who had a bad back, would often be forced to issue his orders lying down as a masseuse attended to him. To those who witnessed this, he resembled a man flattened by pressures.

Without a playwright around to update *Golden Boy,* the criticism turned to Peter Coe, the director. Many of the Negroes in the company, emboldened while reading civil rights headlines and watching television newsreels on a daily basis now, wondered if Coe's British sensibilities were stopping him from realizing the true dramatic leaps the play would have to take to be credible. Sammy—a longtime Anglophile—had hardly a word of criticism for Coe. There were days when Coe seemed unsure and unsettled. Hilly did not like seeing his director indecisive, and wondered if it was just exhaustion. Then he convinced himself that Coe was having a nervous breakdown. Hilly suggested to Coe he take some time off.

Again, Hilly and Sammy conferred. They needed another playwright. And maybe another director. They kept their game faces on; they did not want the company to see them sweat.

It was the silken-faced champ himself, Sugar Ray Robinson. Sammy hired him as a "consultant" to the play, immediately giving the fight scenes in rehearsal a certain verisimilitude. He had Sammy in a corner, teaching him moves—how to throw a punch, how to duck a punch. The entertainer and the fighter. Two Negroes long on the other side of the mirror into which gangster America peered, extracting its coins and profit. "Sammy tried to get everything to be authentic," says Lola Falana, who was herself awed at the sight of Robinson teaching Sammy about the sweet science.

And now it was Hilly swinging—in search of, at long last, a playwright.

William Gibson had achieved fame with his 1959 Broadway production of *The Miracle Worker.* The play, about a teacher called upon to instruct a blind and deaf six-year-old child—and based on the life of Helen Keller—starred Anne Bancroft and a precocious young actress by the name of Patty Duke.

Both gave astonishing performances, and the play ran on Broadway for 719 performances.

Gibson, who lived in Stockbridge, an hour's drive from Boston, had been out walking when his wife yelled at him that there was someone phoning from Boston. "My wife said, 'Do you want to take a call from Hilly Elkins?' " recalls Gibson. "I knew the play was trying out in Boston and wasn't doing very well." After the phone call, Gibson turned to his wife and asked: "Well, do you want to go to Boston?"

William Gibson, in fact, had a deep and spiritual connection to Odets. Years earlier, when he was starting to embark on a writing career in New York, Gibson had taken a writing course taught by Odets, and found that those early teachings had helped shape him as a writer. News of the playwright's illness touched him, and he had visited Odets just before his death in California. As a memento for his emotional support as Odets lay dying, Gibson was given Odets's writing desk.

Upon arriving in Boston, and meeting with Elkins, Sammy, and Coe, who had now returned, Gibson quickly saw for himself that the production was struggling to find an identity. He thought the troubles began with the director. "Coe hadn't the faintest idea of what black culture was like," says Gibson. "He asked, 'Why does the lead character want to get out of Harlem?' " To Gibson, such ignorance was unbelievable, and it was all he needed to hear. Gibson told Hilly that Coe should be allowed to direct *Golden Boy* only "if the play ever goes to the moon"—but no longer on earth.

Hilly pleaded with Gibson to tackle the rewriting Odets had begun. Gibson—tall and raw-boned—found himself warming to the idea. (There was also a sentimental reason: Odets had left two children behind; they would be entitled to *Golden Boy* royalties.)

William Gibson was also curious about America, about what he knew and hoped to learn. He knew enough to know of Negro conditions in Harlem; he did not truly know about Negroes in all of America. He did know that there was anger on the streets. Peter Coe was not at all worried about the rioting going on in the urban centers of America. "This black crisis will pass away," Coe predicted. Gibson thought that by working on a musical drama with Sammy, he would be pulled right into the racial gulf of the country, and that he couldn't help but learn things. "I thought I would get a glimpse of America I wasn't familiar with. On the other hand, all the people in the production end were white." Coe's lack of identification with America was one thing, Gibson felt, but he considered it even stranger that the production itself seemed to be operating in a kind of vacuum, as if, beyond Hilly, they all lacked the artistic vision to adapt the play to the times. There was fear, and nerves were on edge: Godfrey Cambridge had been axed. Who would be next?

Gibson thought the play had a "schizophrenic quality" going that could be ruinous. He believed much of that schizophrenia began with Sammy, whom Gibson wished to mentally unravel for himself: "He was married to May Britt, the whitest girl you ever saw." Gibson had to traverse tricky ground, and he knew he couldn't avoid Sammy while doing it. "Sammy was the one who mattered. He was the economic power behind it. Sammy was the law."

The more Hilly and Sammy listened to the insightful Gibson, the more they realized that Coe would have to go. "Hilly and Sammy told me I had to tell Peter Coe he was fired," says Strouse. "I hated to do it." An exhausted Coe left without an argument.

Hilly and Gibson had indeed begun whispering about a replacement director. Hilly invited Arthur Penn, who had directed Gibson's *Miracle Worker* on Broadway, to come to Boston. He told Penn he merely wanted him to watch the play and offer his reactions, but he had every intention of trying to persuade Penn to direct *Golden Boy*.

Gibson was now officially aboard. He returned to his home in the woods of Stockbridge and set about rewriting the play on the desk of its original author. He figured the only way he could do it was to bring the racial issues of the play out into the open. He told himself there would be more heart and more aching in the play. "I rewrote it day and night. I redid the whole first act."

In the woods, with the death of Odets and the living and breathing Sammy in his mind, William Gibson felt energized. For him, race may have been virgin intellectual territory, but it was also intoxicating because there was so much to explore. He returned to Boston and showed Hilly and Sammy the first act, which he had rewritten. They were mightily impressed.

The more Gibson watched Sammy, watched him interact with the cast, bounce in and out of the theater, the more he listened to the beatniklike language rolling from his mouth, watched Sammy unloose himself from the white world to glide into the Negro world, only to—just like a finger snap—glide back into the white world again, the more entranced he found himself. "Sammy was one of the most extraordinary guys I ever met in my life," Gibson says. "When I went to Sammy, I talked to him and told him what I thought was wrong with the play. Sammy said, 'Hilly, I want that guy.' Hilly put pressure on me to do the script. After I came back to Boston, I remember I said to my wife, 'I have to get rid of some of my prejudices against nightclub performers.' "

Sammy liked new, and he liked invention. Gibson was new. The focus on *Golden Boy* as a racial drama made Sammy nervous, but the nervousness lost out to excitement about the newness, to witnessing the creation of something.

Gibson raced back to his home in Stockbridge while the *Golden Boy* company remained in Boston. He vowed to complete the rewriting of the second act. Going back and forth, it took him ten days of feverish work to rewrite the entire play. It was no longer a play about a boxer grappling with giving up his life because he felt wronged by the world. Now it was a play about a boxer who no longer wanted to live because of a love affair that couldn't be consummated because the disease of racism was far more lethal and destructive than his fists. Sammy didn't want to be a Negro in the play; he simply wanted to be Sammy. But Gibson—his wife, Margaret, was a noted psychoanalyst—knew better. "Once you had Sammy, you couldn't ignore the fact of interracial romance in the play," recalls Gibson.

In the rewritten play, Gibson had now put Sammy's real-life infatuation with white women onstage, for all the world to see. It was, sure enough, art imitating life—only it was far richer.

Sometimes Sammy, sleeping next to his white wife at night, worried if Gibson might be reading too much into his life. Gibson, sleeping next to his psychoanalyst wife, slept like a baby.

"The play," says Gibson, "now seemed about the black and white allegory of America."

Arthur Penn sat watching the play in rehearsals, making notes, his eyes twittering. But he would make no commitment to direct. His indecision did not amuse Hilly Elkins.

Hilly sat watching the play night after night, answering the worries of investors, who were hearing the mixed reports from the road. Like many producers, Hilly began spending money out of his own pocket. "I was in such deep shit," he recalls. "I was literally a quarter million dollars over" budget. Hilly was still jittery enough to consider wholesale changes. He and Gibson began worrying if Paula Wayne would be up to the added dramatic emphasis in the new version of the play. They decided she would not, so they invited Anne Bancroft to come to Boston and consider taking over the female lead. Bancroft came, and declined the offer. Mel Brooks, her husband, told her she would be "cheapening" herself to jump into the role. Wayne was safe.

Late one night—around two a.m., as Hilly Elkins remembers—Arthur Penn found himself sitting in Elkins's hotel suite. Penn began mumbling to himself—in Hebrew. Hilly now realized Penn did not particularly like the play. And Hilly had had enough of Penn's indecisiveness; they were being pilloried in the press; money was on the line. Hilly, his complexion growing redder by the second, grabbed Penn by his shirt collar.

"Are you going to direct this motherfucker, or what?" he yelled at Penn.

Hilly was grimacing. His back was in pain. His hands were still at Penn's neck.

"Of course," Penn replied.

So now they had a director.

. . .

It was off to Detroit, with both Arthur Penn and William Gibson aboard. Sammy was his usual calm self, a man at home on the move, at total ease entering and exiting old theaters. He had a way of making up a family whenever he had to. "When you were in a show with Sammy," says *Golden Boy* dancer Sally Neal, "everybody was important—the usher, the person selling the tickets."

In Detroit, they unloaded at the Fisher Theatre, an old structure in that gritty city. Between Boston and Detroit, there had, of course, been no way, or time, to adapt *Golden Boy* to Gibson's rewrites. So the company adopted a grueling plan: they would give the Detroit theatergoers the Odets version of the play in their scheduled evening performance. But during the day, they would rehearse the new Gibson version. "Finally," recalls Elkins, "at some point, we had most of the show changes in place."

Penn was driving Sammy and Paula Wayne hard. Sammy always had a glass in his hand, sipping from it. It was liquor. (Penn asked him one day if he could get rid of the glass. "No way," Sammy answered.) Arthur Penn intended to get dramatic performances from both Sammy and Paula. *Golden Boy* was a musical, true enough, and Penn did not question their singing voices; it was their acting range that worried him. He would tell the two of them to go off by themselves and concentrate and focus. Sammy found it difficult to sit still, had no idea what Penn was talking about. Focus? Sammy was Sammy, and his splintered mind was his genius. But if Arthur Penn wanted Sammy Davis, Jr., the actor, instead of the nightclub musical performer, then Sammy would give Penn what he wanted. "He learned so fast," Elkins remembers. As for Paula Wayne, some days she did seem fragile. There were those who thought it just a performer's fussiness. Gibson thought otherwise: "Paula was in love with Sammy."

There were some beautiful moments taking place, and both cast and crew could feel it. Many began noticing Johnny Brown, the understudy who had taken over for the fired Godfrey Cambridge. In the early rehearsals, the chubby Brown "couldn't get two feet together," says Elkins. But somehow the feet got lighter. "The first night he went on, he was bloody marvelous," remembers Elkins, of Brown's out-of-town tryout. The Strouse and Adams musical number, "Don't Forget 127th Street"—about remembering one's Harlem roots—was bringing down the house. "I think it was some of our best work," Strouse says.

Gibson would be sitting in the theater, watching a rehearsal, and all of a sudden Sammy would slide across the stage floor and hop, in one fluid slithery motion, atop the piano. Gibson's back would arch up: he just couldn't understand how a one-eyed man could make such a move. Sammy was so hyper Gibson believed he didn't sleep. "He was filled with energy all the time."

In Detroit, Sammy vanished some evenings to a recording studio, where he was laying down tracks on an album with Count Basie. And then there were those times when Sammy just vanished, leaving everyone nervous. "When we were on the road," remembers Gibson, "Sammy would take off for a weekend and do a concert somewhere. He would go do these shows and come back rejuvenated." Once back, having settled everyone's nerves, Sammy had stories to tell. He regaled the cast and crew with stories of his life. Sammy would brag to Gibson about future plans. Gibson listened wide-eyed. "Sammy wanted to be a big shot in the dramatic world. He was always hankering for a big movie role." Sinatra sailed in and out of many of Sammy's conversations. "I remember," recalls Gibson, "Sammy saying to me about Frank, 'He's my leader. He's my leader.' He said it like they were a Boy Scout troop. He would say it with a certain satirical bent." More and more, Gibson felt Sammy Davis, Jr., was "twelve different guys."

But it was in Detroit where Hilly, Sammy, and William Gibson began realizing they had a play worthy of Broadway. The ticket lines were long, and the buzz was not only good, but spirited as well.

During the road turmoil, many of the Negroes in the cast quit: there were death threats; there was the death of Odets; there were worries about the leading lady. But if Sammy had quit, he would have thrown them all out of work. For staying, some of them thought him courageous. And some of them wanted to give themselves to him, wrap their long, long legs around his tiny waist. They wanted to comfort the tired but tireless star. It was infatuation. It was sex. It was love. It was a late-night rendezvous with Sammy in Detroit. It was fucking. "We were all living in a hotel. I'd see one of the showgirls coming out of Sammy's room at three in the morning," says Gibson.

Yes, it was his show, and Sammy would save the whole damn production, and he'd lick the sugar while doing it.

Dancer Sally Neal heard about the sex parties. She stayed away. "They were wild, bizarre, sick."

The more the play righted itself, the wilder with joy Sammy became. He gave Arthur Penn a gold watch. And he gave William Gibson a gold watch. They had taken care of him. They had listened to him when he gave advice. He gave lovely pieces of jewelry to the female dancers in the chorus. Sammy was an old theater pro, and the old pros knew the value of generosity. He gave other cast members gifts: bits of jewelry he found lying around in his dressing room or at home.

From city to city, Sammy went on radio. He visited nightclubs that he only recently had performed in, publicizing his play. There he was, whistling through the theater, in argyle sweater, in square wire-rimmed glasses, in pointy-toed shoes, in sharkskin slacks. Then, onstage, bare-chested, jumping rope, sweating, a man in love, Odets's fighter, singing and dancing, the whiff of

sex spewing from him, from those little hips, ugly offstage, but onstage, dancing, singing, he was beautiful—schooled by the great Sugar Ray Robinson
himself. And the kids in the play began loving him, even the ones who had
doubted him from what they had heard about his obsession with white—
white people, white women, Sinatra. So he kept it all swirling. "Sammy was the
magnetic center of this whole operation," says Gibson.

Dancer Marguerite DeLain knew there was another reason for the constant
curiosity about the play, even during tryouts. "This was 1964. Here was a white
woman being kissed by a black man."

After his daily performance, Sammy didn't have the heart to clear out his
dressing room, so the visitors would stay, until Murphy, his assistant, would
have to beg them to leave, even as Sammy was bent and wrapped around them
like a piece of licorice.

Hilly Elkins had fixed the cracks in his play, and made it look so good that to
see it, one never would have thought it had ever been broken. Negroes on the
march? Photos of deputies spraying tear gas and dogs yapping at the heels of
Negroes in Alabama and Mississippi and Newark, New Jersey, on the front
pages of the *Washington Post*, the *New York Times*? The battle for civil rights?
Well, Hilly had a little dramatic tonic: he'd march little Sammy right up onto a
Broadway stage, a maroon boxing glove on one hand, a white woman on the
other. And right there, out in the open, it would be boxer Joe Wellington's civil
right to parade his sexual appetite onto a white woman in front of everyone's
eyes.

Hilly still cursed the critics in his sleep, though. At some of the out-of-town
theaters he had stood at curbside hurling insults at them! They wanted him
dead before he reached Broadway, and he wouldn't have it.

So, they both had been left for dead on the road. But they had fought back,
mano a mano, with the public and the critics, Hilly and Sammy, against the
world, spreading the gospel about their play. Two five-foot-six-inch men. They
had the white girls and they had the Negro girls. They had sex and they had
drama. They had the ghost of Clifford Odets. The entertainer and the producer. They were heading for Broadway, and they were armed like Napoleon's
army.

As usual, Murphy arrived in New York City ahead of Sammy. He set up a suite
for Sammy at the Gorham Hotel.

In New York City, on the ground where they would live or die, cast and crew
grew a little nervous. "The anxiety in New York before we opened was very
high," remembers Gibson.

The 1964–65 Broadway season was shaping up to be quite interesting. There was the much-anticipated *Fiddler on the Roof*, which would open the week before *Golden Boy*. Also expected to make noise were two other musicals, *Half a Sixpence* and *Oh, What a Lovely War*.

Hilly had New York City plastered with *Golden Boy* posters. Huge pictures of Sammy rose like silky question marks above women dressed in sequins and falling at his knee. Negro women, white women. Sammy always the lone male in the blown-up photographs. He looked like a man being swallowed by sex.

In the evening there were three children and a wife at home awaiting Sammy's arrival. But his nights were long. He convinced himself May would understand why he couldn't rush to their apartment after rehearsals—it was business, it was Broadway. Actually, it was all that and more. The young dancer Lola Falana happened to be drawing more and more of Sammy's attention. May was becoming suspicious of Sammy's carousing, but her quiet and reserved Swedish demeanor stopped her from questioning him.

Sammy understood, just as Hilly did, that the critics were sharpening their knives in anticipation of opening night. Everyone knew Sammy could dance, and everyone knew Sammy could sing. But could Sammy act? Could he become Joe Wellington? Could he exude the pain and suffering endured by one of Odets's most memorable characters? In previous incarnations, Elia Kazan had played the boxer; John Garfield had played him. It was not a role to trifle with.

There were six days to opening. William Gibson felt his own reputation was on the line now. He had written right into the teeth of the play. "From the beginning, I was writing a feisty character for Sammy. Stokely Carmichael would have liked it. Martin Luther King, Jr., wouldn't have liked it." Gibson had not sought to turn the cheek on the issue of race in the play.

Then there were five days. Then four.

On the fourth day from opening—October 16—the stage manager reported that Sammy was late for the Saturday matinee. It was forty-five minutes until curtains, and the clock was ticking. Necks craned, hoping they'd see him whirring into view from the alleyway entrance of the Majestic Theatre. No Sammy. It was a long-running joke, but William Gibson gave Hilly one dollar every time Sammy was late for a curtain call. A lot of one-dollar bills went from Gibson's palm into Hilly's palm. But this was ridiculous, and no one was chuckling. There was worry that something might have happened to him. "We called May," remembers Gibson. "She said she didn't know where he was." Hilly was running around, making calls. Lamont Washington, the understudy, was reciting his lines. "I got onstage," recalls Elkins, "and said, 'Ladies and gentlemen, Sammy Davis won't be performing today.' " He hardly finished before he noticed bodies rising, muffled voices, the shaking of heads. They left even though the play had not yet officially opened. They had come to see Sammy. Without him, there was no reason to stay. Evening came, and everyone felt sure he would show, or at least they would hear something from him. A pre-opening crowd was still a crowd. But Sammy did not show, and there wasn't a word. Dark thoughts began to swirl. After all, there had been death threats. Maybe the bigots had gotten to him. Maybe he had been kidnapped. Hilly started calling some of his Mafia contacts. He wanted to know if they knew anything, if they had heard anything. But nothing. The Shuberts themselves, owners of the Majestic—at 245 West Forty-fourth Street and their showcase theater—came down to lend emotional support. "We didn't know if Sammy would return to the show," recalls Gibson. They called May again and again. She had nothing new to tell them, save how her own worries were increasing. Margaret Gibson, the playwright's wife, went on her own looking for Sammy. Margaret had grown up hanging around Negro musicians. She knew Negro culture. She had grown fond of Sammy. He liked to drink, so she scanned bars. "I felt so sorry for him," she recalls.

One day turned to two. The police were alerted. Now it was the last day of rehearsals before the opening. William Gibson's phone rang. It was Sammy; he said he was fine and would be returning for that evening's performance. Gibson forgot his anger and anxiety; he was thrilled. He rushed to tell Elkins and Penn. "I went to meet him outside the stage door," says Gibson. "He had given me and Arthur gold watches. Arthur said, 'I feel like throwing that watch back in his face.' " Then there he was, the star, alighting from a taxi. He walked right into the theater without saying a word to Gibson or Penn.

Sammy later confided to Margaret Gibson why he had fled. "He told me he thought he was a terrible actor and could never go through with being in *Golden Boy* if it had any kind of a run," she remembers. "He was terrified." Margaret Gibson, the psychoanalyst, let Sammy cry on her shoulders. "He said to me, 'Margaret, I love you.' I said, 'Come on, Sammy, showbiz people say that all the time.' He said, 'Oh, I don't mean it that way at all.' And he began to weep. I apologized."

October 20, 1964. Opening night.

The set is a stark boxing gym. A light shines on one fighter, jumping rope. With each jet-quick slapping of the rope on the ground, an orchestral sound echoes: *ssss, ssss, ssss,* a hissing of rope, over and over as the rope goes over the fighter's head and slaps the gym floor. Then another light cranks on, highlighting another fighter, who is jumping rope in another spot, sweat glistening from his body like the body of the first fighter. Then another light, and another fighter, jumping rope: *ssss, ssss, ssss,* like tree branches smacking the ground, over and over again, all three fighters now, three tight-bellied fighters. The music is almost fiery now, a rumble keeping up with the fighters and the ropes, which are turning fast now, in a rhythm. It is almost a dance. It all looks so bal-letic. A door suddenly swings open. And there he is. The star everyone has come to see. He lingers at the door. (Let the folks get their applause in. They have paid good money, and they have packed the Majestic because of him.) It is Sammy; in the program it says the figure at the door is Joe Wellington, a down-on-his-luck Negro boxer living in Harlem. He is in street clothes, a long coat. The look on his face is hard and serious; he is all business. Joe Wellington starts striding across the gym floor. He has to see his manager.

The action unfolds fast.

There's a scene in the office of Tom, Joe's manager. Joe feels Tom has been shortchanging him. Tom fast-talks Joe: he's doing the best he can, he'll get more money when the knockouts come. Joe has a winning record, but always on technical knockouts. Tom tells Joe maybe he'd get more money if he flat out knocked fighters out. Joe meets Lorna, Tom's girlfriend. There are exchanges, the whiff, right away, of something forbidden, something Joe can't have—a sensuous white woman—and never will have, because he's a Negro.

Another scene, Joe singing to himself, to the world, of his frustrations, about being poor, a fighter, a Negro. He is moving across the stage with cat quickness; his voice is large and throaty:

> *Who do you fight*
> *When you want to break out*
> *But your skin is your cage?*
> *Uptown*
> *Just another joe—*
> *Downtown*
> *Where you gonna go?*

The managers want to take Joe on the road. Joe is leery, always believing he'll get gypped when it comes to money. Lorna is slightly flirtatious, chats with Joe. She is wondering why he fights, she is curious about his life. They're in a park. Lorna tells Joe that traveling as a boxer will be wonderful.

"Go on a tour, see the country—ever travel?" she asks.

"Sure, thousands of miles," Joe says. "All in Harlem."

Joe confides to her that he is confused and sad about life. "My poppa's a junkman and thinks that's fine, my brother works for CORE and gets his head kicked in—and my whole life seems like one long night I've been standing in alleys looking across the park at these buildings, the lights of this city, my God,

it's like diamonds in the air, why can't I pick some too?" This is not Clifford
Odets's writing; it is savvy William Gibson's writing. (The giveaway is the reference to the civil right group, CORE—the Congress of Racial Equality.)

Some young punks—white—stroll into the park and spot Joe and Lorna.

"Hands offa the lady, nigger," one says to Joe.

He shies from a fight, he tries to shoo them away with words. There is Lorna
to think of. But they want a fight. Three against one, and Joe battles them until
they scatter. He is bruised but not down. In the melee, Lorna has tumbled to
the ground. Now she sees a different America, it is Joe's America, and it is full
of daily insults and meanness and unpredictabilities. She has never been a witness to this particular America. She looks at him now not as just a boxer, or a
meal ticket for her boyfriend. She now looks at him as one who has to fight for
his dignity daily. He looks at her shyly. She asks him if girls frighten him.

"White girls," he answers. (Again, the pen of Gibson.)

Joe hits the road—Erie, St. Paul, Akron—and fights. He can't get Lorna out
of his mind. Before leaving, he told her he'd win on the road—for her.

Back from the road, there is a battle brewing between Tom and Eddie, a
Negro promoter and Harlem numbers runner. Eddie has a shady past. Eddie
wants Joe under his wing: he promises riches, women, fame. Tom laughs him
off. Eddie glides through his scenes like ether: it is Billy Daniels, the nightclub
singer, playing the hell out of a role that really isn't much of a stretch for an old
smoothie such as himself, but he still has to play it, he still has to get his cues,
and he does.

There's another dance number, Joe now torn between Harlem and the outside world, between Tom, the white man, and Eddie, the Negro, the soul
brother. The leggy dancers—the sugar that Sammy, now hiding inside of Joe,
had been licking at will on the road—are now swirling around him as he sings
and belts another number. Then comes a dancer, dressed in gold. She manages
to widen eyes in the audience a little more. She is sauntering one moment,
leaping the next. They check their programs. Her character's name is Lola, they
see; and they also see her real name is Lola Falana. They have never heard of
her, and already they are whispering about her.

There are more fight scenes, and they are staged with such verve and skill.
Joe Wellington looks to be getting pummeled one instant, then rallying with a
ferocious round of punches the next. He falls, he rises, he falls, he rises.

The fight game is starting to bewilder Joe. He has no idea where it is leading,
or where he is going with it. Lorna has become a friend he feels he can talk to.

She confesses that she is not in love with Tom. She has, in fact, fallen for Joe,
and she too feels trapped. She wonders, deep inside, if her white skin will allow
her to love Joe. She becomes emotional. "Joe, take me somewhere, take me
somewhere—oh my God, I'll fall apart if you don't hold me," she pleads.

Joe wants her. He knows he can't have her. Why, she is his manager's lady. And she is white. Joe is spinning.

Eddie, the hustler, keeps making promises to Joe—money and more money, TV sets, diamonds. Joe leaves Tom. Now he'll have both Eddie's promises and Lorna, his former manager's girl. Now he will hop over the whole complex racial divide because he has seen the way to his heart. Boxing won't give him love; Lorna will.

Tom finds out about Lorna's expressed love for Joe. He is furious, calls Joe brutal names. Lorna cries.

Time passes, and when it does, Lorna is back, telling Joe she has married Tom after all. Joe is crestfallen.

There is soon the announcement of the big fight, the biggest fight of Joe's career, the fight Eddie has promised. He will be fighting Pepe Lopez—"the pride of Puerto Rico."

The big fight scene is at Madison Square Garden. The fight is under way. Joe is getting beaten, badly, punch after punch, the head, the midsection, the orchestra accentuating the punches, the theatergoers cupping their mouths. Then he rallies, and he throws fiery punch after fiery punch, and there is the exalted feeling he is punching for himself, and for Harlem, and for the right to love the white woman that he has lost. He is punching and bleeding and punching until finally the pride of Puerto Rico is down, and quiet, and his eyes are closed and Joe Wellington is jumping up and down and running from corner to corner. A knockout. A rare knockout in the career of Joe Wellington, always more artist in the ring than knockout puncher.

His manager and boxing corner follow him into the dressing room; fans are trailing like victorious soldiers. In his room Joe is quickly surrounded: photographers, reporters, the fans, flashbulbs popping. "I'm going to go outside my weight and beat up the whole damn world!" Joe yells with mirth and venom. Lorna is gone, and the world is a mess, but he has glory now. Finally, a knockout. Then a boxing official comes into the dressing room. He tells Joe that Lopez is still out, and Joe says of course he's still out. There are snickers and snickers.

"I mean he's dead," the official says.

There is stunned silence. Nothing can fill the hole that the silence has dropped into. Joe has killed a fighter. Eddie Satin reels, then quickly tells the fighter it is not his fault, but faces are drawn. The horrible news spreads. The punch from Joe Wellington has killed Pepe Lopez. Other photographers and reporters rush in; Eddie yells them out. Lorna makes it through. She wants to console Joe. She is on her knees, in blouse and sweater and skirt and high heels, telling him it is not his fault, it was just a terrible accident. And Joe is mumbling, prancing the room, mumbling, staring, charging at one wall, then another.

"Oh, Lorna," he finally says, tears in his voice, "why couldn't you love me right."

In the next scene, there is, at first, only the wail of police sirens. There has been a one-car crash. There are no survivors. Joe Wellington was driving. Joe has committed suicide from behind the wheel. He has died for his boxing, and he has died for his Lorna. He has died for Harlem and all the things he could not get his hands on in life. Joe's father stands with his other son. And there is Lorna, with them, all remembering Joe. Joe's brother tells his father they'll take Joe home. Home, says the father, is exactly where Joe belongs.

"Oh my God," Lorna says, "he belonged anywhere—anywhere a human being could—walk."

And they stroll downstage, the three of them, two Negroes and a white woman, into the darkness, making Joe even bigger in death than he was in life, allowing the audience to feel some of the racial fears that have haunted a country.

The lights dim into darkness.

There is applause, and it is thunderous, and it goes on and on. There is something akin to currents of electricity shooting into and out of the audience. The curtain calls begin.

First, the dancers—really just kids, but on Broadway now—and they are beaming. Hell, Johnny Brown, up from understudy to replace Godfrey Cambridge, went to school right down the street, at the New York High School for Performing Arts. And here he stands, onstage, with family in the audience. Then the old pros come out—Kenneth Tobey and Ted Beniades. Charles Welch and Roy Glenn. They're stage vets with Hollywood experience behind them. Jamie Rogers, who played Pepe Lopez, the pride of Puerto Rico, glides out. Then Lola Falana, in her gold pants, a blazing look in her eyes: she'll never be just a gypsy again. The applause keeps coming. Billy Daniels floats out, the veteran nightclub performer making his Broadway debut, having given a performance as wicked and hard as it was meant to be. "It's *real*," Daniels had told Gibson at one of the final previews. He was trying to tell William Gibson that Negroes would not be ashamed; that Harlem could identify with this *Golden Boy*. There is Paula Wayne. She never knew how close she came to losing the role. But she has performed more than ably; the bigots hurling the insults at her during the out-of-town tryouts never forced her to quit. There is only one performer left. And the other actors spread, because here he comes, bouncy, cat-quick, the star, Joe Wellington, Sammy Davis, Jr., and everyone rises, and he looks around the Majestic, and even if he has been doing this all his life, even if this is the only life he truly knows, it still gives him chills, the joy he can bring from a stage, the way it lifts him up.

"I am what I am," Joe Wellington the boxer had said.

The man standing before them—elfin, fool, Uncle Tom, genius, Negro, brilliant, nigger, Jew; twelve guys, in fact, to William Gibson—is what he is: a star. Because of his one eye, he has to swivel his neck hard right to left to bring the whole audience into view.

Hilly is beaming, and so too are William Gibson and Charles Strouse and Lee Adams. Negro hands touching white hands onstage—and in the audience. Eyes are becoming moist. Maybe there were no more places that taught kids how to bow onstage. But Sammy Davis, Jr., knows how to bow. He can bow like an English gentleman. And he does. The cast can't take their eyes off him. Paula Wayne now loves him more than she ever imagined she could. Lola long ago told herself he was the reason she got into show business. Johnny Brown loves him and Billy Daniels loves him. May, his wife, sitting in the audience, loves him. He is nothing but beautiful, bowing and bowing. Maybe more than the mere wonderful execution of a play is swirling around everyone, onstage and off. Maybe it has something to do with what is going on outside the theater, across America, in the ghettos, in Harlem. There are woes, racial woes. Just months before the *Golden Boy* opening, there were riots in Harlem: a white policeman had shot a Negro youth. Nearly five hundred were arrested. There are civil rights workers who have been murdered, who are as dead as Joe Wellington is dead, down in Mississippi, in Alabama, Georgia, Louisiana. America is not at peace. And maybe this—this night, theatrical as it is—is something of an antidote.

Did they really doubt that he'd give them his best, as he had always done? Arthur Penn, who had floor-managed some of those early Eddie Cantor shows, now was seeing the same Sammy he had seen back then: inventive, thrilling, surprising. Arthur Penn is beaming. They are roaring now in their seats. *Golden Boy* smells like a hit. Hilly knows it. The motherfucker smells like a hit.

They wait—friends, autograph-seekers, family—outside his dressing room. The line stretches and stretches. They wait and they cry. They cry for themselves and for America. They whisper his name as they cry. Sammy. Oh Sammy. His mother, Elvera, is moving like a shark around the theater. She is still a stranger to him. But success and victory soften things—at least for a while they do. Inside the dressing room, they come, and he can't stop hugging the staff; and Hilly, especially Hilly, because it was Hilly who came to London, and it was Hilly who—in Boston, Philadelphia, and Detroit—had taken the racial insults so personally. Sammy wants to see everybody. He hands out gifts to cast and crew: jeweled radios shaped like pianos. (Hilly has no intention of being outdone by Sammy: he gives everyone silver Tiffany key rings.) May is smiling gloriously and nearly wordless. May, the white lady married to the Negro who had died in the play for his love of a white woman. Maybe it is just too much for her to digest, to take in.

William Gibson had seen his allegory long before the others. "In the play," he would recall, "if you're going to kill the guy by suicide, it's because love has failed him. White failed black."

Then they're all out the door into the limos heading to Danny's Hideaway for the after-party. They want to see the reviews. They can't wait for the *Times* to hit the streets, and the *Herald Tribune*. They pour into Danny's, stars and stars. Robert Mitchum is there. So is Shirley Jones. The showgirls are dressed divinely. Danny is Danny Stradella: he loves Sammy too. For so long Sammy had been bringing business to his restaurant. Danny could sense this was a special night. The corks kept popping. "They took the place apart," he would recall. Charles Strouse can't wait for the reviews; he is too antsy. Then he got some news. "Harold Arlen, the songwriter, called me and said the first reviews were terrific." The first reviews were the TV reviews. But television is television, its own transparent medium. Everyone is waiting for the newspapers. They start coming. "The theatrical form of *Golden Boy* as a musical is as crisp as a left jab and as jolting as a right uppercut," writes Howard Taubman in the *Times*. The critics are not bashful about letting their fight metaphors fly. The *Times* man goes on to praise Davis's acting. "For Mr. Davis is a lot more than a nightclub performer. He can act as well as sing and dance." They wanted Sammy Davis the actor, so he gave them Sammy Davis the actor. Hours pass. More reviews; more shrieks of joy; more champagne. "We read the reviews that night at Sardi's, and Sammy cried and cried," remembers his friend Amy Greene. She watched and listened as Hilly read some reviews aloud. Now Hilly was all peacock. "May was sitting next to Sammy," remembers Greene, "glowing like a white snow maiden."

The night folded around them all. The boxer Joe Wellington had referred to all the lights twinkling above New York City as "diamonds in the air."

A day later New York columnist Dick Schaap would write a column, a retrospective look at what had taken place: "Death Watch with the Golden Boy," the column is titled. It is about the disappointment of some of those who had been rooting for *Golden Boy* to fail. And how hurt they were now. "The death watch is a standard Broadway ritual, and it must have been designed to bring out vultures," Schaap wrote. "The vultures had a chance for a big kill this time." Schaap went on to theorize that that was perhaps why Sinatra, or Dean Martin, or Peter Lawford, or Joey Bishop—the Rat Pack—hadn't shown up: they imagined a disaster; they heard about the out-of-town reviews; they didn't want to throw failure in Sammy's face. Instead, it all had come out another way. "There are some people," Schaap wrote in a memorable turn of phrase as he finished off the column, "who can not stand the sight of no blood."

. . .

The phones were ringing. Ticket orders were escalating. Hilly looked brilliant now. The sellout performances were stacking up. He had a hit. And he also had Sammy under contract for two years, which was a coup. "You had to take Sammy whenever you could get him, because you might not be able to get him for another twenty years," Gibson said. Hilly ordered more publicity pictures, more billboards. He had to order a replacement billboard for the picture of Sammy and Paula embracing in jubilant laughter that was behind glass in front of the Majestic, though: someone had riddled it with bullets. The bigots. Hilly cursed, had the picture removed and replaced. More pictures and more radio spots and more photo layouts, whatever it took to keep the fever running high and higher. Someone sent human feces in the mail to Sammy. Hilly couldn't bear to tell him, so he didn't.

May was happy. At least many thought so. Sammy was her life now. She had let one dream die—her film career—to make a family. No one blamed her. Hollywood forgot her.

Sammy walks New York City now like a king. The diamonds in the air are everywhere, and they are shining upon him.

Every night, backstage, there were stars. Sinatra finally came. He had to; the buzz was too magnificent to stay away. Martin Luther King, Jr., came. A song in the show—"No More"—had caught his attention, and he told Charles Strouse how much he liked it. No more agony; no more second-class citizenship; no more sitting in the back of the bus: you were free to make any number of metaphorical allusions to the song. "Dr. King said to me that was his favorite song," recalls Strouse. Dancer Sally Neal had rushed to get a glimpse of King. "I remember following him out the door, watching him walk across the street." Cassius Clay, not yet Muhammad Ali, came, shadowboxing, gliding, looking pretty and creamy and huge. Sammy shrank like a child. He couldn't help himself: stars bedeviled him still, even though he too was a star. Jerry Lewis came. "He made it something it wasn't," Lewis felt of Sammy's performance. Evelyn Cunningham, the writer for the *Pittsburgh Courier,* came. She had written something critical of Sammy, though not *Golden Boy.* It had upset Sammy. "Sammy, I don't care what you think, I still love you," she said on the night she came. And that was all he needed to hear to hug her, to forgive her. She was moved by the play. Burt and Jane Boyar came. They were doubly excited—for Sammy and his performance, and because his autobiography, *Yes I Can,* which they had ghostwritten, would be published soon.

One evening came another guest. An old man, and he seemed to glide along the walls. He was in from California, the sunshine. Sammy fussed over him, showed him around, showed him the big dressing rooms with all the congratulatory telegrams. Will Mastin had lived most of his life in theaters. Inside them, he felt kingly. Most of the cast members had never seen Mastin, only read about him in Sammy's cast-listing biography. They knew Will Mastin was where Sammy began. "He came down to the basement and said hi to everybody," remembers dancer Lolly Fountain. "Very nice."

Sammy liked Lolly's mind, which he could bend, and Lola Falana's bravery, which reminded him of his own.

Even in the midst of all the goings-on, Sammy remained worried about his personal safety. Hilly Elkins couldn't keep all the news of the death threats from Sammy. Sammy conferred more and more with Joe Grant, his personal bodyguard. The marine veteran (Korean War) with the black belt in karate could be heard at times in the basement of the theater grunting—he was practicing his chops, he was breaking boards. When he mingled with the cast, he shared with them obscure volumes of books about Negro history. The combination of lethal skills and a probing intellect gave Grant a countenance that Sammy found intriguing. He'd often catch himself smiling at Grant's presence: a bodyguard; someone who could hurt someone; a bone-crusher like Sinatra's bone-crushers.

Lola Falana had told Sammy about her having left Philadelphia, no one believing in her except herself, how her friends and family warned her against it, told her she'd flop. "When I left home, I told Sammy, a lot of people were laughing at me. They said, 'She'll be back, she won't amount to anything.' Well, during *Golden Boy*, I told him I was going home to visit. He said, 'Let me go back with you.' He said, 'I understand people saying you ain't going to be nothing.' "

He called for the limousine. An easy ride, Manhattan to Philadelphia. The limo turned onto her street in the Germantown section of the city. Solid and sturdy homes. Her roots—something Sammy never had. Lola popped out, her family waiting on her, shrieking and giggling. Sammy was there standing, the oohs and aahs of neighbors' voices rising upon spotting him. He loved it, how she was being recognized, how cars were slowing, all the waves. Of course the waves were mostly for him, but he threw them back at her, so generously, telling those gathered around how wonderfully she had been performing in *Golden Boy*—then, like a star, he invited many of those gathered to come see the show—as his and Lola's personal guests! She was not just Lola anymore, but Lola of *Golden Boy*. Sammy signed some autographs, hugged her relatives as if he'd known them for years. Lola's eyes became warm—as did her mother's. "He came to Philadelphia," recalls Falana, "to show them that a star of his magnitude respected me."

Then Sammy and Lola climbed back into the limo and rode away—as in a fairy tale, only Sammy had really made it happen.

. . .

More and more Sammy started sleeping at his suite at the Gorham. And the girls came, and he bedded them. Lola Falana, who had turned into a New York Broadway sex symbol almost overnight, became a lover. She couldn't help it. "As a rule, hanging around Sammy was fun," Falana says. "You couldn't be around Sammy and not learn. Sammy was a teacher. I learned what not to do, as well as what to do. He schooled me on the status of a star. Sammy was from the old school: 'You don't go out the door unless you look a certain way.' " She thought he was the bravest man she had ever met. She too grew wide-eyed the day Martin Luther King, Jr., came to see *Golden Boy*. She knew enough to know it wasn't all about celebrity. "Martin knew the battle was color. He knew Sammy was in the throes of that because of the show. He saw Sammy as a brave warrior. They threatened to shoot Sammy down. While we were onstage, we would always be ready, listening for gunshots. Sammy had guts, that's the basic word."

Sammy's energy fascinated Falana. His days blended into nights and *Golden Boy,* and after the curtains closed he couldn't stop. He wanted to go some more. The world might, in the blink of an eye—as he well knew—vanish, and then what stage would he have to dance upon? "Sammy was very much alive with life," Falana says. "He had that joie de vivre. He was curious about everything he didn't know." Sometimes he would mention books, the books he had read, then he'd sulk in the same breath about not having gone to school. "We—all those around him—would tell him that we've got, yes, school experience, teacher experience, class experience, but you've got life experience."

Like all the women in Sammy's life, Falana became acquainted with Sammy's camera lens. "With Sammy," she says, "I wasn't allowed to show up someplace and look like I wasn't ready for a photograph. Sammy thought if you were gonna climb a mountain, then every move should be a picture." She could be standing someplace, and she'd see him, and he wouldn't see her, and she would watch him move, quick jerky movements, looking around as if the heat of other human beings was more important to him than life itself, moving as if the world were getting away from him: where was everyone? And she'd find herself falling in love with him so deeply it stunned her. She'd wonder where he got his genius. "He wasn't tall and thin and handsome and gorgeous. God chose this man with handicaps, with no education, no solid family encouragement. God chose all these handicaps and sent him out into the world to climb his mountain." She wanted to laugh with him, hold him, love him. She wanted to wrap herself around him. The world was cold—so he let her.

They'd go shopping in Manhattan, leaving the limo behind, all walking, Sammy, dancer Lester Wilson, and Lola. Giggling as if they were floating. "So many people were following him," Falana recalls. "He wanted some adventure."

Shrewd in the ways of keeping a theatrical company happy, Sammy sent members of the company on quick out-of-town trips. He had Murphy deliver gifts to dressing rooms, accompanied by a little Sammy note. Murphy wrote the note, owing to Sammy's self-consciousness about spelling. "Sammy gave people trips to Bermuda," Charles Strouse would recall. "He wouldn't give me anything. I felt left out."

William Gibson was amazed at how Sammy's world kept turning, one day more fascinating than the next. There Sammy stood, teaching members of the company how to fence—touché! There he sat, teaching them foreign accents. "Around the play, there was all this glamour," he remembers. "Joe Louis would be in the lobby, saying hello to Sammy."

Margaret Gibson—William Gibson's psychoanalyst wife—seemed unable to stop herself from quizzing Sammy about Negro life, Negro culture. She was curious about why he adored Sinatra so much, why he seemed to be running from his own culture. She wondered about his hair, why he had it greased to look like a white man's hairdo. "I used to plead with Sammy: 'Please don't slick down your hair. Leave it natural. It looks better that way.' " He listened and didn't hear her. His hair was fine; the seats at the Majestic were filled to capacity. Lolly, the dancer, loved his hair, Lola loved his hair, May loved his hair. All the women handing those seductive notes to Murphy to pass along to Sammy thought his hair was just fine. There was white culture and there was Negro culture. There was also the culture of success. That was the best culture of all to Sammy. He and Hilly fighting each other over restaurant bills, the limo waiting at curbside, the long legs of Lola folding herself into the limo, she and Sammy off into the night.

The young Hollywood television director Richard Donner, a Brooklyn native, was visiting New York City at the time. He bumped into a friend who told him he just had to see Sammy in *Golden Boy*. "He was gorgeous," remembers Donner. "It was brilliant acting." The crosscurrent of racial imagery in the play deeply moved Donner: "[Sammy] was really playing reality." Donner rushed backstage after the performance. "I see Sammy. I had tears in my eyes."

It was a dizzying and powerhouse performance, emotional and kinetic. Broadway had been struck by lightning. It was a play about race and love, and boxing. Joe Louis was in the lobby, but the dead Jack Johnson—undone by his love of white women—was, if you looked deep enough, in the shadows. It was all about victory and defeat of the soul, about chicanery. It was, as well, all about what was left unsaid across the boundaries of black and white America. Sammy and the Golden Boy seemed—like King and Montgomery—the perfect constellation of performer and message. There seemed no one else in the

Black begets white begets golden.
(COURTESY SALLY NEAL)

country who could have performed the role like Sammy, with his very own demons and insecurities and obsessions; his mother's hurtful love, his rambling vaudevillian's life, his white wife, his wondrous gifts. In the ring, his boxer moved like a feral, lethal tap dancer. And, on a deeper level, he did not have to imagine blackface—hiding behind one face to offer another—because he had worn the burnt cork! He had shaken something loose on Broadway, and what he had shaken fell upon those who saw his performance like the bruised leaves of history. It mattered little that he did not totally realize what he was doing. Nor did Will Mastin when he plucked a little child from his father's arms and sent him out onstage to stomp at ghosts.

What now ailed the country—fear, pain, paranoia, the madness of sex—all seemed to be inside Sammy. He was dispensing it like some great pharmacist of feeling—all our racial paranoias. Pull back the curtain and, for the simple price of a Broadway ticket, there it was, all on display. What had killed Bert Williams and haunted Jack Johnson only enlivened Sammy. Race and sex were the American sword. He knew it—he was smarter than he let on—and he could not stop himself from dancing, tap-dancing, across that sword, laughing, and bleeding, and crying, and laughing.

Chapter 14

FADE TO BLACK

The role of Joe Wellington was punishing. It was soon taking its toll on the 120-pound Sammy. During the first week of July 1965, Jamie Rogers, who played the Puerto Rican prizefighter in the play, accidentally kicked Sammy in the chest during a scene. Sammy crumpled to the floor. When he stayed there, audience members sensed something amiss. They began bringing their hands to their mouths, as if gasping for air. Sammy was finally lifted up and taken offstage. Hilly told the *New York Times* that Sammy had suffered "bone bruises in the ribs on the left side, as well as muscle and ligament damage." The star missed several performances before returning; when he did return, the theater seats filled up again.

Sammy's dressing room was just above the dressing room of the gypsies. Sometimes dancers wanted to get to him—to talk about their futures, life, him—and it wasn't always easy to reach him. So he'd hop downstairs via the stairway to chat with them, taking in their rooms, the heat and juice of so many female bodies, the one eye darting around, then he'd dash away. "He typified what the word 'star' means," says Lolly Fountain. "Like this luminous energy."

When Sammy became interested in a dancer, he let them know very clearly. "He would meet you on the backstairs case. He'd give you a kiss, a flower. Sammy made it very apparent he was interested," recalls Fountain. He made it very clear to Fountain he was interested. She couldn't resist. "Sammy was warm, attentive, romantic. He would sing to you in bed sometimes. He had a song from *Dr. Dolittle*—'Look at That Face.' He would sing something that had meaning for you."

Lolly Fountain would run into other Negroes during the play. She'd be up in Harlem having something to eat. She just knew they wanted to talk about Sammy, how beautiful he was in *Golden Boy*. "Oh," someone said to her one day, "you're working with that one-eyed monkey." The words stunned her. She wondered if Negroes hated Sammy the way bigots did. "I think Sammy was smart enough to know he had no common link to blacks."

Sammy couldn't, and didn't, keep still. A play on Broadway might have been enough to keep Hilly and Arthur Penn and Lee Adams and Charles Strouse occupied, but not Sammy Davis, Jr. He had no idea how to waste time, how to shove time out the window for a few hours, half of a day. Time would be seized, even if, at certain moments, Shirley Rhodes could see the play—the very psychology of it—wearing on Sammy. "It was real tough," she says. "It worked on him mentally." But he powered himself onward.

And he pushed himself right before the cameras for his movie. Sammy hired Ike Jones to coproduce *A Man Called Adam* alongside him. Jones was an anomaly in Hollywood: a black producer. He had been a famed athlete in college out in California. He was handsome enough to be a Negro leading man, but there were virtually no roles for Negro leading men. The tiny few that were available went to Belafonte or Poitier. Jones had something in common with Sammy—his love of a white woman. Her name was Inger Stevens and she was a Swedish-born actress. Jones and Stevens had married in 1961. The marriage received no publicity because it was done in secret. It was only after Stevens' death—from an overdose of barbituates in 1970—that word seeped out she had been married to a black man. The subterfuge seemed only to add to the tragedy. She was thirty-six years old.

Sammy brought together a fine cast for the movie. Louis Armstrong, Ossie Davis, Cicely Tyson—a young New York television actress—Mel Torme, Peter Lawford, and Frank's boy, Frank Sinatra, Jr. Sammy hired Leo Penn to direct. For supporting the Hollywood Ten—that iconoclastic and brave group of actors and directors who threw caution to the wind during the McCarthy scare—Penn had been blacklisted. In 1957 he started working his way back into the business with a notable role in a Clifford Odets movie, *Story on Page One.* Hollywood did not give out statuettes for moral bravery, but the town could sometimes be strangely sentimental: it was the allegiance-switching Odets himself who had first turned Penn's name over to the HUAC. Sammy just showed up for work and turned most of the day-to-day work on the movie over to his producers. During that time, the studio tried to fire Ossie Davis. "I made a statement about Vietnam," Ossie Davis recalls. "They were going to fire me. Sammy said, 'If you lose one Davis, you'll lose another.' I have a great deal of admiration for Sammy."

The movie was filmed fast, in six weeks, a blurry shooting schedule that mostly took place between midnight and four a.m. Some of the locations Sammy used to film were quite familiar: his penthouse at the Gorham Hotel, and Small's Paradise, the kitschy Harlem nightclub owned by basketball star Wilt Chamberlain. The youngsters in the *Golden Boy* cast—Lola Falana, Johnny Brown, Lolly Fountain—loved it when Sammy waved them all onto the movie set. They played extras—with the exception of Lola. She played a real character and got listed in the credits. All received their coveted Screen Actors Guild cards. They couldn't thank Sammy enough. Sammy's mother, Elvera, still working in Atlantic City as a barmaid, was also given a role in the movie: barmaid. Shirley Rhodes would look at Sammy some evenings riding to the movie set in the back of the limo after doing his Broadway show, and she'd feel like mothering him: he'd fallen asleep again. But there were parties, champagne, little time for sleep.

Ann Froman designed cowboy boots for Sammy. "They were pewter baby alligator boots that made him look five inches taller. I put a two-inch heel on the outside, and inside the boot I put a platform." Froman remembers taking her boyfriend—a young and very gifted actor by the name of James Earl Jones, whom she called "Jimmie"—to a party given for the cast of *A Man Called Adam*. "We were at Small's Paradise in Harlem. Jimmie wanted to meet Sammy. Sammy came over and went out of his way to spend time and talk with us. He wouldn't look around to see who he might be missing. You felt very loved the minute you met him." Froman couldn't figure out how Sammy kept going—from his nightly *Golden Boy* performance to the movie shoot to yet another party. "He always acted like he was on uppers," she says.

And so he was going and going, as Will Mastin and Sam Sr. had taught him—going and going, as if the pretty things and true things of the world would escape his grasp if he dared close his one eye.

The eye was wide as he stood in the offices of the William Morris Agency in early August and signed a $1 million contract to appear at Harrah's Club, in Stateline, Nevada. The deal was for eight weeks' worth of work over a four-year period. "I can look up there at Harlem where all this started," he said as he gazed from the twenty-first floor of the Morris agency. "Thirty years ago, I was going around doing one-nighters at ten dollars a night."

Sammy couldn't resist the invitation. Never mind that it came during the height of his Broadway run. It was the ever-present thunder in his soul. Harry Belafonte wanted Sammy—along with Sidney Poitier—for a televised tribute to old Harlem. With the country convulsing racially, television executives were suddenly willing to acknowledge that Negroes had a history. Harlem—birthplace of a Negro cultural renaissance decades earlier; at one time home to Elvera Sanchez and Sammy Davis, Sr.—was rife with dramatic and musical possibilities. Executives at CBS gave Belafonte the go-ahead. "I've always felt,"

Belafonte said before the show's airing, "that television missed a splendid opportunity because it never really did anything on Negro life." Belafonte's cast was eclectic. In addition to Poitier and Sammy, there were Duke Ellington, Diahann Carroll, singer Joe Williams, and comedian Nipsey Russell. Belafonte used Langston Hughes's *The Big Sea* as inspiration, and also hired Hughes as scriptwriter. The result was *The Strollin' Twenties,* a touching and colorful tribute to the Harlem of a bygone era. There were spirited dance numbers, inventive skits (with Poitier leading the tour), plenty of dancing, and a vocal duet by Sammy and Diahann Carroll. Sammy enjoyed the goings-on, appearing as he did onstage with the very two—Poitier and Belafonte—whom he had always felt he was competing against. Belafonte had always possessed an ability to probe Sammy's psyche. He knew Sammy would be wonderful in *The Strollin' Twenties,* and he was not disappointed. "When you looked at Sammy and what a song-and-dance man's evolution was," Belafonte says, "no one could hold a candle to him when it came to walking out into an audience and getting to their jugular vein. It was his greatest comfort zone. But once he stepped offstage, all the evils fell back into him."

The show also presented Langston Hughes to a national television audience. The poet, whose verse had long offered a lyrical song to the odyssey of Negro America, would be dead within fifteen months. At rehearsals for the show, Hughes watched with a gleam in his eyes—his gaze darting from Harry to Sidney to Sammy. He sat dressed in a dark shirt, beige tie, and dark tweedy jacket. The Negro Buddha of verse. He wore horn-rimmed glasses. He smoked a cigarette. Arguably, he was America's first Negro writer to earn his living solely on his words. He never had to teach, nor scrub his way across the fields of daily journalism. He wrote poetry, plays, librettos, fiction, and nonfiction. He wrote autobiographies. He translated the work of foreign writers. Langston Hughes had invested his art in Negro culture before it became vogue to do so.

"Put down the 1920s," Hughes would write, "for the rise of Roland Hayes, who packed Carnegie Hall, the rise of Paul Robeson in New York and London, of Florence Mills over two continents, of Rose McClendon in Broadway parts that never measured up to her, the booming voice of Bessie Smith and the low moan of Clara on thousands of records and the rise of that grand comedienne of song, Ethel Waters, singing 'Charlie's elected now! He's in right for sure!' " (Ethel Waters was now touring the country with evangelist Billy Graham, singing, crying out, reviving the faithful. Those gathered to hear her might have been disappointed that, since 1957, she had stopped singing her famous "Stormy Weather." She said her life was sunny now.)

Such was the excitement about *The Strollin' Twenties* that Sammy and Harry and Sidney were invited to shoot a *Life* magazine cover heralding the telecast. The photographer was Philippe Halsman, who had shot the photos for *Yes I Can,* Sammy's soon-to-be-published autobiography.

"GREATEST NEGRO STARS TEAM UP," the *Life* cover of February 4, 1966, proclaimed. In the cover shot, Poitier and Belafonte are dressed conservatively; Belafonte is in a suit, Poitier in a vest, shirt, tie, and slacks. The two are leaning on a ladder, with Sammy to their left, his look completely different: he is dressed in a beige suit and a red satin bow tie, and he's wearing a white derby hat at a rakish angle atop his head. His mouth is in a wide grin; his eyes are closed. It is the look of a vaudevillian. He seems to still be in character—from his childhood. Unbeknownst to both Poitier and Belafonte, Sammy has never left vaudeville.

The *Golden Boy* ensemble recorded their cast album for Capitol Records. The album impressively captured the sweaty and rhythmic sounds of boxing, the hissing of rope jumping and training, the sureness of voices—Sammy's, Paula Wayne's, the crooner Billy Daniels's. The Broadway cast recording was listed as an Epic production "in association with the Will Mastin Trio, Inc."

The year 1965, however, would bring to an end the Sammy–Will Mastin legal entanglement, and Sammy couldn't be happier.

Hilly did not want to bother Sammy with the latest rumor—that someone intended to kidnap him. It was silly, insane, but the times were bizarre and strange. Hilly alerted the New York police about the kidnapping threat; an extra security guard was posted at the theater.

The theater was a salve for Sammy—at least for the most part. "He'd call me so many nights from New York," recalls Jerry Lewis. "Not to tell me that he was doing this great show, but that there was a letter in his dressing room where someone had called him 'nigger.' And someone else saying he should die. I said, 'If one letter stops you, they win.' "

When the Tony Awards were announced, Sammy and Hilly were ecstatic. *Golden Boy* was nominated for best musical, Sammy for best lead performance in a musical. Hilly was nominated for best producer of a musical. And Donald McKayle, the young Negro choreographer Elkins had taken a chance on, was nominated for choreography. Sammy and Hilly had effectively dulled the critics' knives. Hilly wasted little time in ordering yet another publicity blitz, touting the nominations. While there were four nominees in the best musical performance category, there was a feeling that the competition would be between Sammy and Zero Mostel, star of *Fiddler on the Roof.*

Three months into the run of *Golden Boy,* 1964 turned over into 1965. In reality, more got turned over during those months than just household calendars. The sixties suddenly became "the sixties." Old women, young men, children gave of themselves to a cause. Negroes were boycotting businesses in southern towns. In January and February of 1965, ministers and civil rights activists were trying to register voters in Selma, Alabama. "Our cry to the state of Alabama is a simple one," Martin Luther King, Jr., said. "Give us the ballot!" President Lyndon Johnson sent Lady Bird Johnson on a train throughout the South, where she pleaded with her fellow Southerners to abide by the new desegregation laws of the land. She was met with deaf ears. America was suddenly a land of Negroes who were rising and falling and, sometimes, shot and bloodied only to rise again. Medgar Evers fell and stayed down. But Fannie Lou Hamer of Mississippi kept rising, and so did King. In many households, King had become a king overnight after his 1963 Lincoln Memorial address. (J. Edgar Hoover of the FBI concluded, however, that King was little more than a villain.) And there was the Muslim Malcolm X, of the clinched teeth, the angular body, the finger perpetually pointing outward from an outstretched arm. "I'm a field Negro," Malcolm X cryptically announced, offering an analogy. "If the master won't treat me right and he's sick, I'll tell the doctor to go the other way."

On March 7, a group of Negroes—minus Martin Luther King, Jr., who had, at his staff's pleading, stayed away because of a series of death threats—convened in Selma and began to march. They aimed themselves toward Montgomery, fifty miles away. The weary and the brave—beauticians, janitors, students, teachers. They'd go as far as their legs would take them, just one foot in front of the next. John Lewis, a young Student Nonviolent Coordinating Committee stalwart, would recall that the beginnings of the march made him think of "Gandhi's march to the sea." When they reached the Edmund Pettus Bridge, the marchers noticed a convoy of Alabama state troopers. Other men had been deputized and had joined them. Confederate flags were held aloft. The marchers were ordered to turn around. On either side of them rose bridge railings; down below, water. Some of the marchers, up front, noticed something strange: troopers with tear gas masks. Instead of turning around, the marchers decided to kneel and pray. But before their knees touched the ground, the troopers set upon them. Billy clubs were swung, heads cracked, whips swung, tear gas canisters opened. Men and women screamed and tried retreating, tripping over one another, but the troopers kept coming, swinging. Newsmen in the distance were stunned. The marchers had to run, as fast as they could, to get back into Selma, to one of the Negro churches. They were chased by men on horseback, the hooves of horses slapping at ankles. When they finally reached a church, and gathered themselves, and looked around, the sight was miserable: blood everywhere. Mothers crying, fathers looking for sons and daughters. At a church meeting later that evening, John Lewis addressed the gathering. Blood was matted in his hair. "I don't know how President Johnson can send troops to Vietnam," he said. "I don't see how he can send troops to the

Congo. I don't see how he can send troops to Africa, and he can't send troops to Selma, Alabama."

Later that night, ABC Television cut into its showing of *Judgment at Nuremberg* to report the clash. It seemed a cruel and bizarre bit of cinema: newsreel footage of Negroes being beaten amid shouts of "Get those goddammed niggers!" sliced in between a television movie about Nazi atrocities.

Johnson sent Justice Department officials to Selma to investigate. King and his deputies quickly arrived, now determined to hold a massive Selma-to-Montgomery march. When Harry Belafonte found out, he knew he would have to be a part of it. Then came the familiar King refrain—"Get Sammy"—as he had told Belafonte in the past when the movement needed Sammy's presence.

It took only days, and with a court victory ensuring their safety for another march, Belafonte had to get Sammy—quick. No one, however, in the spring of 1965, could get Sammy quick. He was on Broadway. Belafonte phoned Hilly Elkins.

"Hilly," Elkins recalls Belafonte saying, "I'm calling on behalf of Dr. King. King would like Sammy and you to come with us."

Hilly was flattered. He admired King; like everyone, he followed the movement in the papers, on television. He'd have to tell Sammy right away. Elkins's office, which was in the Lincoln Hotel—"a real shithole"—happened to be attached to the Majestic. Hilly could walk from his office to the stage door of the Majestic in only minutes. "I go down to the dressing room, tell Sammy that Dr. King wants us to join him in Selma," says Elkins. "Sammy said, 'I ain't going to Selma.' I say, 'Why?' He said, 'They're going to kill me.'" And "they," of course, were all the folk who had sent him and May hate mail, who had turned their noses up at him walking through airports, who had sneered at him at the swank clubs and restaurants, who were far to the other side of the thumping American civil rights movement. They were out there, in full force. He knew. Listening, Elkins blanched. He had to think fast, a disposition that came easily to him. He had seen the death threats that came to the Majestic for Sammy, so he could not laugh away Sammy's fears. And yet, he had to give a plausible answer to Belafonte. He bid for time to think by asking Sammy what he should tell Belafonte. "Tell them you can't afford to close the show," Sammy told Elkins.

Hilly felt ashamed that Sammy wanted him to reduce the choice to dollars when he knew moral positioning was at stake. He felt torn inside. He got Belafonte on the phone. He told Belafonte what Sammy wanted him to tell him: "I tell him I can't afford to close the show."

"Can't you?" Belafonte asked, in a tone that didn't so much question Hilly's clout as his nerve.

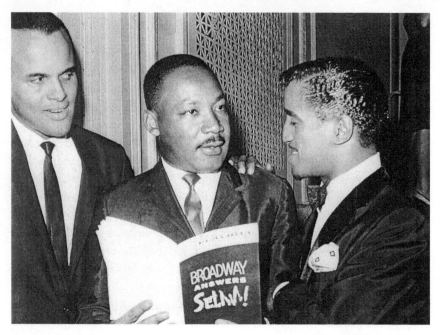

The preacher who blasted the moral conscience of a nation wide open needed Sammy—his money and his name. All those fund-raisers. "Get Sammy," King would cry out, and his lieutenants knew exactly what he meant. (BETTMANN ARCHIVE)

"Of course I can't," Elkins replied.

"I'll *buy* the night," Belafonte then said, speaking as one of the few Negro entertainers in America who could afford to make such a vow. Hilly suddenly brightened. Belafonte had given him the perfect answer. The show wouldn't lose any money. Now Sammy had to go to Selma.

In Selma, tension and fear remained high. A week after Lewis and the others were attacked on the Pettus Bridge, Reverend James Reeb, of Boston, was viciously attacked in Selma during another painful attempt at a march. Two days after he was beaten, he died.

The new Selma-to-Montgomery march was announced for March 21. Belafonte told King and the others that he had Sammy's commitment. On the morning they were to depart, Belafonte went to the Gorham Hotel to pick up Sammy. Murphy, Sammy's assistant, told Belafonte that Davis wasn't around, that he never came in during the previous night. But as he said it, Murphy nodded his head upward, motioning to Belafonte that he should go upstairs and knock on the door. Altering his distinctive and gravelly voice, Belafonte knocked on the door, pretending to be a bellhop. Sammy's female guest—it was not May—opened the door, and Belafonte saw Sammy cowering beneath the bedspread, petrified at going to Selma. Belafonte's voice rose as he spoke to Sammy—scolding like a father to an errant son. He made Sammy feel ashamed of himself. Sammy rose and began to dress for the trip to Selma.

His nerves finally strong enough—Belafonte was not allowing him to back out. Sammy went to get George Rhodes, his musical conductor, who had already agreed to go south. But Rhodes suddenly had a change of mind and backed out at the last minute. "Have a good trip," Rhodes said. "I ain't going."

Americans were being attacked and murdered in Selma. Governor George Wallace was vowing to wage a war against the federal government. Men in small towns were stockpiling weapons. George Rhodes would leave Selma to itself.

Sammy still needed a musician. Charles Strouse, a veteran of the movement before it was a movement—he had accompanied Butterfly McQueen on her southern tour years earlier—volunteered. On the plane, then, it was Sammy, Hilly, Strouse, and Sheila Sullivan, who was Paula Wayne's understudy in *Golden Boy*—and Hilly's current girlfriend. In the air, Sammy began knocking back brandy. He talked about women, about his life, the places he had been. "He was reflective," Strouse recalls. "But he was high." The plane landed in Atlanta; from there, the group boarded a charter flight that would take them to Selma. When they landed in Selma, and as they were preparing to leave the plane, Sammy, in one of those unconscious and sweet little moments that marked him, grabbed the arm of Sheila Sullivan. Sullivan was as white, and as blond, as Paula Wayne, as May Britt herself. Hilly noticed the scene, of Sammy and his arm around Sullivan, of the waiting media, of the Negroes outside the window awaiting them, and thought better of Sammy's debut into the Selma twilight with a white lady on his arm. He whispered to Sammy, who dropped his arm. They all began striding through the terminal. "There was an old black man," remembers Strouse. "He said, 'You're Sammy Davis, Jr.' Sammy said, 'No, I'm the FBI. I'm here to infiltrate.'"

Ha ha ha.

This time, America would be watching, and the brave souls who had been on the Pettus Bridge would be joined by thousands more. The event lasted three days. George Wallace could not stop this march, not this time. There were speeches, brave and defiant words, touching words spoken about those who had died. On the final day there was music. Shelley Winters, the actress, borrowed some lights from a nearby air force base. Elaine May and Mike Nichols—the comedy team soon to become an important writing and directing force—were there. So were Leonard Bernstein and Tony Bennett. The musical organizers needed a stage for a concert event and didn't have one, so they turned to Negro undertakers, who supplied coffins, which, placed side by side, became a makeshift stage. Charles Strouse set up some musical instru-

ments on it. Leonard Bernstein had turned to Hilly and said, "You're a producer, so produce!" Elkins needed dressing rooms for the performers; he got
some buses, and the performers dressed inside them. King spoke. Sammy
performed—first singing "The Star-Spangled Banner"—at a nighttime event.
"He was scared shitless," remembers Elkins. But surrounded by so many brave
common folk, Sammy became struck by their gallantry, their defiance. He had,
during the run of *Golden Boy*, given an interview to Oriana Fallaci, the Italian
journalist. He had spoken of "a man who, halfway between the worlds of
whites and the Negroes, feels at ease with neither the whites nor the Negroes
and [is] rejected by both whites and Negroes." Sammy was, upon the red dirt
of Alabama, not halfway between anything; he was just on the side of justice,
and embraced. He could feel how much Negroes needed him, needed and
wanted him to help them get across all the painful dusty righteous roads. The
plain folk of Selma were hanging on to their undocumented courage. They
thanked Sammy for coming, they thanked him for his courage.

On the final night of the Selma event, Sammy walked over to Belafonte.
"Thank you," he said softly to Belafonte. And as Belafonte looked down at
Sammy Davis's face, he saw tears.

Back in New York, Sammy and Hilly, still doing wonderful business with
Golden Boy every night—they were into the six-month run of the production—could not forget Selma. It had introduced them to the movement from
a front-line perspective. It had seeped into them. So they decided to do something: they'd host an event, bringing together Broadway performers to raise
money for Martin Luther King, Jr., and his movement. Sammy and Hilly
would produce it, and Sammy would play host, right at the Majestic Theatre.

Broadway Answers Selma took place Sunday, April 4, right on the stage of
the Majestic. The theater was packed. Stars of the stage were everywhere,
joined by a sprinkling of politicians. Sammy laughed, hugged, doubled over,
talked movingly of his Selma journey. He was so proud that he had climbed
down off the stage and trekked to Selma—albeit reluctantly. But as movingly
as the gathered stars gazed at Sammy, he gazed just as movingly right back at
them. Celebrities wowed him so. His fawning adulation of others befuddled
Strouse, who began wondering what really lurked in the blueness of Sammy's
soul.

"Sammy was one of the most complicated men I ever met," recalls Strouse.
"I never could feel what he was really feeling."

Barbra Streisand, Jack Benny, Alan Alda, Diana Sands, Maurice Chevalier,
John Gielgud, Richard Kiley, Jack Albertson, they were all there, on the stage of
the Majestic, kissing Sammy, being hugged by Sammy. And more: Martin

Sheen, Walter Matthau, the old cowboy movie star Dan Duryea. Everyone in theatrical circles seemed to know Duryea had a serious drinking problem. But he—so unexpectedly—did a soft-shoe dance number across the stage, and it was so sublime it was gorgeous—"one of the most beautiful things I'd ever seen," recalls William Gibson.

The event at the theater raised $150,000. Martin Luther King's command—"Get Sammy"—had come to have a powerful cachet.

Those in the *Golden Boy* cast noticed a change in Sammy after Selma—an ever-so-slight change. Gone were the British affectations. "He went and brought me an Afro wig," says Lola Falana. "He said, 'Hey, I got something in the bag for you.' I said, 'Sammy, where am I going to wear this?' He said, 'You never know, you might need a little more *flair*.' He said, 'You gotta be in step with the times.' There was one white wig, and one platinum wig."

It was considered de rigueur for the *Golden Boy* cast members to rush out and purchase a copy of Sammy's autobiography, *Yes I Can*. Hilly bought a bunch and gave them out as gifts. Why, it was a wonderful world, this show business: Sammy, the Tony-nominated actor, was, within weeks, a best-selling author.

The fact that he was now an author hardly prohibited Sammy from trumpeting other books. He had additional hardcover recommendations. At the Majestic Theatre one afternoon he asked Lolly Fountain if she had read anything by the Marquis de Sade. She had not. Sammy—his eyes gleaming—gave her the complete works of that French chronicler of lust and debauchery.

The Negro dancers were circling Sammy. His marriage vows had weakened beyond repair. May looked the other way. And stopped coming to the theater.

"He always wanted to be a part of, to be accepted," dancer Lola Falana says. Sammy told Falana—who had created so much buzz with her breakthrough role—that he'd manage her, a mere complement to his secret dream of managing prizefighters. He'd send her out into the world—like some beautiful soaring bird. He'd make her a star. "Sammy said, 'You're not just a little dancer, are you?' I said, 'No sir, I'm not.' He said, 'Well, if you're gonna go out there, you're not gonna do it without my help. They'll eat you alive.'"

He was talking about the sharks, the critics. He knew where they swam.

Rumors were rumors. And May Britt turned an ear away from them. She had been in show business for years—she knew to steel herself against them. She busied herself with the kids.

Roger Straus, Sammy's publisher, worried what effect marital discord and a possible breakup—he had also heard the rumors—might have on sales of *Yes I Can*, but, of course, there was nothing he could do.

Sammy had started telling friends that May's lifestyle bored him.

It was becoming apparent that it was all about more than the Afro wigs Sammy had bought for Falana. He simply could no longer resist the black girls, with their Negroness, their large bobbing Afros, their seductiveness, their pride.

Whenever there was an audition for a new dancer to replace one who had left the production, the tryout session would be crowded, crew members ogling the dancers. One Negro dancer who arrived was Altovise Gore. She had been in several New York productions and was a graduate of New York City's High School for Performing Arts. Musical actor Robert Guillaume, who befriended Gore, thought of her as "one of these fresh unspoiled girls full of life and humor." Sammy took notice of the new arrival, his interest in Negro girls now quite constant.

Sammy's interest in Negro girls paralleled something else far more profound.

Sammy's America had changed right before his eye. Epic events had unfolded. *Yes I Can* was finished in 1962. It lay unpublished for three years. And during those three years, up to 1965, nothing less than a cultural and social revolution had occurred across the American landscape. Negroes were now on the march. A movement had gotten under way, in Mississippi, in Alabama, in Los Angeles, in New Orleans, at the old slave market in St. Augustine, Florida. Old men were marching, old women, children—Sammy. It wasn't so much the "but thank God we ain't what we was" of Sammy's epigraph in *Yes I Can* anymore, in itself a kind of acceptance of the status quo. Now the epigraph was up from the streets and it was something far bolder—"We Shall Overcome." There were now few urban areas in America where racial violence had not erupted; and where it had not erupted, it was simmering.

Negro churches were burned to the ground in the South. Alabama governor George Wallace was drawing large white rallies. Change was everywhere, sudden change. If Sammy had looked, he would have noticed it off-Broadway, in downtown New York, at the St. Marks Playhouse. There, a playwright by the name of LeRoi Jones had two plays, *The Toilet* and *The Slave*, which, when they opened in 1965, had shocked the senses. They attacked racism with a fierceness rarely evidenced on the New York stage. The *New York Journal-American* said that to witness them was "a terrifying evening in the theatre this season, or any other for that matter." There was another play that season, *Day of Absence*, by Douglas Turner Ward. In it, the Negro actors wore whiteface—a satirical variation of blackface. If they'd looked uptown, they'd have seen a Negro actor by the name of Sammy Davis, Jr., who had worn blackface as a little child. Not for satire—but for keeps.

Everywhere, change.

Medgar Evers, dead. Shot with an Enfield rifle close to midnight on June 11,

1963. The voting rights crusader was alighting from his car in the driveway of his Jackson, Mississippi, home. The fragrance of mint julips in the air, blood in the driveway.

Those three young men—Goodman, Schwerner, and Cheney—dead in Mississippi.

Malcolm X, dead. Shot sixteen months after Evers while giving a talk in Harlem at the Audubon Ballroom. "When Malcolm died we had a benefit," remembers Ossie Davis. "We asked Sammy to be on the benefit program. He flew in. He said all he could do was walk onstage and walk off. He stayed fifteen minutes."

In the air, revolution.

Singer Curtis Mayfield released "People Get Ready" in 1965, a soul-stirring tune that took on the weight of a Negro anthem. "People get ready / there's a train a-comin'."

In 1965, Sammy released five albums—*When the Feeling Hits You! Sammy Davis Jr. Meets Sam Butera & the Witnesses; Sammy Davis • Count Basie (Our Shining Hour); If I Ruled the World; The Nat King Cole Songbook;* and *Sammy's Back on Broadway.* Admirable albums, but not a political lyric to be heard.

Martin Luther King, Jr.—recipient of the 1964 Nobel Peace Prize for his nonviolent protests, which ushered him into a far more messiahlike sphere— seemed to be everywhere; often Harry Belafonte was not far behind.

The events of the day seemed to be outrunning an ability to understand them. James Baldwin, his pen mightier by the day now, had written an essay back in 1963, "The Fire Next Time," that had been widely praised. Something about that essay two years later, in 1965, seemed prescient.

> This past, the Negro's past, of rope, fire, torture, castration, infanticide, rape; death and humiliation; fear by day and night, fear as deep as the marrow of the bone; doubt that he was worthy of life, since everyone around him denied it; sorrow for his women, for his kinfolk, for his children, who needed his protection, and whom he could not protect; rage, hatred, and murder, hatred for the white men so deep that it often turned against him and his own, and made all love, all trust, all joy impossible—this past, this endless struggle to achieve and reveal and confirm a human identity; human authority, yet contains, for all its horror, something very beautiful.

Beauty?

For Sammy, the word represented such confusion.

Kim Novak was beautiful. May—and it was one of the reasons he had married her!—was beautiful. Ava Gardner was beautiful—dangerous, but beautiful. Even Sinatra was beautiful—the way he controlled his press agents, the way he sauntered, the way he sang, the way he ducked into his very own airplane, the cameras clicking, the plane enveloped in blue clouds. Frank, in fact, had a new wife, willowy, just nineteen years old, blond—and beautiful. Her name was Mia Farrow, and she was a budding television actress appearing on *Peyton Place,* an evening soap opera.

Frank was singing to the young.

White America, with its swinging and jangly and unpredictable power—Frank with a flower child!—was so beautiful.

"The first time I went up to the house he gave me a hug," actor Peter Brown says of Sammy. "The only time I can remember being hugged by a guy was by a bullfighting friend—that's the Latin way. Sammy felt a little hesitation from me. He took me by the shoulders, grabbed me and rubbed me cheek to cheek. And he said, 'Now look [in the mirror]. See? It doesn't come off.' "

"Black women," says dancer Billie Allen, "would say of Sammy: 'He reminds me of a trained mosquito—in a tux.' "

Whatever happened to be going on around him, Sammy could not help jumping when there was a phone call from Sinatra.

This time it was something out in St. Louis, a benefit for the Dismas House, a halfway house where ex-convicts lived. Sammy flew to Missouri. Dean Martin was coming. Joey was scheduled to host the event, but was felled by back problems, so Johnny Carson, the young, cool, and agile talk-show host, flew in to take his place. Anything for Frank. Even the June heat of a St. Louis summer.

"Joey slipped a disc backing out in Frank's presence," Carson quips in his opening remarks to the audience that had filled St. Louis's Kiel Opera House. Guffaws all around. The late-night talk-show host already had honed a habit of wiping at his brow and under his nose with the forefinger of his right hand, giving him the countenance of a shy kid whose wit surprises even himself. Dean performs first, ambling out like a man strolling on a sunny beach. He is smoking a cigarette, he has a drink in his hand. Later, after several smooth and sunny songs, he tosses the cigarette onto the stage and puts both fingers in his ears as if it would explode. "Frank asked us to come," Dean says, pausing. "Actually, he *told* us to come." Ha ha ha. Dean sings some more, mangling songs with bawdy jokes, doing it all smoothly, and segueing into "Everybody Loves Somebody."

Carson introduces Sammy, who zips onto the stage with snakelike energy. Sammy introduces the Count Basie Band, who are backing him. Then Sammy's snapping his fingers, already off into song. After his first number, he confesses that it is "a tremendous thrill for me to represent the ethnic groups." This is not uttered as a joke. Then he tells the audience it has been fourteen years since he was in St. Louis, performing with his dad and Will Mastin. He tells them that the theater where they had performed is now torn down; he sounds nostalgic. He plugs *Golden Boy*. He could easily have sung a song from it but doesn't, instead choosing a song from another Broadway play, *The Roar of the Greasepaint—The Smell of the Crowd*. It's the big-hearted entertainer in him, wanting to give credit elsewhere. To the audience, before every song, he says, "With your kind permission—" and then he launches into the song. He bows after a song, always beautifully. He does a scat number with Michael Silver, his drummer, Sammy's voice tangoing with the beat of the drums. All for Sinatra. "Marvelous," Sammy says to the audience about Frank, "how he can pick up the phone and say, 'Be there.' I immediately picked up the phone and called Martin Luther King, and he said it was okay." Guffaws again. Well-to-do couples are seated in the audience, gentlemen in fine suits, their wives in evening dresses and white gloves stopping at the elbows. It is a lily-white audience. "Found myself marching with some cats with pillowcases on their heads one day," Sammy goes on, unable to stop himself now, because he has already heard laughter and he wants to keep them laughing and appreciating him and loving him. "My conductor said, 'Uh, Sammy, I believe you marching with the wrong group.' " This last part is delivered in a Pigmeat Markham antebellum voice. More guffaws.

"With your kind permission . . ."

He does a Fred Astaire impersonation, a Dean Martin impersonation, walking and singing in their voices, slurring a song just like Martin. He does Nat King Cole, then Billy Eckstine, then Tony Bennett, then Mel Torme, all dazzling bits of mimickry. He's hardly finished. He does Louis Armstrong, bringing out a hanky and wiping his brow just like Armstrong. He does Jerry Lewis. Then he crawls back inside himself, back to Sammy. "Ladies and gentlemen, thank you for giving me the privilege to be in St. Louis for such a worthy cause."

A gig for Frank, and he's dazzling.

At the time, no one—save those in the audience and a select closed-circuit television audience—saw the show. Among Rat Pack chroniclers, it became a lost taping. But then, in 1997, it was rediscovered in the basement of the Dismas House. It enjoyed a ballyhooed run at the Beverly Hills Museum of Radio & Television. *Variety* reviewed it in 1998 and noted, of the three principals, Frank, Dean, and Sammy, that their "humor is loaded with ethnic digs and putdowns, but a shared love of talent and personality imbues each playful backstabbing moment." It goes on: "Bottle humor gives way to Sammy Davis's gratifying drum-and-vocal rendition of 'I've Got You Under My Skin' and a hilarious version of 'One for My Baby'" that features a good ten impressions. The dig at Dino, natch, is dead on."

It is exactly the ethnic joking part of that performance, however, that makes so many Negroes around the country recoil in 1965 when they see various other examples of it floating from their television screens. But Sammy isn't playing to them. He's playing to the couples in the seats in the audience. He's playing to the couples who have come all these years to see him at the Copacabana, at Bill Miller's Riviera. He jauntily skips off the St. Louis stage, past the white audience, skipping like a man needing to suck up all the air around him just to stay alive.

Manhattan tossed plenty of bon mots in Sammy's direction. *Cue* magazine—referring to him as a "Renaissance Man"—named Sammy "Entertainer of the Year." (Barbra Streisand received the honor the year before.) "He switches from theatre to films to nightclubs to television to recordings with an engaging and seemingly effortless agility," the magazine said in its citation. Sammy took his photography skills seriously. So did the Japan Trade Center on Fifth Avenue, which mounted an exhibition of his work. Not to be outdone, Willoughby-Peerless, another gallery, on West Thirty-second Street, also presented a Sammy exhibition.

On the eve of the first anniversary of *Golden Boy,* Hilly had plastered New York with billboards and juicy ads marking the occasion. So what that they lost out at the Tony Awards; the theater was still packed.

With such a long run, *Golden Boy* cast members began leaving and new ones arrived. Robert Guillaume, a veteran of Cleveland's fabled Karamu House theatrical troupe, arrived to take the place of Johnny Brown. "There was an aura in the company, people wanting to be close to Sammy," Guillaume recalls. "He encouraged that closeness. While at the same time he was wary of who was going to be part of his coterie. If he figured you weren't going to be part of that coterie, you got short shrift. He was extremely theatrical." Guillaume couldn't penetrate Sammy's camp: "I was never able to be part of his inner circle. You had to have a fawning personality, and you had to self-efface."

Guillaume was astonished at Sammy's proclivity for bounding back out onstage to perform after the evening's performance. "I always had the feeling that he hated to go to bed. He hated to bring down the curtain on the night."

It took Guillaume—formally trained and proud of it—little time to realize Sammy's competitive streak. It did not frighten him. "I remember one time I went on as Eddie Satin. It was a flamboyant role. I got to lord over [Sammy] as the character, and one time we were singing 'This Is the Life.' We both have on body mikes. His goes out. I continue to sing lustily, putting him at a disadvantage. I never heard the end of it. He said, 'Goddammit, there's no agent out there. You're not going to be discovered!' Very petulantly. I was unknown, but I was not untalented." The beautiful women in the cast caught Guillaume's eye, particularly Lola Falana: "She was a full woman, the first glamour girl I remember. If you weren't somebody, you knew not to mess with Lola. You couldn't afford the tab."

Guillaume would sit and wonder how Sammy did what he did with just one eye. He'd ponder how that might have wounded anyone's psyche—his own included. "That to me was where his *cojones* were. Sammy was a bad mother-fucker. The missing eye was formidable."

While it was true that many of the Negro dancers were awed by Sammy's Rat Pack reputation, Guillaume saw it through another lens. "Sammy was competitive. He welcomed competition. What must that have cost him when he had to submerge some of that working with Sinatra? You say, 'How the hell do you do this—merge your personality with his?' While Frank did not have the incandescent flair Sammy had, Frank was supremely in charge, and he was allowed to play that position."

When an actor or dancer left the production, Sammy's mood would swing. "When I left the show—when anyone left—Sammy considered it some kind of betrayal, a breach, disloyal," says Guillaume.

Now and then Sammy would get a call from Club Harlem, over in Atlantic City. The owners would want to know if he could maybe pay a visit, a quick stage performance. It would do wonders for business. Sammy would get over to Atlantic City whenever he could. Shirley Rhodes would sometimes accompany him. And sometimes, of course, they'd pay a visit to the Little Belmont nightclub. "His mother would be working behind the bar," she says. And he'd sing—as close to living with his mother as he'd ever be—right there in the edgy bar, in Atlantic City.

"I've gotta be me . . ."

If there was one unmistakable thing about Elvera Davis, it was her work ethic, which was powerful. And what son wouldn't do a little something for his mother standing on her feet all those hours like that?

"Mammy, don't you know me? It's your little baby!"

Chapter 15

MIRRORS

G *olden Boy* closed in the spring of 1966. It had had a phenomenal run. During one week alone, the play had taken in a whopping $94,000. Hilly hated to close.

Actually, Hilly Elkins merely retreated, telling himself that *Golden Boy* was not yet dead. America was a big country—and Sammy was hot.

Sammy's disposition—in both childhood and adult life—was the road. So he welcomed the end of the *Golden Boy* run. Back to the road. "He loved hotels," says Shirley Rhodes. "He loved being away. He liked room service. Far as he was concerned, it never cost anything."

He carried things on the road:

> A pair of six-shooters
> A cape
> A genuine sword—a gift from a bullfighter
> Tape recorders
> Three different record players
> An assortment of radios in varying sizes
> Cases of Scotch
> Cartons of cigarettes
> A set of barbells—which no one ever saw him use
> A shoehorn that he used onstage while slipping into his tap
>   shoes—all the while letting audiences know it had been
>   carved for him from a sword once possessed by one of
>   the queen's guards in London

Musical instruments—horns, drums, tambourines
A four-season wardrobe
A prop case—an essential tool for any serious vaudevillian
An assortment of glass eyes

There were a scant number of feature writers who happened to be Negro on mainstream American magazines in the mid-1960s. They were so few in number that Sammy was rarely—save with the Negro press—interviewed by a black writer. Most of the known black writers—James Baldwin, Ralph Ellison, Richard Wright—concentrated on fiction, even if, now and then, they took breaks for the occasional essay. One Negro writer who had broken through to mainstream nonfiction magazine work was Alex Haley.

Haley, born in 1921 in Ithaca, New York, spent most of his childhood among maternal relatives in Henning, Tennessee. He was precocious enough to finish high school by the age of fifteen. But college bored him, and he left after just two years to join the coast guard. Sailing at sea, he began writing—letters, stories, memories of his southern upbringing. By the time he left the coast guard, in 1959, he had convinced himself he could make a living as a writer. He moved to Greenwich Village, in New York City. He wrote for *Harper's*, for the *New York Times Magazine*, for *Reader's Digest*. He became adept at hustling up assignments on his own. In 1962, Haley tracked down Miles Davis—whose 1959 recording *Sketches of Spain* was still the rage—and spent hours and hours with the musician. Haley sold the piece to *Playboy*, and the magazine shaped it into a longish question-and-answer profile. The reaction to the Q & A format was huge and favorable. It was so positive, in fact, that *Playboy* decided to make it a monthly feature—the *Playboy* interview.

To keep the *Playboy* interview newsworthy, editors would scan the country for newsmakers—the more controversial and edgy, the better—then assign a writer to interview them. *Playboy* had assigned Haley to interview Malcolm X in 1962. The Malcolm X interview was nuanced, full of insight, the first piece for the general public that showed a multidimensional Malcolm X, a figure undergoing transformation regarding some of his radical racial ideas. Exiled by Black Muslim leader Elijah Muhammad, and constantly besieged with death threats, Malcolm X came off as a man both revolutionary and vulnerable. The piece garnered wide attention. Haley and Malcolm X would soon begin collaboration on the latter's life story. *The Autobiography of Malcolm X*, published in 1965, would become a best-seller, demanding a reevaluation of Malcolm X's life. It also saw Haley's reputation as a writer soar.

In 1966 the editors of *Playboy* thought of another figure for Alex Haley to go after: Sammy Davis, Jr. But Sammy was not easy to catch up to. Haley fired off letters, and the letters trailed Sammy, from Los Angeles to New Jersey to New York City. Murphy handled media in his usual laissez-faire manner. Haley's letters took on a more pleading tone. The quarry was elusive: "I had been trying to get his ear, and his confidence, for two weeks, dogging his tracks from city to city, trying to penetrate both his shell of reticence and the cordon of cronies and coworkers with whom he surrounds himself, waiting in vain for Sammy to alight anywhere long enough to buttonhole him for anything more than a wave and a greeting."

Sammy finally told Haley to meet him in Philadelphia. Even before they met, Haley had his own reservations about Sammy, about the persona: "I had gone to the assignment secretly feeling that nobody could be that good."

Upon reaching Philadelphia, Haley got himself to the Forrest Theatre, where Sammy was scheduled to begin an engagement. It took Haley only a short time inside Sammy's dressing room before he realized he had stumbled upon a unique entertainer indeed. The goings-on reminded Haley of "a jug band accompanied by an animated Ray Charles." Sammy bounced, moved about, refused to sit down; he'd let his one eye zone in on Haley, only to, seconds later, yank his attention elsewhere. Haley's eyes widened, and he made notes of it all: "Sammy puts on dressing room shows that should be recorded, doing sketches of everything he does on stage." The writer's curiosity continually rose in Haley. Days with Sammy left him in awe: "Even his dancers watch him night after night, as if to find his secret." One evening Haley sat spellbound as Sammy ordered fried chicken for twenty-eight people and viewed a screening of *The Chase*. (Sammy's *Golden Boy* director, Arthur Penn, had shot the movie, which starred Marlon Brando, Jane Fonda, Robert Redford, and Angie Dickinson. Lillian Hellman wrote the screenplay, based on a Horton Foote novel. Penn and Hellman—and producer Sam Spiegel—all had volatile creative differences during the making of the movie, and those differences made their way into the gossip columns, intriguing many, including Sammy.) Sammy's screening ended at three a.m. Haley wasn't accustomed to such late hours. "I get so incensed when you see a picture like tonight and then you see a picture like *High Noon*. So simple, so brilliant," Sammy explained to a tired Haley. The movie-watching prompted Haley to ask Sammy for a list of the movies he deemed great. Sammy rattled them off: *Gunga Din, The Roaring Twenties, Stage Coach, Cover Girl*, and—little surprise—*Wuthering Heights*. They were movies earmarked by themes of dreaminess, battle, guns, and love—all favorites of Sammy's cinematic mind. Just before five a.m., Sammy shared something else with Haley. He told him he thought *Panhandle*, a little-known 1948 movie with Rod Cameron and Blake Edwards—who would go from acting to a distinguished career as a director—was "a classic." The kid vaudevillian who had grown up in theaters watching films had willed himself a historian of little-seen movies.

Haley got a peek in Sammy's book bag and spied, in addition to three James Bond novels, the following: *Basic Judaism, Yes I Can, A Treasury of Great Poems, The American Indian Wars, A Gift of Prophecy, The Marquis de Sade,* and *Wuthering Heights.* Sammy later confided—and he seemed here to be trying to make a literary connection with Negro writer Haley—that he had read the works of novelist Richard Wright. "They made me feel something about being black that I had never really felt before," he explained to Haley. "It made me uncomfortable, made me feel trapped in black, you know, in a white society that had created you the way it wanted, and still hated you."

Sammy lamented that there were not more hours in the day. If there were, he'd read more books! As it was, he carried what he could and read them simultaneously. A boring passage from one book would force him to drop that book aside and immediately snatch another one up.

Haley went riding in Sammy's limousine. It had an assortment of buttons, varied features. Sammy twisted and touched every button within reach. Haley took notes: "intercom drive, console bar, stereo/45 rpm, ice bucket, holders records/armrest taperecorder, television—moves up and down, telephone, no glare windows—to keep glare off television." So many tricks! Haley seemed amused that a Negro could live so lavishly; at Haley's amusement, Sammy could only smile. He lived like Sinatra. The world—at least nearly so—on a string.

Two Negroes, the writer and the entertainer, lapping it up in America. Haley couldn't stop from cackling. Ha ha ha. Alexander Palmer Haley was a long way from Henning, Tennessee.

Sammy's humor, however, was another thing, a painful mixture of slapstick layered over race. "If I'm in the dark," he told Haley, "and I hear a chain rattling, I will say 'Who dat?'"

On any given moment, Sammy could sound as if his touchstone to slavery were humor. He sounded not unlike Bert Williams, the blackface vaudeville comedian.

Sammy took a phone call from Vice President Hubert Humphrey while in Haley's presence. He saw Haley scribbling the exchange down. Humphrey asked Sammy if he'd consider going to Vietnam to entertain the troops. Such a request served to elevate Sammy's sense of self. Raising his voice so Haley could get it all down, he quickly agreed. (Since the passage of the Tonkin Gulf Resolution, on August 7, 1964, Johnson had escalated American involvement in the Southeast Asia conflict.)

Haley watched Sammy perform onstage and was transfixed. When Sammy knew someone was watching him for the first time, he exhausted himself— even more than his usual exhaustive effort. It was another child-held vaudevillian curse—to overperform, lest you be disliked, booed, chased away. After one show, Haley, worn out, looked forward to relaxing with Sammy in the dressing room: the great entertainer would surely need to relax. Instead, there was energy, noise, commotion, analysis. "Alex," Sammy told the writer, "these are our most productive hours. After a show our minds are sharpest."

Haley the Tennessee hick and late-night Sammy. Sammy had Haley right where he wanted him: awed and beguiled.

Glancing one moment down at Sammy's feet, Haley made a note of Sammy's shoes: "Go go boots . . . black suede."

"I got a little depressed the other day, and I went out and bought me something," Sammy said to Haley on yet another occasion, holding out three new watches for him to admire.

Ha ha ha. Just like Sinatra.

Sammy riffed with Haley about his own life, about his work ethic, his marriage (already irreparably damaged, even if, to Haley, he did sound giddy as a newlywed), movie roles. "Until we get to the point where a Negro can play a heavy—as [Richard] Widmark plays a heavy—then we haven't arrived. . . . [E]very time I get to play a heavy, I do. [And] not a Negro heavy just because he's a Negro."

Haley trailed a bopping Sammy into a March, 16, 1966, press conference. "Nobody said anything about my suntan," Sammy cracked.

Haley seemed genuinely surprised when Sammy told him he carried a gun. Sammy reminded Haley that Dick Gregory had gotten shot, out in Los Angeles during the Watts riots. "They let me carry one in New York, the hardest state to get a gun permit in, because they realized that I get some kind of threat about every day of my life," he told Haley.

Another day—Haley spent two weeks trailing Sammy—the writer sat in a corner listening as Sammy went about untying his bow tie and crooning:

> *Why can't I cast away*
> *This mask of play*
> *And live my life?*
> *Why can't I fall in love*
> *Til I don't give a damn?*
> *And maybe then I'll know*
> *What kind of fool I am.*

Haley thought one of the more poignant moments was watching while Sammy signed autographs, the patter of rain beating outside, Negro and white admirers circling the entertainer.

The *Playboy* interview, which Haley had begun conducting in the spring, appeared in the magazine's December 1966 issue. Haley had been presented with a list of questions by *Playboy* editors to throw at Sammy. More than a few zingers made it into the published version.

"Have you ever wished that you weren't a Negro?"

"You'd just like to look like everybody else so that people wouldn't automatically start hating you a block away," Sammy answered in the magazine's pages. "White cat sees you walking down the street, maybe from across the street, and he never saw you before in his life, and he's not even close enough to distinguish anything about you except that you're not his color—and just for that, right there, snap, bop, bap, he HATES you! That's the injustice of it, that's what makes you cry out inside, sometimes, 'Damn, I wish I wasn't black!' "

Another question: "As you know, there was a widespread feeling among both whites and Negroes that you were marrying May in order to gain status in white society."

The question seemed to genuinely unnerve Sammy. "For the information of those who may not have been able to figure out yet why I DID marry May—despite everything we knew we were letting ourselves in for—it was love, sweet love, baby."

And yet another question—just like certain others in the interview—which threaded right into Sammy's wobbly sense of racial identity: "Your night-club and theater audiences are predominantly white," Haley asked. "Do you think there may be some element of race consciousness in your compulsion to win their approval?"

"No question about it," Sammy answered. "I always go on stage anticipating what people out there may be feeling against me emotionally. I want to rob them of what they're sitting there thinking: NEGRO."

By the time Sammy's *Playboy* interview appeared, May had left New York City and flown to California with the children. By then "love, sweet love, baby" was a thing of the past. The turn of events hardly surprised Sy Marsh, Sammy's agent: "He was on the road fifty weeks a year. He was fucking everything he could get his hands on."

May Britt had finally realized that her husband—trapped in black—no longer wanted to be married.

It had been a difficult year. NBC canceled *The Sammy Davis Jr. Show* that spring; the last telecast aired April 22, 1966. It had been the first variety show hosted by a black in the 1960s, and it had been an uphill battle from the beginning. There were several weeks, following the show's premiere, that Sammy himself could not appear on his own show because of a previous contract with ABC. "I thought the best thing I could do was get everybody to tune in," recalls Jay Bernstein, who did publicity for Sammy and the show. "It was the worst thing I could have done. Everybody tuned in." And when they did, there was no Sammy. Viewership fell off. It hardly helped that the show was pitted against two highly popular CBS comedies—*Hogan's Heroes* and *Gomer Pyle.*

The initial episode, however, was quite memorable, featuring Hollywood's extravagant couple Richard Burton and Elizabeth Taylor. Judy Garland appeared on two other shows. Inasmuch as the show was taped during Sammy's *Golden Boy* run, Sammy made it somewhat of a family affair: he brought his *Golden Boy* musical conductor, George Rhodes, aboard, along with some *Golden Boy* dancers. Despite the show's failure, it certainly pointed up Sammy's stamina.

So May was gone. Other painful shadows and realities were now upon him. His grandmother Rosa died in 1966. And she was the one woman he knew had loved him unconditionally. "When Rosa died, he was devastated," says actress Madelyn Rhue. "Rosa was a Jewish grandmother, and she was the nanny everyone wanted." The last year of Rosa's life had been simple and sweet: she only wanted to be driven around now and then, mostly down from Beverly Hills into South Central Los Angeles. She'd see plenty of Negro faces there, like her friend Virginia Capehart. Capehart was living a spinster's life now, happy to see Rosa's car pulling up to her apartment. "Rosa would sit in the dining room and look at the traffic," Capehart remembers. "It made her think of New York." After her outings, Rosa liked climbing back in her car, and there she'd be, rolling home and hoping that Sammy might be back from the road. But he was rarely there. It was just like in the old days: her little Sammy, gone into the wind. Rosa's car, her driver, her medical bills—everything was paid for by her Sammy. The car was a bone white Cadillac sedan—that dream car of the American Negro.

There were times, in the aftermath of Rosa's death, when the phone would ring in Sammy's house and Rudy, the valet, would pick it up, and it would be Elvera. Why, she was out at the airport, at LAX. No one had realized she was coming. She'd tell Rudy—in that no-nonsense voice of hers—to come fetch her. And he would, and soon after leaving the airport, he would have to inform her that Sammy was out on the road, and when he did, she'd tell him, her voice sharpening, that she did not want to get in anyone's way. Then, suddenly glancing at Rudy and taking umbrage at his innocent sharing of Sammy's whereabouts, she'd change her mind. And instead of going to the house, she now wanted to be dropped off at the Beverly Wilshire Hotel. And now Rudy felt awful. No matter how much he'd beg her to come stay at the house, she was insistent: the Beverly Wilshire. And he'd pull up to the front door of the hotel and escort her inside, fussing over her. After a few days of sitting around, ordering room service, Elvera would summon Rudy again, and he'd come take her back out to LAX, where she'd board the plane and return home.

On such unannounced visits, it was as if Elvera Davis—with Rosa now dead—was trying to be a mother again. And, in walking up that trail, she'd become entangled in her own emotions. Rudy remembers several other visits, when she'd be at Sammy's, and a misunderstanding would occur, over the slightest comment, and it was up and out of there and back to the Beverly Wilshire to wait for her flight home.

It was as if Elvera Davis sometimes possessed the pull of motherhood, but never quite the mettle.

The Beverly Wilshire always sent the bills to her Sammy, as she instructed them to.

The civil rights movement that Sammy had only been glimpsing—unlike Poitier and Belafonte, who seemed spiritually invested in it—was now fully upon the country. It was a movement to celebrate a different kind of beauty from what Madison Avenue advertisers had been flaunting for generations. And included in this beauty was a demand for rights, respect. For Sammy, confusion about such things as the word "Negro" was vanishing. The word that had so much belonged to Sammy's generation—a *Negro* entertainer, a *Negro* teacher, a *Negro* dance act—was gone. Those kids protesting on college campuses and marching in the South had started demanding another word, one as stark against the word "white" as existed in the English language.

Black.

There had been all those schoolchildren—everywhere, anywhere—made especially famous when Negro psychologist Kenneth Clark had been testifying on behalf of Negro lawyers fighting in the renowned 1954 *Brown v. Board of Education* lawsuit which originated in Kansas: the Negro children themselves preferred the white—not black—dolls! And what did that say about a lack of self-esteem?

Now black was dignified. It was the balled fist. It was the Afro. It was Langston Hughes and Curtis Mayfield and Fannie Lou Hamer. It was Martin and Malcolm. It was the struggle in Harlem and the war in Mississippi. It wasn't "Yes I can"; it was "Yes we will." And now, black was also beautiful.

"Negro" was old, suddenly antique.

Poof.

Welcome to black America.

The *Golden Boy* fanfare had seeped deeply into Sammy. He began asking the questions about professional fighters, attending boxing matches, placing bets, weaving through Las Vegas fight nights with his entourage. He was juiced up. He was *Golden Boy* down from the Broadway stage, out into the open.

The young actor Harry Belafonte, on left, would often browbeat Sammy into a position of social activism. Here they are attending the 1957 "Prayer Pilgrimage" in Washington, D.C. Actress Ruby Dee is on Sammy's left. Sammy seemed a peculiar sight at the event, snapping photographs in a tireless effort to fit in. Forevermore, he would be considered a latecomer to "the movement."

(© THE WASHINGTON POST. REPRINTED WITH PERMISSION.)

"All I need is a manager," the boxer Sonny Liston announced in 1967. "Somebody with a nice clean record."

Sammy started bragging, telling those around him he'd manage Liston. Yes, a manager. He was managing Lola Falana, and also a bevy of backup singers. He had watched Will Mastin manage others all his life. He saw no reason why he couldn't manage the volatile Liston. For years Liston had been linked to gangsters—a puppet, albeit a menacing one, to their dirty dreams.

"Why would Sammy want to get involved with managing a guy nobody wants any part of?" Dick Young, the *New York Daily News* columnist, begged to know.

Ideas flew into Sammy's mind, and then they flew out. The curse of the vaudevillian. He and Liston never connected. And *Golden Boy* Sammy kept moving.

. . .

In whatever city he happened to be in between 1963 and 1967, the staff abided Sammy's obsession: they'd sit with him and watch *The Fugitive*, an ABC drama that starred David Janssen. The murder mystery didn't intrigue Sammy as much as the lead character's rootlessness did. Always on the run, always in motion.

Many blacks had started sporting Afros, a large and bushy hairstyle, a fashion ornament taken from the Africans. Earmark of the Afro was to eschew grease, which straightened the hair. Negroes were now proud to sport a "natural" look. And, in another fashion owed to the African, they started wearing dashikis, loose-fitting shirts seen now on the backs of the protesters at many of the demonstrations going on around the country.

Frank had the Italians, as Dean had the Italians. Their blood lay in the old country. And that blood had powered its way into *l'America*. But what did Sammy have? Some vaudeville memories; a checkered family history in Wilmington, North Carolina; a mother's brutal Cuban heritage; a vision of old Will Mastin swinging a cane. And he had three children—Tracey and the two adopted boys, Mark and Jeff. (He played the role of father, however, like a well-known actor making cameo appearances in films—brief moments here and there.) Tracey—half black, half white, a child of Hollywood and all the spoils that would come to apply—recalled in later years only one breakfast with her father in her entire life: "But in years to come, whenever I doubted my father's love, I thought back to that morning, to the smothered pork chops and the shared smiles, and knew the answer. Still, it's sad in a way that one of the only memories I have of being with my father as a child is that we actually had breakfast together. I had breakfast with Mom just about every day, but I only recall that one time with Pop."

Sam Sr. never bent to family obligations. Nor did Will Mastin. Nor did Sinatra. Sammy simply could not picture Sinatra driving the kids off to school in a station wagon.

So he let May go without waging any kind of a battle to keep his marriage intact. There was no attempt at reconciliation.

She was so beautiful in *Blue Angel*, even more so in *The Young Lions*. The wide screen—as it had his father and Will Mastin—bewitched Sammy. May came down off the screen and gave herself to him, and he could not stop himself from falling in love with her image. If only he could have frozen the frame when he spotted her on celluloid. Only life didn't work like that. He would tell those interviewers during the course of their marriage that May was going to get back onscreen. After all, who could walk away from the glittery lights? But it was his hunger, not hers. The deeper into marriage she went, the more she figured her film career had been an accident, a series of flukes. She found real magic in domestic life, in her children. She was the antithesis of Elvera, her mother-in-law. She believed nothing could replace her children galloping into her arms.

Sammy had no idea of the breadth of May's happiness. She wanted to live happily ever after, with her children and her Sammy. But like his father and Will Mastin, he was rarely home. Even when idle on the road, instead of flying home, he'd go off—to gun shows, to film festivals; he'd go visit auto dealers in obscure locales to look at new European cars. He needed the exhaustion of constant movement.

Friends had seen the end coming.

"Sammy openly wanted a movie-star wife," says his friend and ghostwriter Burt Boyar. "He wanted people to say, 'Hey, there's May and Sammy!' He wanted to step out of a limo at an opening and have everybody scream. He wanted it to be two movie stars."

There were those who were aghast that he had abandoned her.

"She deserved better than what she got," says Amy Greene.

"May, to her credit, wanted to be a housewife," says Boyar. "She began resisting what Sammy wanted. She wanted to have the kids in the back of the station wagon and take the kids off to school. It wasn't obvious to Sammy that that was who he was marrying."

Jerry Lewis sat listening to Sammy talk about the end of his marriage, and shook his head.

"He tried to be a family man," says Lewis. "He told me it wasn't fun. I said, 'Sammy, a cunt at night with Chinese food is fun. Family is hard work. It can be a joy, but it is hard work.'"

All the while he was fearful of family dynamics, fearful that, as he put it, his life would be "taken over by them."

May left him; he left May. The press accounts were echoes of surprise and bewilderment at the breakup of their marriage. She said he must not want a family life any longer, because he never came home. She retreated into her family—minus Sammy. "She became almost an overnight hausfrau," Shirley Rhodes says. "She wanted kids, dinner at six, let's go to the zoo, let's get a motor home and drive across country."

He did not imagine life as she imagined it. And she had no sense of the clawing he had done to get where he was.

So the words at the end of *Yes I Can* were so much palaver:

> *I stood up and kissed her beautiful face and*
> *vowed I'd never let anything take away that smile.*

He simply never understood the eyes she saw him with, the pride she got from imagining him not as entertainer, but as man. If she saw in him a certain nobility—and she did—he saw in her a certain American victory, the lovely white woman walking in the same sands he walked, the great white feminine shark, beached unto him. "Wasn't it every black man's fantasy to have a white woman?" asks Helen Gallagher, Sammy's onetime beautiful, pre-May, blond lover.

Whether he wanted it to or not, Sammy's celebrity kept pulling him into the political forces blowing through America. There were discussions with Vice President Humphrey about the urban crisis in America; there were fund-raisers for Martin Luther King, Jr., to keep the civil rights movement in motion; there was a budding friendship with New York senator Robert Kennedy. And still, there were constant musings about the depth of his commitment. The white Sammy and the black Sammy were always at war with each other. "I think Sammy was afraid of the fact—a lot of my colleagues were—of sitting at the table of power," says Harry Belafonte. "They were nervous about what their image was with those people who held their life strings."

King, having determined which Hollywood celebrities he could count on to help foster further acceptance of his mass movement, knew he had steady commitments from Marlon Brando and Tony Franciosa in addition to Poitier and Belafonte. Both Brando and Franciosa—attendees at the 1963 March on Washington—had found a moral yardstick within themselves and aimed it directly into the movement.

There were times when Sammy heard of white celebrities preparing to participate in a movement event or rally, and he would grow suspicious and start wondering why he wasn't approached, wondering if the organizers were doubtful of his own commitment.

Brando was concerned about reports that blacks in Gaston, Alabama, were being mistreated and kept from certain jobs. "Marlon approached me and asked would I like to go with him to Gaston," Franciosa remembers. "He said he had heard doors were being shut to blacks wanting to work in the factory there. I said yes. Next thing I know Sammy is coming along. I was expecting to buy a ticket for the plane. Sammy said, 'No no, I'm going to rent a Learjet.' "

Sammy's fear of the Deep South was palpable. He had a gnawing feeling he would be assassinated, and that feeling bemused him as he pondered how blacks might react. "I don't care whatever move I make, some of my own people won't like it," he had told Alex Haley. "Maybe they'll like me when I die. But I can't die like normal; I got to be shot in Mississippi. Like Dick Gregory got shot at Watts. Shoot me—bam! Then they'll say, 'I guess he really was on our side.' "

"My sense," says Franciosa,

> was that Sammy felt he was walking into a war zone—and as
> a rookie infantryman, he was scared stiff. Not so much that
> he was going into this area, but that he was going to be phys-
> ically assaulted. All Sammy talked about on the plane was the
> hot water we'll be getting into. Marlon was constantly mak-
> ing Sammy feel that everything was going to be okay. When
> we arrived—this Learjet arrived at this tiny airport in Gas-
> ton, there's a group of people waiting for us—people in pain,
> the saddest faces you'd ever want to see. Here we are, a Holly-
> wood contingent in a Learjet at this tiny airport.

It turned out to mostly be a kind of question-and-answer session, with
Brando asking most of the questions, Sammy staring about like a lost child,
only happy when his jet was aloft once again. "Sammy sort of disappeared
down there," says Franciosa.

The black female dancers had been trying to tell him in ways subtle and not so
subtle during both the *Mr. Wonderful* and *Golden Boy* runs that there was such
unexplored juice in his own culture. Now Sammy felt it. He felt it in the kinetic
music coming out of the Detroit music publishing offices known as Motown.
He felt it in the moxie of Hilly Elkins, how Hilly had felt these political winds
and gone crashing into them.

Black was now beautiful. And *Golden Boy* was one of the few recently produced plays that had some of the temper of the times coursing through it—
race, sex, edgy drama, beautiful black girls.

Well, why not reassemble *Golden Boy*? Hilly and Sammy could show America what they had done on Broadway.

Hilly scanned the country—finger to the winds—and found his city. He'd
take *Golden Boy* right into the heart of civil rights demonstrations and activity;
he'd take it, and its interracial cast, into what many believed to be the most segregated city in all of America: Chicago.

The cast and crew convened in New York City early in the year to begin
rehearsals. Sammy had told Hilly he wanted Lolly Fountain—his former
lover—to be among the cast. Hilly had to buy Lolly out of another Broadway
contract: what Sammy wanted, Sammy got.

The news came in the early evening of April 4: Martin Luther King, Jr.,
had been assassinated in Memphis, and the assassin was on the run. It happened while King had been standing on the balcony of the Lorraine Motel

near downtown Memphis. He had gone to the city to assist striking garbage workers.

The murder stunned Sammy and only tightened his already firm beliefs in the dangers that lurked in America. That evening he made appearances on all three major television networks, reminding the viewers, even as the flames were already shooting upward from the rioting, of King's nonviolent message. Sammy's eye looked exhausted, his face drawn. Joe Grant, his bodyguard, stuck even closer to him now.

There were riots and protests in more than one hundred cities. There was looting in the nation's capital. President Johnson ordered out the National Guard.

America's political leaders had been painfully slow to hear the cries from the inner cities, from the ghettos. The mainstream media had inklings. A month before King's murder, *Life* magazine had run a cover article: "The Negro and the Cities: The Cry That Will Be Heard." (The term "black" had not yet been wholly adopted by the media.) The pictures were by longtime *Life* photographer Gordon Parks, who caught hungry Harlem children with lips swollen from eating plaster; going-nowhere youth high on pot in Brooklyn; and Chicago families besieged with poverty.

Black was beautiful, all right—and also angry. A lot of the anger was palpable in Chicago. There was fire in Chicago, and Hilly wanted to be where the fire flamed. On to Chicago! Sammy—sadness and anger sifting inside him as well—became emboldened.

"Sammy had a meeting," remembers Lolly Fountain, on her way to Chicago with the cast. "He wanted to change the show, make it more relevant to the times."

The times: they were full of paranoia and disillusionment. The war in Vietnam had left President Johnson in anguish. But the numbers kept rattling from the Department of Defense—that the war was winnable, never mind the body bags. Anguish turned to arrogance and hubris. Johnson sent in more troops, and then more. The kids were marching on college campuses. Johnson seemed to be in some kind of primordial pain. And then he surprised many by announcing he wouldn't be running for president again.

It would be Nixon versus Humphrey. It would be the youth movement versus whoever stood in their way—parents, politicians, Nixon's army, Humphrey's machine, anything to do with the old dogma was to be challenged.

As for the old guard, they didn't always understand. Sinatra didn't understand the Rolling Stones, or the Beatles. But they were here to stay. From Berkeley to Greenwich Village, poets were in coffeehouses railing against war, the government, discrimination. Poetry and bullets. Sammy went onstage now with love beads draped around his neck.

The president's National Advisory Commission on Civil Disorders had issued its report on the 1967 riots. It presented a cornucopia of statistics and proof that America continued to exist in two societies, one black, one white—and vastly unequal for blacks. And now a Negro, a dreamer, Martin Luther King, Jr., lay dead. His had been the first death of a Negro that wobbled the spiritual senses of the country.

With King dead, many wondered if his dream of racial unity would die. The forces behind *Golden Boy* didn't think so. Sammy and Hilly gathered their integrated cast. They would run with their own dream straight for Chicago. And just wait til Chicagoans heard "No More!"—the very anthem in the play that King himself had liked so much!

If any figure could be imagined standing upon Chicago's mountaintop in 1968, it was Mayor Richard Daley. For years he had delivered Chicago and much of Illinois to Democratic presidential hopefuls. In turn, he expected to be treated with respect. But in the mid-1960s his administration—in the form of his police department—had begun clashing with protesters over civil rights. Justice Department lawyers from the Johnson White House had pointed out the city's segregationist housing policies. Daley, who had become mayor in 1956, winced at criticism of his social policies. He was fond of telling Washington officials that they could stack him up against any southern redneck and he'd come out on top; he was fond of reminding them that he ran his city with control and his city worked. Negro activists were unswayed. In 1966, Martin Luther King, Jr.—making his most robust foray into northern politics—launched the Chicago Freedom Movement. Its immediate aim was a call for fair housing. Riots erupted that very year in Chicago, further shining a spotlight on the city's warring factions. In Daley's mind, rigid segregation was but a way to keep a city running efficiently.

Many of the black inhabitants of Chicago could trace their roots to the epic Great Migration of the 1920s and 1930s, when droves of Negroes poured into the city looking for jobs. With Daley's ascendancy to City Hall, there began a housing boom. The boom, however, resulted in the growth of housing projects on the South Side, where black families were crowded—the Henry Horner Homes, Stateway Gardens, Cabrini-Green, the Robert Taylor Homes. During the boom, Daley slapped down the Dan Ryan Expressway—it kept the blacks from the whites: blacks were on one side of the expressway, whites on the other.

For years, the Negro newspaper the *Chicago Defender* had constantly been at war with the mayor. When young blacks began to suspect that Daley was not moving quickly enough on civil rights, many formed groups—gangs, hodgepodge organizations that not only skirted and mocked the law but broke it. In time, the reality of gang life permeated some of the rougher black neighborhoods of Chicago. One of those gangs became known as the Blackstone Rangers.

Hilly and Sammy booked their *Golden Boy* production into Chicago's Civic Auditorium. As soon as the cast arrived, they sensed a city on edge. Chicago's burgeoning black rights movement was a mishmash. It had King acolyte Jesse Jackson spearheading an antipoverty effort known as Operation Breadbasket. Jackson took an athlete's delight in challenging Daley's policies on nearly a daily basis. The legitimate activists mixed in with the illegitimate. And now the Black Panthers swerved into view in their black leather jackets, further complicating the racial life of the city.

"We get off the plane," remembers Hilly Elkins, "and the newspaper says, 'Daley Orders Troops to Shoot Looters.'" Hilly was a battler, but even he was suddenly besieged with doubts. "I call the NAACP, Harry Belafonte, Sidney Poitier. I said, 'Hey guys, I want to know, if we do the show, is it good or bad [for Chicago]? I don't want to incite riots!'" He heard the encouragement he needed. And actually, in the days ahead, he and Sammy found that the brew of it all thrilled them.

"Chicago looked like it had been burned down," remembers Lolly Fountain. "Daley's men were like these big redneck cops. They had these high black boots on, mirrored sunglasses, these hats."

Sammy felt both saddened and newly emboldened by King's death. He believed the death provided him with new opportunities: he'd introduce his America—white America—to this new black America. Cultural juices were loose inside him now, and he salivated with Chicago as an outlet.

Police officers were stationed near the theater—they were actually on citywide alert—and cast members were required to show identification to enter. "It was like harassment," Fountain felt.

But the winds Sammy felt were not kind. That phrase "Uncle Tom" was being hurled at him once again. It was a tricky city and time for a black man to be in love with a white woman—even onstage. In black Chicago, Sammy's interracial love affair onstage didn't seem progressive; rather, with the tides now shifting regarding racial pride, it seemed regressive! If black was beautiful, why was Joe Wellington, the *Golden Boy* boxer, willing to sacrifice everything for the love of a white woman? Sammy, feeling pressure, began making additional changes to the play. "It was much more militant," Fountain says of the changes. At one point in the play, even the American flag—just as the Vietnam protesters were doing—was mocked.

To ingratiate himself to the city's militant political forces, Sammy began inviting inner-city youths to see the show for free. "We'd sit onstage answering questions about theater," remembers Fountain. "We had meetings with black writers, leaders in the community. Of course they all wanted money." Sammy dispensed money—running to his briefcase to grab hundred-dollar bills—in the form of "political contributions." Ha ha ha. Let them laugh at him now; let them call him an Uncle Tom. He was Sammy—rainmaker!

The black and white controversy, however, was hardly bad for *Golden Boy* business. Theatergoers flooded the Civic Auditorium. Every night was the same: "We sold out," says Elkins, who was intoxicated by it.

Sammy, as always, drew the curious backstage, especially other Negro stars and performers. It had been happening for years: in city after city, Negro performers would seek him out. It wasn't because of his politics—which they often considered bewildering—or the Sinatra fawning, or even the conversion to Judaism, but because he was Sammy, and they wanted to pay homage to his beginnings, his vaudeville odyssey, and his talent. He was an *insider*. Sammy was the brilliant puppet swinging from the string of white consciousness. Sammy had overcome. Not, mind you, in ways the "brothers and the sisters" always admired, but he had overcome. Trumpeter Miles Davis was a frequent *Golden Boy* backstage visitor in Chicago. He'd watch Sammy from behind his dark glasses—nodding, with a faint little smile at his lips.

Giddy with energy during the Chicago run and growing ever more curious about the Black Power movement, Sammy would often invite blacks onstage after the show's performance—the times were too serious for him to offer more song and more dance as he had done in days gone by—and they talked about whatever the gathering wanted to talk about. Even local black leaders were happy to come to the theater and meet with him. "They discussed politics, ways to defuse what was going on," remembers Fountain. Sammy began disbursing free tickets like confetti. Hilly didn't mind, at least up to a point. He wanted Sammy to realize he wasn't exactly running a charity.

Then in walked the Blackstone Rangers. They wanted to talk to Sammy about everything: politics, working within the system, revolution. And sometimes Sammy would just riff, ruminating about his boyhood memories of playing Chicago; race; the death of Martin. Sometimes he sounded a little melancholy—as if he himself were searching.

The Rangers were one of the most notorious criminal gangs in Chicago, battling with other gangs from the myriad city housing projects. They also, however, had an intuitive leader, Jeff Fort, who managed to bag a federal job-training grant in 1967 from the Office of Economic Opportunity. Fort's position—he was a master at manipulating white guilt—was that he could keep a lid on the simmering racial tensions in the city. Sammy gave the Rangers a financial contribution, and they heartily accepted—although some of them secretly wondered if he was trying to compromise them. Sammy seemed confused, and knew better not to hand over jewelry. The Rangers had already begun discussing possible business dealings Sammy could enter with them. Sammy's eye glinted. These were real gangsters—the blood of Sammy's imagination! And, in no time at all, Sammy invested in a liquor store run by the Blackstone Rangers. "Sammy," remembers Lola Falana, who was in Chicago with the *Golden Boy* cast, "seriously wanted to get *down* and be black."

The Blackstone Rangers wanted to honor Sammy, and they invited him to become an honorary member. It meant he would have to go through an initiation process. More eager than ever to dive into black culture—any realm of it, now—thrilled Sammy.

Dancers Lester Wilson and Falana accompanied Sammy to the initiation ceremony, held at a secret Chicago location. Walking into the room, Sammy, Falana, and Wilson all noticed that the faces on the Blackstone Rangers were serious, some grim. There was not the usual bonhomie that greeted Sammy upon entering a room. Celebrity worship did not appeal to the Blackstone Rangers. Falana noticed that Sammy quickly adopted a macho posture—the back arched, the shoulders firm, his own face hardening. The gang members stood in two lines, facing each other—the formation of a gauntlet. "Part of the initation," recalls Falana, "was he had to go through this long line, like an aisle." Falana and Wilson stood back, out of the way. Every member would guide Sammy in the secret Blackstone Ranger handshake. That hardly worried Falana, but what followed the handshake did: it was a hard punch to Sammy's chest. By the third punch Falana began looking at Lester Wilson. "The line was so long." Bam. She could not only see but hear the fists slamming into Sammy's bony chest. Bam. Wilson's eyes widened with worry. Bam. When Sammy finished going down one side of the line, he was turned to face the other line, then he proceeded down it. He was silent, and seemed to be shrinking within himself. Bam. Bam. Bam. "Me and Lester stood there and wondered if Sammy was going to make it," Falana recalls. "We kept saying to each other, 'You think he can make it?' He didn't blink, kept a stiff upper lip." When Sammy had traveled the gauntlet, it was time for him to go. The Blackstone Rangers did not want to engage in small talk. Falana and Wilson instinctively grabbed Sammy's arms, but he pulled away.

"Sammy, you all right?" Falana asked him once he was seated in the car.

"I'm all right," he said, unconvincingly.

When he reached his hotel room, Sammy looked as if he might collapse.

"I got to sit down," he said, touching his upper body and chest. Falana worried she might have to call medics. "I got tired of those niggers hitting me in the chest," Sammy finally said, his voice stern. "I thought I might have to kill one of those motherfuckers." Falana and Wilson looked at each other, and stifled their laughter—at least until they were outside of Sammy's room, where they doubled over laughing.

Sammy was left alone to take a much needed nap.

. . .

Early in the Chicago run, Hilly had begun talking to Sammy of extending the musical, taking it to other cities. But Sammy told Hilly he was exhausted, tired of playing the same role night after night. He wanted to get back to nightclubs; he wanted to travel, to once again be upon—as DuBose Heyward of *Porgy and Bess* fame had put it—"the warm, brown lap of the earth." Hilly had other plans. He told Sammy he was not going to close *Golden Boy,* and reminded Sammy that he had him under a long-term contract. Sammy said he'd just quit. "I'll sue your ass," Hilly told him. But in seconds Hilly thought to himself: "There was no replacing Sammy."

"Okay," Hilly finally said, "I'll tell you what. We'll close the show."

But Hilly had already decided he'd close the show only under one condition, which he shared with Sammy. "You've got to agree to do *Golden Boy* in London," he said to his golden boy, who in turn said that he'd do it under one condition: "You've got to do it at the Palladium."

Of course Sammy the Anglophile knew London, and he knew the Palladium. It was London's classiest venue. It was first class, just as Sammy traveled and lived.

Sammy's Joe Wellington was smashing his way through Richard Daley's riot-torn Chicago—and with a beautiful blonde on his shoulder. At least onstage. At night he was, wisely, seen with Lola Falana. Chicago was no place to challenge the rising black-is-beautiful mantra. Sammy was fully conscious of operating in the backyard of Chicago-based *Ebony* and *Jet* magazines, both longtime chroniclers of his predilection for white women and high white society. The show being a smash, Sammy had become—politically—as intoxicated as Hilly Elkins.

He went out one more time into the mean streets of Chicago. He tried telling some of the Afro-wearing blacks that he had marched; why, he told them he had marched in the mid-1960s in both Alabama and Mississippi. Pride rose in his voice.

"Don't mean shit today," one of the black radicals scowled at him. "This is '68."

Indeed it was.

He was galloping now, and fast, adopting manners of the movement in both speech and style—the return of the mimic—his words tumbling forth almost musically. He was moving through the movement now, baby; grooving with the soul brothers and soul sisters; getting high on some weed in the early morning hours after performances; sipping on some Scotch, loving on Lola, sweet Lola. It was, baby, the new—poof—all-black Sammy. And the kid from vaudeville was now an honorary Blackstone Ranger!

Draw!
Draw!
Draw!

There was little doubt that Hilly Elkins would come through with Sammy's demand to book him into London's renowned Palladium, and he did. *Golden Boy* was scheduled to open June 4, 1968.

Cast and crew packed to go across the ocean. "Being the unpretentious fucker I am," recalls Hilly Elkins, "I rented a 747." Sammy and Hilly, black and white, bound for London. The plane lifted, and blue clouds were in view. Someone started rolling some weed. Before long the plane held the pungent smell of marijuana. "By the time we took off," remembers Hilly, "you could get a 'contact' high anyplace on the airplane."

As always, upon landing, Sammy purchased gifts for the *Golden Boy* cast in anticipation of opening night. Racing store to store, his arm waving over and selecting items, he'd then turn to his assistant Murphy to complete the purchases because he was rushing and rushing.

Having been a longtime friend of *Playboy* magazine founder Hugh Hefner, Sammy took a suite in London at the Playboy Club, his Gucci and Louis Vuitton luggage, musical instruments, and bric-a-brac crowding the suite.

There were new cast members for the London production. Gloria DeHaven was signed to play the role of Lorna, Sammy's love interest. DeHaven had been a child vaudeville performer, and had made her screen debut in 1936 at the age of eleven in Charlie Chaplin's *Modern Times*. In the 1940s she appeared in a series of Hollywood musicals; her sultry beauty cast a glow from the screen. But the decline of the Hollywood musical forced her to turn to the stage for work. There was another reason Hilly Elkins matched her with Sammy: she was petite, the prerequisite for Sammy's leading ladies. Lon Satton would be playing the role of Eddie Satin that had been played by Billy Daniels in New York. Satton had appeared on the American screen in the Sidney Poitier vehicle *For the Love of Ivy*. He also would be understudying Sammy's Joe Wellington. Physically, the role would not be a stretch for Satton. He had boxed professionally while an undergraduate in college. Lolly Fountain and Altovise Gore had also come to London. And so did Lola Falana, whose stature was now prominently billed: ". . . and Lola Falana."

Given that Emily Brontë was his favorite author, and her novel *Wuthering Heights* his favorite book, it is little wonder that London was Sammy's favorite city. He had long considered his 1961 and 1962 Command Performances before the queen highlights of his show-business career. He liked the fact that William Shakespeare was an Englishman. The audiences touched him. "You know they don't applaud you until the end of the show," he said of Londoners. "You work hard and they sit there . . . you know they are digging you but no applause, they just enjoy you quietly . . . and then you are engulfed in a wave of applause." London's sartorial fervor—men smoking pipes, swinging walking sticks, wearing derbies, dressed in tailor-made suits from Saville Row— appealed to Sammy's sense of style. He wasted little time in discarding his Chicago wardrobe—jeans and dashikis—for the sophisticated threads of London. He was soon hobnobbing with friends—Peter O'Toole, Anthony Newley, Leslie Bricusse—and carousing in and around Piccadilly Square. His English accent, perfected by mimicry, resurfaced. "He'd speak with an English accent in a minute," recalls Falana.

The London production was directed by Michael Thoma, but Sammy awarded himself an unbilled codirecting title. It meant little more than the waving of his arms and the nodding of his head during rehearsals. He was at play, and quite enjoying himself. Well-dressed Londoners flocked to Sammy's June 4 opening at the bulb-lit Palladium.

Then, just two days into the run, grim news came from America. Presidential candidate Robert Kennedy, having swept the California primary in the race for the White House, was fatally shot on June 6 in Los Angeles. Sammy had campaigned for Kennedy, had visited with him and his family at Kennedy's Hickory Hills estate in Virginia. Kennedy, drawing on the poor and disenfranchised, on blacks and Indians, Chicanos and migrant workers, had appealed to Sammy's sense of inventiveness and tender spirit. Black and white seemed a cure-all to Robert Kennedy. (Often, before his journeys into the Deep South, Sammy would phone Kennedy, telling him where he was headed, leaving the impression—especially in his own mind—that if harm came to him, Kennedy would, like a game of cowboys and Indians, direct a rescue party to go get him.)

It was clear to cast members that the assassination stunned Sammy. He looked depressed and overwhelmed. He took a night off. Then he resumed performing.

Performing was how Sammy coped. It was how he survived.

One evening Sinatra sat in the audience. Yes, it was a small world: back in 1944, Frank had appeared onscreen with Gloria DeHaven in *Step Lively*. Frank Sinatra never looked as easy on English soil as Sammy. He didn't understand the music. The Beatles, their offices right on Savile Row, still confused him. After the show, Sinatra took Sammy and DeHaven and other cast members out to dinner at the White Elephant, one of London's finest restaurants. The night was long, and the next day he was gone.

Sammy had nothing on Frank when it came to disappearing.

When Sammy escorted a group of cast members out to dinner, there would often be a kind of pleading look in his eyes as dinner wound down, as if he would crumble if his guests left too early. "Sammy was very needy," recalls Marguerite DeLain, another *Golden Boy* dancer who followed the show from New York to London. "He did not want to be alone. He had a sense of abandonment. People who have that need applause. All those things you don't get from parents, you try to get from the world." Other times—to keep a crowd around him—he'd rent out whole movie theaters. "We'd get these movie prints sent from the United States," recalls Fountain. "You'd go to this private theater. He'd have sandwiches, food, drinks. He'd sit down and show one picture after another."

And it was in London that Sammy began an affair with dancer Altovise Gore. It made for interesting chatter among the company, inasmuch as there were now, on the scene, three paramours: Lola Falana, Lolly Fountain, and Gore. Sammy no longer had doubts: black was beautiful. "I used to say," recalls DeLain, who saw the goings-on, " 'Mr. Davis loves confusion.' "

London itself had changed since Sammy's last visit, in 1962, in part because Africa had begun the process of decolonization. In Nigeria, the Biafran War was taking place, covered widely in the British press. A Pan-African conference took place in London during Sammy's *Golden Boy* run, and he hustled over to it, excited as a child. African students were there in large numbers; tension was in the air. Lolly Fountain remembers spotting Wole Soyinka, a Nigerian exile and writer, at the conference. Just as he had long been torn between white and black, Sammy now had to ponder his old London—pipes and Savile Row suits—and the new London: rebellion fueled by African students and fiery liberals. He hated to lose one in favor of another.

For the first time in modern times, the policies of the British government were being questioned. The protest movement, however, unleashed another movement—a white Nazi brigade. Sammy, paradoxically, was caught between a nascent black Pan-African movement and the bobbing heads of racists. It hardly helped that tabloids had seemed to portray his quandary in advance, excerpting, as they did, portions of Sammy's *Yes I Can,* and not just any portions, but the parts of the book about Sammy and May. Billboards trumpeting the excerpts had shown Sammy and May Britt; there were even photos splashed about of Sammy and Kim Novak! The potency of interracial sex was titillation enough for the Nazis, and they began to picket Sammy at the Palladium, spewing epithets at cast members and at the star himself.

Slowly but surely, resentment began building against *Golden Boy.* During changeover scenes—lights out, everyone dressing in darkness—odd things began to happen. Actors were knocked down, unaware of where the belligerent blow had come from. Sandbags suddenly fell from the ceiling. Cast members grew frightened and sensed conspiratorial goings-on. "Taxi drivers spit on you," remembers Fountain. It was still the London where, in the sixties, during a bout of campaigning, a Tory candidate had uttered: "If you want a nigger neighbor, vote Labour."

Sammy and Hilly constantly tried to reassure the cast. More bodyguards were placed at the theater. Any odd movement toward the stage from a member of the audience would draw quick attention from the bodyguards. Fountain and others, however, could be forgiven their fright on the night when a man glided down the aisle, and, freezing cast members, walked right up onstage. The man served Sammy with a summons. It turned out that several London department stores—oh how he loved those Turnbull & Asser shirts, those Savile Row suits!—were exhausted trying to collect the money Sammy owed them. "Sammy went on with the show," Fountain recalls of the moment. "But he was really shaken." (To take care of his debt, Sammy phoned Prince Spencer—his dancing buddy from the 1940s—and his wife, Jerri, whom he considered family. "He needed money," recalls Jerri. "He was too proud to go to Sinatra. We wired him several thousand dollars." Not long after returning stateside, Sammy made his way to Chicago to visit the Spencers. "He came into the room, pulled up his dashiki, and laid all the money on the table," says Jerri.)

When Fountain left the London production of *Golden Boy,* Sammy gave her a pendant. It was from Asprey, the store that made jewelry for the royal family.

When Sammy returned to America at the end of his *Golden Boy* London run, he knew he was returning to a different and now ever-spinning America. Robert Kennedy—gone. Martin—gone. Both within two months of each other. Whenever asked, Sammy had swung his puppet's body around the country for both, raising money. Almost daily now, there were antiwar protests on college campuses and street corners. The Black Power movement was in full flight. Taking earnest measure of its reality, Sammy reappeared sporting an Afro—and with a black girlfriend, Altovise Gore. Drawing on his mimicry skills, he quickly dropped the tendency to use British inflections in his language and began speaking, once again, in the voice of the urban black.

Helen Gallagher, his former blond lover, ran into Sammy in 1968 at the Copa in New York City. He spotted her and sent her a note to come backstage. "I go backstage," she remembers. "Everybody's black. He says, 'This is my soul brother, this is my soul sister.' I said, 'Why, you little black bastard. I knew you when you were white.'" There was awkard silence, the soul brothers and soul sisters looking at Sammy, wondering what he might say, how he might put the blond white lady in her place. Then it comes, the rising whoosh and spread of Sammy's unctuous laughter to rip away the embarrassment.

With President Johnson battered by the Vietnam War—"Johnson's War," the protesters were now dubbing it—Hubert Humphrey received the Democratic presidential nomination that summer in Chicago. But the event was a disaster. Mayor Daley's riot policemen—Sammy's *Golden Boy* cast had spied them up close months earlier!—attacked convention goers and even the media. Blood spilled. On television the spectacle looked ghastly. "The kids screamed and were beaten to the ground, rapped in the genitals by cops swinging billies," one reporter noted. The Republicans nominated former vice president Richard Nixon. Sammy knew Nixon better than Humphrey. As for Humphrey, he lacked animation on the stump. The citizenry seemed somewhat bewildered by him; his years in LBJ's shadow had not properly illuminated his natural gifts. It did not help that George Wallace, running himself and ricocheting across the Deep South—uttering fiery and code-worded racist oratory—was yapping at Humphrey's heels. Humphrey also fretted about how quickly he should distance himself from the administration's Vietnam policies. He waited until September, which proved too late. Nixon bested Humphrey in a squeaker—43.4 to 42.7 in the popular vote—becoming the thirty-seventh president of the United States.

The atmosphere on the streets alarmed Sammy so much that he decided to, once again, beef up his security detail.

There was hardly a month where Sammy wasn't seen on the American television screen. His appearances were mostly on comedy specials, sitcoms, and talk shows. Rather than ingratiate himself deeply, he fell back on what he knew: the quip from the stage, mocking the volcanic times upon the land, making fun of race, of black and white.

In the days of the antebellum South, cartoonists often drew Negroes sitting on picket fences, eating watermelon. The image portrayed was of the happy Negro, watermelon seeds dripping from mouths. The watermelon would become a rather bizarre piece of fruit in the annals of the Negro and stereotype.

When Sammy—accompanied by Jay Bernstein—showed up in Moab, Utah, for the start of filming on *Sergeants 3*, both noticed something large and green outside the door of his hotel room. They stared hard. It was a watermelon. A little something from Sinatra, who admitted to the prank. Sammy howled. Ha ha ha.

Appearing on the variety show *Laugh-In*, Sammy is seated at a piano, playing a tune. A flower vase on the piano suddenly breaks. "Now that's black power!" he howls out to the nationwide audience. America on fire. Ha ha ha. And you can almost hear the giddy laughter from the suburbs—and the anguish from the inner-city living rooms.

And yet, Sammy was money, and no one knew that better than the NAACP. They'd write those fundraiser letters and he'd scribble his name at the bottom, and the letters went out and the cash rolled back in. He'd been doing it since the early '50s. And so many times there he'd be on a stage in Kansas City, in Boston, in New York, performing, raising money—and publicizing Sammy.

In 1969, Sammy received the Spingarn Medal from the NAACP. It represented the organization's highest award. All those benefits! All that money for "the movement." Sammy showed at the ceremony wearing a Nehru suit. He resembled an escapee from a high-level cabinet meeting in India. Roy Wilkins, NAACP director, had to raise his arms up and over Sammy's head—so as not to trifle with the star's stylishly coiffed Afro—as he draped the medal around the honoree's neck.

Soul brother Sammy.

Chapter 16

SAMMY AND
TRICKY DICK

S ammy Davis, Jr., might have become a fine movie actor, but there were two things that conspired against him. First, he lacked the patience it took to sit on a movie set inside a trailer waiting to be summoned for his performance. Great movie actors—Spencer Tracy, Laurence Olivier (from whom Sammy dreamed of taking personal tutorials)—focused inside their idleness. The staccato rhythm of movie acting—scenes shot out of sequence—did nothing to undermine their performances. But that very process bored Sammy. Vaudevillians, who were itchy creatures, didn't idle; they performed. The second, and perhaps more damaging, was Frank Sinatra, whom Sammy allowed to hijack what might have been an admirable movie career. Before Sinatra came along, Sammy had given two nuanced performances—in *Anna Lucasta* and *Porgy and Bess*—working, on both occasions, with directors who challenged him. More movie roles, however, did not follow. He took to the road; he had mouths—his retinue—to feed! But he loved Hollywood and wanted a movie mogul behind him. His courting of Goldwyn for his *Porgy and Bess* role had been shameless. But along came Sinatra, offering up a string of movies in which Sammy costarred: *Ocean's 11, Sergeants 3, Robin and the 7 Hoods* (the latter, it must be said, featured Sammy in a fervid dance-and-gun routine atop a bartop that alone was worth the price of a ticket).

Sinatra, for all his renown in Hollywood, for his *From Here to Eternity* Oscar, never took his film career seriously. He needed—as did Sammy—the warm flesh and presence of bodies, a stage with hungry faces peering up at him, the music of a live audience. In a way, both Sinatra and Sammy Davis, Jr., considered movies a little beneath them, the trick of holding an audience in the palm of a hand their highest self-salute. Sammy appeared in only one movie in 1965, the forgettable *Nightmare in the Sun,* and one movie in 1966, *A Man Called Adam,* the vehicle he produced and starred in while appearing in *Golden Boy* on Broadway. At the time of filming that movie, he was not only onstage but doing his short-lived television series as well. Little wonder his performance in the movie seems disjointed. Sinatra wanted Sammy's follow-up to *A Man Called Adam* to be Sinatra's own *Tony Rome*. "Frank calls me," recalls agent Sy Marsh, "says, 'Listen, I want Sammy to do *Tony Rome* with me.' I say, 'He can't. He's committed to *Sweet Charity*.' I call Sammy and tell him. He says, 'Do what you have to do.' I tell Frank. He says, 'Okay, fuck him, it's the last time I'll do something for him.' "

Sinatra aside, Sammy's best performances always occurred when he was whirring before the camera—in *Porgy and Bess, Robin and the 7 Hoods, Sweet Charity.* In those films, he offered dazzling bits of performance; he appears both kinetic and sinewy. A musical figure in his offscreen life, Sammy needed to feel and act musical in reel life to cement his confidence that the screen was for him.

The director Richard Donner first gained attention in Hollywood directing episodic television. A onetime actor, he had a feel for performers. Among his earliest efforts was directing episodes of *Wanted Dead or Alive,* a CBS television Western that aired from 1958 to 1961 and made a star of Steve McQueen. Donner liked directing Westerns, and got additional work directing episodes of *The Wild Wild West,* starring Robert Conrad. Sammy agreed to a guest starring role on *The Wild Wild West* but wanted Peter Lawford to appear as well. On his guest stint, Sammy played an undercover Secret Service agent. Donner was beguiled at Sammy's insistence that his skin color have nothing to do with the role. "It wasn't a black secret service agent—it was Sammy. It wasn't a black actor—it was Sammy Davis, Jr. It's a big difference," notes Donner. The episode gave Sammy just what he wanted—yet another opportunity to showcase his dazzling quick-draw skills. "I had a crazy time with them," Donner recalls of the friendship he formed with Sammy and Peter Lawford. Carousing together, the three began joking about opening up a nightclub, then did just that. "We called it 'Mutha'—for 'Motherfucker,' " says Donner. "I found the building on La Pierre, between Santa Monica and Melrose [in Los Angeles]. It was the old Mitchell camera factory. But we changed the name from 'Mutha' to 'The Factory.' It was the most 'in' private club in the world. I met Ike and Tina Turner at a wedding in Texas. They came and played at the club." Sammy would swoop into the club, the music blaring, his bony shoulders twisting and turning to the beat, in love with the scene he himself had helped create. It was an ode to a new and hipper Hollywood. At times Donner would find himself just staring at Sammy as he crisscrossed the floor of the nightclub. "Sammy was like a puppet when he walked. But it was wonderful to watch."

Sammy and his two co-owners were shrewd about the club's clientele. "You couldn't get in," says Donner. "Every major model and airline stewardess got free membership. We'd get phone calls from the State Department saying a sheikh was coming with twenty women. We made it so exclusive it was ridiculous. Minnesota Fats used to play [pool] there. Sammy was king. Every once and a while he'd get up and sing—or grab the mike and be the emcee."

And every once in a while the three—Sammy, Peter Lawford, and Donner—would talk of movies. Sammy confided to Donner that he had ambitions to direct. He still hungered to direct a remake of *The Scarlet Pimpernel,* a 1935 British production that starred Leslie Howard, who played two roles in the film: an ordinary British fop, and a brave soul who rescued those undone by the French Revolution. Sammy loved double lives.

Sammy and Lawford sometimes hashed out movie ideas for themselves. ("Sammy and Peter wanted to show people they were stars *without* Frank," says Jay Bernstein.) One evening the two turned to Donner with something on their minds. "They said, 'We'd love to do a movie with you,' " Donner says. Their idea was a film about two London disco-club owners and their run-ins with nightclub rivals. It would be a comedy, a farce. Inside the Factory they began imagining scenes, bits of dialogue. Sammy longed to play a Londoner. "We were writing *Salt & Pepper*" inside the club, Donner says. Donner finally hired Michael Pertwee, an English playwright and screenwriter, for the major writing job. "While the writing was being done," Donner recalls, "Sammy was on the road all the time. We joined him in Oahu [Hawaii]."

As he got to know Sammy, Donner found something rather strange in the entertainer's voice: "He always talked 'white.' I think at that point that was just Sammy. I don't think it was an affectation."

Donner went to London in 1968 to prepare for filming of *Salt & Pepper*—Lawford was salt, Sammy pepper. Ha ha. The movie would be shot at Shepperdon Studios. When Sammy arrived, he was giddy, as ever, to be back in London. Among the items in his prepared wardrobe were derbies, pinstriped suits, narrow trousers, and walking sticks. "The wardrobe on the picture disappeared fast as it was made," says Donner. Sammy was seen on the streets of London in costume. A modern-day Heathcliff! Sammy immediately hit the nightspots. In fact, they had jolly good fun. And they gave young Donner reason to worry:

> They would come to work and not have any idea what we were doing. You'd walk them through the movie. They'd say, "Okay baby, okay baby. Let's go." Here I was, my second movie. I was directing Sammy Davis and Peter Lawford. The Beatles were happening. There was a restaurant called El Vino. The main table was under a clock, and Sammy had it. It

was his. You'd come in and Sammy would go, "Here comes my director!" Everyone would show up because it was Sammy. He loved it. He wore it well. He'd buy for everybody all the time. I guess I kind of loved him in a strange way. At that time he was the most fascinating person who ever came into my life.

Donner simply found it impossible to ignore Sammy's charm, his astounding energy. Restaurant bills, nightclub tabs—Sammy said send the bills to him! "They owed everybody," Donner says of Sammy and Lawford. "Money burned a hole in Sammy's pocket." Donner would sit in the restaurants where Sammy sometimes gathered cast and crew members and he'd listen to the racial jokes. With Sammy around, it was open season on racial verbal patter. Donner would listen to the jokes and nearly squirm—wondering how Sammy could raise himself up with his powerful talent, then alternately lower himself by succumbing to the demeaning put-downs: "That's the genius," believed Donner.

The London street crowds—friend or foe—energized Sammy. "I remember him getting out of cars in London," says Donner. "He'd walk out there. It wasn't artificial happiness. He loved it. It was like insulin in his arm."

There was the matter of acting discipline, which Donner found wanting. "They would become childishly temperamental," he says of Sammy and Lawford. "Peter bent to Sammy's demands." The two Rat Packers knew Donner was director, but they were—as Sinatra had so often been—the producers! "Filming was brutal," Donner says.

> They were both nuts. Sammy would rent a theater every night and run movies. There was a lot of drugs, booze. They would never show up on time. Ninety percent of the time they didn't know what we were doing. It was painful. That was my second feature. They were the producers. I always thought I would acquiesce to some of their offbeat ideas. But I knew when I got to the cutting room, I would take the things out. When the picture was over, they fucked me without giving me the final cut. I went out looking for them, and in the condition I was in, I was looking for blood.

Donner was left with one thought about Sammy when filming ended: "I think he would have given anything to be white." In a strange way, the revelation endeared Sammy to him. "To know him was to love him. To experience him was to know his pain."

. . .

Even as good movie roles eluded Sammy, he continued to dream. He had announced plans in February 1973 to film *The Legend of Isaac Murphy*. Murphy was a black jockey who won the Kentucky Derby in 1884—and went on to tally many other notable victories, among them three American Derbies, becoming one of the most celebrated jockeys of his time. Sammy, of course, needed to look no further than his own family circle for insight into the racing profession: Will Mastin and Sam Sr. had always been drawn to horses and stables. But in 1973, Hollywood was swooning over its production of a stream of urban-oriented films featuring blacks far removed from historical figures. These were the so-called black exploitation movies, and they featured the meanderings of a mélange of characters—pimps, thieves, con artists, hustlers, and Robin Hood criminals. Their titles were rather exotic—*Superfly, Friday Foster, Cleopatra Jones*. Having traveled in the rarefied world of working with such A-list names as Otto Preminger, Sinatra, and Harry Belafonte, Sammy steered clear of the black exploitation films. Never mind that these movies provided many blacks with their first starring roles, the movies themselves seemed to grate on Sammy. "We should show all the sides," he said of the black-themed movies and their propensity for glorifying crime. He had a point, but not a true understanding of blacks in Hollywood and the travails of the past.

So Sammy wanted to play Isaac Murphy. He had the requisite physical attributes for a jockey—Sammy flinging the whip, kicking the stirrups! But the Murphy legend meant nothing to the Hollywood power brokers. Those exploitation movies were profitable. The studios turned Sammy down.

Isaac Murphy died at his Kentucky home on February 12, 1896. He had left his wife, Lucy; the couple never had children. In his later years he was bedeviled by drink and debt. It was estimated that during his lifetime Murphy won 530 races; his winning percentage was put at 34 percent, an astonishing rate for a jockey. For years after his death, Murphy remained as distant from the public mind as Bert Williams, as Florence Mills. But in 1967—in the swirl of the civil rights movement and in an effort to reclaim the Murphy legend—he was reburied at Man O' War Park, near Lexington, in a public ceremony. "I am as proud of my calling as I am of my record, and I believe my life will be recorded as a success, though the reputation I enjoyed was earned in the stable and saddle," Murphy once said. "It is a great honor to be classed as one of America's great jockeys."

Sammy's presence in the civil rights movement grew more and more hypnotic. Just as he had brought juice and a byzantine gallantry to Sinatra's Rat Pack, he brought similar qualities to the growing struggle for equal rights. "Sammy brought a constituency of power and visibility," says Harry Belafonte. "Dr. King said, 'Let us not alienate people.' America watched Sammy Davis, Jr. People tuned in to Sammy. If you told people, 'Sammy Davis, Jr., will be at this or that benefit,' you got more people coming."

Sammy never asked for money to perform at a benefit. But having slept in bungalows and one-room motels as a struggling vaudevillian, he did have one request: that he and his crew be given suites in a hotel. In larger cities, the presidential suite was demanded. Little Sammy would not be treated as Will Mastin and his father had been treated.

Would Sammy marry Jean Seberg?

The Iowa-born actress had caught his eye. She first caught the public's attention in 1957, when Otto Preminger cast her in his *Saint Joan*. Two years later she starred in Jean-Luc Godard's *Breathless* and became genuinely famous, especially in Europe. In America, Seberg became more notable for something other than her film roles: she had a real fascination with the Black Panthers and their cause. The white actress's obsession ensured that she was followed by FBI agents. She took Sammy to a Black Panther gathering. She seemed so much more comfortable than he did. Sammy's lack of radicalism did not appeal to the black-white Jean Seberg, and the two drifted apart.

Would Sammy marry Romy Schneider?

The international screen star—she galloped among French, Italian, and German cinema—came to the attention of American audiences in *The Victors*, a World War II drama released in 1963 that also starred Peter Fonda, George Peppard, Senta Berger, and Albert Finney. Sammy met her in Paris: "We would laugh, we would giggle. There's something about staying up late in Paris, drinking French 75s, being upstairs at the Calvados, coming down to the bar after dinner and the cat's playing the piano late, it was like a movie."

He would not marry Seberg or Schneider. Sammy's black friends began telling him he had to marry a black woman. Image was at stake. Black America was coming on now.

Lola Falana—appearing in her own nightclub dates now—was once in the audience of a Los Angeles club, listening to comedian Redd Foxx. When Foxx spotted Falana, he went on to tell the audience that she had been linked romantically in the past with Sammy. Foxx sounded a little snarly; he sounded a little jealous of Sammy. "Sammy's a white guy in black skin," Foxx said by way of a punch line. Falana rose and left.

Sammy's musical director, George Rhodes, had gotten into several heated arguments in bars about Sammy's racial preference: men swirling their beers wanting to jawbone with him about Sammy and white women.

Just as he lifted himself out of vaudeville, and just as he lifted himself out of a life without religion into Judaism, now he'd lift himself up and away from white America. Sammy had a chameleon's abilities, along with his slyness of a mimic. Black looked to be going mainstream, where Sammy had always been. So black looked to be so beautiful now.

There was no one better at survival than Sammy.

"After May, white women were out," says Lolly Fountain. "He told me that. Sammy let me know he was going to marry a black woman."

Sammy thought Altovise Gore might be just another fling—flesh upon flesh—something that began in London during the *Golden Boy* run. In London he had even suggested she room with his costar, Lola Falana, and how he loved that: the three of them seen out in London, two tall leggy Negro girls and Sammy. Cruising Piccadilly Square. They kept him giggling; he kept them feeling fussed over, admired, cherished. Bottles of champagne to the room! "Altovise," says Lolly Fountain, "didn't want to be famous. She wanted to be 'moneyed.' "

Once back in the States, Sammy started traveling around to his engagements with Altovise. She had cocoa-colored skin, large expressive eyes, and he said she reminded him of an Egyptian queen—of Queen Nefertiti, to be exact. He'd look at her and just marvel. Frank had a young girl; Dean had a young girl. Youth was the coin rolling down the boulevard of American life now. Altovise Gore was twenty-two years younger than Sammy. She was like some feral creature rising and reflecting in his glass eye. The gift-buying began— jewelry and more jewelry. And there were trips, zooming through the clouds.

His Queen Nefertiti was actually a child of Queens, New York. Altovise Gore—father a career navy man, mother a homemaker—attended the High School for Performing Arts. Afterward she found work in the theater as a gypsy dancer, once dancing in a production alongside Harry Belafonte, once getting a dancing role in *High Spirits,* a Noël Coward play. But now she was with Sammy Davis, Jr. "I fell for him because of his mind," she would say.

She was partial to high-heeled boots, in which she stood nearly six feet tall. She had the chirpy voice of a little girl—a voice that charmed the childlike Sammy. And yet the voice was so at odds with her physical countenance. (Some dancers—out of earshot—had taken to calling her "Baby Huey," after the cartoon character.) Gliding through airports, tall and short, they looked odd, trailed by loads of luggage, Queen Nefertiti drawing stares and taking long strides, her Sammy double-stepping to keep up. The more he bought for her, the more he felt she was becoming his creation. Whereas May had shrunk from attention and publicity, Altovise reveled in it.

He introduced her to everyone—Shirley and Murphy, his father, Will when he came around. He introduced her to his Hollywood friends, to Swifty Lazar, Lucille Ball, Loretta Young, of course Sinatra. He took her to his tailor, Sy

Devore, and then there they were, in his-and-hers matching outfits. On the streets, the soul brothers went wild at the sight of Altovise. She wasn't a classic beauty, but there was no one who could have told her that. Her own self-confidence was quite seductive. Sammy did not grow jealous at the attention she drew from men. In that manner, he was so unlike Sinatra. He swooned at the lasciviousness; he was sweetly giddy at the sight of her in hot pants, and thrilled as other men looked at her with raw lust in their eyes. (Hot pants notwithstanding, Sammy bragged that he was going to turn Altovise into something he believed did not yet exist—"the black Jacqueline Kennedy," as he told Molly Marsh, Sy's wife.)

Wherever they were—Philadelphia, New York, Los Angeles—he'd ball a fist, showing his Black Power salute, and raise it to the soul brothers eyeing him and Altovise. Ha ha ha. Black Power, baby.

Altovise found it amazing how he could sleep on airplanes. They would take off, and he'd be out, next to her, in first class. The world in Technicolor one moment, dark the next—the entertainer weary and asleep to the world.

In Philadelphia on May 11, 1970—he had just completed an engagement at the Latin Casino—Sammy was invited by his longtime friend Jerry "the Geator" Blavat, the local radio personality, to join him at his home for dinner. Sammy arrived at 5859 Overbrook Avenue along with Altovise and Elvera, his mother, who had come over from nearby Atlantic City. Blavat's mother cooked wonderful Italian dinners—"She cooked for Frank, Sammy, all of them," says Blavat.

"Geator, what are you doing tomorrow?" Sammy asked the deejay.

"Why?" said Geator.

"I wanna get married," Sammy blurted, turning to Altovise. "Altovise, let's get married tomorrow."

Altovise began to shriek with howls of joy. There were looks of stunned surprise at the table as Sammy and Altovise embraced. Blavat, seated next to Elvera, felt a swift kick under the table. It was Elvera getting Blavat's attention. "That stupid-ass son of a bitch doesn't know what he's doing," she whispered in his ear.

Sammy told Blavat he wanted to go right to the courthouse the next day, and there they all stood—Blavat; the justice of the peace; Carl Barry, a comedian friend of Sammy's; and Sammy and Altovise.

Later that night there was a dinner party at Cinelli's Restaurant in Cherry Hill.

Blavat and others were surprised that Sammy had married Altovise. "Everyone thought he would marry Lola," Blavat says.

Sammy's two other marriages—to Loray White and May Britt—had been elaborate ceremonies, and what did that guarantee? Not a thing. So he settled

In Altovise, his last wife, Sammy had someone in lockstep with the power-
ful flavor of the sixties: she was black, prideful, and über-stylish.
(ASSOCIATED PRESS)

for a bare-bones courthouse affair. There had been no family present. Elvera
had been at the dinner the night before, but on the day of the wedding, she
skipped away, back to Atlantic City, unwilling to participate. It was what it was:
Elvera had now been absent from all three of her son's weddings.

The marriage surprised Sy Marsh and made him suspicious. "Jesse Jackson
thought it would be good if he married a black woman," says Marsh of Sammy.
"He thought blacks would come around."

Jerry Lewis knew quite well Sammy's preference in women, and the marriage also surprised him. "I never saw him with a black chick until he married
Altovise," says Lewis.

Sammy's wedding gift to Altovise—as it had been to Loray—was a mink.

There was, however, a slight difference: Loray's mink was white; Altovise's black. In for a dollar, in for a diamond. Love was love, and glitter was glitter.

Altovise loathed the gold-digger talk. Why, she fell for him because of his intellect, as she had reminded one and all. Actually, he had tons of questions for her. "He'd always quiz me: 'Who was the thirty-seventh president of the United States?' I'd say, 'I don't know.' He'd say, 'You went to school!' "

The newlyweds needed a home.

For years Sammy had visited Tony Curtis and Janet Leigh at their Spanish-style house on Summit Ridge Drive in Beverly Hills, which they had purchased in 1958. It had a circular driveway, a lovely view of the hills. One had to drive past the old Mary Pickford–Douglas Fairbanks mansion to get there. "Sammy was there all the time," remembers Leigh. "He lived in that house. He said to me, 'Someday I'm going to buy this house.' "

After the breakup of the Leigh and Curtis marriage, the house was purchased by actress Constance Towers. After Towers's ownership, the house was sold to Joan Collins and Anthony Newley. When Collins and Newley put the house on the market in 1970, Sammy began negotiations. "The minute it was done," says Leigh, "he called and said, 'Guess what? I bought 1151.' "

Sammy now had a fabulous address. Old Hollywood had long been in his bones, and the ghosts of Mary Pickford and Douglas Fairbanks were neighbors. He summoned decorators, designers, and watched gleefully as Altovise gave instructions, whizzing around the property like a mannequin come to life. While the decorators went to work, the newlyweds retreated to the Ambassador Hotel for a respite.

The sixties had now closed around him. That explosive and unpredictable and history-making decade had opened with Sammy having a white bride, and closed with his taking a black one. All his life, rummaging for respect and acceptance, he had been able to impersonate any decade: in his youth he had been as bouncy as the 1940s; as dreamy and homespun (*Mr. Wonderful*) as the 1950s; as wickedly inventive—given his Chicago *Golden Boy* incarnation—and conscience-touched as the 1960s. "He always sort of embraced what was new, what was 'in,' " says Janet Leigh. "I always thought he incorporated all of that so he wouldn't seem old hat."

As a singer, Sammy sang from the neck up. The peerless Sinatra, on the other hand, seemed to sing from the heart up. Sammy was a throat singer. His mimicry controlled the singer inside him. "He always seemed to be doing Billy Eckstine," says producer Buddy Bregman—by way not of criticism but explanation. Eckstine, of course, was an amazingly gifted singer. "To me a singer had to put you into the picture," Bregman adds. "I don't think [Sammy] ever did that. He performed. He was the world's 'best' performer."

Sammy's oeuvre consisted of jumpy Broadway show tunes, old jazz standards ("My Funny Valentine," "April in Paris"), and ballads. He did have a
thing for the lushness of a tune, but he was also quick to make a tune over, as
he had done with "Hey There," his first hit. Never a popular singer, he
remained, during his career, one who relished the mechanics of singing. It can
be said that he genuinely gave his voice to a song, but a great deal of the
giving was in the enunciation and theatrics—not to be confused with what lay
inside the heart. Sammy could not—and here is but another of the contradictions that coursed through his life—read music, and yet, he sang like a
conservatory-trained singer.

If Sammy did not receive proper direction in his singing career, he had only
himself to blame. Having allowed Sinatra to march through his life like a commanding general—dispensing advice, movie scripts, record deals—he
remained loath to rebel against his principal ally. A string of albums—*At the
Coconut Grove, The Sounds of '66, That's All! Sammy Davis Jr. Belts the Best of
Broadway, Dr. Dolittle*—were all under Sinatra's Reprise label. On November 7,
1962, Reprise released the single "Me and My Shadow," a Sammy Davis–Frank
Sinatra duet. The song was written by Billy Rose, Dave Dreyer, and Al Jolson.
(Jolson, the blackface artist, seemed to be trailing Sammy's life like smoke
through curtains.)

Sammy's agent, Sy Marsh, chafed at the Reprise arrangement. "He got the
leftover shit," he says of Sammy. "All these guys wrote for Frank. When I came
in the picture, I started making demands." When his demands were not met,
Marsh encouraged Sammy to leave Reprise, convincing him he'd find another,
more agreeable label elsewhere. It took time, but the phone finally rang. The
caller stunned Sy Marsh: it was Berry Gordy, of Motown Records. Marsh was
shrewd enough to recognize the psychological tensions of Sammy's racial persona—he knew few blacks purchased Sammy's records, or attended his nightclub performances, for that matter—and simply could not imagine such
realities being in harmony with the Motown Record company.

In 1959, former auto-plant worker Berry Gordy had founded Motown
Records in Detroit. Gordy decided he'd recruit local talent, and would aug-
ment their natural gifts by sending them to the Motown in-house "charm
school." Among Gordy's first hires was Cholly Atkins, who would teach the
singers dance steps. (It was the same Atkins who had toured with the Will
Mastin Trio decades earlier. What Atkins would begin teaching at Motown,
Sammy already knew.) Among the label's first hits was something Gordy himself wrote—"Lonely Teardrops"—sung by a young Jackie Wilson. Gordy soon
had a unique roster of talent—Smokey Robinson and the Miracles, the Contours, Martha and the Vandellas, the Four Tops, Marvin Gaye, Diana Ross and
the Supremes, "Little" Stevie Wonder, and the Temptations. Within a few short
years, most would be famous and wildly successful. Gordy called his music the

"Sound of Young America." It had its millions of white listeners, to be sure, but Motown had the synergy of black America in its veins. Not all of its tunes were ballads and love songs; in 1970, Motown singer Edwin Starr recorded "War!" one of the earliest of the anti-Vietnam songs. That same year the label also released "Why I Oppose the War in Vietnam," a speech that had been recorded by Martin Luther King, Jr. It would be honored with a Grammy Award.

On the surface, the mingling of Sammy and Motown seemed as unlikely as Sammy and the Blackstone Rangers. Motown had soul singers; Sammy's sound was difficult to categorize—a fusion of nostalgia, jazz, bebop, and Broadway; "middle-of-the-road shit," in Sy Marsh's mind—and he sang it to the suburbs. Sammy's favorite songwriters were Anthony Newley and Leslie Bricusse—two Brits; Motown's galaxy of singers were partial to Eddie Holland, Lamont Dozier, and Brian Holland, young black songwriters who had written many of the label's hits for Diana Ross and the Supremes. And yet, the more Sy Marsh thought about Berry Gordy and Motown—and Sammy's distant relationship with black America—the more his mind began clicking. He saw a wonderful opportunity: "Here's a chance to go with the hottest record label for blacks in the world."

Sammy and Sy hustled off to a meeting with Gordy. Sammy sat listening. For Marsh, his earlier revelation deepened during that meeting: "Here I am with the world's number one producer—black—and Sammy, the greatest entertainer." Gordy made a pitch about his stable of songwriters, about how Motown could broaden Sammy's appeal. Gordy's label indeed had produced more than two dozen number 1 hits in the past decade. The record mogul offered a two-record deal. "Think about it," he said, as Sammy and Sy rose to leave.

They didn't need very long to think. Sinatra was the 1940s and 1950s, the past; Berry Gordy was the 1960s—and the future. A press conference was called. "I believe I can make Sammy Davis the world's biggest recording star," Gordy announced.

As for Anthony Newley and Leslie Bricusse, they were—poof—gone.

A black wife.

A black recording label.

Sammy's conversion was streaking.

There were few places across the American landscape where social change had taken shape so vividly as in the Deep South. Blacks had been elected to school boards, to city councils. Sometimes it felt like the walls of Jericho were cracking.

Since 1947 the town leaders of Wilmington, North Carolina, had hosted their annual Azalea Festival. It consisted of parades, garden exhibits, and plenty of music. The old southern city, hugging the Atlantic Ocean, dressed itself up every springtime to host the festival. In 1978, the event's organizers invited Sammy Davis, Sr., to be one of its marshals. They contacted Charles Fisher, Sam Sr.'s cousin, who still resided in Wilmington.

Sam Sr. was leading a life of leisure in Beverly Hills, tooling along in his Jaguar with his wife, Rita. He was an old retired tap dancer who played the horses and stopped off at his son's Hollywood offices now and then. His waist had widened, but he still looked a dandy in his suits. When Charles Fisher reached Sam Sr. and told him that the organizers of the Azalea Festival in his hometown of Wilmington wanted him to be one of the guest marshals, he simply could not believe it. After all, he had left the town as a young man decades before with his heart beating fast, believing police officers were about to arrest him for the confrontation he had had with the white store owner. Sam Sr. listened to Charles, and he pelted him with questions, not believing any of it. And Charles kept talking, trying to sell the city to Sam Sr., telling him it was a changed city, an integrated city now. "Sam thought they were planning a lynch party for him for what had happened" in the past, recalls Fisher. But Sam Sr. finally agreed to the return. (After his conversation with Fisher, however, he phoned another Wilmington relative to make sure the invitation was legit and that there was no trickery involved.)

Sam was greeted by family and festival officials upon his arrival. He fairly beamed. (The festival would run from April 6 to 9.) Rita held his hand. Inasmuch as he had never returned to the city since he'd left, it was a homecoming. Charles, having played intermediary, was delighted—in himself, for pulling Sam Sr. back to his hometown, and also in Wilmington. Sam exchanged pleasantries with festival organizers, then Charles ushered him into his station wagon. "He said, 'Charlie, take me over to Brooklyn [a section of Wilmington] so I can show Rita where I was born.'" And there he stood—the boy who had fled town by train, who had danced the Charleston all over the country, who had sent for his mother to leave Wilmington and come to New York City, who married a showgirl, who raised a boy who became a star. Watching Big Sam show Rita around touched Charles. Everyone got emotional. A meal was prepared; Charles couldn't help complimenting Sam on the beauty of his wife.

The concert, which featured soap opera stars and singer B. J. Thomas, was held the following evening in the auditorium that had formerly belonged to the all-white high school. A local black fraternity, AKA, performed. Sam Sr. cackled, enjoying it all. "Big Sam danced that evening," remembers Charles. "Old as he was, he got up and stole the show."

Before he left Wilmington, Sam Sr.—a son of North Carolina—wanted to leave something behind for the people of his hometown to remember him by.

He left his tap shoes.

. . .

In a concession to the youth movement, Sy Marsh figured it was wise to have someone youthful and black on Sammy's office staff. Sy always feared someone from the Negro press dropping by and seeing only white faces. So he hired Ann Slider, a young black aspiring actress, to be an office assistant. She began work in 1970 at the office on Sunset Boulevard.

Slider, short and perky, was thrilled to be working for Sammy Davis, Jr. Before long, she was greeted with a rather charming, if peculiar, sight: old show-business people—vaudevillians—marching in and out of the office. They were dragging themselves now because of age. They had worked with Sammy when he was with the Will Mastin Trio—in Detroit, in Chicago, in Washington, D.C., in Syracuse. They'd rattle off names of cities, and Ann would just smile. But they were not only there for a trip down memory lane. They also wanted to know if there was a check—some money. When Slider would exhibit confusion and sorrow—there was no check; of course there was no check; why would there be a check for someone not currently working with Sammy?—they insisted she keep looking, because they knew there was a check. And in a drawer, or a stack of mail, she would find one check, then another, and another. "I couldn't believe all the people on the payroll," she says of the comics, mimics, dancers who danced no more. "Pigmeat Markham was on the payroll. All these vaudeville people." They would hug her—Sammy was not often around—and simply shuffle on away with a gift from Sammy.

Now and then Will Mastin or Sam Sr. would come to the office, old dignified men, still dressing sharply. "Mainly, they were there to pick up checks," says Slider. She'd engage them in small conversation. "I said to Will one day, 'Teach me how to tap-dance.' He got up and showed me some steps." When Sam Sr. would bump into Mastin at the office, he'd start talking about "family," and beg Will to come spend the holidays with him and Sammy. Will listened, nodded, and went about his way. They'd be lucky to see him in a year's passing.

Sam Sr.—unlike Will—adored the public. He did quite a bit of fishing now. He'd get himself down to Redondo Beach, and climb aboard the public boat with his fishing gear. It wasn't just any fishing gear, it was Abercrombie & Fitch. A five-hundred-dollar rod and reel. And he wasn't one for scruffy fishing attire. "The dad was dressed impeccably," recalls Mike Green, a young UCLA medical resident then who used to go on the fishing boat along with his buddies and who befriended Sam Sr. The aging entertainer would regale them with vaudeville stories. There was warmth in his voice as he talked about Sam Jr. "Here we were dressed in Levi's, and the dad was out there in a two-piece suit," says Green. But the trips would always end embarrassingly; Sam Sr. would always get drunk. "He would be unconscious by the time we'd get off the boat," says Green. "They literally had to carry him off the boat."

. . .

Ann Slider found it hard to get used to the volume of phone calls ringing in Sammy's office concerning old bills. "When I first started there, I was appalled at the phone calls that came in from creditors," she says. "Sy would say, 'We're going to take care of it.' "

But she found a huge amount of joy in opening up Sammy's fan mail. The volume of mail so astonished her that she finally decided to do something. "There was so much mail, boxes and boxes of mail that was never looked at. So I started the Sammy Davis Fan Club. I had posters made, jewelry, medallions."

On the occasions she tried telling Sammy about the fan club, he'd hunch his shoulders, seem a little uninterested. She didn't exactly realize he'd been gathering fans since the age of five.

"People were just in love with him," says Slider. "There was some little girl who had been in a coma and her mother put a Sammy tune on for her. And she began to move. I told him that story one day. He was in the office shooting pool. He just had no idea people loved him so much."

But the longer Ann Slider worked for Sammy, the more his name came up outside the office, mostly in little asides made to her by her friends. And those little asides were not salutes but criticisms. They were denigrating comments about all the times Sammy allowed himself to be the foil of racial jokes on the television screen. Slider's friends thought they were but insults covered in laughter. So her friends asked her about Sammy's mind-set. And the constant questions thrown at her began to make Ann herself pay closer attention to his television appearances. And she began, like her friends, to wonder about the self-deprecation; how Sammy seemed to be actually embracing the mockery. She was youthful, and her youth propelled her to take risks: she was going to talk to Sammy about the image he was portraying on television—the image he was portraying to America. But first she talked to Jackie, the other secretary in the office—who happened to be white. Jackie's reaction surprised Ann: "She was in agreement about the way he acted." Jackie also thought he demeaned himself.

Slider found herself in a quiet moment with her boss. "I told him that when I see him on shows and he's grinning, well, it really isn't necessary for him to do that." She told him her friends felt uneasy—especially her black friends. Then, just as quickly, she told him Jackie—the white secretary—felt the same way. Sammy seemed perplexed, searching for words, an answer. "He started to tell me these are people who helped him and opened doors for him," she says of those she thought were mocking Sammy—the talk show hosts, the aging white comedians. The moment became even more awkward, until all there was left was a strange silence, suddenly overtaken once again by office noises.

It had to hurt Sammy—the king of the empire—to be assailed in such a manner. The black secretary and the white secretary—both peering right into him. He was confused, so he did what he had long done in the past. He reached for gifts. "The next day he sent me a Sony tape recorder," Slider says. "He was on his way to Japan. And when he came back he gave Jackie a beautiful Omega watch and he gave me a hand-carved bracelet watch. I had it appraised later. It was worth $5,000."

So he bought the kids off. What did they know of the doors vaudevillians had to pry open? What did they know of blackface? Of dancing on street corners? Of sleepless and motherless nights?

Jack Carter in 1972, during that year of war and revolution: "Sammy cares about his people." Long pause. "And black people, too."

There was something else that bewildered Ann Slider about working for Sammy: the gentlemen who sometimes walked through the door, and began whispering, and took seats and remained seated in silence until Sammy arrived. "The mob guys would come in the office, sitting there, talking, waiting for Sammy," she says. "They'd scare me."

Sammy made only one movie in 1970, a forgettable venture that he co–executive produced, titled *One More Time*. It was a sequel to *Salt & Pepper*, the equally forgettable crime caper that had starred Sammy and Peter Lawford. What was unique about *One More Time* was its director—Jerry Lewis. It would be the only movie Lewis directed in which he himself did not star. As his career tumbled in various incarnations, Lewis came to imagine himself as something of a Charlie Chaplin figure—an unappreciated auteur. The movie was shot in London. Lewis insisted his sets be open to the public, so *One More Time* had a gaggle of Londoners constantly popping in and out during filming. Lewis worried little about concentration, believing a movie achieved true verisimilitude with ad-libbing and improvisation. Ad-libbing was a dimension of Sammy's arsenal, and he let loose. He laughed, Jerry laughed, Peter Lawford laughed. They were housed at the tony Mayfair Hotel—where the laughing continued. Alas, the movie studio honchos did not laugh. The film was a mess—although Sammy's wardrobe, featuring such classic outfits as velvet smoking jacket with high collar—effortlessly caught one's eye, as did his puffy Afro. "Working with [Sammy], I had ten weeks of ecstasy," Lewis would remember of that film. (It was on this film set that Sammy offered Lewis the job of directing his autobiography, *Yes I Can*, for the screen. Lewis exuberantly accepted, and loudly announced himself the only man alive who could properly bring the project to the screen. Tsk, tsk, not to be.) As for *One More Time,* the critics were harsh. Like Chaplin, Lewis hated critics. They all became his mortal enemies. So fuck the critics. "It was a great joy," he says of the film. "Problem was, Metro released it but didn't sell it. They just let it come and go."

In May 1970, Motown released its first Sammy Davis, Jr., album. Titled *Something for Everyone,* it boasted nine singles and was an unmitigated disaster. The album had a beguiling tone, in both content and art design. Among the singles were "Spinning Wheel," "You've Made Me So Very Happy," and "In the Ghetto," the latter the blatant attempt to introduce Sammy to the black audience— those who might well be living *in* the ghetto. The cover featured Sammy in long robe—the Afro, of course—tinted glasses, a drink and a cigarette in hand. He is surrounded by more than two dozen women. The women—white and black, though mostly white—are dressed in long modish attire, and the fashion effect seems to evoke a commune, or a hippie haven. On the album's cover there appears a striking blonde who is sucking on a multicolored lollipop. Hovering body-close to Sammy is a soul sister in a gigantic Afro, her arm seductively resting on Sammy's shoulder. Opening the slipcover, one is treated to a double-truck photo of Sammy, seated, in his robe—only now he has the robe's hood over his head. He holds a bust, a sculpture—it looks to be Beethoven's head— in his lap. Sitting behind tinted glasses, surrounded by curvaceous beauties, Sammy resembles a woozy pharoah. It is an album that, with little regret, one might judge by its cover: confusion reigns both inside, in the recordings, and outside, in the artwork. Five years earlier Sammy had recorded *Our Shining Hour* with Count Basie. Now this: he has gone from jazz and jumpy Broadway melodies to Berry Gordy's musical invention—the black Sammy.

The album received scant airplay and did not yield a single hit. (Gordy asked Marvin Gaye to come up with original songs for Sammy to record. But during this time Gaye—who possessed epic gifts, as evidenced by his landmark 1971 album, *What's Going On,* in which he sang with rapture about ecology, the Vietnam War, and race—had a not-so-small problem: an addiction to cocaine. His concentration waned, and his songs for Sammy never materialized.)

Sammy worried. There was another album to deliver. "You know, I'm not a Motown singer," he finally confessed to Sy Marsh. "I can do it, but I'm not comfortable."

Sy Marsh told him not to worry, to just sing. Sammy went back into the recording studio. Tracks were laid down for the follow-up album. Motown executives seemed preoccupied. Marsh could feel it. "We're recording, but nothing is coming out," Marsh says of the company's refusal to release

Sammy's follow-up singles and album. He requested a meeting with Gordy. "I say, 'Berry, when the fuck you going to put out our records?' Berry says, 'I got a problem. Our salespeople say Sammy doesn't have the Motown sound.' I said, 'Fuck the Motown sound. What about the Sammy sound?' " Marsh's face turned red. "I want all the masters back," he snapped at Gordy before meeting's end, referring to the unreleased demo tapes.

When Sy Marsh told Sammy that he had ended the Motown arrangement—a move Motown executives hardly tried to stop—Sammy told him it might be a struggle to get the demo tapes back. A short while later, much to Sammy's surprise, Gordy had the tapes returned. "You must have caught that nigger in the bed fucking somebody," Sammy told Marsh.

Sy Marsh was still determined to revive Sammy's flagging singing career. The Motown fallout also had an effect on Shirley Rhodes. A native of Detroit, where Motown was headquartered—and one of the few black road managers in the country—she had an open line of communication with Berry Gordy. In a chat with Gordy, he suggested Sammy's music team might be more comfortable with someone like Mike Curb, a young record producer.

Mike Curb's best-known talent was a young sister-and-brother duo—Marie and Donny Osmond—whose record *One Bad Apple* had made its way onto the R & B charts. The Osmonds were white; Mike Curb was white; the Osmonds were on the R & B charts. "Berry appreciated competition," Curb says, trying to explain Gordy's advocacy on his behalf.

Curb was born in Savannah, Georgia, but spent much of his youth in Compton, California. His father was an FBI agent. Young Curb, in a community populated mostly by blacks, listened to a lot of black music while growing up. He was wild for the Drifters, Clyde McPhatter, and Fats Domino, among others. He dropped out of college when he was nineteen, wrote some advertising jingles, made some money, and started Curb Records, his own label. (He produced the music for Roger Corman's 1966 film *The Wild Angels,* which starred Peter Fonda and Frank's daughter Nancy Sinatra. A movie critic would say of the film that it was fine to watch "after about twenty-four beers.") One of Curb's wiliest creations was the Mike Curb Congregation, a group of gospel singers he formed to back up his artists. They provided a rather stumping and soulful beat to his label's music tracks. In 1969, when he was a twenty-five-year-old successful music mogul, Curb merged his label with MGM Records.

Shirley Rhodes got the Mike Curb Congregation to appear with Sammy on a couple of dates. Curb and Sammy struck up a friendship. Sammy confided to Curb how unhappy he had been with Motown. "Sammy really didn't like R & B music," says Curb. "I think he felt he had passed it [by]." Curb's gospel congregation had already recorded "The Candy Man," an Anthony Newley–Leslie Bricusse composition, but it had not done well. "I was disappointed," says Curb of the single's failure. He had another idea. "We were back-stage one night at Caesar's Palace. I said, 'Hey Sammy, why don't you do "The Candy Man"?'" Sammy didn't make a commitment, but Curb felt he was intrigued. Curb had another point to make as Sammy pondered the possibility, and he wasted no time in sharing it. "I said, 'You remember "High Hopes" with Sinatra?' That was Sinatra singing with kids. I said, 'Sinatra did a fun song like that. Why don't you do a fun song?'" The Sinatra link touched Sammy where he was most vulnerable. "Next time I saw him," says Curb, "he said, 'Maybe it will be a fun song to do for the kids.'"

Sammy and his entourage showed at Curb's studio space on Fairfax and Melrose in Los Angeles to record "Candy Man." Curb ushered his congregation into the studio. With the congregation swaying and Sammy singing, Curb felt good. "The thing I learned about Sammy was if he could snap his fingers to something, he could do it." Curb and those gathered around began snapping their fingers. "After he left, we took the finger snaps and put a Motown-like drum over it real hard. It almost sounded like a combination of 'High Hopes' with a Motown drum." (Sammy never was one for doing more than one recording of a song. He did one take of "Candy Man," and then bolted.)

It was treacly. It was kiddielike. Children's voices are everywhere on the tune, yelping sweetly. It was corny. It had a fairy-tale lilt to it:

> *Who can take a sunrise*
> *Sprinkle it with dew*
> *Cover it with chocolate*
> *And a miracle or two?*
> *The Candy Man*
> *Oh, the Candy Man Can*
> *Cause he mixes it with love*
> *And makes the world taste good . . .*

And the disc jockeys began playing it. No, it wasn't being piped into Berry Gordy's urban America. But the kids liked it, and what the kids liked, their parents had to buy. And out there in the suburbs their parents bought "Candy Man." And they kept buying it. And who is to say that against the backdrop of the Vietnam War and racial unrest—so much strife, so much disenchantment—that a fairy-tale tune didn't have a place? A fairy-tale tune sung by a middle-aged vaudevillian who never had a childhood of his own. The tune started climbing the *Billboard* charts. It became infectious, both a joke and a surprise hit. With a hit, one has to hit the road, and Sammy did. Shirley Rhodes couldn't believe it. Sy Marsh couldn't believe it: the middle-of-the-road shit was hot. Berry Gordy reached Sy Marsh by phone. "He says, 'I see your guy's on the charts.' I said, 'Berry, you called our stuff "white bread." Well, this is white bread. But we're on the charts."

From Berry Gordy back to Anthony Newley and Leslie Bricusse, from black back to—poof—white bread.

Out on tour, singing "Candy Man," Sammy would be holding the mike in one hand, a bucket in the other. In the bucket there was candy, hundreds of pieces of wrapped candy. He'd start flinging the candy into the audience, all the while singing. The crowds went wild. "I was going to milk the fuck out of it," says Sy Marsh, who came up with the idea.

Growing more and more stunned by the record's success, Berry Gordy phoned Marsh again. "Are you guys buying up all those records?" Gordy asked Marsh.

On March 11, 1972, "Candy Man" reached number 1 on the *Billboard* charts. "The one thing he always wanted," says Mike Curb, "was a number one record." Curb joined Sammy on tour in celebration. "It was euphoric," he recalls. "When you get the number one record with a legend like Sammy—and with your own group—it's like something you think about the rest of your life."

Sammy had no intention of losing sight of Mike Curb. "Sammy said, 'What's that song about the vaudeville guy?' " recalls Curb. "I said, ' "Mr. Bojangles" ?' He said, 'Yes.' I went out and bought it for him."

"Frank Sinatra has a cold," went the famously titled Gay Talese *Esquire* article about the singer.

Well, Sammy Davis, Jr., has a high-spending wife.

In "Candy Man" he had a hit record, and it was a good thing. Sammy always spent money he didn't have; absent Will Mastin he spent foolishly, in part because he simply had more money to spend.

"I said to him one day," recalls Jerry Lewis, " 'Sammy, at the end of this week you'll be $20,000 richer. Now tell me, why have you gone out and bought $30,000 worth of jewelry?' "

"Why not?" answered the vaudevillian who had had so little early in life.

Now Sammy had a wife who was in lockstep with his spending sprees. She didn't marry him for his money. Of course she didn't. One grocery bill—and there would be many, many other bills—caught the attention of Sy Marsh. It was for $5,200. A lot of caviar, a lot of lobster; a lot of a lot of things. The bills—food, furniture—worried Marsh. And they worried Shirley Rhodes. They did not worry Sammy: "She was in my league," he felt of his wife's spending habits. "I was almost proud of her."

He showed her how proud. In the driveway for his wife sat a Rolls-Royce and—because, well, maybe some mornings she'd like to zip along a little faster, maybe along the Pacific Coast Highway, which hugged the ocean—a Maserati.

Sammy described Altovise to *Women's Wear Daily* as "my rock and my reason."

She wanted to be an actress. Sammy put her in touch with agents. The contacts yielded no roles. So he bought an empty building in Los Angeles and said he'd use it as space to make—direct—his own movies. And he'd cast and direct his wife in those movies!

Yes I can.

He adored Reno, Nevada. It had an edge, it had landscape, it had the Sierra in the distance. And it had Bill Harrah, who owned Harrah's. Bill Harrah took care of Sammy because Sammy always packed his place. Harrah put Sammy up in a house, and the house looked out onto a lake. And inside the house there was the finest food, the best champagne. "One day I get a call from Bill Harrah," says Sy Marsh. "He said, 'I want to do something for Sammy. What would get him excited?' " Marsh's loss for words caused Harrah to interject: "He said, 'Sy, do you know about the Duesenberg? It's a handmade car. Doesn't go on the assembly line. It'll take a year to make.' I said, 'Terrific.' He said, 'Don't tell him.' "

One evening, a year later, the car arrived. Sammy was onstage, the car sitting out back of the hotel. Between the first and second shows, Marsh pulled Sammy aside. "I said, 'Bill wants to meet with you,' We go out back. There's a spotlight, and there's this candy-apple red convertible Duesenberg. Sammy looks at the thing and goes, 'Holy shit!' He thought it was Bill Harrah's car. Sammy said, 'Bill, that's a son of a bitch!' Bill said, 'Sammy, you like it that much, it's yours.' He handed him the keys. Sammy is practically crying."

Sammy never told Bill Harrah, but his feet couldn't reach the pedals. So he gave the Duesenberg to Altovise, to go beside the Rolls and the Maserati he had already given her.

Love was such a wonderful thing.

As an everyman of entertainment, Sammy had elevated his celebrity to the point that, from the mid-1960s on, he'd play himself on television. In a curious fashion, he had already outgrown the medium despite the fact he was never commercially accepted by it.

In 1968, the Hollywood television producer Norman Lear began imagining a way to adapt the popular British series *Till Death Do Us Part* for American television. Lear's version would highlight the comical and social ruminations of a bigoted father and his family living in Queens, New York. A pilot was filmed for ABC, but the network turned it down. Lear was undaunted. He had cast, in the lead roles, Carroll O'Connor, a veteran motion picture character actor, and, as his wife, Jean Stapleton, a stage actress. Lear pleaded with the two to remain available. Finally, CBS picked up the show. Its first airing came on January 12, 1971. Just before the first night's airing, the network issued a statement to the national viewing audience: "The program you are about to see is *All in the Family*. It seeks to throw a humorous spotlight on our frailties, prejudices, and concerns. By making them a source of laughter we hope to show—in a mature fashion—just how absurd they are." The unusual comedy, which addressed issues such as homosexuality, abortion, racism, and interracial marriage, caught on, and by summer's end, was America's number 1–rated show. Its nervy appeal was the undeniable attention it paid to race, thrusting the issue right out into the open. Archie Bunker, the name of O'Connor's character, became, for many blacks, a kind of bogeyman behind a laugh sound track, a dim-witted white man who would never fully respect blacks or other minorities as evidenced by the words—"coon," "spic," "dago," and "spade"—that were often sprinkled into his conversations. The heightened and sensitive insights offered by his more liberal family members raised the show's laughter. The show's theme song was titled "Those Were the Days," a sweetly nostalgic piece of music that harkened back to a simpler—more segregated—America. (Interestingly enough, the song had been written by Lee Adams and Charles Strouse, musical collaborators on *Golden Boy*.)

Volumes of mail about *All in the Family* poured into the CBS mail room. The mail cut sharply along racial lines. Many whites had taken to the crusty Archie Bunker character. "Archie Bunker for President" buttons began showing up in many trinket shops across the country. Blacks were alternately amused and alarmed by a show which showed the mental wanderings of an open bigot such as Bunker. Whitney Young, Jr., esteemed head of the National Urban League, derided the series and its showering of racial epithets. Nothing, however, could derail its popularity.

The craze reached the White House. President Nixon watched an episode on May 13, 1971. It was sex, not race, that seemed to unnerve the president. "Archie is sitting here with his hippie son-in-law, married to the screwball daughter. . . . The son-in-law apparently goes both ways," Nixon scoffed, his words dropping into his secret tape recorder. Another character Nixon deemed as "obviously queer. He wears an ascot, and so forth." (Ironically, Archie was quick to heap praise upon "law-and-order" President Nixon.)

Lear was quick to defend the show, explaining that by showing racist attitudes so openly, one could then begin to understand the folly of them. The reasoning didn't always catch on. "It's a very dangerous show" is how Harvard psychiatrist Alvin Poussaint—himself black—felt about *All in the Family*. The ratings remained high, and the *All in the Family* rage hardly escaped Sammy. Given his own life, Sammy became an instant fan. And thirteen months after the show's premiere, he became a guest star.

In the episode, which aired February 19, 1972, Archie is seized with excitement as Sammy Davis, Jr.—played by Sammy Davis, Jr.—having left his briefcase in Archie's taxi, is on his way to the Bunkers' house to retrieve it. As Sammy enters the Bunker household, there is verbal interplay about having him in the house. Sammy takes a seat. Before long, amid the chatter, the conversation turns to race:

ARCHIE:
> If God had meant us to be together, he'd have put us together. But look what he done? He put you over in Africa and he put the rest of us in all the white countries.

SAMMY—A LOOK OF COMICAL RAGE ON HIS FACE:
> Well, you must have told him where we were, 'cause somebody came and got us.

The quick history lesson seems to stun Archie Bunker.

Sammy, as he's leaving with his briefcase, poses with Archie for a picture. And in that one magical moment just before the flash goes off, Sammy leans over and—black lips to white cheek—kisses Archie Bunker on the cheek. The laughter on the sound track explodes.

It wasn't just a kiss. It was more like the thunder hooves of history rolled up into a kiss. Blacks and whites did not kiss on American television. It was taboo. That one man had kissed another man was an even deeper taboo. That Sammy Davis, Jr.—much of his own life mired in episodes involving interracial sex and matrimony, enraging both blacks and whites over the years—had kissed Archie Bunker, celebrated as archetype of the American bigot, seemed a joke so majestically cruel that many did not know whether to laugh or cry. One thing was for sure: many millions watched. The Sammy Davis–Archie Bunker episode of *All in the Family* became one of the highest-rated television half hours in the medium's history.

The mail into CBS—and into Sammy's office—came with lightning speed. And it was nasty. The network had imagined a sophisticated response to its creative history lesson, as Norman Lear himself did. But they imagined wrong. The controversy bewildered Sammy. He had a black wife! Didn't they read the papers? Didn't they scan the magazines? *All in the Family* was entertainment!

Four months after the show's airing, the fissures could still be felt. One black-oriented magazine featured a photo of Sammy and Archie inside and asked: "Is Archie Bunker the Real White America?"

Altovise Gore may not have known the answer to the question Sammy had so gleefully asked her—"Who is the thirty-seventh president of the United States?"—but Sammy himself knew, and for someone who never went to school, it made him proud he knew: Richard Milhous Nixon. The same Richard Nixon who had come to visit Sammy at the Copa so many years before; the same Nixon who had invited Sammy to visit the White House when he was vice president.

Richard Nixon did not come as easily to glitter and stars as Jack Kennedy, his nemesis and the first modern president who openly courted Hollywood. Against Kennedy's savoir faire, Nixon appeared but a foil for satirists: he was the man seen on the beach in wing tips. His body language was stiff, his smile frozen. He seemed a man constantly emerging from a wall of alabaster. And yet, in terms of cinema, consider his roots: he was born in a place called Yorba Linda, a mere twenty-five miles from Hollywood, that land of film and the tricky camera. "You see," Nixon wrote in a 1938 letter to actress Patricia Neal, "I too live in a world of make-believe."

The whiff and struggle of the 1960s still lay upon the Nixon White House. He had Vietnam to grapple with—he had vowed to end the war—and the youthful culture in the streets. Blacks, almost universally, loathed the thirty-seventh president of the United States. Nixon had nominated two southern judges—Clement Haynesworth and Harold Carswell—to the Supreme Court and watched as an uproar flared about their past links to segregationists. The two nominees were rebuffed. That only enlarged the wound felt by blacks when Nixon refused to name a black to his cabinet—unlike LBJ, who had been the first to do so. (It was Robert Weaver, as LBJ's HUD secretary.) In 1971, the Congressional Black Caucus—the symbolic representative on Capitol Hill of black America—boycotted Nixon's State of the Union address to protest his policies, which they felt were undermining the War on Poverty, an earmark of Lyndon Johnson's administrations. "Flush Model Cities and [the] Great Society along with it," Nixon had once directed an aide.

But to those who felt Nixon suffered from cultural myopia, there was always trickling evidence to prove otherwise. He invited Elvis Presley to the White House. Presley showed in sequins and sunglasses—the outfit had a carnival-like look—and pridefully left with a badge, Nixon having made him an honorary law enforcement official. And Nixon had invited James Brown—the soul-singing James Brown of the ear-catching lyric "Say it loud / I'm black and I'm proud"—to the White House. If Nixon could get the King of Soul into the

White House, primping with the very song that had been adopted by blacks as a kind of anthem, well, what did that say to the Congressional Black Caucus and his other black critics? The White House hadn't been shy in letting fly the photos of Nixon and Presley, and they certainly were not shy in releasing the photos of Nixon and Brown.

Nixon believed that criticism that painted him as out of touch with culture—high or low—had been unleashed by Kennedy partisans. He would never be able to claim Sinatra—nor did he wish to. Sinatra was too shady: the gangster scent. Sammy was a different matter.

Nixon dispatched Bob Brown, one of the few blacks working in the White House, to Beverly Hills to ask Sammy if he would accept a seat on the National Advisory Council on Economic Opportunity. Every president had put together such councils: little bite, but great public relations. "We've got Jim Brown [the football star] with us, and we've got James Brown, we've got good people, but the president wants you," Brown said in his pitch to Sammy.

Sammy did not think of Carswell and Haynesworth, whose very nominations had struck fear into the heart of black America. And he did not think of the Congressional Black Caucus and their animus toward Nixon. Sammy thought of none of that.

The White House was power! The president needed him! The vaudevillian who had never attended school couldn't resist.

Sammy arrived at the White House on July 1, 1971, to officially accept his position on the council. He yuk-yukked with Nixon as the camera flashes went off. (Within hours, the White House photo of Sammy and Nixon was out on the wires.) In subsequent visits as a member of the council, Sammy loved sweeping into the Executive Office Building. Pulling open his Gucci briefcase, chatting up Bob Brown and the other black businessmen on the council, Sammy walked like Sinatra: summoned by presidents. Nixon's contribution to black America was business opportunity upon business opportunity. Successful businesses yielded money. Republicans knew money. And Sammy couldn't argue with the sweetness of money. When the meetings adjourned, Sammy would hobnob with James Brown and other council members. Hearty slaps and soul-brother handshakes—the thumb slapping against the palm of the other hand, then the viselike grip. Ha ha ha. Nixon's soul brothers.

Nixon—ever thinking of reelection, of votes, and also mindful of how long and full of heartbreak his journey to the White House had been—was hardly finished with the courting of Sammy.

When gospel singer Mahalia Jackson died of a heart attack in Chicago on January 27, 1972, the White House, reaching Sammy in Las Vegas, where he was performing, asked him if he'd represent President Nixon at the funeral. Sammy immediately agreed—it was the president calling!—but told

In Black and White

the White House he'd have to be back in Las Vegas after the funeral to continue his engagement. The White House told Sammy they'd take care of all transportation.

Mahalia Jackson, born in New Orleans in 1911, was raised listening to Bessie Smith's blues and so-called sanctified music—music of the black church. Jackson's mother died when she was four years old, and Jackson moved to Chicago in 1927 to live with relatives. In Chicago she formed the Johnson Gospel Singers and became its featured soloist. She launched her gospel recording career in 1937 with Decca Records. More than two dozen albums would follow. In Chicago, radio show host Studs Terkel, wild about her voice, constantly played her music. She played before a Carnegie Hall audience in 1951; many were brought to tears. Many more trembled when she sang at the 1963 March on Washington, King nodding his head so reverently at the sound of her pretty voice.

In Chicago, where Jackson's funeral was held on February 1, at McCormick Place, Sammy—as befitting his status as President Nixon's representative—was seated between Mayor Daley and his wife. Thousands were in attendance. After the ceremony, Sammy was driven back to the private plane on which he'd flown to Chicago—compliments of the Nixon White House.

Early in her career, Mahalia Jackson had begun singing a song that always seemed special to her. She'd sing it time and time again in that full-throated voice of hers. The song was called "Sometimes I Feel Like a Motherless Child."

The images—of body bags, bamboo swinging in the Vietnam countryside, rice paddies and billowing smoke from bombs, TV reporters and their staccato voices trying to explain the conflict back into American homes, and more body bags—wouldn't go away. Nixon had come into office promising a secret plan to end the Vietnam War. But he was dealing with an emotional public, and he knew it. In November 1969—Nixon's first year in office—700,000 antiwar demonstrators had massed in the nation's capital. Two years later, war was still being waged in Southeast Asia. The Paris Peace Talks, orchestrated by Nixon and Secretary of State Henry Kissinger, had gotten under way, but without conclusive results. So the war, despite intermittent American troop withdrawals, droned on.

On May 4, at Kent State University, antiwar protesters torched the ROTC building. National Guard troops stormed the campus. Before they departed, they had killed four students, among them an ROTC cadet. The tragedy sparked wide protests on college campuses nationwide. Nixon agonized. One night he left the White House to go visit the Lincoln Memorial. He saw an assortment of demonstrators camping out, dressed in the eye-catching multicolored dress of the day. "I know that most of you think I'm an SOB," Nixon said, pumping flesh, "but I want you to know that I understand just how you feel." At one point Nixon talked of the gulf that existed between blacks and whites in America. The kids stared in bewilderment. Various mentions of the event would seep out to the media, all giving an indication of an incoherent Nixon.

Nixon's shrewd courting of Sammy continued. The president had another mission: he asked Sammy if he would go to Vietnam to entertain the soldiers. From Mahalia Jackson to 'Nam; Sammy nearly swooned from the request, and quickly accepted. "Wasn't a black cat important who ever went to Vietnam," he bragged rather strangely to Sy Marsh. (Actually, singer James Brown had already visited the troops.)

Putting together a traveling variety show was one of Sammy's gifts. His Vietnam-bound retinue included upward of two dozen, among them Shirley Rhodes, her husband, George, Altovise (she'd choreograph the shows), Sy Marsh, folk singer Lynn Kellogg, soul singer Blinky Williams, a gaggle of female dancers, and Timmie Rogers—Sammy's cohort from vaudeville. "Sammy," remembers Rogers, "said, 'Timmie, we're going to Vietnam. The reason I'm asking you is there ain't no money. Altovise and I are getting a hundred dollars a day and everybody else is getting twenty-five dollars a day.'"

Murphy, Sammy's assistant, was not included on the traveling list. Shirley Rhodes stood next to Sammy as he explained why: "It's too dangerous, Murphy. You can't go."

Sammy loved Murphy, and Murphy loved Sammy. But now Blackstone Ranger Sammy had a job to do. He had to get himself over to Vietnam.

Draw!

Draw!

Murphy begged Shirley to keep an eye on his Sammy.

They loaded up from the Ambassador Hotel in Los Angeles. "Went in an army transport plane," remembers Shirley Rhodes. "We had box lunches. It was awful. From there we went to Hawaii, then Guam, and on to Vietnam." Sammy looked jittery upon landing—but game, also. "We both were scared," remembers Altovise.

They roomed in a small house; dinner that first day was fried chicken. And the second and third days also: Shirley started feeling that the Vietnamese cooks thought black folk ate only fried chicken. "We stayed in a little Vietnamese house," Shirley says. "Sammy and Altovise on one side, George and I on the other."

In Danang the army built a stage and supplied Sammy with an army band. Sammy performed several shows before large groups of soldiers at a time. He sang and told jokes. He shrank back and watched Lynn Kellogg sing country tunes. He drenched himself in exhaustion. "He did extra-extra," says Altovise. He'd tear off his shirt, strut across the stage in his GI getup. He started doing the Black Power salute. He was with the brothers, in the jungle, in 'Nam; he was as black as they were now. Altovise served as mistress of ceremonies. The GIs ogled her. In hot pants, in Vietnam, on a stage before hundreds of soldiers, she was suddenly the star she had never been in the States. "Hey!" Sammy screamed at the soldiers at one site, "You gotta ease up on my wife. That ain't my old lady, that's my wife, man. Don't let me come out here and have to cut somebody."

Whoops of laughter from the GIs.

In the distance, at night, artillery could be heard. "You could hear bullets flying," remembers Shirley.

They performed at hospitals, rehab centers. Sometimes his audience numbered upward of ten thousand soldiers, waves of men on the ground, their legs crossed, faces upturned to Sammy.

In Long Binh, a UPI reporter trailed the troupe. "The relationship between black and white is better," Sammy told the reporter. "I saw some things yesterday I wish people could see at home. Like two cats standing around, one black and one white. These cats are talking and one lights the other's cigarette— because when they go out in the bush together they face the same thing."

Sammy, as usual, snapped hundreds of photos while walking down dusty roads with army personnel. He encouraged his hot-pants-wearing dancers to mingle with the troops. And they did. "They're very lonesome, and some of them have families that don't write," dancer Gigi Gamble confided to Sammy.

Sammy's mission was twofold: entertain the troops, but also check up on reports of drug abuse. Civil rights leaders back in America were complaining that a disproportionate number of black GIs were being singled out for punishment when caught using drugs. Sammy aimed to check up on the black soldiers. He went to a detoxification center.

"Motherfucker, w[hat] you doin' here?" a black GI asked him.

Sammy explained his mission, told them President Nixon had sent him, and they snorted. Back in America, Nixon had meant law and order to a lot of young blacks, the same young blacks in Vietnam.

The white GIs—just as their parents had done—guffawed at Sammy, slapping their knees, gazing. Many black GIs distrusted him. They read the Negro press; they knew Sammy's image. Several in the detox unit—never mind his marriage to Altovise—made loud noises about his marriage to May Britt. Sammy pleaded for understanding. But many rolled their eyes, complained to him about "the white man," about Nixon, about being hooked on dope. Standing next to Sammy, listening to him offer counsel against drug use, Sy Marsh, who knew of Sammy's own drug use, could hardly barely stifle a chuckle.

Some afternoons, rising in a helicopter—plenty of military protection for Sammy, on orders from the State Department—Sammy would arrive at a small camp with American GIs. As soon as the chopper landed, he'd hop out, wade into a group of soldiers, put out the cigarette, and just start strumming his guitar, just singing. He had a canteen on his belt loop. "See a kid, he'd sing a song," remembers Sy Marsh.

There were moments when Sammy would get lost in himself, in performing on dirt around some soldiers who'd rather be a million other places than Vietnam. He was a vaudevillian all over again. He'd work tirelessly to get smiles. And yet, there were times when he'd turn to Timmie Rogers and start wondering—in a fearful voice—if the Vietcong were going to sneak up on them at night.

Before Sammy left, he asked some of the soldiers if there was anything he could do for them. Someone answered it'd be nice if they could get some ice cream. Ice cream in the jungle. Ha ha.

There was little doubt, when the trip came to a close, that it all had thrilled Sammy. The cinema-loving cowboy versus Indian, good guy versus bad guy—Sammy.

When Sammy arrived back in America in March, he couldn't wait to tell friends about his experience in Vietnam. Madelyn Rhue, the actress, sat listening. He told her about the blacks and whites, about how they were bonding in the jungle, at war; he told her about the boys on dope; he told her about the songs he sang. And as he sat telling her, his eyes welled. "When he went to Vietnam, he came back and cried," she says. Some of the soldiers had given him phone numbers and pleaded with him to call their loved ones when he reached the States. He made as many calls as he could. Most of the parents didn't believe it was him; when they were convinced it really was, he'd deliver a greeting from their son or daughter.

He was invited back to the White House to give his report about his Vietnam trip. "I can't discuss too much about my findings there, but I've already made my report to the president," he said later, sounding like a member of the president's inner circle. "I made some promises to some people in Vietnam and I mean to keep them. We'd have rap sessions with no officers present—just enlisted personnel. I'd sit and talk with them and after an hour or so they felt there was a rapport, that I cared enough, and then they'd rap with me. They told me the good things and the bad. I wanted to find out because I wanted to come back knowledgeable."

A group of black Republicans had coaxed Sammy earlier, so at his meeting with Nixon, Sammy invited the president to a Washington dinner organized by those same black Republicans. Nixon shied from all-black events—even those staged by Republicans. He told Sammy he had to think about it. And when he surprisingly came, black Republicans, their heads swiveling in amazement, had to concede that Sammy had done something no black had ever been able to do: he had, in some strange, beguiling, unfathomable way, touched Richard Nixon. At the dinner, Sammy was introduced to Brigadier General Daniel "Chappie" James, the highest-ranking black in the armed forces. Sammy asked that powerful man—Altovise with him—if there was any way to get ice cream to the troops in Vietnam. James, long known as a severe man, looked strangely at Sammy.

Although Nixon performed behind the curtains, in the shadows—a fiend for secrecy—and Sammy operated out in the open—a fiend for the lights—one's genius sucked at the other's. They were both entertainers. Nixon understood power; power made Sammy vulnerable. Race confused Nixon, and caught Sammy in its web. Nixon needed Sammy's aura—the white Sammy—and Sammy welcomed Nixon's power to salve his insecurities—the black Sammy. In a way they were both homeless men, spirits set loose in the world. They had long proved themselves eternal searchers, hungrier than their demons. "He never learned where his home was," Henry Kissinger had once remarked of Nixon.

Nixon threw yet another bouquet to Sammy: a job promoting UNICEF. They were, Nixon and Sammy, entertaining each other. And when Nixon asked Sammy if he'd be willing to campaign for his reelection, again Sammy rushed out an answer.

It was such an honor; how could he say no; of course he would! He'd give a performance in a city, then go to some stalwart Republican's home—$500 a plate—and be waltzed around the home with his vaudeville grin. "There was no selling in campaigning for Nixon," as Sammy would recall. "I would simply attend Republican affairs. I'd be in a town and the man there would call and say, 'Sam, we're having a fund-raising cocktail party, will you come by?' 'Of course I will,' and I would go by . . . and socialize. Sometimes, it was 'Sam, will you sing a song?' 'Yes, of course.' "

Given that Sammy's relations with the Negro press were often prickly—and that Nixon's relations with blacks were acrimonious—one might have thought Sammy's budding alliance with Nixon might anger the owners of the Negro press. But hardly. The Negro press, while striking notes of advocacy journalism when it came to civil rights, had, since the days of Republican Abraham Lincoln, remained sentimental toward the Republican Party: it was the Republican Party that so often—and still—contributed generously to the advertising budgets of the Negro press barons.

Senator George McGovern of South Dakota was the front-runner for the

Democratic ticket. His task would be formidable: in some polls, Nixon was ahead of all Democratic challengers by at least twenty points. What Frank Sinatra had done for Kennedy, Sammy was now doing for Nixon. Spreading the gospel.

In the wee hours of the morning, on June 17, 1972, there was a break-in at the Democratic National Committee headquarters in Washington at the Watergate complex. The police arrested five men. Among the items confiscated from them were cameras, tear-gas guns, lock picks, and rolls of film. Given that it was an election year, the summertime story drew attention, and the *Washington Post* put it on the front page. The first words in an ocean of words to come.

The Democrats had a strange campaign season. McGovern—who Nixon charged was fostering an aura of "amnesty, acid and abortion"—had chosen Missouri senator Thomas Eagleton as his running mate. The revelation that Eagleton had once undergone shock treatments for depression alarmed many, and McGovern was forced to drop him in favor of Kennedy in-law Sargent Shriver. The Republicans prepared for their Miami Beach nominating convention as if it were a mere formality before four more years in the White House. Nixon's lead in the polls remained in the double digits. The war in Vietnam, as Nixon had promised, was ending.

Sammy's "Candy Man" was still humming on the airwaves. It yielded him, in 1972, his first gold record. After all those years, all those recording sessions. Sammy and Sy Marsh were both overwhelmed.

Mike Curb had intriguing musical tastes, and, as the son of an FBI agent, a political affiliation that was hardly surprising: he was a devoted Republican. The White House knew the name Mike Curb, and it was the White House on the telephone. "Nixon, the president, called me and said his favorite record was 'Candy Man,'" recalls Curb. "He asked me if Sammy and the Curb Congregation would perform in Miami at the Republican convention. I said, 'My group will perform. I don't manage Sammy. Sy Marsh does.'" But before he hung up the phone, Curb told President Nixon that his record company was thinking of a suitable venue to present Sammy with his gold record. Curb mentioned that Miami Beach, during the convention, might be a possibility, then he asked the president if he'd phone Sammy and invite him down. "[Nixon] said, 'I'd love to do that. I love Sammy Davis, Jr.'"

The Republicans booked Sammy into a suite at the Playboy Hotel in Miami. He flew in on an oil company's private jet. The business moguls arrived like geese. And on the second day of the convention, Sammy was seated not just

A camera's click, and a click heard around the world. Both men held demons, and those demons washed over each other in 1972 when Sammy was wooed and won over by President Nixon. Sammy failed to understand blacks' distrust of Nixon's ultraconservative views. The hug at the Republican National Convention, in the glare of the nation's spotlight, seemed too close to minstrelsy. It seemed to stun large segments of the public. To blacks, it seemed like something out of an Al Jolson scrapbook. The price for Sammy was dear. As for Nixon, the bulb of Watergate would be in high wattage soon enough. (ASSOCIATED PRESS)

anywhere, but in the private Nixon family box, with Edward Cox and his wife, Tricia, the president's daughter; Tricia's sister, Julie, and her husband, Lt. David Eisenhower; and First Lady Pat Nixon herself. Sammy Davis, Jr., in a plaid tailor-made suit, white shirt, and dotted tie, his lapels festooned with buttons ("I'm from Montana," "Try a Virgin"), a cigarette in his hand, two jeweled rings on each hand, sat with the whitest family in America. This was better than being Harry Belafonte or Sidney Poitier. This was power. This was salve for the hurt from the Kennedys. This was better than hamming it up with Frank and Dean. Hell, this was power and entertainment—the elixir that made color vanish!

Two nights later the Republican delegates—with whoops and cries—nominated President Nixon for reelection. Afterward, he made his way over to the Republican Youth Rally, where Sammy was performing, was sweating, was singing, was joking. He was in a shirt, opened to a naked chest and tied at the waist, and thin pants with X's as belt loops: it looked like an outfit a Spanish bullfighter might wear. When Nixon came into view, with his phalanx of Secret Service men, amid shouts of FOUR MORE YEARS! FOUR MORE YEARS! Sammy knew exactly what to do. He'd been in show business all his life. He quieted the crowd. Then: "Ladies and gentlemen, young voters, the president of the United States." And they went wild. Nixon was grinning. It was his night. And Sammy, at the other end of the stage, crouched a bit, then leaped over to Nixon and clasped him. It was all so beautifully vaudeville, Sammy suddenly upon the president, a touchy-touchy hug. Why, the public had rarely seen Nixon in such an embrace with his own wife! And Nixon, letting loose with a slow widening grin, towering over Sammy, wrapping his arms across his own chest so awkwardly and yet tenderly like some flushed teenage kid; and all those white delegates and all those Nixon placards and Sammy leaning on the president's shoulder as if Nixon were kin, family. And who knew how far they went back—to the days of wine and roses and Jules Podell's Copacabana nightclub!

Nixon and Sammy, in full embrace: the camera flashes blinked with the furiousness of a movie premiere.

Freeze the frame.

Imagine a vaudeville kid—the young Sammy, who used to be required to carry a pass to stroll segregated Miami Beach when he and his father and Will Mastin were performing—who had broken his way into Ciro's, into television, onto Broadway, into Las Vegas; who had been booed by the southern Democrats at the Kennedy convention in Los Angeles in 1960; who wished only to be loved; who had the strange and beguiling ability to wipe the emotions of black America out of his psyche; who had touched this most impersonal of presidents, made him smile and laugh as he was now doing. Now imagine that kid on a stage with the most powerful man in the whole wide world!

Imagine: the wide hard grins of two survivors—Nixon and Sammy—both with their Kennedy-inflicted pain lodged inside them like a switchblade.

When Nixon finally got around to talking—"Sammy, I want to apologize for interrupting your performance . . ."—he had a little remembrance he wished to share with the audience:

> I have a cute story to tell the people, if I may. Years ago, when I was a senator in California, I came to New York. Sammy was appearing at the Copa. It was winter and snow was around the block. The limo dropped me off. I said, "I'm Senator Nixon and I was wondering if there's a chance to see Sammy." They said, "There's not a seat in the house." I said, "Is there any way for me to get a message to Sammy Davis?" Just then, one of the guys got ahold of Sammy, said Senator Nixon's out there, he can't get in. Sammy got ahold of the owner of the Copa and said, "Senator Nixon and his wife are out there. I know there are no seats. Put them at my table." And Sammy, you performed. It was an evening I'll never forget. I want you to know you're still the greatest.

The audience howled and whooped and hollered. And Nixon was hardly finished. The shouts seemed to have unleashed something in him. He talked of Sammy's critics, the ones who, Nixon said, felt Sammy had "sold out" for supporting his presidency. "Well, let me give you the answer: You aren't going to buy Sammy Davis, Jr., by inviting him to the White House." Sammy seemed to melt.

More camera flashes blinked into the night, Mike Curb smiled on the bandstand, and how many in the crowd believed that this—Nixon and Sammy—must be but black America's approval of Nixon?

Sammy knew well the staying power of a photograph. Within a day, a fortnight, the photo—of Sammy and Nixon, of the embrace—was popping up everywhere: in the Negro press, in the white press, even in the Jewish press. The photograph, taking on its own life, became fixed in the populace's mind like some kind of cultural ornament.

Television, particularly when tied to a political convention, sent out a powerful message. One of Nixon's campaign vows was to keep up his attack on busing—to stop the effort being made to get black children into decent school districts. His antibusing crusade had been adopted by Alabama governor George Wallace and a host of other segregationists. So in the span of six months—the February 19 airing of *All in the Family* and the Republican convention in August—Sammy had aligned himself with both Archie Bunker, a symbol of everyman-as-bigot, and Richard Nixon. Who could forget those Supreme Court nominees?

So many wonderful, frozen moments to be captured by the camera's flash: Sammy in the White House; Sammy in 'Nam for the president; Sammy and Archie; Sammy at the riotous GOP event—his eye dreamily cascading over all those states' righter conventioneers! Every time he had entered the convention hall there was rising applause, and whispering, and pointing, and the turning of heads—because if Sammy was good enough for their law-and-order nominee, for their antibusing nominee to undo what LBJ had done, and that was to march the federal government right into their lives—then, by God, why weren't other blacks beginning to understand the virtues of Nixon?

Sammy kissed Archie Bunker. He hugged Richard Nixon. All in front of tens of millions of people!

"Isn't that a hell of a thing," Nixon would say at one point in his life, "that the fate of a great country can depend on camera angles."

The Republicans' unofficial envoys to Hollywood were Donald Rumsfeld, an aide to Nixon, and his wife, Joyce. After the Miami Beach convention, Sammy invited the Rumsfelds back to Las Vegas with him. And there they all were, sitting around the pool, whacking at tennis balls. While in Vegas, Sammy took the Republican couple over to the Hilton to meet Elvis Presley. Donald Rumsfeld thought there was something "weird" about the way Elvis smiled. Leaving the Hilton, out of earshot of Presley and his entourage, Sammy began mimicking the King—the hip-swiveling, the accent. Joyce Rumsfeld howled.

"What are we going to do with you, Sammy?" she said.

"Well," Sammy answered—in just the right, prideful, Republican tone—"you're stuck with me for the next four years."

Ann Slider kept opening the mail in Sammy's office. And, in the aftermath of the GOP convention, it was brutal. It quickly unnerved her. The volume of mail was so heavy that she hid some of the stacks, lest Sammy stumble upon them. "A ton of it" came in, Slider says. "Calling him 'nigger,' 'Uncle Tom.' " She told Sy Marsh. "Sy said, 'We can't tell him.' I said, 'He could get killed.' " As the days passed—more mail, more hateful phone calls, all because of that moment, that photo, Nixon and Sammy—Slider became defensive, even protective of Sammy. She blamed Curb and his associates: "They used him, and I blame Sy for letting them use him." The mail kept coming, faster, even nastier. Slider had no choice but to alert the authorities about the death threats.

Sammy would tell interviewers that the president's programs were good for blacks. Blacks were aghast. The Negro press seemed slightly tickled at Sammy's predicament—blowing the picture up as if it were some kind of irreversible coronation. Eartha Kitt found herself on a plane with Sammy. She wanted to have words with him, but not on the plane, not to cause a commotion. Kitt was on Nixon's infamous enemies list, along with Gregory Peck, Bill Cosby, Jane Fonda, Dick Gregory, Edward Kennedy, Paul Newman, Steve McQueen, and many, many others. They were Democrats, and they were liberal, and they opposed both Nixon and the Vietnam War. Those on the list were often subjected to audits by the IRS. As soon as the plane landed, Kitt marched right over to Sammy.

"I said, 'Why? Why?' " she remembers of the first words to blurt from her mouth. "I said, 'So, did you have to kiss him?' "

Sammy was befuddled, searching for words as airport strollers gawked at the two celebrities. Kitt pressed on; she was livid; her voice kept rising. And it only rose more when Sammy tried to tell her that Nixon cared about blacks. Then she stormed off.

Sy Marsh had a public relations fiasco on his hands, and he knew it. "Black people would be in the elevator with us, and they'd turn their heads."

Julian Bond, a member of the Georgia House of Representatives and an ardent opponent of the war, referred to Sammy's endorsement of Nixon as "unbelievable, an irrational act."

Amy Greene, Sammy's friend for three decades now, was livid about the Sammy-Nixon alliance. "I loathed Richard Nixon," she says. "I didn't speak to [Sammy] for nine months. He'd call, and I'd say, 'I'm not going to talk to you until I get over this.' "

Ann Slider cried.

Madelyn Rhue hurt for him but kept quiet. "I never said anything to him about it," she says of the Nixon imbroglio. "But he got phone calls and he'd say, 'That's not what I meant! I meant love, peace, and togetherness.' "

Shirley Rhodes became defensive, wondering just what Sammy owed to blacks. "Blacks didn't support Sammy. White America made him."

Sammy grew ever more fearful. At one time having lived in mortal fear of white southern bigots, he now worried about black militants. Having once told Alex Haley he felt "trapped in black," Sammy now faced a different conundrum: trapped in Nixon.

In Atlantic City, Elvera argued with customers who berated her son for his support of the president. "You would have thought Sammy was the only black to support Nixon," she would say.

Nixon's appointment of Sammy to the UNICEF board came in handy. It got Sammy out of America and to Europe, where he gave concerts and promoted UNICEF for several weeks before returning stateside.

Flying was still considered a rather luxurious way to travel, and Sammy never saw a lot of black air travelers in the 1960s and early 1970s. He did see plenty of black bellhops. They'd rush and slap his back, shake his hand: *Hey Sammy! Brother Sammy! Sammaaayyy!* Only now they were not doing that anymore. They were ignoring him, as were the few black travelers he did see. Maybe it was Nixon. Maybe it was Archie Bunker. Maybe it was the frozen camera image of him and May Britt. Maybe it was all of it combined. Mostly, it was Nixon.

Sy Marsh contacted Jesse Jackson.

Ever since King's death, Jackson had been rising as a black leader. He was coltish and young in 1968 when the bullets took King. He was also brash, and with a galaxy of civil rights leaders—Whitney Young, Roy Wilkins, A. Philip Randolph—showing telltale signs of age, Jackson galloped into the spotlight. He played the role of hearty nemesis to Chicago mayor Richard Daley, then saw fit to anoint himself troubleshooter across urban America, wading into confrontations, quelling riots. With his large bobbing Afro—and, often, his leather jacket, with a medallion bouncing upon his chest—he had the insouciance of a soul singer looking for a stage. An older generation was respectful of his presence because of his links to King, even if some members of King's camp thought him too hungry for media attention. He had marched, he had been there when the bullets came, and he could preach—an important source of pride to Southerners. Jackson's sermons had the lilt of both poet and rebel. From his base in Chicago, he often depended on celebrities—Ossie Davis, Bill Cosby, Roberta Flack, B. B. King, Sammy—to fund his operations and ventures. With Sammy having given Jackson's Operation PUSH plenty of money in the past, a desperate Sy Marsh told Jackson that Sammy really needed help. He needed a way out of the Nixon mess. "Jesse said, 'If you can come up with $25,000 for my charity, then [have Sammy] come to Chicago.' "

There was one problem: Sammy didn't have $25,000 in his account.

"I had to borrow the money from Vegas," says Marsh.

With Jesse's money in hand, Sammy, a few of his musicians, Altovise, and Sy Marsh headed east. Sammy would perform. He'd kill Jesse's people—the brothers and the sisters—with kindness. And once he was performing, they'd like him; they'd understand about politics and entertainment.

There were seven thousand on hand at the PUSH convention. Some had attended the Democratic convention at Miami Beach with Jesse—carrying their placards, pushing for a more open party plank. They were eager and energized, vowing to march against any more cuts Nixon was proposing in his domestic budget that might affect the poor and the disenfranchised. Sy Marsh slipped Jesse the check for twenty-five grand backstage. And then there was Jesse. To see him onstage, before his people, was like seeing a minister before a large and swaying congregation. A decade earlier he was participating in student sit-ins at the Woolworth's in Greensboro, North Carolina. Who knew then how history would arc itself? King down; freedom ringing; Jesse rising. He raised the microphone to his mouth: "Ladies and gentlemen, I have a surprise. Brother Sammy Davis is here." Jesse motioned for Sammy with a raise of the arm. Sammy strode out into a sea of black faces in their Afros, many wearing their dashikis. Democrats, to be sure, although there were some third-party dreamers. Brother Sammy now among them.

"Sammy walks out," recalls Sy Marsh, "and they booed him. Sammy is in a state of shock."

Sammy swung his head from side to side of the building, looking for the boos, the anger, the one eye like a laser beam. "It struck me as with physical force, knocking the wind out of me," Sammy would recall. "It grew louder." Jesse seemed momentarily startled. He quickly flung his arm around Sammy—like a big bear protecting a threatened cub. Jesse's ferocious grip was so full of on-the-spot love it seemed to weaken Sammy. He seemed to be shrinking inside his denim jacket. The boos and catcalls rained on. "Brothers," Jackson said, waving his arm upward for quiet, "if it wasn't for people like Sammy Davis you wouldn't be here, we wouldn't have PUSH today. Now, I expected some foolish people were going to react like this because the man hugged the president of the United States. So what? Look at what this gigantic little man has committed himself to over all these years."

As the boos erupted anew, Jackson realized he had underestimated the anger. Sammy's body began twisting. He wanted to bolt. Jesse could feel his angst, and only held Sammy tighter. Then he told Sammy to sing something, and suggested Sammy sing "I've Gotta Be Me." Given the surroundings, the circumstances, it was a request both funny and meaningful—and nearly Freudian. Sammy had no time to ponder the meaning; he simply began singing. Words caught in his throat; there was snickering. Sy Marsh felt terrible. "Sammy sang a song, came off, said, 'Fuck 'em. They don't want me. I don't want them.' He got blind drunk that night, and cried."

The wounds could not but take their toll. Sammy could use a friend. He need look no farther than the White House, where President Nixon again reached out for him. In for a dollar, in for a president. On March 3, Sammy gave a one-man performance at the White House. It was what President Nixon and the first lady billed as one of their "Evenings of Entertainment." Nixon beamed and tapped his wing-tipped feet; tuxedoed Sammy sang and gyrated onstage. Members of the cabinet and Senate were in attendance, as well as the *Apollo 17* astronauts and their families. Among Sammy's musical offerings were, of course, "Candy Man," "Mr. Bojangles"—a tender ode about a vaudevillian who loses everything at the end of his life—and "I've Gotta Be Me," which Sammy was now singing as a kind of personal anthem. He didn't care about Jesse and his cohorts now; Sammy was grooving in the White House. There was dancing afterward. Sammy—who could, in a mimic's flash, become an English dandy—squired Pat Nixon across the dance floor as Shirley and George Rhodes beamed. From all those years on the vaudeville circuit, it had come to this moment. Sammy knew it was special: "This is about as far uptown as I'm ever going to get," he had quipped before beginning his performance.

Later that night Nixon gave Sammy and Altovise a tour of the White House, pointing out art and artifacts. If only his enemies, black and white, could see him now. Then the Davises prepared for their overnight in the Lincoln Bedroom. They cackled together. In the middle of the night, Sammy became hungry and tiptoed to the kitchen. He saw some blacks, made eye contact with one. "Brother," he said, "can I have me a little sandwich upstairs?" There was a nod yes, but no conversation. Just a black butler moving about, carving up some pieces of a Virginia ham. Now why would a black man not wish to make idle chatter with the great Sammy Davis, Jr.? Let them all snicker. He was nibbling on good country ham in the Lincoln Bedroom.

Thirteen days after Sammy's performance at the White House, on March 16, the Senate began its televised Watergate hearings. They were presided over by North Carolina senator Sam Ervin, a courtly bulldog of a Democrat.

Nixon's courting of Sammy had proved to be shrewd—and methodical. On May 25, Nixon had Sammy back to the White House, this time with Bob Hope, to entertain returning POWs. This time Nixon hugged Sammy, two grinning men—both in obvious pain, however—captured by the camera's flash.

In July came testimony that Nixon secretly taped White House conversations.

In October, Nixon fired Archibald Cox, the Watergate special prosecutor. Elliot Richardson, the attorney general, and William Ruckelshaus, his deputy, abruptly quit over the firing. The dragon of Watergate was fully loose now, and the end of Nixon's presidency irreversible.

Richard Nixon had no curiosity about blacks or ethnic minorities in America. The domestic populace—be they young, long-haired, or black—rattled him. Jews frightened him, sending his paranoia into dark, shameful quarters. (His White House recordings are full of anti-Semitic as well as homophobic rantings.) But the movies and make-believe thrilled him. "Despite all the polls and all the rest, I think there are still a hell of a lot of people out there, and from what I've seen they're—you know, they, they want to believe, that's the point, isn't it?" Nixon asked an aide in the spring of 1973. Nixon wanted to believe that Sammy was black America: If Sammy could make it, then why all the black poverty? Why so many blacks hemmed into inferior housing? Why the drumbeat of complaints from the ghetto? Sammy became Nixon's envoy to a world Nixon did not understand. Inasmuch as Sammy himself had been fairly new to the rhythms of black America, it was a choice both curious and comedic. (In the White House one afternoon, Sammy took it upon himself to explain to Nixon how the word "colored" had changed to "Negro," which had now changed to "black.")

The closer Nixon got to Sammy, the more apparent it became he did not understand the entertainer at all. "You aren't going to buy Sammy Davis, Jr., by inviting him to the White House," Nixon had said in Miami Beach. But Nixon was wrong: you could buy Sammy. Not in a vicious or completely immoral manner—not, say, in the manner Nixon would seek to buy off Watergate conspirators. But if you *could* get to the soft spot in Sammy's heart—insecurity—and linger there, shadowing him with threat (Sinatra) or power (Nixon), then his heartstrings would race to his head, leading him to dangerous and sentimental conclusions that had little to do with reason. And those conclusions—he was being loved!—set him up to be bought. Nixon and Sammy played against each other's torments. With Watergate draping all around him, Nixon needed friends. He sulked along the corridors of the White House, many nights alone. But then, there, within reach—within a camera's flash—was his old Copa pal, Sammy. Webbed between black and white, Sammy reached in desperate romantic directions—Judaism in the mid-'50s, Black Power in the mid-'60s, Nixon now—to stabilize his insecurities. It was the quick thinking of a stage veteran, the light of survival.

But this particular light was quickly turning black, with all the meanings inherent in that word—that one word that was so frightening and confusing to Sammy.

Chapter 17

ODE TO THE VAUDEVILLIAN

The constant and shrill voice of blacks deriding Sammy for his support of Nixon was one thing. The Watergate prosecutors were quite another. The evidence was astonishing; "high crimes and misdemeanors" had taken place. Nixon held on in the early summer months of 1974. The cartoonists had a high good time. There was one cartoon in the form of a "Ten Most Wanted" poster—Nixon's face in all ten frames. On August 8, 1974, the thirty-seventh president of the United States announced his resignation. The next morning he helicoptered away from the White House lawn, his arm awkwardly waving a farewell.

Those who had shuttled past Sammy earlier with bewildering looks on their faces—as if they were right on the lip of a cutting comment about him and Nixon—now were nervy enough to bring their questions out into the open. An autograph-seeker coming his way? Not exactly—just another Nixon-hater. Sammy squinted the one eye, and looked for his able assistant Murphy to drag him away from the inquisitor. But time after time he was corralled, and quizzed. "The flak got so hot at one stage," Sammy would come to recall, "I think I was pretty close to a nervous breakdown."

The truth is that not since President Theodore Roosevelt had invited Booker T. Washington to the White House on the evening of October 16, 1901, had a president and a black man been so entangled and talked about in a slice of national discourse. History, however, had now turned over on itself: in 1901, Roosevelt was pilloried for the invitation to Washington, as evidenced by a dispatch in the *Memphis Scimitar:*

> It is only recently that President Roosevelt boasted that his mother was a Southern woman, and that he is half Southern by reason of that fact. By inviting a nigger to his table he pays his mother small duty. . . . No South-

ern woman with a proper self-respect would now accept an invitation to the White House, nor would President Roosevelt be welcomed today in Southern homes. He has not inflamed the anger of the Southern people; he has excited their disgust.

Seventy-one years later it was the guest himself—Sammy Davis, Jr.—who was being assailed.

With the vanishing of Nixon, Sammy decided it best to dust his hands of Republicans. Four more years of Republicans, he had gleefully told the Rumsfelds! Ha ha ha! Not anymore. Back to the Democratic fold! He began bragging up Senator Edward M. Kennedy for the next presidential sweepstakes.

The world was changing—again—and Sammy could see it and feel it. "Fucking youth freaks," is how he derisively referred to the kids in the streets. He turned fifty on December 8, 1975. Where did all those yesterdays go?

For his fiftieth birthday, Altovise threw a party. Everyone had to come in costume—children's costumes. Tina Sinatra, Frank's daughter, came with Wes Craven, a young screenwriter and aspiring film director. They were both in blackface, and wearing wigs. Sammy stamped his feet and laughed out loud. (Sammy was costumed in a pair of children's pajamas.) Late into the evening, the birthday celebrant wanted to treat everyone to a movie, and so they all settled down and watched a porn flick, glancing back and forth between the screen and the star of the movie, who sat among them.

Sammy rarely saw his own kids. Seeing his friends dressed in children's costumes at the party only made him feel older. He started drinking more. He began playing more golf. So many contradictions.

Two years earlier he had lent his name to a golf tournament in Hartford, Connecticut. It was now known as the Sammy Davis, Jr., Greater Hartford Open. Golf was just another stage and microphone. But it was a shrewd stage: middle America and rich America—white America—played golf, lots of it. Sammy danced around the course like an elastic gnome, swinging a gold-plated club at balls, bending over in laughter, his wrist jewelry glinting. He was making history again—the first black to have corporate sponsorship of his own golf tournament. But after Nixon, not a lot of blacks were mindful of Sammy's history-making ventures.

"Sammy and I played together," Jack Carter recalls of an outing at Sammy's tournament. "When we got to the eighteenth hole, a mob [of people] was around. I took the golf bag off my cart. We picked up Sammy and put him in the bag. The crowd was screaming. We took him over to Frank, in the bag. The crowd screamed [for] three hours."

In the end—poof—Sammy decided it best to be in the company of those so-called youth freaks. The wave of youth, of everything young, was so colossal, and he had no intention of being left behind. He sought out new friends, and these new friends were far younger than himself. Many were actors and actresses—only they acted in various stages of undress. Sammy had become fascinated with the world of porn. He instructed Ann Slider, his office assistant, to keep a Rolodex of the studios in town that specialized in making porn films. She'd call from the office—her voice pitched low—and they'd send their latest movies for Sammy to view. At home, Rudy, the valet, would set up the projector. And then Sammy, Altovise, and friends would loll on the couch, the naked bodies bouncing onscreen, Sammy studying them like a scientist looking at molecules. Once things had seized him—gadgets, Sinatra in his youth, tap dancing, now pornography—he grabbed ahold of them fiercely until they adequately spent his sense of wonder and curiosity.

In 1972, an X-rated movie titled *Deep Throat* was released. (*Washington Post* reporters Carl Bernstein and Bob Woodward used the movie title to identify their unknown source who helped them crack the Watergate scandal, insuring that "Deep Throat" would enter the vernacular beyond the world of film.) The movie quickly became a kind of sneering classic. Its freckle-faced female lead, Linda Lovelace—Bronx-born, and the daughter of a policeman—possessed alarming skills at fellatio, a man's organ wholly disappearing inside her mouth. Because she did not gag, the act seemed something akin to magic. "How does she do it?" no less an authority than Vincent Canby of the *New York Times* wondered. "The film has less to do with the manifold pleasure of sex than with physical engineering."

The place to see porn in Hollywood—and Sammy wanted to see *Deep Throat* on the large screen—was the Pussycat Theatre, over on Santa Monica Boulevard. He would not, of course, enter the theater with the flick showing. The autograph hounds! So to watch *Deep Throat* he rented the place out, and, along with Altovise, accompanied a gaggle of friends. The movie enthralled Sammy, so much so that he got in contact with its star and invited her to his home, first for his fiftieth birthday party—she was the porn star in attendance that night—then on many other occasions. It wasn't long before Lovelace—with Altovise's approval—was sharing a bed with Sammy. Nights at the house became fun-filled hours of bacchanalia. Little Sammy, the onetime critic of the wild youth movement, now one of its captains. "And I liked it," he would come to confess, "having everyone thinking that there wasn't a porn star on the screen that I hadn't partied with or didn't know—clutching on for dear life to the image of swinger."

John Souza, working security for Sammy, would sometimes wheel the limousine right up to the Palomino Club—a strip club in Las Vegas—and park it. He and Sammy would stride inside and take seats at a table. "We'd come back with six girls," remembers Souza. "First thing out of his mouth was, 'Watch the jewelry.' He said to me, 'Pick one of these broads.' I said, 'I'm not interested, Sammy.' I was married."

When a night of revelry was about to turn a corner, into the arena of debauchery and naked bodies, Sammy would nod to the innocents that it was high time for them to leave. "Whenever there was that kind of thing, I wasn't allowed to remain in the house," says actress Madelyn Rhue. "Sammy always looked out for me."

He invited porn stars to his own shows—free admission; a seat at Sammy's table!—and they came, trailing him around Los Angeles, all the way to Las Vegas, hitching themselves to his entourage. A gaggle of young whites— the porn world was overwhelmingly white—in Nehru suits and polyester. Their unashamed freedom excited Sammy. He was swinging, and swinging maniacally.

"He loved strip shows," says Molly Marsh, Sy's wife. "He would send champagne backstage."

Champagne in their blood, the strippers would soon be at Sammy's Beverly Hills home. Everyone would bundle into the Rolls. Strippers in the Rolls, and life was a gas.

He'd tell the comely porn stars that they had met in another life—Sammy believed in reincarnation—and when they would look at him quizzically, completely bewildered, he'd change tactics, telling them they would meet in the afterlife! With the porn stars, Brontë's Heathcliff was out; references to mysticism and the occult were in. Dexterity had served him well all his life. Sammy told Linda Lovelace he'd manage her career. "Linda Lovelace would come over," recalls Souza. "Her husband would be sitting downstairs, and she'd be up in the bedroom with Sammy."

"Sammy never asked me much about my past, about my growing up, but that would have seemed as ordinary to him as it does to me," Lovelace would write in *Ordeal,* her honestly titled autobiography. "He was interested in now, in what I was doing with my career at the moment. For a time he seemed intrigued by the thought of my becoming part of his show, but that never came about. He did suggest that I put together a big Las Vegas act."

Sammy's aides smirked and laughed coldly, but Sammy was sincere in his sentiments. He could see it: Linda Lovelace onstage, in Las Vegas. Sprung from a world of vaudeville, he imagined most things possible. He could remember as a child seeing fire-eaters and cyclists upon the stage. Sammy contacted Frances Davis, who had appeared in his taped—but aborted—television series back in the 1950s, and asked her to teach the porn star the rudiments of acting, of stage presentation—everything! "He wanted to get something going for her, but she didn't have any talent," remembers Frances, who took Sammy's assignment seriously. She began with voice, then went on to movement, followed by dance lessons.

Ha ha ha. Linda Lovelace needing pelvic movements? Lovelace finally just stopped showing up for classes.

Never mind. Sammy gave her gifts—gold jewelry, trinkets—whatever he whimsically grabbed from yet another jewelry store. Lovelace respected Sammy, not just his generosity, but his morals: "He had his own code of marital fidelity—he explained to me that he could do anything except have normal intercourse because that, the act of making love, would be cheating on his wife. What he wanted me to do, then, was to deep-throat him. Because that would not be an act of infidelity."

Sammy was never ashamed of his pursuits, and least of all his acquaintances. "We're out to dinner at an Italian restaurant," recalls Ann Slider. "This woman comes in. Sammy introduces her. All of a sudden it dawns on me: 'You're Linda Lovelace!' " Laughter all around. "Okay, Ann," Sammy broke in, "that's why we don't take you anywhere."

The kids—the youth—seemed so energetic. And sometimes he'd get tired. But he had to keep going. And to keep going he began snorting cocaine. It boosted his energy levels. The candy man was now into the white candy.

Jack and Roxanne Carter—longtime friends—went by the house one evening. They were a witty and charming couple. The door opened, then the door closed. They decided not to enter. "He had heavy-metal-music people over," says Carter.

Sometimes, for days on end, Sammy would disappear, over to Palm Springs, up to San Francisco, somewhere, anywhere, snorting coke, drinking, stretching out a childhood. When he returned once from San Francisco, there was talk of devil worship, the occult. (Both Sammy and Murphy believed in ghosts, and they often—after oh-so-many sips of bourbon—would discuss visions, wispy configurations they swore they had seen in the dark, scurrying down hallways. In his spare time, Murphy walked through cemeteries, and showed up at the funerals of complete strangers.) Sammy began inviting the devil-worshipers to the house, giddily questioning them about their beliefs. Clothes were shed, candles lit, days and nights hazily drifted by. He painted his nails red. The world was suddenly a space odyssey. Why, the entire world had caught up to his world of vaudeville! "I remember one day at the house, those devil-worshipers came," says Madelyn Rhue. "Altovise and I left and went to the Beverly Wilshire Hotel."

Fear gripped the entourage. Might Sammy accidentally kill himself? Such an event would never happen on purpose, for, as all knew, he loved himself far too much. But there was no denying that devil-worshipers were in the California hills. Shirley Rhodes adopted an attitude: "It's better to just wait it out."

Sammy emerged like a woozy child from a briar patch. And when he did, Sy Marsh, now his manager, as Sammy had convinced Marsh to work exclusively for him, was waiting. There were bills, and more bills. Bills for the lobsters for the parties that Sammy couldn't quite remember had taken place. Construction bills for the new additions to the property. Jewelry bills from Cartier and Dunhill and fancy Parisian stores. Sometimes Shirley could do little but howl at the shopping sprees. George once had an itch for a slot machine. No one, however, could purchase a slot machine. "One day the door rings and there's a slot machine," recalls Shirley. "It was against the law to own them. Sammy bribed someone."

He had a line of credit with Sy Devore, his personal tailor.

He had a line of credit at Gucci.

John Souza, Sammy's security man, had a dog, and the dog died. Souza was crestfallen. To help ease the pain, Sammy gave him a gift, a Gucci watch: "To my main man John," it said on the back.

"We'd go into Gucci, here in Beverly Hills," remembers Sy Marsh. "Sammy sees a black leather couch. He says, 'Damn, look at that couch. I'd like to buy that! Get me the manager.' [The manager says] 'It's not for sale, Mr. Davis.' Sammy said, 'Call Mr. Gucci, tell him I want to buy the couch.' They call Emilio Gucci. Gucci, in Italy, says, 'If Sammy Davis, Jr., wants to buy the couch, sell it to him.' Sammy then said, 'I want to be liberal. You got a white couch?' "

The couches—one black, one white—sat in his sunken living room. Guests commented exuberantly about them. Sammy would grin: Gucci, baby. Gucci.

Money grew on trees. Sy Marsh told Sammy the trees were getting bare. There were tax bills.

Having come up in the world of vaudeville—the pay often given in cash, in brown envelopes—Sammy continued to see money as a mere game, and he had been playing and winning at the game for so long. There was always a place to get money to stay in the game—nightclub owners, other entertainers; money flying from one pocket was simply replaced by the money coming into another pocket. He had money in his alligator briefcase—tens and twenties, hundred-dollar bills.

"More champagne!" Sy Marsh recalls Sammy hollering as the strippers would cavort around the house.

Sammy would throw the strippers hundred-dollar bills. It was just money, and it grew inside vaudeville dreams, and on the stages of Las Vegas, and in the hushed backrooms of the Copa, and beneath the roof of Bill Miller's Riviera. It grew in the pockets of Broadway producers. It grew in the dirt that lay over the graves of Bert Williams and Bill "Bojangles" Robinson. It grew in the shadowy eyes of nightclub owner Skinny D'Amato: Need anything?

When Liza Minnelli married Jack Haley, Jr., in 1974—two children of Holly-

wood celebrity, such a sweet boon to Sammy's sense of tinseltown history!—
Sammy gave them a little gift. It was $25,000.

Twenty-five Gs.

It was just money.

He'd whistle while being driven in and out of Nevada. The desert was so open,
and the owners took care of him in Lake Tahoe, in Reno, in Vegas. Plenty of
casino owners were Republicans. Republicans were businessmen, and hadn't
they seen him on TV, hugging Nixon?

He changed his shows. He used to close with the song "I've Gotta Be Me."
But now he was closing them with remembrances of a ghost.

Record producer Mike Curb had not disappointed Sammy in his vow to
make it possible for him to record "Mr. Bojangles."

Because of its title, there were those who thought the song a tribute to Bill
Robinson, the famed tap dancer who died in 1949. In reality, the only connection was to the Robinson nickname—Bojangles—which was a nickname
many street-corner performers were prone to adopt. Robinson himself, while
having been a vaudevillian, died with money. He lived his life in high hat and
tails; once he had made it, he never fell from grace. The "Mr. Bojangles" of the
song Sammy was now singing had something of the Will Mastin in him, something of the Sammy Davis, Sr., in him—and it circled Sammy like a sky full of
memory.

The song was written by Jerry Jeff Walker, a young songwriter who had a
fetching way with a lyric. Walker left his New York home in 1959, a seventeen-
year-old on the doorstep of the '60s—and roamed the country in a cowboy
hat. He had a guitar. He performed in minstrel shows—they were more like
county fairs. Road musicians, with their vagabond nature, would sometimes
find themselves in jail, and it was in jail in New Orleans that Jerry Jeff Walker
met a man who had once performed on the streets. The image of the man
stuck with Walker, who wrote a song about him and called it "Mr. Bojangles."
In 1968, he got it recorded while taping a radio show in New York City on
WBAI-FM. It was a sweet, plaintive tune about a vaudevillian. It really caught
on in 1971 when it was recorded by the Nitty Gritty Dirt Band, a group of Tex-
ans in straw hats who sang hip country music.

The narrator of the song rhapsodized about having met Mr. Bojangles in
that cell in New Orleans:

> *He looked to me to be the very eyes of age as he spoke right out*
> *He talked of life, Lord he talked of life*
> *ha ha ha . . .*

Bojangles was a hoofer in ragged clothes. He confessed to drinking—"I drinks a bit"—and being reduced to singing for bar tips.

> *He laughed and slapped his leg, he said his name was Bojangles*
> *And he danced a lick right across the cell . . .*

Sammy sang it with studied precision, whistling at the beginning of the song, as if whistling back through the ages.

> *He told me of the times he worked for minstrel shows*
> *traveling throughout the South . . .*

When performing this song, Sammy, who usually sang to the back of the audience, altered his voice to such a gentle tone that it seemed as if he were singing to himself. "When he did 'Bojangles' the first time onstage," recalls Sy Marsh, "he came off, looked at me, and said, 'I'll never do it again.' I said, 'What are you talking about? They gave you a standing ovation.' He said, 'I don't want to be the guy standing around at the end and the parade passes him by.' "

But Sammy could not stop singing the song. It was as if a gravitational pull had claimed him.

Let Bob Dylan and the Nitty Gritty Dirt Band and Frankie Laine record "Mr. Bojangles," as they all did. But it was Sammy who raised the vaudevillian from the dead into flesh. It was Sammy who had been there.

Yes, a song about a ghost. An old gray-haired hoofer reminiscing in a Louisiana jail cell, left with memories of his minstrel shows, ghosts upon the memory. Some of those ghosts were still walking into Sammy's office in Hollywood and picked up checks from his secretary Ann Slider.

Sammy began closing his shows standing in the middle of the stage, a derby atop his head, in a stilled pose, his hands spread wide, one foot flat, the other on its tippy toe, the band's last bars of the song fading gently. Imagine—he seemed to be saying to his audiences—an old broken-down vaudevillian; broken down yet prideful; imagine him—and know he does not need your pity, because he remains capable of doing a little bit of lovely soft-shoe. And then, from the frozen pose, came movement: a twirl, one foot crossing in front of the other, the arms akimbo, a quick pirouette across the stage, the cane in hand. And he'd freeze again, and start whistling. He'd stay frozen for a while. And audience members would drop tears.

They had many songs among them, hundreds and hundreds of songs. It is true that some songs they seemed to yawn through, as if slouching toward the beating of yet another contractual deadline. A lot of going-nowhere singles on Frank's Reprise label. One for the road, baby. And another, and another. But many songs were different. Some they went deeper on. Some could now stop the populace in its tracks. You'd hear the song, walking beneath an open window as it floated from the radio, or maybe echoing from the black-and-white television set. Wherever, you'd know it was one of them.

"New York, New York"—Frank.

"Everybody Loves Somebody"—Dean.

"Mr. Bojangles"—Sammy.

Now each had a song that would follow him into—and beyond—death.

Women and love and fame, they sometimes felt, had betrayed them, hurt them. The world was crazy: some fool kidnapping Frank's boy, Frank Jr., like that back in 1963, scaring the bejesus out of Frank until the boy got released unharmed. The world was puny: the feds busting Dino Jr. like that, back in 1974, for trying to sell those combat rifles. The arrest got wide publicity. "The whole thing was innocent," the elder Martin felt compelled to say. The world was hypocritical: all those blacks coming after Sammy, anguishing his heart, because of Nixon! After all that money he had helped raise for the movement!

They were men who spent a lot of their lives in hotel rooms. And never mind the people around them—stalwart Murphy, always by Sammy's side, setting up the fruit tray, pouring the bourbon; Frank's people, Dean's people— hotels and hotel rooms tended to be sad places. The songs, however, were a constant. The songs never betrayed them. Never the songs.

I knew a man, Bojangles, and he danced for you, in worn-out shoes
With silver hair, a ragged shirt, and baggy pants, the old soft-shoe
He jumped so high, jumped so high
Then he lightly touched down.

Sammy's film career now seemed to be unofficially dead. There would be three years between the Jerry Lewis–directed fiasco, *One More Time,* and Sammy's next screen appearance. And even that film—the 1973 *Save the Children*— wasn't a starring role but a collaborative effort made at the behest of Jesse Jackson. The movie, released a year after it was made, was a filmed concert of Chicago's 1972 Operation PUSH Exposition. Jackson, turning on efforts to promote black economic strength while still engaging in King-like spiritual crusades, rarely held events without a plan to make money for his antipoverty crusade. *Save the Children* then became a rocking and swaying concert, as an assortment of musical artists performed during Jackson's Expo. Among the headliners were Isaac Hayes, Wilson Pickett, Gladys Knight, Marvin Gaye, the

Temptations, Roberta Flack, and Sammy. Sammy moved about awkwardly in such soul-stirring, mostly black environments, wondering if he were truly respected or slyly mocked, given his dilettante-like associations with black folk. Such confusion saw him sharing his Black Power salute in Chicago in a kind of macho pantomime, which drew chuckles.

"What we want is white folks' technology with black folks' love," is how Jesse Jackson put it regarding his efforts to raise economic consciousness among blacks.

In 1974, Sammy made no movies. He decided to turn his attention to a smaller medium.

He was always a fan of television, peering for hours on end into the black box. But he was also a fan of celebrity culture, as starstruck as any fan. In 1975, ABC gave Sammy a ninety-minute talk show, and there he sat, mimicking Mike Douglas and Johnny Carson, hosting his own show, *Sammy and Company*. Johnny Brown, from the *Golden Boy* production, was a member of the show, dovetailing, as it did, into a kind of variety hour as well. There was gabbing, and there were skits. The show aired on Sunday nights. The producers realized the tapings would have to be done around Sammy's nightclub dates, and the show aired from a variety of locations: New York, Palm Springs, Las Vegas, Los Angeles, even Honolulu. The show was syndicated, which meant it was apt to be seen at any given hour of the late night. A nocturnal denizen might turn the set on and catch Sammy jawboning with his guests, united in their silliness, guffawing into the camera, Sammy slapping his knee, the jewelry gleaming, Bob Hope sliding out of view as if he had mistakenly stumbled onto the set of a talk show gone awry. Sammy had been around so long that he could summon potent guest stars. One show featured not only Billy Eckstine, but Sarah Vaughan, Count Basie, and Dizzie Gillespie as well.

Going into its second year, however, the show—always a part-time venture for Sammy—seemed to be gasping for air. Viewership declined. In 1977, ABC yanked it, and Sammy complained not one bit. Hell, that was the business, and Sammy knew what Frank knew: riding high in April, shot down in May. Many were surprised it lasted as long as it did.

If May Britt had tired of her budding film career, Altovise went in the other direction—trying to ignite hers. She appeared in *Kingdom of the Spiders* in 1977. Few saw it; fewer still remember it. It starred William Shatner, of *Star Trek* fame, and Woody Strode, an aging black actor who had appeared in *Spartacus* alongside Kirk Douglas, and in some John Ford Westerns. The movie was about a veterinarian who uncovers a horde of tarantulas causing havoc in the Arizona desert. It was what it was.

. . .

Alex Haley—the writer *Playboy* had sent to interview Sammy back in 1966—
had been working, for years, on his family lineage. Haley was fascinated by his
Tennessee hometown and his ancestral roots. To piece together his family history on his mother's side—all the while working between magazine assignments and the occasional speaking engagement—he combed archives near
and distant, and interviewed relatives, and trekked to Africa, all to answer a
question: How did the Haleys reach America's shores? Tracing his family's
roots to a village in Gambia, Haley set about writing his narrative.

It was in the year of America's Bicentennial when *Roots: The Saga of an
American Family* was published. The reviews were stunning. "It suggests, with
great power, how each of us, however unconsciously, can't but be the vehicle of
the history which has produced us," James Baldwin would write in his review
of the book. In workmanlike prose, Haley traced his family's odyssey from
capture in Africa, slave-ship crossing, to slave-cabin living in America. The
book received prizes and acclaim. Haley became a celebrity.

The year after its publication, on January 23, 1977, ABC aired the first night
of an eight-night showing of the dramatization of Haley's book. By the end of
the telecast, a nation seemed mesmerized, shocked, and stilled. Slavery, in all
its horror, had been shown for the first time to mass audiences. The Nielsen
ratings showed that parts of the series had been watched by upward of 130 million viewers. Characters from the series—Kunte Kinte, Toby, Kizzy, "Chicken"
George, Fiddler—became fodder for touching commentary across the nation.
Large questions that had haunted the country—black illiteracy, racism,
poverty—suddenly seemed, if not completely answered, then at least partially
understood. So colored maids did have a history. And Isaac Murphy, the forgotten black jockey who had won Kentucky Derbies, had a history. And so, too,
did Negro cabdrivers everywhere; likewise those souls who had been gathered
around Sammy in Alabama, in Mississippi, at the foot of the Lincoln Memorial to hear Martin Luther King, Jr. And so did the old broken-down vaudevillians walking into 9000 Sunset Boulevard—Sammy's office; they had a
history indeed. The black butlers working in the Nixon White House had a history. Rudy Duff, driving Sammy's grandma around Los Angeles, back and
forth to the market before her death, had a history.

Blacks and whites across America, who had, for so long, ignored each other,
began talking, discussing *Roots*.

There was something else notable about *Roots*. It provided a bevy of black
actors—many of whom had been toiling in their craft for years—with their
juiciest roles ever. Among them were Louis Gossett, Jr., Olivia Cole, Leslie
Uggams, Ben Vereen, Cicely Tyson, John Amos, and Scatman Crothers. Never

before, in the history of television, had so many black actors been featured in roles with dimension. (The network, realizing how unfamiliar audiences were with black-themed programs, especially of a historical nature, shrewdly cast a wide assortment of known white stars—Ed Asner, George Hamilton, Lorne Greene, Lynda Day George, Chuck Connors, Vic Morrow—and featured them prominently in promos trumpeting the miniseries.) The struggle for decent roles for black actors had been a huge one: Olivia Cole had studied at London's prestigious Royal Academy of Dramatic Arts, and was widely deemed an estimable actress, but Hollywood couldn't find roles for her.

It began as a kind of quip, Sammy introducing himself to audiences as the only black actor who *didn't* appear in *Roots*. Ha ha ha. But the more he repeated it, the more a kind of sadness crept into his voice. It hurt that he had not been asked. Still, watching the series, he felt some gratification: years earlier he had cast Cicely Tyson as his love interest in his film *A Man Called Adam*. Louis Gossett, Jr., had appeared in his *Golden Boy* in New York. And Ben Vereen had appeared in his *Golden Boy* in London.

Roots.

There was something missing in Sammy's life now. Frank Sinatra was nowhere around. First it went on for weeks, then months and months. A painful chill had entered the relationship between him and Sammy.

It wasn't just the *Tony Rome* film role offer that Sammy snubbed that hurt Sinatra. It was that one thing that you were never, ever to betray regarding Francis Albert Sinatra—his loyalty. Sammy had begun complaining to friends that Frank was a bully, and too demanding. The East Coast gossips started dropping hints of Sammy's rebellion into their columns. It had painful echoes of 1959, when Sammy told Chicago radio host Irv Kupcinet virtually the same thing. "You don't do that to Sinatra without repercussions," Cindy Bitterman, said, recalling the genesis of the earlier impasse between the two. "Sammy knew better than to do a thing like that." Sinatra's memory seemed shorter then; he forgave Sammy in time to be best man at his wedding to May Britt. But the latest infraction was compounded by something else: Frank had heard about the wild parties at Sammy's house, and the drug use, which he loathed.

And just like that it was over. The two free-falling away from each other as if all the years mattered no more. To be cold-shouldered by Frank Sinatra—by the Sinatra who had aided and assisted you—was no small thing. Imagine some massive ocean liner that had always provided your security suddenly turning wide and abandoning you, dropping you into the sea—such was the power of a Sinatra dismissal. It looked as if each was trying to turn the other into a stranger.

Neither would seek to mend things. Sometimes they'd be at the same black-tie social event. They kept their distance. Frank's body language said one thing: Fuck Sammy.

Sammy's body language was no different: Fuck Frank.

Acquaintances of both men could see that personal pride heaved out of them like swords.

Sammy was performing in Lake Tahoe when word came.

The police estimated the old man had been dead a couple of days. Neighbors knew him to be extremely quiet. He lived on Irolo Street, and sometimes he'd be seen walking around his Hollywood neighborhood, alone. Matter of fact, he was always alone. It was March 1, 1979, when Tom Erlich, a friend, knocking on the door of Will Mastin's apartment and, getting no answer, became worried. Inside, the old vaudevillian lay breathless. Will Mastin was dead. Sammy and Shirley and her husband, George, and the entire entourage left Nevada to return to California.

In his own way, he was a vaudeville giant. Will Mastin had hoarded his money while working in pickaninny shows in rural Alabama. In those early years he had scuffled with the cockamamie idea of producing Negro vaudeville

He was born fourteen years after the abolition of slavery, and something about that time of torment seems to have cautioned him against harboring too much happiness or joy. He seemed burdened by melancholy, and was a man who lived completely inside himself. He was a loner. He rarely drank. Will Mastin possessed odd contrasts for a showman. Now and then he'd raise a cigarette to his lips. His lifelong habits were meticulous— arrival at the theater, the laying out of his clothing, the checking of his taps. He believed in the Almighty, but his church was the theater. Here, backstage, he irons a garment. (JESS RAND COLLECTION)

shows. He bested the 1920s, and—with a kid in tow—the '30s as well. He had lived in an age of great invention—the automobile, the airplane, the telephone. It was as if he had walked through a great billowing curtain—starkness and woods and dusty towns on one side, and, on the other, fine wardrobes and his name in lights. He had lived through the passage of profound civil rights laws. But he never participated in one protest march. Will Mastin's whole life was a march. For years he had worked his face into the kindly smile of the non-threatening Negro as he stepped from train to motel to theater. For years he had dealt with mobsters and fast-talking theatrical operatives, and never conceded his dignity, or authority, over the trio that bore his name. There were a wife and two children, but he was married to show business.

Upon his death, all the accessories of his trade were still in his apartment—the canes, the hats, the many pairs of cuff links, the lovely suits. And, of course, the tap shoes in which, for decades—and against unimaginable odds—he had clicked his heels and danced the old soft-shoe.

It was a shame, upon his death, that there was no one around to take measure of his life. He had outlived the obituary writers who might have offered the proper tributes. His obits were criminally short. The *Variety* obit, printed March 14, 1979, was a mere three paragraphs. It took less than sixty seconds to read. The Associated Press notice, which ran in a series of newspapers on March 16, 1979, was but seventy-nine words. It was as if he didn't have a history. It was as if he didn't have roots. At his death, Will Mastin was one hundred years old.

He died owing no one, free of debt. Not long before his death he had begun giving away much of his money to churches in the Hollywood area.

The funeral was held March 19 at the Little Church of the Flowers in Glendale, California. Following scripture and prayer, there was an organ medley: "As Long As He Needs Me," followed by "I've Gotta Be Me." Later in the ceremony, Billy Eckstine sang "Dearest." (Back in the 1940s, when times had been hard for the Mastin trio, Eckstine was generous: he'd drop a little money into Sammy's palm. Sammy remembered.) Among the final organ selections were "Liza" and "My Daddy, My Uncle and Me."

When they finally got his stone in the ground—it lay flat—the wording was simple:

Will Mastin Sr.

HE WAS A VAUDEVILLIAN

Undated. As if he were but a ghost.

· · ·

Sammy began the 1980s just as he had begun the decade before, and the decade before that—on the road. He opened January 17 for a three-week engagement at Caesars Palace. On Valentine's Day he strolled onstage at Harrah's in Reno. He rested his weary body at night by the house on the lake given to him to stay in while performing. On March 5 he opened in Phoenix. On March 13 he opened at the Arena Theatre in Houston. Days sleeping and resting, listening to his music.

In 1980, Sammy entered into a business partnership with his manager, Sy Marsh. "Sammy," says Marsh, "used to say, 'There are two captains on this ship.' " They named their company SyNI—Sy & I. "Sammy said, ' "SyNI," now that's a hell of a name for two Jewish guys,' " says Marsh.

Now, for the first time, Sammy would own a part of himself, of the business that promoted and marketed Sammy. Only Sammy hated business, or money matters; he loathed things in the mail that needed his immediate attention; he hated overdue bills. Will Mastin used to take care of money matters. But now Will was dead. Now Sammy trusted Sy Marsh.

Marsh wore a Corum solid gold watch on his wrist, a little something Sammy picked up during a shopping spree in London. On the back, in small lettering, it said:

> To Sy
> Til Death do us Part
> Sam

They'd split the profits; it was all kind of wonderful; it was all kind of hazy. Sy would take care of things. Numbers were so cumbersome—and what was a man who never went to school to do about it?

"He had no concept of money," Marsh says of Sammy. "He had no idea that with $100,000, you'd be taxed $40,000."

Betty Belle had worked fifteen years as a bookkeeper for CBS when she joined Sammy's office in 1970, in that same role. She saw the money come in, and she saw the money go out. For years it worried Betty how the books were being kept. The money seemed to be flying in various directions. "When I got a few chances to talk to him about his financial problems," she says of Sammy, "he would say, 'I'm not interested in that, I'm interested in my art.' "

His art was hardly cheap. It cost $200,000 a year to run the office. "All these salaries to people who were playing handball and shooting pool," says Belle.

Sammy didn't mind. Money sat in the alligator briefcase he carried, stacks of it. The only thing, however, was that the stacks of money in the briefcase did not make the debts go away. In the old days, he'd cash in a marker, huddle with a nightclub owner. Bill Miller or Skinny D'Amato. Yes, the old days were beautiful. But those men were mostly out of the nightclub business. This was a new era, a new decade. There were bean counters. There was accountability.

So he took out another mortgage on his twenty-two-room home.

It was just like 1966 all over again, when the IRS hounded him and his father for those back taxes. There had been tax woes plenty of years. Money that was made was often spent before it was taxed, and so debts accumulated.

When Sammy was worried with exhaustion, the good eye hurt. It became red, and it sagged. Now it was doing both.

Why, it was Amy Greene's birthday. Sammy would never forget her on such a special day. Only she wished he had; he was broke, she had heard. "He slips me this baby blue velvet case and there is a three-strand pearl necklace with a wonderful antique clasp," she remembers. "I said, 'I am not going to take it.' He said, 'Yes you are.' "

Betty Belle didn't know what to do. "Many times my own salary check would bounce," she says. "There were two sets of books—Sammy's and the corporation's [SyNI]."

All the bad habits—all the borrowing today against future earnings, all the vaudeville escapades he had dragged with him from the past to the present—were catching up to him. Shirley Rhodes realized things had to be tightened up. "He never had anybody say, 'No, you can't, this is it,' " she says. "I have taken jewelry back to Cartier and said, 'He doesn't want it.' I took a $13,000 necklace back to Gucci. They said, 'He liked it when he left.' I said, 'Well, he doesn't like it anymore.' "

In the spring of 1980 Sammy and Altovise threw a party. There was no special occasion; it was just a party. Some tents on the lawn; a catered affair; the usual. The guest list, showing Sammy's taste, was, as always, eclectic: Fred MacMurray and his wife, June Haver; Jack Haley, Jr., and his wife, Liza Minnelli; Edmund O'Brien; Loretta Young; porn star Marilyn Chambers—and an assortment of "obscure white and black actors," as Sammy put it. Altovise looked ravishing, gliding about the festivities in a Galanos gown. In a corner, there stood MacMurray and Marilyn Chambers, chatting away. The avuncular father of television's *My Three Sons* and the porn starlet.

Let Frank have New York, New York; Hollywood was Sammy's kind of town.

The party bill came to $100,000. Shirley couldn't get a cent of it back. She cried to Sammy.

When he didn't understand the accounting is when Sammy really wished he'd gone to school. Then maybe he could understand what Sy Marsh was talking about; what the IRS was trying to explain to him. They were all just words to him. Why worry? He'd get the money. He'd just take to the road.

He didn't get smaller, but the rooms damn sure seemed to get bigger. He couldn't sell out. Two shows, and sometimes the audience for the early show was a little on the thin side. There sat Fred Hull, the doctor who had performed the eye surgery, along with his wife. (Backstage, Hull lectured Sammy about the drinking.)

He was boozing too much. He wouldn't eat. Shirley flew his personal cook into Las Vegas. It was actually Lessie Jackson, who had been his children's nanny. If anybody could get Sammy to eat—other than his late grandmother Rosa—it was Lessie. Her specialty was southern cuisine—fried chicken, collard greens, pudding, sweet potatoes, hush puppies. And he began to eat, though still not enough.

Sammy complained to Murphy that his side hurt, so Murphy accompanied him to a doctor in Reno. It was jaundice of the liver. Boozing too much indeed. The doctors told Sammy that he'd have to quit. He put the warning into his shows, joking about having to stop drinking, swirling the contents of a cup in his hand: soda pop. Ha ha ha.

And he sang "Mr. Bojangles."

. . . I drinks a bit.

One afternoon, while in Vegas, Sammy got a sudden, childlike hankering for a dog. John Souza drove him over to the dog pound. One of the workers pointed out a mutt. The mutt had a handicap: it was blind in one eye. Sammy took the one-eyed mutt home. Between dog and dog owner, two eyes.

It did not surprise doctors that drinkers with small bodies—150 pounds or less—suffered greater liver damage than drinkers with larger bodies. Often the drinkers with smaller bodies had no appetite; they were malnourished without realizing it. "He was the first one," says Shirley of Sammy, "to say, 'Let's eat! Let's go to lunch.' And he wouldn't eat anything." What was paradoxical to medical professionals was that only one in ten drinkers—those who drank more than just casually—seemed to suffer liver damage. It was as if the other nine had the light of medical luck shining upon them. For Sammy, the dice had come up craps: he was the one in ten. The liver was on its way to killing him.

On the road now, Sammy became a fan of soap operas, idling in hotel rooms, gazing in silence at the TV screen. (At home he'd keep several televisions going at once.) The soaps appealed to him because they were as close to live television as one could get. It was stand-around vaudeville, performers in nice suits playing at their twisty plots and cliffhangers. "I'd call Sammy, say I needed a gig," remembers pianist Rudi Eagan. "He'd say, 'Come over after three, I watch the soaps.'"

Money tight, Sammy came up with bizarre moneymaking ventures. As the mailing stated:

> Sammy Davis Jr. would like you to enjoy these new products with his compliments. He wanted you to be one of the first to receive them. They reflect Sammy's personal tastes—and his passion for casual cooking. Once you try them, you'll understand why Sammy and his Cleveland food partners formed SDJ Food Corporation. Enjoy.

Barbecue sauces, spices, other sauces. He was listed as chairman of the board. Finally—like Frank—chairman of the board. The venture went bust. (Friends snickered behind Sammy's back that he had become obsessive with cooking Italian food for one reason: Frank cooked Italian.)

John Souza tried to implore Sammy to explore grilling food—chops on the grill. "He'd say, 'I don't do charcoal. I don't like charcoal.'"

In the days of vaudeville, Negro performers used to carry around little sacks of charcoal. They'd use it to "black" their faces up darker—just like white performers.

So the hell with charcoal.

The money Sammy made from his television appearances—the guest spots on the half-hour shows, the comical turns on someone's variety show—was nothing: $10,000 here, $10,000 there. "Sammy would do a television show and spend more on the wrap party than he made for the show," says Madelyn Rhue.

He sold the Rolls.

But he purchased an Andy Warhol original, the famous one of the Campbell's soup can. He paid $12,000. Betty Belle, the bookkeeper, couldn't believe it. "Twelve thousand for a painting of a Campbell's soup can!"

He sold the building he had purchased years earlier with an eye toward directing Altovise in her own movies.

Things were not so good between him and Altovise. They had begun arguing about just how "open" an open marriage should be. "She would call from L.A.," John Souza says, "and say, 'Tell Sammy I'm coming in and to get rid of whoever he's got with him there.'"

Sy sent over a script. It was a far cry from *The Scarlet Pimpernel*. Sammy went to Atlanta in 1981 and shot a Hal Needham–directed movie, *The Cannonball Run*, with Burt Reynolds as the marquee star. It was a reunion of sorts for Sammy: Dean Martin also starred. Dean was always simpatico with Sammy, and never liked the manner in which Sinatra dominated him. There would be Dean slyly rolling his eyes as Frank engaged in yet another putdown of Sammy. Sammy never saw the denigration; he only saw the past: Frank at the Capitol Theatre, 1942, sending for the Will Mastin Trio.

"In the Rat Pack, it was Dean who Sammy felt love from," says actress Madelyn Rhue. "Dean didn't call him 'Smokey.' He loved Sammy, and Sammy knew it."

Everybody loves somebody.

In *The Cannonball Run*, he and Dean played crooks—masquerading as priests—on a cross-country escapade with an odd assortment of characters in chase. Among others in the cast were Terry Bradshaw, Peter Fonda, Jackie Chan, and Roger Moore. Sammy was slumming—again. In the old days the movie slumming was for Frank, now it was just for laughs. He was the only black with a sizable role in the cast. The critics howled at the movie, which was a mess. But it turned a robust profit, grossing $37 million.

All his life, he told himself, he had worked for a home like the one he had in the Hollywood Hills. Twenty-two rooms, the stretch balcony, the sunken living room, the dozen closets, the maid and butler quarters. It did not really matter to him that he wasn't there a lot. Others were. His house became a kind of haven for writers, musicians, various performers. Those in need.

There was certainly a need in Atlanta. Black children were missing, some being murdered. The story began to dominate nationwide news in March and April of 1981. The missing children, you might say, helped bring Frank and Sammy back together. They forgot about the anger—actually, Frank forgot, allowing the mending to take place. And there went the big beautiful Sinatra arm around Sammy's shoulders, bringing him back into the fold.

Clearing the deck of everything in sight, just him and Sammy. And just Frank inside Sammy's one eye. "The state of Georgia had never before exhibited so intense an interest in Black life or Black death," the writer James Baldwin said—rather cryptically. A reward fund was set up. Sammy—he'd show the "brothers and the sisters" how much he cared—flew to Atlanta with Sinatra to give a concert, with the proceeds going to the reward fund. David Levering Lewis, who had written a well-received book, *When Harlem Was in Vogue*, about the Harlem Renaissance, happened to be in Atlanta, working on a book about the administration of Mayor Maynard Jackson. "Somehow," says Lewis, "I was assigned to travel with Sammy. We spent an evening going about. Had lunch, sat, and talked. For me, it was wonderful. He was a fabulously interesting guy. *When Harlem Was in Vogue* had just come out. I tried to get him interested in the book. Of course this was all in his blood. He talked about 'Bojangles' and the impact he had on him. It was like, 'You want to tell me about the Harlem Renaissance? Well, let me tell *you* about the Harlem Renaissance.' " On June 21, 1981, Atlanta police arrested a freelance photographer by the name of Wayne Williams in connection with the murders. He was convicted of just two of the killings, enough to put him behind bars for life. (There were twenty-two other missing and presumed murdered at the hands of Williams. The killings both saddened and befuddled black Atlantans, many of whom had wondered if some bigot were behind the murder. Williams was black.)

When Madelyn Rhue confided to Sammy in 1974 that she had been diagnosed with multiple sclerosis, he insisted she move in with him. His staff would watch over her. The invite—so generous, so quickly given—left her speechless, and she feigned indifference. But he insisted, and she came. Her bedroom was "the Kennedy room"—a room Sammy had decorated in lovely pink tones. Rhue so enjoyed Sammy's home. "Sammy would have these wonderful parties with the Nicholas Brothers and the comic Redd Foxx. Everyone would be black but me. I loved it. They had stories they would spellbind you with. They'd talk about the old days at MGM. They tapped in the living room. Sammy would get up and tap. They were like history lessons." When Rhue's health deteriorated, Sammy bought a van for her, equipped for a wheelchair.

In 1981, Jim Davis, a writer who Sammy met through Amy Greene, was working on a book about Myrna Loy and was on his way to Los Angeles. Sammy invited him to live in the guest house on his property. "Sammy was never there," Davis remembers. "The staff was so thrilled if I'd go eat something. Altovise would stop and get lobster at Nick's Fish Market for fifty bucks."

Looking around the home, taking Sammy's lifestyle in, made Davis wonder about certain things. He once asked Sammy, during one of his rare visits home, everyone sitting by the pool, if he knew how much it cost monthly to heat the pool. Sammy had never heard such a question.

"No," he answered.

"It's $10,000 a month," Jim Davis told him.

Sammy didn't give a hoot about how much it cost to heat his swimming pool. Hell, he didn't even know how to swim. He cared only if those diving into the pool were happy. And if they loved him, well, that was nice also.

All those activists from SNCC, from SCLC, from "the movement," who'd bunk at his house. His marriage was not the only thing open; so was his home.

And now the IRS was talking to Sy Marsh about taking the houses—Sy's *and* Sammy's. It was SyNI: they were not paying taxes, and the books were a mess. Rudi Eagan, the pianist who sometimes traveled with Sammy, saw a strange scene in Sammy's hotel room one evening while on the road. "Sammy's jewelry was spread all over the room—the bed, the rug—estimating the cost of it for the IRS."

In 1984, Sammy did another movie—*Cannonball Run II*. It was worse than the first, and it made less money. But for sentiment and nostalgia, it was worth a peek: along with Dean again, Shirley MacLaine was in the cast—and Sinatra himself. Sinatra didn't act much anymore. It was his first movie since 1980. Shirley looked fine; the others did not. Dean appeared lackluster and—even given his usual lushlike stage appearances—genuinely inebriated. Sammy's face was drawn in. During filming, his hip had been in pain. Sinatra looked embarrassed in his scenes. (It would be his last movie.)

Sammy got enough money to pay some of the IRS debt, and he began to feel sunny again, owing to a string of engagements that awaited him. But then he began to break apart physically. He began hobbling through airports, leaning on a cane, leaning on Murphy, leaning on Shirley. It was the hip; he needed reconstructive surgery. Altovise stayed home. More and more, she remained at home. The marriage was faltering. Sy Marsh suggested a divorce. "I can't divorce her," Sammy told him. "We can't give up what we worked our asses for." Sammy was referring to himself and Sy—till death do us part.

He went into Cedars-Sinai Hospital. Sinatra called.

"Who's your doctor?" he snapped, demanding to know.

Just as in the old days. But now Sammy put him off, as gently as possible—and kept his own doctor.

Sy Marsh convinced Sammy to invest in tax shelters. To Sammy it was all mumbo-jumbo: tax shelters; investments; barbecue sauces on the market. Tax shelters were a fancy way of playing hide-and-seek with whatever money one might owe to the federal government.

He gave the go-ahead.

And he picked up another obsession. It was Pac-Man, the video game. He'd sit for hours, playing alone. He was the kid who never got to play such games. "We had one everywhere we went," says Shirley of the Pac-Man game. "Or the club owners would get one."

It seemed like yesterday when he and Will and Sam Sr. and George and Shirley were out there, rolling in a bus across the hinterland. Only yesterday. And yet, time could move like a bullet.

Sammy added "Ol' Man River" to the stage repertoire.

The calendar said 1985.

Christmas morning. Shirley was on the phone.

"Sammy, George is gone," she said.

"Where'd he go?" Sammy wanted to know.

"He's dead."

It was a heart attack. Sammy rushed over—still in his pajamas—and cried with Shirley. He told her he'd take care of everything.

He wanted Jesse. This was Shirley and George. Frank had the Italians, like Dean had the Italians. Sammy had Shirley and George.

When a black dignitary died in America now, it was Jesse Jackson who was called upon. He was becoming a kind of professional eulogist. He was still flying on the aura of Martin Luther King, Jr., and no one begrudged him that, because he worked so tirelessly. Where Jesse went, so did the media—television, radio, the white press, the Negro press. Jesse came out to California and preached beautifully, talking about George's career as a musician. Sammy rode in the passenger seat—shotgun—as the hearse took George's body out to the Glendale Cemetery, where he was laid to rest on a hillside.

Shirley thought of retiring. She wondered if she could go on without George.

Sy Marsh wondered if they would be able to go on at all. "The government came into the office—the IRS," says Marsh. "They said, 'You cannot be hiding behind a veil.' " The tax shelter scheme had been exposed. "I lost a $2 million estate," says Marsh. " 'Piercing the veil,' they called it."

Sammy would not lose his house. The house meant so much to him. He had dreamed of it when Janet Leigh and Tony Curtis owned it, and he had dreamed of it when Joan Collins owned it. He called Sinatra; he called Jerry Lewis. "Frank and I tried to lessen the load," says Lewis. "Moneywise, we had come full circle." (Because in the beginning—in the 1940s and 1950s—they had loaned him money on his advances. He always repaid—to the day he was supposed to, to the dollar he owed.)

Sy and Molly Marsh moved into an apartment.

On the road, Sammy and Murphy, after the shows, would sit and rest. They'd play Pac-Man. He'd watch the soaps during the day. There was always a local police officer outside his door—security.

The young kids; the youth freaks. They'd catch glimpses of him and gawk. He was like some creaking gnome. Sammy Davis, Jr.: the name meant quite a bit in the American mind-set. He had endured. He'd been in the business for decades. A tap dancer. A singer. And didn't he write some best-selling book— *Yes I Can*—a long time ago?

Everywhere the young kids. There was one by the name of Billy Crystal. He had joined the cast of *Saturday Night Live* in 1985, and began touring college campuses as a stand-up. A limber young comedian, he had the insouciance of an Al Jolson. Crystal began doing an imitation of Sammy: hunched shoulders, nasal voice, squinting eyes, some hepcat lingo: hey baby, what a gas, hey chickee. It got laughs. Impressions involved exaggeration, and Crystal milked Sammy's physical mannerisms. What did those young audiences know of Sammy's eye incident? What did they know of the massive amounts of dental surgery that gave him that strange overbite?

Some white kid doing black Sammy. Ha ha ha. What goes around comes around: he had made his own name in those early years doing impersonations.

Sammy would look at this impersonator riffing on him, and he'd wonder: did he really look like that—hunched over, the eyes squinting?

There was another young kid—Leon Isaac Kennedy. Sammy started inviting him up to the house.

Kennedy arrived in Hollywood in 1972 from Cleveland, where he had been a popular deejay, known as "Leon the Lover." It was his intention, upon landing in Hollywood, to become a leading man—a lofty dream for any black actor. He had wormed his way into one of Sammy's parties, and his moxie touched Sammy. "Sammy was the first big star who befriended me," Kennedy says.

Sammy kept inviting him back. "You could go by Sammy's house and on any given night meet the biggest people in the world," Kennedy says. "The first time I met Liza Minnelli was at Sammy's. His big parties were the best of the best of the melting pot. Because, no matter, if a black person had a party, it was a 'black party.' If a white person had a party, it was a 'white party.' At Sammy's, it was a party of everybody coming together. At Sammy's house you would have Jim Brown, Red Skelton, Milton Berle, Caesar Romero. All these people. They were great parties."

Kennedy peppered Sammy with questions about the business, and Sammy was happy to explain some secrets: "He said, 'Other artists have to worry about hit records. You don't have to have hit records if you work Vegas.'" Kennedy was impressed with Sammy's ability to identify with young talent. "I remember talking to him about Michael Jackson when *Thriller* came out [in 1982]. He said, 'I'm going to work that into the Vegas act.'"

In 1979, Kennedy got a starring role in *Penitentiary,* a low-budget vehicle in which he played a wrongfully imprisoned boxer. The movie acquired something of a cult following. "Sammy mentioned it on *The Tonight Show,* and that was a great plug." Kennedy became a leading man, but they were B movies. They played in drive-ins. He didn't mind, and his hubris soared. (When Kennedy initially arrived in Hollywood, he was carrying *My Wicked, Wicked Ways,* Errol Flynn's autobiography.) In 1981, Kennedy starred in *Body and Soul,* a remake of the 1947 classic John Garfield boxing movie directed by Robert Rossen. With Garfield, critics raved; with Kennedy, they howled. The cast, along with Kennedy, was an eyebrow-raiser: his beautiful real-life wife, Jayne Kennedy; Rat Packer Peter Lawford; and Muhammad Ali in a cameo.

Five years after *Body and Soul,* Kennedy found himself coproducing and starring in *Knights of the City*, which he imagined, rather grandiosely, as a "modern-day *West Side Story*." He wrote a part especially for Sammy. "I'm sitting, and thinking, and I said, 'This will be the Academy Award–winning performance for Sammy,' " recalls Kennedy. Sammy was still ailing a bit from hip surgery, but he was in need of money and accepted the role. "I call him and tell him about the role," says Kennedy. "He said, 'I love it. I trust you.' "

Before filming got under way, and before Sammy arrived, Kennedy phoned him. There was a little problem: money. He told Sammy he could afford to pay him only $15,000. Ha. Fifteen grand: Sammy's wrap parties cost as much. The conversation ended. But then Kennedy's phone rang. It was Sammy. "Leon," he said, "I'm going to do the movie for you, but it can never be said somebody got Sammy Davis for $15,000. You keep it. When the movie comes out, if it does well, you give me what you want."

Kennedy thought his movie could pick up some of the steam of the 1983 hit *Flashdance*. It had dancing; it would appeal to a young audience. He believed if his movie caught on it could gross $30 million.

Filming began in Ft. Lauderdale. Sammy arrived with Murphy. "We film three days with Sammy," recalls Kennedy. "I'm really thinking he's gonna be nominated for an Academy Award. That's how great his performance was." During postproduction, the shenanigans began. One of the producers was arrested and found to owe the IRS millions. The government took possession of the movie prints. After legal wrangling, Kennedy and another producer were finally able to wrest back control of the film. But the new producer wanted the final edit. "He comes out," says Kennedy, "with the most outlandish idea I ever heard of: We need to cut Sammy out of the film because his character slows the film down."

Never in his life had Sammy Davis, Jr., wound up on the cutting-room floor.

"I go to Sammy and say, 'Sammy, I've run into all types of personal problems with this movie.' He says, 'I've heard.' I say, 'Its worse than that. They've cut you out of the film.' He says, 'How could you allow that to happen? You're the producer and the star.' " The conversation degenerated from there.

For his work on the movie, Sammy never received a dime. He was an entertainer, and he had gone slumming in a B movie, and paid the price.

He now hated outdoors, especially the cold winds whipping—it was as if those winds were directed right at his hip joints. And his eye hurt. He missed George, his musical conductor. Sometimes he and Shirley would start reminiscing about George. There'd be a torrent of laughter, a flood of tears.

He was spending hours in the kitchen while on the road, cooking in the presidential suite of the hotel, mixing his sauces, stirring his creations in his large pots and pans. Invited guests raved about his chili. "He took an entire kitchen on the road," says Shirley.

But he still wouldn't eat.

When the White House phoned, his spirits lifted.

He would be receiving the Kennedy Center for the Performing Arts' 1987 Gold Medal for Lifetime Achievement. An announcement of any award charmed Sammy—blowing away, at least temporarily, some of the ash of his insecurity. He shared the news with Sam Sr., who was quite happy. Big Sam had been ailing. It was his heart; he had been fitted with a pacemaker.

President Ronald Reagan and his wife, Nancy, would host the Kennedy Center event. Along with Sammy, the honorees included Perry Como, Bette Davis, Nathan Milstein, and Alwin Nikolais.

There was something about those Republicans. They bestowed such affection on Sammy! First Nixon, now Reagan. How could he—ever searching for love—not be appreciative? But an overwhelming majority of blacks held no affection for Reagan, who often told anecdotal stories about "welfare queens" and poor inner-city men driving Cadillacs, tales interpreted by many blacks as offensive and full of stereotype. But to Sammy, who was such a chronicler of Hollywood, Reagan was the actor from *Kings Row* and *Knute Rockne—All American*. Sinatra, now a Republican too, used to drag Sammy to those political fund-raisers when Reagan was governor of California. Reagan and Nixon: two longtime denizens of that land of make-believe; California dreamers. (Years earlier, when Sammy was just getting his start in Hollywood as an actor, and was so happy to get a role on General Electric Theater, it was Ronald Reagan who had introduced the episode he appeared on. Reagan and Nixon both knew quite a bit about camera angles.)

Sammy came to Washington, checked into the hotel, sat facing a *Washington Post* reporter, and that name came out, rolling like a boulder: Nixon. "First of all, I'm not the only black celebrity that was involved in campaigning for the president," he said, feeling such a need to explain. "Secondly, I wasn't bucking for publicity or anything else." Sammy was in the autumn of his years as a performer now. He confided to the reporter how he admired the way Maurice Chevalier lived his life. "When he didn't want to work, he'd go sit in his beautiful villa outside of Paris. There he'd sit, for two or three years, and when the urge hit him, he'd come back to do nine o'clock theater in New York, two pianos, you know? He'd put his straw hat on, and he was charming, and beautiful, and then he'd disappear again. He didn't do it for the money."

Sammy, however, did it for the money.

He was thrilled at the Kennedy Center honor, and he had Altovise on his arm. His face beamed; his hip hurt. (Harry Belafonte would receive the Kennedy honor in 1989; Sidney Poitier in 1995. But Sammy, the vaudeville kid, had beat both to the honors! Ha ha.)

Afterward, Sammy returned to California for a second hip operation.

. . .

In 1988, Sammy made a guest appearance on *The Cosby Show*, comedian Bill Cosby's highly rated family sitcom. He played a father worried incessantly about his daughter, who was soon to give birth. Sammy came up with the name for his daughter in the episode. Her name was Luisa Sanchez—the name of Sammy's real-life grandmother, his mother's mother. Sammy, it seemed, was trying to acknowledge his roots.

Chapter 18

THE IDES OF TIME

O n May 21, 1988, in these Hollywood Hills, Sam Sr. died. Went in his sleep, his Jag in the garage. Like Mastin, he had lived a lifetime on the road, hustling and dancing across the American landscape.

"After Sam Sr. died, we were at Sammy's house," recalls Virginia Capehart, the longtime family friend. "He had a little alcove, and was sitting in there all alone. He said, 'I wish I could find someone to love me for me, not for what I can do for them. Love me for me.' I said, 'Rita [Sammy's stepmother] did.' He said, 'Yes, Rita did.' "

Years earlier, in retirement, Sam Sr. had given his tap shoes to the city of Wilmington, North Carolina, place of his birth. Upon his death, the shoes were given to the local historical society. They are still there, protected in a glass case.

Where have you gone, Rat Pack?

There had been, over the years, sightings. There they were on May 22, 1978—Frank and Sammy and Dean—at the Santa Monica Civic Auditorium, appearing together for a SHARE charity event. In February 1983, they popped up for a hospital charity event in Palm Springs. Some songs, some memories, some drinks—then they split, going their separate ways. Toward the end of 1987, Sammy and Dean found themselves in Palm Springs, visiting with Frank and Barbara. "We've got to do something together again," Sammy offered. Sinatra had an idea: the three of them could go on the road. Dean listened, resisted work as always, then came around: "How much longer have we got?" he was moved to wonder himself. The ghosts. Sammy knew: time was so wickedly swift. Days later Sinatra was on the phone to Sammy. "Smokey, let's do it. It will be hard work, but it could be exciting. And I think it would be great for Dean. Get him out. For that alone it would be worth doing." Dean's son, Dino, had gone missing on March 20, 1987, flying in an Air National Guard jet over the San Bernardino mountains. Five days later the crash site was located; he and a copilot had died on impact. For days Dean sequestered himself with Jeannie, his ex-wife, mother of his boy. Dino had been, as Sammy knew, his father's "golden child."

Sinatra—taking charge, playing chairman—said they'd go by train, tuxedoed barnstormers, a long elegant train. But after more thought, such a mode of travel was deemed too cumbersome, so it would be by air. Thirty cities, taking in March and April of 1988, followed by a break, then a resumption for September and October.

Word had actually leaked out about the tour in late December. Sammy imagined what the public might be thinking: "This is the last hurrah."

The official press conference, announcing the tour, was held at Chasen's. They arrived in tuxedos; the press were gathered like geese.

"You start it off, Sam," Sinatra whispered to Sammy.

"Ladies and gentlemen, we thank you for coming here today . . ."

Dean interrupted: "Is there any way we can call this whole thing off?"

Was he joking? Why of course. But who knew for sure? Sammy shot him a strange look.

"We want to officially announce that we're going to be 'Together Again,' the first time since Las Vegas in the sixties . . ." Sammy continued.

A little later someone asked if they could pack the big arenas they were being booked into. It touched a nerve in Dean. "This country has not seen us," he began. "They've seen rock 'n' roll and all this other—not that I . . ." He trailed off.

Their schedule was announced: Cincinnati and Pittsburgh, Detroit and Cleveland, Vancouver, of course New York, New York, Providence, Washington, D.C., Seattle, Bloomington. Sinatra imagined other cities would be added once the act caught on.

They'd open in Oakland.

Shirley asked Sammy how much money he'd reap from the tour. She had to keep an eye on the books. Sammy didn't know. Sinatra's office told Sammy not to worry about money just yet. That was just it; squeezed by debtors, Sammy had to worry about money right now.

Later, Sinatra sought to assure him: "The accountants say you should come out of this with from six to eight million dollars."

Sammy refinanced the house again.

They rehearsed in Hollywood. Singing, bantering, joking. Shirley saw something she did not like at the rehearsal: there was not a black face in the forty-piece orchestra. Sammy mentioned it to Sinatra.

"What the fuck is this snow-white orchestra," Sinatra hollered out. "That stinks."

Sinatra was told it would cost money to hire more musicians, especially with such short notice. "Pay what we have to. Fix it!" In 1941, it was *The House*

I Live In, Sinatra's Oscar-winning documentary about racial tolerance. It was still, at times, the house he lived in.

They flew to Oakland. Sammy and Murphy; Sammy and Dean and Frank; years and years and years. It was March 13, 1988. There were sixteen thousand sitting at the Oakland Coliseum.

FRANK, DEAN, SAMMY, SOLD OUT.

That was the marquee in Oakland.

Dean would be followed by Sammy, who would be followed by Frank.

Dean came on, heard the words "Can't hear you. Louder." This wasn't Bill Miller's Riviera; it wasn't even the Sands. This Oakland venue was a huge gaping wound in the earth. Sammy's youth freaks loved this kind of setting.

Dean made it through seven songs.

Then came Sammy, bouncing, even on the bad hip. Bouncing as in the old days, grabbing the mike, the jewelry glinting, twisting open the mouth, only he couldn't get anything out, because the people had begun to rise, they were standing, it was for him, Sammy, and he slow-motioned himself through the moments. The kid from vaudeville. A standing O; how sweet. His hip hurt. The lights were glinting. And he said, at long last, "Good evening, ladies and gentlemen." Then he began—"I've Gotta Be Me"—happy as can be. "For me," he told the crowd, "it's one day at a time now." He was talking about the drinking, the liver, life.

Sinatra closed it out, then all three of them were onstage for a medley. Dean threw a cigarette into the crowd after the medley. Frank didn't like it, and they both exchanged harsh words about it.

Sammy loved it all, every second. He had no complaints.

A week later in Chicago Frank blew up because—while they each had quite spacious hotel suites—they were placed on different floors.

"Don't unpack," Frank said. "We're going to get the hell out of this dump. Get Dean and Sammy in here." Dean didn't move; Sammy came running.

Then and there, Dean made up his mind. No more. He got a private jet and split, leaving at night through the dark clouds. He couldn't take Sinatra anymore.

Eliot Weisman, one of the tour sponsors, frantically went about seeking a replacement.

Now it was just the two of them—Frank and Sammy. It had been three wars ago when they first met; a lot of ballads ago; plenty of hotel rooms ago. Six children and seven wives were between them now. Years and years: the years gone like a snap of Frank's finger—1942, when they first met, to now, finger snap, 1988; gone like the speed of Sammy's quick draw. In some quarters back then it was the dago and the nigger. Now, Ol' Blue Eyes and Sammy Davis, Jr.

Now, a lot of songs, and a lot of memories. Jack Kennedy, Peter Lawford, Dean's boy, Will, Martin Luther King, Jr., Rosa, all gone. Forty-six years. Imagine—nearly half a century. And now here they stood, on a stage in Bloomington.

Frank: "The Lady Is a Tramp."
Sammy: "I've Gotta Be Me."
Frank: "The Summer Wind."
Sammy: "Mr. Bojangles."

Old lions, no; old poets, yes.

One night on stage Sammy had a funny feeling in his throat. Murphy pampered him, kept hot tea nearby. Frank didn't remember every word to every song. It was like that: the wounds of the road, of time. But they enjoyed themselves, leaning against the piano, bowing to each other, the magic of it all.

Eliot Weisman, tour sponsor, looked no further than his own client list. He handled Liza Minnelli, and she joined the second half of the tour. Sammy hugged her as a child does a parent. Cacophony and controversy: the vaudevillian in him could withstand all of it.

They altered the order in which they came onstage. Now it was Sammy who came out first, then Liza, then Frank. Then everyone taking off, after concert's end, in the plane. They were in New Jersey one night. Frank wanted to go to New York City, get some dinner. He summoned a helicopter, saw the lights down below. Sammy and Liza—Judy's girl—and Frank, floating. Then down to earth and a limo took them off to eat.

The tour ended in May and picked back up in August. They played Boston; they played Landover, Maryland, and Charlotte and Greensboro in North Carolina. By October, Sammy was back home, and tired. The throat was scratchy. Nothing seemed to help. Shirley and Murphy begged him to see a doctor. Altovise was gone as much as she was home. She was drinking heavily; the house had become so lonely.

A box for Sammy was delivered to the house. Murphy opened it; it was from Sinatra, and it was a beautiful gold watch—and along with it a note thanking him for going on the tour. Sammy was nearly speechless. That's why he was Sinatra.

It wasn't the smartest thing to do, given his physical ailments, but Sammy couldn't resist. All his life a performer, he needed things to do, movement.

A shot of bourbon and a song. A duet, a duo, a tandem. Never ever just strangers in the night. The association began at the Paramount, in New York City, before World War II. It lasted through the years, through the arguments and silences and misunderstandings and this reunion event in 1988. They knew what the audiences wanted, and they could deliver.
(© THE WASHINGTON POST. REPRINTED WITH PERMISSION.)

Filmmaker Paul Mazursky wanted Sammy for a role in his *Moon Over Parador*, a farcical film about an actor in a Latin American country who gets a "job" to play the dictator when the dictator himself dies. Mazursky trooped to the Sands in Las Vegas to talk to Sammy about the part. "He was outrageously wonderful," Mazursky would recall of meeting Sammy. "Huge glass bowls of Pall Mall cigarettes and candy bars were all over Sammy's monster suite at the Sands. I promised him that we would take good care of him in Ouro Preto." Ouro Preto was the Brazilian city where the film would be shot. The cast included Richard Dreyfuss—playing the actor who would be playing the dictator; Raul Julia; Sonia Braga; Jonathan Winters; and Sammy—who would be playing Sammy Davis, Jr., an entertainer who performs for the dictator.

The travel—from Las Vegas to Miami, and from there on to Rio, and from Rio by car to Ouro Preto—was brutal on Sammy and Murphy. They were exhausted when they finally reached their hotel rooms. And Sammy was disappointed with his accommodations: he did not have a suite. It was, however, the best hotel accommodations Mazursky could get in the small town. Mazursky and his assistant went to Sammy's room to welcome him: "There were trunks everywhere, their goods displayed for all to see: dress shirts, cuff links, trousers, cigarettes, videos, shoes, stockings, cans of strawberry soda—all of the paraphernalia someone on the road might deem necessary. Then I saw Sammy—in the middle of the king-sized bed. He seemed tiny. I began to worry. I knew that he was having severe hip problems, and now he had to deal with this room." But they were laughing, and hugging.

Sammy had one big scene in the movie. He'd be singing the national anthem of this imaginary Latin American country at an outdoor plaza. "My only real concern," Mazursky would recall, "was Sammy's hips. He used a cane most of the time, and it was obvious that he was in great pain." On the night his scene was to be filmed, Mazursky went by Sammy's trailer to check on him. "His tuxedo shirt was open to the fourth button. He smiled at me, looking about as tired as a man could be." Mazursky informed Sammy the technicians needed more time to set up, maybe three hours; Sammy said he'd nap. Mazursky returned again.

"Ready, kid?" Sammy said at his trailer door.

"Yes, Sammy. But let me prepare you. There are about seven thousand dancing Brazilians out there."

The entertainer—performing since he was four, having performed all over the world—could only giggle.

"I've played bigger rooms," Sammy said.

And Paul Mazursky was astonished at what he witnessed next. It was Sammy, turning into Sammy the entertainer, handing off his cane to Murphy, hobbling but with less of a hobble—willpower—and taking his place onstage. "I steered him to one of the floats and said I wanted him to stand in between half a dozen gorgeous women with perfectly formed Amazonian bodies," Mazursky would remember. "He practically hopped onto the float. For the next three hours Sammy sang perfect renditions of 'Besame Mucho,' Parador style, never off a beat. He had the body language of a man of thirty. The crowd went wild. It was impossible to get them quiet."

And Sammy sang and sang, and Murphy stood out of camera's view watching him. He hurt because Sammy's hip hurt, and he just wanted to get him home, and here they were, in some Brazilian outpost, at night, because they were pros, he and Sammy. "When I finally called a wrap about five in the morning, I saw Sammy's body sag," Mazursky would recall. "They helped him off the float and handed him his cane. He was limping again, badly, and suddenly an old man."

Mazursky hugged Sammy soon as he was down off the stage. Sammy then asked him a question with a childlike need for an answer: "Just tell me one thing, kid. Did I do good for your movie?"

"You were magnificent," Mazursky assured him.

And with that Murphy gently led Sammy away.

A limp, a cane, the hour late. Home for Mr. Bojangles.

The years had piled up, in broken marriages and disenchanted children. But he forged on, pulling on the gold the way he had seen his father and Will Mastin do so many evenings before. The stage was still his, even if the rooms were smaller.

.   .   .

Sammy was feeling mighty nostalgic. The last week of October 1988, he joined Jerry Lewis onstage in Vegas for a string of performances. They referred to themselves as "the last of the down-fronters," which meant guys who could walk right down in front of the stage and let you see them up close and not fear it. "Sammy was carrying Jerry," says Jim Delaney, the former record producer, now turned news columnist, who saw the show.

Director Nick Castle and actor Gregory Hines asked Sammy to be in their movie *Tap*. Filming got under way in 1988, and the movie opened February 10, 1989. Sammy did the promotional movie junket. It was his first one—he never had the time!—since *Porgy and Bess*. "This movie represents a real part of my life," he told a journalist in New York City. "There's a line of honesty in the film, which I like." Sammy played Little Mo, an aging dancer with dreams of putting together a tap revue.

Critics were mostly kind to the movie, out of deference, it seemed, to its reverence for the lost art of tap. Our first glimpse of Sammy is atop a roof, gardening. The sound of taps brings him downstairs. He walks with a cane. One scene is maudlin but sweetly powerful: a bevy of old tap dancers—Bunny Briggs, Sandman Sims, and Harold Nicholas—do solo tap numbers. Little Mo squares off with the Hines character in a feverish sixty-second duet. And Little Mo dazzles.

In an earlier scene—and here the cinematographer seems to glaze the movie in sepia tones—the Hines character pauses in a room, halted there by the photos on the wall. There are Sammy and Eartha Kitt from *Anna Lucasta*; and Sammy in *Mr. Wonderful*; and Sammy, his father, and Will onstage in yet another photo. It is a kind of ode, an homage to the Will Mastin Trio and the kid who sprang from it.

"If I'm gonna die"—he said in *Taps*—"I wanna die with my tap shoes on."

Finally he went to Cedars-Sinai Hospital, accompanied by Shirley and Murphy, to have his throat checked. Doctors decided to do a biopsy. He was stoic when the diagnosis came: throat cancer.

His voice began to turn hoarse. His weight dropped. He had no desire to eat. He began a revolving-door round of visits to the hospital for radiation treatments. One day, when he was back home, there was a visitor. It was Dean Martin, who himself had been ailing: liver, ulcers. "He came around to see Sammy," Shirley says. "They hugged and cried. I don't know if they thought they'd see each other again."

Sammy made a commitment to do a TV movie—*The Kid Who Loved Christmas*—and it was to be filmed in Chicago. He'd now have to cancel. "The doctor called me and said, 'He shouldn't go,' " says Shirley. "I said, 'You call him.' He did. Sammy called me back, and said, 'We're going.' "

It was the hoofer in him. Sickly and weak, he boarded a plane for Chicago. Right into the winter. It was a small role. He played a musician, and soldiered through his scenes, then it was back to Los Angeles. But not for long. He had given his word: "Then we went to San Diego for a benefit," says Shirley. "It was the last thing we did."

George Schlatter—who had been working the floor the night at Ciro's when Sammy returned from the eye injury, and was now a successful Hollywood producer—started coming by the house to visit. He had never seen Sammy so weak. He told himself he'd put together a Sammy television special. George didn't care about the past controversies. "I didn't give a fuck that he hugged Nixon."

On January 25, Sammy was readmitted to Cedars-Sinai. The doctors told him they had to do a tracheotomy. He told Shirley without his voice he'd rather die. Out of sight from him, she broke down.

His eye, his hip, now his voice. He wanted to try radiation first; maybe save the voice despite the odds given by the doctors.

George Schlatter did what he promised himself. The evening's event—to be televised later as *Sammy Davis Jr.'s 60th Anniversary Celebration*—was held on November 13 in Hollywood.

Murphy helped Sammy get dressed. Sammy had asked the doctors if he could forgo radiation treatments that day. The treatments zapped his strength.

It was an array of stars, old Hollywood and new. There were Clint Eastwood and Goldie Hawn. Whitney Houston and Stevie Wonder. Michael Jackson. Of course Sinatra. Sammy was still Hollywood's biggest fan, and he couldn't stop himself from looking around. The gathering of so many celebrities deeply touched him. There were montages of him tapping, movie clips. Black-and-white clips of him and Frank and Dean. Carousing at the Sands. Ha ha. Years ago. Watch the draw of the gun; now it's back in the holster. The years had gone just like that—fast. Sammy bopped his head a bit. The one eye welled up.

Everyone struggled to keep it from feeling like a eulogy; still, at times it did. It was because of his physical appearance. He seemed smaller than ever. He seemed almost weightless.

Afterward, he invited certain guests over to his house. He looked happy, but weak. After they had left, Sammy turned to Murphy. He wanted to go for a ride; Murphy was befuddled. And there they were, in the limo. Sammy wanted to go back over to Cedars-Sinai. There was someone he wanted to see. He glided right by the nurses. No one asked him a question. He walked right into Madelyn Rhue's room. (The multiple sclerosis had sent her back to the hospital.) She was shocked to see him. And he started to tell her, with such unabashed joy, using his hands for emphasis, and his whispery voice, of the event just held for him, and of the party going on at his home. He told her who was there. "He said to me, 'Clint Eastwood was in my house! He had a drink in my house!' " He hugged and kissed Madelyn Rhue, and then he and Murphy glided through the night, back home.

Back home that night, Murphy put Sammy to bed.

It was a lovely little question, and they asked it between themselves often, especially upon greeting, though Frank asked Sammy more than Sammy asked Frank: "You got your shoes?"

Translation: You okay?

No one who heard it outside the business really understood it. It wasn't exactly a question about dancing shoes—tap shoes—at all. It was a question about life—about the family, the bank account, health. It covered everything. If you were okay, then of course you had your shoes. They weren't in somebody's glass case.

Days later, Sammy returned to Cedars-Sinai. The radiation treatments couldn't halt the cancer. They had to take the voice, and scheduled the surgery. He spent weeks hospitalized. Even with the surgery, his condition did not improve. The cancer had him in its grip.

On March 12 he went home, back up into the Hollywood Hills.

Chapter 19

THE FINAL CURTAIN

S hirley came by every day. He asked for a video monitor because he was so curious about who had gotten by the front gate and was coming to visit. February and April came and went.

On any good afternoon in May—the April rains having come and gone—the climb up to Sammy's house could be lovely. The flowers—the hyacinths and poinsettias, the irises and tulips—were in such bloom. That first week of May, a great many cars were coming up to Summit Ridge Drive. Hollywood never made any apologies that it was a furtive town.

Sammy was dying. He had stopped eating. He was tiny as a pillow. The rumors of his death slithered like snakes.

He was alive, but bedridden. Some days he was simply knocked out: the morphine. Because he was moody about eating, a feeding tube was inserted, which he frequently pulled out. Friends began sending over food and fruit trays. There was enough to feed a regiment. Someone sent a mogul-like spread: turned out to be from Merv Griffin, the mogul.

The month of May might be a poet's month, but it was a harsh month for the Davis men. Sam Sr. went May 21, 1988. Now, in May 1990, Sammy lay dying.

Elvera was in New Jersey, and they told her she ought to come on out.

Murphy, as expected, was taking it quite hard. He moved about like a mime. All his dreams—of being a comic, a singer—had been abandoned so he could spend his life with Sammy.

"Shirley was holding court, saying who could go up and see him and who couldn't," remembers Steve Blauner. Blauner climbed the stairs, and there lay Sammy, the Sammy who had dressed in long tweed and beatnik glasses back in Manhattan in the '50s; the same Sammy who had adopted him—the hulking Blauner—like a kid brother. Blauner sat and gazed long as he could take it. "I went outside and cried like a baby."

Robert Blake came by. Day after day he came. He said little, and he'd sit for

hours. Blake had been a child actor and sometime movie star who gave a powerful performance as one of the killers in the 1967 film *In Cold Blood*, based on
Capote's book. Blake's career, however, sagged. The television series *Baretta*,
which debuted in 1975 and ran to 1978, seemed to revive it. Sammy sang the
show's theme song—"Keep Your Eye on the Sparrow." But the show was
yanked after three years, and Blake went into a depression.

Back in the early 1950s, before Blake achieved any kind of film success, and
was often between roles, he'd take off, traveling for a spell around the country
with three Negro dancers—the Will Mastin Trio. Shirley and George got a kick
out of his company. He seemed so kind, and he seemed in need of emotional
comfort. Bobby Blake—whose real name was Michael Gubitosi—knew vaudeville, and his story was far from pretty. His parents forced him upon the stage,
sometimes administering beatings. He was one of the child actors in the *Our
Gang* series. His parents took most of his money. He'd tell all of these stories
later in life in the midst of his drinking and drug woes. Little Michael Gubitosi
had suffered unto the dreams of others. Now he'd come up to the house and
ask Shirley if she needed anything—anything at all. Then he'd take his seat
near Sammy's bed. He sat there looking at another ex–child actor. "I remember
Robert Blake was sitting there waiting for Sammy to die," says Blauner.

It was Lola; Lola Falana. She wanted to see Sammy. She had been battling
multiple sclerosis. Once, before Sammy's illness, she had started showing signs
of improving, and she called Shirley. She was living, quietly, in Las Vegas.
Sammy was appearing at Caesar's Palace. She wanted to show him she was
walking again. "I called Shirley and said, 'Do you think it'll be all right if I come
to say hello to Sammy?' They said, 'We'll have our people bring you up.' " She
stood outside the dressing-room door, and someone swung it open. Sammy
was inside, jawing with friends.

"I was in white boots, white pants, white top. He looked at me. If all the
emotions of a heart and soul could be in one perfect eye, it was there. He stood
up, slowly, as if the wind might blow him over. He said, 'You okay? You need
help?' I said, 'Stay there, Sammy.' He was crying. I was crying. Everybody was
crying. I think whatever weaknesses there might have been in his faith, he
thanked God right there." She credited Sammy with some of her physical
revival. "I believe, with all my heart, that Sammy prayed for me. When I got
multiple sclerosis, he said to me, 'I don't pray that much, but I said to God, "I
know I've tried your patience, but this friend of mine, if you would just heal
her, if you would help her, I'd turn my face to you the rest of my life." ' As I got
well, he was so happy."

Now Sammy was dying, and she wanted to see him. Before she went into the
room, Shirley pulled Falana aside. "When you go in, don't be upset if he
doesn't recognize you. We just think he's now in that twilight place. But at least

you can say you came to say good-bye." Shirley bent and told Sammy that Lola was in the room. "His eyes came to me," Falana recalls. "Once again, with that one eye, he smiled the biggest smile—the brightest light I ever seen on his face. Then his eyes just went back up into his head."

Burt and Jane Boyar were still coauthoring books, still traveling—Paris, Monaco, London. They didn't come to the house. They had visited Sammy earlier, at the hospital, shortly after the tracheotomy. "He looked gorgeous, dressed in silk pajamas. True to form, being Sammy," says Burt Boyar. "He received us looking like a little king." The Boyars had sat smiling at Sammy, at each other, memories of Manhattan and the Copa and staying up all night working on the book about a rising Negro entertainer that had seized them in their youth and was titled *Yes I Can*. They knew they'd never see him alive again. "We kissed him good-bye."

The cars kept coming up the driveway.

Jack Carter and his wife, Roxanne, came. It pained Roxanne that Altovise was often not around. "When Sammy was dying, Altovise was running off to the islands," she says. "She had a disease." It was her drinking, which had become heavy, which everyone seemed to know about.

Sinatra came. When he was on your side, and if you were in need, in distress, he would give anything to help. But health and life were not his to give. After his visits, other guests would see him out in the driveway, standing, alone, the head down.

The summer wind. And Sammy lay dying.

At night, the last thing Sammy would see during all the years he lived in this house—because he kept it on a stand next to his bed—was a picture of ten-year-old Judy Garland. At that age, just like him, she was out on the road, hustling, working, helping to put food on the table, trying to make the grown-ups who said they loved her happy. She was a child in glass slippers trying to get home. As for those ruby-red slippers Judy Garland wore in *The Wizard of Oz*, well, Sammy had those in a glass case in his house.

There were some camera trucks circling outside the driveway. Awaiting word.

May Britt, who lately had begun spending more and more time back in her native Sweden, came by. She and Sammy had remained cordial since the divorce.

Peter Brown, the cowboy, came by. Shook some hands, hugged Shirley, looked in on Sammy.

Jerry Blavat, the Philadelphia radio personality who had known Sammy since 1956, and was right there when Sammy married Altovise, stopped by almost daily. During one visit Blavat was toting some holy water. "They sent it from Rome," Blavat says. He asked Sammy's nurse to apply the holy water to

Sammy's neck. No one questioned the request. "They unwrapped his neck," remembers Blavat. "And they applied the holy water."

Sammy's weight slipped to sixty pounds.

Mark, Jeff, and Tracey, his children, came. Tracey, who had her mother's beauty, was working in television. She had gotten married; her husband was white. The boys were finding it hard to keep steady jobs, and May would some-times go weeks without seeing or hearing from them.

One morning Sammy was stirring around in bed a lot. Shirley understood: he wanted to go outside. So she wheeled him out to the back patio. Side to side he turned his head, off into the distance, all around. They were the hills he had conquered.

To have seen him in his twenties, carving up a stage; and to have seen him in his thirties, holding up two aging hoofers; to have seen him hugging the bony chests of old vaudevillians and slipping them money; and to have seen him singing before the queen of England; to have seen him at his sister's side, pleading with her to hold on as she grappled with her own demons about fam-ily pain; and to have seen him kiss his father on the lips and wonder to himself why he wasn't a better parent himself; to have seen him shining his own shoes—he said it relieved stress; to have seen him get emotional over a news-paper story about a family in distress because of fire or flood and insist they be sent money, not tomorrow, but now, immediately, money from his account, and flowers as well; and to have seen him express his joy at America—her nightclubs, her military bases, which he relished visiting, her women, black and white, whom he loved loving; to have seen him go from black to white, and white, to black, to Sammy, was all amazing. And Shirley had seen it all.

"I'm vaudeville," Sammy had said to a Radio City Music Hall crowd in 1977, aligning himself with that pantheon of entertainers who now were mostly dust.

She wheeled him back inside.

He didn't have his shoes on.

On May 16, 1990—it was 5:59 a.m., the sun up—the heart of Sammy Davis, Jr., stopped.

Throughout the day, the house filled with tears and sometimes shrieks. The child in blackface, the child inside the photo that hung in the foyer, had died. He was sixty-four years old.

Shirley and Murphy did not want the media—namely the tabloids—to get photographs of Sammy being taken from the house, as his body was so emaci-ated. Jerry Blavat had arrived at the house shortly after Sammy died. Noticing all the flowers in the home, Blavat came up with the idea to call the florist and have them send a truck, explaining that they wanted to cart some of the old flowers away. The truck soon arrived. Inside the home, Sammy was gingerly placed in a small black bag, and the bag was zipped up. Then he was carried out and set in the flower truck. The driver was given strict instructions to take his body to the funeral home. And when the truck rode out through the gates, the media unaware, Sammy was making his last ride down the sloping road, swathed in flowers.

Family members approached the gates and announced the death—and revealed that Sammy was already gone from the home.

And by midmorning, Sammy's mother, Elvera, was in the air, on her way.

The news immediately went out over the airwaves. Across the country and throughout Europe they began playing his songs on the radio—"Mr. Bojangles," "Birth of the Blues," "I've Gotta Be Me." At dusk that evening, the lights along the Strip in Las Vegas were dimmed for a minute in his honor.

Peggy King, the singer with whom he had fallen in love during the 1950s—Catherine to his Heathcliff—was in Philadelphia giving a USO performance that night. "A friend of mine that I loved died today," she told them about Sammy, "and I'd like to sing a song." She sang "I'll Be Seeing You," and as she was singing it, bodies started to rise from seats. "Generals were standing up," she remembers. "It was wild."

The worldwide obituaries recapped his career, mostly drawing information from *Yes I Can* and magazine articles.

"It was a generous God who gave him to us for all these years," said Sinatra.

"I'll see him later," promised Bill Cosby.

The evening before the funeral, on May 17, a private service was held at a small chapel in the Hollywood Hills. It was for family only. The casket was open; it would not be at the funeral. Sammy lay in a dark suit, red tie, red handkerchief. Altovise, his widow, and Murphy—who was family—and Shirley and his children got their last glimpse of him.

The sun was so bright on the day of his funeral that many wore sunglasses. Elvera sat in between May Britt and Altovise. Jess Rand, who had been out on the road with the Will Mastin Trio all those years ago, became agitated because he had to talk his way into the proceedings: Jess who? There were more than a few young teenagers milling around, tap shoes flung over their shoulders, who had come to pay respect to Sammy. An array of celebrities were in attendance. Milton Berle, Little Richard, Carroll O'Connor, Cicely Tyson; many more—Speaker Willie Brown of the California Assembly; Robert Wagner; Gregory Hines; Dick Gregory; of course Frank; of course Dean. Jerry Lewis didn't go to funerals. They struck him as hypocritical—but there he sat. Jesse Jackson—who but Jesse—stood next to Rabbi Allen Freehling.

"To love Sammy," Jesse said, "is to love black and white."

Lanes of two freeways were closed as the caravan of cars—more than three hundred—made its way out to Glendale.

He was laid to rest behind a gray stone wall, behind lock and key. His father lay next to him, Will Mastin three feet away.

SAMMY DAVIS JR.

"THE ENTERTAINER"

HE DID IT ALL

DEC. 8, 1925—MAY 16, 1990

Before his casket had been closed in that quiet Hollywood chapel the evening before his funeral, Murphy bent down and put something around Sammy's wrist. It was the gold watch Sinatra had sent him after that final tour. Sammy had left instructions that he wanted to be buried wearing it. Of the many things Sammy Davis, Jr., believed in—art, jazz, old performers, cinema history, photography, Emily Brontë's Heathcliff, Romanticism, English royalty, the memories of Al Jolson and Eddie Cantor, the proper way to bow onstage, the voice of Mahalia Jackson—he also believed in the supernatural, in the afterlife. He took out subscriptions to periodicals that told of such things.

The watch that Murphy slipped onto Sammy's wrist was glittering, and it was running. Maybe there were performances where he was going; maybe he'd need a good timepiece.

MOTHER OF A
MOTHERLESS CHILD

Mammy, don't you know me? It's your little baby!
AL JOLSON

Since he led a life without financial discipline, it is little wonder that there was such disarray following the death of Sammy Davis, Jr. Bills piled high; IRS debts went unpaid. There were overdue mortgage payments on the twenty-two-room home. Having no income of her own, Altovise, his widow, had no idea what to do. There were whispers of an auction of personal belongings. Of course, it would never come to that—only, of course, it did. The auction was conducted by Butterfield & Butterfield. Among the items were photographs, jewelry, a pair of tap shoes, the autograph book that Sammy—ever the fan—had inside his home. Long lines began forming outside the auction house that morning. Shirley Rhodes watched with fascination and without—she would have one believe—much sadness. "He would have loved it," she says of Sammy. "It was crowded. He wanted fans to have his stuff. It was standing room only."

Sammy's pearl-handled six-shooters were not put on the auction block. He had bequeathed them to Burt Boyar. Those six-shooters, still holstered, lie inside a glass case in Boyar's Los Angeles home.

Sammy's tap shoes were auctioned by Butterfield & Butterfield and went for eleven grand.

Eventually, Altovise lost the home she and Sammy had lived in.

Two of Sammy's children—Tracey and Mark—married young and suffered through divorces. Mark, strangely enough, went through three marriages before he reached thirty-five. There is no attempt here to make any connection to their father's marital history; the heart tends to go its own way, as it should. But a trend is a trend, something a biographer must acknowledge. In 1996, Tracey Davis wrote a book, *Sammy Davis Jr.: My Father*. It is a book by a child of Hollywood about a father whose persona remained a mystery to her. Tracey Davis would recall just that one solo breakfast with her father: it was hardly enough. Nor could the missed birthdays and graduation ceremonies be forgotten. "I know you love me Pop," she says at one point in the book to Sammy. "But where were you?" It is full of pain—a little girl lost from her father, angry at her stepmother, suffering the trials of her own identity.

I had one interview, in 1999, with Altovise Davis in New York City. There had been various reports of her living in poverty. If so, I couldn't tell. She looked rather elegant. She was, however, strangely guarded, and kept inquiring, in between my questions, if I were interested in helping her write a book about *her* life. I told her I was not; that I was otherwise engaged. Not long thereafter, I received a letter from Altovise in which she said if I wished any future interviews to take place, I would have to pay her. Thus we never spoke again.

In late 1998, I began a search to look up the obituaries of Sammy Davis, Sr., and Elvera Davis. The obits for Sam Sr. were easy enough to locate. But not so with Elvera. There was nothing. Then I realized that sometimes she used Elvera Sanchez, her maiden name. Still nothing. I called Congressman Charlie Rangel of New York, whom I had met while working on a previous book. I told him I was having trouble finding the obit of Elvera Davis, Sammy's mother, and asked him if she perhaps had passed away unnoticed. "She's not dead," he said. "That's the reason you can't find her obit."

She lived alone on the East Side of New York City in a town house. She was ninety-three years old. I was fortunate that the Sanchez women lived long lives. (Elvera's mother, Luisa Sanchez—Sammy's grandmother—had lived to be 112.) Upon seeing Elvera Davis for the first time, I couldn't help but see where her son's nose and angular features sprang from. There was certainly something of the Latina in Elvera, owing to her Cuban heritage. Her voice had a chill; she was wary of me. She wanted to know why I was interested in writing a book "about Sammy." I imagined she would shoo me away any moment. But she did not, and she started to talk—about her days as a showgirl, about Harlem, about the smoky nights of vaudeville. As I would inch up on a question about her and Sammy—it was as if she could smell the question I most wanted to ask: Why the gulf between the two of them?—she'd stare hard and unblinkingly at me. The stare signaled her oncoming quiet. There was a cane propped between her legs, which she rubbed periodically. Then came a small opening as she began talking of bad blood between her and Sam Sr., of letters written to Sammy in her hand that were returned unopened. I asked her about the long gaps, the long months, when she heard nothing from her son, when he was out there on the road: Did that bother you? After all, he was your baby, your child. She snapped; the interview was over; I had overstayed my welcome. I rose to leave. But then a strange thing happened: Elvera Davis asked me when I would be returning to New York City. And there was something in the back of her throat, something I sensed: it struck me that she might be a little lonely, that she hankered for company. I told her I'd return in a month, and wondered if we could perhaps have dinner. She said she would like to go out—*out,* as in to see some kind of entertainment. (Her grandnieces would later tell me that Elvera, in her ninety-third year, still went dancing.) I suggested something a little more sedate, perhaps a Broadway play; she mentioned *Ragtime.*

On my return, there she was, in the lobby of her apartment building. She was dressed in gold lamé and black, and wearing loopy earrings—they did not look cheap—several bracelets, rings on both sets of fingers, and a necklace around the throat. Truly bejeweled. Well, her Sammy loved jewelry, wore too much of it, in fact. Inside the lobby of the theater, she glittered in sparkles of light, idling and looking around with a showgirl's curiosity. She leaned on me with one hand, on her stylish cane with the other.

We reached the elevator to go downstairs, where theatergoers could have a bite to eat, or a refreshment. The elevator was out of order. "You should have called ahead and found out about this," she snapped to me, a sudden coldness in her voice building. I felt wobbly; I had angered the mother of Sammy Davis, Jr.!

I hustled through the crowd, wanting to find the stairs and the shortest possible route for me to walk her to them. I was breathing heavily, wondering if something might happen to her out of my sight. I got back to her, and there we were, finally, at the stairwell. "You really should have taken care of this! I don't appreciate this at all." Walking down the stairs, I held her for dear life. Those steps became my descent from Mt. Everest. I did not want Elvera Davis to slip, and fall, and break a bone. We were finally down, seated in a small room where refreshments were served. We each nibbled on fruit slices. I was practically shaking.

Halfway through the opening act of *Ragtime,* I looked over at Elvera. She was asleep. Perhaps the commotion around an inoperative elevator had exhausted her. But as she slept, I wondered anew why she remained out of Sammy's sight; why she didn't make even a feeble attempt to go rip him away from those two dream-hungry men. At first act's end, the applause woke her. "It's beautiful, isn't it?" Her voice was tiny as it fought against the rising applause. She had told me, during our first meeting, that she loathed the parents of famous entertainers who took advantage of their offspring.

At the end of *Ragtime,* Elvera wanted to meet Brian Stokes Mitchell, the show's star. But outside, the line at the stage door was frightfully long. We wouldn't get to see Mitchell; any fool could see that. So gliding along the line I suggested dinner. (I had more questions to ask, anyway!) Then, in a flash, Elvera Davis raised her cane above her head and started moving and elbowing up the line. The cane poked a man in his rear end; I looked away as his head jerked around. "Move, please!" Elvera hollered out. "I'm Sammy Davis's mother. Please move. I'm the mother of Sammy Davis, Jr.!" She stood at a glass booth, next to the stage door, and identified herself. The man behind the glass listened, seemingly drawn to her spiel. "Tell Brian Mitchell I want to see him. I'm Sammy Davis's mother." And there we were, in Mitchell's dressing room. He hugged Elvera and shook my stranger's hand and grinned at us both. He was in between performances; it was the matinee; of course he needed his rest before the evening show, and as there were others who wanted to meet him, we needed to go. But Elvera rested her cane, then herself, giving Mitchell no choice but to entertain us. He summoned his wife, who was also appearing in the play, and we all idled in his dressing room.

Afterward, Elvera and I went to dinner. On the way, she had sharp words for the taxi driver, whom she accused of taking the long way back to the East Side, needlessly hiking the fare. She sat mostly in silence at dinner. She had had enough of my line of inquiry about her and Sammy, and would direct the conversation elsewhere.

During the last months of her life, Elvera Davis began confiding to her niece Gloria that she needed to talk to someone, a professional. When her niece asked why, Elvera told her that she was beginning to worry why she hadn't cried at Sammy's funeral. They found a psychiatrist for Elvera to talk to. At the end of her first visit, the psychiatrist suggested a follow-up; he told her it would be wise. Elvera told him she could not schedule it right then because she had to check her appointment book, which was at home; she did not want to schedule a visit and have it conflict with her upcoming manicurist appointment. The psychiatrist thought the manicurist visit—whenever it happened to be—was not important, told her so, and waited for her to suggest a follow-up date. Elvera Davis did not approve of his tone, or his suggesting that her manicure date was unimportant. She rose, left, and never returned to see the psychiatrist again.

The last I saw of Elvera Davis, she was walking back inside her apartment building. She was leaning on the cane that had been given to her by Sammy— and given to Sammy by Will Mastin.

Elvera Davis died, at home, on September 2, 2000. She was ninety-five years old. None of Sammy's children attended her funeral. Mark Davis, Sammy's adopted son, actually confided to his aunt Gloria that he was intimidated by his grandmother's demeanor.

Maybe we are all lonely. And maybe we all suffer—more than we let on— under the gods of our own families.

Elvera's nieces and grandnieces went to clean out her apartment. In the apartment, they came across a box filled with mementos—cast listings from her showgirl wanderings; precious photos of her Cuban-born ancestors; other

Sammy, age five. In black (face) and white.
(COURTESY LORELEI FIELDS)

photos. Elvera in flapper dress; Elvera tending bar; Elvera standing pridefully next to the only man she married. There was a picture of Sammy Jr. and Sam Sr., side by side, in pinstriped suits. They were somewhere on the road. The year 1937 is etched on the photo. Little Sammy would have been twelve.

Despite what we would like to believe, sweetness and light does not fall from the womb of all mothers. Sammy would always wonder if his mother truly loved him. Who knows? Who are we to ask? Elvera Davis, like her own mother, lived her life at an emotional remove. When the world of show business snapped their children up, there was nary a motherly voice raised. They were tough Catholic women who mothered with coldness; they were descendants of Cuba's internecine wars; they both had lost husbands early. Of course they wished their children well, but they had no intentions of tarrying after them. Through the years, Elvera's children—Sammy and his sister, Ramona— would have questions for each other about their mother, each curious what the other knew. They were like sightless adults trying to stack chess pieces upright on a board. They realized that each was in too much darkness to help the other.

I had one long meeting with Ramona in a Harlem restaurant. She was quite formal. The only time she smiled was when she told me of the true joy of her childhood—seeing her little brother, Sammy, come through the door, off the road of vaudeville, and plop on the floor with her, where they would play, as brother and sister. At the time of our meeting, Elvera was still alive, but Ramona did not want to talk of her mother. She surprised me now and then by sending things through the mail. On two occasions, tapings of Sammy's concerts. And once she sent a photo of her and Sammy on a rare vacation together—1987, Hawaii. They've got their arms flung around one another. They're facing the camera—a brother and sister who were mostly separated at birth—and smiling.

Ramona James died in New York City on April 10, 2001.

Still waters run deep, all right; they can also be dangerous. There were many things Sammy triumphed over in his life, not the least his mother. His money could not come close to unraveling her hard life. But she had given him something quite significant: the dark and ferocious wind at his back. Elvera Davis was the love that haunted her only son, and the devil that drove him.

SOURCE NOTES

The bulk of this narrative has been shaped by interviews, of which all—more than 250—were conducted by the author. I was fortunate, during these five years, to come across nine individuals who had a decades-long relationship with the elusive Sammy Davis, Jr., and had rarely, if ever, talked about him. Especially warm thanks to: Cindy Bitterman, whom I thank not only for the long hours she talked to me about Sammy, but also for her godmothering grace; Jess Rand, for trusting me and spilling it all forth (not to mention the wonderful photo archive); Steve Blauner, for his candor, hospitality, and the Sammy film moments; Rudi Eagan, for his amazing concern about both book and author—and for the Las Vegas insights; Amy Greene, for all the doors she helped open; Burt Boyar, for the *Yes I Can* story and his graciousness; Shirley Rhodes, for her faith; and Peggy King and Helen Gallagher, for breaking their silence.

Others whom I thank for interviews: Jay Bernstein, Dick Gregory, William Gibson, Margaret Gibson, Hugh Benson, Judy Balaban, Rudy Duff, Jim Davis, Ernie Farrell, Dean Green, Carl Green, Jerry Blavatt, Randy Phillips, Bobby Short, Danny Stradella, David Levering Lewis, Jerri Spencer, Joe Stabile, Gregg Geller, Francis Davis, Jack Carter, Roxanne Carter, Johnny Brown, Altovise Davis, Marguerite DeLain, Al Grey, Lillian Cumber, Mary Louise, Bill Britten, Abe Lafferty, Pudgy Barksdale, Harry Belafonte, Mike Green, Peter Brown, Robert Guillaume, Lolly Fountain, Eileen Barton, Tony Franciosa, Doug Benton, Lola Falana, Ramona James, Mike Curb, Cholly Atkins, Billie Allen, Dorothy Dicker, Evelyn Cunningham, Elvera Davis, Steve Allen, Buddy Bregman, Charlotte Dicker, Warren Cowan, Jean Flemming, Carl Brandt, Lee Adams, Dee Dee Cotton, Betty Belle, Virginia Capehart, Joe Delaney, Sally Neal, Hilly Elkins, Charles Fisher, Richard Donner, Abe Ford, Frank Bolden, DeForest Covan, Tony Curtis, Milt Gabler, Will Jordan, Jerry Lewis, Miriam Nelson, Olga James, Frank Military, Pat Marshall, Virginia Henderson, Elliott Kozak, Lionel Hampton, Maggie Hathaway, Peggy Miller, Fayard Nicholas, Norma Miller, Elliott Norton, Phoebe Jacobs, Eartha Kitt, Dr. Fred Hull, Mabel Robinson, Marilyn McAdoo, Howard Koch, Bill Miller, Lenny Hirschan, Betty Isard, Sy Marsh, Molly Marsh, Leon Isaac Kennedy, Janet Leigh, Maurice Hines, Billy Kelly, Leroy Myers, Bonnie Rand, Albert Popwell, Luddie Waters, Philip Yordan, Paul Winik, Barbara Rush, Paula Wayne, George David Weiss, Gloria Williams, Tara Arthur, Lorelei Fields, Madelyn Rhue, Annie Stevens, George Schlatter, John Barry Ryan, Ann Slider, William Smith, Keely Smith, Pierre Turner, Margaret Styne, Prince Spencer, Timmie Rogers, Lloyd Richards, Chita Rivera, Claude Thompson, John Souza, Charles Strouse, Arthur Penn, Roger Straus, Bill Reed, and Josephine Premice.

Prologue: Yes He Can

When Sammy Davis, Jr.'s autobiography, *Yes I Can*, was published in 1965, it created something of a sensation. It made best-seller lists, it was widely reviewed. There had never been a book quite like it in American letters. But when I began peeling away the layers, probing the origins of the book, I became fascinated by what was *not* in *Yes I*

Can: no Davis family history, little if anything about Sammy's psyche. Thus I became more than a little curious about the book's genesis, inasmuch as the book itself had seemed to fasten itself upon the American reading public just as the door to the civil rights movement was swinging open.

Burt and Jane Boyar were the coauthors of *Yes I Can.* I wrote Burt—his wife, Jane, had died—and when I didn't hear back, I wondered if he had simply felt there was nothing else to discuss, that, for him at least, everything was in *Yes I Can.* My letter had actually wound its way across the ocean: Boyar was living in Spain at the time. When his reply arrived, he said he'd be more than happy to talk about Sammy and the creation of *Yes I Can.* He happened to be in the process of relocating to Los Angeles. There was much, he allowed, that never made it into the book. And thus began a kind of literary investigation on my part into the making of a book that, because of its litany of editors who came and went, was in constant peril of never being published. Burt Boyar sat for several interviews in his Los Angeles home. He prepared a delicious lunch once; he battled with me over a dinner bill on another occasion. My gratitude to him is large.

Others who were interviewed for this chapter: Carl Brandt, Roger Straus of Farrar, Straus and Giroux (publisher of *Yes I Can*), Jess Rand, Peggy Miller, Eartha Kitt, Cindy Bitterman, and Dick Gregory. (The notes cited here and in subsequent chapters are given where there is no obvious citation in the text.) **4:** "But you don't": Odets and Gibson, *Golden Boy,* 98; **4:** "Is his gun": *Hue,* 5-58; **5:** "the world's greatest": *Ebony,* 7-90; **5:** "Can it be": *New York Times,* 9-19-65; **10:** "We played the": Davis, *Yes I Can,* 74; **11:** "Baby, you'd better": ibid., 252; **12:** "I'm not going": ibid., 281; **19:** "Can I get": Odets and Gibson, *Golden Boy,* 74; **23:** "New York is": Kluger, *The Paper,* 701; **24:** "Something very nice": Plimpton, *Truman Capote,* 245; **26:** "an adroitly balanced": *New Yorker,* 10-30-65; **26:** "After the show": Davis, *Yes I Can,* 84–85; **27:** "So it does": *Christian Science Monitor,* 9-30-65; **27:** "I didn't write": Boyar interview; **27:** "tiny rejected spirit": *Negro Digest,* 1-66; **29:** "Strip him of ": *New York Review of Books,* 1-20-66; **29:** "Are you that": Branch, *Pillar of Fire,* 509; **30:** "Now, the plane": Davis, *Yes I Can,* 430–31; **31:** "It goes a": Ellison, *Invisible Man,* 15; **31:** "I turned on": Davis, *Yes I Can,* 6.

Chapter 1: Vaudeville Dreams

Upon the death of Elvera Sanchez Davis, Sammy's mother, I received a phone call. It was from Tara Arthur, a grandniece of Elvera's. She said that she had been cleaning out Elvera's apartment, sorting things, and had come across a letter I had written to Elvera. "Did she tell you about the Cuban side of the family?" Cuban side? "Yes, she was Cuban, not Puerto Rican." The revelation stunned me. Days later I sat in an apartment in upper Manhattan surrounded by women—one was Gloria Williams, Elvera's niece and Sammy's aunt—who not only told me of the family's Cuban roots, but shared photographs and dates of Cuban ancestry with me. Sammy had sought to keep this part of his family history secret. ("Families are strange," Williams said to me.) I am deeply grateful that Tara and her sister, Lorelei Fields, took the time to explain this family dynamic to me, which shed wonderful light upon Elvera and her own mother. I also benefited from three interviews with Elvera Davis herself. (An interview she gave to the Hatch-Billops Collection on March 25, 1990—it is a research library housed at 491 Broadway, New York, New York—proved helpful as well.) Steve Blauner invited me into his home in Marina Del Rey and showed me the rare and precious copy of *Rufus Jones for President,* Sammy's first film performance. Blauner's kindness seemed endless.

The interviews that proved most helpful for this chapter: Elvera Sanchez Davis, Tara Arthur, Lorelei Fields, Gloria Williams, and Virginia Capehart. **34:** "My mother was": *Playboy*, 12-66; **34:** "My mother was born": ibid.; **36:** "I am Cuban": Lorelei Fields interview; **36:** "the spectacle of ": Morris, *The Rise of Theodore Roosevelt*, 607; **37:** "have this war": ibid.; **37:** "Now, Senator, may": ibid., 608; **39:** "within five years": Courtney, *The Intimate Biography of Laurette Taylor*, 129; **39:** "We don't serve": Lorelei Fields interview; **40:** "One day I": Hatch-Billops, 31; **40:** "bloodthirsty black men": Lewis, *When Harlem Was in Vogue*, 4; **41:** "The tide of": ibid., 5; **41:** "Before Jim Europe": Ward and Burns, *Jazz: A History of America's Music*, 70; **42:** "You knew": ibid., 142; **42:** "Up in Harlem": Anderson, *This Was Harlem*, 157; **42:** " 'Gladys Bentley' was": ibid., 169; **43:** "a sociological El Dorado": Lewis, *When Harlem Was in Vogue*, 164; **43:** "Right around the": Hatch-Billops, 30; **43:** "We'd go there": ibid.; **43:** "In some places": Lewis, *When Harlem Was in Vogue*, 103; **44:** "We would do": Hatch-Billops, 32; **45:** "I don't want": ibid., 31; **46:** "Little kids would": ibid., 31; **47:** "Sharp as he": ibid.; **47:** "emboldens bad Negroes": Gates and Appiah, *Africana*, 2002; **47:** "Our experience": ibid.; **49:** "Negro life is": Anderson, *This Was Harlem*, 202; **50:** "almost an addiction": Douglas, *Terrible Honesty*, 288; **50:** "Get the fuck": Lewis, *When Harlem Was in Vogue*, 183; **50:** "Damn it man": ibid., 99; **53:** "How do I": Buckley, *The Hornes*, 84; **54:** " 'Where is the' ": Lewis, *When Harlem Was in Vogue*, 35–36; **55:** "Look for me": Evans, *The American Century*, 195; **55:** "a little monkey": Virginia Capehart interview.

Chapter 2: Long Shadows

Anyone writing about vaudeville—especially Negro vaudeville and blackface minstrel performers—owes a great debt to Henry Sampson. He has written several books—they are mostly tucked away in the special-collections archives of select libraries—about early Negro performers. His *Blacks in Blackface* has been extraordinarily helpful to me. Sampson has tracked various early twentieth-century vaudeville troupes back and forth across the country. One hopes his books reach a wider audience, though that does not seem to be the joy of his mission. He simply wants to provide a road map into the lost pages of history, which he has done.

57: "a true copy": Hughes and Meltzer, *Black Magic*, 24; **58:** "NATIONAL THE-ATRE": ibid., 37; **58:** "a passel of darkies": ibid., 33; **59:** "On Billy Kersands": Sampson, *Blacks in Blackface*, 391; **60:** "State all that": ibid., 60; **61:** " 'Tommy' meant prostitute": Stearns, *Jazz Dance*, 128; **61:** "His name was": ibid., 254; **61:** "Is we all": Douglas, *Terrible Honesty*, 328; **62:** "I have no": *New York Age*, 12-29-18; **62:** "Give me ten": Cantor, *My Life Is in Your Hands*, 160; **62:** "Bert Williams was": *Amsterdam News*, 5-30-23; **62:** "He was the": Cantor, *My Life Is in Your Hands*, 159; **63:** "We greet you": *Amsterdam News*, 4-18-23; **64:** "Many theatres have": Muse, *Way Down South*, 22–23; **65:** "five times as": Anderson, *This Was Harlem*, 242; **65:** "By 1930, Harlem": ibid., 243; **65:** "as if reluctant": Douglas, *Terrible Honesty*, 464; **65:** "A night club": Lewis, *When Harlem Was in Vogue*, 266; **66:** "The West Coast": Douglas, *Terrible Honesty*, 467; **68:** "Sammy used to": *Boston Globe*, 8-2-55; **68:** "I think the": undated Earl Wilson column in *Porgy and Bess* archives (Robert Breen Collection, folder #2), Ohio State University; **71:** "You're Just a": Courtney, *The Intimate Biography of Laurette Taylor*, 27; **71:** "You see a": William C. Young, *Famous Actors and Actresses on the American Stage*, vol. 2 (New York: R. R. Bowker, 1975), 1042; **72:** "Sometimes on a": Short, *Black and White Baby*, 82; **73:** "My spine tingled": Davis, *Hollywood in a Suitcase*, 39; **73:** "We moved from": Davis, *Yes I Can*, 20; **73:**

"When I was": Sampson, *Blacks in Blackface,* 404; **74:** "talented": Sampson, *Black and White,* 422; **75:** "I never was": Waters, *His Eye is on the Sparrow,* 1; **75:** "Only the details": Davis, *Yes I Can,* 17; **77:** "coon shouting from": Stearns, *Jazz Dance,* 254; **77:** "The melancholy spirituals": Sampson, *Blacks in Blackface,* 23; **78:** "Momma, squeeze me": Virginia Capehart interview; **78:** "Little Florence, so": Sampson, *Blacks in Blackface,* 402; **80:** "There is a": Evans, *The American Century,* 248; **80:** "I wasn't invited": Gates, *Africana,* 1472–73.

Chapter 3: The Kid in the Middle

The vaudeville dancers who shared their memories of watching the young Sammy dance were Billy Kelly, Paul Winik, Pudgy Barksdale, Prince Spencer—who became famous in his own right—and Leroy Meyers. I thank them all. I found Abe Ford, one of the earliest of the agents for the Will Mastin Trio, in Boston. He was still working out of his theatrical office on Tremont Street in 2001. (Ford died, at the age of eighty-nine, in 2002.) Other interviews that proved helpful: Mabel Robinson, Elvera Davis, and Abe Lafferty. **82:** "Hey! Here they": Earley, *Sammy Davis Reader,* 468; **84:** "A couple of": *Providence Journal Bulletin,* 3-25-40; **88:** "I used to": Davis, Hatch-Billops, 35; **88:** "You had a": ibid.; **88:** "Those were good": *Montreal Gazette,* 8-24-77; **89:** "And we were": ibid.; **89:** "a mecca for": ibid.; **99:** "persuade, embarrass, compel": Gates, *Africana,* 2029; **99:** "You say we're": ibid.; **100:** "the right to": ibid., 2027; **100:** "You niggers were" ibid., 2028; **100:** "We look to": Morris, *The Rise of Theodore Roosevelt,* 453; **100:** "executive lynch law": Louis R. Harlan, *Booker T. Washington, The Wizard of Tuskegee* (New York: Oxford University Press, 1983), 311; **101:** "I ain't arguin' ": Davis, *Yes I Can,* 52; **102:** "How many white": ibid., 55; **102:** "Awww, don't carry": ibid., 57; **102:** "Overnight, the": ibid.; **103:** "My talent was": ibid., 54; **104:** "I dug down": ibid., 75; **104:** "It was the": *New York Times,* 5-16-98.

Chapter 4: And Sammy Shall Lead Them

Others—in addition to the aforementioned Amy Greene—who were quite helpful in this chapter were Judy Balaban, Steve Allen, Timmie Rogers, Keely Smith, and Lionel Hampton. **109:** "Now that's a": Davis, *Yes I Can,* 99; **110:** "I don't know": Rooney, *I.E., An Autobiography,* 50–51; **112:** "OPEN CAPITOL THEATRE": Davis, *Why Me,* 37; **112:** "I'll never forget": Kelley, *His Way,* 115; **113:** "I can lick": ibid., 117; **113:** "You sound too": *Down-Beat,* 8-56.

Chapter 5: White Sammy, Black Sammy

In distilling the dual worlds in which Sammy Davis, Jr., operated—he was truly one of our earliest crossover artists—it was crucial that I find those who pulled him into their (white) world. Inasmuch as Sammy hungered for female acceptance, these women were of great interest to me. Those interracial assignations also offered powerful hints of danger. As mentioned earlier, I'm thankful for the time Helen Gallagher and Peggy King chose to spend with me—Gallagher in New York City, and King in Philadelphia. (King appears in Chapter 6.) Both women also shared illuminating photographs. Others who were important to this chapter were Tony Curtis, Janet Leigh, Jess Rand, Bonnie Rand, Arthur Penn, Eartha Kitt, and Francis Taylor. As well, I will not soon forget my hours-long session with Jerry Lewis on his houseboat in the San Diego harbor. **116:**

"The resemblance of": *The American Heritage Dictionary of the English Language*, 3d ed. (Boston: Houghton Mifflin, 1992); **119:** "I just don't": *Ebony*, 12-50; **119:** "Hollywood is": *Vanity Fair*, 4-98; **121:** "I knew it": Reed, *Hot from Harlem*, 169; **121:** "Once in a": Davis, *Yes I Can*, 132; **129:** "I'm not saying": *Ebony*, 12-50; **130:** "My format for": Cantor, *My Life Is in Your Hands*, 246; **132:** "the whitest black": ibid., 159; **139:** "We started in": Kitt, *Thursday's Child*, 190; **144:** "As Sammy Davis' ": letter dated May 5, 1954, in personal files of Jess Rand; **144:** "Results offered sharp": Bogle, *Prime Time Blues*, 9; **145:** "Hazel Scott has": ibid., 16; **145:** "We should not": Wil Haygood, *King of the Cats: The Life and Times of Adam Clayton Powell, Jr.* (Boston: Houghton Mifflin, 1993) 162; **146:** "white folks kitchen": Bogle, *Prime Time Blues*, 25; **146:** "There are three": Watkins, *On the Real Side*, 278; **146:** "I done told": ibid., 317; **147:** "An entire race": ibid., 322.

Chapter 6: Through a Glass Eye Brightly

It seemed improbable to be sitting in the San Bernardino living room of Dr. Fred Hull, the eye surgeon who removed Sammy's eye back in 1954. But there we were. I am grateful to Dr. Hull for the long interview, as well as his allowing me to look at the notes he wrote on a yellow pad immediately following the Davis surgery. (It seemed a bit haunting to me when Hull picked up a large magnifying glass to read: "I'm losing my sight," the eye surgeon said, matter-of-factly.) It was Virginia Henderson, the admitting nurse that night in 1954, who led me to Hull. She, too, was of immense help in piecing together Sammy's hospital stay. Others who were quite helpful in this chapter: Frank Military, Jess Rand, Cindy Bitterman, Eileen Barton, Jerry Lewis, Janet Leigh, Judy Balaban, Keely Smith, Roxanne Carter, Amy Greene, Maurice Hines, and Peggy King. **153:** "And what is": Cadillac ad, owned by author; **157:** "I had no": Davis, *Yes I Can*, 7; **163:** "I just got": ibid., 29; **171:** "Onstage he": Greene interview; **171:** "Let us not": Evans, *The American Century*, 447; **171:** "The truth": Halberstam, *The Fifties*, 568; **172:** "The show is": Stott, *On Broadway*, 244; **172:** "You see, young": Branch, *Parting the Waters*, 119; **172:** "Whenever he's": *San Bernardino Sun*, 11-25-54; **174:** "No longer did": Salamon, *Facing the Wind*, 83; **179:** "Fainting, which": Herr, *The Big Room*, 131; **179:** "Ava does strange": Rooney, *I.E.*, 126; **179:** "The night we": ibid., 144; **184:** "When he was": Gabler, *An Empire of Their Own*, 305; **184:** "When I met": ibid., 306; **184:** "Let me caution": Davis, *Yes I Can*, 292; **185:** "Though the notion": Baldwin, *The Price of the Ticket*, 7; **185:** "It is part": ibid., 8; **194:** "too damned old": Davis, *Yes I Can*, 233; **194:** "It was Sammy": *Variety*, 1-11-55; **196:** "Never dug you": telegram in Rand personal files; **197:** "In a time": *Time*, 4-18-55; **200:** "Photographs, which": Sontag, *On Photography*, 68; **201:** "It is as": Brontë, *Wuthering Heights*, viii (Modern Library edition).

Chapter 7: The Great White Sammy Way

Tracking down members of a Broadway show more than four decades old presented challenges. And yet, they were wondrous challenges, inspired more so by various members of the *Mr. Wonderful* cast themselves, who would lead me to other members, and those members on to yet other members. Sally Neal, a gypsy dancer in that cast, was remarkably warm and generous with both time and photographs. My two visits with the still-beautiful Olga James provided inestimable insights into Sammy, his father, and Will Mastin: the trio. Jule Styne's widow, Margaret, helped me understand her husband. Jack and Roxanne Carter had me to their Beverly Hills home for a holiday dinner. (Jack was one of Sammy's *Wonderful* costars.) Others who were interviewed for this chapter: Claude Thompson, Josephine Premice, Dorothy Dicker (for years Jule Styne's top assistant), George David Weiss, Harry Belafonte, Jess Rand, Dean Green, Carl Green, Chita Rivera, and Steve Blauner, whose contributions have been spoken of elsewhere. **207:** "those two West": Poitier, *This Life*, 261; **208:** "More or less": Taylor, *Jule*, 37; **209:** "The big-band": ibid., 49; **210:** "Please, Nan": Stott, *On Broadway*, 154; **211:** "Someday, somehow": ibid., 14; **211:** "It was apparent": Taylor, *Jule*, 188; **211:** "The sooner": ibid., 181; **212:** "they were going": Weiss interview; **212:** "We're going to": ibid.; **213:** "an opera": Taylor, *Jule*, 189; **213:** "I'm going to": Weiss interview; **213:** "Give it a": ibid.; **215:** "a force of": Douglas, *Terrible Honesty*, 292; **215:** "Oh mama, mama": Evans, *The American Century*, 255; **216:** "For hour after": Kefauver, *Crime in America*, 11; **216:** "A nationwide crime": ibid., 12; **216:** "Wish you were": ibid., 3; **216:** "Infiltration of": ibid., 16; **216:** "disreputable persons": Tosches, *Dino*, 162; **217:** "I spent a": *The New Yorker*, 11-3-97; **218:** "a Miami Beach": Sammy Davis, Jr., FBI files, document #100-450712, 3; **220:** "emissary to the": Rose, *The Agency*, 180; **220:** "Sign!": Jess Rand interview; **223:** "What would you": Taylor, *Jule*, 189; **224:** "Abraham Lincoln": Blumenthal, *The Stork Club*, 159; **224:** "I didn't want": Taylor, *Jule*, 189; **225:** "Are we casting": ibid., 190; **226:** "greatest significance": Ward and Burns, *Jazz*, 386; **226:** "Time moves by": Stott, *On Broadway*, 259; **227:** "a crossroads Marilyn": Halberstam, *The Fifties*, 432; **227:** "Have you ever": ibid., 436.

Chapter 8: The Wonder of It All

I am quite grateful to Dean Ward for sharing with me his historical knowledge of the Friars Club. **233:** "a tedious two-hour": *Philadelphia Daily News*, 2-22-56; **233:** "Major innovation": ibid.; **234:** "I don't want": Taylor, *Jule*, 190; **234:** "Unless you listen": ibid., 191; **234:** "Don't worry": ibid.; **234:** "In the show": ibid.; **235:** "The youthful Davis": *New York Journal-American*, 3-23-56; **235:** "Don't get me": ibid.; **235:** "On exit the": Taylor, *Jule*, 191; **235:** "The time was": Stott, *On Broadway*, 279; **237:** "They don't do": ibid., 284; **238:** "blood would flow": Gabler, *Winchell*, 429; **244:** "I believe you": Halberstam, *The Fifties*, 562; **249:** "the relief of": Stephen Bogart, *Bogart: In Search of My Father* (New York: Dutton, 1995), 55; **250:** "Sammy Davis Jr.": *Variety*, 12-25-57; **250:** "definitely": *Variety*, 3-18-58.

Chapter 9: A Hitchcockian Affair

Janet Leigh, Steve Blauner, Harry Belafonte, Tony Curtis, Buddy Bregman, Cindy Bitterman, Jess Rand, Annie Stevens, and Jerry Lewis all were helpful in my understanding the Sammy–Kim Novak relationship. Luddie Waters, a former assistant to Novak, had made a promise to the actress that she'd never talk about the affair. Still, I had a long conversation with Waters in Los Angeles: she kept her promise to Novak, but offered valuable insights into Sammy's early years in Hollywood and the operations of his business office. (Waters preceded Shirley Rhodes as Sammy's office manager.) **254:** "Bring your sick": *Look*, 10-12-57; **256:** "And in the": Goodman, *The Fifty-Year Decline and Fall of Hollywood*, 273; **257:** "the proverbial quality": Katz, *The Film Encyclopedia*, 1026; **262:** "Lynch her!": Halberstam, *The Fifties*, 675; **270:** "Wedding of Sammy": *Ebony*, 4-58; **270:** "Well, it only": *Vanity Fair*, 4-99; **272:** "When audiences left": Davis, *Hollywood in a Suitcase*, 46; **272:** "I'd proud": *Look*, 11-12-57.

Chapter 10: On to Catfish Row

Playwright Philip Yordan was not up to a personal visit, but he indulged me in a long phone conversation about *Anna Lucasta*. Jess Rand, Virginia Henderson, Jean Flemming, Lenny Hirschan, and Buddy Bregman were all helpful to this chapter. 274: "portray Negro life": Gates, *Africana*, 83; 274: "Go ahead": Stott, *On Broadway*, 69; 274: "I remember watching": Davis and Dee, *With Ossie & Ruby*, 157; 274: "People began to": Stott, *On Broadway*, 69; 274: "In St. Louis": Poitier, *This Life*, 118–19; 275: "Chicago, at that": Davis and Dee, *With Ossie & Ruby*, 158; 275: "The company had": ibid., 165; 275: "Hollywood's lavish": ibid., 167; 275: "Opportunity's golden door": ibid.; 275: "He told me": *Arna Bontemps–Langston Hughes Letters, 1925–1967*, ed. Charles H. Nichols (New York: Dodd, Mead & Company, 1980), 270; 277: "blatantly portray": Gevison, *American Film Institute Catalog*, 130; 278: "The story has": ibid., 38; 278: "There is no": ibid.; 278: "racial grounds": ibid.; 280: "It was doomed": Early, *Sammy Davis Reader*, 494; 280: "We want a": Collier-Thomas and Franklin, *My Soul Is a Witness*, 103; 280: "colored help on": ibid.; 281: "I was completely": ibid., 107; 281: "Negroes in long": Alpert, *The Life and Times of* Porgy and Bess, 22; 281: "The best novel": ibid., 39; 282: "I think he": ibid., 89; 282: "You've done it": ibid., 111; 282: "When the cries": ibid., 112; 282: "a Bess of": ibid., 171; 282: "Uncle Toms": ibid., 224; 283: "Ve have dem": ibid., 225; 283: "Samuel Smalls, who": ibid., 17; 283: "Just think of": ibid., 17; 283: "To Smalls, I": ibid., 784; 284: "Porgy lived in": Heyward, *Porgy*, 16; 284: "I had a": Berg, *Goldwyn*, 480; 285: "quiet boycott": Gevison, *AFI Catalog*, 784; 285: "In a period": ibid.; 285: "Him?": Berg, *Goldwyn*, 479; 286: "No one is": ibid., 482; 286: "trespasses upon my": Gevison, *AFI*, 785; 286: "I believe that": *New York Times*, 8-7-58; 287: "I won't be here": Early, *Sammy Davis Jr. Reader*, 62; 291: "undoubtedly the greatest": *San Bernardino Sun*, 11-16-58; 291: "In previous stage": Gevison, *AFI*, 786; 291: "The most articulately": *Variety* ad, Jess Rand collection; 292: "It's hard for": *Montreal Gazette*, 11-6-59; 292: "I love her": ibid.

Chapter 11: The Sands of Las Vegas and Beyond

The great theatrical director Lloyd Richards was instrumental in my understanding Sammy's desires to constantly take artistic risks. Paula Wayne, Sammy's *Golden Boy* costar, invited me to Florida. Hilly Elkins filled in the *Golden Boy* drama: a play that became a drama unto Sammy. Others who were so helpful: Warren Cowan, Bill Miller (we sat in the shade of his Palm Springs home, by the pool, as Sammy and the Pack used to do), Shirley Rhodes, Jay Bernstein, Charles Strouse, and Lee Adams. 298: "It won't be": Early, *The Sammy Davis Jr. Reader*, 237; 298: "Here she is": *New York Herald Tribune*, 6-7-60; 300: "Mob Routs Nazis": *Los Angeles Mirror*, 10-26-60; 301: "This award just": Joey Bishop interview; 304: "if Richard Nixon": Branch, *Parting the Waters*, 219; 311: "Mama, it is": Hansberry, *To Be Young, Gifted and Black*, 109; 313: "American Negroes through": Reeves, *President Kennedy*, 462; 313: "It looks like": ibid., 464; 313: "What's he doing": ibid.; 313: "more fictional than": ibid., 463; 314: "its worst case": Branch, *Pillar of Fire*, 131; 316: "Sammy Davis' Mother": *Carolinian*, 6-15-1963.

Chapter 12: Sammy and Hilly

Playwright William Gibson, sitting in the sunroom of his Stockbridge, Massachusetts, home, explained so very well the competitive juices that flowed between Sammy and Hilly Elkins. Gibson's wife, Margaret, a renowned psychoanalyst—and Odets scholar—also offered a shrewd assessment of how she viewed Sammy and his racial conundrum. Lola Falana might not have talked were it not for the nod from Shirley Rhodes. Sally Neal was again helpful. Others interviewed for this chapter were Johnny Brown, Elliott Norton, Arthur Penn, and Marguerite DeLain. **327:** "I'm going to": Elkins interview; **328:** "burlesque without": Hughes and Meltzer, *Black Magic*, 232.

Chapter 13: Golden

333: "an archangel who": William Gibson, *Sammy Davis Jr.: Golden Boy* (New York: Bantam, 1965), 10; **334:** "All of the": *Boston Globe*, 5-19-64; **334:** "a joke can": ibid., 7-28-64; **335:** "I don't have": ibid.; **337:** "This black crisis": William Gibson interview; **345:** "Who do you": Odets and Gibson, *Golden Boy*, 37; **345:** "Go on a": ibid., 46; **345:** "Sure, thousands": ibid., 47; **345:** "My poppa's a": ibid.; **345:** "Hands offa": ibid., 48; **346:** "White girls": ibid., 49; **346:** "Joe, take me": ibid., lines attached to flyleaf, following p. 64; **347:** "the pride of": ibid., 118; **347:** "I'm going to": ibid., 120; **347:** "I mean he's": ibid., 121; **348:** "Oh, Lorna": ibid., 123; **348:** "Oh my God": ibid., 125; **350:** "The theatrical form": *New York Times*, 10-21-64; **350:** "The death watch": *New York Herald Tribune*, 10-22-64.

Chapter 14: Fade to Black

Shirley Rhodes, Hilly Elkins, and Robert Guillaume were quite helpful in this chapter. **357:** "bone bruises in": *New York Times*, 7-2-65; **359:** "I can look": ibid.; **359:** "I've always felt": *Life*, 2-4-66; **360:** "Put down the": ibid.; **362:** "Our cry to": Branch, *Pillar of Fire*, 555; **362:** "I'm a field": ibid., 579; **362:** "Gandhi's march to": Lewis, *Walking with the Wind*, 325; **362:** "I don't know": ibid., 330; **366:** "a man who": Oriana Fallaci, *The Egotists: Sixteen Surprising Interviews* (Chicago: H. Regnery, 1968), 232–33; **368:** "a terrifying evening": Hughes, *Black Magic*, 252; **369:** "This past, the": Baldwin, *The Price of the Ticket*, 376; **371:** "humor is loaded": *Daily Variety*, 4-20-98.

Chapter 15: Mirrors

The Alex Haley–Sammy Davis, Jr., interview (conducted for *Playboy*) is at the Schomburg Center for Research in Black Culture, the New York Public Library, listed under "Alex Haley Papers." The collection is as yet uncatalogued. Attached to the interview— and unnumbered—are notes Haley kept of the interview. The helpful interviews for this chapter: Virginia Capehart, Jerry Lewis, Harry Belafonte, Shirley Rhodes, Tony Franciosa, Lolly Fountain, Altovise Davis, Hilly Elkins, and Lola Falana. **376:** "I had been": *Playboy*, 12-66; **376:** "a jug band": ibid.; **376:** "Sammy puts on": ibid.; **376:** "Even his dancers": ibid.; **376:** "I get so": ibid.; **376:** "a classic": ibid.; **377:** "They made me": ibid.; **378:** "They let me": ibid.; **382:** "All I need": Tosches, *Dino*, 226; **382:** "Why would

Sammy": ibid.; **384:** "taken over by": Davis, *Why Me,* 177; **384:** "I stood up": Davis, *Yes I Can,* 630; **385:** "I don't care": *Playboy,* 12-66; **392:** "Don't mean a shit": Davis, *Why Me,* 214; **393:** "You know they": Early, *The Sammy Davis Jr. Reader,* 237; **397:** "The kids screamed": Evans, *The American Century,* 551.

Chapter 16: Sammy and Tricky Dick

I am grateful to Mark Feeney—one of my former colleagues at the *Boston Globe*—for sharing with me his shrewdly insightful (though yet to be published) book, "Nixon and the Movies." It proved a wonderful guide into the cinematic mind-set of President Richard M. Nixon. Jess Rand, Jay Bernstein, Richard Donner, Sy Marsh, Molly Marsh, Lolly Fountain, Jerry Blavat, Altovise Davis, Charles Fisher, Ann Slider, Shirley Rhodes, Timmie Rogers, Mike Curb, and Madelyn Rhue were all also helpful here. **403:** "We should show": *Hartford Courant,* 2-20-73; **404:** "Sammy's a white": Sy Marsh interview; **416:** "after about twenty-four": Leonard Maltin, *Leonard Maltin's 2002 Movie & Video Guide* (New York: Penguin Putnam, 2001), 1535; **418:** "She was in": Davis, *Why Me,* 248; **419:** "my rock and": *Women's Wear Daily,* 10-10-72; **420:** "The program you": McNeil, *Total Television,* 26; **420:** "obviously queer": *Washington Post,* 3-21-2002; **420:** "It's a very": *Ebony,* 6-72; **421:** "If God had": *TV Guide,* 1-23-99; **422:** "Is Archie Bunker": *Ebony,* 6-72; **422:** "You see, I": Feeney, "Nixon," 1; **422:** "Flush Model Cities": Evans, *The American Century,* 570; **423:** "We've got Jim": Davis, *Why Me,* 249; **425:** "I know that": Evans, *The American Century,* 557; **426:** "You gotta ease": Davis, *Why Me,* 255; **426:** "I saw some": *Boston Globe,* 2-24-72; **426:** "They're very lonesome": *Ebony,* 6-72; **426:** "Motherfucker": Davis, *Why Me,* 253; **427:** "I can't discuss": *Ebony,* 6-72; **428:** "He never learned": Feeney, "Nixon," 1; **428:** "There was no": Davis, *Why Me,* 258; **429:** "amnesty, acid": Evans, *The American Century,* 571; **431:** "Ladies and gentlemen": Davis, *Why Me,* 261; **431:** "Sammy, I want": Sy Marsh interview; **432:** "Well, let me": Davis, *Why Me,* 263; **433:** "Isn't that a": Feeney, "Nixon," vi; **433:** "What are we": *New York Times Sunday Magazine,* 10-15-72; **434:** "unbelievable": ibid.; **435:** "Ladies and gentlemen": Marsh interview; **436:** "It struck me": Davis, *Why Me,* 267; **436:** "Brothers, if it": ibid.; **436:** "This is about": ibid., 271; **437:** "Brother, can I": ibid., 272; **437:** "Despite all the": Feeney, "Nixon," unnumbered page before introduction; **438:** "You aren't going": Davis, *Why Me,* 263.

Chapter 17: Ode to the Vaudevillian

Jack Carter, Shirley Rhodes, John Souza, Sy Marsh, Jim Davis, Madelyn Rhue, and Leon Isaac Kennedy all sat for interviews and have my gratitude. **439:** "The flak got": Early, *The Sammy Davis Jr. Reader,* 539; **439:** "It is only": Morris, *The Rise of Theodore Roosevelt,* 54; **440:** "Fucking youth": Davis, *Why Me,* 274; **441:** "How does she": *New York Times,* 4-24-02; **441:** "And I liked": Davis, *Why Me,* 280; **442:** "Sammy never asked": Early, *The Sammy Davis Jr. Reader,* 86; **443:** "He had his": ibid.; **447:** "The whole thing": Tosches, *Dino,* 426; **448:** "What we want": Frady, *Jesse,* 256; **449:** "It suggests": Baldwin, *The Price of the Ticket,* 556; **454:** "obscure white and black": Davis, *Why Me,* 300; **457:** "The state of": Pomerantz, *Peachtree,* 485; **463:** "Secondly, I wasn't": *Washington Post,* 12-6-87; **463:** "When he didn't": ibid.

Chapter 18: The Ides of Time

Sy Marsh, Shirley Rhodes, and George Schlatter were all helpful. **465:** "We've got to": Davis, *Why Me*, 364; **465:** "How much longer": Tosches, *Dino*, 451; **465:** "Smokey, let's": Davis, *Why Me*, 364; **466:** "golden child": ibid., 365; **466:** "This is the": *Washington Post*, 12-6-87; **466:** "You start it": Davis, *Why Me*, 367; **466:** "Ladies and gentlemen": ibid.; **466:** "We want to": ibid.; **466:** "This country has": Tosches, *Dino*, 453; **466:** "The accountants say": Davis, *Why Me*, 368; **466:** "What the fuck": ibid., 370; **466:** "Pay what we": ibid.; **467:** "Can't hear": Tosches, *Dino*, 453; **467:** "For me": ibid.; **467:** "Don't unpack": ibid., 454; **471:** "the last of": Jerry Lewis interview; **472:** "This movie represents": *Boston Globe*, 2-10-89.

Chapter 19: The Final Curtain

I thank Shirley Rhodes for accompanying me to Sammy Davis's grave site in Glendale: one needs a key to enter the gated site. Lola Falana, Steve Blauner, Burt Boyar, Peter Brown, and Jack Carter all shared their memories of Sammy's last days. **478:** "I'm vaudeville": *New York Times*, 10-3-77; **479:** "It was a": *Los Angeles Times*, 5-17-90; **479:** "I'll see him": ibid.; **479:** "To love Sammy": *Ebony*, 7-90.

Epilogue: Mother of a Motherless Child

Elvera Davis, Gloria Williams, and Ramona Davis—all, like Sammy, touched by Cuban blood—had memories to share.

SELECTED BIBLIOGRAPHY

Alexander, Michael. *Jazz Age Jews*. Princeton, N.J.: Princeton University Press, 2001.

Alpert, Hollis. *The Life and Times of* Porgy and Bess: *The Story of an American Classic*. New York: Knopf, 1990.

Anderson, Jervis. *This Was Harlem: A Cultural Portrait, 1900–1950*. New York: Farrar, Straus and Giroux, 1983.

Appiah, Kwame Anthony, and Henry Louis Gates, Jr. *Africana: The Encyclopedia of the African and African American Experience*. New York: Basic Civitas Books, 1999.

Atkins, Cholly, and Jacqui Malone. *Class Act: The Jazz Life of Choreographer Cholly Atkins*. New York: Columbia University Press, 2001.

Auiler, Dan. *Vertigo: The Making of a Hitchcock Classic*. New York: St. Martin's/Marek, 1985.

Baldwin, James. *The Price of the Ticket: Collected Nonfiction 1948–1985*. New York: St. Martin's/Marek, 1985.

Berg, A. Scott. *Goldwyn: A Biography*. New York: Knopf, 1989.

Blumenthal, Ralph. *Stork Club: America's Most Famous Nightspot and the Lost World of Café Society*. Boston: Little, Brown, 2000.

Bogle, Donald. *Prime Time Blues: African Americans on Network Television*. New York: Farrar, Straus and Giroux, 2001.

———. *Toms, Coons, Mulattoes, Mammies & Bucks*. New York: Bantam Books, 1974.

Branch, Taylor. *Parting the Waters: America in the King Years 1954–1963*. New York: Simon and Schuster, 1988.

———. *Pillar of Fire: America in the King Years: 1963–1965*. New York: Simon and Schuster, 1998.

Brontë, Emily. *Wuthering Heights*. New York: Random House Modern Library, 2000.

Buber, Martin. *On Judaism*. New York: Schocken Books, 1967.

Buckley, Gail Lumet. *The Hornes*. New York: Knopf, 1986.

Cantor, Eddie, with David Freeman and Jane Kesner Ardmore. *My Life Is in Your Hands & Take My Life: The Autobiographies of Eddie Cantor*. Published as one edition. New York: Cooper Square Press, 2000.

Chaplin, Lita Grey, with Morton Cooper. *My Life with Chaplin: An Intimate Memoir*. New York: Bernard Geis Associates, 1966.

Collier-Thomas, Bettye, and V. P. Franklin. *My Soul Is A Witness: A Chronology of the Civil Rights Era 1954–1965*. New York: Henry Holt, 1999.

Courtney, Marguerite. *Laurette: The Intimate Biography of Laurette Taylor*. New York: Limelight Editions, 1984.

Davis, Christopher. *The Producer*. New York: Harper and Row, 1970.

Davis, Ossie, and Ruby Dee. *With Ossie & Ruby: In This Life Together*. New York: William Morrow, 1998.

Davis, Sammy, Jr. *Hollywood in a Suitcase*. New York: William Morrow, 1980.

Davis, Sammy, Jr., and Jane and Burt Boyar. *Why Me? The Sammy Davis Jr. Story.* New York: Farrar, Straus and Giroux, 1989.

———. *Yes I Can: The Story of Sammy Davis Jr.* New York: Farrar, Straus and Giroux, 1965.

Davis, Tracey, and Dolores A. Barclay. *Sammy Davis Jr.: My Father.* Los Angeles: General Publishing Group, 1996.

Douglas, Ann. *Terrible Honesty: Mongrel Manhattan in the 1920s.* New York: The Noonday Press, 1996.

Early, Gerald, ed. *The Sammy Davis Jr. Reader.* New York: Farrar, Straus and Giroux, 2001.

Ellison, Ralph. *Invisible Man.* New York: Vintage, 1995.

Evans, Harold. *The American Century.* New York: Knopf, 2000.

Feeney, Mark. "Nixon at the Movies." (unpublished.)

Fein, Irving A. *Jack Benny: An Intimate Biography.* New York: G. P. Putnam's Sons, 1976.

Frady, Marshall. *Jesse: The Life and Pilgrimage of Jesse Jackson.* New York: Random House, 1996.

Frank, Rusty E. *Tap! The Greatest Tap Dance Stars and Their Stories 1900–1955.* Revised edition. New York: Da Capo, 1994.

Gabler, Neal. *An Empire of Their Own: How the Jews Invented Hollywood.* New York: Anchor Books, 1989.

———. *Winchell: Gossip, Power and the Culture of Celebrity.* New York: Knopf, 1994.

Gerard, Philip. *Cape Fear Rising.* Winston-Salem, N.C.: John F. Blair, 1994.

Gevison, Alan. *American Film Institute Catalog—Within Our Gates: Ethnicity in American Feature Films, 1911–1960.* Berkeley: University of California Press, 1997.

Gibson, William. *A Mass for the Dead.* New York: Atheneum, 1968.

Goodman, Ezra. *The Fifty-Year Decline and Fall of Hollywood.* New York: Simon and Schuster, 1961.

Halberstam, David. *The Fifties.* New York: Ballantine, 1994.

Hanna, David. *Ol' Blue Eyes Remembered.* New York: Gramercy Books, 1997.

Hansberry, Lorraine. *To Be Young, Gifted, and Black.* New York: New American Library, 1970.

Harvey, James. *Movie Love in the Fifties.* New York: Knopf, 2001.

Herr, Michael, and Guy Peellaert. *The Big Room.* New York: Summit, 1986.

Heyward, DuBose. *Porgy.* Jackson: University Press of Mississippi, 2001.

Hotaling, Edward. *The Great Black Jockeys.* Rocklin, Calif.: Prima, 1999.

Hughes, Langston, and Milton Meltzer. *Black Magic.* New York: Da Capo, 1967.

Katz, Ephraim. *The Film Encyclopedia.* Third edition. HarperCollins, 1998.

Kelley, Kitty. *His Way: The Unauthorized Biography of Frank Sinatra.* New York: Bantam, 1987.

Kefauver, Estes. *Crime in America.* Garden City, N.Y.: Doubleday, 1951.

Kitt, Eartha. *Thursday's Child.* New York: Duell, Sloan and Pearce, 1956.

Kluger, Richard. *The Paper: The Life and Death of the* New York Herald Tribune. New York: Knopf, 1986.

Lemann, Nicholas. *The Promised Land: The Great Black Migration and How It Changed America.* New York: Knopf, 1991.

Levy, Shawn. *King of Comedy: The Life and Art of Jerry Lewis.* New York: St. Martin's, 1996.

Lewis, David Levering. *When Harlem Was in Vogue.* New York: Knopf, 1981.

Lewis, Jerry. *The Total Film-Maker.* New York: Random House, 1971.

Lewis, John, with Michael D'Orso. *Walking with the Wind: A Memoir of the Movement.* New York: Simon and Schuster, 1998.

Mailer, Norman. *An American Dream.* New York: Vintage, 1999.

Mazursky, Paul. *Show Me the Magic.* New York: Simon and Schuster, 1999.

McNeil, Alex. *Total Television.* New York: Penguin, 1980.

Mordden, Ethan. *The Hollywood Studios.* New York: Knopf, 1988.

Morris, Edmund. *The Rise of Theodore Roosevelt.* New York: Ballantine, 1980.

Muse, Clarence, and David Arlen. *Way Down South.* Hollywood, Calif.: David Graham Fischer, 1932.

Odets, Clifford, and William Gibson. *Golden Boy.* New York: Bantam, 1966.

Petkov, Steven, and Leonard Mustazza, eds. *The Frank Sinatra Reader.* New York: Oxford, 1995.

Plimpton, George. *Truman Capote.* New York: Doubleday, 1997.

Poitier, Sidney. *This Life.* New York: Knopf, 1980.

Pomerantz, Gary. *Where Peachtree Meets Sweet Auburn: The Saga of Two Families and the Making of Atlanta.* New York: Scribner, 1996.

Reed, Bill. *Hot from Harlem: Profiles in Classic African-American Entertainment.* Los Angeles: Cellar Door Books, 1998.

Reeves, Richard. *President Kennedy.* New York: Simon and Schuster, 1993.

Rooney, Mickey. *I.E., An Autobiography.* G. P. Putnam's Sons, 1965.

Rose, Frank. *The Agency: William Morris and the History of Show Business.* New York: Harper Business, 1995.

Salamon, Julie. *Facing the Wind.* New York: Random House, 2001.

Sampson, Henry. *Blacks in Blackface.* Metuchen, N.J.: Scarecrow Press, 1988.

Short, Bobby. *Black and White Baby.* New York: Dodd, Mead, 1971.

Sobel, Bernard. *A Pictorial History of Vaudeville.* New York: Citadel Press, 1961.

Sontag, Susan. *On Photography.* New York: Doubleday, 1989.

Stearns, Marshall, and Jean. *Jazz Dance: The Story of American Vernacular Dance.* New York: Da Capo, 1994.

Stott, William, with Jane Stott. *On Broadway.* New York: Da Capo, 1978.

Stowe, Harriet Beecher. *Uncle Tom's Cabin.* New York: The Modern Library, 2001.

Taylor, Theodore. *Jule: The Story of Composer Jule Styne.* New York: Random House, 1979.

Tosches, Nick. *Dino: Living High in the Dirty Business of Dreams.* New York: Dell, 1993.

Ward, Geoffrey C., and Ken Burns. *Jazz: A History of America's Music.* New York: Knopf, 2000.

Waters, Ethel, with Charles Samuels. *His Eye Is on the Sparrow; an Autobiography.* Garden City, N.Y.: Doubleday, 1951.

Watkins, Mel. *On the Real Side.* New York: Simon and Schuster, 1995.

Williams, Alan D. *Fifty Years: A Farrar, Straus and Giroux Reader.* New York: Farrar, Straus and Giroux, 1996.

ACKNOWLEDGMENTS

Peter Gethers, my editor, made this book so much better by bringing uncommon smarts and gracenotes to it. When I was deep into the project, and told him, with a burst of excitement, that the story of Sammy was the story of America itself, he said—as if he knew all along—Yes, it is. Year to year, his implorings were: Explore what made Sammy Sammy. Peter and Sonny Mehta of Alfred A. Knopf were out in front of the Sammy renaissance, and met me at the crossroads five years ago. I am more than grateful to both. Claudia Herr, assistant to Peter Gethers, was unflappable and wise. Others whom I thank at Knopf for their much-appreciated contributions: Abby Weintraub, Anthea Lingeman, Kathy Zuckerman, and Paul Bogaards.

Esther Newberg is my literary agent. She has cared unfailingly about my writing life. She works hard and with style, returns every phone call, and simply gets it done.

The following comprises those whom I have known over the years, before this book, but who were there, during this book, swinging a lantern in my direction, never too busy to offer a kind word, an ear. My sincere thanks to: Gerald Bell, Tina Moody, Jonathan Kaufman, Jack Winchester, Jerry Roberts, Matt Storin, Ceil Hendrickson, Elizabeth Graceffo, Peter Sheehan, Marty Berg, Michael D'Orso, David Warsh, Suzanne Kreiter, Sabrina Goodwin Monday, Lisa Frazier Page, Howard Manly, Dick Lehr, John G. Craig, Jr., Patty Bailey, Sue Callahan, Jim Vandervort, Greg Moore (now editor of the *Denver Post*), Ann Scales, Sanj Kharbanda, Paul Hendrickson, Elizabeth Calderone, Tony Stigger, Larry Young, Steve Flannigan, Mitch Zuckoff, David Lieber, Bob Hart, Tom Mulvoy, Carol Tyler, Serena Williams, Debra Dickerson, Ginger Rhodes. Kindnesses also came from Kathy Megan, Tyler Bridges, Julia Keller, Mary Jo Green, Jerry Hammond, Warren Tyler, Jim Gavin, Peggy Curran, John Weeks, Mike Curtin, Peter Guralnick, D'Lana Lockett, and Sean Mullin.

Tommy Spurlock, and Susan Hicks Spurlock, provided a home away from home. Always an extra chair at the dinner table—"oh come on over!"—Sammy crooning on the stereo.

Dick Rhodes believed in this project from the beginning.

Lynn Peterson saved the day.

Phil Bennett indulged my long talks about Sammy, read parts of the manuscript when asked, and offered scintillating insights.

Andrew Sheehan was ferocious in his support.

Stan Grossfeld, and Stacey Kabat: bless you.

The Yaddo Foundation provided a fellowship to write in the woods.

For years I had a writing space—ever grateful for it—at the *Boston Globe*. Now I'm at the *Washington Post*. The landing was made especially gentle by my immediate editor, the estimable Gene Robinson—and also by Len Downie, Steve Coll, Milton Coleman, Deb Heard, Steve Reiss, Linton Weeks, Marcia Davis, Jabari Asim, Don Graham, Bo Jones, and Kevin Merida. They each have my gratitude.

INDEX

A Note about the Author

Wil Haygood is a staff writer for the Style section of the *Washington Post.* For seventeen years he was a feature writer, and national and foreign correspondent at the *Boston Globe.* He is a native of Columbus, Ohio. Among his honors are: the New England Associated Press Award; the Sunday Magazine Editors Award for feature writing, which he was awarded twice; and the National Association of Black Journalists Award for Foreign Reporting, which he was also twice awarded. Haygood has also received the James Thurber Literary Fellowship, a Yaddo Fellowship, and an Alicia Patterson Foundation Fellowship. In 2001 he was a visiting Foster Distinguished Writer at Penn State University. He is also the author of *Two on the River; King of the Cats: The Life and Times of Adam Clayton Powell, Jr.* (named a *New York Times* Notable Book); and *The Haygoods of Columbus: A Family Memoir,* which was awarded the Great Lakes Book Award. He lives in Washington, D.C.